London

The travel guide

Footprint

Handbook

Charlie Godfrey-Faussett

The Clock Room

I looked for you in the Clock Room
of the British Museum -
the Ship's boom and the Scythe's whirr
told me their mechanism
but you were not there.

You were not there and when
the clocks began to slow
I watched Time's stiffened wing unbend -
love gone among the shadows
where the dials tend.

Gabriel Gbadamosi

London Handbook
First edition
© Footprint Handbooks Ltd 2001

Published by Footprint Handbooks
6 Riverside Court
Lower Bristol Road
Bath BA2 3DZ. England
T +44 (0)1225 469141
F +44 (0)1225 469461
Email discover@footprintbooks.com
Web www.footprintbooks.com

ISBN 1 900949 88 1
CIP DATA: A catalogue record for this
book is available from the British Library

Distributed in the USA by
Publishers Group West

Credits

Series editors
Patrick Dawson and Rachel Fielding

Editorial
Editors: Alan Murphy and
Felicity Laughton
Maps: Sarah Sorensen

Production
Typesetting: Richard Ponsford, Emma
Bryers and Leona Bailey
Maps: Robert Lunn and Claire Benison
Colour maps: Kevin Feeney

Cover: Camilla Ford

Design
Mytton Williams

Photography
Front cover: Impact Photo Library
Back cover: Robert Harding
Picture Library
Inside colour section: British Museum
Press Office, Eye Ubiquitous, James
Davis Worldwide, Pictures Colour
Library, Robert Harding Picture Library,
The Travel Library.

Print
Manufactured in Italy by LEGOPRINT

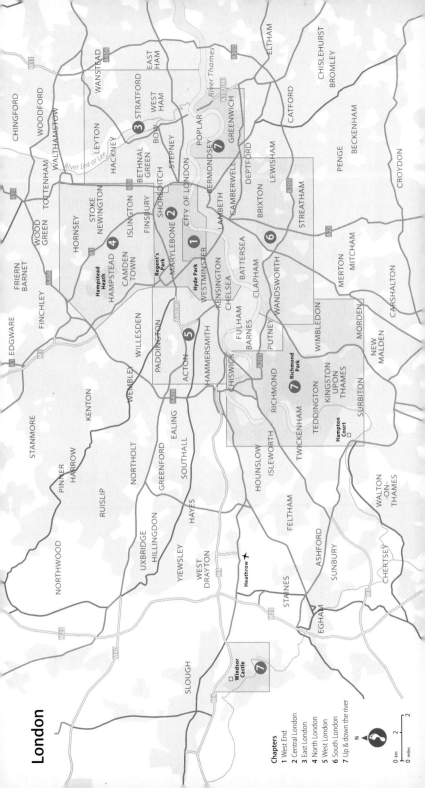

London

N

0 km   2
0 miles   2

Contents

Left: *The much-lauded new Great Court of the British Museum presents an impressive juxtaposition of old and new.*

Right: Big Ben, one of the capital's great landmarks and a face once familiar to millions of British news-watchers.

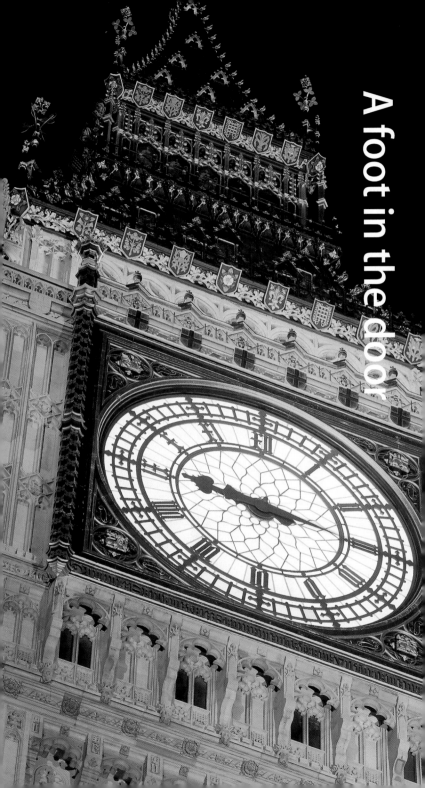

A foot in the door

Right: The London Eye: one of the biggest all-round successes among the city's new attractions. ***Below***:The much-maligned Millennium Dome framed by the Thames Barrier: white elephant meets guardian angel.

Above:The Millennium bridge – minus its infamous 'wobble' – connecting St Paul's cathedral across the Thames with the massive new Tate Modern. ***Right***:Lloyds building, a feature of London's ever-changing skyline and architectural symbol of its bright, shiny future.

London calling

London is more a great big jumble than a wild urban jungle. Like the British weather, it has difficulty making up its mind whether it's coming or going: seldom either baking hot or freezing cold, the city is a hotch-potch of subtle differences, an endless anonymous sprawl that can all of a sudden be vivid, distinct and charming, riddled bit by bit with immense diversity and character. First impressions are likely to be decidedly mixed: broadly low-rise, it's far from low-rent. And it does have problems, many of which directly affect visitors: the underground transport is unreliable and overcrowded; too much traffic and too many people regularly clog its polluted streets; decent accommodation can be unaffordable or booked solid; and at the end of every working week many parts of town get hopelessly drunk. And yet for all that, with its ethnic mix, street markets and multinational business, its political pragmatism and creative chaos, London remains one of the most global, engaging and invigorating places on the planet.

Every kinda people

It's still governed by the clock. Every morning Monday to Friday the population almost doubles as millions stream into work. Despite embracing European attitudes to all-day and most-of-the-night bar and café culture, lots of people only use the city to earn a living, choosing to sleep somewhere else several hours away by train. At weekends the whole place is noticeably more empty. And though the streets are fairly safe during the day, they're hardly very friendly. Like most large cities, London can give the impression that it doesn't have much time for strangers and has more important matters in hand. Warm-hearted Londoners do exist though and are responsible for sustaining the method in the city's apparent madness. Unlike Parisians, New Yorkers, or Romans, they may not immediately own up to the fact. Most were probably not born here – may not even be proud or fond of the place – but have been drawn into the grip of a city that manages quite successfully to mean all things to all people: hedonists, ascetics, glamourpusses, Cockneys, country weekenders, civil servants, raving clubbers and any number of other characters think of it as home.

Village people

With as many different reasons to live or work in the place as there are reasons to visit it, London usually wins people over eventually. Just getting about the city can be an ordeal or an adventure in itself. Unless you happen to be a courier or taxi driver, it takes years to build up a mental map of the city above ground, gradually piecing together well-known areas within walking distance of a familiar tube station or bus stop. Slowly it becomes clear that everything connects. It is really many different and discreet towns and villages all lumped together, surprisingly close to each other and often still fiercely protective of their identity and social status. Bewildering enough for its inhabitants, London can be made more accessible and enjoyable by focussing on the strengths – and some of the weaknesses – of its most individual parts, even though they may not divide up neatly into separate blocks, districts, or neighbourhoods.

North-south divide

The one great divide is the river. On this issue, everyone living in the city eventually makes a stand. North Londoners especially never seem to tire of comparing the perils and vices of the south with their own. The city was founded on the north bank near London Bridge, and since then the badlands in the south have always been treated with suspicion. As a result, most of the oldest tight-knit communities and the majority of London's attractions are on the north side.

In the city

West End thrills In pole position between these two cities, at the heart of modern London, Trafalgar Square and the West End are understandably top of the pops with visitors. The pivot on which the city swings, the West End is a relatively well-defined mish mash north and west of the square, glued together around the theatres, cinemas and clubs of Piccadilly Circus and Leicester Square, involving at least five other places with distinct identities: the Strand, Soho, Covent Garden, Mayfair, and St James's. All are within walking distance of each other. Before the Victoria Embankment was built in the 19th century, pushing the river back, the Strand was a famous society prom along the north bank connecting Westminster with the City. Today the reclaimed land is a massive main road rushing past Victoria Gardens and the vestiges of a few great houses. Most impressive though, near the Aldwych, is the 18th-century pile of Somerset House, facing south across the river and now home to several magnificent art collections. North of the Strand is Covent Garden, blissfully free of the traffic but rarely of the crowds descending on its shops, cafés, restaurants around its old Victorian market place. North of Leicester Square and Shaftesbury Avenue, the narrow streets of Soho are even more of a seething nightspot, packed with fashionable clubs, bars and cheerful restaurants heaving with humanity. Just over Regent Street though, Mayfair boasts broad avenues, big empty squares, upmarket eateries and some very smart hotels. Bijou examples of the latter can be found in the terribly upper-crust enclave of St James's, close to Royalty at St James's Palace and Buckingham Palace.

Pose codes Tucked behind the Palace, Victoria station and its environs disturb the creamy stuccoed dignity of Belgravia – practically the only part of London where everyone is as wealthy as each other – and its less pompous little neighbour Pimlico, home to the national collection of British art in Tate Britain on the river. Knightsbridge tries to maintain the tone of Belgravia westwards south of Hyde Park and north of the Brompton Road, with London's poshest department store, Harrods, the splendour of the Brompton Oratory, and also the wonders of Museumland. Its cheeky but just as affluent southern neighbour is Chelsea, where the charming old streets off the King's Road are freshened by river breezes. These two are divided by their postcodes, letters followed by apparently random numbers of incomprehensible significance to strangers but provoking limitless prejudice in the natives: any number preceded by SW – South West – or W has always been considered superior, hence Belgravia SW1, Knightsbridge SW7, Chelsea SW3. Mayfair's postcode is W1 which also embraces Marylebone north of Oxford Street, the newest must-have destination for the glitterati, and includes rundown, media-friendly and upwardly mobile Fitzrovia.

Nice & EC does it Across the Tottenham Court Road to the east, Bloomsbury's severe brick and stone streets and squares, housing the University of London and the exceptional antiquities of the British Museum are in WC1. Holborn is caught in the no-man's-land of WC2, between west and east, bordering the City of London. Here the codes become much more straightforward and businesslike, simply cutting up the old Square Mile into four quarters – EC1, EC2, EC3, EC4 – clockwise from the top near cutting-edge Clerkenwell. Then again, to the south over London Bridge, Southwark, Bankside, the South Bank and Waterloo are all proud to be in SE1. Bankside especially has become the talk of the town since Tate Modern opened in the great brick hulk of Bankside Power Station. On the South Bank, across the river from the Strand, the big wheel of the London Eye offers a bird's eye view of its plum location in the middle of town next to Westminster Bridge.

Left:The seamy side of the teeming media village that is Soho. **Below**:Tourists swarm around Covent Garden like bees after nectar, filling its myriad pubs and restaurants, its fashion shops, its market and, with any luck, its Royal Opera House.

Above: Oxford Street, loved and hated in equal measure but impossible to ignore, a retail wonderland or consumer hell, depending on your point of view.
Left: Camden canalside: where pop kids come to buy trendy gear by day and get wasted in an alcohol-fuelled frenzy by night.
Previous pages: Mornington Crescent – an old tube station near Camden renovated at long last, but to BBC Radio 4 listeners it means so much more…

14

Right:The Docklands, well-connected and a paean to Mammon, a place where Fritz Lang's Metropolis meets Aldous Huxley's Brave New World. *Below*:Not a billiard table on its back, but Battersea power station's distinctive and disused chimneys, one of the most evocative London landmarks at sunset.

Above: Away from the centre, some of London's quieter corners offer a change of pace and a peaceful haven from the urban clamour. *Right*: Workin' nine till five – or rather seven till eleven in the case of the City of London's terminal workaholics.
Previous pages: For a couple of days every summer, Notting Hill lets its hair down and brings the Caribbean and urban beats into the heart of West London.

One step beyond

Beyond Central London and the City, east London inspires local loyalties even more fiercely than the north or south. With its street markets, urban decay and poverty, the East End around Bethnal Green is 'proper' London and often not a pretty sight. That said, immigrants to the city have long made it their first port of call – although the Docklands have been redeveloped as a soulless and glimmering testament to the power of money – while the fashionable arty areas of Shoreditch and Hoxton on its margins have seen a boom in latenight bars and clubs, turning their desolate streets into a hip tourist destination.

East Enders

To the north, strangers have never been much of a surprise either to the polite heath-clad hilltop 'villages' of Hampstead and Highgate. Their grand houses, fine views and quaint sloping streets have harboured artists and emigrés for centuries. At the bottom of the hill, nearer the centre of the city, Camden Town could hardly be more different, with its crowded weekend street markets, late-night music and may-hem. On the other side of the tracks to the east, Islington is the birthplace of New Labour. It likes to look to west London for inspiration, especially to super-hip Notting Hill with its multicultural mix of old money and new media. At the bottom of that hill, and much more staid, is High Street Kensington, lent social cachet by Princess Di's for-mer home, Kensington Palace. Bayswater and Paddington, just to the north of Hyde Park, are an odd mixture of cheesy shops, palatial houses and dodgy hotels, roughly similar in character to Earl's Court, south of High Street Kensington.

The cool, the trad & the lovely

In south London, Brixton is the most happening town, sometimes for all the wrong reasons, while Clapham's wide common is ringed with genteel residences whose inhabitants party hard on their old high street. At Battersea, spread wide open with its park and power station, just across from Chelsea, we're back on the river again. The one constant in London's cityscape, the meandering Thames rises and falls peacefully enough thanks to the Barrier in the east, downstream from grand old Greenwich. Upriver it glides past the seasonal glories of Kew Gardens, picturesque Richmond and the beautiful palace at Hampton Court.

Southern comforts

In the end though, apart from the constant reminders that almost every part of the city suffered extensive bomb damage during the Second World War – its redevelopment forcing the very rich into ever closer proximity with the very poor – unifying features of any kind have always been thin on the ground in this city. With its brave new Lot-tery-funded Millennium projects – some (like the Dome) already dead on their feet – its wealth of renovated or rusting great museums and galleries, its multicoloured cabs and deregulated buses, London still rejects any attempt to make it conform to expec-tations. Large enough to require several lifetimes to know much of it well, but small enough in parts to become familiar in a day, the only certainty is that it must be one of the most extraordinary and surprising cities in the world to go rummaging around.

It's London, innit?

Next page: *Little Venice may have ideas above its station, but London's canals present a refreshing, and often surprisingly bucolic, aspect of this sprawling city.*

Essentials

2

Essentials

Planning your trip

Essential London

London is a city often seen in a hurry. If time is very limited, then the one unmissable sight is **Tate Modern**. Whatever your reaction to the contents or industrial style of this huge new gallery of contemporary art, its position on the river puts it at the heart of the beast. If you really want to 'do' as many other sights as possible in one day, then the shiny new **Millennium footbridge** across the river to **St Paul's Cathedral** from the gallery means that wheeled transport of any kind is best abandoned altogether.

A circular three-mile walk starting at Piccadilly Circus could take in Trafalgar Square, St James's Park and its views of Buckingham Palace, the Houses of Parliament and Westminster Abbey, Westminster Bridge and Big Ben, the London Eye, the South Bank, Tate Modern, the Globe Theatre, the Inns of Court, Somerset House, Covent Garden and the National Galleries before you finally collapse breathless, confused and exhausted somewhere in Soho. Add half a mile or so and you could have popped your head into the Great Court at the British Museum too.

Less energetic and just as rewarding perhaps would be to spend the morning at Tate Modern, the afternoon at St Paul's, and the evening in a bar or restaurant somewhere near Smithfield. With an extra day, the half-hour skyride on offer at the London Eye is definitely worth the ticket price, although even with its sophisticated boarding system, precious time can still sometimes be lost in the queue.

Alternatively, the new **Great Court at the British Museum** has divided expert opinion but the public has been enthusiastic. It's not hard to see why: the airy lattice-work of the great glass roof round the central reading room defies old-fashioned fustiness and casts the Museum's frankly mind-boggling collection of antiquities in a new light. A visit here can also easily be combined with a taste of the peculiar small-scale charm and beauty of **Sir John Soane's Museum** in Lincoln's Inn Fields.

On a similar scale to the British Museum, the **Victoria and Albert Museum** in South Kensington is an extraordinary neo-gothic shrine to art and design packed with innumerable marvellous things. Less aesthetic and more historical insights can be found either at the **Imperial War Museum** or the **Tower of London**. Both are a little off the main tourist track, and both have sorry tales to tale. At the gateway to south London, the Imperial War Museum is the most disturbing, its new exhibition on the Holocaust putting the antique military hardware and World War memorabilia on display into perspective. The Tower of London, downriver near the splendid Tower Bridge, is a proper medieval castle, a very well-preserved relic riddled with stories of the pursuit and abuse of Royal power.

With more time, essential destinations further afield are the venerable old Tate Gallery of Modern Art near Victoria, now rechristened **Tate Britain** and dedicated to the latest in British contemporary, modern and historical art including Turner's dramatic oil paintings; the superhip bars, restaurants and shops of **Notting Hill** in the west; either the loud and grungey music mecca of **Camden** and its market or the views of the city from genteel **Hampstead** in the north; and the nightlife of **Shoreditch** to the east. Day trips south to the revamped Dulwich Picture Gallery or a river trip to Kew or Hampton Court also rank with the best that London has to offer.

British Tourist Authority offices abroad

The BTA represents the London Tourist Board (LTB) abroad. Information can be obtained from their **website** *(www.visitbritain.com), or from the offices listed below:*

Australia *Level 16, Gateway, 1 Macquarie Pl, Sydney NSW 2000, T02-93774400, F02-93774499.*

Belgium *Ave Louise 140, 1050 Brussels, T2-6262580, F2-6462726.*

Canada *5915 Airport Rd, Suite 120, Mississauga, Ontario LV4 1T1, T905-4051840, F905-4051835.*

Denmark *Montergade 3, 1116 Copenhagen K, T33-330142, F33-140136.*

France *Maison de la Grande-Bretagne, 19 rue des Mathurins, 75009 Paris, T1-44515622, F1-44515621.*

Germany *Westendstr 16-22, 60325 Frankfurt, T69-971123, F69-97112444.*

Ireland *18/19 College Green, Dublin 2, T1-6708000, F1-6708100.*

Italy *Via Nazionale 230, 00184 Rome, T06-4620221, F06-72010086.*

Netherlands *Stadhouderskade 2 (5e), 1054 ES Amsterdam, T20-6077705, F20-6186868.*

New Zealand *17th Flr, 151 Queen St, Auckland 1, T09-3031446, F09-3776965.*

South Africa *Lancaster Gate, Hyde Park Lane, Hyde Park 2196, Johannesburg, T011-3250342, F011-3250344.*

Switzerland and Austria *Limmatquai 78, CH-8001 Zurich, T01-2662166, F01-2662161*

USA *7th Flr, 551 Fifth Ave, New York, NY 10176-0799, T212-986-2200/ 1-800-GO-2-BRITAIN.*
10880 Wilshire Blvd, Suite 570, Los Angeles, CA 90024, T310-4702782, F310-4708549.
625 North Michigan Ave, Suite 1510, Chicago, IL 60611, T1-800-4622748, F312 7870464.

When to go

Climate
For recorded weather information, T0891-500401

The English obsession with the weather can largely be put down to its unpredictable nature. The climate in London is generally milder than in the rest of the country and although temperatures rarely drop to freezing or below, they can fluctuate considerably from one day to the next, with temperatures averaging around 6°C (43°F) in winter and 18°C (64°F) in summer, although in July and August it is not unusual for them to soar to 30°C (86°F). Despite its reputation, the average annual rainfall is fairly low – around 60 cm (24") – although visitors should come prepared for wet weather at any time of year.

Two excellent weather forecast websites are **www.met-office.gov.uk** and **www.bbc.co.uk/weather**

Organized tours

See also Sightseeing tours, on page 38

There are hundreds of tours of London offered by companies organizing sightseeing by coach, mini-coach, bus, boat, taxi, private driver-guides or on foot. These tours can last for anything from 2-3 hours to a full day. Sightseeing tour coaches should carry the LTB 'Approved Sightseeing Tour' sticker and it is advisable to make sure that your guide is a trained Blue Badge Guide. For details of operators and guide services see page 38. The *British Tourist Authority*, the *London Tourist Board* or local travel agents will also have information.

A recommended British company aimed at the more mature traveller is *Saga Holidays*, Saga Building, Middelburg Square, Folkestone, Kent CT20 1AZ, T0800-300500. *Saga* also operates in the USA, at 222 Berkeley Street, Boston, MA 02116; and in Australia, at Level 1, 10-14 Paul Street, Milsons Point, Sydney 2061.

Essentials

Other **specialist tour operators in the USA** are *Abercrombie & Kent*, T1-800-3237308, www.abercrombiekent.com, *Especially Britain*, T1-800-8690538, www.expresspages. com/e/especiallybritain, *Golden Tours*, T510-2626965, www.goldentours.co.uk, *Prestige Tours*, T1-800-8907375, www.prestigetours.com and *Sterling Tours*, T1-800-7274359, www.sterlingtours.com

A London-based company offering a wide variety of specialist holidays is *Exodus Travels*, T020-8772 3882, www.exodus.co.uk There are many other companies catering for any number of special interest holidays in London for students and young people, seniors and veterans, disabled travellers, gays and lesbians, singles, couples or families. A wide range of themes includes antiques, historic houses, theatre and the arts, boats, barges and canals, murder and mystery, religious, movies and garden tours.

Finding out more

The best way of finding out more information for your trip to London is to contact the British Tourist Authority (BTA) in your country or write (or email) direct to the head office of the London Tourist Board (LTB). The BTA and LTB can provide a wealth of free literature and information such as maps, city guides, events calendars and accommodation brochures. Travellers with special needs should also contact their nearest BTA office.

For a list of useful websites, see page 55

The official London Tourist Board site, **www.londontown.com** contains information on accommodation, transport and tourist sights, events and attractions. It has a very useful page with tips and ideas for travellers on a tight budget (www.londontown.com/free).

Essentials

Learning English in London

Thousands of people come to London each year to study English as a Foreign Language (EFL), but finding the right course can be confusing and time-consuming. First of all make sure you choose an organization that is **accredited by the British Council**. There are about 100 accredited schools, colleges and universities in London offering a range of courses at all levels and for all ages. They can all arrange accommodation and many organize social activities for students as well. Type of course, cost, class size and location of college may influence your decision. Executive courses, for example, are normally more expensive, in small groups, or one-to-one, and they usually offer more expensive accommodation arrangements. There are general programmes, examination courses, or those specializing in business or other kinds of English. Courses can be part time, full time, intensive, or you can opt for an 'in-tuition' placement which means you live in the house of a trained EFL teacher. Summer courses are often held in the universities and colleges.

The **English in Britain** website, www.englishinbritain.co.uk, lists the accredited schools and colleges in London and the rest of the UK. From the website you'll be able to search the database, contact the schools and colleges, visit their websites, and book a course. www.educationuk.org/www.britishcouncil.org The British Council's Education Information Centre gives guidance on studying in the UK; British Council, 10 Spring Gardens, SW1, T020-7389 4383.

Before you travel

Entry requirements

Visas Visa regulations are subject to change, so it is essential to check with your local British Embassy, Consulate or High Commission before leaving home. Citizens of all European countries – except Albania, Bosnia, Bulgaria, Macedonia, Romania, Slovakia, Yugoslavia and all former Soviet republics (other than the Baltic states) – require only a passport to enter Britain and can generally stay for up to three months. Citizens of Australia, Canada, New Zealand, South Africa or the USA can stay for up to six months, providing they have a return ticket and sufficient funds to cover their stay. Citizens of most other countries require a visa from the commission or consular office in the country of application.

The **Foreign Office's website** (www.fco.gov.uk) provides details of British immigration and visa requirements. Also, the **Immigration Advisory Service** (IAS) offers free and confidential advice to anyone applying for entry clearance into the UK: County House, 190 Great Dover Street, London SE1 4YB, T020-73576917, www.vois.org.uk/ias

Longer stays & work permits
A good place to begin a job search is www.transdata-inter. co.uk/jobs-agencies

For **visa extensions** contact the Home Office, Immigration and Nationality Department, Lunar House, Wellesley Road, Croydon, London CR9, T020-8686 0688, before your existing visa expires. Citizens of **Australia**, **Canada**, **New Zealand**, **South Africa** or the **USA** wishing to stay longer than six months will need an Entry Clearance Certificate from the British Embassy or High Commission in their country.

Citizens of **European Union** (EU) countries can live and work in Britain freely without a visa, but **non-EU residents** need a permit to work legally. This can be difficult to obtain without the backing of an established company or employer in the UK. **NB** Visas should be obtained from a British mission overseas before entering the UK.

British embassies abroad

Australia High Commission: Commonwealth Ave, Yarralumla, Canberra, ACT 2600, T02-62706666, www.uk.emb.gov.au

Belgium rue d'Arlon 85, 1040 Brussels, T2 2876211, www.british-embassy.be

Canada High Commission: 80 Elgin St, Ottawa, 5K7, T613-2371530

Denmark Kastelsvej 36/38/40, DK-2100 Copenhagen, T35-445200, www.britishembassy.dk

France 35 rue du Faubourg St Honoré, 75383 Paris T01-4451 3100, www.amb-grandebretagne.fr

Germany Wilhelmstrasse 70, 10117, Berlin, T30-204570, www.britischebotschaft.de

Ireland 29 Merrion Rd, Ballsbridge, Dublin 4, T01-2053700, www.britishembassy.ie

Israel 192 Hayarkon St, Tel Aviv 63405, T3-7251222, www.britemb.org.il/

Italy Via XX Settembre 80a 1-00187 Roma RM, T06-4220 0001, www.ukinitalia.it

Netherlands Koningslaan 44, 1075AE Amsterdam, T020-6764343.

New Zealand High Commission: 44 Hill St, Wellington 1, T04-4726049, www.britain.org.nz

South Africa High Commission: 91 Parliament St, Cape Town 8001, T21-4617220.

Spain Calle de San Fernando el Santo 16, 28010 Madrid, T91-7008200, www.ukinspain.com

USA 3100 Massachusetts Ave NW, Washington DC 20008, T202-5886500, www.britainusa.com

Essentials

Visitors from **Commonwealth countries** who are aged between 17 and 27 can apply for a working-holidaymaker's visa which permits them to do casual (ie non-career oriented) work for up to two years in the UK. Ads for typical working-holidaymaker jobs (pub or restaurant work, clerking, book-keeping, etc) can always be found in the pages of *TNT*, *SX*, or other magazines distributed free outside train and tube stations in London.

An option for citizens of some **non-Commonwealth** countries is to come to the UK on an `au pair' placement in order to learn English by living with an English-speaking family for a maximum of two years. In return for helping in the home (up to a maximum of five hours per day), the au pair is given a `reasonable allowance' and two days off each week. Au pairs too must be aged between 17 and 27, and come from one of the following countries: Andorra, Bosnia-Herzegovina, Croatia, Cyprus, Czech Republic, The Faroes, Greenland, Hungary, Macedonia, Malta, Monaco, San Marino, Slovak Republic, Slovenia, Switzerland or Turkey. This can be a very good way to learn English and to live rent free in London, but check out the precise conditions of your placement (as far as possible) before you take it up.

If you want to **study** in the UK you must first prove you can support and accommodate yourself without working in the UK and without recourse to public funds. Your studies should take up at least 15 hours a week for a minimum of six months. Once you are studying, you are allowed to do 20 hours of casual work per week in the term time and you can work full time during the holidays if you want. The type of job you do will depend largely on how much English you speak; students with very little or no English often do office cleaning or similar work.

In **North America**, **full-time students** can obtain temporary work or study permits through the Council of International Education Exchange (CIEE), 205 E 42nd Street, New York, NY 10017, T212-8222600, www.ciee.org Also, **Commonwealth** citizens with a parent or grandparent born in the UK can apply for a **Certificate of Entitlement to the Right of Abode**, allowing them to work in Britain.

Overseas embassies in London

Australia *T020-7379 4334.*	**Netherlands** *T020-7590 3200.*
Canada *T020-7258 6600.*	**New Zealand** *T020-79308422.*
Denmark *T020-7235 1255*	**South Africa** *T020-74517299.*
France *T020-7201 1000.*	**Spain** *T020-7589 8989.*
Germany *T020-7824 1300.*	**Sweden** *T020-7917 6400.*
Italy *T020-7312 2200.*	**Switzerland** *T020-7616 6000.*
Japan *T020-7465 6500.*	**USA** *T020-7499 9000.*

For more details, contact your nearest British Embassy, Consulate or High Commission, or the Foreign and Commonwealth Office in London, T020-7270 1500.

Customs regulations and tax

Visitors from EU countries do not have to make a declaration to customs on entry into the UK. The limits for **duty-paid goods** from within the EU are 800 cigarettes, or 1 kg of tobacco, 10 litres of spirits, 20 litres of fortified wine, 90 litres of wine and 110 litres of beer. There is no longer any duty-free shopping. Visitors from non-EU countries are allowed to import 200 cigarettes, or 250g of tobacco, two litres of wine, and two litres of fortified wine or one litre of spirits.

There are various import restrictions, most of which should not affect the average tourist, and tight **quarantine restrictions** which apply to animals brought from overseas (except for Ireland). For more information on British import regulations, contact HM Customs and Excise, Dorset House, Stamford Street, London, SE1 9PJ, T020-79283344, www.hmce.gov.uk

Many goods in Britain are subject to a **Value Added Tax** (VAT) of 17.5%, with the major exception of books and food. Visitors from non-EU countries can save money through the Retail Export Scheme, which allows a refund of VAT on goods to be taken out of the country. Note that not all shops are participants in the scheme and that VAT cannot be reclaimed on hotel bills or other services.

Insurance

It's a good idea to take out some form of travel insurance, wherever you're travelling from. This should cover you for theft or loss of possessions and money, the cost of all medical and dental treatment, cancellation of flights, delays in travel arrangements, accidents, missed departures, lost baggage, lost passport and personal liability and legal expenses.

Insurance companies
There isn't one site for all travel insurance companies, but www.travelinsurance.co.uk is a good place to start shopping around

There are a variety of policies to choose from, so it's best to shop around to get the best price. Your travel agent can also advise you on the best deals available. *STA Travel* and other reputable student travel organizations often offer good-value travel policies.

Travellers from North America can try the International Student Insurance Service (ISIS), which is available through *STA Travel*, T1-800-7770112, www.sta-travel.com Some other recommended travel insurance companies in North America include **Travel Guard**, T1-800-8261300, www.noelgroup.com, **Access America**, T1-800-2848300, **Travel Insurance Services** (1-800-9371387), **Travel Assistance International**, T1-800-8212828 and **Council Travel**, 1-888-COUNCIL, www.counciltravel.com Another company worth calling for a quote is **Columbus Direct**, T020-73750011.

Older travellers should note that some companies won't cover people over 65 years old, or may charge high premiums. The best policies for older travellers are offered by *Age Concern*, T01883-346964, though these can be expensive.

Points to note You should always read the small print carefully. Some policies exclude 'dangerous activities' such as scuba diving, skiing, horse riding or even trekking. Not all policies cover ambulance, helicopter rescue or emergency flights home. Find out if your policy pays medical expenses direct to the hospital or doctor, or if you have to pay and then claim the money back later. If the latter applies, make sure you keep all records. Whatever your policy, if you are unfortunate enough to have something stolen, make sure you get a copy of the police report, as you will need this to substantiate your claim.

What to take

You'll be able to find everything you could possibly need for your trip in London, so you can pack light and buy stuff as you go along. Given the climate, however, you should bring a lightweight waterproof jacket and a warm sweater whatever the time of year. Also bring light clothes in the summer.

A padlock can be handy for locking your bag if you are staying in one of London's *Youth Hostel Association* (www.yha.org.uk) hostels. All necessary linen is provided in the cost of the room so it is not necessary to take a sleeping bag or sheet. Other useful items include an alarm clock and an adaptor plug for electrical appliances.

Money

The British currency is the pound sterling (£), divided into 100 pence (p). Coins come in denominations of 1p, 2p, 5p, 10p, 20p, 50p, £1 and £2.

Travellers' cheques The safest way to carry money is in travellers' cheques. These are available for a small commission from all major banks. *American Express* (Amex), *Visa* and *Thomas Cook* cheques are widely accepted and are the most commonly issued by banks. You'll normally have to pay commission again when you cash each cheque. This will usually be 1%, or a flat rate. No commission is payable on Amex cheques cashed at Amex offices. Make sure you keep a record of the cheque numbers and the cheques you've cashed separate from the cheques themselves, so that you can get a full refund of all uncashed cheques should you lose them. It's best to bring sterling cheques to avoid changing currencies twice. Also note that in Britain travellers' cheques are rarely accepted outside banks, so you'll need to cash them in advance and keep a good supply of ready cash.

Credit cards & ATMs Most hotels, shops and restaurants in London accept the major credit cards Access/MasterCard, Visa and Amex), though some places may charge for using them. Some smaller establishments such as B&Bs will often only accept cash. You can withdraw cash from selected banks and ATMs (or cashpoints as they are called in Britain) with your cash card. Your bank or credit card company will give you a list of locations where you can use your card. Visa card and Access/MasterCard holders can use all major High Street banks (*Barclays*, *HSBC*, *Lloyds TSB*, *NatWest*, *Royal Bank of Scotland* and *Bank of Scotland*). Amex card holders can use the *HSBC*, the *Royal Bank of Scotland* and any other bank or building society displaying the 'Link' symbol.

Banks & bureaux de change Branches of the main High Street banks – *Barclays*, *HSBC*, *Lloyds TSB*, *NatWest*, *Royal Bank of Scotland* and *Bank of Scotland* – are easily found throughout London. Bank opening hours are Monday-Friday from 0930 to 1600 or 1700. Some larger branches

Essentials

may open later on Thursdays and on Saturday mornings. Banks tend to offer very similar exchange rates and are usually the best places to change money and cheques. Outside banking hours you'll have to use a **bureau de change**, which can be easily found in central London and also at the airports and train stations.

Note that some private *bureaux* charge high commissions for changing cheques; those at international airports, however, often charge less than banks and will change pound sterling cheques for free. Another option is *Exchange International* which has over 20 branches throughout central London and offers good exchange facilities; Thomas Cook and other major travel agents also operate bureaux de change with reasonable rates. Avoid changing money or cheques in hotels, as the rates are usually very poor.

Money transfers If you need money urgently, the quickest way to have it sent to you is to have it **wired** to the nearest agent via *Western Union* (T0800-833833) or *Moneygram* (T0800-89718971). Charges are on a sliding scale, ie it will cost proportionately less to wire out more money. Money can also be wired by *Thomas Cook* or *American Express*, though this may take a day or two, or transferred via a bank draft, but this can take up to a week.

Cost of living/ travelling London is not a cheap city to visit – accommodation and restaurant prices are high and public transport is expensive. However, by staying in YHA youth hostels – some include a substantial breakfast in the price – and by getting around on foot or using London Transport Travelcards (see box page 42), costs can be kept to a minimum of around £30 per person per day. Those staying in slightly more upmarket B&Bs or guesthouses, eating out every evening at pubs or modest restaurants and visiting tourist attractions, such as castles or museums, can expect to pay around £60 per person per day. Single travellers will have to pay more than half the cost of a double room in most places and should budget on spending around 60% of what a couple would spend. In order to enjoy London to the full then you'll need at least £70 per day, without being extravagant.

Youth & student discounts There are various official youth/student ID cards available. The most useful is the **International Student ID Card** (ISIC), which soon pays for itself through a series of discounts, including most forms of local transport, cheap or free admission to museums, theatres and other attractions, and cheap meals in some restaurants. US and Canadian citizens are also entitled to emergency medical coverage with the card, and there's a 24-hour hotline to call in the event of medical, legal or financial emergencies.

If you're aged under 26 but not a student, you can apply for a **Federation of International Youth Travel Organizations** (FIYTO) card, or a **Euro 26 Card**, which give you much the same discounts. If you're 25 or younger you can qualify for a **Go-25 Card**, which gives you the same benefits as an ISIC card. These discount cards are issued by discount travel agencies (see pages 28 and 29 for addresses) and hostelling organizations (see page 41).

Tipping Tipping in London is at the customer's discretion. In a restaurant you should leave a tip of 10-15% if you are satisfied with the service. If the bill already includes a service charge, you needn't add a further tip. Tipping is not normal in pubs or bars. Taxi drivers expect a tip, usually of around 10%. As in most other countries, porters, bellboys and waiters in more upmarket hotels rely on tips to supplement their meagre wages.

Getting there

By air

The majority of overseas visitors arrive at one of London's five airports. The largest of these, Heathrow, is the busiest airport in the world and is a main routing point for international flights in Europe. As a result, it is possible to fly direct to anywhere in Europe and to most other major international destinations. There are also good air links to all parts of the British Isles.

For airport information, see page 33

Essentials

Those wishing to fly on to other parts of Britain should note that it may be cheaper if you use an Airpass or Europass bought in your own country. They are offered by British Airways and British Midland and are valid only with an international scheduled flight ticket. Alternatively, there is a growing number of low-cost airlines which offer cheap air tickets on the internet and on back pages of weekend national newspapers.

There are a mind-boggling number of outlets for buying your plane ticket and finding the best deal can be a confusing business. **Fares** will depend on the season. Ticket prices are highest from around early June to mid-September, which is the tourist high season. Fares drop in the months either side of the peak season – mid-September to early November and mid-April to early June. They are cheapest in the low season, from November to April, although prices tend to rise sharply over Christmas and the New Year. It's also worth noting that flying at the weekend is normally more expensive.

Buying a ticket

It is always worth spending a bit of time researching the various options available and starting early, as some of the cheapest tickets have to be bought months in advance and the most popular flights sell out early.

One of the best ways of finding a good deal is to use the internet. There are a number of sites where you can check out prices and even book tickets. You can search in the travel sections of your web browser or try the sites of the discount travel companies and agents and the budget airlines listed in this section. Also worth trying are: **www.expedia.co.uk lastminute.com e-bookers.com cheapflights.co.uk deckchair.com flynow.com dialaflight.co.uk**

Cheap flight tickets fall into two categories; official and unofficial. Official tickets are called budget fares, Apex, super-Apex, advance-purchase tickets, or whatever a particular airline chooses to call them. Unofficial tickets are discounted or consolidated tickets which are released by airlines through selected travel agents. They are not sold directly by airlines. Discounted tickets are usually as low or lower than the official budget-price tickets. **Return tickets** are usually a lot cheaper than buying two one-way tickets. London is ideally situated for a round-the-world itinerary and **Round-the-World** (RTW) tickets can be a real bargain, with prices ranging from between £500 and £1500.

When trying to find the best deal, make sure you check the route, the duration of the journey, stopovers allowed, any travel restrictions such as minimum and maximum periods away, and cancellation penalties. Many of the cheapest flights are sold by small agencies, most of whom are honest and reliable, but there may be some risks involved with buying tickets at rock-bottom prices. You should avoid paying too much money in advance and you could check with the airline directly to make sure you have a reservation.

You may be safer choosing a better-known travel agent, such as *STA*, which has offices worldwide, or *Trailfinders* in the UK, or *Council Travel* in the USA. These and other reputable discount companies and agents are listed above.

Essentials

Airlines flying from North America

Air Canada, T1-888-2472262, www.aircanada.ca

American Airlines, T1-800-4337300, www.americanair.com

British Airways, T1-800-2479297; in Canada T1-800-6681059, www.british-airways.com

Continental Airlines, T1-800-2310856, www.flycontinental.com

Delta Airlines, T1-800-2414141, www.delta-air.com

TWA, T1-800-8924141, www.twa.com

United Airlines, T1-800-5382929, www.ual.com

Virgin Atlantic Airways, T1-800-8628621, www.fly.virgin.com

Discount travel agents in North America

Air Brokers International, 323 Geary St, Suite 411, San Francisco, CA 94102, T1-800-8833273, www.airbrokers.com Consolidator and specialist on RTW and Circle Pacific tickets.

Council Travel, 205 E 42nd St, New York, NY 10017, T1-888-COUNCIL, www.counciltravel.com Student/budget agency with branches in many US cities.

Discount Airfares Worldwide On-Line, www.etn.nl/discount.htm A hub of consolidator and discount agent links.

International Travel Network/Airlines of the Web, www.itn.net/airlines Online air travel information and reservations.

STA Travel, 5900 Wilshire Blvd, suite 2110, Los Angeles, CA 90036, T1-800-8364115, www.sta-travel.com Discount student/youth travel company with branches in New York, San Francisco, Boston, Miami, Chicago, Seattle and Washington DC.

Travel CUTS, 187 College St, Toronto, ON M5T 1P7, T1-800-6672887, www.travelcuts.com Specialist in student discount fares, IDs and other travel services. Branches in other Canadian cities.

Travelocity, www.travelocity.com Online consolidator.

All tickets are subject to a passenger service charge and airport tax. For economy-fare flights within the UK and from EU countries the tax is £5. For all other flights it is £20. Taxes on first or club-class flights are £10 for UK and EU and £40 for other destinations. The service charge varies from one airport to another.

The cheapest flights usually arrive and leave from London's Luton or Stansted airports. They are often subject to rigid restrictions but the savings can make the extra effort worthwhile. Cheaper tickets usually have to be bought at least a week in advance, apply to only a few mid-week flights and must include a Saturday night stayover. They are also non-refundable, or only partly refundable, and non-transferable. A standard flexible and refundable fare can be as much as two or three times a budget fare.

For flights within the UK, specialist agencies such as *Usit Campus* or *STA* (see above) offer Domestic Air Passes on *British Airways* and *British Midlands* flights to full-time students and travellers under 26 years old. These give substantial discounts on flights from Heathrow and Gatwick to specified destinations in England, Scotland, Northern Ireland and Jersey, in the Channel Islands. Flights work out at between £28 and £32 each, with a minimum of four flights per person.

Discount charter flights to **Continental Europe** are often available to young travellers aged under 26 and holders of ISIC cards through the large student travel agencies listed above. The London listings magazine *Time Out* is a good place to look for cheap fares, as well the back pages of some national weekend newspaper

Airlines flying from Australia and New Zealand

Air France, T02-9321 1030 (Sydney), www.airfrance.com
Air New Zealand, T09-3573000 (Auckland), 02-9937 5111 (Sydney), 03-9670 3499 (Melbourne), www.airnz.co.nz
British Airways, T02-9258 3200 (Sydney); T09-3568690 (Auckland), www.british-airways.com
Cathay Pacific, T02-9931 5500 (Sydney), www.cathaypacific.com
Gulf Air, T02-9244 2199 (Sydney).
Japanese Airlines (JAL), T02-9272 1111 (Sydney); T09-3799906 (Auckland).
Korean Air, T02-9262 6000 (Sydney); 09-3073687 (Auckland).

Qantas, T09-3578900 (Auckland), www.qantas.com.au
Singapore Airlines, T02-9350 0100 (Sydney), T131011 (reservations); T09-3793209 (Auckland).
South African Airways, T02-9223 4448 (Sydney), www.saa.co.za
Thai Airways, T02-9251 1922 (Sydney); T09-3773886 (Auckland), www.thaiair.com
United Airlines, T02-9292 4111 (Sydney) T131777 (reservations); T09-3793800 (Auckland), www.ual.com
Virgin Atlantic, T02-9352 6199, www.flyvirgin.com/atlantic

Discount travel agents in Australia and New Zealand

Flight Centres, 82 Elizabeth St, Sydney, T13-1600; 205 Queen St, Auckland, T09-3096171. Also branches in other towns and cities.
STA Travel, T1300-360960, www.statravelaus.com.au 702 Harris St, Ultimo, Sydney, and 256 Flinders St, Melbourne. In New Zealand: 10 High St, Auckland, T09-3090458. Also in major towns and cities and university campuses.

Travel.com.au, 80 Clarence St, Sydney, T02-92901500, www.travel.com.au
UK Flight Shop, 7 Macquarie Place, Sydney, T02-92474833, www.ukflightshop.com.au   They also have branches in Melbourne T03-9600 3022, and Perth, T08-9226 1222.

supplements and also free magazines such as *TNT* which you can find outside train and tube stations in London.

There are several daily non-stop flights to Heathrow and Gatwick from many US and Canadian cities, including Boston, Calgary, Chicago, Denver, Las Vegas, Los Angeles, Miami, Montreal, New York, Philadelphia, San Francisco, Seattle, Toronto, Vancouver and Washington. Transatlantic carriers are listed above. **Flights from North America**

For low-season Apex fares expect to pay around US$400-600 from New York and other East Coast cities and around US$500-700 from the West Coast. Prices rise to around US$700-900 from New York and up to US$1000 from the West Coast in the summer months. Low-season Apex fares from Toronto and Montreal cost around CAN$600-700, and from Vancouver around CAN$800-900, rising to $750-950 and $950-1150 respectively during the summer.

The cheapest scheduled flights to London from Australia or New Zealand are **via Asia** with *Gulf Air*, *Royal Brunei* or *Thai Airways*. They charge A$1300-1500 in low season and up to A$1800 in high season, and involve a transfer en route. Flights via **Africa** start at around $2000 and are yet more expensive via **North America**. Flights to and from Perth via Africa or Asia are a few hundred dollars cheaper. **Flights from Australia & New Zealand**

Essentials

Airlines within Britain and Ireland

Aer Lingus, Ireland T01-8444777; UK T0645-737747, www.aerlingus.ie, flies from Heathrow, Gatwick and London City to Dublin and Cork with connections to Shannon, Sligo, Galway, Kerry and Donegal.

British Airways, T0845-7799977, www.britishairways.com, flies from Heathrow and Gatwick to most parts of the UK. They also fly from London's Stansted Airport to Manchester.

British Midland, T08706-070555, www.britishmidland.com, flies from London Heathrow to East Midlands, Leeds/Bradford, Manchester and Teesside, in England; to Aberdeen, Edinburgh and Glasgow in Scotland; and to Belfast in Northern Ireland.

easyJet, T08706-000000, www.easyjet.com, is a budget airline which flies from London's Gatwick, Luton and Stansted airports to Belfast, Liverpool, Aberdeen, Edinburgh, Glasgow and Inverness, from £30 one-way.

Go, T0845-6054321, www.go-fly.com, is a low-cost airline which flies from London Stansted to Edinburgh, Glasgow and Belfast. Return fares fluctuate between £50 and £140.

Ryanair, T08701-569569; Ireland T01-609-7800, www.ryanair.com, is a low-fares airline with flights from London Stansted to Glasgow (Prestwick) from £40 return. They also fly from Stansted, Gatwick and Luton airports to Dublin .

Scot Airways, T08706-060707, www.scotairways.co.uk, flies from London City airport to Dundee, Edinburgh and Glasgow.

Buzz, T08702-407070, www.buzzaway.com, is a low-cost internet-based airline that flies from London Stansted to 13 destinations in continental Europe.

KLM AirUK, T08705-074074, www.klm.com, flies to Amsterdam from London's Stansted and City airports and from 11 other regional UK airports.

The cheapest scheduled flights from **New Zealand** are with *Korean Air*, *Thai Airways* or *JAL*, all of whom fly via their home cities for around NZ$2000-2300. The most direct route is via North America with *United Airlines*, via Chicago or Los Angeles. Fares range from around NZ$2800 in low season to NZ$3200 in high season.

A **Round-the-World** (RTW) ticket may work out just as cheap as a return ticket. Good deals are offered by *Qantas/British Airways*.

Land and sea travel

Passengers arriving from Europe by coach, rail, car or on foot will have to cross the English Channel either by ferry or the Channel Tunnel. Hovercraft services no longer operate.

By train
For any other continental rail tickets, contact Rail Europe, T0990-848848, www.raileurope.co.uk, or European Rail Travel, T020-7387 0444, www.europeanrail.com

Since 1994, when the Channel Tunnel finally linked Britain to continental Europe, **Eurostar**, T0990-186186, www.eurostar.com, has been operating high-speed trains to London Waterloo from Paris (three hours) and Brussels (two hours 40 minutes) via Lille (two hours). Between December and April, there is also a weekend ski train service between Waterloo and the French Alps. Standard-class tickets to Paris and Brussels range from £70 for a weekend day return. A standard, mid-week return ticket costs £300 (£165 one way). There are substantial discounts for children (4-11 years) and for passengers who are under 26 years on the day of travel. It is worth keeping an eye open for special offers, especially in the low season.

"Le Shuttle"
If you're driving from continental Europe you can take the *Eurotunnel Shuttle Service*, T0800-969992, www.eurotunnel.com, a freight train which runs 24 hours a day, 365 days a year, and takes you and your car from Calais to Folkestone in 35-45 minutes.

Essentials

Discount travel agents in London

Big Save Travel, Rutland House, 44 Masons Hill, Bromley, Kent BR2 9JG, T020-8353 8888, F020-8353 8889. Particularly good for fares to Australia and New Zealand.
Council Travel, 28a Poland St, London W1V 3DB, T020-7437 7767, www.destinations-group.com
STA Travel, 86 Old Brompton Rd, London SW7 3LH, T020-7361 6161, www.statravel.co.uk They have other branches in London, as well as in Brighton, Bristol, Cambridge, Leeds, Manchester, Newcastle-upon-Tyne and Oxford and on many university campuses. Specialists in low-cost student/youth flights and tours, also good for student IDs and insurance.
Trailfinders, 194 Kensington High St, London W8 7RG, T020-7938 3939.
Usit Campus, 52 Grosvenor Gardens, London SW1 OAG, T020-7730 3402, www.usitcampus.co.uk Student/youth travel specialists with branches also in Belfast, Brighton, Bristol, Cambridge, Manchester and Oxford. The main Ireland branch is at 19 Aston Quay, Dublin 2, T01-6021777 or 6778117.

Essentials

Fares range from £84 to £165 per carload, depending on the time of year or how far in advance you book. For bookings, call T08705-353535. Foot passengers cannot cross on the Shuttle.

The closest continental ferry port to London is Dover, in Kent. **P&O Stena Line**, T087-0600 0600, www.posl.com crosses the Channel from Calais in 1 hour 15 minutes. For bookings in Calais, call T(33)802-010020. Fares vary enormously according to the season, time of day and duration of stay. Foot passengers can pay as little as £5, while cars pay anything between £42 (for a 12-hour, off-peak return with up to five passengers) and £299 (for a fully flexible return in the high season with up to nine passengers).

By ferry
www.ferrysavers.co.uk is for booking ferries with cars only

For visitors wanting to travel to or from other parts of France or Spain, **Brittany Ferries**, T0990 360360, www.brittanyferries.com, operate out of Portsmouth, Poole and Plymouth to Caen, St-Malo, Cherbourg, Roscoff and Santander. Bookings in France should be made on T(33)299-828080; in Spain, call T(34)942-360611. **P&O European Ferries**, T0870-2424999, run services between Portsmouth and Le Havre, Cherbourg and Bilbao.

National Express' **Eurolines**, T0990-143219, operates services between London's Victoria Coach Station and many European destinations. Channel crossings are made by both the ferry and Eurotunnel and tickets are cheaper if booked at least seven days in advance. This is a good option for travellers on a tight budget, as fares are less than half those on the Eurostar.

By coach

Getting to London from within the UK

There are four main companies operating frequent rail services between London and other towns and cities in England, Scotland and Wales: **GNER**, T0345-225225, leave from Kings' Cross and run up the east coast to the East Midlands, Yorkshire, Northeast England and Scotland; **Virgin** trains, T08457-222333, operate a cross-country and a west coast service from Euston to the Midlands, the northwest and Scotland. **Scotrail**, T08457-550033, www.scotrail.co.uk, operate the Caledonian Sleeper service if you wish to travel overnight to Scotland. Trains to Wales and the west of England are run by **First Great Western**, T0845-7000125, www.great-western-trains.co.uk, from Paddington Station in London.

By train

Essentials

Discount railcards

*For people wishing to travel out of London by train, there are variety of railcards which give discounts on fares for certain groups. Cards are valid for one year and most are available from main stations. You will need a passport photo and proof of age or status. For further information, contact **National Rail Enquiries**, T0345-484950, www.railtrack.co.uk*

***Young Person's Railcard**: for those aged 16-25 or full-time students in the UK. Costs £18 and gives 34% discount on most train tickets.*

***Senior Citizen's Railcard**: for those aged over 60. Same price and discount as above.*

***Disabled Person's Railcard**: costs £14 and gives 34% discount to a disabled person and one other. Pick up application form from stations and send it to: Disabled Person's Railcard Office, PO Box 1YT, Newcastle-upon-Tyne, NE99 1YT. It may take up to 21 days to process, so apply in advance.*

***Family Railcard**: costs £20 and gives 34% discount on most tickets (20% on others) for up to four adults travelling together. Up to four accompanying children receive an 81% discount with a minimum ticket price of £1.*

Fares

National Rail Enquiries, T0345-484950, www.railtrack.co.uk, are very helpful for information on rail services and fares

The system of rail ticket pricing is very complicated. There are a series of discounted fares, but restrictions can be prohibitive, which often explains the long queues and delays at ticket counters in railway stations. The cheapest ticket is a **Super Apex**, which must be booked at least two weeks in advance. Next cheapest is an **Apex** ticket which has to be booked at least seven days before travelling. Other discount tickets include a **Saver** return, which can be used on all trains, and a **Super Saver**, which costs slightly less but cannot be used on a Friday or during peak times. You can book tickets online at **www.thetrainline.com**

For details of various **discount rail passes** and rail services within the United Kingdom, see box above.

Bus

This is the generally the cheapest form of travel in the UK. Road links between major cities are excellent and a number of companies offer express coach services day and night. The main operator, *National Express*, T08705-808080, www.gobycoach.com, operates out of Victoria Coach Station and has a nationwide network with over 1000 destinations. Tickets can be bought at bus stations or from a huge number of agents throughout the country.

Bus travel passes

Full-time students or those aged under 25 or over 50, can buy a **Coach Card** for £9 which is valid for one year and gets you a 20-30% discount on all fares. Children normally travel for half price, but with a **Family Card** costing £18, two children travel free with two adults. The **Tourist Trail Pass** offers unlimited travel on all *National Express* services throughout Britain. Passes cost from £49 for two days' travel out of three up to £190 for 15 days' travel out of 30. They can be bought from major travel agents, at Gatwick and Heathrow airports, as well as from bus stations.

In **North America** these passes are available from *British Travel International*, T1-800-3276097, www.britishtravel.com, or from *US National Express*, T502-2981395.

Touching down

London is served by two major international airports, Heathrow (mostly scheduled flights) and Gatwick (charter and scheduled flights). Stansted and Luton are smaller airports to the north of London, dealing with regular and budget flights, while London City Airport is used mostly by business commuters travelling to destinations within Europe.

Coaches leave from Heathrow & Gatwick to other cities in the UK

Essentials

London Heathrow Airport

London Heathrow Airport (LHR), Hounslow, Middlesex, TW6 1JH, T0870-0000123. The world's busiest international airport, Heathrow has four terminals: generally speaking, all domestic flights operate out of Terminal 1; Terminal 2 deals mostly with European flights, while Terminals 3 & 4 are mainly international, handling flights from Canada and the USA and some European ones too. When leaving London, it's important to check which terminal to go to before setting out for the airport.

A London Tourist Board information centre is located in the underground station (Terminals 1, 2 & 3) and London Transport and British Rail also have travel information points in Terminals 1, 2 & 4. Bus and coach sales/information desks are located in all four terminals. There are hotel reservations desks in the arrivals area of each terminal (a booking fee is charged).

For general enquiries, passengers with special needs should contact the Call Centre, T0870-0000123. If further help or advice concerning travel arrangements is required call Heathrow Travel-care T0208-745 7495.

The airport is on **London Underground**'s Piccadilly Line, which runs trains every 5-9 minutes to the centre of London and beyond, with an approximate journey time of 50 minutes. There are two stations: one serving Terminals 1, 2, and 3; the other for Terminal 4. The first train from central London arrives at Terminal 4 at 0629 (0749 on Sun) and the last arrives at 0107 (0008 on Sun). Allow a further five minutes to reach the station for Terminals 1, 2 & 3. Details of timetables and fares are available from London Transport: T020-7222 1234 (24 hours), www.londonunderground.co.uk

Getting there
Several transport options are available for the 15-mile journey between central London & Heathrow

Heathrow Express, T0845-6001515, runs non-stop to and from Paddington Station in central London. The journey takes 15 minutes to Terminals 1, 2 and 3, and 20 minutes to Terminal 4. Trains depart every 15 minutes between 0510 and 2340, 365 days a year. There is plenty of luggage space and wheelchairs and pushchairs are catered for. Some airlines have check-in facilities at Paddington. Tickets cost £12 (single), £22 (return). A £2 premium is charged for tickets purchased on board the train. Discounted fares are available and tickets purchased on the internet (www.heathrowexpress.co.uk) are also cheaper. Children (0 - 15 years) travel free when accompanied by an adult.

By bus An *Airlinks*', T0990-747777, `Hotel Hoppa' shuttle service serves most major hotels near the airport. *Airbus A2* (T020-8400 6655) runs every 30 minutes throughout the day to and from a number of stops in central London. During the night, the **N97** bus (see Night Buses page 43) connects Heathrow with central London. *National Express* coaches run from Victoria Coach Station every 30 minutes. Airlinks also operates frequent coach services between Heathrow, Gatwick, Luton, Stansted and other airports.

By taxi From Heathrow Airport to central London takes approximately one hour and should cost around £40. There are taxi desks in the Arrivals area of all four terminals (Terminal 1: T020-8745 7487; Terminal 2: T020-8745 5408; Terminal 3: T020-8745 4655; Terminal 4: T020-8745 7302).

Essentials

 ## Touching down

Electricity *The current in Britain is 240V AC. Plugs have three square pins and adapters are widely available.*

Emergencies *For **police**, **fire brigade** and **ambulance** dial 999.*

Laundry *Coin-operated launderettes are easy to find in residential areas of London. The average cost for a wash and tumble dry is about £4. A service wash where someone will do your washing for you, costs around £6.*

Time *Greenwich Mean Time (GMT) is used from late October to late March, after which time the clocks go forward an hour to British Summer Time (BST). GMT is five hours ahead of US Eastern Standard Time*

and 10 hours behind Australian Eastern Standard Time.

Toilets *Public toilets are found at all train and bus stations. They may charge 20p but are generally clean with disabled and baby-changing facilities. Those in the main train stations also have showers for around £4. Those in department stores, pubs or restaurants are usually better – and easier to find – than public toilets in the street.*

Weights and measures *Imperial and metric systems are both currently in use. Distances on roads are measured in miles and yards, drinks are poured in pints and gills, but generally nowadays, the metric system is used elsewhere.*

By car Head west out of London on the M4 and exit at Junction 4 for Terminals 1, 2 and 3 and at Junction 3 for Terminal 4. Parking is easy but expensive. There are two petrol stations at Heathrow, both open 24 hours a day, seven days a week.

London Gatwick Airport

London Gatwick Airport (LGW), Gatwick, West Sussex, RH6 0JH, T01293-535353, London's second airport 28 miles south of the capital, has two terminals, North and South, with all the usual facilities including car hire, currency exchange, 24-hour banking, Flight Shops (T08000-747787), Hotel Reservations Desks (T01293-504549) and a Travel Shop in the South Terminal (T01293-506783). There are numerous help points for passengers with special needs and free wheelchair assistance or help with baggage to reach check-in.

Getting there   **By train**   All trains arrive at the South Terminal where there is a fast link to the North Terminal. A number of airlines offer check-in facilities at London's Victoria Station. The fastest service is the non-stop 30-minute *Gatwick Express*, T0990-301530, which runs to and from London Victoria every 15 minutes during the day, and hourly throughout the night. Standard tickets cost £10.50 single and £20 return; first-class and cheap-day returns are available. *Connex South Central* runs a less expensive but slightly slower service to Victoria. *Thameslink* rail services run from King's Cross, Farringdon, Blackfriars and London Bridge stations. For further information call National Rail Enquiries, T08457-484950.

By bus   *Airbus A5* operates hourly from Victoria Coach Station and Pimlico underground station. For further information call the Airport Travel Line, T0990-747777.

By car   From Junction 7 of the M25 London Orbital Motorway, take the M23 south, coming off at Junction 9 for the airport. Otherwise take the A23 London-Brighton road. There are 24-hour petrol stations at both terminals.

London City Airport

London City Airport (LCY), Royal Dock, London E16 2PX, T020-7646 0000, is situated 6 miles (15 minutes' drive) east of the City of London. Continually updated flight information is available at www.londoncityairport.com/index.wml

Take the Jubilee line or Docklands Light Railway (DLR) to Canning Town for a connecting shuttle bus service. An *Airbus* shuttle service also runs every 10 minutes to and from Liverpool Street via Canary Wharf Underground and DLR stations until around 2130. London sightseeing bus services are also available from the airport.

Getting there

London Luton Airport

London Luton Airport (LTN), Luton, Bedfordshire, LU2 9LU, T01582-405100, about 30 miles north of central London, deals with charter and scheduled flights (particularly those operated by the budget airline *easyJet*) to a variety of domestic and European destinations. All the usual facilities are available plus fax, internet and email, a children's play area and an airport chapel. There is also a Skyline Travel Shop (T01582-726454).

By train Regular *Thameslink* trains leave from London Bridge, Blackfriars, Farringdon and King's Cross stations to Luton Airport Parkway station; a free shuttle bus service operates between the station and the airport terminal. The Thameslink station at King's Cross is about 100 yards east of the main station, along the Pentonville Road.

Getting there
For information,
call National
Rail Enquiries,
T08457-484950

By coach *Green Line* coaches run to and from Victoria Coach Station, Hyde Park Corner, Marble Arch, George Street and Baker Street in central London.

By car The airport is situated southeast of Luton, 2 miles off the M1 at Junction 10.

Stansted Airport

Stansted Airport (STN), Stansted, CM24 1RW, T08700-000303, 30 miles northeast of London, serves domestic and European destinations, including many of the short-haul economy flights; long-haul flights to the USA are due to start later in 2001. Terminal facilities include car hire, ATMs, 24-hour currency exchange, shops, restaurants and bars. There's a *Book and Go* Travel Shop (T08700-102015), a hotel reservations desk (T01279-661220), and AAS Assistance (T01279-663213), for passengers with special needs and also for left luggage.

By train *Stansted Skytrain*, T08457-484950, runs trains every 30 minutes from London's Liverpool Street Station to the station located directly below the main terminal building.

Getting there

By bus *Airbus A6* runs every hour from Victoria Coach Station, Hyde Park Corner, Marble Arch and Baker Street. *Airbus A7* also runs an hourly service from Victoria Coach Station, Embankment and Aldgate. The journey takes around 1 ½ hours. *Jetlink*, T08705-747777, operates a frequent service between London's four main airports.

By car The airport is situated north of London by Junction 8 of the M11.

Disabled travellers

Most visitors should not experience too many problems on arrival as all London airports are modern and equipped to help passengers with special needs. Express service
transport from the airports to the city centre (ie via Heathrow or Gatwick Express) is
also easily accessible for wheelchair users. Eurostar trains and Waterloo International
(the Eurostar terminal) are also accessible, although each train takes a maximum of
only two wheelchairs).

Accommodation in London can be problematic. Many of the large, modern and
more expensive hotels do have disabled facilities, but most of the smaller hotels are
not designed to cater for people with disabilities or can only accommodate people
with limited mobility. Of the seven YHA youth hostels, only the **Rotherhithe** hostel
(see page 446) has access for wheelchairs. *Holiday Care Service*, T01293-774535,
www.holidaycare.org.uk, is an organization that provides information on holidays
and accommodation suitable for disabled visitors. They operate a three-category
system for hotels whereby Category 1 hotels are suitable for independent wheelchair travellers; Category 2 are suitable for wheelchair users travelling with a helper;
and Category 3 are suitable for wheelchair users who are able to walk a few paces
and up a maximum of three steps.

Public transport is still quite bad too: access to most **underground** stations is via
numerous steps and extreme crowding at peak times make things difficult for anyone
with mobility problems. However, some newer tube stations and the DLR stations are
wheelchair accessible, and an increasing number of low-floor accessible **buses** are
being introduced. *London Transport* publishes a booklet with information on access
to buses and the tube as well as Braille maps and recorded guides (all free). They also
give information and advice to disabled travellers on T020-7918 3312.

Most, if not all, London **taxis** are now wheelchair accessible (look out for the illuminated chair symbol when the 'for hire' symbol is on). If ordering a taxi in advance from
one of the hire services, you must state it is needed for a disabled person. People with
impaired mobility are welcome on **Thames river services** and step-free access is now
available from most major piers. Newer craft have dedicated wheelchair spaces.

On the national rail network, wheelchair users, and blind or partially sighted people are
automatically given 30-50% discount on train fares; those with other disabilities are eligible for the **Disabled Person's Railcard**, which costs £14 per year and gives a third
off tickets for the disabled person and one other. There are no reductions on national
buses, however.

The London Tourist Board website, www.londontown.com, has an informative *Guide
to Disabled London* with information and tips on accommodation, attractions, nightlife, shopping, travelling and sightseeing in the capital. There are ideas for everything
from easy-access walks along the Thames, suitable for wheelchair users, to listen-
ing-and-touching tours of St Paul's Cathedral aimed specifically at blind and partially
sighted visitors. For further ideas of suitable walks and tours, see pages 38 and 46.

Public toilets Britain has a system of keys to open many of the public toilets available
for disabled people. To purchase a key (£3.50), contact RADAR (see below). A guide
book detailing locations of these disabled toilets across the UK costs £5.00 (p&p
included). If you're only visiting London, however, it's not worth buying a key and
guide; many of the large department stores have wheelchair access, lifts and disabled

loos. Some, such as *John Lewis* and *Selfridges* in Oxford Street and *Peter Jones* in Sloane Square, will also provide carers for a wide range of customers with special needs. In *Harrods* there are wheelchairs for hire.

Information and organizations If you are disabled you should contact the travel offi-cer of your national support organization before travelling. They can provide literature or put you in touch with travel agents specializing in tours for the disabled. In London, tour operator *Can Be Done*, T020-8907 2400, www.canbedone.co.uk, will arrange holidays for disabled visitors in a range of accommodation to suit individual requirements.

For more information, contact **The Royal Association for Disability and Rehabili-tation (RADAR)**, 12 City Forum, 250 City Road, London EC1V 8AF, T020-7250 3222, F020-7250 0212, www.radar.org.uk, who publish *Holidays in Britain and Ireland*, an annual guide on travelling in the UK (£8.00 including p&p within UK; £11 to Continen-tal Europe, £15 rest of the world).

Another useful contact is **Artsline**, T020-7388 2227, www.dircon.co.uk/artsline, which has detailed information and publications on arts, attractions and entertainment for disabled people in London. The **Royal National Institute for the Blind**, T020-7388 1266, publishes a *Hotel Guide Book* for blind and partially sighted people. They also have maps for the blind of London and other cities.

Gay and lesbian

The Soho area, and particularly Old Compton Street (see page 85), is the hub of Lon-don's gay community and is probably a good place to head for initially. Meeting places, clubs and bars are widely advertised in listings magazine *Time Out*, and in gay publica-tions such as the free weekly *Boyz*, *Pink Voice* or *Outcast Magazine*. *Rainbow Tickets* publishes weekly listings of gay events. Gay maps of London are also available.

London has a flourishing gay scene & is generally an easy place for gay travellers to feel safe & comfortable

London's calendar of gay and lesbian events is busy, particularly in the spring and sum-mer with the **London Lesbian and Gay Film Festival** (from 28 March, 2001), and the **Mardi Gras Parade and Party** (30 June, 2001) which, after 30 years, has become somewhat of an institution. It is preceded, in the last two weeks of June, by the **Mardi Gras Arts Festival**, which won't happen in 2001 but is back in 2002.

For the London Lesbian & Gay Film Festival: www.llgff. org.uk For Mardi Gras T020-7494 2225

For a good selection of gay events and venues, check out **www.whatsonwhen. com** or the London and UK gay-scene index at **www.queenscene.com** which has information on clubs, gay groups, accommodation, events, HIV/AIDS and cultural and ethical issues. It also has listings and information on sightseeing, museums, markets, emergency services and many others, and a useful directory of about 70 London cybercafés in different areas of the capital listed by area, postcode and tube station.

Other good sites include: **www.gaybritain.co.uk** a collection of websites with infor-mation and entertainment especially for gays in Britain; **www.rainbownetwork.com** a magazine-style gay and lesbian site; and **www.gaypride.co.uk**

Further listings of gay and gay-friendly holiday accommodation are published at **www.londongay.co.uk**, **www.kitsch.freeserve.co.uk/hotel/london.htm**; and at **www.gaytravel.co.uk**

Essentials

Essentials

Sightseeing tours

Big Bus Company, 48 Buckingham Palace Road, SW1, T020-7233 9533, www.bigbus.co.uk   Daily sightseeing tours from hop-on, hop-off, open-top double-decker buses. Tickets include a free river cruise and a choice of walking tours. The commentary is live, or else digitally recorded in 12 languages. £15 adults, £6 children.

Black Taxi tours of London, T020-7289 4371, www.blacktaxitours.co.uk Sightseeing tours in licensed taxi cabs. Commentary from trained London 'cabbies'. Two-hour day and night tours. Pick-up and return to hotel. Costs £70 for up to five people.

Evans Evans Tours, T020-7950 1777, www.evansevans.co.uk Half- and full-day coach tours of London with stop-offs at key sights. Prices start at £17 for adults (£14.50 for children between 3 and 16). Sightseeing trips to major tourist destinations outside London also available, as are tours in Japanese and Spanish.

London Frog Tours, T020-7928 3132, www.frogtours.com Starting at County Hall, these 'road and river' tours of London last 80 minutes in bright yellow amphibious vehicles. The Frogs 'splash down' into the Thames at Lacks Dock Vauxhall and the river part of the tour lasts about 30 minutes. Tours cost £12 for adults and £9 for children; family tickets are also available.

Driver-guides operating general and special-interest tours for individuals and small groups in and around London are another option. The Driver-Guides Association (DGA), T020-8874 2745, www.driver-guides.org.uk, can provide details of professional blue-badge driver-guides throughout the country.

William Forrester, T01483-575401, a museum lecturer and London **Blue Badge Guide** leads tours in London and the UK for **able bodied and disabled people** (groups and individuals). The guide is himself a wheelchair user.

Safety

Generally speaking, London is a safe place to visit, though, like in any big city, sensible precautions need to be taken to guard against pickpockets. Even at night you should feel relatively safe as there are usually plenty of people milling about, especially around Soho, Leicester Square and Piccadilly. Places to be especially vigilant against pickpockets are in tube stations and while travelling on the tube. Assault in Central London is comparatively rare, though women travellers are advised never to get into an empty tube carriage on their own. You should also avoid deserted and unlit streets at night.

The greatest annoyance in Central London is likely to be the unwanted attention of drunks, particularly at the weekend. Depending on your sensibilites, you'll probably find this amusing, or at worst, slightly irritating. It often consists of someone sitting next to you on the night bus or last tube, off their face and trying to chat you up before falling asleep on your shoulder and dribbling, or perhaps puking up on your shoes. Rather more worrying is if you're stuck in a tube carriage on your own with a nutcase screaming obscenities in your general direction. Best thing to do in this situation is to simply get off at the next populated station platform. Other popular places for freaks, or those intent on harm, are any of the city's parks or open spaces, and these should be avoided after dark.

Trafalgar Square late at night can be a bit chaotic, as this is where most revellers congregate to try and remember which night bus they should be taking, but in reality the most dangerous people around here are those selling distinctly dodgy-looking hot dogs.

London Tourist Board's Phone Guide

*The LTB has a **recorded information service**, available 24 hours a day (from within the UK only), with up-to-date information on events, exhibitions, theatres, places to visit, etc. **Calls cost 60p per minute**. To access this service, dial T09064-123 plus the last three digits as shown:*

What's on

What's on this week	400
What's on - next three months	401
London parks	406
Christmas & Easter	418
Changing the Guard	411
Current exhibitions	403
Rock & pop concerts	422
Lord Mayor's Show, State Opening of Parliament & Trooping the Colour	413

Out & about

Travel in London	430
River trips/boat hire	432
Guided tours & walks	431
Getting to the airports	433
Shops & stores	486
Street markets	428
Eating out	485
Gay & lesbian London	09068 141120

Theatre

West End shows	416
Non-West End shows	434

Where to take children

What's on	404
Places to visit	424

Places to visit

Museums & galleries	429
Palaces (including Buckingham Palace)	481
Attractions in Greenwich	482
Famous houses & gardens	483
Other attractions	480
Day trips from London	484

Accommodation

General advice	435

To receive information by fax on the following topics, dial the number on a fax machine and press start/receive after the tone, or set the fax machine to polling mode.

Major events	09068 353715
Events in London	09068 353716
Changing the Guard	09068 353718
Booking a tour guide	09068 353719
River trips schedule	09068 353720
Shops and stores	09068 353721
Eating out	09068 353722

Essentials

Tourist information

All tourist offices provide information on accommodation, public transport, local attractions and restaurants. They also sell books, guides, maps and souvenirs. Many provide free street plans and leaflets describing local attractions. They can also book accommodation for you for a small fee.

Contact the London Tourist Board (LTB), T020-7932 2000, www.londontown.com or drop in at one of the following centres:

For details of the LTB's recorded information service, see box above

Britain Visitor Centre, 1 Regent Street, SW1. Open all year, Monday 0900-1830, Tuesday-Friday 0930-1830, Saturday and Sunday 1000-1600 (June-October Saturday 0900-1700).

Heathrow Terminals 1,2,3 Underground Station Concourse, Heathrow Airport, TW6 2JA. Open daily 0800-1800 (1 June-30 September 0800-1900, Sunday 0800-1800).

Liverpool Street Underground Station, EC2. Open daily 0800-1800 (1 June-30 September 0800-1900, Sunday 0800-1800).

Victoria Station Forecourt, SW1. Open Easter-31 May Monday-Saturday 0800-2000, Sunday 0800-1800; 1 June-30 September Monday-Saturday 0800-2100, Sunday 0800-1800; 1 October-Easter daily 0800-1800.

Waterloo International Terminal, Arrivals Hall, SE1. Open daily 0830-2230.

Travel information is available at London Transport Travel Information Centres, see page 41.

Discount passes

The **London Pass** covers entry to over 60 varied attractions from the Tower of London and the London Dungeon to river boat rides and ten-pin bowling. Prices start at £17.50 for a one-day adult pass and £12 for children. It can be purchased online at www.londonpass.com or at London Transport and Tourist Information Centres and at Exchange International bureaux de change.

The **GoSeeCard**, www.london-gosee.com, a one-, three- or seven-day discount pass gives visitors access to around 17 London museums and galleries. The card costs £10, £16 or £26 per adult; a family card (two adults and up to four children) is also available at £32 for three days or £50 for seven days. But before buying it, make sure you will get you money's worth, you'd need to see at least two museums per day (check prices in individual entries) - bear in mind that some of the big museums and galleries don't charge, and that in other cases (for example the Natural History and Science Museums) entry is free for children and senior citizens.

Where to stay

For a full list of accommodation, see Sleeping on page 439

London is not a cheap place to visit, and this is particularly the case when it comes to finding a place to stay. Accommodation will represent a substantial proportion of your budget. In fact, aside from the air fare, it will be your greatest expense.

For disabled facilities, see page 36

Those with plenty of cash to spare will some find wonderful hotels to choose from, many of which boast very fine restaurants, but those on a tight budget will be hard pushed to find reasonably comfortable accommodation for less than £25-30 per person. If you fall into the latter category, then you're best bet is Earl's Court, where there are numerous hotels at the cheaper end of the market, especially on Barkston Gardens. The area around Victoria train station is also full of small hotels, and there are there are several very cheap options near King's Cross, though this is not the most salubrious of districts.

www.yha.org.uk Youth Hostel Association (YHA) website with information & on-line booking facilities for London's seven YHA hostels

Those trying to get by on the tightest of budgets should try the The seven YHA London hostels, which are well spread out around the city. All are open 24 hours and charge between £20 and £24 per night; some include breakfast in the price; some provide rooms with en suite facilities. Also check out the halls of residence of the various universities, where student rooms are let during vacation. Details are given under the individual halls of residence listing in the Sleeping chapter.

Getting around

Public transport is generally fairly efficient, although it can be expensive. Fortunately, there's a whole raft of discount passes and tickets which can cut the price considerably (see page 42). **London Transport Travel Information Centres** provide free travel advice, maps and timetables. They also sell travelcards and bus passes as well as guide books, sightseeing tours and entry tickets to many London attractions.

Youth Hostel Associations

Australia *Australian Youth Hostels Association, 422 Kent Street, Sydney, T02-92611111.*
Canada *Hostelling International Canada, Room 400, 205 Catherine Street, Ottowa, ON K2P 1C3, T800-6635777.*
England & Wales *Youth Hostel Association (YHA), Trevelyan House, 8 St Stephen's Hill, St Albans, Herts AL1 2DY, T0870-8708808, www.yha/england/wales/org.uk*
France *FUAJ, 7 Rue Pajol, 75018 Paris, T1-4498727.*
Germany *Deutsches Jugendherbergswerk, Hauptverband, Postfach 1455, 32704 Detmold, T5231-74010.*
Ireland *An Oige, 61 Muntjoy Street,*

Dublin 7, T01-8304555, www.irelandyha.org
New Zealand *Youth Hostels Association of New Zealand, PO Box 436, Christchurch 1, T03-379970.*
Northern Ireland *Youth Hostel Association of Northern Ireland, 22 Donegal Road, Belfast BT12 5JN, T01232-324733.*
Scotland *Scottish Youth Hostel Association (SYHA), 7 Glebe Crescent, Stirling FK8 2JA, T01786-451181, www.syha.org.uk*
USA *Hostelling International-American Youth Hostels (HI-AYH), 733 15th Street NW, Suite 840, PO Box 37613, Washington DC 20005, T202-7836161, www.hostel.com*

There are five Travel Information Centres in London underground stations (Heathrow 1,2,3, King's Cross, Liverpool Street, Oxford Circus and St James's Park), three at National Rail stations (Euston, Paddington and Victoria), several at bus stations, including Hammersmith, and also in the arrival halls of Terminals 1, 2 and 3 at Heathrow Airport.

For 24-hour information about London Transport, call T020-7222 1234, or T020-7918 3015 (recorded information), www.transportforlondon.gov.uk Travel information and advice for **disabled travellers** is available on T020-7918 3312.

By tube

The London underground, or tube, is the fastest way of getting around town and most Londoners use it. The 12 lines are colour coded, the map (see page 512) is easy to follow and the system is relatively straightforward to use. However, it is worth avoiding during rush hour (0800-0930 and 1700-1830) if at all possible. Crime is not a serious problem on the tube in Central London although, as with anywhere else, beware of pickpockets and don't choose an empty carriage, especially at night. Services run from 0530 until just after midnight. Fewer trains run on Sundays and public holidays.

The underground is divided into six **fare zones**, with Zone 1 covering central London. Travel between two stations in Zone 1 costs £1.50 (child 60p); a journey crossing into Zone 2 will cost £1.90 (child 80p). Anyone planning to make more that two journeys in one day will save money by buying a Travelcard (see box page 42). Tickets can be purchased from a ticket machine or ticket office at any underground station. Keep hold of your ticket after you have passed through the electronic barrier, you will need it to exit at your destination.

Smoking is not permitted on the underground

The **Docklands Light Railway (DLR)**, operating as part of the tube system, runs from Bank and Tower Gateway to the Cutty Sark for Maritime Greenwich and beyond. It is a scenic route, passing through the revived Docklands area and Canary Wharf and can be used by travelcard holders (see box page 42). Guided tours on weekend services make a good (and cheap) tour option.

Essentials

London Transport Travelcards

London Transport issues several types of Travelcard which allow you to make unlimited journeys within the zones you have selected on the underground, buses, Docklands Light Railway (DLR), Tramlink and most National Rail sevices within Greater London. The cost of your ticket depends on the number of zones your journey covers.

One-Day Travelcards cost £4 for Zones 1 and 2 and are valid from 0930 Monday-Friday on the day of validity (0001 on Saturday, Sunday and public holidays). They can also be used on night buses.

Weekend Travelcards cost £6 for Zones 1 and 2 and are valid all day on Saturday and Sunday (from 0001 on the first day of validity). They can also be used on two consecutive days during public holidays and are valid on night buses (during the night following the first day of validity only).

Family Travelcards are well worthwhile for groups of one or two adults travelling with up to four children. Members of the group must travel together at all times. For Zones 1 and 2, the cost is £2.60 for adults and 80p for each child.

Seven-Day Travelcards costing £18.90 (£7.70 for children over 5) can be used at any time for seven consecutive days. Photocards are needed.

Carnets are books of 10 single underground tickets for use in **Zone 1 only**. They cost £11.50 (£5 for children), saving £3.50 on the cost of buying 10 single adult tickets, and £1 in the case of children.

Bus passes costing £3 (£1 for children) for one day, or £11.50 (£4 for children) for seven days give unlimited bus travel but are not valid on the night buses (ie after 0030). You'll need a photocard for the seven-day pass.

DLR Sail and Rail tickets combine one day's unlimited travel on Docklands Light Railway (T020-7363 9700) with a riverboat trip from either Westminster Pier or Greenwich Pier. Tickets cost £8.30 (£4 for children), can be bought from Tower Gateway information point or Westminster Pier, and give discounted entry at various attractions.

Child rates apply to anyone between 5 and 15; 14 and 15 year olds need a child photocard for most passes and travelcards.

Youth passes are available for 16 and 17 year olds (photocard needed). **Groups** of more than 10 people are also eligible for discounts. **Monthly** and **annual** travelcards are also available.

By bus

The No 11 bus route is one of the best sightseeing trips in town, see page 150

The big, red double-decker buses, introduced in 1959, are a London institution, part of the fabric of the city. But other buses now run alongside them and, no matter where you are in London, there will always be a bus route nearby. Bus stops are either compulsory or request stops. Buses always stop at **compulsory stops** (red symbol on a white background) unless they are full; at **request stops** (white symbol on a red background) they will only stop if you put out your hand. To get off at a request stop, ring the bell once and in good time to let the driver know.

Daytime buses, like the London underground, run until about 0030. After that, an extensive system of **night buses** takes over. Most areas of Greater London are within easy reach of at least one night bus service. All night bus route numbers start with the letter 'N'. All stops are treated as request stops at night so remember to signal clearly when you want to get on or off the bus. Most of the central London night buses pass through Trafalgar Square (see box). The standard single Zone 1 night bus fare is £1.50.

Buses are a great way of getting to know the city, especially from the top deck, but please note that traffic congestion is a serious problem in London and it may take substantially longer to reach your destination by bus than by tube.

Night buses

Night buses run hourly along more than 50 routes from about 2300 until dawn; most pass through Trafalgar Square, a good place to head for if you are unsure of which bus you need. The **Central London Bus Guide**, which includes a night bus map, is provided free at Travel Information Centres (see previous page). Alternatively, call **London Transport Information**, T020-7222 1234 (lines are very busy).

The following is a selection of ten popular routes:

N5 Trafalgar Sq – Hampstead – Hendon – Edgware

N9 Aldwych – Trafalgar Sq – Hammersmith – Putney – Richmond – Kingston

N11 Liverpool St – Trafalgar Sq – Fulham – Hammersmith – Wembley

N12 Notting Hill Gate – Trafalgar Sq – Elephant – Camberwell – Peckham – Dulwich

N14 Tottenham Court Rd – Piccadilly Circus – Fulham – Putney – Roe Hampton

N31 Camden Town – Kilburn – Kensington – Earl's Court – Chelsea – Clapham Junction

N52 Victoria – Trafalgar Sq – Notting Hill – Ladbroke Grove – Willesden

N97 Trafalgar Square – Earl's Court – Hammersmith – Hounslow – Heathrow Airport

N159 Marble Arch – Trafalgar Sq – Brixton – Streatham – Croydon – New Addington

N207 Holborn – Shepherd's Bush – Ealing – Southall – Uxbridge

By boat

Daily services operate from most central London piers. Riverboats travel to and from Greenwich and the Thames Barrier in the east, and as far as Hampton Court in the west. There are over 20 piers along this stretch of the Thames and apart from Hampton Court Palace and the sights at Greenwich, the river gives access to Kew Gardens, Richmond Park and many of the central London attractions. Tickets for most trips can be bought at the pier or, in some cases, on the boat.

Sail and Rail tickets (see box, page 42) can be used on the direct, 50-minute Westminster to Greenwich route, operated by **Westminster Passenger Services**, T020-7930 4097. Otherwise a single adult ticket costs £6.30 (return £7.60). There are concessions for children and senior citizens and family tickets are also available. The 50-minute 'Multilingual Circular Cruises', with a taped commentary in seven languages, operate from Waterloo and Embankment piers and are run by **Catamaran Cruisers**, T020-7987 1185, www.catamarancruisers.co.uk Tickets cost £6.70 (adults), £4.70 (children) with concessions for students and senior citizens. Other one-hour long **Circular Cruises**, T020-7936 2033, leave from Westminster Pier and cost £5.80 for adults and £2.90 for children. For the 3½-hour Westminster-Kew-Richmond-Hampton Court route, contact **Westminster Passenger Service Association (Upriver)**, T020-7930 2062, www.wpsa.co.uk This service doesn't run between 30 October and 1 April. Shorter 25-30-minute trips between Westminster Pier and Tower Pier are operated by **City Cruises**, T020-7237 5134. Adults pay £4.80 single, £6 return; children are £2.40 single and £3 return.

Other riverboat options are the **lunch and dinner cruises** operated by: **Woods River Cruises**, T020-7480 7770, www.woodsrivercruises.co.uk; **Bateaux London**, T020-7925 2215, www.bateauxlondon.com; and **City Cruises**, T020-7237 5134, www.citycruises.com

For further information, go to www.canalmuseum. org.uk/tripboat.htm

Several companies offer trips on traditional narrow boats along **Regent's Canal** between Camden Lock and Little Venice taking in Regent's Park and London Zoo: *London Waterbus Company*, T020-7482 2660; *Jenny Wren*, T020-7485 4433 (also operate a restaurant boat, *My Fair Lady* for private charters); and *Jason's Canal Boat Trip*, T020-7286 3428.

By taxi

The famous London black cabs are almost as much of an institution as the old, double-decker buses. Licensed cabs can be hailed in the street when the yellow 'For Hire' sign is displayed; they all have meters which start ticking as soon as you get in, and fares increase by the minute thereafter. Surcharges are added late at night and for luggage or extra passengers. Most 'cabbies' will expect a tip of between 10 and 15%. Any comments or complaints should be made to the Public Carriage Office, T020-7230 1631, whilst lost property should be reported to T020-7833 0996 (make a note of your taxi's licence number and the driver's badge number). For 24-hour **Radio Taxis**, call T020-7272 0272.

If in doubt, it's best to stick to black cabs – at least they know their way around the city

As well as black cabs there are also regular taxis, which are known as minicabs. It is advisable to book these directly from the cab office, as there are many unlicensed cab drivers operating in Central London. Minicabs can be more economical, especially during busy times, as they charge a flat fee for the journey instead of using a meter, but you will need to know the going rate for a particular journey in order to avoid being ripped off.

By car

If you are only planning to spend a short time in London, don't bother hiring a car, it's not worth it. Traffic-clogged central London is a nightmare to drive in. Indeed, Londoners themselves tend to use public transport during the day, saving their cars for night and weekends. Apart from the heavy traffic and complicated web of one-way streets, parking is hard to find and exorbitantly expensive. Beware of parking illegally as you are likely to get a ticket or else be clamped or towed away and impounded (in which case you should call T020-7747 4747). This can set you back anywhere between £60 and £205 (although there's 50% reduction for prompt payment of parking tickets). Driving in London at weekends is less daunting and there is no problem finding free parking spaces in central London on Sundays and bank holidays.

Rules & regulations
www.dvla.gov.uk has details on every aspect of driving in the UK

To drive in the UK you must have a current driving licence. Although foreign nationals may use their own licence for one year, international driving permits, available from your country of origin, may be required for some rentals, especially if your own licence is not in English. Visitors importing their own vehicle should also have their vehicle registration or ownership document. Make sure you're adequately insured. In all of the UK you **drive on the left**. **Speed limits** are 30 miles per hour (mph) in built-up areas, 70 mph on motorways and dual carriageways and 60 mph on most other roads.

Motoring organizations
The AA & RAC websites are excellent for route planning

It's advisable to join one of the main UK motoring organizations during your visit for their **24-hour breakdown assistance**. The two main ones in Britain are the *Automobile Association* (AA), T0800-444999, www.theaa.co.uk, and the *Royal Automobile Club* (RAC), T0800-550550, www.rac.co.uk. One year's membership starts at £43 for the AA and £39 for the *RAC*. They also provide many other services, including a reciprocal agreement for free assistance with many overseas motoring organizations. Check to see if your organization is included. Both companies can extend their cover to include Europe. Their **emergency numbers** are: *AA* T0800-887766; *RAC* T08000-828282. You can call these numbers even if you're not a member, but you'll have to a pay a large fee.

Car hire companies

Britain Avis, T0870 6060100; Budget, T0800-181181; Best Hire, T020-7720 3535; Europcar, T0345-222525; Hertz, T0990-996699; Holiday Autos, T0870-4000011; National Car Rental, T020-7278 2273; Thrifty, T0990-168238.
North America Alamo, T800-5229696, www.goalamo.com; Avis, T800-3311084, www.avis.com; Budget, T800-5270700, www.budgetrentacar.com; Dollar,

T800-4216868, www.dollar.com; Hertz, T800-6543001, www.hertz.com; Holiday Autos, T800-4227737, www.holiday/colauto.com; National, T800-CAR-RENT, www.nationalcar.com; Thrifty, T800-3672277, www.thrifty.com
Australia Avis, T1800-225533; Budget, T1300-362848; Hertz, T1800-550067.
New Zealand Avis, T09-5262847; Budget, T09-3752222; Hertz, T09-3676350.

Essentials

Car hire/rental is expensive in London and you may be better off making arrangements in your home country for a fly/drive deal through one of the main multi-national companies. The minimum you can expect to pay is around £150 per week for a small car. Always check and compare conditions, such as mileage limitations, excess payable in the case of an accident, etc. Small, local hire companies often offer better deals than the larger multi-nationals. Most companies prefer payment with a credit card - some insist on it - otherwise you'll have to leave a large deposit (£100 or more). You need to have had a full driver's licence for at least one year and to be aged between 21 (25 for some companies) and 70. **Motorcycle hire** is very expensive, ranging from around £200 up to £350 per week.

Car hire

By bike

Cycle lanes are still not the norm in London and, compared with some European or Scandinavian cities, London is not an easy ride for cyclists. Make sure you always wear a helmet and never leave your bike unlocked. A 1000-mile cycle network is planned for the city and several organizations and direct action groups are continually pressing for improvements and to convince the Greater London Authority of the importance of making London more bicycle friendly.

Cycling.uk.com is a cycling information station with over 200 links to other useful sites

The best known is the **London Cycling Campaign**, T020-7928 7220 (Mon-Fri, 1400-1700 only), F020-7928 2318, www.lcc.org.uk Their magazine *London Cyclist*, publishes a diary of rides and related events for all London. They also publish the *Brand New Central London Map* (£4.95), a cycling map with traffic-free routes, safe cycle crossings and bike shops. Other publications include the *Ordnance Survey Cycle Tours Around London* (£9.99), which has 24 one-day routes within a 60-mile radius of the capital; and the *London Cycle Guide* by Nick Crowther (£8.99), which details 25 routes in and around the city.

The **London Bicycle Tour Company**, T020-7928 6838, www.londonbicycle.com, rent bikes with full insurance (helmets provided), and operate guided cycle tours along four different routes: *The Royal West Tour* (9 miles, 3 ½ hours on Sunday afternoons); *The Middle London Tour* (6 miles, 3 hours on Wednesday and Friday mornings); *The East Tour* (9 miles, 3 ½ hours on Tuesday and Thursday afternoons); and *The Market Excursion* (20 miles, 6 hours on Saturday mornings). Tours all leave from the company's base at Gabriel's Wharf, SE1, and cost between £11.95 and £14.95. You are advised to book in advance.

One other option for bike rentals is **Wheelie Serious**, T020-7487 3233 (see page 103).

Every summer thousands of people take part in long-distance cycle rides (often in aid of charity) from London to cities as far afield as Brighton, Paris and Brussels.

On foot

Be careful at all times of traffic travelling on the left-hand side of the road (ie look to your right before stepping off the pavement)

Walking is an excellent way to get to know London whether it be on your own with a map or book or as part of a group on an organized tour. More and more companies are running these tours, either pre-booked or regular, turn-up-and-go walks that leave from the same place at a fixed time every week. There are walks in the morning, after-noon or evening, seasonal walks, and dozens of special-interest walks, from Dickens and Jack the Ripper, to Bohemians and Bluestockings, to Bishops, Brothels and the Bard. There are also ghost walks, haunted pubs, mystery pubs, Clubland, and the Bee-tles, or perhaps Beautiful Belgravia, Hidden Hampstead and Little Venice... Most of these walks last between 1½ and 2 hours and cost about £5 for adults with discounts for students (accompanied children usually go free).

Also try www.london.walks.com

One of the best-known companies, *The Original London Walks*, T020-7624 3978, F020-7625 1932, www.london.walks.com, have over 40 walks to choose from. Some other companies are: *Guided Walks in London*, T020-7243 1097, www.walkslondon.co.uk; *Mystery Walks*, T020-8558 9446, www.mysterywalks.co.uk; and *Stepping Out*, T020-8881 2933.

Guided historical tours of the Houses of Parliament (see page 145) were introduced for the first time in 2000. For information, T020-7219 4272 (commons) and T020-7219 3107 (Lords).

Other enjoyable walks, if the weather is good, are around London's many parks, gardens and cemeteries. One of these is the circular **Diana Princess of Wales Memorial Walk**, a 7-mile route through St James's Park, Green Park, Hyde Park and Kensington Gardens. For more information: T020-7298 2000.

Police New Scotland Yard, Broadway, SW1, T020-7230 1212. Metropolitan Police HQ.

Entertainment and nightlife

Music

For a comprehensive guide to music venues in London, see the Entertainment & nightlife chapter, on page 403. It's also well worthwhile checking the newspapers & listings magazines to see what's on

It's true to say that in the field of popular music if you can't find what you're looking for in London then you probably won't find it anywhere. For London is without a doubt the musical capital of Europe offering every conceivable form of music in its various bars, clubs and auditoriums. Whether it's dance clubs or live music you want, you'll never be short of options. From the sixties through to the eighties London was known primarily for its live music, with the city being the main centre for pop and rock music outside America. Over the last decade live music, and rock in particular, have been taken over by dance music and nightclubs with clubbing now established as the pre-ferred social activity for London's young people.

Aside from clubs and dancing there is still a lot of live music to be enjoyed in the capital. If there is a centre for **rock music** in London then it's definitely **Camden Town** in North London. Famous primarily for its weekend market, Camden also has a number of pubs which feature live music in their back rooms and present new groups on the first step of the ladder. Such well known groups as Blur, Travis, Elastica, Suede and The Stereophonics, all got started by playing early gigs at Camden pubs and clubs like *The Dublin Castle* (Parkway, NW1), *The Monarch* (Chalk Farm Road, NW1), *The Underworld* (Camden High Street, NW1) and *Dingwalls* (Camden Lock, NW1). All of these venues can be found within a short walk of Camden Town tube station and feature live bands most nights of the week. Entrance will be no more than around £5 and drinks are at pub prices.

In the **West End** of London there's a mixture of different-size venues featuring rock music. *The Astoria* (Charing Cross Road, WC1) plays host to big name groups from the UK and abroad, whilst smaller venues like *The Borderline* (Orange Tree Yard St, WC1) feature up and coming groups. The centre of London and particularly **Soho** is definitely the place to head if you want to hear jazz in London. The main venue is the world famous *Ronnie Scotts* (Frith Street) which has been open for over 30 years and plays host to many of the biggest and the best of the jazz world. There's also *The Pizza Express Jazz Club* (Greek Street) in Soho where you can eat pizza and listen to very good jazz. Outside Soho the main jazz venue is the excellent *Jazz Café* in Camden (Parkway, NW1). This beautifully designed venue usually has more funky jazz, Latin music and soul with very good food served upstairs. On the weekends DJs also perform at the *Jazz Café* also features DJ's.

For those wanting **folk and blues** there's a number of long-standing small venues which cater exclusively to these types of music. The *12 Bar Club* has been running for decades and is situated in a back alley off Denmark Street in the West End hidden amongst the street's renowned selection of guitar and musical equipment shops. Here you can find would-be folk pickers and blues players most nights of the week in a very sympathetic and charmingly low-key environment.

London is one of the best places in Europe to hear excellent **classical music**. As well as being home to four world class orchestras and numerous notable ensembles, it also boasts some great venues, such as the South Bank Centre (which is really three venues in one), the *Royal Albert Hall* and the Wigmore Hall, to name but a few. **Opera** is best served by the *Royal Opera House* and the English National Opera at the *Coliseum*.

Calendar of events

Flora London Marathon 2001, from Greenwich, SE10, to The Mall, SW1; 22 April.   **Spring 2001**
Nearest tube: Greenwich/Embankment.
Chelsea Art Fair, Chelsea Old Town Hall, SW3; 26-29 April. Nearest tube: South Kensington.
Royal Windsor Horse Show, Home Park, Windsor; 9-13 May.
Chelsea Flower Show, Royal Hospital, Chelsea, SW3; 22-25 May (general public 24-25 May). Nearest tube: Sloane Square.

Biggin Hill International Air Fair, Biggin Hill Airfield, Kent; 2-3 June (date to be con-   **Summer 2001**
firmed). Nearest railway stations: Bromley South, Kent; Oxted, Surrey.
International Henley Royal Regatta, Henley-on-Thames, Oxfordshire; 4-8 June.
Royal Academy Summer Exhibition, Royal Academy of Arts, Piccadilly, W1; 5 June-13 August (date to be confirmed). Nearest tube: Piccadilly Circus.
Royal Academy Summer Exhibition, Royal Academy of Arts, Piccadilly, W1; 5 June-13 August. Nearest tube: Piccadilly Circus.
20th-Century Art & Design Fair, Olympia, W14; 6-10 June. Nearest tube: Kensington (Olympia).
Derby Day, Epsom, Surrey; 9 June.
The Queen's Birthday Parade - Trooping the Colour, Horse Guards Parade, SW1; 9 June. Nearest tube: Westminster.
Royal Ascot Race Meeting, Ascot, Berkshire; 19-22 June.
Covent Garden Flower Festival, Covent Garden Piazza, WC2; 20-24 June. Nearest tube: Covent Garden.

Essentials

Wimbledon Lawn Tennis Championships, All England Lawn Tennis Club, SW19; 25 June-8 July (no play on Sunday 1 July). Nearest tube: Southfields.

City of London Festival, various venues in the City of London; 26 June-19 July.

Hampton Court Palace Flower Show, Hampton Court Palace, Surrey; 3-8 July.

Greenwich & Docklands International Festival, various venues in Greenwich, SE10; 6-15 Jul. Nearest tube: Cutty Sark DLR (for Maritime Greenwich).

BBC Henry Wood Promenade Concerts, Royal Albert Hall, SW7; 20 July-15 September. Nearest tube: High Street Kensington.

Kensington Antiques Fair, Kensington Town Hall, W8; 17-19 August. Nearest tube: High Street Kensington.

Teddies 2001: British Teddy Bear Festival, Kensington Town Hall, W8; 26 August. Nearest tube: High Street Kensington.

Notting Hill Carnival, Ladbroke Grove, W10; 26-27 August. Nearest tube: Notting Hill Gate/Ladbroke Grove.

Autumn 2001   **Chelsea Antiques Fair**, Chelsea Old Town Hall, SW3; 14-23 September. Nearest tube: South Kensington.

Great River Race, Richmond to Island Gardens, River Thames; 15 September. Nearest tube: Richmond.

Thames Festival, between Westminster Bridge and Southwark Cathedral, River Thames; 16 September. Nearest tube: Waterloo/London Bridge.

Horse of the Year Show, Wembley Arena, Wembley; 26-30 September. Nearest tube: Wembley Park.

London Motor Show, Earl's Court, SW5; 17-28 October. Nearest tube: Earl's Court.

Trafalgar Day Parade, Trafalgar Square, WC2, 21 October. Nearest tube: Embankment.

London to Brighton Veteran Car Run, Hyde Park, W2; 4 November.

Lord Mayor's Show, through the streets of the City of London; 10 November.

Remembrance Day Service & Parade, Cenotaph, Whitehall, SW1; 11 November. Nearest tube: Westminster.

Fine Art & Antiques Fair, Olympia, W14; !2-18 November. Nearest tube: Kensington (Olympia).

Winter 2001-2002   **Christmas Without Cruelty Fayre**, Kensington Town Hall, Hornton Street, W8; 2 December (date to be confirmed). Nearest tube: High Street Kensington.

Christmas Tree, Trafalgar Square, WC2; 6 December-6 January. Nearest tube: Embankment.

New Year's Day Parade, Parliament Square, SW1 to Berkeley Square, W1; 1 January. Nearest tube: Westminster/Green Park.

48th London International Boat Show, Earl's Court, SW5; 3-13 January. Nearest tube: Earl's Court.

Chinese New Year Celebrations (Year of the Horse), Soho, W1, 17 February (date to be confirmed). Nearest tube: Leicester Square.

Spring 2002   **Head of the River Race**, Mortlake to Putney; 23 March. Nearest tube: Putney Bridge.

Flora London Marathon 2002, from Greenwich, SE10, to The Mall, SW1; mid-April (date to be confirmed). Nearest tube: Greenwich/Embankment.

Royal Windsor Horse Show, Home Park, Windsor; 15-19 May.

Summer 2002   **Biggin Hill International Air Fair**, Biggin Hill Airfield, Kent; 1-2 June (date to be confirmed).

The Queen's Birthday Parade - Trooping the Colour, Horse Guards Parade, SW1, 8 June (date to be confirmed). Nearest tube: Westminster.

Wimbledon Lawn Tennis Championships, All England Lawn Tennis Club, SW19; 24 June-7 July (no play on Sun 30 June). Nearest tube: Southfields.
International Henley Royal Regatta, Henley-on-Thames, Oxfordshire; 3-7 July.
BBC Henry Wood Promenade Concerts, Royal Albert Hall, SW7; 19 July-14 September. Nearest tube: High Street Kensington.
Farnborough International Exhibition & Flying Display, Farnborough Airfield, Hampshire; 22-28 July (date to be confirmed; last two days open to the public).
Notting Hill Carnival, Ladbroke Grove, W10; 25-26 August. Nearest tube: Notting Hill Gate/Ladbroke Grove.

Horse of the Year Show, Wembley Arena, Wembley; 2-6 October. Nearest tube: Wembley Park. **Autumn 2002**
Trafalgar Day Parade, Trafalgar Square, WC2; 21 October. Nearest tube: Embankment.
London to Brighton Veteran Car Run, Hyde Park, W2; 3 November.
Lord Mayor's Show, through the streets of the City of London; 9 November.
Remembrance Day Service & Parade, Cenotaph, Whitehall, SW1; 10 November. Nearest tube: Westminster.
Royal Smithfield Show, Earl's Court, SW1; 24-27 November. Nearest tube: Earl's Court.

Christmas Without Cruelty Fayre, Kensington Town Hall, Hornton Street, W8; 1 December. Nearest tube: High Street Kensington. **Winter 2002-2003**
Christmas Tree, Trafalgar Square, WC2; 5 December-6 January. Nearest tube: Embankment.

Food and drink

London is one of the world's great gastronomic centres. Here, you can sample the delights of pretty much every national and regional cuisine on this planet – from Welsh lava bread to Eritrean *injera*. The traditional view of British dining habits goes out the window in London and eating out in style is an essential part of any visit to this most cosmopolitan of cities.

Good (or rather bad) old-fashioned British stodge still exists and is served up as an excuse for a meal in all too many pubs. But fear not. If you follow the advice given in this guidebook, and stick to the many restaurants, cafés, bars and pubs recommended under the Eating and drinking sections of each district you won't be disappointed. In fact, you may return home to amaze your friends and families with the news that the British have learned how to enjoy good food.

Like any major tourist centre, London has its fair share of overpriced mediocrity, but this is easily avoided. For example, if you're shopping in the West End, a slight detour into the streets of Soho, choc-full of excellent bars, cafés and restuarants, offers refuge from the culinary wasteland of Oxford Street. Similarly, Chinatown's myriad restaurants are an appealing alternative to the bland chains of Piccadilly and Leicester Square. Just across Charing Cross Road, Covent Garden may look like a tourist trap, but has some tasty secrets up its sleeve, and if money's no object, then Mayfair's finest can deliver the goods with impeccable manners and no shortage of style. Red-blooded carnivores, meanwhile, should head for trendy Clerkenwell, where several chic eateries are taking advantage of neighbouring Smithfield meat market.

Beyond the West End and Central London there are many more treats in store. Wealthy areas such as Clapham in South London, Islington and Hampstead in the north and

★ Five of the best: markets

Those who love rooting around for a bargain won't be disappointed by London's markets. Everyone has their own favourite, but here are five of the best.

Spitalfields Market, Commercial Street, E1. Open Sunday 1100-1500. Clothes, books, paintings, organic food, jewellery, antiques, bric-a-brac.

Brick Lane, E1, Sundays 0700-1300. Mainly second-hand, including clothes, bric-a-brac, books, records and some furniture.

Camden Market, Camden High Street, NW1, Saturday and Sunday 0900-1700. Everything under the sun, with an accent on techno-clubby gear and retro clothing.

Greenwich, SE5, Sundays 0900-1700. Retro clothes, bric-a-brac, antiques, more for the retro purists than Camden.

Portobello Road, Notting Hill, W11. Fridays and Saturdays 0800-1800. Antiques at the beginning, then retro clothes, records, junk and books. Prices drop as you head into Golborne Road.

Notting Hill in the west boast many excellent eating establishments. Take note, however, that in some of the more painfully hip joints, style may rule over substance. Not so much 'you are what you eat' as 'you are where you're seen to eat'.

Alternatively, you can always set off in search of Britain's favourite dish – curry. Two districts in the city are *sans pareil* when it comes to Asian cuisine. Brick Lane, in the East End, is jam-packed with seriously good curry houses, where a full meal may stretch your waistline but not your budget. While way out west in Southall authentic Indian food comes so cheap they're practically giving it away.

Restaurants listed in the main text are divided into three categories: **expensive** (£40 and above); **mid-range** (£20-40) and **cheap** (£20 and under). These prices are based on a three-course meal for one, including service charge and one drink. Places which are considerably cheaper than £20 are described as such in the listing.

Shopping

There's little doubt that London is the shopping capital of Europe. Retail junkies can get their fix in any number of outlets specializing in everything from Cuban cigars to kinky underwear. If you can't find it here, then it probably doesn't exist.

Oxford Street is the most famous of the city's shopping streets and, judging by the sheer volume of people choking its pavements, the most popular, though its mainstream, and slightly tacky, approach may not be to everyone's taste. Rather more upmarket is the King's Road, Chelsea, a name once synonymous with the swinging sixties. It still boasts many stylish fashion shops though lacks the street cred of Camden and other parts of North London. Knightsbridge, meanwhile, is not for the faint-hearted, with chic designer outlets selling clothes at prices designed to shock. A good place for dedicated followers of fashion to head for is Covent Garden, whose narrow streets are full of trendy little shops, many selling cheap retro clothing.

If it's books rather than looks you're after, then get down to Charing Cross Road, where second-hand booksellers stack 'em (and occasionally price 'em) high, but which is a must-visit for specialist one-offs. Off Charing Cross Road is Denmark Street, London's number one for musical instruments, where lank-haired lads from the suburbs can be heard playing endless renditions of *Stairway to Heaven*. Nearby, Tottenham Court Road is lined with hi-fi shops catering for those who prefer to listen rather than play.

Sports

Whether it be the Oxford and Cambridge Boat Race in spring, strawberries and cream   Spectator
at Wimbledon in the summer, or a rugby match at Twickenham in the autumn, spectator sports in London can keep you on the edge of your seat at any time of the year.

Essentials

Football   For Londoners, football (soccer) is still the most popular spectator sport, at
least for men, that is. Tickets to see Premier League London clubs like Arsenal, Chelsea,
Tottenham Hotspurs or West Ham can be pretty hard to come by; for information try
calling the Football Association, T020-7262 4542, the Premier League, T020-7298 1600
or the Football League, T01772-325800, for games in one of the other three League
divisions. Tickets for Premiership matches start at about £20.

The Oxford and Cambridge Boat Race   You can witness this traditional contest for
supremacy between England's two most famous universities from either bank of the
Thames along the whole length of the course, but the best viewpoints are Putney
Bridge, Putney Embankment and Bishops Park at the start of the race, Hammersmith
and Barnes in the middle, and Dukes Meadows and Chiswick Bridge at the finish.

Rugby   Twickenham Rugby Football Ground, T020-8744 3111 (ticket information
line), hosts the main national and international matches. The season last from early
September to April (although a few matches may run into May).

Cricket, the definitive summer sport, is played from April to September. London's two
main grounds are the Oval, SE11, T020-7582 7764, and Lord's Cricket Ground, NW8,
T020-7432 1066. Test Match tickets usually need to be bought well in advance, but you
should be able to get seats for county matches on the day.

Greyhound racing   makes for a fun and different night out. Most tracks hold two or
three meetings a week and the first race is usually at around 1930. Most easily accessible from central London are the tracks at Walthamstow, Chingford Road, E4,
T020-8531 4255 (Walthamstow Central tube), and Wimbledon, Plough Lane, SW19,
T020-8946 8000 (Wimbledon Park tube). Both have restaurant and bar facilities.

Horse racing   You'll need to travel a bit further to put your money on the horses. The
nearest racetracks to the capital are a shortish train ride away at Ascot, T01344 622211;
Epsom, T01372-726311; Sandown Park, T01372-463072; and Windsor, 01753-865234.
Admission prices for the general public start at about £6.

Tennis   If you want Centre Court or Court 1 seats for **Wimbledon** you'll need to contact
the All England Lawn Tennis Club, Church Road, SW19, T020-8946 2244, at least six
months in advance. Otherwise you can get there early and queue on the day (some people camp out overnight) to watch play on the outside courts. Determined fans can usually buy cut-price returned tickets later in the afternoon for some Centre Court action.

London's parks are a good place to head for if you want outdoor sports. There are ath-   Participant
letics tracks, public tennis courts, cycling and rollerblading tracks, football, rugby,   *Details of sport &*
cricket, hockey and softball pitches. **Horse riding** in Hyde Park, T020-7723 2813, is   *leisure facilities are*
available at £30 per hour (with an escort). You can also ride in Richmond Park and on   *given under each area*
Hampstead Heath. **Boating** is popular too on the lakes in Hyde Park, Regent's Park and
Battersea Park.

For further information on available sports in London, contact Sportsline, T020-7222 8000.

Indoor sports such as badminton, squash and swimming are available at public sport and leisure centres. The local tourist board will tell you which is the nearest, or you can call Sportsline. Most leisure centres have fitness rooms and gym facilities and run martial arts, yoga, exercise and other classes. **Outdoor swimming** is available in the summer only in Hyde Park (Serpentine Lido, T020-7298 2100), Hampstead Heath Ponds (T020-7485 4491, entry free) and Richmond Pools on the Park (T020-8940 0561).

To find out about sports facilities for disabled people, call the London Sports Forum, T020-7354 8666 (minicom 020-7354 9554)

For the first time, in 2000 winter **open-air ice skating** was possible for a couple of months in the 18th-century courtyard at Somerset House (see page 71). Tickets cost £6 for adults and £4 for children including skate hire. It is likely to become a regular feature, but check first on T020-7845 4600. The Broadgate Ice Rink, near Liverpool Street tube station, T020-7505 4068, is another open-air option (open until April). Entry costs £5 for adults (plus £2 skate hire) and £3 for children (plus £1 for skates). There are also year-round **indoor ice rinks** at Broadgate, T020-7505 4068 (Liverpool Street tube); Leisurebox, T020-7229 0172 (Queensway tube); and Streatham, T020-8769 7771 (Streatham Station, South London).

There are several options for **dry-slope skiing** too: Alexandra Palace Ski Centre, T020-8888 2284; Crystal Palace Ski School, T020-8778 0131; Hillingdon Ski Centre, Uxbridge, T01895-58506; Profiles Ski Centre, Orpington, T01689-78239; Woolwich Ski Slope Army Barracks, T020-8317 1726.

For **watersports** such as sailing, canoeing, rowing and Chinese dragon-boat racing (no power sports), contact Docklands Sailing & Watersports Centre, T020-7537 2626 (Crossharbour and London Arena DLR station).

Serious runners wanting to enter the **Flora London Marathon** (26 miles from Greenwich and Blackheath to The Mall), in April each year, should apply to enter a ballot. Entry forms are distributed in *Marathon News* (a free magazine available in specialist sports stores). Overseas visitors wanting to receive copies of the entry form should send a self-addressed envelope (stating the number you require), with two international reply coupons to: Overseas Entry Co-ordinator, 91 Walkden Road, Walkden, Manchester, M28 7BQ, England. All entry forms for the 2002 Marathon must be submitted for ballot between 1 August and 19 October 2001.

Keeping in touch

Communications

Internet
Many hotels now have email access. Some hostels also offer Internet access to their guests. Websites and email addresses are listed where appropriate in this guide. The British Tourist Authority (www.visitbritain.com) and London Tourist Board (www.londontown.com) have their own websites. A few of London's many **cybercafés** are listed on the next page.

Post
Most **post offices** are open Monday-Friday 0900 to 1730 and Saturday 0900 to 1230 or 1300. Many smaller sub-post offices operate out of a shop.

Stamps can be bought at post offices and from vending machines outside as well as from many newsagents and supermarkets. A first-class letter to anywhere in the UK costs 26p and should arrive the following day, while second-class letters cost 19p and take between two and four days. Airmail letters of less than 20g cost 36p to Europe. To

Cybercafés

The are Internet cafés all over London where you can access the internet and pick up your email. **easyEverything**, probably the biggest and cheapest option (access from £1), has five locations in central London (open 24 hours). 9-16 Tottenham Court Road (Oxford Street end); 7 Strand (Trafalgar Square end); 358 Oxford Street (opposite Bond Street tube station); 9-13 Wilton Road, Victoria (opposite main line station); 160-166 Kensington High Street. **Dotcom Café**, 3-5 Thorpe Close, W10, T020-8964 5484, www.dotcom.uk.com As well as internet facilities, this is a snooker club, restaurant and bar, with live music,

near Ladbroke Grove tube station. **Global Café**, 15 Golden Square, W1, T020-7287 2242, www.globalcafe.net Fully licensed and with food as well, this is a good option if your in Piccadilly. Prices range from 50p for 5 mins. A £5-per-year membership fee gives free access. **For other options**, www.queenscene.com has a directory of about 70 cybercafés in different areas of the capital listed by area, postcode or nearest tube station. Local libraries often provide cheap or free internet access.

Essentials

the USA and Australia costs 45p for 10g and 65g for 20g. For more information about Royal Mail postal services, call T0845-740740.

Most public **payphones** are operated by British Telecom (*BT*) and are widespread throughout London. *BT* payphones take either coins (20p, 50p, £1 and occasionally £2) or **phonecards**, which are available at newsagents, post offices and supermarkets displaying the *BT* logo. These cards come in denominations of £3, £5, £10 and £20. Some payphones also accept credit cards (Delta, Visa and Diners Club). Calls are cheapest between 1800 and 0800 Monday-Friday and all day Saturday and Sunday.

Telephone
*Operator: T100
International
operator: T155
Directory enquiries:
T192 Overseas
directory enquiries:
T153*

The **phone code** for the whole of London is **020**. All old 0171 and 0181 phone codes have been replaced by 020; previous 0171 numbers are now prefixed with a 7, while 0181 numbers now begin with 8. You don't need to use the area code if calling from within London. Any number prefixed by **0800** or **0500** is free to the caller; **0345** and **0845** numbers are charged at local rates and **0990** numbers at the national rate. Premium rates, charged on numbers prefixed by **090**, vary from number to number and can be very high (up to £2 per minute from a public payphone); the operator (T100) will tell you how much your call will cost.

To **call London** from overseas, dial 011 from USA and Canada, 0011 from Australia and 00 from New Zealand, followed by 44, then 20 (ie the area code, minus the first zero), then the number.

To **call overseas from London** dial 00 followed by the country code and the number (minus the fist zero). Country codes include: **Australia** 61; **France** 33; **Ireland** 353; **New Zealand** 64; **South Africa** 27; **USA** and **Canada** 1.

Media

London is media central for the UK and you just can't escape it. There is a huge variety of national newspapers and competition between them is fierce. The national dailies are divided into two distinct camps; the **tabloids**, which are more downmarket; and the **broadsheets**, which are generally of a higher standard. Foreign visitors may find the broadsheets easier to understand as they tend to use less slang than the tabloids.

Newspapers

The broadsheets include *The Times* and *The Daily Telegraph*, which are politically conservative, and *The Guardian* and *The Independent*, which have more of a liberal/left-wing leaning. There's also the distinctively coloured and very serious *Financial Times*, which focuses on business and finance. The Saturday editions of these papers carry their own listings guides with useful reviews of movies, clubs, restaurants, theatre, etc. The broadsheets' Sunday versions are huge and would take most of your holiday to read thoroughly. They include the *Independent on Sunday*, *Sunday Times*, *Sunday Telegraph* and the *Observer* (a stablemate of *The Guardian*).

The list of tabloids (known also as redtops) comprises *The Sun* and *The Mirror* which are the most popular and provide celebrity gossip and extensive sports coverage, the *Daily Mail* and *Daily Express* which are right-wing and aimed directly at 'Middle England'. Then there's the *Daily Star* and *The Sport* and the less said about them the better. The tabloids have their own Sunday versions, which, are, if anything, even more salacious: these include the notorious *News of the World*; the *Sunday Mirror*, *Sunday People* and *Sunday Sport*.

London's daily is the *Evening Standard* with local news and views and a useful *ES Magazine* on Friday's which contains some good features.

Free publications, usually distributed at tube stations, include the daily *Metro*, which has listings for that evening including free things to do, or the magazines *TNT* and *Southern Cross* which also have listings and ads for good travel deals.

Foreign newspapers and magazines, including *USA Today* and *International Herald Tribune*, are available in larger newsagents. *Time* and *Newsweek* are also widely available.

Magazines   There are thousands of mags available and the choice is bewildering. The women's market is particularly saturated, and men's titles are growing, too. If you've got any kind of social consience, then you should buy *The Big Issue*, which is sold exclusively on the streets by the homeless and which also happens to be a good read. The best for a guide to what's on in London is *Time Out*, which also has some interesting features. Those looking for political comment of a left-wing nature should read the *New Statesman*, while *The Spectator* provides a right-wing viewpoint on the world. For a satirical, and very funny, look at British politics, check out the weekly *Private Eye*.

For music fans the *NME* gives reviews of gigs and new releases. The dashing gentleman about town should pick up his copy of *The Chap*, which provides the last word on sartorial elegance.

Television   There are five main television channels in the UK; the publicly funded BBC 1 and 2, and the independent commercial stations, Channel 4, Channel 5 and ITV. The ITV network in London includes Thames Television and London Weekend Television.

The rather limited offerings of the main five channels is greatly expanded by the various digital cable TV companies, such as *Sky Digital*, which currently has 170 channels, and *ONdigital*. These include movie channels such as *FilmFour*, *Sky Movies* and the *Movie Channel*, as well as sports-only channels like *Sky Sports*.

Radio   The BBC network also broadcasts several radio channels, most of which are based in London. These include: *Radio 1* (98.8 FM) aimed at a young audience; *Radio 2* (89.1 FM) targeting a more mature audience; *Radio 3* (91.3 FM) which plays mostly classical music; *Radio 4* (93.5 FM) which is talk-based and features arts, drama and current affairs; and *Radio 5 Live* (693, 909 MW) which is a mix of sport and news. *BBC London Live* (94.9 FM) is a talk-based station, a poor replacement for the much-missed *GLR* which was far and away the most intelligent radio station in the capital, if not the world (please bring it back!)

Hospitals and emergency services

Charing Cross Hospital, Fulham Palace Road, W6 8RF, T020-8846 1234

Chelsea Royal Hospital, Royal Hospital Road, SW3, T020-7730 0161

Guy's Hospital, St Thomas Street, SE1 9RT, T020-7955 5000

St Thomas's Hospital, Lambeth Palace Road, SE1 7EH, T020-7928 9292

Bliss Chemist, 5 Marble Arch, W1, open 0900-2400 daily.

In case of an emergency, dial T999 for an ambulance

Essentials

There is also a large number of local **commercial radio stations**, including *Capital FM* (95.8 FM) which is London's biggest station playing mainstream chart stuff. There's also *Jazz FM* (102.2 FM), which is far more eclectic than the name implies, and *XFM* (104.9 FM) for dedicated indie-kids.

Health

No vaccinations are required for entry into Britain. Citizens of **EU** countries are entitled to free medical treatment at National Health Service hospitals and health centres on production of an E111 form. Also, Australia, New Zealand and several other non-EU European countries have reciprocal health-care arrangements with Britain. You should encounter no major problems or irritations during your visit to London.

Medical emergency: dial 999 or 112 (both free) for an ambulance

Citizens of other countries will have to pay for all medical services, except accident and emergency care given at Accident and Emergency (A&E) Units at most (but not all) National Health hospitals. Health insurance is therefore strongly advised for citizens of non-EU countries.

Pharmacists (or chemists) can dispense only a limited range of drugs without a doctor's prescription. Most pharmacies are open during normal shop hours, though some are open late; *Bliss Chemist*, 5 Marble Arch, W1, open till midnight every day.

Doctors' surgeries are usually open from around 0830-0900 till 1730-1800, though times vary. Outside surgery hours you can go to the casualty department of the local hospital for any complaint requiring urgent attention. For the address of the nearest hospital or doctor's surgery, T0800-665544.

Useful websites

www.loot.com Over 100,000 adverts for bedsits, flats and houseshare; also jobs and personal chat on Loot café.

Accommodation

www.artguide.org Easy to navigate; organized by region, exhibition or museum.
www.tate.org.uk Good site with good-quality pictures.
www.nationalgallery.org.uk Very comprehensive.
npg.org.uk National Portrait Gallery site and one of the biggest on-line galleries. Extensive on-line shop for prints to buy.
www.sothebys.com Site of the prestigious art dealers; only for connoisseurs.
www.christies.com Tells you what's on but can't buy or sell on-line.

Art

Eating & drinking	**www.goodguides.com** Easy-to-use regional UK guide to the best pubs. **www.dine-online.co.uk** Good selection of recommended restaurants in London and rest of the UK.
Family history	**genuki.org.uk** Great place to start genealogical research, with loads of links.
Government	**http://open.gov.co.uk** Huge site devoted to UK government. It lists the top 10 sites and has a monarchy section at **royal.gov.uk**
Health	**www.healthfinder.com** US-based, with links to every conceivable health/fitness site. **www.patient.co.uk;** and **www.netdoctor.co.uk** Both excellent UK-based sites. **www.medinex.com** The best for up-to-date information.
Language courses	**www.englishinbritain.co.uk** Database including over 1500 English language courses offered throughout the UK. You can search by region, type of course, town/city or institution.
News	**www.bbc.co.uk/news** Excellent news service in several languages. The BBC site is the most popular in the UK and also features health, sport, education and history. **www.sky.co.uk/news** Another excellent news site. **www.thisislondon.com** With up-to-date news, business information and weather for London.
Sports	**www.bikemagic.com** Excellent site for cyclists with loads of links to other biking sites. **www.footballnews.co.uk** In-depth coverage. Also good is **www.football365.co.uk** **www.uk.cricket.org** Superb site for cricket. **www.sporting-life.com** Comprehensive site for all UK sports. **www.scrum.com** Rugby Union site; also see **www.planet-rugby.com** **www.wimbledon.org** Official Wimbledon tennis site.
Travel	**www.britishtravel.com** British Travel International has information and booking lines (in the USA) for transport in London and the rest of the UK. **www.thetube.com** The London Underground's webiste enables you to plan journeys and print out itineraries.
What's on	**www.bbc.co.uk** Huge site which includes an excellent what's on guide. **www.bigmouth.co.uk** UK's most comprehensive gig guide. Excellent search engine and you can buy tickets on-line. **www.localtoday.co.uk** Provides details of local events and allows you to search by village, town or city under 17 different event categories. You can also receive updates by email. **www.london.co.uk** Wacky tips and features on what's going down in the city. **www.ticketmaster.co.uk** Can book tickets for just about anything that's happening in London. Searches by venue or date. **www.timeout.com** The ultimate listings guide to what's on in London. **www.whatsonwhen.com** A world events guide with listings for London by date, interest and venue.

The West End

The West End

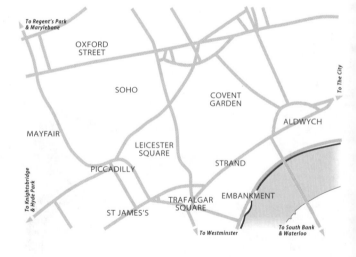

Trafalgar Square

Trafalgar Square is the centre of London, avoided by Londoners if at all possible.
It's the lynch pin of the West End's tourist triangle between Piccadilly Circus and
Leicester Square. On its north side, Pall Mall slides west while St Martin's Place
wiggles northwards to become Charing Cross Road. The Strand hurtles in the
from the east, but it's the breadth of Whitehall approaching from Westminster
and the south that explains the prominence of the square in London's geography.
This is where the administrative offices of government meet the people, and the
monarch comes too, with The Mall marching straight up from Buckingham Pal-
ace into the southwest corner through Admiralty Arch.

Charing Cross is the nearest tube & train station

   Nelson's Column*, Landseer's lions and the two large fountains give the*
square some dignity, inspiring a sense of occasion, and the fluttering flocks of dis-
ease-ridden pigeons are surprisingly popular pests. In a controversial move the
last birdseed sellers have recently had their licences revoked; it remains to be seen
how long the birds will stay on. Best of all though, if the planned pedestrianisation
of the north side of the square goes ahead, the whole place will become the grand
*front forecourt of the **National Gallery**, appropriate to one of the most impressive*
*collections of fine art in the world. Along with the **National Portrait Gallery***
behind it, these two treasure houses are the best reasons for a visit here, unless you
just want to sit around in the centre of things. During the day the square must be
one of the most polyglot places in town, teeming with visitors from every corner of
the globe. At night it becomes less inspiring, the embarkation point for night
buses, the last stage of an evening's entertainment for lots of drunken Londoners.

The West End

History

This area has always been an important crossroads and has become the place
from which all distances to London are measured. Seven hundred years ago, the
Abbot of Westminster's fields and gardens lay to the southwest, while Whitehall
was no more than a track heading south to the abbey itself. A road west, over the
River Tyburn and through fields, led to Knightsbridge. In Henry II's reign, the
church of St Martin-in-the-Fields in the northeast corner would have lived up
to its name. The king's mews occupied the area, housing falconers, clerks
(Geoffrey Chaucer among them), and later, under the Stuarts, court officials.

   The original site of the Charing Cross, the last of a series of crosses placed by
Edward I to commemorate the 12 resting places of his beloved Eleanor's
funeral procession (a 19th-century imitation of it now stands on the forecourt
of Charing Cross Station), is marked by a statue of Charles I, looking majesti-
cally down Whitehall towards his place of execution, Banqueting House. Propaganda is nothing new – Charles I was 5' 4", but the sculptor, Le Sueur, was
obliged by contract to ensure that 'the figure of his majesty King Charles pro-
portionate six foot'.

The area first won the title Trafalgar Square in 1835 in celebration of Horatio
Nelson's defence of British naval supremacy against Napoleon's navy at the
Battle of Trafalgar in 1805 – its redesign was the product of John Nash's
Charing Cross Improvement Scheme of the 1830s. Sir Edwin Landseer's lions
only finally settled at the column's base in 1867. They had caused the sculptor
endless difficulties after the ageing lion posing for him died, forcing Landseer
to use the decomposing corpse as a model.

Naval power has a recurring theme here, with statues of Admirals Cunningham, Jellicoe and Beatty, and Admiralty Arch – once the offices of the First Sea Lord – framing the entrance to The Mall. The square also has a history of political activism: the Chartists demanded constitutional reforms here in 1848; artist and writer William Morris and George Bernard Shaw joined a march against the Reform Bill in 1887, an event known as Bloody Sunday; the socialist writer George Orwell slept here in the course of his research for *Down and Out in Paris and London* and this is where the Poll Tax demonstration of 1990 turned nasty. Most recently, the 24-hour anti-apartheid vigil outside South Africa House was accorded gratitude by President Nelson Mandela.

Sights

Around the square

The square itself, hardly very beautiful, well designed, or even a proper square, does at least have a focal point in **Nelson's Column**. Admiral Horatio Nelson is just about the only military commander ever to have been truly taken to heart by the British people. Even so, it took 40 years after he was mortally wounded while defeating Napoleon's navy at Trafalgar before his Column was finally erected. In a fit of patriotic fervour in 1843, two days after the anniversary of the battle, 14 people ate a dizzy supper of rump steak on the top. Then the statue of the one-armed hero, three times life size and sporting his eye-patch and three-cornered hat, was hoist into position on his granite Corinthian column, facing southwest so that he could review the fleet in Portsmouth. Around the base the bronze relief sculptures were cast from captured French cannons, celebrating his sea victories at Copenhagen, the Nile, and Cape St Vincent, as well as Trafalgar.

Several other monuments in the square are more easily missed. In fact it's been suggested that some of the more obscure generals and admirals adorning the square be removed to a less central location to make way for more familiar characters. Set into the **north wall** on a bronze plate, between the statues of Admirals Jellicoe and Cunningham, are the definitive Imperial Standards of Length: the inch, the foot and the yard, solemnly marked out between stubby brass pegs. The inscription claims that the thing is accurate 'at 62 degrees Fahrenheit'. In the **southeastern corner** is 'the smallest police station in the world', a stone box that once contained a telephone linked to Scotland Yard, topped by a lamp from Nelson's flagship, 'The Victory'. In the **northeastern corner**, the equestrian statue of George IV in a toga was originally intended for the top of Marble Arch but no one has ever bothered to put it there.

Trafalgar Square

● Eating	● Pubs & bars
1 Cranks Express	3 Sherlock
2 Hampton's	Holmes
Wine Bar	

Walkabout in the West End

A common mistake many visitors to London make is to slavishly take the tube everywhere, when it would be far quicker to walk. This is especially true around the West End. For example, it only takes ten minutes to walk from Piccadilly Circus to Covent Garden, by which time the tube traveller would still be queuing for their ticket. Similarly, Tottenham Court Road tube station is only a ten-minute walk from Leicester Square, and Oxford Circus is a mere ten minutes on foot from Piccadilly Circus. However, on a Saturday afternoon you may want to consider taking a tube from Oxford Circus to Tottenham Court Road to avoid the hordes of shoppers.

The long-empty pedestal in the **northwest corner**, now known as the Fourth Plinth, has recently hosted a series of contemporary sculptures, the most controversial being Mark Wallinger's all-too-human life-sized 'Ecce Homo', a man wearing a loincloth and crown of thorns, dwarfed by his monumental position. The artist's request that the sculpture be illuminated for Christmas 1999 was denied. The Greater London Assembly hopes to preserve the site as a unique temporary public space for national and international contemporary art.

By spring 2001, Rachel Whiteread's 'Plinth' should be on show, an inverted & extruded version of the pedestal itself

The oldest and finest of the buildings surrounding the square is the **Church of St Martin-in-the-Fields**. Like St Mary-le-Strand nearby, but on a larger scale, it's an impressive fusion of classical and baroque by James Gibbs, dating from 1722-26. The interior is less remarkable, although beautifully proportioned, and includes a font from the original medieval church. There's a tacky tourist market in the churchyard at the back, near where notables such as Joshua Reynolds, Hogarth, and Charles II's mistress Nell Gwynne are buried. Regular concerts are also given here (see page 416) and there's an excellent café in the crypt (see Eating below) and brass rubbing centre. ■ *Open Mon-Fri 0745-1800, Sat 0845-1800, Sun 0745-1930. T020-7766 1100.*

Over Duncannon Street to the south, opposite the entrance to the church's crypt, is **South Africa House**, the home of the South African High Commission. Built in 1933, the exterior features various African animals carved in stone. The recently refurbished interior can be visited by pre-arranged groups. ■ *Open Mon, Wed & Fri 1100-1300, 1400-1600. T020-7451 7299.*

Anyone is welcome to use the library of all things South African in the Visitor Bureau

Continuing clockwise round the square, beyond Northumberland Avenue and Whitehall, is Admiralty Arch. Designed by Aston Webb in 1910, the triple-arched building provided a grand gateway to The Mall and Webb's new east front for Buckingham Palace as well as offices for the First Sea Lord, the commander of the Royal Navy. He has now moved out and the Arch has become government offices. Traffic goes through the arches on either side, the central arch being reserved for royal processions.

Canada House, at 5 Trafalgar Square, is the cultural arm of the Canadian Embassy. Formerly Royal College of Physicians and Union Club, it hosts art exhibitions in two galleries, with Canadian artists, Canadian music, library, Canadian newspapers, email for use by Canadians or anyone doing Canadian research. There might be free movies twice a week (for more information T020-7258 6421). ■ *Open Mon-Fri 1000-1800; library open Mon-Fri 1000-1300. T020-7258 6600 Canadian High Commission, www.dfait-maci. gc.ca/london*

National Gallery

Erika Langmuir's 'Companion Guide' to the collection is an excellent investment

Stretching along the north side of the square, and easily its most unmissable attraction, is the National Gallery, housing more than 2000 Western European paintings dating from the 13th century to 1900. The collection began with the purchase by the government in 1824 of 38 paintings from the financier John Julius Angerstein. Originally housed in Pall Mall, the present building was purpose built and completed by 1838. Artificial lighting, to extend the winter opening hours, was introduced as recently as 1935. The Sainsbury Wing, specially designed to house the earliest paintings, was finished in 1991. Today the gallery is pushed to cope with about five million visitors a year. Although it may not possess as many masterpieces as the Louvre, the Prado or the Hermitage, it glories in a comprehensive selection of outstanding work from all the great schools of European painting down the ages.

The main entrance is one of central London's favourite meeting places

The main entrance, up the steps beneath the grand portico and 'pepperpot' dome, overlooks Trafalgar Square, well above the traffic, and there's a great view past Nelson's Column down Whitehall towards the Palace of Westminster, enough to make you feel as though you really have found the middle of London. Unsurprisingly, it can get impossibly busy. Once inside, the bustle of bag-checking and orientation tends to distract visitors from the curious floor mosaics by **Boris Anrep**, on the stairway leading up to the central hall. Only completed in 1952 after nearly a quarter of a century's labour, they depict a weird cavalcade of early and mid-20th century celebrities personifying the Muses and 'Modern Virtues' such as Lucidity and Defiance. They're also the only examples of modern art permanently on show in the gallery. If you want to put them in the correct chronological order in which the rest of the Gallery's collection is arranged you'll need to save them for your exit, by starting a visit instead at the much less cramped side entrance at street level in the Sainsbury Wing.

The Sainsbury Wing: paintings from 1260-1510

On the ground floor of the Sainsbury Wing is the Gallery's main shop while the basement is reserved for special exhibitions. The stairs up to the main galleries take you past the Micro Gallery and Restaurant on the first floor. The **Micro Gallery** provides a free computerized pictorial database of the entire collection that allows visitors to find the locations of their favourite pictures, plan and print out a personalised tour, or browse through genres, periods, themes or artists. The 12 workstations are at their busiest during school term-time, at the weekends, and in the afternoons between 1300-1600, when access may be limited to 20 minutes.

The 16 rooms of the Sainsbury Wing, on the left at the top of the stairs, are broadly arranged in chronological order. In the first room, 51, the most significant exceptions are two masterpieces of the early Renaissance by **Leonardo da Vinci**. In a special alcove of its own, behind his *Virgin of the Rocks*, is the gallery's most fragile and precious possession, a charcoal and chalk cartoon on paper of *The Virgin and Child with St Anne and St John the Baptist*. Carefully restored after being attacked by a maniac with a shotgun in the 80s, the dim lighting establishes a suitably devotional mood. Most of the pictures in this wing have religious and devout themes, with a strong Italian and Dutch emphasis. Painted at a time when all western nations were under the Pope, they would look best in flickering candlelight.

One of the most significant early works, **Giotto**'s *The Pentecost*, executed in 1306, was the last in a series of seven panels for an Italian church altarpiece. The two figures in the foreground were almost certainly painted by the artist himself, as opposed to his assistants, and demonstrate the early moves he made towards three-dimensionality and psychological accuracy. One of the first oil paintings in the collection, **Jan van Eyck**'s meticulous *Arnolfini Marriage* uses the play of light to astonishing effect, right down to the tiny reflection of the painter himself at his easel in the convex mirror behind the complacent newly weds. The same artist's *Man in a Turban* could well be a self-portrait, inscribed with the motto 'As I can', an abbreviation of the Flemish proverb 'As I can, not as I would wish'.

> **Five of the best: West End sights**
>
> - *National Portrait Gallery*, Trafalgar Square.
> - *Courtauld Gallery*, Somerset House, Strand.
> - *Institute of Contemporary Art* (ICA), The Mall, St James's.
> - *Royal Opera House*, Covent Garden.
> - *St James's Park*, St James's.

Pierro della Franscesca's *Baptism of Christ* is unmissable, hung in a key position at the far end, showing the most important moment in the life of John the Baptist, with the Holy Spirit hovering overhead, a dove that could almost be a cloud. **Crivelli**'s *Annunciation, with St Emidius,* nearby, is an extraordinary study in deep architectural perspective. **Botticelli**'s *Mystic Nativity* is the only surviving painting with his signature, a strange composition based on the book of Revelations that the artist probably used for his private devotions. His *Venus and Mars* is one of the few secular paintings in the wing.

Another brilliant and moving piece of composition is **Raphael**'s *The Ansidei Madonna*, with St John looking up at the source of the light, his pose reflected by the Christ-child's posture in the lap of the Virgin as they gaze upon a book, leading the viewer on to St Nicholas on the right, also rapt in study. The same artist's *Saint Catherine of Alexandria* shows the influence of Leornardo in the saint's twisting pose. The peculiar *Wilton Diptych* was probably commissioned by Richard II as an affirmation of his divine right to rule, showing the king in the company of angels and his saintly predecessors. Cleaning in 1992 revealed a castle on a green island in a silver sea painted onto the tiny orb above the banner of St George, the patron saint of England.

Leaving the Sainsbury Wing, the High Renaissance begins in the West Wing, in the the main body of the gallery, starting with the Wohl Room and three outstanding **Titian**'s, *Bacchus and Ariadne, Noli Me Tangere* and the possible self-portrait *Portrait of a Man*. This last work makes interesting comparison with **Raphael**'s beautiful portrait of the soldier pontif *Pope Julius II*. In the same wing, *The Entombment* and *The Manchester Madonna* are both exceptionally rare things, paintings by **Michelangelo**, both unfinished. Look out too for **Tintoretto**'s dynamic *Saint George and the Dragon* and **Holbein**'s *Christina of Denmark*. Henry VIII commissioned Holbein to paint his prospective bride full face so that all her blemishes would be revealed. Even though there were none, the marriage came to naught. Ten years earlier, the same artist's *Lady with a Squirrel and a Starling* is more fun, the squirrel's tail modestly covering his demure subject's cleavage. The Venetian master **Correggio**'s *Madonna of the Basket* is one of the most perfectly preserved paintings in the gallery, while the sombre hue of **El Greco**'s *Christ Driving the Traders from the Temple* has been taken to reflect the seriousness of the

The West Wing: paintings from 1510-1600

The West End

counter-reformation. Mythological subjects also became increasingly popular at this time, such as **Bronzino**'s impressive *Allegory with Venus and Cupid*. Other paintings here mark the birth of landscape painting.

The North Wing: paintings from 1600-1700

The North Wing, comprising the back rooms of the gallery, houses 17th-century paintings, with a stronger emphasis on landscapes and especially rich in the Spanish and Dutch schools, including **Velázquez**'s extraordinary play on the nature of 'looking', *The Rokeby Venus*. The first room (15) includes two remarkable paintings by **Claude Lorrain**, *Seaport with the Embarkation of the Queen of Sheba* and *Landscape with the Marriage of Isaac and Rebekah*. Thanks to a clause in Turner's will, that 19th-century British landscape painter's *Sun Rising through Vapour* and *Dido Building Carthage* hang alongside those of his hero. This wing is also home to the collection's wonderful array of Rubens, Poussin and also Rembrandt paintings, including the delightfully light touch of the latter's *Woman Bathing in a Stream*, the thoroughness of *Self Portrait Aged 34* and the atmospheric and dramatic *Belshazzar's Feast*. Look out too for **Frans Hals**' spontaneous rendition of a *Young Man Holding a Skull* and **Caravaggio**'s compelling *Supper at Emmaus*.

The East Wing: paintings from 1700-1900

Unsurprisingly, the most crowded part of the gallery is often the East Wing, where the collection of works by **Van Gogh**, **Gauguin**, **Cézanne**, **Degas**, **Monet** and **Renoir** draw in admirers of the Impressionists and Post-Impressionists. 18th-century British landscape and portraiture are also well represented, with some beautiful family portraits by **Gainsborough** and **Stubbs**, and also several works, including *The Haywain*, by **John Constable**, the greatest landscape painter the country has ever produced. **Goya**'s lively portrait of the Duke of Wellington is also worth seeking out, as is **William Hogarth**'s irresistible and satirical *Marriage Settlement*. No visit to the gallery is complete without a look at **Turner**'s shimmering *Rain, Steam and Speed*.

The late opening on Wed is often a good time to avoid the crush

Despite the popularity of the gallery, it's just large enough to mean that there are always some rooms away from the bustle of visitors jostling to find their favourites. Equally, there's far too much to see in one visit. Plans are afoot to provide more areas for quiet contemplation in an attempt to prevent the gallery from becoming too crowded for its own good.

■ *Open daily 1000-1800, Wed 1000-2100. Admission free. T020-7747 2885, www.nationalgallery.org.uk*

National Portrait Gallery

The National Portrait Gallery attracts fewer visitors than the National Gallery & is much smaller, but can be almost as rewarding

Tucked away behind the National Gallery, up Charing Cross Road, the National Portrait Gallery is a shrine to British history pictured in the portraits of those who have shaped it. A six-year lottery-funded project has resulted in the excellent new **Ondaatje Wing**, opened in May 2000. Directly beyond the old main entrance, visitors arrive in a soaring lobby, ready to be whisked up an escalator to the earliest pictures in the collection, now hung in purpose-built rooms on the second floor.

It might come as a disappointment that there are no medieval works here, the earliest being an impressive portrait of Henry VII, but the new **Tudor Galleries** more than make up for their absence. Modelled on an Elizabethan Long Room, they include the only portrait of Shakespeare known to have been taken from life, **Holbein**'s Henry VIII, several striking images of Elizabeth I and many of her famous courtiers. Further on, the Stuarts are even more colourful and extraordinary: a leggy full-length celebration of James I's toyboy, George Villiers, Duke of Buckingham; **Van Dyck**'s weird allegorical portrait redeeming the nymphomaniac Venetia, Lady Digby; a sensitive picture of the philosopher Thomas Hobbes, most famous for his assertion that life is 'nasty, brutish and short'; and a vivid likeness of a jaded Charles II.

On the same floor, the vibrancy of those early years gives way to the formal elegance of the 18th century, with works by **Joshua Reynolds**, **Thomas Gainsborough** and **Hogarth**. One floor down, the galleries given over to the Victorians are powerfully evocative of the age of Empire, full of Roman-style busts and severe expressions, including a haunting picture of Charles Darwin. A surprisingly modern-looking Henry James ushers in the 20th century, a wavy see-through gallery design marking a significant change in mood. In the small room before it, in a massive and strange picture of First World War statesmen, Winston Churchill takes centre stage lit by a prophetic shaft of sunlight.

The West End

The new **Balcony Gallery** in the Ondaatje Wing displays images and sculptures of movers and shakers in Britain since the 60s. Look out for **Helmut Newton**'s huge black and white photo of former PM Margaret Thatcher, gazing out of the dark like some awe-inspiring figurehead on the prow of a ship. On the way back to the ground floor, which is given over to special temporary exhibitions, the entire collection can be searched in the comfort of the IT Gallery and favourite pictures printed out.

The gallery also runs a series of lectures, opens late on Thu & Fri, & has a smart new restaurant & bar with great views over the old roofs of the National Gallery towards Big Ben

■ *Open Mon-Wed, Sat, Sun 1000-1800, Thu and Fri 1000-2100. Free. T020-7306 0055, information ext 216, recorded information T020-7312 2463, www.npg.org.uk Lectures: Tue & Thu 1310, Sat & Sun 1500, free; Thu 1900, admission charge. Fri music nights 1900; free. IT Gallery does print outs; black and white free, colour postcard £5.50, colour A4 £17.50.*

Eating and drinking

Mid-range The new *Portrait Rooftop Restaurant*, on the top floor of the National Portrait Gallery (T020-7312 2490), is run by Corrigan-Searcey's, doing a fine modern British menu, but the views are really what people come for. Open 1000-1715 Mon-Wed and at the weekends, and from 1000 until 2200 with last orders at 2015 on Thu & Fri. The same hours apply to the bar, where you can also enjoy some fairly expensive snacks and are allowed to smoke.

● *on map, page 60 Trafalgar Square is not really the place to look for good restaurants. Better to try St James's or Covent Garden nearby, although there are a few interesting exceptions*

Cheap For less of an occasion, there are a surprising number of good-value options close to the Square. The *Café in the Crypt* under St Martin-in-the-Fields, Trafalgar Square, T020-7839 4342, closes at 1930 daily but is an atmospheric location to enjoy some reasonably priced salads, hot soups and meals served canteen style to the strains of classical music. The *Portrait Café* in the basement of the Portrait Gallery serves excellent coffee, cakes and sandwiches during the day. *Cranks Express*, 8 Adelaide St, T020-7836 0660, is a branch of the healthy-eating vegetarian chain, open until 2000, closed on Sun. *Hampton's Wine Bar*, 15 Whitcomb St, WC2, T020-7839 2823 (closed weekends) is a middle-of-the-road wine bar and restaurant doing the likes of Eggs Benedict for under a tenner, tucked away in a new development beside the National Gallery and popular with local office workers. In the National Gallery itself, the *Brasserie* in the Sainsbury wing provides a pleasant spot for lunch and there's also a busy *Prêt à Manger* café in the basement.

The West End

Log on at any time with a coffee at the easyEverything Internet Café opposite Charing Cross Station

Pubs and bars Again, this is not the best place to look for a drink, although the *Portrait Gallery's Rooftop Bar* makes an interesting venue. *The Sherlock Holmes*, 10 Northumberland Ave, WC2, T020-7930 2644, is a cosy, very busy pub with a central bar surrounded by Holmes memorabilia. ▶▶ Go to page 416 for entertainment and nightlife.

Shopping

The *National Gallery* has three shops, the main one in the Sainsbury Wing, T020-7747 2870, with an extensive array of books on art and art history, postcards and gift ideas like Van Gogh sunflower umbrellas or oven gloves. A new edition of the Companion Guide is due out in 2001. The *National Portrait Gallery Shop* T020-7306 0055 (ext 223) is smaller, packed with postcards and posters of famous Brits down the ages. *Waterstone's*, The Grand Building, Trafalgar Square, T020-7839 4411, on the corner of the Strand, has a *Coffee Republic* on the first floor, and is open until 2100, Mon-Sat, 1200-1800 Sun, with three floors of books and specializing in business and travel. *Europa Food and Wine* is a useful late-night supermarket on the corner of Whitehall and Trafalgar Square.

Transport

Buses   Too many to list here, but most parts of London can be reached by bus from Trafalgar Square 24-hrs a day, seven days a week. **Night buses** run once or twice hourly from midnight until 0600 daily: to North and East London from Stop C, outside the National Gallery; to South and Southeast London from stop V, outside Canada House on the west side of the Square; to West London from stops T and W, on Cockspur St outside the Scottish Tourist Board on the south side of the Square.

Taxis   Whitehall is usually a better place to hail a cab than the Square itself

Trains   Charing Cross station, serving the Southeastern suburbs, Kent and Sussex. Also frequent trains to Waterloo East and London Bridge.

Tubes   Charing Cross (Northern and Bakerloo lines).

The Strand, Embankment and Aldwych

🚇 *Nearest tube stations are Charing Cross, Embankment & Temple (closed Sun)*

*Once one of the most important streets in town, linking Westminster with the City, the Strand has seen much better days. Upstaged in the late 19th century by the building of the Victoria Embankment, its theatres have largely disappeared and its famous coffee shops closed down. Even so, this north bank of the river is much more than just the southern border of Covent Garden. **The Savoy, Simpson's-in-the-Strand restaurant, Somerset House**, along with the other grand government buildings around the Aldwych, are all sterling examples of the architectural legacy of the Empire and its administration. The **Courtauld Gallery** is one of the most exceptional small collections of Fine Art in the city.*

*The Strand itself has some interesting old-established specialist shops like Stanley Gibbons and Twinings Tea, while the Embankment provides great views of the South Bank and Waterloo Bridge. **Somerset House**, one of London's finest 18th-century buildings, was opened up fully to the public for the first time in 2000* *and promises to become one of the riverside's more exotic attractions. It combines the art hoard of the Courtauld Gallery and the glitz of the Gilbert Collection with a high-tech waterjet display and a glimpse in the Hermitage Rooms of treasures from the great St Petersburg museum. Other discoveries waiting to be made here include the Queens Chapel of the Savoy, the York Water Gate, the Royal Society of Arts and a 'Roman' bath.*

History

The Strand was the link between the City and the village of Charing, and thence on to Whitehall. Streams flowed gently into the Thames across its path as the Strand tracked its way through fields from the edge of the City at Temple Bar to what is now Trafalgar Square. In the 10th century a Danish community settled here, probably those who had married Englishwomen before Alfred the Great drove the Danes out. St Clement Danes now occupies the site of their church.

Medieval mansions sprung up in the 13th century the grandest of which was the Savoy Palace along the south side. The **Savoy Chapel** is on the site of the original chapel (incidentally, the first church in London to be lit by electricity), while the grand **Savoy Hotel** (the largest in Europe when it opened in 1886) now covers the site of the original palace. It was finally destroyed by the Peasants' Revolt in 1381. Mansions for bishops and nobles and the inns of court swept down to the Thames, and although they were torn down by the 17th-century entrepreneur Dr Nicholas Barbon, today's street names indicate those who once resided here (Durham, Exeter, Devereux, Sussex). The current Somerset House is an 18th-century replacement of the palace built by the Lord Protector Somerset in 1547-50, and the York Watergate remains an elegant monument to the grand residences that lined the street.

During the course of the 16th and 17th centuries, when Whitehall and Parliament emerged as the focus of political power, so the Strand's traffic grew. Barbon's transformation of the street to more wood-framed, modest housing saw the Strand develop into a haven for taverns, alehouses, coffeehouses and chophouses (*Twinings Tea*, at No 216, settled here in 1706, and has yet to move). Meanwhile, pickpockets and prostitutes exploited the narrow alleyways. During the course of the 19th century theatres emerged (the *Adelphi*, *Vaudeville* and *Savoy* remain), hotels set up residence, and restaurants (*Simpson's*), music halls, and smoking rooms made it popular not only with lawyers (the Royal Courts of Justice were erected in the 1870s), but also among literary figures. Pepys, Coleridge, George Eliot, Shaw, Galsworthy and Hardy all lived on or around the street.

Meanwhile, in the late 19th century, London resumed expanding into the Thames. According to Tacitus, the growth of the River's banks began with the Romans, and underwent further development at various points thereafter. The Embankment was the creation of London's drainage king, Sir Joseph Bazalgette, who in the late 1860s began to build the Albert, Victoria and Chelsea embankments. The delays over the construction of the District line held up proceedings until Bazalgette lost patience and

In 1917, Cleopatra's Needle earned the odd distinction of being the first London monument to be hit by an air attack

Hotels in the area

AL *The Savoy*
AL *One Aldwych*
A *Waldorf Meridien*
B *Strand Palace*
C *Royal Adelphi*
E *Strand Continental*
▸▸ *Go to page 441*

The West End

went ahead regardless. The gardens were integrated into the plans, and **Cleopatra's Needle**, a gift from the Turkish viceroy of Egypt, arrived in 1878. This granite obelisk from c1475 BC was intended to stand proudly before Parliament, but the ground was subsiding, so it now watches over the river. Below it is buried a time-capsule, containing, among the obvious newspapers, coins and bible and photos of the best-looking women of the day – no doubt Cleopatra herself would have featured in her day.

The 20th century saw the more notable additions of Bush House, synonymous with the voice of the BBC World Service, and the commonwealth High Commissions such as Australia and Zimbabwe (the male nude statues on the front of Zimbabwe House were 'modified' in response to popular outrage). Disraeli described the Strand as 'perhaps the greatest street in Europe' – it would be an ambitious claim now, but its renown is certainly well deserved.

Sights

Emerge from Charing Cross train or tube station and you'll find yourself on the Strand. Apart from its width, first impressions reveal little of this vital thoroughfare's glory days in the 18th and 19th centuries, when it was every fashionable Londoner's favourite riverside prom. To catch a glimpse of those times, turn right down Villiers Street, and then right again through **The Arches**, an atmospheric sunken shopping arcade beneath the station.

The Benjamin Franklin museum should be open some time in 2001, but it can be visited before then by arrangement (T020-7930 9121)

Craven Passage, at the end, which oddly enough cuts the Ship and Shovel pub in half, brings you into **Craven Street**, sloping down towards Northumberland Avenue and the river. Here is one of the most complete rows of Georgian houses in the centre of the city. Number 36 was Benjamin Franklin's home in the 1750s; it's now a Grade I listed building and is in the process of being transformed into a 'dynamic' museum by the Friends of Benjamin Franklin House.

Left at the end of Craven Street, past the Playhouse Theatre, you're directly beneath postmodernist Terry Farrell's **Embankment Place**, one of his love-'em-or-loathe-'em '90s developments, spectacularly lit at night. Passing beneath it brings you out in front of Embankment tube station at the foot of Villiers Street. From here you can walk through the station, past the flower and fruit'n'veg stalls, onto the Embankment itself (see below) and then over the river via **Hungerford Bridge**.

Probably the ugliest river crossing in London, this railway bridge has long been ripe for redevelopment. It was originally built to replace the Hungerford Suspension Bridge, which went on to provide the ironwork for Brunel's bridge over the Avon at Clifton in Bristol. As long ago as the 1940s, there were plans to scrap it and move Charing Cross station south of the river. They came to nothing and now the dirty, cantilevered monster is to be given a new lease of life. The narrow walkway on its north side has long provided some of the finest views of the City, but becomes very crowded at rush hour and flooded in wet weather. The idea is to sling two much wider walkways either side of the bridge, offering spectacular views to the west, and more than doubling the bridge's capacity. The project was supposed to be complete by late 2000, but work has been delayed by unexploded Second World War bombs found on the riverbed. Eventually it should provide much improved pedestrian access to the South Bank and Waterloo.

Constructed in the late 1860s, the Victoria Embankment between Westminster and Blackfriars bridges was an amazing feat of engineering led by Sir Joseph Bazalgette, commemorated here with a bronze bust. Its 8 ft-thick granite walls still protect both the Circle and District tube line and the largest sewer the world had yet needed from the brunt of the current on this outside bend of the river. The road above soon became the most popular route between the City and Westminster. Today it is lined with noble plane trees but its sunny south-facing views are spoiled by the continual roar of traffic.

Victoria Embankment

Cleopatra's Needle is easily the oldest thing around here, and just about the oldest monument in London exposed to the weather. The pink granite obelisk is one of a pair that once stood in Heliopolis, around 1500 BC, long before the Egyptian queen with the famous nose, although the inscriptions on the stone apparently refer to her. It was given to George IV by the viceroy of Egypt in 1820 but only made it to the banks of the Thames over 50 years later after an extremely hazardous voyage in which several sailors' lives were lost. Its companion is in New York's Central Park. The First World War bomb-scarred bronze sphinxes are late 19th-century, replaced the wrong way round after cleaning in the 1920s.

Cleopatra's Needle

The West End

Strand, Aldwych & Embankment

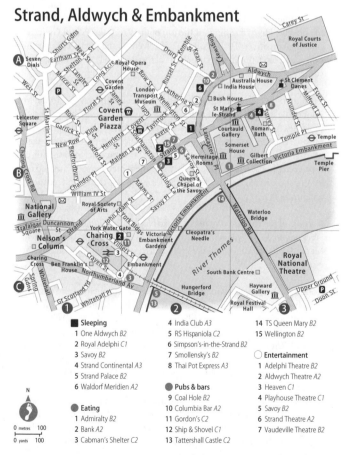

■ **Sleeping**	4 India Club *A3*	14 TS Queen Mary *B2*
1 One Aldwych *B2*	5 RS Hispaniola *C2*	15 Wellington *B2*
2 Royal Adelphi *C1*	6 Simpson's-in-the-Strand *B2*	
3 Savoy *B2*	7 Smollensky's *B2*	◯ **Entertainment**
4 Strand Continental *A3*	8 Thai Pot Express *A3*	1 Adelphi Theatre *B2*
5 Strand Palace *B2*		2 Aldwych Theatre *A2*
6 Waldorf Meridien *A2*	● **Pubs & bars**	3 Heaven *C1*
	9 Coal Hole *B2*	4 Playhouse Theatre *C1*
● **Eating**	10 Columbia Bar *A2*	5 Savoy *B2*
1 Admiralty *B2*	11 Gordon's *C2*	6 Strand Theatre *A2*
2 Bank *A2*	12 Ship & Shovel *C1*	7 Vaudeville Theatre *B2*
3 Cabman's Shelter *C2*	13 Tattershall Castle *C2*	

N

0 metres 100
0 yards 100

Victoria Embankment Gardens
The gardens are a pleasant place to take a picnic

Escape the fumes in Victoria Embankment Gardens, where the free lunch-time and evening entertainment manages to make itself heard above the din of the road. In high season, afternoon and evening events in the old bandstand range from dance, mime and poetry to world music and brass bands, organised by *Alternative Arts*, T020-7375 0441. They can be enjoyed from the comfort of ranks of stripy blue deckchairs. You'll be surrounded by lunching office workers and statues of famous folk, notably the great Scottish bard, Robert Burns. There's also a basic tearoom and café with plastic tables and chairs outside; open throughout the year 0730-1930 daily.

On the north side of the gardens, near Villiers Street, the **York Water Gate** is all that remains of York House, the 17th-century home of James I's favourite, George Villiers, Duke of Buckingham. He has left most of the many parts of his name on the surrounding streets. Before his time, York House was also the birthplace and later the home of the great natural philosopher Sir Francis Bacon. The grand old stone gate was probably designed by Inigo Jones. Its main interest today is its position, showing how much wider the river was before the construction of the Victoria Embankment. Today the foot of the gate is lapped not by the Thames but by the waters of an ornamental pond.

Buckingham Street, overlooking the watergate, has also been home, at different times, to Samuel Pepys, Peter the Great, David Hume, Rousseau and the novelist Henry Fielding. At the top of the street, the **Proud Galleries**, 5 Buckingham Street, T020-7839 4942, is a lively young media-driven exhibition space, often putting on controversial shows, usually of photography and contemporary art.

Royal Society of Arts
There's an interesting view of the back of the building from the Strand

Turning right takes you into John Adam Street and brings you to the front door of the **Royal Society of Arts**, at No 8. One of the few remaining original buildings from the Adam brothers' ambitious Adelphi development, it was purpose built by Robert Adam for the 'Royal Society for the Encouragement of Arts, Manufactures and Commerce' in 1774. A product of mid-18th-century 'coffee house' culture, the Society's eminent members still meet up regularly to share ideas, discuss the latest issues in the arts, design and technology, and promote new projects.

■ *Tours of the 18th-century interior take place at lunchtime on the first Fri of every month T020-7451 6874 and for groups by appointment T020-7451 6825 (or for details of the regular series of public lectures and lunchtime events staged by the RSA).*

Queen's Chapel of the Savoy
This was the place for fashionable weddings in the 19th century

Round the corner, back on the Strand, pass the Savoy Hotel and then duck right beneath it down Savoy Buildings, through its white-tiled bowels, past the staff entrance into Savoy Hill. Here stands the incongruous little stone tower of the Queen's Chapel of the Savoy, and an often unremarked little piece of Royal London. Built on the site of John of Gaunt's Savoy Palace, which was burnt down during the Peasants' Revolt of 1381, it was restored by Queen Victoria and became the chapel of the Royal Victorian Order in 1937. Heraldic copper plaques mark the pews of the different knights in the splendid late-Gothic interior, its flat ceiling decorated with the Royal Arms above the monarch's seat at the west end. The BBC broadcast its first daily radio programmes in 1922 from the building over the road, moving to Broadcasting House 10 years later. ■ *Open Tue-Fri 1130-1530 (closed Aug/Sep) T020-7836 7221. Services on Sun and Wed.*

Somerset House

Further east along the Strand, on the right, stands Somerset House. It was designed by Sir William Chambers in 1776 for George III's Naval office, with the wings on the Strand purpose-built for the fledgling Royal Academy of Arts (which was founded in 1768 but moved to Piccadilly in 1837), the Royal Society, and the Society of Antiquaries. Appropriately enough, since 1990, this northern wing has been occupied by the **Courtauld Institute and Gallery**. In 2000 the southern buildings were opened up to display the **Gilbert Collection** and **Hermitage Rooms**, providing access for the first time to the river frontage. The terrace, which can also be reached from Waterloo Bridge, is a sunny spot to take some tea, slightly marred by the traffic noise from the Embankment below. The entrance to Somerset House on the Embankment takes you through the original watergate, past a royal barge on loan from the Maritime Museum in Greenwich.

Somerset House is acclaimed as one of the most important 18th-century buildings in Europe

The West End

Founded by the textile magnate Samuel Courtauld in memory of his wife Elizabeth, who died on Christmas day 1931, the Courtauld Institute, now attached to the University of London, has become the foremost academy of fine art history in the country. The Courtauld Gallery, on the right-hand side as you enter Somerset House from the Strand, gains its special character from its role as a teaching aid to the Institute as well as from the beautifully proportioned rooms that it now occupies. Ascending the wonderful winding stairway, apparently designed to inspire the terror that the time considered necessary to the appreciation of the Sublime, the 11 rooms afford a delightful potted introduction to Western art.

Courtauld Institute & Gallery

The ground floor begins with European medieval art, including the Master of Flemalle's triptych of *The Entombment*, a masterpiece of early Dutch painting. On the first floor, four rooms move through the Renaissance in Italy and Northern Europe, via Rubens, to the Baroque and 18th-century British portraiture. Among the many remarkable works on show, look out for **Botticelli**'s altarpiece for the Augustinian convent of Sant' Elisabetta in Florence; Martin Luther's friend **Lucas Cranach**'s *Adam and Eve*; **Bruegel**'s dramatic *Landscape with the Flight into Egypt*; **Rubens**' strange, star-studded *Landscape by Moonlight*; and **Gainsborough**'s *Portrait of Mrs Gainsborough*.

For many the highlight of a visit comes on the second floor, in Room 9, the gallery originally designed for the Royal Academy, where Courtauld's own collection of Impressionists and Post-Impressionists are hung. A copy of **Manet**'s *Déjeuner sur l'herbe* and, even more extraordinary, his *Bar at the Folies-Bergère*, vie for attention with famous works by **Degas**, **Pissarro**, **Monet**, **Renoir**, **Seurat**, **Gauguin**, **Van Gogh** and **Cezanne**. Smaller rooms on this floor focus on British art up to 1950, 20th-century French painting up to 1925, and temporary exhibitions.

■ *Open Mon-Sat 1000-1800, Sun 1200-1800. Admission £4, under 18s free, concession £3. Joint ticket with Gilbert Collection £6; £5 OAPs. Free on Mon 1000-1400 except Bank Holidays. T020-7848 2526, www.courtauld.ac.uk*

The great central courtyard of Somerset House has recently been re-christened the **Edmond J Safra Fountain Court** and blessed with a diverting but controversial computer-operated water feature. Fifty fountains arranged in 10 rows of five spurt straight up out of the ground with varying force, reaching a height of about 15 ft. In daylight the effect is more comical than impressive, but the display is best seen after dark when the lights in place beneath the waterjets transform them into sparkling columns of luminesence. The reservoir for the fountains is located in the two storeys beneath the courtyard, a reminder that Somerset House was built facing the river, its front three times higher than its back. The fountains have been criticized for upsetting the intended effect of the quad's classical proportions, but they make an appropriately wacky introduction to the wonders of the Gilbert Collection now on display in the riverside wings of the building.

■ *The fountains operate from 1000-2300, with short displays on the hour and half hour, and main displays at 1300, 1800, and 2200. For details on ice skating in the courtyard in winter, see page 52.*

For details on ice skating in the courtyard in winter, see page 52.

The Gilbert Collection

An audio guide tells the history of some of the items which often proves more interesting than the objects themselves

This is London's latest museum of decorative art. Arthur Gilbert was born in London in 1913 and moved to California in 1949. With the profits from his successful adventures in real estate he began an extraordinary and costly collection of gold and silverware, precious snuff boxes and peculiar Roman micromosaics, among other things. Described as the single most generous gift ever made to the nation, his collection went on display in purpose-built galleries in the southern wing of Somerset House in 2000.

The effect of so many expensive objects gathered together and lovingly lit in the darkened designer galleries is fairly overwhelming. They include one of the earliest gold vessels in the world, from Bronze Age Anatolia, a Maharajah's silver howdah from Rajasthan, and a pair of silver-gilt royal gates given to a monastery in a Kiev by Catherine the Great. The most bizarre exhibit must be the recreation of Gilbert's study, complete with a waxwork replica of the collector himself.

■ *Open Mon-Sat 1000-1800, Sun 1200-1800 (last entry 1715). Admission £4, under 18s free, students £3, disabled and helpers £2 (joint ticket with Courtauld Gallery £7, OAPs £5). T020-7240 4080, www.gilbert-collection.org.uk*

The Hermitage Rooms

The most recent addition to the exotic collections at Somerset House are the contents of The Hermitage Rooms, designed to exhibit changing selections of artefacts from the great St Petersburg museum. The five rooms have been decorated in the Imperial style of the Winter Palace, with replica chandeliers, gilded chairs and marquetry floors. The first room shows a live feed to St Petersburg, looking across Palace Square, and a six-minute video taking you on a tour of the Hermitage itself. The inaugural exhibition (until September 23, 2001) displays the 'Treasures of Catherine the Great', Russia's 18th-century Empress, including portraits, medals, clocks, precious gems, porcelain and even her wig, woven entirely from silver thread. The last gallery is dedicated to her taste for chinoiserie, with 23 very rare gold hairpins gifted to her by the Emperor of China. There's also a shop selling souvenirs inspired by the Hermitage.

■ *Open Mon-Sat 1000-1800 (last admission 1715), Sun and Bank Holidays 1200-1800. Admission £6, concession £4, under-5s free. T020-7845 4630.*

Back on the Strand, the church marooned on its traffic island in front of King's College London is **St Mary-le-Strand**. A striking blend of Italian baroque and renaissance, it was the first public building designed by the Scotsman James Gibbs, from 1714-17. Free lunchtime recitals are usually given here on Wednesdays at 1300. The pulpit was carved by Grinling Gibbons and oddly

The West End

enough, this is where Bonnie Prince Charlie secretly converted to Anglicism after his disastrous defeat at Culloden. ■ *Open Mon-Fri 1100-1530.*

Bush House, now the home of the BBC World Service, was designed by Americans in 1920 and sensitively embraces the church. The shop (see Shopping below) sells World Service merchandise, BBC videos, books, CDs and cassettes, and technical books on radio production. Next door is the mighty façade of **India House,** dating from 1930. **Australia House** is on the other side of Melbourne Place. Built during the First

Five of the best: West End cafés and restaurants with outside seating

· *The Admiralty*, Somerset House, Strand.
· *TS Queen Mary*, Waterloo Bridge, Strand.
· *The Garden Café*, Newburgh Street, Soho.
· *Market Café*, Apple Market, Covent Garden.
· *Giovanni*, James Street, off Oxford Street.

The West End

World War, Australian stone, wood and marble were used in its construction. The entrance is decorated with statues of Exploration and Shearing and Reaping; up above are the Horses of the Sun.

The other church at the end of the Strand is **St Clement Danes** (T020-7242 8282). Named after the Danish settlement at Aldwych in Saxon times, this is probably not the St Clement's whose bells say 'Oranges and Lemons' although tradition would have it so. This was also Dr Johnson's church. It was badly bombed in the Blitz, and became the RAF church; the USAF donated the organ. ■ *Open Mon-Fri 0830-1630, Sat 0900-1530, Sun 0900-1230.*

Just down the hill from here is London's only **'Roman' Bath** at 5 Strand Lane, off Surrey Street. Whether or not you've booked an appointment, you can peer through grubby windows at ground level at its sunken brickwork, fed by the Holy Well nearby. It has been known about since at least the late 18th century and Dickens mentions it in *David Copperfield*. No one has yet proven that it is Roman, although it almost certainly does date back at least to Shakespeare's day. ■ *Open May-Sep, every Wed 1300-1700 by appointment only, with 24 hrs notice during office hours. Admission free. T020-7641 5264 .*

Eating and drinking

With Covent Garden just up the hill, there's little reason for restaurants to flourish here. *Simpsons-in-the-Strand*,100 Strand, WC2, T020-7836 9112, has been the exception to that rule for longer than most its clientele could possibly remember. It can be relied upon to provide good old-fashioned English food in a formal, upper-crust environment any day for lunch and dinner. Pretty much the same is true of the *Savoy Grill, in The Savoy Hotel*, Strand, WC2, T020-7836 4343. It's closed in Aug and insists on jacket and tie, no denims or trainers.

More of a buzz and a significantly more modern approach can be found at *Bank*, 1 Kingsway, on the corner of Aldwych, WC2, T020-7379 9797. Brave the designer shards of plate glass suspended from the ceiling of this bank-branch-conversion to enjoy some top-quality fish and modern European dishes. The set pre-theatre and lunch menus are particularly good value at £13.50 for 2 courses. Booking is essential. It's also open on Sun, for brunch, lunch and dinner.

Easily the best option at the top end of this bracket is *The Admiralty*, which opened in 1999 in Somerset House, T020-7845 4646. The French regional cooking here deserves

Expensive
● *on map, page 69*

Mid-range

high praise and a few hiccups in the standard of the service have been ironed out, making booking for one of the 62 covers essential. The 3-course pre-theatre menu available 1800-1900 is £17.50.

Staying with French food, albeit less inspired, and a nautical theme, the *RS Hispaniola* is an unusually comfortable restaurant ship moored beneath Hungerford Bridge on the Victoria Embankment, WC2, T020-7839 3011. Another smaller restaurant ship, *El Barco Latino*, Temple Pier, Victoria Embankment, WC2, T020-7379 5496, is a Spanish party boat open until 0300 Mon-Sat and until midnight on Sun. Admission is £6 after 2100 for non-diners, 'ladies are free on Fri'. A 3-course set meal (£13.50) sets you up for the salsa. Booking advisable.

Smollensky's on the Strand, 105 Strand, WC2, T020-7497 2101, has become an institution. It's a reasonably good-value family restaurant, American in style and generosity, though heaving with kids. Jazz bands play here on Sun evenings, as well as a pianist throughout the week and DJ's from Thu to Sat.

Cheap A world apart from the area's many funky cafés and fast-food joints, the *India Club*, 143 Strand, WC2, T020-7836 0650, is easily the most characterful place to eat cheaply around here. Pay up to £10 for old-style curries at formica tables on linoleum floors with yellow walls. A very Indian institution, since 1950. It also has the unusual advantage (in central London) of being unlicensed: take your own booze and they won't even charge you 'corkage'. Open Mon-Sat 1200-1430, 1800-2250. Next door, *Thai Pot Express*, 148 Strand, WC2, T020-7497 0904, is a smart, new, woody place for slightly more expensive Thai food.

Cafés & Top-notch teas can be taken at the *Savoy*, Strand, WC2, T020-7836 4343, daily
sandwich bars between 1500-1730. They cost about £20. Othewise there are plenty of options along the Strand, including *Aroma*, 125 Strand, WC2, T020-7836 8852, *Coffee Republic*, 80 Strand WC2, T020-7836 6660, and at the bottom of Villiers St, or the popular sandwich chain *Prêt à Manger*, 135 Strand, WC2, T020-7836 7576 (also at 421-422 and 192 Aldwych). Another more interesting option is the *Cabman's Shelter* in Embankment Place doing low-price takeaway teas and very basic rolls.

Pubs & bars *The Ship and Shovel*, in Craven Passage, is the best traditional pub in the area. It survived the renovation of Charing Cross in the 90s and opened another version of itself across the passage a year ago. *No 1 Craven* is a new old-fashioned little place with a snug. Both do good beers and food. *Gordon's*, 47 Villiers Street, WC2, T020-7930 1408, is a subterranean wine-bar at the bottom of Villiers St. Exceptional wines can be enjoyed in the candlelit gloom of its convivial vaults. It also does fairly expensive salad bar-style food.

▶▶ Go to page 403 for entertainment & nightlife

Other pubs around here tend towards the big, busy and commercial. The best of them is still the *Coal Hole*, 91 Strand, WC2, T020-7836 7503, which has real ales, tables outside and lots of decorative plasterwork. *The Wellington*, 351 Strand, WC2, T020-7557 9881, is another good bet, on a prominent corner sight at the end of Waterloo Bridge. Its standard pub grub is very reasonably priced. *The Columbia Bar*, 69 Aldwych, WC2, T020-7831 8043, is a new pub run by the excellent Young's brewery (so good beer here) where the food is of a slightly higher quality and price.

Otherwise this is an area that excels in sophisticated and expensive hotel bars. The *American Bar* at the *Savoy*, Strand, WC2, T020-7836 4343, has a dress code, no smoking area and claims to be the first place a Martini was put together in Britain (shaken, not shtirred, of courshe). Less stuffy and more trendy is the *Lobby Bar* at *One Aldwych Hotel*, 1 Aldwych, WC2, T020-7300 1000, somewhere to enjoy sculpture and design as well as good-value cocktails. In the same hotel the *Axis Bar* is smarter, above the restaurant and done up in art deco style. Unusually for a hotel, *The Club Bar* at *Le Meridien Waldorf*, Aldwych, WC2, T020-7836 2400, pulls a very good if expensive pint and the atmosphere is not as formal as you might expect.

Two pub-clubs on ships are also worth investigating, especially during the day when the sun is out. The *TS Queen Mary*, T020-7240 9404, moored just by Waterloo Bridge. A place for baguettes and chips on the sundeck. Hornblower's club nights Thu-Sat can be rowdy but fun. Smaller and more convenient, *The Tattershall Castle*, T020-7839 6548, does bar food with a barbecue on deck through Jul and Aug. There are good views of the Eye from its position upstream of Hungerford Bridge.

Shopping

Davenport's Magic Shop, 7 Charing Cross Underground Arcade, Strand, WC2, T020-7836 0408 (closed on Sun), in the tube station, is a family business that has been catering to the needs of magicians amateur and professional since 1898. Another old family business, on a much grander scale, is *R Twining & Co*, 216 Strand, WC2, T020- 7353 3511. They've been importing and exporting fine tea and coffee on this site since 1706 and won't let you forget it. There's even a museum.

When the theatres on the Strand closed down, the philatelists and numismatists that had colonised the street stayed on. Nowadays only two stamp emporia are left: *Stanley Gibbons International*, 399 Strand, WC2, T020-7836 8444, was founded in 1856, and is the Harrods of world stamp collecting. *The Stamp Centre*, 79 Strand, WC2, T020-7836 2579, has less cachet and hence lower prices. *A H Baldwin & Sons*, 11 Adelphi Terrace, WC2, T020-7930 6879, open by appointment during the week, is the UK's second largest numismatist. They're the fourth generation of a family firm dealing in coins and medals.

Under the wing of the World Service in Bush House, scribblers of the world can unite at *Penfriend*, Bush House Arcade, Strand, WC2, T020-7836 9809, which has a wide selection of antique and new pens. In the same place, the *BBC World Service Shop*, T020-7557 2576, has videos and cassettes, books, souvenirs and umbrellas. *The London Camera Exchange*, 98 Strand, WC2, T020-7379 0200, is a reliable independent dealing in new and second-hand cameras.

For a special thank you present perhaps, *Woodhams at One*, 1 Aldwych, WC2, T020-7300 0777, do the flowers for the designer hotel, and also do spectacular bouquet deliveries in a smart box complete with their own water for £30-£50. *Body Active Fitness Superstore*, Charing Cross Underground Arcade, Strand, WC2, T020-7240 1363, sells fitness equipment, specialist clothings, books, videos and lots of nutritional supplements.

This isn't an area that you'd choose to mount a shopping expedition but there are several interesting specialist shops worth a look if you happen to be passing

The West End

Transport

Westbound from Aldwych along the Strand:
No 6 to Kensal Rise via Oxford Circus and Marble Arch.
No 9 to Hammersmith via Hyde Park Corner and Knightsbridge.
No 13 to Golders Green via Oxford Circus and Baker St.
No 23 to Paddington via Oxford Circus.
No 77A to Wandsworth via Westminster and Vauxhall Bridge.

Along the Strand eastbound:
No 11 to Liverpool St via St Paul's.
No 15 to Limehouse via St Paul's and Tower of London.
No 91 to Crouch End via Euston, King's Cross and Caledonian Rd.
No 176 to Penge via Waterloo and Dulwich.

Buses
There are no buses along the Embankment

Along the Strand westbound:
No 11 to Fulham Broadway via Victoria and Sloane Square.
No 15 to Paddington via Oxford Circus.
No 176 to Oxford Circus via Charing Cross Rd..

River transport   **Embankment Pier to Greenwich**, via the Tower and St Katherine's, taking about 1 hr, Apr-Oct, daily from 1030 every 30 mins until 1600; Nov-Mar, daily at 1030, 1115, 1200, 1245, 1330, 1415, 1500. Approx return fare £7.50, under 15s £4.10. T020-7987 1185.

    Embankment Multi-lingual Circular Cruise: to view Westminster and the Tower, taking 50 mins, mid-Mar-Oct, daily from 1100 every hr until 1700. Approx fare £6.70, under-15s £4.70. T020-7987 1185.

    Central London Fast Ferry: from Embankment to Canary Wharf, via Festival, London Bridge and Nelson Dock, taking 40 mins, Mon-Fri at 0700, 0740, 0815, 0850, 0925; then including Bankside, taking 50 mins, every 40 mins from 1122 until 1950 and bank holidays (T01474-566220).

Taxis   Cab ranks at the Aldwych, Waldorf Hotel, Number One Aldwych, Carting Lane (Savoy Place). There's a major one at Embankment Place on Villiers St, also on the Strand at Villiers St, St Clement Dane's Church and The Mall at Charing Cross station.

Trains   Charing Cross Station, at the west end of the Strand next to Trafalgar Square, serves London's southeastern suburbs and Kent.

Tubes   Embankment tube (Circle, District, Bakerloo and Northern lines) is right on the river next door, the jumping off point for Hungerford Bridge and often the best way to reach the South Bank. Temple tube (Circel and District lines) is closed on Sun but is the closest to Somerset House and the east end of the Strand.

Leicester Square and around

⊖ *Leicester Square tube station is on Charing Cross Rd. Piccadilly Circus tube is almost as close to Leicester Square itself, just down Coventry St*

Leicester Square always gets bad press, written off as a charmless tourist-trap rife with pickpockets, bagsnatchers and mediocre buskers. The criticisms are still justified – not too many of the businesses round here expect to see the same face twice – but since the little square's pedestrianization and then refurbishment in the early 90s it has increasingly provided a much-needed focal point for the entertainment scene in the West End. Just about everyone looking for fun in central London ends up passing through here eventually, as Soho, Covent Garden, Piccadilly and Mayfair are all within easy reach. During the day Leicester Fields, the gardens in the middle, are usually packed with people sitting about deciding what to do next. This is where they gravitate to get their bearings, away from the traffic if not from each other.

    In the evenings the crowds can make crossing the square almost impossible. The two main draws are the cinemas, not only the blockbusting first-run multiscreens surrounding the square, but also places like the cult rep the Prince Charles, or the fashionable Curzon Soho, and the nightclubs, like Home, the Wag, Sound and Limelight. And then there's the Comedy Store, the place that set many comedians on the road to stardom in the 70s. Just north of the square lies **Chinatown**, *only a couple of streets of restaurants but still an area with one of the*

A hare-raising tale

Perhaps Leicester Square's most entertaining claim to fame (apart from being the venue for one of Shelley's sleepwalking excursions), was the humiliation of one of its more distinguished 17th-century residents, the anatomist Nathanael St André.

He brought a certain Mary Tofte to his surgery here, to investigate her claim to have given birth to a litter of fifteen rabbits following a shock encounter in a field in Surrey. St Andre supported her story, claiming to have delivered two further bunnies himself; George I sent a physician, who made similar claims. It was only when she was caught trying to buy a rabbit at a market stall that Mary Tofte confessed her ruse.

*most distinctive cultural identities in the capital. It squeezes into a little niche between the square itself, **Shaftesbury Avenue**, the high street of 'Theatreland', and **Charing Cross Road**, the bookseller's favourite address.*

The West End

History

Leicester Square derives its name from the grand Leicester House that dominated the area in the mid-17th century. The fields sloping south were slowly surrounded by grand houses, creating a square, while in the latter part of the century the area behind the Earl of Leicester's house was developed by Nicholas Barbon, the entrepreneur who tore down the mansions that lined the Strand. It remained primarily residential until the mid-18th century, when the construction of New Coventry Street led to the emergence of coffee houses, taverns, hotels and hotel restaurants. Nevertheless it remained a distinguished address – John Dryden, Edmund Burke and Sir Joshua Reynolds lived here, while Hogarth executed many of his more notable works in a gallery he built off his house at No 30.

As the area became less residential, the Survey of London observed "Leicester Square was essentially masculine – its popularity with the demi-monde meant that there was no place for unescorted ladies". In later Victorian times oyster rooms and theatres, such as the Alhambra and Empire, emerged, and Turkish baths became the vogue. The Hippodrome became a venue of almost Roman proportions – watershows were put on here, as well as music-hall and circus acts. The central garden's fortunes also fluctuated. Originally available to commoners to graze their livestock, its heyday was in the mid-19th century when the Great Globe was constructed by James Wylde, a geographer, to capitalize on the mass of visitors drawn by the Great Exhibition of 1851. Standing 60 ft high and 40 ft in diameter, visitors ascended a four-stage gallery constructed on the inside, viewing the world's surface reproduced on a scale of one inch to one mile. It was sold for scrap 10 years later. Despite a cleaning up of the garden itself in 1992, the square's current status as a popular tourist attraction continues to mystify Londoners.

The area north of the square, now called **Chinatown** (although a pale imitation of its namesake in New York), has only relatively recently become the focal point for the city's Chinese community. Before that, Gerrard Street and the smaller streets

Hotels in the area

AL The Radisson Edwardian Hampshire
AL St Martin's Lane
C Manzi's
▶▶ **Go to page 441**

around housed nightclubs, strip-joints and other such clubs – the author Graham Greene commenting that "half the blackmail or swindling cases lived in Gerrard Street". Although opium dens run by the likes of Brilliant Chang existed in the 20s, it is only since the '50s that Chinese businesses began moving in from their earlier community near the docks in Limehouse.

Leicester Square & around

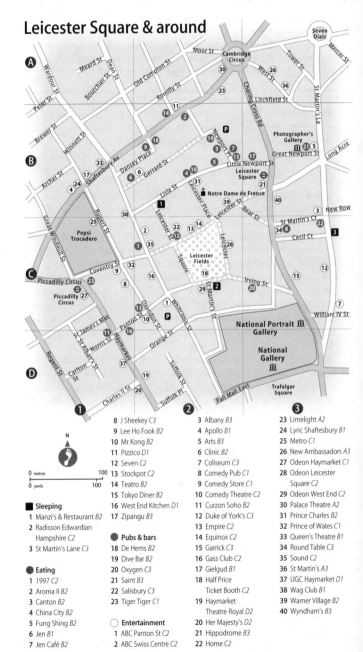

0 metres 100
0 yards 100

N

■ **Sleeping**
1 Manzi's & Restaurant *B2*
2 Radisson Edwardian
   Hampshire *C2*
3 St Martin's Lane *C3*

● **Eating**
1 1997 *C2*
2 Aroma II *B2*
3 Canton *B2*
4 China City *B2*
5 Fung Shing *B2*
6 Jen *B1*
7 Jen Café *B2*

8 J Sheekey *C3*
9 Lee Ho Fook *B2*
10 Mr Kong *B2*
11 Pizzico *D1*
12 Seven *C2*
13 Stockpot *C2*
14 Teatro *B2*
15 Tokyo Diner *B2*
16 West End Kitchen *D1*
17 Zipangu *B3*

● **Pubs & bars**
18 De Hems *B2*
19 Dive Bar *B2*
20 Oxygen *C3*
21 Saint *B3*
22 Salisbury *C3*
23 Tiger Tiger *C1*

○ **Entertainment**
1 ABC Panton St *C2*
2 ABC Swiss Centre *C2*

3 Albany *B3*
4 Apollo *B1*
5 Arts *B3*
6 Clinic *B2*
7 Coliseum *C3*
8 Comedy Pub *C1*
9 Comedy Store *C1*
10 Comedy Theatre *C2*
11 Curzon Soho *B2*
12 Duke of York's *C3*
13 Empire *C2*
14 Equinox *C2*
15 Garrick *C3*
16 Gass Club *C2*
17 Gielgud *B1*
18 Half Price
   Ticket Booth *C2*
19 Haymarket
   Theatre Royal *D2*
20 Her Majesty's *D2*
21 Hippodrome *B3*
22 Home *C2*

23 Limelight *A2*
24 Lyric Shaftesbury *B1*
25 Metro *C1*
26 New Ambassadors *A3*
27 Odeon Haymarket *C1*
28 Odeon Leicester
   Square *C2*
29 Odeon West End *C2*
30 Palace Theatre *A2*
31 Prince Charles *B2*
32 Prince of Wales *C1*
33 Queen's Theatre *B1*
34 Round Table *C3*
35 Sound *C2*
36 St Martin's *A3*
37 UGC Haymarket *D1*
38 Wag Club *B1*
39 Warner Village *B2*
40 Wyndham's *B3*

Buying tickets for a West End show

Any number of ticket touts and unofficial booths offer cut-price theatre tickets around Leicester Square and they should definitely be avoided.

Only one outlet can be relied upon to sell the genuine article that guarantees last-minute access to the big shows. What was once known as the 'Half Price Ticket Booth', in the clocktower building on the south side of the Square, has been relaunched by the Society of London Theatres as 'tkts' in an attempt to avoid confusion with its dodgier imitators in the area. Half-price and discounted tickets for many of the West End's most popular

shows go on sale here on the day of performance only at 1000 sharp Monday to Saturday and 1200 on Sundays. The famous queue for these bargains has often formed well before then. The booth closes at 1900 Monday-Saturday and at about 1530 on Sundays.

More details can be found at www.OfficialLondonTheatre.co.uk

Other ways of seeing plays on the cheap include checking out individual theatres for standbys, pay-what-you-can nights and returns, usually on sale half an hour before the performance at the box office - again, expect to queue.

Sights

Leicester Square itself is surprisingly small, and since being cleaned up is in fact quite attractive. Sloping downhill from the Empire cinema, it's ringed by big cinemas catching the eye with the titles of the current Hollywood block-busters. Contemporary art installations are shown on a large Global Multimedia Imaging screen outside *Home*, the megaclub that opened here in the late 90s. **Leicester Fields** is the leafy garden in the middle, with a statue of Shake-speare, a copy of the one in Westminster Abbey. He's surrounded on the edge of the garden by busts of famous locals like Hogarth, Newton, and Joshua Reynolds as well as a modern statue of Charlie Chaplin with the mawkish inscription 'the comic genius who gave pleasure to so many'.

The big film premieres at the Empire cinema on the northside of the Square regularly draw huge crowds of stargazers

Dedicated sightseers won't want to miss the church of **Notre Dame de France**, in Leicester Place on the north side of the Square. Originally a pan-oramic playhouse, explaining its unusual round design, it became the Eglise Française Catholique de Londres in 1865. Bombed out in 1940 it was almost entirely rebuilt in 1955 and Jean Cocteau was commissioned to decorate the Chapelle du Saint Sacrement. His mural still merits a look, an energetic depic-tion of the Annunciation, Mary at the foot of the Cross, and the Assumption. An Aubusson tapestry hangs over the altar and Boris Anrep did the mosaics.

Leicester Place and Leicester Street both head north into Chinatown. It may be tiny in comparison to other cities', but then this is not really the home of London's Chinese community, more like its market place. **Lisle Street** is lined with restaurants and supermarkets, while pedestrianized **Gerrard Street** has been 'themed' with Chinoiserie street furniture and gates to complement another stretch of busy restaurants. Both streets meet in **Newport Place**, where a little bandstand-cum-pagoda has become a bustling meeting point.

Chinatown
For a list of restaurants here, see page 80

Shaftesbury Avenue runs along the northern boundary of Chinatown, from Piccadilly Circus to High Holborn. Since the late 19th century, this street has most famously been the heart of West End 'theatreland', as the street signs now indicate. Six theatres were opened up along its west side in the decades

Shaftesbury Avenue
For theatre listings, see page 419

either side of 1900, including the *Lyric*, the *Apollo*, the *Globe* (now the *Gielgud*), the *Queen's* and the grand *Palace Theatre* on Cambridge Circus. Before then, the most important theatres were on the Haymarket, being *Her Majesty's* and the *Theatre Royal, Haymarket*.

Charing
Cross Road

Cambridge Circus is where Shaftesbury Avenue crosses the Charing Cross Road as it heads north to Tottenham Court Road and south to Trafalgar Square. Charing Cross Road has long been to books what Shaftesbury Avenue has to theatres. South of Cambridge Circus, almost every shop on the east side is stacked full of books new and second-hand, while small pedestrian alleyways like Cecil Street and St Martin's Court run through into St Martin's Lane lined with some of the city's foremost specialist booksellers. **The Photographer's Gallery**, 5-8 Great Newport Street, WC2, T020-7831 1772, mounts regular exhibitions of promising new work and has a good café.

Eating and drinking

If you're not a fan of Chinese cooking, either splash out on some celebrity dining or head for Soho or Covent Garden

The obvious destination around here is Chinatown, although the choice can be bewildering. The best bet is to join a crowded restaurant, especially if the crowd is Chinese, and don't insist on too much English explanation from either menu or staff. A traditional feature of Hong Kong/Cantonese cuisine, dim sum, are tasty little dumplings and snacks, often excellent value but not usually served after about 1700.

Expensive
● *on map, page 78*

J Sheekey, 28-32 St Martin's Court, WC2, T020-7240 2565, is a name that has long been associated with fish, and has now been given a sympathetic overhaul by the people responsible for *The Ivy* and *Le Caprice*. Now it's the most stylish place around for top-quality seafood, fairly traditional and exclusive. *Teatro*, 93-107 Shaftesbury Ave, W1, T020-7494 3040, owned by footballer Lee Chapman and actress Leslie Ash, is a discreet, sleek venue for some fine modern European food, favoured by B-list celebrities who quaff their aperitifs at the private members bar. More loud and lively and just about as star-studded is *Asia de Cuba*, 45 St Martin's Lane, WC2, T020-7300 5588, in *St Martin's Lane Hotel*, with an imaginative menu fashionably fusing Asian and Latin American cuisine. All three need booking well ahead for the weekend.

Mid-range
Two restaurants very close to Leicester Square stand out in this bracket: *Seven*, on the 7th floor of *Home* at 1 Leicester Square, T020-7909 1177, is a large modern European restaurant that has been widely praised, not least for its views over the square towards Big Ben and the Eye. *Manzi's*, 1/2 Leicester St, WC2, T020-7734 0224, has been around for years, drawing in a generally sedate crowd of regulars, often an elder statesman or two, who come for its old-fashioned Italian service and traditional ways with fish.

Effectively on the same street, in Chinatown, *Fung Shing*, 15 Lisle St, WC2, T020-7437 1539, www.ipi.co.uk/funshing, has also long had a good reputation for its seafood and Cantonese cooking. It was one of the first restaurants in London to serve up Chinese haute cuisine and standards reportedly remain high.

At the lower end of this price range, but also taking their cookery seriously, two Chinatown restaurants are exceptional: *Aroma II*, 118-120 Shaftesbury Ave, W1, T020-7437 0377, on a busy corner opposite the Curzon Soho cinema, is a large, modern restaurant with a very wide choice of Cantonese and, more unusually, Peking dishes. *China City*, White Bear Yard, 25a Lisle St, WC2, T020-7734 3388, another large restaurant, hidden away in the tranquility of its own courtyard off Lisle St, does very good dim sum until 1700 as well as good value Cantonese dishes.

Five of the best: late-night food in the West End

- *Mr Chung's*, Wardour Street, Leicester Square.
- *1997*, Wardour Street, Leicester Square.
- *Café Boheme*, Old Compton Street, Soho.
- *Tesco Metro*, Oxford Street.
- *Belgo Centraal*, Earlham Street, Covent Garden.

At the upper end of this price range, the *Canton Restaurant*, 11 Newport Place, WC2, T020-7437 6220, is a reliable old-timer. Jen, 7 Gerrard St, W1, T020-7287 8193, is a newcomer that has successfully cut a dash. *Mr Kong*, 21 Lisle St, WC2, T020-7437 7923, does some excellent Mandarin dishes and is open until 0300. Another newcomer, *1997*, 19 Wardour St, W1, T020-7734 2868, named after the year of Hong Kong's handover, is open 24 hrs for consistently good-value Cantonese cooking.

For some authentic barbecued duck at bargain prices, seek out *Lee Ho Fook*, 4 Macclesfield St, W1, T020-7734 0782. Easily confused with the more conventional restaurant of the same name on Gerrard St, this one is basic, caff style with brisk service. Equally true to its roots is the *Jen Café Tea Specialist*, 4-8 Newport Place, T020-7287 9708, a basic place for a cuppa of chrysanthemum tea. Mr Chung's, Wardour St, Leicester Square, a small and highly rated latenight Chinese restaurant, open till 0200.

Of the Japanese restuarants in Chinatown, the *Tokyo Diner*, 2 Newport Place, WC2, T020-7287 8777, remains many people's favourite, as much for its cheerful service as its sushi and noodles. *Zipangu*, 8 Little Newport St, WC2, T020-7437 5042, is another.

For something other than Oriental food, make for Panton St, where a branch of the *Stockpot* chain at 40 Panton St, SW1, T020-7839 5142, has been doing inexpensive, unfancy British food for years, as has its former partner over the road, the *West End Kitchen*, 5 Panton St, SW1, T020-7839 4241. Altogether more upbeat and contemporary, *Pizzico*, 66 Haymarket, SW1, T020-7839 3641, is a new venture by the Spaghetti House chain, where the pizzas are excellent value for the area. Open all day until 2330 Fri and Sat, 2300 other nights, Sun 2230.

Oxygen, 17 Irving St, WC2, T020-7930 0907, is open late, the ground floor is large and dark, the first floor brighter, and you can buy its namesake here if you're having trouble breathing in the crush. *De Hems*, Macclesfield St, T020-7437 2494, is also a very lively place, unusual for being the only authentically Dutch pub in London. Another good party venue is *Tiger Tiger*, 29 Haymarket, SW1, T020-7930 1885, a huge place decorated in a weird mock-North African style that's quite fun.

Much more fashionable, restrained (and expensive), *Saint*, 8 Great Newport St, WC2, T020-7240 1551, is open until 0200 during the week and 0300 Fri and Sat, a subterranean designer dive bar with a good range of cocktails and a Pan Soho menu (modern British with an Asian twist). Just off Charing Cross Rd, on Cranbourn St, almost opposite the Warner Village cinema, is the *Cork and Bottle*, a long-established subterranean wine bar which is a good place to enjoy some oysters washed down with a good bottle of Chablis, very popular with office workers on Fri nights.

Stride confidently or book into *The Light Bar* in the St Martin's Lane Hotel, T020-7300 5599, if you are looking for an awesome designer drinking experience surrounded by models and media darlings. For somewhere at the other extreme of style-consciousness or smart, *The Dive Bar*, beneath the King's Head on Gerrard St, really does live up to its name but comes with added cool points. Easily the grandest old boozer in the area is *The Salisbury*, 90 St Martin's Lane, WC2, T020-7836 5863, its gleaming Victorian interior fully renovated and as popular as ever (sometimes too popular), especially with tourists, theatregoers and thesps, darling.

Cheap
Many Chinatown restaurants can serve a meal for under £10, although the quality varies widely

The West End

Leicester Square has no shortage of cafés but some of them can charge £3.50 for a coffee. One of the several ice cream parlours might be a better bet

Pubs & bars
There are plenty of loud & lairy places to go for a drink - quiet pints are in much shorter supply.
▶▶ Go to page 417 for entertainment & nightlife

Shopping

Books   Books, books, books! Charing Cross Rd is still the best place in London to rummage around for any and every out-of-print, remaindered or second-hand book as well as new titles. Most special and antiquarian items of interest can be found just off the road on Cecil Court, St Martin's Court and Caxton Walk.

Stage Door Prints, 9 Cecil Court, WC2, T020-240 1683, has one of the best stocks of theatre-related volumes and prints in the capital. *Dance Books*, 15 Cecil Court, WC2, T020-7836 2314, do the same for ballet and dance. *Watkins Books*, 19 Cecil Court, WC2, T020-7836 2182, are specialists in mysticism and the occult. *Motor Books*, 33 St Martin's Court, WC2, T020-7836 5376, stock a range that will satisfy the most frustrated or devoted mechanic while further up just beyond Cambridge Circus, *Sportspages*, Caxton Walk, 94-96 Charing Cross Rd, WC2, T020-7240 9604, cover every sport imaginable.

South of Cambridge Circus, on Charing Cross Rd itself, there are three branches of *Zwemmer's*: at 80 Charing Cross Rd, WC2, T020-7240 4157, for photography and film, across the way at 24 Lichfield St, T020-7240 4158, for fine art, and at 70-80 Charing Cross Rd, T020-7240 1559, for design. Further down the street, *Shipley Art Booksellers*, 70 Charing Cross Rd, T020-7836 4872, is an independent that has been around for over 100 years, specializing in new, rare and out of print books on the fine arts. *Silver Moon Woman's Bookshop*, 64-68 Charing Cross Rd, WC2, T020-7836 7906, specializes in new books on women's issues. *Any Amount of Books*, 62 Charing Cross Rd, WC2, T020-7240 8140, and *Charing Cross Rd Bookshop*, 56 Charing Cross Rd, T020-7836 3697, are run by the same people, both rambling treasure troves of battered second-hand. *Henry Pordes Books*, T020-7836 9031, is another good general second-hand, specialiszing in art, literature and cinema.

Bookshops apart, smokers should not miss *G Smith and Sons*, 74 Charing Cross Rd, WC2, T020-7836 7422, traditional tobacconist extraordinaire.

Transport

Buses   **Along Shaftesbury Ave eastbound west of Cambridge Circus**:

Charing Cross station is a 10-min walk from Leicester Square. The British Museum is only a 15-min walk from Cambridge Circus

No 19 to Finsbury Park via Bloomsbury, Islington and Highbury.
No 38 to Hackney via Bloomsbury (for British Museum) and Islington.

Along Shaftesbury Ave westbound west of Cambridge Circus:
No 14 to Putney via Hyde Park Corner, Knightsbridge, South Kensington and Fulham Broadway.
No19 to Battersea, via Hyde Park Corner, Knightsbridge, Sloane Square, and Chelsea.
No 38 to Piccadilly Circus, Hyde Park Corner and Victoria.

Along Charing Cross Rd northbound south of Cambridge Circus:
No 24 to Hampstead Heath via Warren St and Camden Town.
No 29 to Camden Town via Warren St.
No 176 to Oxford Circus.

Directory

*There's an **internet café** at Home, 1 Leicester Square, where £1 will buy 15 mins online.*
***Post offices** on William IV St, off St Martin's Lane, near Trafalgar Square, and on Jermyn St.*

***Libraries** Westminster Central Reference Library, St Martin's St, on the site of Newton's house, Mon-Fri 1000-2000, Sat 1000-1700. Business library T020-7641 4634; general reference T020-7641 4636; arts and design library T020-7641 4638.*

Along Charing Cross Rd southbound south of Cambridge Circus:
No 24 to Pimlico via Trafalgar Square, Westminster and Victoria.
No 176 to Dulwich, via Trafalgar Square, Aldwych, Waterloo and Camberwell.

Everyone tries to hail a cab at Cambridge Circus. Gazumpers move further down **Taxis**
Shaftesbury Ave or Charing Cross Rd.

Leicester Square tube station (Northern and Piccadilly lines) is only a few mins walk **Tubes**
from covent Garden and Piccadilly Circus.

Soho

The West End

Soho has always been the West End at its least respectable and most lively, and now it's the only part of central London that really comes close to keeping the same hours as New York. Long considered to be shifty and disreputable, this small well-defined area south of Oxford Street, east of Regent Street, west of the Charing Cross Road and north of Shaftesbury Avenue has more character (and characters) per square yard than all those big names put together. That's mainly because people still actually live here and are proud of the place. Unlike New Yorkers though, they need their sleep. The recent influx of late-night partygoers, chain bars and mega restaurants has received almost as much opposition as the sex industry that once pervaded the area, though currently that opposition looks as if it will be less successful, posing a serious threat to the balance of the neighbourhood.

⊖ *Leicester Square or Tottenham Court Rd tube for east Soho, Oxford Circus tube for west Soho, Piccadilly Circus tube for both*

History

The name Soho derives from a medieval hunting or coursing cry, 'So-ho'. The farmland belonged to the Abbot and convent of Abingdon, before being handed over to Henry VIII in the course of the Dissolution of the Monasteries, and was briefly a royal park for Whitehall Palace. By the end of the 17th century, however, parts of the land were sold off to various nobles and the 1670s and 1680s saw rapid development, and with it the influx of refugees from abroad. Greeks fled here from persecution under the Ottomans – hence Greek Street, and French Huguenots sought refuge from Louis XIV's intolerance.

The French connection was to last through to the Second World War, with the French House restaurant on Dean Street serving as the unofficial HQ of the Free French Forces. Although the wealthier residents headed west to Mayfair towards the end of the 18th century, the area grew famous for its craftsmen and artisans – the Soho Tapestries flourished, the Soho Bazaar on the site of King Square (now Soho Square) housed stalls and counters for jewellery, millinery, gloves and lace for much of the 19th century, and Josiah Wedgwoods's London warehouse lay on Greek Street.

Predictably, the cosmopolitan flavour of the area attracted writers and artists to both live and drink in its taverns and coffee-houses. Canaletto had a studio in Beak Street; William Blake was born on Marshall Street and returned to the area later in life; Shelley was sent down from Oxford and came to Poland Street; William Hazlitt's house (now a cosy and exclusive hotel) remains on Frith Street; and a seven year-old Mozart touted his

•••••••••••••••••••••••••••

Hotels in the area

AL *Sanderson*
A *Hazlitt's*
▸▸ *Go to page 441*

Highs and lows of Soho

Soho divides neatly into two halves either side of Wardour Street. Both are a maze of little streets lined with shops, cafés, bars and restaurants that can take years to get to know and have become a popular but by no means exclusive stamping ground for the gay scene. Old Compton Street and the streets running south from Soho Square are the heart of 'high' Soho, while 'low' Soho, west of Wardour Street has

now been branded West Soho, picking up on Carnaby Street's doubtful fashionability, with seedy Brewer Street continuing the line of Old Compton Street. Both parts are top destinations for anyone and everyone looking for a long night out, joining the frantic buzz of London's media, advertising and film industry that fills the place by day. Respect due to the residents.

talents on Dean Street. Karl Marx lived at No 28 Dean Street in dingy attic rooms (three of his children died here), while Verlaine and Rimbaud lodged briefly on Old Compton Street following the fall of the Paris Commune.

The Hospital for Diseases of Women in Soho Square was the first of its kind in the world, although it had to change its name to simply the Hospital for Women since many people thought it only dealt with Venereal Disease

By the mid-18th century Soho had become severely overcrowded – there were 327 inhabitants per acre in 1851, so the cholera epidemic of 1854 spread voraciously. The burial ground of St Anne's Church is set 6 ft above the ground to accommodate some 10,000 bodies and six hospitals were built in the area. The area also became a centre of entertainment. Restaurants such as the Café Royale opened, and were frequented by the likes of Beardsley, GB Shaw, DH Lawrence, and Katherine Mansfield, while Kettner's bedrooms were visited by Wilde with his young acolytes, and Edward VII and Lillie Langtree.

The 20th century saw a further broadening of Soho's international flavour. Germans, Italians, Polish and Russian Jews, Greeks and Swiss were included among the residents, but Soho also began to gravitate towards a centre for the media. John Logie Baird gave the first demonstration of television in his rooms above what is now *Bar Italia*, publishers such as Bloomsbury, and film companies like Twentieth Century Fox set up in Soho Square – the *Groucho Club* on Dean Street continues this tradition. The sex industry took hold in the 1960s, but the Soho Society managed to restrict its spread. Soho is now known as a 'gay' area, with several gay bars dotting Rupert Street and Old Compton Street; one, the *Admiral Duncan*, was bombed in 1999 by a lone bigot.

Sights

Shopfronts, restaurant windows, doorways, alleys and, most important of all, other people are the sights of Soho, all packed so close together that somewhere somehow here you can reasonably expect to find your heart's desire.

Soho Square

Soho Square is one of the few breathing spaces, formerly the site of Monmouth House, the home of Charles II's bastard son James Scott, who rebelled unsuccessfully against James II, crying 'soho!' as he went into battle. Now a weather-beaten statue of his father by Caius Gabriel Cibber stands in front of a mock tudor toolshed, and the gardens are the favourite summer lunchtime snackspot of office workers and resting cycle couriers.

On either side of the square stand the French protestant church and St Patrick's Catholic church. The **House of St Barnabas**, on the corner of the square where it meets Greek Street, is a beautiful Georgian building with a

Sex and clubs and rock 'n' roll

Soho has long been associated with sex and vice. Central London's notorious one-square-mile district was home to some 300 prostitutes in the 1950s and when they moved elsewhere in the 60s, Soho turned to other methods, such as 'clipping' (which involves getting the customer to pay before sending them to a fictitious address and then disappearing). Around this time, the number of strip clubs and drinking clubs increased dramatically. The most famous, Raymond Revuebar, is still doing business, though most have now closed.

From the late 60s Soho became the centre of the porn industry. While pornographic magazines were shipped over from the continent in Danish Bacon lorries, the Obscene Publications Squad (OPS) was being bribed to turn a blind eye. But in 1972 a new commissioner of the Metropolitan Police was appointed to clean up Soho and the OPS was suspended. In the early 80s new legislation requiring all sex shops to be licensed came into effect.

Soho was also one of the centres of British bohemia as well as the culinary capital of Britain. Its drinking clubs are still famous: The Colony Room, on Dean Street, has always been a favourite haunt of hard-drinking British artists, from Francis Bacon to Damien Hirst, and the Groucho, once the epitome of Thatcherite excess, still serves the inflated egos of medialand.

Soho also has mighty impressive music credentials. Ronnie Scott's was the first outlet in the capital for modern jazz, while the Marquee (now closed) played host to the Yardbirds and the Rolling Stones. Its dance clubs, such as The Wag and Beat Route were at the cutting edge of late 70s/early 80s music and its most famous late-night coffee bar, Bar Italia on Frith Street, still gives homeward-bound clubbers the coolest of caffeine kicks.

Soho's most recent cultural incarnation, as the capital's big gay heart only confirms its status as London's Left Bank or Greenwich Village.

The West End

very old mulberry tree in the garden. It's been a hostel for single homeless women since 1851. Tours of the fine interior, including the charming Victorian chapel, in 13th-century French Gothic style, usually take place on Tuesdays and Thursdays. ■ *Open by appointment Tue 1430-1630, and Thu 1100-1230. Call to check details, T020-7437 1894.*

Running south down to Shaftesbury Avenue from Soho Square, roughly parallel to the Charing Cross Road, are **Greek Street** and **Frith Street**. The **Frith Street Gallery**, at 59-60 Frith Street, W1 (T020-7494 1550), picks up on their tone by putting on shows of cutting-edge contemporary art. The length of **Dean Street** lies one block further west. Even though each is crowded with highly individual shops, restaurants and bars, these three streets and the alleyways between them are so similar in atmosphere and appearance that they can easily baffle the inexperienced Soho partygoer.

Greek Street, Frith Street & Dean Street *These streets form the core of 'high' Soho, with Dean St perhaps the most happening of the three*

Just before reaching Shaftesbury Avenue they all cross **Old Compton Street**, the area's unofficial high street. A recent attempt to pedestrianize this main drag failed due to problems policing the late-night hordes. The street has also become the main artery of the gay scene, while its junction with Greek Street and Moor Street must be one of the most characteristic and crowded spots in the area.

Old Compton Street

Meard Street, a fine row of Georgian houses, links Dean Street with **Wardour Street**, the main north-south axis dividing this part of the area from 'low' Soho to the west. Wardour Street is still synonymous with the film industry,

Wardour Street

Soho

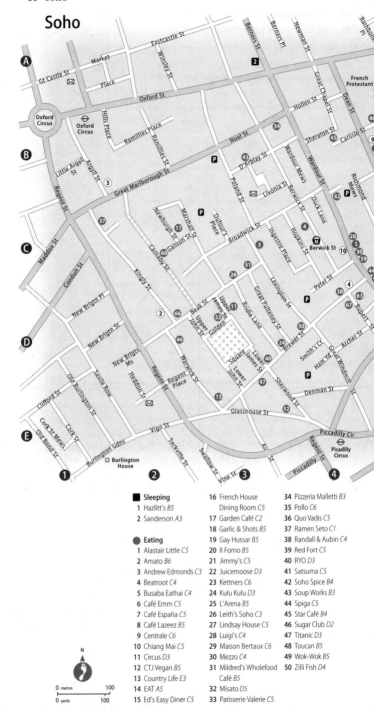

■ **Sleeping**	16 French House	34 Pizzeria Malletti *B3*
1 Hazlitt's *B5*	Dining Room *C5*	35 Pollo *C6*
2 Sanderson *A3*	17 Garden Café *C2*	36 Quo Vadis *C5*
	18 Garlic & Shots *B5*	37 Ramen Seto *C1*
● **Eating**	19 Gay Hussar *B5*	38 Randall & Aubin *C4*
1 Alastair Little *C5*	20 Il Forno *B5*	39 Red Fort *C5*
2 Amato *B6*	21 Jimmy's *C5*	40 RYO *D3*
3 Andrew Edmonds *C3*	22 Juicemoose *D3*	41 Satsuma *C5*
4 Beatroot *C4*	23 Kettners *C6*	42 Soho Spice *B4*
5 Busaba Eathai *C4*	24 Kulu Kulu *D3*	43 Soup Works *B3*
6 Café Emm *C5*	25 L'Arena *B5*	44 Spiga *C5*
7 Café España *C5*	26 Leith's Soho *C3*	45 Star Café *B4*
8 Café Lazeez *B5*	27 Lindsay House *C5*	46 Sugar Club *D2*
9 Centrale *C6*	28 Luigi's *C4*	47 Titanic *D3*
10 Chiang Mai *C5*	29 Maison Bertaux *C6*	48 Toucan *B5*
11 Circus *D3*	30 Mezzo *C4*	49 Wok-Wok *B5*
12 CTJ Vegan *B5*	31 Mildred's Wholefood	50 Zilli Fish *D4*
13 Country Life *E3*	Café *B5*	
14 EAT *A5*	32 Misato *D5*	
15 Ed's Easy Diner *C5*	33 Patisserie Valerie *C5*	

N

0 metres 100
0 yards 100

Pubs & bars
51 Alphabet *C3*
52 Atlantic Bar & Grill *E3*
53 Café Boheme *C6*
54 Coach & Horses *C6*
55 Dog & Duck *B5*
56 Downstairs at Phoenix *B6*
57 Edge *A5*
58 French House *C5*
59 Freedom *C4*
60 Freedom Brewing Co *C2*
61 Lab *B6*
62 Mondo *B6*
63 Rupert St *D4*
64 Sak *B5*
65 Three Greyhounds *C6*
66 Two Floors *D2*
67 Yard *D4*

Entertainment
1 Candy Bar *B5*
2 Emporium *E3*
3 London Palladium *E*
4 Madam Jo Jo's *C4*
5 Pop *A5*
6 Prince Edward Theatre *C6*
7 Ronnie Scotts *C5*
8 Salsa! *B6*
9 Soho Theatre & Writer's Centre *B5*
10 St Moritz *C4*
11 Velvet Room *B6*

even though few British film companies can afford much office space here, most of it being taken up by advertising production companies.

On the corner of Wardour Street and Old Compton Street, only the tower of the Church of St Anne survived the Blitz, but it now houses the **Soho Society**; T020-7439 4303. Among the many projects and campaigns in support of the area currently being undertaken by the Society is the quest for the Museum of Soho's new home.

Berwick Street

Brewer Street continues the thrust of Old Compton Street westwards, heading into the newly branded 'West Soho'. Just along here on the right, a seedy little passage called Walker's Court leads through into **Berwick Street**, home to the West End's one and only pukka **fruit 'n' veg market**. Since 1995 the stalls piled high with bargain comestibles have only been allowed on one side of the street, making for more space on the road but threatening the future of the market. Even so, a jostle down this street of a busy weekday lunchtime remains one of Soho's unmissable treats. Apart from fresh fruit and vegetables, look out for the cheese stall and fresh herb barrow. The market does not take place on Sundays.

Carnaby Street & around

The formal gardens in the middle of Golden Square are a pleasant enough place to take a sandwich

This west side of Soho is generally more seedy and money-grabbing than boho high Soho. Nearer Regent Street, around **Carnaby Street**, it also becomes even more fashion-conscious, especially along Newburgh Street. Carnaby Street itself, a bye-word for anything groovy in the 60s, has begun to reclaim some of the cachet that it let slip in the 1980s after becoming a tourist trap trading on its heyday. Other streets nearby well worth exploring for their bars, clubs, shops and restaurants are Kingly Street and Beak Street. Just south of these, **Golden Square** is like a piece of Mayfair that has slipped the

wrong side of Regent Street. Although nothing remains of its early 18th-century origins, it is distinguished by the faceless offices of media multinationals and a few interesting shops on its southern side.

Eating and drinking

Many of the places listed here will need to be booked

Just about every type of cooking under the sun is available somewhere in Soho: the problem is deciding exactly where and how to enjoy what. A clutch of Japanese noodle and sushi bars are the latest arrivals, most being fast, high quality and affordable. Modern European dining is also particularly well represented at a variety of oh-so Soho venues, as well as endless different alternatives, from fashionable fusion and fish menus to tremendous Italian, modern British and Thai restaurants. In fact, the sheer number of good mid-range and cheap restaurants in Soho has been largely responsible for the area's popularity for some time.

Expensive
● *on map, page 86*

The most fun and fashionable smart eaterie in Soho is still *The Sugar Club*, 21 Warwick St, W1, T020-7437 7776. A dressed-up crowd flock here for New Zealand-Asian fusion food in a see-and-be-seen setting. A similar crew can be found at *Titanic*, 81 Brewer St, W1, T020-7437 1912, a stylish bar-restaurant with attitude and door policy to match. Both should be booked. If they're full, try *Circus Restaurant and Bar*, 1 Upper James St, W1, T020-7534 4000. Even more expensive, and stuffed with smart suits and fashionistas, the downstairs bar is lavish and late.

Other gourmet dining options in the area can offer more quiet pleasures, such as *Leith's Soho*, 41 Beak St, W1, T020-7287 2057. Excellent modern European cooking from the world-famous cookery school proprietor is served up in a cool and restrained ambience. For a slightly more zippy dining experience, *Alastair Little*, 49 Frith St, W1, T020-7734 5183, the trailblazer of Anglo-Italian cooking, continues to come up with the freshest of well-prepared goods in his eponymous flagship.

Richard Corrigan at Lindsay House, 21 Romilly St, W1, T020-7439 0450, makes similar waves with his modern British menu. The 18th-century atmosphere of his Soho townhouse may be a little precious but creates an appreciative mood. Much larger and louder, *Quo Vadis*, 28 Dean St, W1, T020-7437 9585, is yet another Marco Pierre White venture, with a typically fine Frenchified menu and considerable buzz.

Spoon Plus, in the super-chic *Sanderson Hotel*, 50 Berners St, T020-7245 0896, is the latest opening to cause a stir with the area's media darlings, doing a pricey pick'n'mix menu for very fussy eaters. The predominantly grey-haired customers at one of Soho's best-loved institutions have no such qualms as they tuck into gigantic servings of Hungarian food in the clubby, old-fashioned intimacy of the *Gay Hussar*, 2 Greek St, W1, T020-7437 0973.

Mid-range

Two modern European restaurants stand out in this bracket: the offal-based delicacies on offer in the excellently laid-back little *French House Dining Room*, 49 Dean St, W1, T020-7437 2477, and the slightly more atmospheric, candlelit wonders of *Andrew Edmonds*, 46 Lexington St, W1, T020-7437 5708. At both the very freshest ingredients go into regularly changing menus that are excellent value. Booking is essential and they can get smokey. Just as popular for fish is the bistro-style *Randall and Aubin*, 16 Brewer St, W1, T020-7287 4447, and slightly more expensive, *Zilli Fish*, 36-40 Brewer St, W1, T020-7734 8649.

Italian cooking achieves new heights in Soho: *Il Forno*, 63-64 Frith St, W1, T020-7734 4545, run by the same people as *Al Duca* in St James's, and *Spiga*, 84-86 Wardour St, W1, T020-7734 3444, both offer excellent contemporary recipes in appropriately spare and stylish settings. For more traditional Italian favourites, try *Luigi's*, 134 Wardour St, W1, T020-7437 6527, which also has a lively bar, or *L'Arena*, 6 Greek St,

W1, T020-7734 2334, even more well-starched.

Urban vampires should keep well away from *Garlic & Shots*, 14 Frith St, W1, T020-7734 9505, a glorified drinking den where garlic is served with everything in casual, almost grungy atmosphere. It's also a great place for some serious brain-cell damage, with 101 various shots on offer. Friendly service but you may have few afterwards.

Five of the best: cheap eats in the West End ★

- *Busaba Eathai*, Wardour Street, Soho.
- *Hammock Café*, Drury Lane, Covent Garden.
- *India Club*, Strand.
- *ICA Café*, The Mall, St James's.
- *Pizzico*, Haymarket, Leicester Square.

The West End

Wok-Wok, 10 Frith St, W1, T020-7437 7080, is one of a small city-wide chain that does interesting Chinese food, here on a big, bustling but friendly scale.

Strangely enough Indian cuisine is not particularly well represented in Soho. The best are both run by the same people, embracing the pomp and pageantry of *The Red Fort*, 77 Dean St, W1, T020-7437 2115, and the more hip and happening *Soho Spice*, 124-126 Wardour St, W1, T020-7434 0808, open until 0300 on Fri and Sat. *Chiang Mai*, 48 Frith St, W1, T020-7437 7444, offers a peaceful, intimate venue for decidedly elegant Thai food.

Terence Conran's massive Soho outfit, *Mezzo*, 100 Wardour St, W1, T020-7314 4000, can usually be relied upon to have a table where some perfectly good modern European cuisine can be enjoyed in a swish atmosphere.

Vegetarians are well catered for. Many make for *Mildred's Wholefood Café*, 58 Greek St, W1, T020-7494 1634, which is licensed, clean and non-smoking. On the other side of Soho, *Country Life*, 3-4 Warwick St, W1, T020-7434 2922, is a very good-value vegan, with no alcohol or smoking, and only open until 2130. Back in High Soho, *CTJ Vegan Restaurant*, 10 Greek St, W1, T020-7287 3714, is an organic vegetarian Thai doing an all-you-can-eat lunch for £5. Altogether more hip, but also busier and slightly more expensive, is *Busaba Eathai*, 106-110 Wardour St, W1, T020-7255 8686, a new 'Thai casual dining room' with large windows onto Wardour St, open 1200-2330. Just down the road, *Satsuma*, 56 Wardour St, W1, T020-7437 8338 is a well-established Japanese doing fine ramen soups and bento boxes.

For healthy-eating 21st-century style though, four Japanese noodle and sushi bars win the day: *Kulu Kulu*, 76 Brewer St, W1, T020-7734 7316, does sushi on a travellator, as does *Misato*, 11 Wardour St, W1, T020-7734 0808, for very quick, high-quality lunches. *Ramen Seto*, 19 Kingly St, W1, T020-7434 0309, and *RYO*, 84 Brewer St, W1, T020-7287 1318, are two efficient noodle bars.

Much more old-school are two Italian fast-food joints, serving up great bowlfuls of comfort food at very low prices. The least hectic is the *Centrale*, 16 Moor St, W1, T020-7437 5513, last orders at 2130, while the best known and biggest is *Pollo*, 20 Old Compton St, W1, T020-7734 5917, last orders at 2330. *Jimmy's*, 23 Frith St, W1, T020-7437 9521, is the Greek equivalent. All three have tremendous brusque and business-like atmospheres and are very popular with students.

More laid-back and sophisticated, *Amato*, 14 Old Compton St, W1, T020-7734 5733, is open until 2200, doing fine patisserie and sandwiches. For a takeaway lunch-time pizza, the authenticity of *Pizzeria Malletti*, 26 Noel St, T020-7439 4096, is hard to beat. The longest-standing home of the pizza around here though is *Kettners*, 29 Romilly St, W1, T020-7734 6112, where no booking is required and the savoury flatbreads are still exceptional value given the faded grandeur of the décor.

Another good cheap choice is the effortlessly informal *Café Emm*, 17 Frith St, T020-7437 0723, where the portions are as huge as its popularity. The dive bar beneath the *Toucan*, 19 Carlisle St, W1, T020-7437 4123, does filling platefuls of

Cheap

good-quality Irish nosh. A good place to take the kids is *Ed's Easy Diner*, Old Compton St, T020-7434 4439, an American-style diner that does it better than most, serving great big greasy cheeseburgers and fries and luscious milkshakes; also at 38 Shaftesbury Ave.

Cafés &
sandwich bars
Soho, along with
Covent Garden, is
the epicentre of
London's café culture

In Soho, almost every other door opens on tempting cakes, coffees, pastries, sandwiches and full meals. Five of the best have all been around a long time: they are the French fancies of *Maison Bertaux*, 28 Greek St, W1, T020-7437 4520, and *Patisserie Valerie*, 44 Old Compton St, and the football and coffee crazy *Bar Italia*, 22 Frith St, open 24 hrs daily (except Mon) and still as hip as ever, the *Café España*, 63 Old Compton St, W1, T020-7494 1271, with an equally self-explanatory name, and the indomitable *Star Café*, 22 Great Chapel St, W1, T020-7437 8778, its check tablecloths presided over by the same family since 1936.

In a newer mould, the branch of *EAT*, at 16 Soho Square, W1, T020-7222 7200, is a particularly good outlet of the new sandwich, soup and coffee chain. The new *Café Lazeez* in Soho Theatre, 21 Dean St, W1, T020-7434 9393, is open until 0100, a functional-looking bar, restaurant and café with huge windows onto Dean St that just about manages to be all things to all people.

On the other side of Soho, *The Garden Café*, 4 Newburgh St, W1, T020-7494 0044, is a sweet place that comes into its own when the sun shines, with its quirky little back garden, while *Beatroot*, 82 Berwick St, W1, T020-7437 8591, is an excellent funky fresh-food café bang on Berwick St market. *Juicemoose*, on Upper St James' St, off Golden Square, can satisfy the most serious craving for smoothies and freshly squeezed juices. For some seriously nourishing modern soups, head for *Soup Works* at 9 D'Arblay St, W1, T020-7439 7687, or 15 Moor St, W1, T020-7734 7687.

Pubs & bars

At weekends the crowds of revellers make streets like Old Compton and Greek almost impassable. After 1800 throughout the week, finding a pub or bar with room to sit down can be a challenge, not just in the new wave of designer and chain bars that are causing the residents concern, but also in those pubs that have been around for years.

The Coach and Horses, 29 Greek St, W1, T020-7437 5920, has long established itself as the archetypal Soho boozer, thanks to its famously rude landlord and alcoholic regulars like the late Jeffrey Bernard. It's still a refreshingly unpretentious place for a plain pint and a very old-style ham sandwich. The other favourite haunt of the Soho set is the cosy little *French House*, 49 Dean St, W1, T020-7437 2799, formerly the *Yorkminster*, where the wine is very good and beer served in halves only.

Usually less crowded, unless pre- or post-theatre, is the *Three Greyhounds*, 25 Greek St, W1, T020-7287 0754, its strange mock-Swiss interior presided over by a formidable landlady serving good home-made food. The film industry's favourite old-fashioned pub remains the *Dog and Duck*, 18 Bateman St, W1, T020-7494 0697, a busy little corner pub on two floors pumping very good beer. *The Toucan*, 19 Carlisle St, W1, T020-7437 4123, is an Irish pub boasting the best Guiness in Soho with plenty of scruffy charm and not too themed. *Propaganda*, 201 Wardour St, W1, T020-7434 3820 , is a brand new designer style bar with a cutting-edge music policy.

Café Bohème, 13-17 Old Compton St, W1, T020-7734 0623, open 24 hrs Fri and Sat, admission £3 after 2200, £4 after 2300 Fri, Sat (last orders for alcohol 0230 daily) was one of the bars that led the way for late-night Soho, a relaxed, continental-style brasserie on a busy corner with a top-notch restaurant attached. Expect to queue if arriving late. Another old-timer, relatively speaking, is *Mondo*, 12-13 Greek St, W1, T020-7734 7157, also open late, a subterranean warren of comfy booths and banquettes. *Lab*, 12 Old Compton St, T020-7437 7820, opened more recently, its 70s design popular with students. *Sak*, 49 Greek St, T020-7439 4159, is another more grown-up designer bar.

Five of the best: late-night bars in the West End

- *Sak*, Greek Street, Soho.
- *St James's Circus* Upper James Street, Soho.
- *Café Boheme*, Old Compton Street, Soho.
- *Zoo Bar*, Winsley Street, off Oxford Street.
- *ICA Bar*, The Mall, St James's.

Freedom, 60 Wardour St, W1, T020-7734 0071, has a predominantly gay clientele but has long made a point of welcoming any sexual persuasion. *Rupert St*, 50 Rupert St, W1, T020-7292 7141, is the most fashionable of the gay bars. Opposite it, *The Yard*, 57 Rupert St, W1, T020-7437 2652, is the most homely and comfortable, while *The Edge*, 11 Soho Square, W1, T020-7439 1313, is a vast five-floor gay pleasuredome.

Most of the bars in Soho welcome gay or straight customers but some are more out & proud than others

In west Soho, the best pub-bar-restaurant hybrid is the *Freedom Brewing Company*, 14-16 Ganton St, T020-7287 5267. The ground floor has tables outside, just off Carnaby St, and downstairs the long bar pumps own-brew beer from the gleaming vats on display. *Two Floors*, 3 Kingly St, W1, T020-7439 1007, pretty much kicked off the boom in style bars in this part of town and remains popular. *Alphabet*, 61-63 Beak St, W1, T020-7439 2190, took up the challenge and has become the favourite place to be seen if you're in advertising. Arrive early to ensure a seat.

▶▶ Go to page 419 for entertainment & nightlife

Still going strong after becoming the most fashionable dive of the 90s, is the *Atlantic Bar and Grill*, 20 Glasshouse St, W1, T020-7734 4888. Book a table at the restaurant if you want guaranteed entry, although the louche comfort of *Dick's Bar* is the main attraction. Back on the other side of Soho, another late bar with plenty of character and an equally uncertain door policy is *Downstairs at the Phoenix*, 1 Phoenix St, WC2, T020-7836 1077. Arrive before 2000 to be sure of gaining access to this bric-a-brac filled cellar just off the Charing Cross Rd.

Shopping

For books, Charing Cross Rd north of Cambridge Circus has several large shops for new books. Above all, there's the inimitable, rambling and extraordinary range of new titles on four floors at *Foyles*, 113-119 Charing Cross Rd, WC2, T020-7437 5660, open until 1930 and also open Sun. Every fairly recently published book could well be here somewhere, but it may take some finding. Nearby there are branches of *Borders*, **Books Etc**, **Blackwells** and *Waterstones*. In Soho itself, the **European Bookshop**, 5 Warwick St, W1, T020-7734 5259, has a wide range of European language books while **Grant and Cutler**, 55-57 Great Marlborough St, W1, T020-7734 2012, is one of the most famous foreign-language bookshops in the city. *A Moroni and Son*, 68 Old Compton St, W1, T020-7437 2847 is a large international newsagent, open until 2000 or 2200 Thu, Fri.

Bookshops

Head for West Soho for the latest street fashions, at shops like *Plum*, 79 Berwick St, W1, T020-7734 0812, for skateboard stuff, labels like Komodo, and jeans, or to *Beau Monde*, 43 Lexington St, W1, T020-7734 6563, and *Idol*, 15 Ingestre Place, W1, T020-7439 8537, or *Carhartt*, Newburgh St, for own-label womenswear. Own-label fashion for men can be found at *John Richmond*, 2 Newburgh St, W1, T020-7734 5782, and there's also a branch on the same street for women, *R12* at 12 Newburgh St. In the same area, *Yesterday's Bread*, 29 Fouberts Place, W1, T020-7287 1929, is a good stop for original 60s clothing.

Clothing & jewellery
Streetwear & fashion accessory shops dominate Soho, especially West Soho

Jess James, 3 Newburgh St, W1, T020-7437 7001, stocks hip designer jewellery displayed round gold fish. *Slinky's*, 10 Walker Court, W1, T020-7434 1716, is one of several fetishwear outlets, full of rubber and bondage stuff. Back in East Soho, fashion shops are thinner on the ground but include *American Retro*, 35 Old Compton St, W1,

T020-7734 3477, and the supercool *Kokon To Zai*, 57 Greek St, W1, T020-7434 1316, for dance music and dance gear.

Food & drink For good coffee there's the *Algerian Coffee Stores*, 52 Old Compton St, W1, T020-7437 2480. Fine wines and spirits can be found at *The Vintage House*, 42 Old Compton St, W1, T020-7437 2592, and *Nicolas*, 21 Berwick St, W1, T020-7494 4287.

Miscellaneous There are also quirky one-offs like *Anything Left-Handed*, 57 Brewer St, W1, T020- 7437 3910, selling exactly what its name suggests, and likewise the *Vintage Magazine Store*, 39-43 Brewer St, W1, T020-7439 8525, although it also has a wide range of old movie posters and postcards. *J Blundell and Sons*, 199 Wardour St, W1, T020-7437 4746, have been dispensing raw precious metals since 1890. *The Eye Company*, Optometrist and Contact Lens Practitioner, 159 Wardour St, W1, T020-7434 0988, is a good place to pick up some fashionable (and expensive) sunglasses by the likes of Oliver Peoples, Paul Smith, or Gucci, and they also do eye-tests. On the same street, *Scribbler*, 104 Wardour St, W1, T020-7439 2199, have a wacky range of cards and wrapping paper, while *Louise Woodhouse*, 100 Wardour St, W1, T020-7494 1144, is a sophisticated florist. Nearby, *Sendean*, 9-12 St Anne's Court, T020-7439 8418, are reliable camera repairers.

Transport

Buses **Along Charing Cross Rd northbound north of Cambridge Circus**:
No 19 to Finsbury Park via Bloomsbury, Islington and Highbury.
No 24 to Hampstead Heath via Warren St and Camden Town.
No 29 to Palmers Green via Warren St, Camden Town, Holloway and Finsbury Park.
No 38 to Hackney via Bloomsbury and Islington.

Along Charing Cross Rd southbound north of Cambridge Circus:
No 14 to Putney via Hyde Park Corner, Knightsbridge, South Kensington and Fulham Broadway.
No 19 to Battersea, via Hyde Park Corner, Knightsbridge, Sloane Square, and Chelsea.
No 24 to Pimlico via Trafalgar Square, Westminster and Victoria.
No 38 to Victoria via Hyde Park Corner.
No 176 to Penge, via Trafalgar Square, Aldwych, Waterloo, Camberwell, Dulwich and Sydenham.

Taxis The Charing Cross Rd, Oxford St, and Regent St are the best bets for finding an available cab in the likely event that all those clogged up in Soho itself are already taken. A good bet at night is to use the taxi firm a few doors west of *Pollo* restaurant, on Old Compton St; they operate shared cabs which greatly reduces the cost of the fare.

Tubes The four corners of Soho are covered by Tottenham Court Rd tube (Central and Northern lines), Oxford Circus (Central and Victoria lines), Piccadilly Circus (Piccadilly and Bakerloo lines) and Leicester Square (Northern and Piccadilly lines).

Directory

Medical Services *Soho Centre for Health and Care, 1 Frith St, W1, T0771-205 1119, www.tropicalscreening.com Soho NHS Walk-in Centre Open 7.30am-9pm Mon-Fri, 1000-2000, Sat, Sun. No* *appointment necessary. Assessment by an experienced nurse.*

Sports *Fitness First, 59 Kingly St, W1 T020-734 6226. £8.50 1 day, £30 for 5 sessions, £55 for 10 sessions. Gym and sauna.*

Covent Garden

Covent Garden has been attracting traders, entertainers, their customers and audiences for at least 300 years but it only became a respectable tourist hotspot about 30 years ago, a fairly successful transformation of one of the oldest meeting places in the West End into one of the youngest. Thankfully it's still largely free of the depressing tat peddled to visitors around Piccadilly Circus and Leicester Square.

⊖ *Nearest tube Covent Garden; nearest train station Charing Cross*

The West End

Sandwiched between the Charing Cross Road, Bloomsbury, the Strand and Holborn, the area is almost as well defined as Soho, but doesn't quite have the buzz that makes its neighbour to the west so vital. The focal point is still what was once London's largest and most famous fruit n' veg market, immortalized in Hitchcock's film Frenzy *before it moved out to Nine Elms in 1974. Now an impressive 'piazza', it still bears a faint flavour of those bustling times thanks to its converted Victorian covered market and the crowds that flock here day and night to shop, eat, drink and enjoy a pleasant place away from all the traffic.*

Like Soho, people not only work but also live in the surrounding streets, despite rocketing rents, and they managed to save the market from the developers when the stallholders moved out. To the east, the **Royal Opera House** *has reopened to great acclaim after its multi-million pound redevelopment. North of Long Acre, what were once narrow streets of warehouses and slums have experienced a boom in youth-orientated shops and bars, led by long-established crowd-pullers like the Donmar Warehouse theatre and Neals Yard wholefood hippy enclave.*

History

The area known as Covent Garden emerged as a focal point for London society in the 17th and 18th centuries. St Martin's Lane had long been the great north road from Charing Cross, but until Henry VIII seized the land during the dissolution, this was pasture belonging to St Peter's Convent, with narrow strips of market gardens running down what is now Long Acre. Henry granted the land to John Russell, Earl of Bedford, but it was 100 years before the area was developed, when the fourth earl commissioned Inigo Jones to build a piazza. Jones produced a courtyard of high terraced houses, with the front doors covered by vaulted arcades, and St Paul's church on one side.

Bedford had asked for the church to be little more than a barn, so Jones promised him "the handsomest barn in England". St Paul's was the first Anglican church to be built in London since the Reformation (up to 100 years earlier), and while it was damaged by fire in 1795, it is essentially still the same today. It has seen some distinguished visitors. Wesley preached here, JMW Turner and WS Gilbert (minus Sullivan) were both baptised here, while Sir Peter Lely, Grinling Gibbons, Thomas Rowlandson and Ellen Terry are among those that have never left.

St Paul's columned front provides the backdrop for Eliza Doolittle's first appearance in Pygmalion

The square was a desirable address among early 17th-century society, and the fruit, vegetable and flower market ensured a lively atmosphere. Streets built up around the square, and coffee-houses such as *Will's*

Hotels in the area

A Covent Garden
A Radisson Mountbatten
B Drury Lane Moat House
C Seven Dials
C Fielding Hotel
C Jubilee Hotel
▸▸ **Go to page 441**

Covent Garden

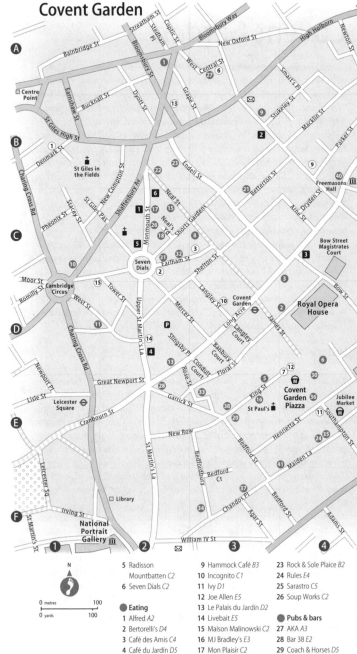

The West End

N

0 metres   100
0 yards   100

■ **Sleeping**
1 Covent Garden *C2*
2 Drury Lane Moat House *B3*
3 Fielding *C4*
4 Jubilee *D2*
5 Radisson Mountbatten *C2*
6 Seven Dials *C2*

● **Eating**
1 Alfred *A2*
2 Bertorelli's *D4*
3 Café des Amis *C4*
4 Café du Jardin *D5*
5 Calabash at the Africa Centre *E3*
6 Chez Gerrard *D4*
7 Christopher's & Speakeasy *D5*
8 Food for Thought *C3*

9 Hammock Café *B3*
10 Incognito *C1*
11 Ivy *D1*
12 Joe Allen *E5*
13 Le Palais du Jardin *D2*
14 Livebait *E5*
15 Maison Malinowski *C2*
16 MJ Bradley's *E3*
17 Mon Plaisir *C2*
18 Neals Yard Bakery & Tearoom *C2*
19 Orso *E5*
20 Plummers *D2*
21 Poetry Society *C3*
22 Punjab *B2*

23 Rock & Sole Plaice *B2*
24 Rules *E4*
25 Sarastro *C5*
26 Soup Works *C2*

● **Pubs & bars**
27 AKA *A3*
28 Bar 38 *E2*
29 Coach & Horses *D5*
30 Crusting Pipe *E4*
31 Detroit *C2*
32 Freedom Brewing Company *C2*
33 Lamb & Flag *E3*
34 Lemon Tree *F3*

The West End

became haunts for the likes of John Dryden, Alexander Pope and Pepys, who saw Dryden there holding forth "with all the wits in town". But as the market grew, the coffee-shops and taverns were supplemented by gambling dens and Turkish baths, (aka brothels), and the wealthy fled west to Mayfair, returning perhaps for a spot of theatre or opera at what is now the Royal Opera House.

The area became increasingly lively – duels were regularly fought in taverns, (Sheridan's third duel over a certain Miss Linley in the Castle Tavern on Henrietta Street resulted in such harsh injuries that the pistol became the preferred duelling weapon), press-gangs and mohocks (aristocratic gangs) roamed the streets, while *Henry's List of Covent Garden Ladies* sold out each edition. Such was the lawlessness that Henry Fielding, Bow Street magistrate and novelist, set up with his blind brother John the **Bow Street Runners**, 'thief-takers' that were precursors of the world's first Metropolitan police force.

The market steadily grew and the theatres began to flourish. The Opera House was twice rebuilt following fires, and sparked riots through its pricing policy. Meanwhile Bow Street magistrates exercised the censor's knife on DH Lawrence's *The Rainbow* – it was found to be obscene – and Oscar Wilde was charged with gross indecency here in 1895. When the market itself moved to Vauxhall in 1974, the area narrowly survived the town planners' toll, and is now a tourist trap of chic shops, restaurants and buskers, but lacks the raw energy that the market provided.

Sights

Covent Garden tube is a popular rendezvous point, where afterwork crowds gather on the corner of Long Acre and James Street before heading off for an afternoon's shopping or an

Covent Garden Piazza

Covent Garden's artistic connections

Naturally, artists and artisans were drawn by Covent Garden's vitality. Chippendale's workshop was in Goodwins Court, Boswell first met Johnson in Davies's bookshop at No 8 Russell Street, Jane Austen stayed with her brother on Henrietta Street, and Thomas De Quincey researched and wrote Confessions of an English Opium Eater *in Tavistock Street. There was also poverty and squalor – the Seven Dials was the setting for Hogarth's* Gin Lane, *where Dickens observed its 'half-naked children that wallow in the kennels'.*

evening's entertainment. Pedestrianized James Street leads directly south towards Covent Garden Piazza, one of the more pleasant and all-too-rare car-free environments in central London. Just beside the tube, Floral Street runs off to the right parallel to Long Acre, lined with the area's most fashionable clothes shops. The Piazza itself is the main event though, London's first planned square although nothing of it remains, its Victorian covered market very much the focal point of the area, now a dinky two-tier shopping arcade packed with tempting tourist-orientated boutiques that mostly aren't too tacky, alongside decent cafés and bars, some with balconies overlooking the courtyards on either side.

The west side is dominated by the classical portico of **St Paul's Church**, a 17th-century box designed by Inigo Jones that has long been known as the actors' church thanks to the plaques inside commemorating bygone stars of the stage and screen. The interior is as simple and modest as the exterior suggests, and it's reached round the back via a charming little back garden with tiny entrances off Henrietta Street, King Street and Bedford Street. The portico on the piazza forms the backdrop to regular street theatre events of widely varying quality throughout the year. ■ *Open Tue-Fri 0930-1630. T020-7836 5221.*

On the south side, the **Jubilee Market** is another covered market with a much lower-rent selection of clothing and jewellery stalls as well as some reasonable snack stops. Things improve here on Mondays when an antiques market sets up shop and at weekends when craftworkers arrive with their wares. The Jubilee Sports Centre (see Sport below) is in the same building.

London Transport Museum
There's also a café & a shop full of London Transport's distinctive & historic merchandising, classic posters, mugs & toys

Next door, in the old flower market in the southeast corner of the piazza, the London Transport Museum is an excellent place to take the kids for free. As well as a host of antique carriages, trams, buses and tube trains, many of which can be boarded and explored, the great glass-roofed hall contains a formidable battery of hands-on exhibits, push-button panels and a cunning labyrinth of aerial walkways. Plenty of opportunities for adults to enjoy themselves too, whether coming over all nostalgic at the smell of an old railway carriage, driving a tube train simulator or discovering how designer Frank Pick arrived at the final version of his classic tube map.

■ *Open Mon-Thu, Sat, Sun 1000- 1800, Fri 1100-1800 (last entry 1700). Admission £5.50, free for under-16s. T020-7379 6344, www.ltmuseum.co.uk*

Royal Opera House
Opposite, in the northeast corner, stands the brand new Royal Opera House, the end result of years of controversy spiced with bitter accusations about squandering public funds on elitist pastimes. In fact the new development has been a huge success, open to the general public throughout the day. It

includes a terrace overlooking the piazza while the refurbished Floral Hall needs to be seen to be believed. The main entrance is on Bow Street (see Essentials below).

Appropriately enough, given the proximity of the Royal Opera House and the Drury Lane Theatre Royal, just down the road on Russell Street is the Theatre Museum. A strange idea perhaps for such a live art form, the museum will probably only really appeal to theatre nuts. The most eye-catching exhibits, antique masks, wigs, costumes and memorabilia are just up the stairs on the right. Downstairs, more pictures and theatre-related objects are pickled in rows of skilfully illuminated glass tanks, tracing the history of the stage from Tudor times up to the mid-20th century. 'From Page To Stage' is a long term exhibition charting the birth of the National Theatre's very popular production of Alan Bennett's *Wind In The Willows*, with plenty of hands-on activities for the kids. The video archive of stage performance is a fascinating collection of never-to-be-repeated performances while temporary exhibitions focus on elements of current theatre practice.

Theatre Museum
The museum entrance is off Russell St

■ *Open Tue-Sun 1000-1800, last entry 1730. Admission £4.50, £2.50 concession; under 16s and over 60s free. T020-7943 4700.*

Back on Bow Street, past **Bow Street Magistrates Court** – where the capital's first police force, the Bow Street Runners, originated – and the front of the Royal Opera House, Great Queen Street heads off to the right, continuing the line of Long Acre. The massive art deco building at the end of Great Queen Street is the Freemasons' Hall, the United Grand Lodge of Freemasonry in England, which despite the powerful society's repeated avowals of openness and good deeds still looks pretty intimidating. The **Museum** contains all kinds of Masonic regalia, clocks, watches and other artefacts, and is open free of charge throughout the week, but it's probably best to join one of the free guided tours which include the Grand Master's Robing Room, the Shrine, and also the Grand Temple, a spectacular edifice with an extraordinary mosaic ceiling and massive brass doors.

Freemasons' Hall

■ *Museum open 1000-1700 Mon-Fri, tours lasting about 1 hr at 1100, 1200, 1400, 1500 Mon-Fri unless a ceremony is in progress. T020- 7831 9811.*

North of Long Acre, Covent Garden becomes considerably less pompous and more intimate, an intricate network of little streets that still retain some flavour of their dubious past. Seven Dials, a seven-arm junction marked by a restored multi-faceted sundial, provides a landmark in the western part of this area while Endell Street cuts north-south in the east. From Seven Dials, narrow little Earlham Street sneaks through to Cambridge Circus and Shaftesbury Avenue.

Seven Dials

Monmouth Street heads north into the area long known as St Giles, once a disease-infested slum much criticized and described by Dickens. On St Giles High Street is the church of **St Giles in the Fields**, which still looks much as it did in the 18th century. In front of it stands the Resurrection Gate, complete with a spectacular relief of the Day of Judgement carved in wood in 1687. The church has a simple interior and interesting history fully explained in a leaflet by the Reverand Gordon Taylor. From here, leading onto the Charing Cross Road, **Denmark Street** is London's unofficial tin-pan alley, lined with musical instrument shops.

St Giles

The West End

Eating and drinking

● *on map, page 94* Covent Garden is an enormously popular destination for dining out but has never quite fulfilled the promise of the 80s gastronomic revolution when it looked like it might become the epicentre of fine dining in London. Now it is overshadowed by Soho, Mayfair, St James's and even Clerkenwell. That said, there are plenty of special exceptions to the complacent mediocrity all too often encouraged by tourist booms.

Expensive Wood pannelling, stained glass, modern art, superb service and Italianate brasserie food have made the tables at *The Ivy*, 1 West St, WC2, T020-7836 4751, the most sought after in London. Long popular with thespians and wealthy families treating themselves, the well-deserved hype has ensured that booking weeks in advance is often the only way of enjoying a meal here in the evenings. Lunchtimes are often booked solid too, but it's well worth having a go.

Incognito, 117 Shaftesbury Ave, WC2, T020-7836 8866, is Nico Landenis' highly acclaimed new venture, doing an excellent modern French menu in a discreet and sophisticated style.

A world apart from all these is *Rules*, 35 Maiden Lane, WC2, T020-7836 5314, one of the oldest English restaurants in Britain and now something of a tourist trap, but nonetheless a highly atmospheric Victorian venue for some classic recipes majoring on game. *Christopher's*, 18 Wellington St, WC2, T020-7240 4222, hasn't been around quite as long but is pretty much the American equivalent, its first-floor dining room reached via an impressive stone staircase making an appropriately theatrical setting for some good meat and seafood.

Mon Plaisir, 21 Monmouth Street, WC2, T020-7836 7243, is another first-rate old-timer, much loved for its shabby charm and French regional cuisine. *Bertorelli's*, 44a Floral Street, WC2, T020-7836 3969, is a classic and cheerful Italian restaurant that isn't afraid to experiment.

Mid-range *Joe Allen*, 13 Exeter St, WC2, T020-7836 0651, is quite hard to find but definitely worth the effort. The American menu served up in this traditional basement diner never fails to please a host of theatre-going regulars as well as tourists in the know and it's open late throughout the week. *Orso*, 27 Wellington St, WC2, T020-7240 5269, is another excellent basement venue for some very good Tuscan cooking. Both should be booked. For some decent seafood in a busy, functional environment, head next door to *Livebait*, 21 Wellington St, WC2, T020-7836 7161, the Covent Garden branch of the Waterloo purveyors of fine fish now owned by the Chez Gerrard chain.

On the same street is the *Café du Jardin*, 28 Wellington St, WC2, T020-7836 4123, a neat and orderly place for some reliable modern European food. Slightly further afield but well worth the walk, *Alfred*, 245 Shaftesbury Ave, WC2, T020-7240 2566, is a no-nonsense British restaurant with a positively spartan formica interior, an appropriate setting for good beer and wine and some well-sourced traditional and innovative recipes.

Back in Covent Garden proper, *Calabash at the Africa Centre*, 38 King St, WC2, T020-7836 1976, is probably one of the best African restaurants in London, in a cosy basement which also hosts excellent African live music in a laid-back atmosphere that's not too expensive either. *Punjab*, 80/82 Neal St, WC2, T020-7836 9787, is a reliable but not cheap curry house that has been around for years in an area not blessed with a particularly wide choice of Indian restaurants. The *Café des Amis*, just off Long Acre at 11-14 Hanover Place, WC2, T020 7379 3444 has long been a tourist favourite and it's easy to see why, it's a cheerful airy venue for an eclectic menu that's good value. Not far away, *Le Palais du Jardin*, 136 Long Acre, WC2, T020-7379 5353, is an equally popular brasserie, often very loud and busy.

Belgo Centraal, 50 Earlham St, WC2, T020-7813 2333, is a huge subterranean celebration of all things Belgian. You can enjoy the mussels from Brussels in a buzzy (and boozy) beer-hall setting, and sample more than 100 types of beer. Open daily 1200-1500, Mon-Thu 1730-0030, Fri & Sat till 0130, Sun till 2330. (Also *Belgo Noord*, at 72 Chalk Farm Rd, NW1, T020-7267 0718 and *Belgo Zud*, at 124 Ladbroke Grove, W10, T020-8982 8400.) *Chez Gerrard at the Opera House Terrace*, 1st floor Opera Terrace, Covent Garden Central Market, WC2, T020-7379 0666, is everything its name suggests, a successful branch of the Frenchified restaurant chain with decent food and views over neat box hedges towards the new Opera House.

Five of the best: rooms with a view ★

· *Royal Opera House Restaurant*, Covent Garden.
· *Rooftop Restaurant in the Portrait Gallery*, Trafalgar Square.
· *Seven*, in Home, Leicester Square.
· *Windows Bar*, in London Hilton Park Lane, Mayfair.
· *Studio Lounge*, Waterstones, Piccadilly.

The West End

Cheap
Finding a snack in Covent Garden is no problem at all, but a cheap meal is much more difficult

Probably the best option for a cheap meal is in one of the cafés listed below. Otherwise though, *The Rock and Sole Plaice*, 47 Endell St, WC2, T020-7836 3785, does famously good fish and chips. *Food For Thought*, 31 Neal St, WC2, T020-7836 0239, is a very good-value vegetarian. *Plummers*, 33 King Street, WC2, T020-7240 2534, is a little more expensive, but an intimate place for good-value set-price British food. Altogether more offbeat, *Sarastro*, 126 Drury Lane, WC2, T020-7836 0101, is a wacky and strange Moorish-style restaurant with a surprisingly inexpensive menu.

Cafés & sandwich bars
Covent Garden has more than enough cafés for everyone & few of them are the kind of rip-off merchants found around Leicester Square

It's pretty safe here to plump for whichever takes your fancy, although those listed below are exceptional. Neal's Yard is a good destination for a healthy lunch, provided either by the vegetarian *Neal's Yard Bakery & Tearoom*, 6 Neal's Yard, WC2, T020-7836 5199, or if that's too busy, the long-standing *World Food Café*, Neals Yard Dining Room, 1st floor, 14 Neal's Yard, WC2, T020-7379 0298 with a self-explanatory name and basic décor. Just round the corner, *Maison Malnowski*, 63 Neal Street, WC2, T020-7836 9779, has tables outside, good coffee and cakes. *The Hammock Café*, 186 Drury Lane, WC2, T020-7404 7808, is an interesting Brazilian place, while *M.J. Bradley's*, 9 King St, WC2, T020-7240 5178, is a decidedly superior sandwich joint. *Soup Works*, 29 Monmouth St, W1, T020-7240 7687, do excellent fresh soups to go or eat in with friendly staff and a funky attitude. The café at the *Poetry Society*, 22 Betterton St, WC2, T020-7420 9880, is an endearing little bar and wholefood café run by reliable poem-promoters.

Pubs & bars
Thanks to the tourist trade & local office custom, many of Covent Garden's old pubs have managed to retain their intimate scale & old-fashioned furnishings

The most famous of the old pubs is the *Lamb & Flag*, 33 Rose Street, WC2, T020-7497 9504, best approached down a tiny covered alley off Floral St, but its warm and woody interior and front courtyard can become impossibly busy. Another is the *Marquis of Granby*, 51 Chandos Place, WC2, T020-7836 7657, a characterful old-timer with its panelled partitions and glasswork intact. Nearby, the *Lemon Tree*, tucked away behind the London Coliseum in Bedfordbury, is a sweet little place adorned with operatic posters. The *Opera Tavern*, 23 Catherine St, WC2, T020-7379 9832, with its grand Victorian interior, pays similar respect to the Royal Opera House. The small Irish bar round the corner at the *Coach and Horses*, 42 Wellington St, WC2, T020-7240 0553, is very cosy, while on the same street, *Speakeasy at Christopher's*, 18 Wellington St, WC2, T020-7240 4222, stays open a little later than most pubs, an American-style basement bar with good-value cocktails. *The Maple Leaf*, 41 Maiden Lane, WC2, T020-7240 2843 is one of London's few Canadian pubs.

The West End

★ **Five of the best: West End DJ bars**

- *AKA*, West Central Street, Covent Garden.
- *The Spot*, Maiden Lane, Covent Garden.
- *The Loop*, Dering Street, Mayfair.
- *Propaganda*, Wardour Street, Soho.
- *Pop*, Soho Street, Soho .

In the Piazza itself, the best bar for its views, value, hours and avoiding the crush is the *Market Café*, 21 The Piazza, WC2, T020-7836 2137, open until 0200 Mon-Sat, in the southwest corner with a small terrace overlooking the courtyard in front of St Paul's. At ground level it's also a coffee bar with outside seating. In the bowels of the market is the *Crusting Pipe*, 27 The Market, The Piazza, WC2, T020-7836 1415, a branch of the Davys wine bar chain, a resolutely British institution popular with the local office crowd.

▶▶ Go to page 420 for entertainment & nightlife Most of the louder party venues and club bars are a little further afield. On the corner of Long Acre, at the gateway to the area, *Bar 38*, 1-3 Long Acre, WC2, T020-7836 7794, is a large, loud and modern chain bar. *Detroit*, 35 Earlham St, WC2, T020-7240 2662, open until 2400 Mon-Sat, has much more character, a subterranean warren of alcoves, excellent cocktails and decent food. Next door, the *Freedom Brewing Company*, 41 Earlham St, WC2, T020-7240 0606, is another underground venue, more airily done out in stainless steel and pale wood where beer is brewed on the premises and there's a separate dining area for food at reasonable prices. Both can get extremely busy. Much larger, but also doing designer-label brews, is *Navajo Joe's*, 34 King St, WC2, T020-7240 4008, with an enjoyably self-conscious Mexican theme.

Other party venues popular with lads and laddettes include the sports bar *Ram-Page*, 32 Great Queen St, WC2, T020-7242 0622, and the dance music bar *Spot*, 29 Maiden Lane, WC2, T020-7379 5900, open until 0100 (admission charge on Fri and Sat). Further north, *AKA*, 18 West Central St, WC2 T020-7836 0110, next door to *The End* nightclub (see page 421), open Thu-Sat until 0300, after 2230 admission £5, has live music and DJs, one big split-level floor with a restaurant, the latest in cool.

Shopping

Bookshops The area also boasts a good selection of bookshops, with the exceptional one being *Edward Stanford*, 12-14 Long Acre, WC2, T020-7836 1321, mapmakers and sellers since 1900, with a comprehensive stock of maps, travel guides and travel literature. There's also *Waterstone's*, 13-19 Garrick St, WC2, T020- 7836 6757. *The Africa Book Centre*, Africa Centre, 38 King St, WC2, T020-7240 6649, has a small but important selection of books from and about that continent. *The Dover Bookshop*, 18 Earlham St, WC2, T020-7836 2111, specializes in the out-of-copyright pictorial archive of Dover Publications for artists and designers. *Mysteries*, 9-11 Monmouth St, WC2, T020-7240 3688, stocks titles on anything New Age. *The Banana Bookshop,* 10 The Market, Piazza WC2, T020-7379 7475, has a good selection of children's books and a fairly wide range of general-interest titles.

Clothes
Covent Garden's main strength is its proliferation of clothes shops, ranging from a few exclusively high-fashion outlets through to second-hand jumble

For men Most of the big designers have congregated on Floral St. Here you'll find *Paul Smith*, 40-44 Floral St, WC2, T020-7379 7133, for smart menswear and accessories, with the *Paul Smith Sale Shop*, just off Floral St, at 7-8 Langley Court, WC2, T020-7379 7133, near *Ted Baker*, 1-4 Langley Court, WC2, T020-7497 8862, packed full of casualwear for men. Also for men, *Robot*, 37 Floral St, WC2, T020-7836 6156, do their own line of shoes as well as Diesel and Patrick Cox shoes, and clothing by Firetrap and Full Circle. *Jones*, 13 Floral St, WC2, T020-7240 8312, is a post-industrialized place for their own-label menswear as well as styles by Prada, Miu Miu, and Helmut Lang; a new ultra-modern branch has just opened at 19a Floral St, WC2, T020-7836 3860.

For women *Question Air*, 38 Floral St, WC2, T020-7836 8220, also have branches in Dulwich Village, Wimbledon Village, and Barnes Village, stocking eccentric lines by the likes of Shiren Guild, Issey Miyake, Ghost, and Maria Chen. *Home*, 28a Floral St, WC2, T020-7240 7077, also do designer label womenswear and some menswear, by labels like Paul Frank, Hysteric Glamour, Roial, and Junk. *Nicole Farhi* is at 11 Floral St, WC2, T020-7497 8713, while next door is *Uth*, 9-10 Floral St, WC2, T020-7836 6390, a newish chain stocking 'High Street Plus' clothes for young women. Beyond the market on the other side, *Stephen Jones Millinery*, 36 Great Queen St, WC2, T020-7242 0770, has an excellent array of extraordinary designer hats for every occasion.

Most of the more affordable fashion shops can be found on the streets north of Long Acre, especially on Neal St, Earlham St and in Shorts Gardens. *Mambo* 37 Earlham Street, WC2, T020-7379 6066, is an Australian street-fashion label for boys and girls, stocking Globes trainers and casual smart dress streetwear, some of it in denim. Just down the road are the throwback street styles of *Diesel*, 43 Earlham Street, WC2, T020-7497 5543. *Kirk Originals*, 36 Earlham Street, WC2, T020-7240 5055, do their own-brand designer sunglasses and specs, also on Floral St. On Neal St the shops are a little more upmarket. *Super Lovers*, 64 Neal St, WC2, T020-7240 5248, is the only European outlet for the Japanese label at the cutting-edge of teenage fashion for boys and girls. *Blakes*, 50 Neal St, WC2 T020-7240 5552, sell stylish own-label unisex leatherwear. *O'Neill*, 9-15 Neal St, WC2, T020-7836 7686, bring surfing and skiing chic off the boards and pistes and on to the streets. *Carhartt*, 56 Neal St, WC2, T020-7836 5659, have made a name for their trendy men's workwear. Crossing Neal St, Shorts Gardens continues the pre-occupation with own-label urban style at the likes of *Boxfresh*, 2 Shorts Gardens, W1, T020-7240 4742, *Duffer of St George*, 29 Shorts Gardens, WC2, T020-7379 4666, and *Hope and Glory*, 30 Shorts Gardens, WC2, T020-7240 3713.

Second-hand and discounted designer clothes With the notable exception of *Koh Samui*, at 65 Monmouth St, WC2, T020-7240 4280, with their highly fashionable range of brand new designer-label womenswear, **Monmouth St** is the place to go for second-hand and discounted designer clothes, sometimes at bargain prices. Good first stops are *The Loft*, 35 Monmouth St, WC2, T020-7240 3807, or the more retro *Pop Boutique*, 6 Monmouth St, WC2, T020-7497 5262. *Bazaar*, 13 Monmouth St, WC2, T020-7240 9314, specializes in jeans and discounted designer labels, while *Cenci*, 31 Monmouth St, WC2, T020-7836 1400, have long been peddling an affordable profusion of second-hand Italian styles.

Foodies might want to check out *Neal's Yard Dairy*, 19 Shorts Gardens, WC2, T020-7379 **Food & drink** 7646, for its exceptional range of home-grown British and Irish cheeses, and meat-eaters should not miss *Portwine*, 24 Earlham St, WC2, T020-7836 2353, an excellent old-fashioned shop with a wide assortment of pies, sausages and other meaty fare. The *Monmouth Coffee House*, 27 Monmouth St, WC2, T020-7836 5272, has turned coffee consumption into an art form, stocking a huge number of different beans complete with a tiny tasting café. *The Drury Lane Tea and Coffee Co*, 37 Drury Lane, WC2, T020-7836 2607, is cheaper, sells mainly to the trade but will happily bag up smaller quantities for personal callers. Nearby, although it wouldn't dream of selling anything that deserved to be put in a cup of coffee, is *Cadenheads Whisky Shop*, 3 Russell St, WC2, T020-7379 4640, a connoisseur of the finest malts and blends. Also an expert in his field, *Carluccios*, 28a Neal St, WC2, T020-7240 1487, is a supremely elegant and expensive Italian deli, with a restaurant for fungiphiles next door: The *Neal St Restaurant*, 26 Neal St, WC2, T020-7836 8368. If you're just looking for picnic materials, head for *Shepherds Foods*, 24 Drury Lane, WC2, T020-7240 1336, or *Tesco Metro*, 21 Bedford St, WC2.

The West End

Gifts

Covent Garden is packed with individual boutiques catering for all kinds of enthusiasms & activities, making it an excellent hunting ground for gifts & quirky one-offs

Octopus, 54 Neal St, WC2, T020-7836 2911, stock a range of eye-catching gifty things by the French designers Pylones. *Orc's Nest*, 6 Earlham Street, WC2, T020-7379 4254, is one of London's busiest role-playing shops, dealing in a mulitude of different-sided dice and little fantasy figures. *The Kite Store*, 48 Neal St, WC2, T020-7836 1666, has long been famous for its comprehensive stock of anything that flies high or low. *On Show*, 19 Shorts Gardens, WC2, T020-7379 4454, is an Aladdin's cave of gifts from around the world, including bonsai trees, oriental lamps and Romanian shawls. *The Australia Shop*, 26 Henrietta St, WC2, T020-7836 2292, stocks all manner of items manufactured downunder, including Drizabone coats, Thomas Cook clothing, and Australian chocolate and biscuits. *The Tintin Shop*, 34 Floral St, WC2, T020-7836 1131, is the only shop in London solely dedicated to everything related to Hergé's boy detective. *The Wild Bunch*, 17 Earlham St, WC2, T020-7497 1200, has an enormous range of strange and exotic fresh flowers and potted plants.

The shops in the old Apple Market itself, in the central covered market of the Piazza, make for good browsing for gifts or clothes, although many are fairly expensive. *The Candle Shop*, 30 The Market, Covent Garden, WC2, T020-7836 9815, sells just about anything that burns wax or oil in all shapes and sizes. *Benjamin Pollock's Toy Shop*, 44 The Market, WC2, T020-7379 7866, specializes in traditional wooden toys, as well as toy theatres, pop-up books and other essentials for an old-fashioned childhood. In the same spirit, *The London Dolls House Company*, 29 Covent Garden Market, WC2, T020-7240 8681, sells repro Georgian and Victorian-style houses and accessories for collectors and children. Like much of the market itself, each of these shops just about manages to avoid being terribly twee.

Leisure activities

On Southampton St, between the Piazza and the Strand, a cluster of shops are a good destination for every rambler, outdoor activist and backpacker. *Karrimor*, 3 Southampton St, WC2, T020-7497 0716, is a branch of the Baker St Field and Trek shop specializing in the famous rucksacks but also doing boots, anoraks and accessories. Next door the *YHA Adventure Shop*, 14 Southampton St, WC2, T020-7836 8541, stocks everything anyone outward bound on a budget might require. For bike hire and repair, there's *Wheelie Serious*, 2 Nottingham Court, off Shorts Gardens, T020-7836 1752.

Snowboard Asylum, 30-32 Southampton St, WC2, T020-7240 5316, stock boards by Slade, Libtech, Palmer, and Burton among many others as well as all the clothes and bindings. Other specialist sports shops in the area include *Speedo*, 41-43 Neal St, WC2,

Directory

Laundry Covent Garden Coin-Op, 35 Betterton St, WC2. Dry Cleaning at Seven Dials, 37 Monmouth St WC2, T020-7240 9274.

Medical Services St Thomas's Hospital, 2 Lambeth Palace Rd, SE1, T020-7928 9292.

Places of worship Church of Scotland Crown Court Church, Russell St, T020-7836 5643. Corpus Christi Catholic Chuch, Maiden Lane, T020-7836 4700. St Pauls Church, Bedford St, T020-7836 5221. Eglise Suisse de Londres, 79 Endell St, T020-7836 1418.

Sports Jubilee Sports Hall, 30 The Piazza, WC2 T020 -836 4835 Mon-Fri

0700-220(last entry 2115), Sat, Sun 1000-1700. Large gym, programme of exercise classes, £6.90 for the gym which can include an hour's induction to the machines, £6 for a class, or £10 for both, circuit, step, aerobics, body blast (body pump), no need for induction, plus café and sunbed. The Sauna Bar, 29 Endell St, WC2 T020 -836 2236 Men only gay sauna, 12- 12 £12. Oasis Sports Centre, 32 Endell St, WC2 T020-7831 1804 two swimming pools, one of them outdoor, gym and fitness classes.

Useful addresses Covent Garden Association www.coventgarden.org.uk

T020-7379 7571, for their branded swimwear and *Slam City Skates*, 16 Neals Yard, WC2, T020-7240 0928, a mecca for serious in-line skaters and boarders. More sedate leisure interests are catered for by the long-established artworld suppliers *Russell & Chapple*, 23 Monmouth St, WC2, T020-7836 7521. *Arthur Beale*, 194 Shaftesbury Ave, WC2, T020-7836 9034, is a well-respected yacht chandler, an old-fashioned shop full of rope, shackles, cleats and pulleys, while *Angels and Bermans*, 119 Shaftesbury Ave, WC2, T020-7836 5678, are probably London's most famous theatrical, film and TV costumiers and have an excellent fancy dress department for the public, although costumes must be hired for at least week, starting from around £80.

Fans of the stage musical should head down the street to *Dress Circle*, 57-59 Monmouth St, WC2, T020-7240 2227 where musical numbers on CD and vinyl go back over 100 years as well as posters and prints. *Ray's Jazz Shop*, 180 Shaftesbury Ave, WC2, T020-7240 3969, is one of the best jazz and blues new and second-hand record and CD shops in central London. *Eukatech*, 49 Endell St, WC2, T020-7240 8060, have two floors of back-catalogue CDs and vinyl and DJ mixed house, electronica and trance.

Music

Camper, 39 Floral St, WC2, T020-7379 8678, is a very popular brand of Spanish casual footwear. *Dr Marten Department Store*, 1-4 King St, WC2, T020-7497 1460, stocks the full range of the much imitated British workboot, while the *Natural Shoe Store*, 21 Neal St, WC2, T020-7836 5254, specializes in eccentric and comfortable footwear, good walking shoes and wide-fitters, also including *Birkenstock*, 37 Neal St, T020-7240 2783 famous for their ergonomically sound sandals. *Sole Trader*, 72 Neal St, WC2, T020-7836 6777 stocks trendy shoes, trainers and accessories.

Shoes
Shoe-shoppers are unlikely to go away disappointed around here, although prices are often high

Transport

Bike hire *Wheelie Serious*, 2 Nottingham Court, off Shorts Gardens, T020-7836 1752.

Buses See under Soho (page 92) and Bloomsbury and Fitzrovia (page 216).

Car parking Shelton St car park, T020-7497 9232.

Taxis Plenty along Long Acre and at the top end of Shaftesbury Ave, cutting through to Seven Dials.

Mayfair and Regent Street

North of Piccadilly, and south of Oxford Street, Mayfair is the West End at its most swanky. Protected from the chaos of Soho to the east by the grand swathe of Regent Street, it still earns its place as the last and most expensive stop on the Monopoly board by boasting the capital's most luxurious hotels, the hautest couture and cuisine, and some of its wealthiest residents. Unbelievably, people of more modest means do still live here, although the daytime and early evening population consists largely of itinerant office workers, business people and tourists.

Lavish and louche, Mayfair smells of money. Even if you don't happen to own a Roller yourself, there will be plenty of free opportunities to observe those that do. Recently Mayfair is supposed to have become less stuffy and more fashionable:

Marble Arch, Bond St & Oxford Circus tubes for North Mayfair, west to east. Hyde Park Corner, Green Park & Piccadilly Circus tubes for South Mayfair, west to east

The West End

Handel and Hendrix

Legendary rock star, Jimi Hendrix lived next door to Handel's old address, at No 23 Brook Street, in 1968, two years before his untimely death from an overdose of sleeping pills.

Remarkably enough, both musicians have been honoured with venerable blue plaques: Hendrix's went up in 1995, the first rock star to receive such recognition.

superficially little seems to have changed, but digging a bit deeper behind those imposing façades is likely to unearth some stylish and affordable surprises. Window-shopping in the Arcades and **New Bond Street**, *inspecting the objets d'art up for auction at Sotheby's, getting measured for a suit in* **Savile Row**, *wondering at contemporary artwork in* **Cork Street**, *sipping lime cordials in luxury hotel bars, and even listening for nightingales in Berkeley Square, all these cost next to nothing.*

History

Mayfair earned its name from the annual fair held in the area that is now Shepherd Market, a boisterous affair that was intermittently banned until its final demise in 1730, when residents prevented its return (see also page 110). From the 1660s building had begun edging northwards along Piccadilly, a reflection of the growing popularity of St James's Palace as the favoured royal residence.

By the mid-18th century almost all of the land we call Mayfair was taken up by houses, most of it owned by six estates, the largest of which was the Grosvenor estate. Three great squares of large Georgian townhouses were built – Berkeley, Hanover, and Grosvenor, the largest of them all. Noblemen's residences emerged, such as Dorchester House and Grosvenor House that overlooked Park Lane, then known as Tyburn Lane, into Hyde Park, and Devonshire House and Lansdowne House close by Berkeley Square. Mews of stables and coach houses were built to house the grooms and coachmen.

Old Bond Street was extended northwards to Oxford Street, and Shepherd Market emerged as a busy network of shops. St George's church in Hanover Square, where Handel was once Church Warden, served the wealthy residents, and became particularly popular for marriages. By 1800, tall townhouses were preferred to large piles, although the Prince Regent, later George IV, employed John Nash to develop Carlton House into the 'most perfect palace in Europe'.

He also demanded a route north to Regent's Park where he planned to build another grand residence. The result is Regent Street, also designed by Nash, which underwent several modifications in the design and building until its completion in the 1820s. It was funded by private money, and the buildings were the product of a range of architects, so there was little uniformity in the façades. The Quadrant however, that great sweep from Piccadilly up to Oxford Circus, boasted a grand colonnade to provide cover for the shoppers, and balconies for the bachelors who took rooms above, while

Hotels in the area

AL *Brown's*
AL *The Connaught*
AL *Claridge's*
AL *The Dorchester*
AL *The London Hilton*
AL *The Metropolitan*
A *Millennium Britannia Hotel*
A *Flemings Mayfair*
A *The Chesterfield*
A *No.5 Maddox Street*
A *Westbury Hotel*
A *Curzon Plaza*
A *Berkeley Plaza*
▸▸ *Go to page 442*

The West End

Shepherd Market

A plaque on the Al Hamra restaurant declares that this was the site of the 'historic' May Fair, which was apparently a riotous and disreputable event lasting about a fortnight, held annually for a little over half a century until the mid 1700s. Another plaque on Stanhope Row fancifully records that here stood 'Mayfair's oldest house, The Cottage, 1618, from where a shepherd tended his flock while Tyburn idled nearby'.

In fact this small and now mercifully traffic-free corner of Mayfair has nothing to do with sheep. Developed by the architect Edward Shepherd during the 18th century in response to the authorities' concern about the licentious nature of the festivities, old habits died hard and it remained notorious for prostitution until quite recently.

Once described as 'a modest little country town… small but busy… a strange survival in this most aristocratic quarter', it now boasts one of the most comfortable cinemas in the city, The Curzon Mayfair; several good pubs, like Ye Grapes; and some attractive ethnic restaurants nestling in the old mock-market building itself.

On Down Street, past the front doors of various South American embassies on Hertford Street, Christchurch Mayfair is now used by the Ethiopian Orthodox Church. Look out too for Knight the fishmonger at No 8, where live lobsters await their fate in the window, and next door the old-fashioned Butwick Pharmacy. On Sundays the railings of Green Park nearby are hung with tremendously tacky paintings. On White Horse Street, once the staging post on Piccadilly for coaches west, the seemy side of the district's past has been reborn in the shape of the swanky new lap-dancing club, For Your Eyes Only.

The West End

the stretch up to Portland Place was designed more for purely residential purposes. The elegant All Soul's church in Langham Place, another Adam product, was built to serve the growing local population.

By 1900, Regent Street had become one of society's most fashionable venues for shopping, theatres and restaurants, but the shops wanted to expand and the buildings revealed structural strains. Despite delays caused by the First World War, the Quadrant was redeveloped by the 1920s, lending the street a more uniform appearance. Meanwhile, in Mayfair itself, the price of maintaining a household forced many of the residents to sell up and move west. Embassies and hotels moved in, and as the devastation of the City during the Second World War created a shortage of office space, so businesses also arrived. More hotels and embassies followed, most notably the American Embassy in Grosvenor Square. It was first established here in 1938, and the square became unofficially known as Eisenhower Platz as American military offices took over many houses in the square during the course of the war. Mayfair retains its reputation for wealth, all the more so since it has become the playground for the global jetset.

Sights

Mayfair's traditional exclusivity has ensured that there's little of the usual 'see and do' variety. At weekends the wide streets can be almost deserted. Instead, this is a good place to take a quiet stroll around, marvelling at the Duke of Westminster's several hundred acre estate (he still owns much of the area, including the land beneath the American Embassy).

Mayfair & Regent St

The West End

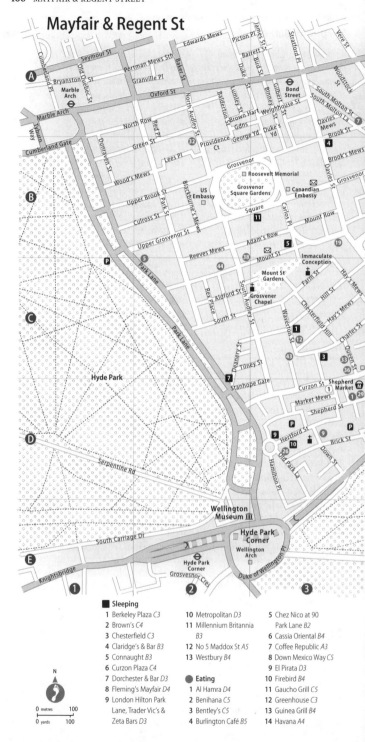

N

0 metres   100
0 yards   100

■ Sleeping
1 Berkeley Plaza *C3*
2 Brown's *C4*
3 Chesterfield *C3*
4 Claridge's & Bar *B3*
5 Connaught *B3*
6 Curzon Plaza *C4*
7 Dorchester & Bar *D3*
8 Fleming's Mayfair *D4*
9 London Hilton Park
   Lane, Trader Vic's &
   Zeta Bars *D3*
10 Metropolitan *D3*
11 Millennium Britannia
   B3
12 No 5 Maddox St *A5*
13 Westbury *B4*

● Eating
1 Al Hamra *D4*
2 Benihana *C5*
3 Bentley's *C5*
4 Burlington Café *B5*

5 Chez Nico at 90
   Park Lane *B2*
6 Cassia Oriental *B4*
7 Coffee Republic *A3*
8 Down Mexico Way *C5*
9 El Pirata *D3*
10 Firebird *B4*
11 Gaucho Grill *C5*
12 Greenhouse *C3*
13 Guinea Grill *B4*
14 Havana *A4*

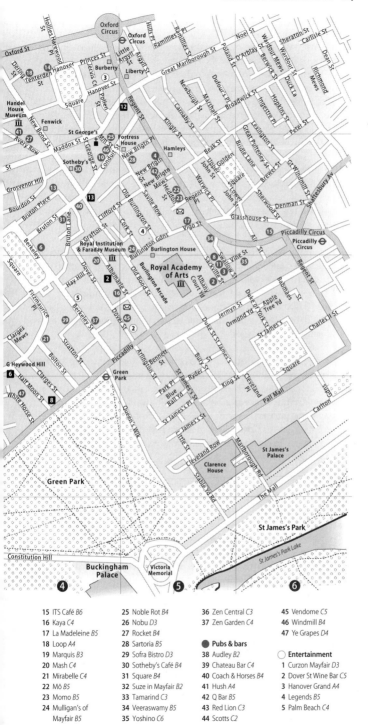

The West End

15 ITS Café *B6*	25 Noble Rot *B4*	36 Zen Central *C3*	45 Vendome *C5*
16 Kaya *C4*	26 Nobu *D3*	37 Zen Garden *C4*	46 Windmill *B4*
17 La Madeleine *B5*	27 Rocket *B4*		47 Ye Grapes *D4*
18 Loop *A4*	28 Sartoria *B5*	● Pubs & bars	
19 Marquis *B3*	29 Sofra Bistro *D3*	38 Audley *B2*	○ Entertainment
20 Mash *C4*	30 Sotheby's Café *B4*	39 Chateau Bar *C4*	1 Curzon Mayfair *D3*
21 Mirabelle *C4*	31 Square *B4*	40 Coach & Horses *B4*	2 Dover St Wine Bar *C5*
22 Mô *B5*	32 Suze in Mayfair *B2*	41 Hush *A4*	3 Hanover Grand *A4*
23 Momo *B5*	33 Tamarind *C3*	42 Q Bar *B5*	4 Legends *B5*
24 Mulligan's of	34 Veeraswamy *B5*	43 Red Lion *C3*	5 Palm Beach *C4*
Mayfair *B5*	35 Yoshino *C6*	44 Scotts *C2*	

Savile Row
The Beatles' famous return to live performance in 1969, captured on film for 'Let It Be', took place on the roof of No 3

If you want to see where the Duke and his kind might buy their suits, walk up Regent Street from Piccadilly Circus, turn left into Vigo Street and you come to Savile Row, a name that has been synonymous with high-quality bespoke tailoring since the middle of the 19th century. Many of the shops retain their old-fashioned standards of style and service: the solicitous or snobbish attentions of their staff towards potential customers have become the stuff of legend, satirised by the TV sketch show catchphrase 'Ooh! Suits you, Sir!' At the northern end of the street is **Fortress House**, the home of English Heritage and hence the place to pick up information leaflets on any and every historic attraction maintained by the state throughout London and England.

Back on Vigo Street, Burlington Gardens is dominated by the back of **Burlington House** with its rows of larger-than-life statues of the great philosophers. Once an outstation of the British Museum for its ethnographic collection, the building will be handed over to the Royal Academy (who own the front on Piccadilly) in 2003.

Cork Street
Just up here on the right is Cork Street, London's most prestigious address for dealers in contemporary fine art. *Victoria Miro's* space at number 21, and *Michael Hue-Williams'* at the same number on the first floor, both show challenging new work, as do *Mayor* at number 22a, *Houldsworth* at numbers 33-34 and, for more mainstream shows, *Alan Cristea* at number 31. Don't be intimidated; all are usually open during the day in the week, they're free and usually welcome browsers.

Burlington Arcade
Beyond Burlington House on the left, the glassy colonnade of the Burlington Arcade stretches down to Piccadilly, guarded by top-hatted beadles. These quaint anachronistic characters are supposed to ensure that no one runs, sings or whistles. Take care, because whistling would be the appropriate reaction to the price tags in some of the shops. Most sell jewellery, with the odd exception like *A la Reine Astrid* at number 27, chocolatier since 1935, doing exceptional pralines, ganaches, marrons glaces and truffles (T020-7499 8558), and *Church's* fine English shoes.

Old & New Bond Street
The Arcade makes as good an introduction as any to the main shopping drag in Mayfair, at the end of Burlington Gardens: turn left into Old Bond Street or right into New Bond Street. You won't find Bond Street W1 in the A-Z. Strictly speaking, round here plain 'Bond Street' only refers to the tube station on Oxford Street. Pedestrianized South Molton Street, running south from the station, hosts probably the highest density of high-fashion outlets in London, but the Bond streets themselves are home to all the big names – Versace, Gucci, Dolce and Gabbana, Prada et al – as well as more staid establishments like the auctioneers **Sotheby's** at 34-35 New Bond St, with its 3600-year-old Egyptian carving of Sekhmet above the door, and the jewellers **Tiffany's** at 25 Old Bond Street. (See Shopping, pages 113-114).

Faraday Museum
Slightly less grand, the Royal Arcade leads from Old Bond St into Albermarle Street near Brown's Hotel. Turn right and you can't miss the classical façade of the **Royal Institution** at number 21, modelled on the Temple of Antoninus in Rome. The Royal Institution was established in the last year of the 18th century to 'facilitate the general introduction of useful mechanical inventions... and the application of science to the common purposes of life'. Under the current directorship of brain scientist Susan Greenfield it fulfills pretty much the

same role today, increasing access to scientific ideas, conducting experiments and staging an interesting programme of public lectures. It's worth looking in to check out the old-fashioned Faraday Museum in the basement. Michael Faraday was the assistant of Humphry Davy, who invented the miners' Davy lamp, and was made a professor of the Institution in 1833 for his research into electricity. Apart from informative wall displays on Faraday's life and works, the small museum's main attraction is an evocative reconstruction of the laboratory where he discovered 'the identity of electricities', including his great electromagnet and an extraordinary hand-operated vacuum pump. ■ *Open Mon-Fri 0900-1700. Admission £1. T020-7409 2992 ,www.ri.ac.uk*

Berkeley Square

Left at the end into Grafton Street and down Hay Hill brings you into the oldest and finest of Mayfair's three great squares. Berkeley Square is an open space preserved since 1696, although these days it's ruined by the hurtling traffic. Nightingales would now be unlikely to stop for long in any of the three dozen magnificent plane trees planted here in the 1780s. The east side of the square was completely re-developed in the 1930s, but numbers 42-46 on the west side remain much as they would have looked 250 years ago. Number 44 was described by Pevsner as 'the finest terrace house in London'. Designed by William Kent, it now houses the Clermont Club, the private gambling club of which 'lucky' Lord Lucan was a member. Unfortunately the public aren't allowed in to see the spectacular staircase. Number 45 is where Clive of India overdosed on opium in 1774, and Winston Churchill spent time as a child in Number 47.

Bruton Street leads back out of the square to the east, lined with smart galleries of antique furniture. The *Timothy Taylor Gallery*, 1 Bruton Place, T020-7409 3344, is an interesting little contemporary art space with its finger on the pulse.

St George's Church

Crossing over New Bond Street into Conduit Street, St George Street heads up past St George's Church, built in the 1720s and the first London church to be graced with a portico. In the 19th century it became the most fashionable place to get married, where Benjamin Disraeli and Mrs Wyndham Lewis, George Eliot and Mr Cross among others tied the knot. Most fatefully, in 1814 the radical romantic poet Shelley and Harriet Westbrook confirmed the vows here that they had made three years earlier in Edinburgh. She drowned herself in the Serpentine in Hyde Park shortly afterwards and Shelley himself didn't live much longer, being lost at sea five years later.

Handel House Museum

George Street brings you into Hanover Square, laid out in the 1720s and unremarkable today except that it has a buzz the others lack, probably because of the proximity of the artworld on Dering Street and the offices of Vogue in its bottom right-hand corner. Turning left leads into Brook Street numbers 23-25 are the Handel House Museum, above the shopfronts of Perla and Regina Rubens. By mid-2001 you should be able to visit a recreation of the house as Handel would have known it, based on his will and the inventory of the house at his death in 1759. He lived here for 35 years after making London his adopted home as composer to the courts of the Georges. ■ *T020-7495 1685 for details of opening times and admission prices.*

Grosvenor Square & around

Brook Street runs straight into Grosvenor Square, taking its name from the Grosvenor family of the Dukes of Westminster. One of London's largest squares, it was the last in Mayfair to be laid out, in the mid-18th century. Nothing much remains of that square today although its scale is still impressive. The west side is taken up with the massive US embassy, put up in the late 50s and topped with an enormous American eagle. Pevsner described the building's effect as 'embarrassing'. There's a not-so-embarrassing statue of President Roosevelt on the north side. In Carlos Place, south of the square, is **Hamilton's Gallery** at number 13, T020-7499 9493, one of London's foremost photography galleries, usually holding an exhibition by one of the camera's great artists like Helmut Newton or Cecil Beaton.

Turn left in the square and left again into South Audley Street. Just beyond Mount Street, the little **Grosvenor Chapel** is as old as the square and has become the favourite church of US ex-pats. It was used by American soldiers during the Second World War and is now a chapel of ease. ■ *T020-7499 1684 for times of services.*

Behind it, Mount Street Gardens are a miniature delight full of trees and the best approach to the **Church of the Immaculate Conception**, a splendid neo-gothic catholic church and the oldest Jesuit church in London: it celebrated its 150th anniversary in 2000. Latin masses sung by a world-famous choir are at 1100 every Sunday and there's a bookshop open on Sunday mornings, Tuesdays and Fridays. ■ *Open 0700-1900 daily. T020-749 3 7811.*

The front of the church is on Farm Street. Turn right out of the door and then left down Chesterfield Hill to find Chesterfield Street, the area's least altered row of Georgian houses, giving a good idea of how Mayfair would have looked in its heyday. Somerset Maugham lived at number six. Cross Curzon Street at the end to find **Shepherd Market**.

Eating and drinking

Expensive
● *on map, page 106*

The best place to treat yourself is undoubtedly *The Mirabelle*, 56 Curzon St, W1, T020-7499 4636. Marco Pierre White re-opened this classic Mayfair restaurant in the 90s to rave reviews. Everything here justifies the average £90 tab for two, from the impeccable service to the presentation of top-notch Frenchified food. Booking in advance is strongly advised, although couples might well be found a table on spec. There's an outside seating area at the back of the elegantly designed basement space. Closed for lunch at weekends.

Another reliable, similarly priced destination is *Chez Nico at Ninety Park Lane*, 90 Park Lane, W1, T020-7409 1290. Nico Landenis has long been famous for combining elegance and precision in his kitchen with non-stuffy service at the smartest address in his chain. Closed on Sun and lunchtime Sat.

More expensive and probably more difficult to drop in on unless just for sushi, is Robert de Niro et al's venture at the super-fashionable *Metropolitan Hotel*, **Nobu**, 19 Old Park Lane, W1, T020-7447 4747. Drag your eyes away from the stars stuffing their faces on some ultra-light Japanese-cum-South American food. Book at least a month in advance for 1900-2200 reservations.

Another Mayfair rendezvous for fashionistas is *Noble Rot*, 3-5 Mill St, W1, T020-7629 8877, which has an African-style members-only basement bar that diners can also enjoy until 0300. The modern European food is good and there's seating outside during the summer months.

Less posing and more cosseting goes on at *The Greenhouse*, 27a Hay's Mews, W1, T020-7499 3331, which does a very good-value (and very busy) set lunch at £10.50 for two courses Mon to Fri. Evenings in the country cottage-style basement are more expensive but the modern British cuisine is worth it.

More sophisticated, airy and popular with power lunchers during the week (closed for lunch weekends) is *The Square*, 6-10 Bruton St, W1, T020-7839 8787. It looks like a car showroom from the outside but the sleek interior is a stylish setting for some excellent French food majoring on fish. For an Italian restaurant with similar aspirations, try *Sartoria*, 20 Savile Row, W1, T020-7534 7000. In summer, book a table by the large windows opening onto New Burlington St.

Several restaurants concentrate on character rather than cutting-edge cuisine and tend to be marginally more affordable as a result. Two of this type are *Mulligan's of Mayfair*, 13 Cork St, T020-7409 1370, and *The Guinea Grill*, 30 Bruton Place, W1, T020- 7499 1210. Both are attached to very good pubs. *Mulligan's* offers interesting dishes with an Irish twist in a woody, masculine basement that gets lively in the evenings. Last orders at 2130 though. *The Guinea* is tucked away behind the Fuller's pub of the same name and is famous for its steak and kidney pies. Cordial service, good food and a pleasant ambience have been keeping a wide cross-section of diners coming back for more since the 1950s.

At the top end of this price range is *Mash*, 26b Albemarle St, W1, T020-7495 5999. What was once the popular 'Coast' has now been transformed into one of the media set's favourite micro-brewery-bar-restaurant concepts. They usually do modern European food expertly in a busy atmosphere. Another interesting newcomer is *Firebird*, 23 Conduit St, W1, T020-7493 7000. Eating at this cosy 'Tsarist Russian' restaurant is given a sense of occasion by the gloriously uniformed waiters and décor that looks like it's been borrowed from the Winter Palace.

Mid-range *It isn't always necessary to take out a loan for a good meal in Mayfair*

The West End

Most of the other good restaurants in this bracket look further east for their inspiration, like *Cassia Oriental*, Restaurant and Bar, 12 Berkeley Square, W1, T020-7629 8886. This is the latest and decidedly the most superior branch of the Zen chain, doing sushi in the comfortable bar area while the ivories are tinkled in the restaurant, offering Japanese, Thai and Vietnamese dishes as well as Chinese staples. £22 for three courses. Nearby is one of its sister establishments, the *Zen Garden*, 16 Berkeley St, T020-7493 1381, a large restaurant doing very good Chinese food at a price. Marginally more ritzy Chinese dining can also be enjoyed at the original branch, *Zen Central*, 20-22 Queen St, W1, T020-7629 8089.

In Shepherd Market, the *Al Hamra*, 31-33 Shepherd Market, W1, T020-7493 1954, serves very good Lebanese food in an attractive room and there are tables outside for those who want to observe the street life of this strange little corner of London. Nearby, and less expensive, the *Sofra Bistro*, 18 Shepherd St, W1, T020-7493 3320, is a reputable Turkish restaurant open until midnight that does sandwiches as well as full meals. *Tamarind*, 20 Queen St, W1, T020-7629 3561, is a very good Indian restaurant, decorated in an opulent modern style, specializing in dishes from the Northwest Frontier that are prepared with a care that justifies their relatively high price. *Veeraswamy*, Victory House, 99 Regent St (entrance on Swallow St), T020-7734 1401, www.realindianfood.com, claims to be the first Indian restaurant in London but only moved into these beautifully clean new premises overlooking Regent St in 1998. The quality of the food certainly demonstrates their years of experience.

Swallow St is also home to what was once London's oldest Spanish restaurant, *Down Mexico Way*, 25 Swallow Street, W1, T020-7437 9895, www.downmexway. com Its sumptuous colourfully tiled interior was donated by the King of Spain in 1926. Nowadays, it does good Mexican food upstairs with drinking and dancing on the ground floor until 0300. Reaching further south in the Americas for inspiration next door is the *Gaucho Grill*, 19 Swallow St, W1, T020-7734 4040, strictly for voracious meat-eaters and wine-lovers: sit on cow-hide-covered chairs in the cellar-like space and consume top-quality Argentine steaks, from £10 with a variety of sauces. Next stop on Swallow St is the haunt of old-fashioned seafood aficionados, *Bentley's*, 11-15 Swallow St, W1, T020-7734 4756. Very good fish dishes have been served here in an antique interior since 1912.

Back in Mayfair proper, *Kaya*, 42 Albemarle St, W1, T020-7499 0622, is the finest Korean restaurant in London. It specializes in table-barbecues and traditional dishes from the region of Seoul.

For some of the most authentic Japanese dining in town, head for *Yoshino*, 3 Piccadilly Place, W1, T020-7287 6622. Tucked away in a corner off Piccadilly and designed by cult architect Rick Mather, the restaurant used only to print its menu in Japanese. Now there's an English translation but the food and service are still as genuine as ever. Also Japanese but a world apart is *Benihana*, 37 Sackville St, W1, T020-7494 2525, the brainchild of former Olympic wrestler Rocky Aoki. It's a party destination for teppanyaki, where your own personal chef shows off his knife-skills as he cooks the meal on a hotplate at your table.

Much hyped but justifiably so is *Momo*, 25 Heddon St, W1, T020-434 4040, a North African dining experience with a distinctly metropolitan approach to taking reservations. Pretending to be famous will guarantee a booking.

Cheap *Finding somewhere cheap to eat in Mayfair is really only for the brave* There are many places where you'll still find overpriced pub-grub, underheated pizza or soggy pasta. More enticingly, *El Pirata*, 5-6 Down St, W1, T020-7491 3810, is open until 2345 and has set tapas menus for £13.75 or £17.50 per person, for a minimum of two people. *The Marquis*, 121a Mount St, W1, T020-7499 1256, is also at the top end of this bracket but does some good Italian and game dishes in a quiet, sedate atmosphere. Slightly less expensive, *Suze in Mayfair*, 41 North Audley St, W1, T020-7491 3237, is an attractive new winebar, owned by New Zealanders, sporting a decent-value menu inspired by that part of the world.

Otherwise, the music bar-restaurants in the area are the best bet: *Havana*,17 Hanover Square, W1, T020-7629 2552, is a clubby Latin music basement bar, open late and serving good-value Mexican *antojitos* until midnight. There's an admission charge after 2200 though. Just around the corner is *The Loop*, 19 Dering St, W1, T020-7493 1003, www.theloopbar.co.uk, is a huge place with four separate bars and a restaurant. Most of the loud party action goes on in the cellars, making the ground floor and upstairs good spots for a quieter bite of interesting fusion food at reasonable prices.

There's also good pizza and Italian dishes to be had above the new bar *Rocket*, 4-5 Lancaster Court, Brook Place, T020-7629 2889. Off Regent St, *Mô*, 23 Heddon St, T020-7434 4040, is an excellent new Moroccan snack bar run by the people at *Momo* (see above).

Cafés & sandwich bars The pick of the many coffee and sandwich shops in Mayfair include *Sotheby's Café*, 34-35 New Bond St, W1, T020-7293 5077, a fairly expensive but very English and genteel establishment for the taking of tea in the old auction house. Last orders are at 1645 and it's closed at weekends. *La Madeleine*, 5 Vigo St, W1, T020-7734 8353, is open until 2000 every day except Sun, a real French patisserie with a brightly lit back area for good omelettes, pasta, quiches, and grills. *Coffee Republic*, 2 South Molton St, W1, T020-7629 4567, was the first, busiest and some say the best of the excellent UK coffee and cake chain. *ITS Café*, Quadrant Arcade, Regent St, W1, T020-7734 4267, is a clean, reasonably priced pizza and pasta joint in an unusual setting off Regent St. Further up towards Oxford Circus, *The Burlington Café*, New Burlington St, W1, T020-7437 0458, does baked potatoes and straightforward sandwiches in a no-nonsense environment for footsore shoppers and weary office workers.

Pubs & bars *If you're looking for that perfect Martini, this is the place to start* Unsurprisingly Mayfair boasts some of the best hotel bars in the country, let alone London. None of them are cheap but some deserve the extra spend, especially these few that are outstanding. *Trader Vic's* at the *Hilton Hotel*, Park Lane, W1, T020-7493 8000, with its South Island Beach bar theme and glamorous oriental waitresses, is an old-timer that still delivers a kick with its famous hot rum cocktails served in shiver-me-timbers skull mugs. Good Chinese oven-roast food too. On the ground floor of the same hotel, *Zeta* is a good-looking, new health-giving fruit juice and cocktail bar that's open until 0300 Mon-Sat and offers a decently priced menu from the Pacific rim.

Nearby, the *Dorchester Bar*, *Dorchester Hotel*, 53 Park Lane, W1, T020-7629 8888, is nothing like as stuffy as you might expect. The charming service and a myriad of mirror tiles make drinking here a many splendored thing. A snug New York-style piano-cocktail bar popular with sundry celebrity musos major and minor can be found at *The Chateau Bar*, *Mayfair Intercontinental Hotel*, Stratton St, W1, T020-7629 7777. Watch out for their famous whisky martini, the Silver Bullet.

For the ultimate in designer drinking, *Claridge's Bar*, *Claridge's Hotel*, Brook St, W1, T020-7629 8860, has won awards from high-chic interiors magazines while the smooth service of some delicious bar snacks is not at all condescending.

Mayfair also excels in the quality of the bars attached to its smart restaurants. The basement cocktail bar at *Scotts*, 20 Mount St, W1, T020-7629 5248 must be one of the most quietly sophisticated places in London to enjoy some expertly mixed concoctions. Immaculate staff glide around the Pierre Chareau sofas while a pianist plays as if she's in love. Less sedate and slightly less expensive, the *Vendôme*, 20 Dover St, W1, T020-7629 5417, captures a hint of Parisian style alongside a busy restaurant popular with power-lunchers. More self-conciously hip than either is *Hush*, 8 Lancashire Court, Brook St, W1, T020-7659 1500, a spacious new venture that boasts a celebrity clientele and good champagne cocktails.

▶▶ Go to page 422 for entertainment & nightlife

A music bar popular with funky Europeans is the *Q Bar*, 12 New Burlington St, W1, T020-7434 3949, open late evenings only, doing Italian food and decorated in a Moorish style.

Many of the old pubs, like the *Audley* 41-43 Mount St, W1, T020-7499 1843, hark back to Mayfair's grand old days and indulge tourist expectations. Its historic and palatial dark red and dark wood décor is reminiscent of a rather run-down gentleman's club. *The Red Lion*, tucked away at 1 Waverton St, W1, T020-7499 1307, famously feels more like a country pub than many pubs in the country, with its snug set of panelled rooms and high-backed wooden benches. No music and an expensive but high-quality restaurant in the back room. Quite often just as crowded is *Ye Grapes*, 16 Shepherd Market, W1, T020-7499 1563. Its tiny exterior belies a louche Edwardian interior decorated with stuffed animals and plush velvet seating.

Surprisingly perhaps, given the area's astronomical ground rents, old-style pubs continue to thrive here

More of a local's local, the *Coach & Horses*, 5 Bruton St, W1, T020-7629 4123, occupies an incongruous little timber-frame building surrounded by smart offices and boutiques. Charmingly tiny, it attracts an affable crowd of shop and office workers. Similar in style but on a larger scale, the *Windmill*, 6-8 Mill St, W1, T020-7491 8050, is a Young's pub with lots of character, if a bit tatty, and it does award-winning sandwiches.

Shopping

All along Old and New Bond streets, many of the big names' shops are gob-smacking attractions in themselves, like *Prada's* gallery-style store at 15 Old Bond St, W1, T020-7647 5000, or *Versace's* massive over-the-top, three-storey shopping palace at 34-36 Old Bond St, T020-7499 1862. Next door is *Gucci*, 33 Old Bond St, T020-7235 6707; *Chanel* is at 26 Old Bond St, T020-7493 5040. Less flash or intimidating than many of them, *Etro* is at 14 Old Bond St, T020-7495 5767. Further up on New Bond St, you'll find *Donna Karan* at No 19, T020-7495 3100; *Versace Jeans* at No 113, T020-7355 2700; *Calvin Klein* at Nos 53-55, T020-7491 9696; *Miu Miu* at No 123, T020-7409 0900; and *Ralph Polo Lauren* at No 1, T020-7647 6510. Chances are that if you don't know what these kind of shops are stocking, you won't want to afford them.

Old & New Bond Streets
Only in Knightsbridge will you find as many high-fashion designer outlets as in Mayfair

Traditional English craftwork in leather & other accessories reaches its peak in Mayfair

Mulberry, 41-42 New Bond St, W1, T020-7491 3900 make very British bags, holdalls and suitcases as well as smart gifts, as do **Tanner Krolle**, 38 Old Bond St, W1, T020-7493 6302, the places to upgrade your wallet or purse by making them about £40 lighter. **Swaine Adeney**, 10 Old Bond St, W1, T020-7409 7277, are saddlers to the horsey set and have also taken over the world-famous Brigg umbrellas, keeping the rain off the rich and famous since 1750. A silk brollie with a crocodile skin handle will set you back £650, or £130 for something more practical. Wonderful occasional hats can be found at the 'Queen's Milliner', **Frederick Fox**, 87-91 New Bond St, W1, T020-7629 5706, while **Smythsons**, 40 New Bond St, W1, T020-7629 8558, are the last word in traditional British bespoke stationery and writing accessories. Finally, much more middle of the road but also very manageable, a trip around Bond St's only department store, **Fenwick**, 63 New Bond St, W1, T020-7629 9161, will turn up some affordable hats, gloves or shoes.

Cheek-by-jowl with the vaguaries of fashion, New Bond St is home to London's two busiest auction houses. **Sotheby's** at 34-35 New Bond St, W1, T020-7293 5000, is the grandest and has been bringing the gavel down on rare and expensive objets d'art since 1744. It's open for valuations from 0900-1630 Mon-Fri, or you can pick up a catalogue (from £10) and view the current sale. Call in advance to find out what's going… going… when, before it's gone. There's also a good bookshop (T020-7293 5856 open 0930-1730, sometimes Sun if there's a sale), and a café. Very slightly more downmarket, **Phillips**, 101 New Bond St, W1, T020-7629 6602, is the other very large and very busy auction house. The showroom of **The Fine Art Society**, 148 New Bond St, W1, T020-7629 5116, one of London's longest-established dealers in paintings, can also make for a rewarding browse.

The Bond St area is also famous for its jewellers, most notably **Tiffany & Co**, 25 Old Bond St, W1, T020-7409 2790, and **Cartier** 175-176 New Bond St, T020-7493 6962. Both feature classic, old-fashioned interiors, sky-high prices and dazzling rocks. **Asprey and Garrard**, 167 New Bond St, T020-7493 6767, is similar but has a few more affordable items, including stationery. If it's fashionable pearls you fancy, head for **Mikimoto**, 179 New Bond St W1, T020-7629 5300. Gifts such as pens with a pearl stud from around £30 as well as strings of the things worth thousands. For less expensive designer jewellery, **Agatha**, 4 South Molton St, W1, T020-7495 2779, is the local branch of the famous French chain, or have a look around the **Electrum Gallery**, 21 South Molton St, W1, T020-7629 6325, which curates a wide selection of international contemporary jewellery makers including big names like Wendy Ramshaw, Gerda Flöckinger, and Tone Vigeland. They hold four feature exhibitions a year.

Savile Row Unless you have a spare couple of thousand, you won't want to be ordering a bespoke suit from the home of the English gentleman's tailors either. Even so, these unique and increasingly timeless institutions can be relied upon to make a visit entertaining: their staff are famous for their sense of humour. **Henry Poole**, 15 Savile Row, W1, T020-7734 5985, is the oldest established on the Row, since 1846. Past customers include the dandy philanderer Edward VII, who changed his clothes three times a day, the Emperor Napoleon III, and more recently the Emperor of Japan. Pick up a pair of braces for £10-£40 or a silk tie for £45. **Anderson & Shepherd**, 30 Savile Row, W1, T020-7734 1420, tailors to Prince Charles, will do you a pair of sheepskin slippers from £35. **Gieves & Hawkes**, 1 Savile Row, W1, T020-7434 2001, has recently launched a more casual range just called 'Gieves' and have superb driving gloves for £45. **Ede and Ravenscroft**, 8 Burlington Gardens, W1, T020-7734 5450, proudly display all four Royal 'by appointments'. Reknowned legal and academic tailors, this shop stocks their overcoats, as well as silk handkerchiefs with a bird of paradise motif for £30. Altogether more cutting-edge in style, **Ozwald Boateng**, 9 Vigo St, W1, T020-7734 6868, does snazzy off-the-peg and bespoke suits and womenswear.

Burberry,165 Regent St, W1, T020-7734 4060, is a traditional English label that has managed to re-invent itself to the extent that their famous check pattern (based on the Thompson clan tartan) is constantly in fashion. *Aquascutum*,100 Regent St, W1, T020-7734 6090, is another in a similar mould. *Austin Reed*, 103-113 Regent St, W1, T020-7734 6789, were bigger in the 60s but still do sophisticated suits at lower prices than Savile Row for business and leisure.

For women, *French Connection*, 429 Regent St, W1, T020-7493 3124, constantly re-invents itself. *Jaeger*, 200-206 Regent St, W1, T020-7200 4000 traditionally cater for women of a certain age but also have some sophisticated lines for girls. *Karen Millen*, 262-264 Regent St, W1, T020-7287 6158, might be a more likely stop-off for bright young things. Of the department stores, *Dickens & Jones*, 224-244 Regent St, W1, T020-7734 7070, is huge, woman-orientated and slightly pedestrian. Much more glamorous but not intimidatingly trendy is *Liberty*, 210-220 Regent St, W1, T020-7734 1234. Its mock-Tudor building on Marlborough St is a joy to wander around and home to many of the latest looks.

Regent St can be a risky place to take the kids. *Hamleys* 188-196 Regent St, W1, T020-7494 2000, still leads the way for toy shops the world over but can become nightmarishly busy. Its famous window displays highlight aspects of its staggering stock, none of which comes cheap. *The Warner Brothers Studio Store*, 178-182 Regent St, W1, T020-7434 3334, and the *Disney Store*,140-144 Regent St, W1, T020-7287 6558, provide as much merchandising and film tie-in material as starry-eyed young fans will insist on buying. *The Teddy Bear Shop*, 153 Regent St, W1, provides more traditional comforters, some handmade, at a price.

Jacobs Photography, 324 Regent St, W1, T020-7637 1237, can provide for all of your photographic needs, including film, cameras, and printing, at very reasonable rates. If your camera is broken, take it to the *Camera Clinic*, 2nd Floor, Room 241, The Linen Hall, 162 Regent St, W1, T020-7437 2484, where repairs are efficient and friendly. *The Pen Shop*, 199 Regent St, W1, T020-7734 4088, has the latest lines for serious scribblers while *Pencraft*, 119 Regent St, W1, T020-7734 4928, is similar but more traditional. Serious walkers and sightseers might want to book themselves a session with the *Scholl Footcare Centre*,185 Regent St, W1, T020-7437 0850. 30 mins with a chiropodist costing £30 will relieve those aching feet. They also sell new shoes.

Grays Antiques Market, 58 Davies St, W1, T020-7629 7034, is always worth a browse, especially for second-hand books. Only the rare and second-hand bookshop is open on Sat. *G Heywood Hill*, 10 Curzon St, W1, T020-7629 0647, a long-established upper-crust bookseller, has a good stock of rare and second-hand books, knowledgeable staff and charming premises.

Dedicated followers of fashion will want to head to *Comme des Garçons*, 59 Brook St, W1, T020-7493 1258, for the latest from Japan's hottest designer, or to *Vivienne Westwood* at 44 Conduit St, T020-7439 1109, for her Red Label day wear. The *Conran Collection*, 12 Conduit St, W1, T020-7399 0710, is a sparkling emporium full of mini things, gadgets and designer gifts, furniture, lighting and bedlinen, glass, pens and watches, exclusive to the indefatigable Conrans. *Armando Pollini*, 35 Brook St, W1, T020-7629 7606, does stylish Italian shoes with elast and microfibre soles.

Some of the most opulent flower displays in London can found at *Kenneth Turner*, 125 Mount St, W1, T020-7355 3880, while *Caviar Kaspia*,18 Bruton Place, W1, T020-7493 2612, is a friendly place to seek out a variety of luxurious international foods, not just

Regent Street
The shops of Regent St are world famous. Listed here are some that justify that claim among the many that don't

The West End

Around Mayfair

the treasured eggs of the sturgeon. *Culpeper*, 21 Bruton St, W1, T020-7629 4559, have been providing herbal everything since 1927, while the olde-worlde *Nelson Pharmacy*, 73 Duke St, W1, T020-7629 3118, has been purveying homeopathic medicines since 1860 and will recommend a local homeopath.

Transport

Buses **Along Oxford St west of Oxford Circus, heading west**:
No 7 to Ladbroke Grove via Paddington.
No 10 to Hammersmith via Knightsbridge and Ken High St.
No 12 to Notting Hill Gate via Bayswater.
No 13 to Golders Green via Baker St (not Marble Arch) and Swiss Cottage.
No 15 to Paddington.
No 23 to Ladbroke Grove via Paddington.
No 73 to Victoria.
No 94 to Shepherd's Bush via Bayswater and Notting Hill.
No 113 to Edgware via Baker St (not Marble Arch) and Swiss Cottage.
No 137 to Clapham via Knightsbridge, Sloane Square and Chelsea Bridge.
No 139 and 189 to Baker St and Lisson Grove.

Along Oxford St west of Oxford Circus, heading east:
No 6 and 13 to Aldywch via Piccadilly Circus and Trafalgar Square.
No 7 to Russell Square via the **British Museum.**
No 10 to King's Cross via Tottenham Court Rd.
No 12 to Dulwich via Piccadilly Circus, Trafalgar Square, Westminster and Peckham.
No 15 to the **Tower of London** via Trafalgar Square, Aldwych and **St Paul's**.
No 23 to Liverpool St via Trafalgar Square, Aldwych and St Paul's (Sat, Sun as far as Aldwych only).
No 73 to Islington and Stoke Newington via King's Cross.
No 98 to Holborn.
No 135 to Archway via Great Portland St and Camden Town.
No 159 to Brixton via Trafalgar Square and Westminster.

Taxis Plenty along Piccadilly, with Berkeley Square a good bet at busy times.

Tubes Marble Arch (Central line), Bond St (Central and Jubilee lines) and Oxford Circus (Central and Victoria lines) serve North Mayfair. Hyde Park Corner (Piccadilly line), Green Park (Piccadilly, Victoria and Jubilee lines) and Piccadilly Circus (Piccadilly and Bakerloo lines) tubes for South Mayfair.

Directory

Embassies and Consulates American Embassy, 24 Grosvenor Square, W1, T020-7499 9000. Canadian High Commission, 38 Grosvenor St, W1, T020-7258 6600.

Medical Services Mayfair Medical Centre, 3-5 Weighouse St, W1, T020-7493 1647. Also a private health centre beneath Gould Pharmacy, 37 North Audley St, T020-7495 6298.

Places of worship Church of the Immaculate Conception, Grosvenor Chapel (see Sights above)

Tourist offices Britain Visitor Centre, 1 Regent Street, Piccadilly Circus, SW1. Open: Mon 0930-1830, Tue-Fri 0900-1830, Sat & Sun 1000-1600; Jun-Oct, Sat 0900-1700. Irish Tourist Board, corner of Bruton St and New Bond St.

Piccadilly and St James's

Piccadilly Circus is the heart of the West End, pumping traffic, commuters and tourists round central London's party zone. Here the pomp of Piccadilly and Regent Street meets the shifty alleyways running into Soho, the milling crowds on Coventry Street coming from Leicester Square, and theatreland's main artery, Shaftesbury Avenue. The Circus's most famous sights are not particularly memorable, neither the neon advertising hoardings on its north side, nor the little statue of 'Eros', but the view down Lower Regent Street towards Westminster is compensation enough. Somehow the place manages to make a satisfactory fist of joining up four of the West End's most distinctive districts: Soho, Mayfair, St James's and Leicester Square.

*Piccadilly itself goes west with considerable panache, down past **Fortnum's**, the **Royal Academy**, the **Ritz** and **Green Park**, heading for the memorials on Hyde Park Corner, and dividing the glitz of Mayfair to the north from London's most exclusive and rarefied enclave, the gentlemen's clubland of St James's. Those stately sanctuaries of affluent indolence are lined up on **Pall Mall** (rhyming with 'gal'), trying to ignore the vulgar roar of traffic rushing out from Trafalgar Square, past the Tudor gates of **St James's Palace**, and up the 18th-century breadth of St James's Street. Just beyond this small quirky quarter long dedicated to keeping the English gent in shirts, shoes and headgear lies the reason for its status, Royal London: the processional splendour of The Mall, the lakeside garden tranquility of **St James's Park**, and the monumental bastion of Buckingham Palace. This is London as millions of tourists expect to find it, which is fine, because unless they're actually storming the Queen's private apartments, they'll hardly be noticed by its cultivated air of effortless superiority.*

⊖ *Nearest tube stations are Piccadilly Circus, Green Park & Hyde Park Corner*

The West End

History

The area that has become synonymous with gentlemen's clubs and fine living was built up, appropriately, around St James's Palace. Little of the original palace remains now, but it was first built by Henry VIII on the site of a leper hospital for young women, and the marshy land to the south where the lepers fed their hogs was drained and developed as a nursery for his deer.

Close to Whitehall, St James's saw many regal dramas. 'Bloody' Mary I died here, Elizabeth I hunted in the park, and James I formalized the gardens with an aviary (hence Birdcage Walk) and an orchard of 10,000 mulberry trees planted on land that is now taken up by Buckingham Palace. (One of the trees, from 1609, remains in the 45-acre garden).

Charles I's last journey to his execution took him from the palace, across the park, to Banqueting House, where his beheading was met with a groan from the crowd. Unperturbed by the area's macabre memories, however, Charles II enjoyed the palace and its grounds. He played an Italian variant of croquet, called pall-mall, on an avenue in the park, and the park was extended over what many believed to be the leper burial ground, now Green Park. (There have long been popular rumours about Green Park –

Hotels in the area

AL *Le Meridien*
AL *The Ritz*
A *Athenaeum Hotel and Apartment*
A *The Stafford*
A *Dukes Hotel*
A *No 22*
▶▶ *Go to page 442*

not least those about the 'tree of death', a haunted tree avoided by birds, but patronized by a mysterious coated figure.)

The area began to attract developers. St James's Square and St James's Street went up in the 1660s and 1670s, Buckingham House, now Buckingham Palace was built over the River Tyburn, and Burlington House, now the Royal Academy, was one of the several grand piles stretching along Piccadilly to Hyde Park Corner. One of the earliest, dating from 1612, was built by Robert Baker, a tailor with a shop in the Strand. Nicknamed Piccadilly Hall (in reference to the source of his wealth, 'picadils'- stiff-collars), the name finally won formal approval over 100 years later.

Over the next two centuries the area became a curious mix of the smart and the seedy. Fashionable shops were to be found in the grand streets – bespoke hats from James Lock, men's toiletries from perfumier Floris, or all manner of

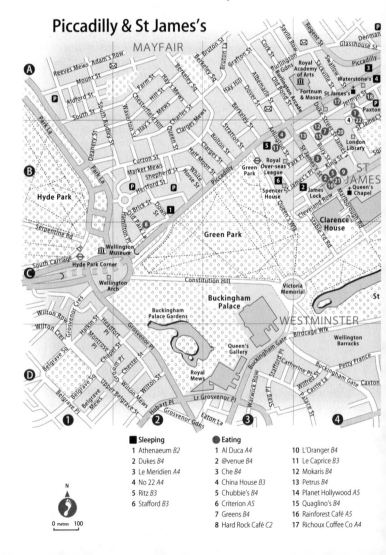

Piccadilly & St James's

N
0 metres 100

Sleeping	Eating	
1 Athenaeum *B2*	1 Al Duca *A4*	10 L'Oranger *B4*
2 Dukes *B4*	2 @venue *B4*	11 Le Caprice *B3*
3 Le Meridien *A4*	3 Che *B4*	12 Mokaris *B4*
4 No 22 *A4*	4 China House *B3*	13 Petrus *B4*
5 Ritz *B3*	5 Chubbie's *B4*	14 Planet Hollywood *A5*
6 Stafford *B3*	6 Criterion *A5*	15 Quaglino's *B4*
	7 Greens *B4*	16 Rainforest Café *A5*
	8 Hard Rock Café *C2*	17 Richoux Coffee Co *A4*

consumables from Fortnum and Mason on Piccadilly. Gentlemen's clubs blossomed, metamorphosing from coffeeshops into exclusive clubs, and in 1721 there were six dukes and sevens earls living in St James's Square. But as one French visitor observed, 'it's a strange sight, in fine weather, to see the flower of the nobility and the first ladies of court mingling in confusion with the vilest populace…'. The vilest populace, as he would have it, included prostitutes, in St James's Park after the gates were locked (there were thousands of keys in circulation), or seeing out the weekend in Haymarket, still a hay and straw market three days a week, but by night 'a spacious street of great Resort, full of Inns and Houses of Entertainment'.

Highwaymen and robbery were commonplace, even along Piccadilly, where you might see late-night parties returning en masse for protection from their various engagements in Kensington or Knightsbridge. Following considerable reconstruction under George IV, Buckingham Palace became

The West End

Victoria's preferred residence, and the houses closed up as the rich moved to Belgravia and businesses moved in. Piccadilly Circus, formed in 1819 to accommodate Nash's Regent Street, soon emerged as a busy intersection and a popular meeting point. One explorer confessed to JM Barrie in the Traveller's Club that the most dangerous part of his latest trip to Africa had been "crossing Piccadilly Circus".

Eros, erected in 1893, became a much-loved statue in the Circus, and until the 1940s attracted flower-girls to its base. Messrs J Lyons established their first tea-house on Piccadilly in 1894, and by 1910 neon lights shone brightly on the circus. The Mall was rebuilt as a grand avenue leading from Admiralty Arch to Buckingham Palace as part of the Victoria Memorial development; and the Ritz was constructed as the first steel-framed building in London. Although it has suffered from relentless commercialization, St James's, as David Piper noted in 1964, is where '…the embodiment, if not the spirit, of the English upper-class male persists'. Even now, a trip to St James's Park at lunchtime will be rewarded with the sight of civil servants in deep discussion, or politicians and bishops heading purposefully across the park from Whitehall for lunch at the clubs.

The West End

Sights

Piccadilly Circus

Piccadilly Circus is usually so relentlessly busy that it's not a particularly pleasant place to linger, but thousands do, gathering around the endearing little monument representing the Angel of Christian Charity. Erected in 1893 in memory of the stern philanthropist Lord Shaftesbury, who did much to help abolish child labour, the winged boy with his bow was so unpopular that the sculptor Sir Arthur Gilbert went into retirement. Persistently taken to be the God of Love, **'Eros'**, as the sculpture came to be known, was recently given loving restoration and has become one of the city's most famous landmarks. Nowadays it is dwarfed by the neon-lit logos of Macdonalds, Nescafé and Coca Cola on the north side. Opposite them is the grand façade of *The Criterion Restaurant*. To its right, there's a strikingly beautiful view down Lower Regent Street past the Duke of York's Column and over the trees of St James's Park towards the Victoria Tower of the Palace of Westminster.

To the left of the *Criterion*, Coventry Street is a tasteless stretch of tourist-tat retailers and 'have a nice day' diners. Its bustling popularity can only be explained by its being the shortest, partially pedestrianized route between Piccadilly Circus and the dubious delights of Leicester Square. This is also the home of the **Rock Circus**, an overpriced outpost of Madame Tussaud's dedicated to all things rock'n'roll. It hardly deserves its place at the centre of the music capital of the world with its feeble rock star waxworks, embarrassing animatronic displays and lame recreations of 'swinging' London streets.

■ *Open Mar-Aug 1000-2000 Mon, Wed, Thu, Sun; 1100-2000 Tue; 1000-2100 Fri, Sat; Sep-Feb 1000-1730, Tue from 1100. Admission £8.25 adults, £7.25 concs. T020-7734 7203.*

Rock Circus shares the block with the **Pepsi Trocadero**, six floors of much more straightforward high-tech entertainment and bottom-drawer commercialism. Cock of the roost is *Segaworld*, spread over all six floors, featuring virtual reality rides and a videogame arcade. *Funland* is more of the same but more 'traditional', while the *Pepsi Max Drop* ride, takes up to seven punters 40 m to the top of the building and lets them fall very fast down to the bottom for £3. Not for very tall or very small people though, or, like the rest of the complex, for the timid. The Trocadero is also home to all the usual suspects of noisy mass-market retailing, including the *Gadgetshop*, the *Bodyshop* and the *Sock Shop*. ■ *Open 1000-2400 Mon-Thu, 1000-0100 Fri, Sat. T09068-881100. Admission £2-3; rides and videogames 30p-£1.*

Along Piccadilly

Progressing westwards for about a mile to Hyde Park Corner, Piccadilly itself is a top-class, if frantic and congested, strip of extraordinary shops, world-class hotels, green space and fine architecture.

St James's
Piccadilly
Church
*Regular concerts are
given (see page 422) &
an Aroma café gives
onto the courtyard*

One of the most beautiful churches in London is on the left a few hundred yards down from Piccadilly Circus, at 197 Piccadilly. St James's Piccadilly, known as the 'visitors' church', was its architect Christopher Wren's personal favourite, a haven set back from the street in its own courtyard dedicated to Londoners who died in the Second World War, now hosting a small craft and antiques market. Completed in 1684, the church sustained severe bomb damage in the Second World War and needed extensive restoration. The interior retains delightful balance and poise, best appreciated in bright daylight, and includes a spectacular limewood altar-screen carved by Grinling Gibbons in the 17th century, who may also have been responsible for the font here in which William Blake was baptised.

■ *Open 0800-1900 daily. Café (T020-7437 9419), open 0800-1900 Mon-Sat, 1000-1900 Sun. Antique market Tue 1000-1730; craft market (T020-7437 7688), Wed-Sat 1000-1730 . T020-7734 4511.*

On the opposite side of the street, a little further along, the Albany is a Georgian mansion block tucked away behind smart iron railings, famous for providing prestigious bachelor pads for the likes of Byron, Macaulay, Aldous Huxley and more recently the late Alan Clark MP. Next door is Burlington House, the home since 1869 of the Royal Academy of Arts, founded by George III in 1768 as the first art school in the country. A modern statue of its first president, Sir Joshua Reynolds, stands in the middle of the palatial central courtyard, which despite doubling as a carpark is a pleasant enough place to escape from the traffic with a picnic. Under the directorship of Norman Rosenthal, the Academy has determinedly cast off its fusty image by mounting popular attention-grabbing exhibitions of contemporary British art, with titles like 'Sensation' and 'Apocalypse'. Even so, the opening of its Summer Exhibition in June and July remains an important event in the social calendar, when a profusion of less controversial and generally more attractive work is selected from an open competition, including some by current Academicians. Michelangelo's *Virgin and Child with the Infant St John* (*The Taddei Tondo*) is one of only four sculptures by the artist outside Italy and is permanently on display outside the Sackler Galleries.

Royal Academy of Arts

The West End

Guided tours of the permanent collection, which includes works by Reynolds, Turner, Constable and Stanley Spencer, are given Tuesday-Friday at 1300 and are free (be there on time).

■ *Open 1000-1800 Mon-Thu, Sat, Sun; 1000-2030 Fri. Admission to exhibitions varies. T020-7300 8000; bookings T020-7300 5959.*

Facing the Academy's massive portico another even older and almost as venerable institution, **Fortnum and Mason,** have been furnishing the upper classes with tea, fine food, glassware, clothes and antiques since it was founded by one of Queen Anne's footmen, Mr Fortnum, in 1707. Above the door, he emerges every hour to greet Mr Mason from a clock installed in the 1960s. The window displays are usually lavish artworks in themselves (see Shopping on page 129 for further details).

More window-shopping (and it's probably best to keep it to that) can be enjoyed a little further along in the **Burlington Arcade**, running north (see page 108), and through the Piccadilly Arcade's great bow windows running south, elegant spaces to gawp at unaffordable jewellery, fine art and antiques.

Past Old Bond Street, St James's Street and just beyond the Ritz Hotel, the buildings on the left-hand side give way to the rolling Green Park. Laid out by Henry VIII, the 53-acre park's name is self-explanatory enough, kept free of formal flower beds out of respect for the lepers from the Hospital of St James's buried beneath. More fancifully, Charles II, who made it a Royal park, is supposed to have picked a flower to give to the next beautiful woman he saw, who happened to be a local milkmaid. Queen Katharine was so furious that she banned flowers from the park for good. Nowadays the plane trees, crocuses,

Green Park

daffodils and deck chairs make it a charming spot to wile away an afternoon in the spring. Chairs can be hired from the corner of the park nearest the Ritz. ■ *Open dawn-dusk daily. T020-7930 1793.*

The Queen's Walk runs down its east side to The Mall and Buckingham Palace's ticket office, behind stately mansions like Spencer House (see next page) and the government offices of Lancaster House. The peculiar bowl of the Canadian Memorial near The Mall was erected in 1994 to commemorate the Canadian dead of the two world wars.

Hyde Park Corner   Piccadilly continues downhill to **Hyde Park Corner**, past the Inigo Jones-designed Devonshire Gates into Green Park. They were removed from Devonshire House, one of the grand houses that once lined the length of Piccadilly's north side. Hyde Park Corner itself terrifies drivers and pedestrians alike. Decimus Burton's **Wellington Arch**, erected in 1828, dominates the roundabout, commemorating victory in the Napoleonic war. It is in the process of being turned into a museum of public monuments that should open in Spring 2001. Nearby there's a disturbing memorial to the Machine Guns Corps of the First World War, a statue of David and two gatling guns, complete with a biblical inscription referring to his slaying in his 'tens of thousands'.

The Wellington Museum   The main reason to come here and not hurry through is a visit to Apsley House, the house that Arthur Wellesley, the Duke of Wellington, bought off his brother after Waterloo. It stands on the north side of Hyde Park corner, by the entrance to Park Lane. Known as No 1 London, for being the first house in the West End on the road from Knightsbridge, it's now The Wellington Museum, administrated by the V&A but also still the London home of the great man's descendants. The Iron Duke resided here from 1817-1852. The place remains a dignified monument to the man and the post-Napoleonic era in Britain, restored in Louis XIV style, and refurbished throughout in its original colour scheme in 1995.

The Iron Duke was so called because of the metal shutters fitted to his windows here to protect him from Reform Act rioters

A small shop sells books, souvenirs, postcards, & a guide for £5.95, although there's also a free audio guide   Of the 10 rooms open to the public, six are on the first floor, the highlight being the Waterloo Gallery, complete with a magnificent chandelier and works by Rubens, Bruegel, Van Dyck and Murillo, alongside the Duke's favourite, Correggio's *Agony in the Garden*, as well as Velázquez's *Water Seller*. The Striped Drawing Room is the most atmospheric, with its striking portraits of Wellesley's military colleagues. Most visitors are also surprised and impressed by the massive 11-ft statue of Napoleon, heroically naked in the stairwell, given to Wellington in 1816 after its diminutive subject had refused it in distaste. The basement gallery displays memorabilia connected with the Duke, including 15 fine cartoons. ■ *Open 1100-1700 Tue-Sun. Admission £4.50, £3 concession & under-16s. Guided tours on request, £30 for groups of up to 25 people. T020-7499 5676.*

St James's

St James's is the land that time forgot, pretty much stuck in a fantasy of the English past, peddling classy airs and graces as though they had never lost influence, or even political favour. Even so, it's well worth exploring for its peculiar air of self-conscious restraint and an awareness that its prestige lies largely in pandering to the mega rich. The layout of its streets little changed since the 17th century, it has preserved a more intimate scale than Mayfair, although the grandeur of its aspirations are forcefully expressed in St James's

Square and along Pall Mall. Above all, this is the part of London that enshrines the idea of the English gentleman.

The smartest address for your club is St James's Street, the main thoroughfare running down from Piccadilly to St James's Palace. Try *White's* (Nos 37-38, the oldest), *Brooks's* (No 60, the poshest), or *Boodles* (No 28, the wackiest), but you're only likely to get in to whichever one suits you anyway because you'll already know several other members. Each club has its own different character, attributes, and politics, bound to go largely unnoticed by the casual passer-by who must settle with being impressed by their grand façades and entrance halls. An exception are the literary, musical and artistic events organised by **ROSL Arts** at the **Royal Over-Seas League**, Over-Seas House, Park Place, St James's Street, SW1, T020-7408 0214 (ext 219). They're well worth looking into in themselves, not least to enjoy the club-like interior of Over-Seas House.

If you want some idea of the type of effect the interiors of these fashionable gambling houses might have hoped to imitate in their heyday, you can visit Spencer House, at 27 St James's Place,the ancestral London home of Princess Diana's family from 1755 until the 1920s. Eight grand rooms are open to the public by guided tour every 15 minutes on Sundays, highlights being the views of the garden and Green Park, the ceiling of the Dining Room, the gilded trees in the Palm Room, and the Great Room. The garden has been returned to its late 18th-century design, complete with plants and shrubs true to the period, and can now be visited separately from the house during spring and summer. Phone for details. ■ *Open Feb-Jul, Sep-Dec 1030-1730 (last tour 1645), Sun only or during the week for groups by appointment in writing. Admission £6, £5 children. Guided tour obligatory. Garden only £3.50. T020-7499 8620.*

Spencer House
The house was restored by its current owner Lord Rothschild's bank in 1990

Parallel to Piccadilly, off St James's Street to the left, Jermyn Street sets the tone for the shops that cater for the area's clubbable gents, passing the back door of Fortnum's (see Shopping below). Any street going south heads into the heart of the area. On Duke Street you'll find the **White Cube**, at 44 Duke Street, SW1, T020-7930 5373. The small conceptual art gallery run by Jay Jopling that helped to kick start several Young British Artists in the 90s. Most of the more traditional commercial art galleries in the area line King Street, headed up by **Christie's**, at 8 King Street, SW1, T020-7839 9060, an auctioneer with a pedigree as ancient as Sotheby's. The main sale season is from September to April. Phone for details of upcoming sales or drop in and pick up a catalogue.

At the bottom of St James's Street, where it turns sharp left into Pall Mall, two fully armed redcoats in their bearskin busbies stand or stomp about like clockwork beneath the red-brick Tudor gatehouse of St James's Palace. Now used as offices for various Royals including Prince Charles and the Queen Mother, the palace is closed to visitors, although the **Chapel Royal** inside is open for Sunday services from October until Good Friday. Like the gatehouse, the ceiling of the Chapel is one of the last traces of the palace that Henry VIII built himself here in 1531, on the site of the Leper Hospital of St James the Less.

St James's Palace

A little way down Marlborough Road, opposite the Ambassador's Court, its name a reminder that modern ambassadors to the UK are still received 'at the court of St James', stands the **Queen's Chapel**, in the grounds of Marlborough House, the HQ of the Commonwealth. The chapel was designed by Inigo Jones for Charles I, done up by Wren, and has a classically proportioned interior that is puritan in its simplicity. ■ *Open only for Sun services Easter to Jul 0830; sung Eucharist on first Sun of the month and Great Festivals, other Suns 1115, Holy Communion on Holy Days 1230.*

Pall Mall & St James's Square

Most of the clubs are on **Pall Mall**, named after the Italian Pell Mell croquet-cum-golf game beloved of Charles II, who installed his mistress Nell Gwynne in a house overlooking the pitch. Architecturally, the street is sombre, grand and restrained, with the exception of Schomberg House, numbers 80-82, in a florid red-brick Dutch style unique in London. Just off it is leafy St James's Square, until relatively recently the favourite London address of aristocrats. The equestrian statue in the middle is of William III, who died in a riding accident.

Today the square is home to clubs and offices. **The London Library**, at number 14, T020-7930 7705, in the northwest corner, was founded by Thomas Carlyle in 1841, in disgust at the poor service offered by the British Library. It's still a private members' lending library, with a wonderful 19th-century reading room and lobby. Membership applications are open to all but usually take about a week to process, ranging from full annual membership, through temporary (four-month) overseas membership (£75), to use of the reading room for a month for reference only (£18.50).

Outside number 5 there is a small plaque commemorating PC Yvonne Fletcher, who was shot from the Libyan Embassy in 1984. On Charles II Street, linking the square with Lower Regent Street, the **Emily Tsingou Gallery**, 10 Charles II Street, SW1, T020-7839 5320, is a cutting-edge contemporary art dealer showing challenging new work.

At the bottom of Lower Regent Street, Waterloo Place crosses Pall Mall, the intersection dominated by the massive **Crimean Monument,** including a statue of Florence Nightingale and an early 19th-century streetlamp. On the right-hand side of the place stands the **Athenaeum club**, designed by Decimus Burton with a replica of the Parthenon frieze over the door, appropriate to a club popular with academics and clerics. Opposite is a matching building, also by Burton, which is now the Institute of Directors.

The most prominent monument among the several dotted around here, including a statue of Scott of the Antartic, is the **Duke of York's Column**. Erected in 1833, it was paid for by taking one day's wages off every soldier in the army in honour of the Duke, the Grand Old one who 'had ten thousand men, marched them up to the top of the hill, and then marched them down again'. Luckily he was a popular commander.

To the right of the column, beneath a tree, is a curious little gravestone inscribed 'Giro, died 1934', commemorating the German ambassador Leopold von Hoesch's dog. The German Embassy until the Second World War was close by at numbers 7-9 Carlton House Terrace. Von Hoesch himself died two years later at the age of 55 under the strain of worsening Anglo-German relationships. From here steps lead down onto The Mall.

The Mall

Walk down the Duke of York's steps and you are entering Toytown. Here is Royal London, with its processional road, its smart soldiers on parade, and in the distance, safe in her palace, its very own Queen. The Mall is an imposing public space, lined with trees and flagstaffs, its pink tarmac matching the forecourt of Buckingham Palace, that comes into its own for ceremonies like Trooping the Colour. Just beyond, St James's Park is the Palace's front garden, one of London's most beautiful parks.

At the bottom of the steps on the left, the **Institute of Contemporary Arts (ICA)**, 12 Carlton House Terrace, was founded in 1948 by the anarchist Herbert Read. Nash's stately Georgian terrace seems an incongruous setting for the radical film, theatre, dance and art shown here. The gallery played an important role in launching the contemporary British art boom of the 90s and has a theatre, two cinemas, bookshop and lively bar and café. Further up on the left, in the same building, is a more traditional exhibition space mounting temporary shows of affordable paintings and watercolours and special exhibitions. ■ *Open 1000-1700 daily, admission £2.50. Day membership £1.50 Mon-Fri, £2.50 Sat, Sun. T020-7930 3647; galleries T020-7930 6844.*

St James's Park is the finest and most carefully laid out of the Royal parks, once again the work of the indefatigable John Nash in the early 19th century. A wander around reveals surprising but carefully orchestrated vistas at every turn. The lake teems with exotic wildfowl, including the pelicans first given to the park by a Russian ambassador in the 17th century, a tradition that has continued to increase their numbers. They're fed at 1500 daily. The view from the bridge across the lake is justly famous, looking over Duck Island towards Whitehall and Westminster. From April to September deck chairs can be hired (£1 for four hours), guided tours of the park are given by its warden, and brass bands play in the bandstand most afternoons. ■ *Open dawn-dusk daily; T020-7930 1793.*

St James's Park

The West End

Buckingham Palace

At the opposite end of The Mall from Admiralty Arch stands the Victoria Memorial, a white marble monument topped with a winged figure of Victory, now best serving as a vantage point from which to view the Changing of the Guard on the forecourt of Buckingham Palace. In 1993 the Queen opened the doors of the palace for two months to the paying public for the first time to raise money for the restoration of the fire-damaged Windsor Castle. Critics have scoffed at the gesture, complaining (with some justification) that tickets are too expensive, queues for entry too long, and the tour itself an anti-climax. That hasn't stopped thousands of people from all over the world lapping up the opportunity every August and September.

Changing of the Guard at 1130 daily Apr 1 to the end of Jul; alternate days the rest of the year

A maximum of 250 visitors are admitted every 15 minutes, in a fairly successful attempt to avoid overcrowding (or perhaps for fear of a rebellion) on a one-way route around 14 state rooms, with the recent addition of the Ballroom, shepherded by 200 extra staff in navy blue and red uniforms who are generally friendly and well-informed.

Entering via the Ambassador's entrance on the south side of the Palace, first impressions are of a place not much more opulent than many West End theatres. Emerging into Nash's central quadrangle of beautifully warm sandstone does create an impression though. 'It ain't much but it's home' was one American woman's wry comment, but then it ain't really 'home' at all. The glossy official brochure (the only floorplan available) emphasises that this is a working palace, although even if the Royal Standard happens to be flying, indicating that Her Majesty is in residence, there's little chance of bumping into her.

Through the red and gold **Grand Hall** and up the Grand Staircase, which lives up to its name thanks to some Carrara marble and Samuel Parker's intricate gilt balustrade, the rooms on show are the roped-off stage set for formal state receptions. The Green Drawing Room gives onto the **Throne Room**, where the two red chairs on their podium behind a baroque proscenium arch represent the climax of royalty as pantomime.

Next comes the real highlight of a visit, the **Picture Gallery**. The Royal Collection is the largest private collection in the world and, until the re-opening of the refurbished Queen's Gallery in 2002, the public must make do with enjoying the works hanging in this 50-m, toplit room, like **Vermeer**'s *The Music Lesson*, **van Dyck**'s *Mystic Marriage of St Catherine*, **Rubens**' *The Farm at Laeken* and **Rembrandt**'s *The Ship Builder and his Wife*, along with others by **Canaletto**, **Guercino** and **Cuyp**.

The gallery leads into the **Ballroom**, the first and only opportunity for a sit-down and a chance to watch a pretty feeble video on the royals at work. The Ballroom looks like a very grand village hall, where state investitures take place, but it's followed, after the **State Dining Room**, by the three finest rooms on show, overlooking the back garden. The **Blue Drawing Room** looks like it belongs in a palace, a sumptuous exercise in Georgian decoration. The **Music Room** has a beautiful parquet floor, domed ceiling and great bow window, while Nash designed a remarkable tent-like ceiling for the **White Drawing Room** above a frieze showing *the Origin and Progress and Pleasure*. Downstairs again, the Marble Hall beneath the Picture Gallery leads into the Bow Room and the garden.

And that's about it, except for the shop, in a tent in the garden, where you can pick up a Buckingham Palace mug, crown keyring, or beanie corgi, among other more expensive items. Overall the lack of any personal touch, which remains one of the keys to the monarchy's staying power, means that the whole experience is rather soulless and dispiriting.

■ *Open 0930-1630 Aug & Sep. Ticket Office in Green Park near The Mall, for tickets on the day, open 0900-1600. Admission £10.50, £8 OAP, £5 under-17. T020-7930 4832; recorded information T020-7799 2331. Tickets in advance (£10.50) by credit card on T020-7321 2233, or by post to The Visitor Office, Buckingham Palace, London, SW1A 1AA.*

Royal Mews   If you've still got a stomach for all things Royal, next door to the Palace are the Royal Mews, open year round, where all the Queen's stately transport is kept, including her gilded State coach and her Windsor grey horses. If anything the array of splendid carriages gives a better value and more atmospheric insight into the pageant of British sovereignty than the Palace itself. ■ *Open Oct-Jul Mon-Thu 1200-1600, Aug-Sept Mon-Thu 1030-1630, last admission 30 mins before closing. Admission £4.30, £3.30 OAP, £2.10 under-17. T020-7930 4832.*

Eating and drinking

Expensive   On Piccadilly Circus, *The Criterion*, 224 Piccadilly, W1, T020-7930 0488, is a grand and
● on map, page 118   beautiful setting for some typically assured Marco Pierre White recipes. The interior of this old dance hall is a symphony in wood and gold, the prices are surprisingly reasonable and the atmosphere quite laid back considering the sumptuousness of the surroundings. The flamboyant restauranteur's flagship is nearby at the more staid (and more expensive, with a dress code) *Oak Room* at the *Meridien Hotel*, 21 Piccadilly, T020-7851 3140.

It comes as some surprise that St James's has become one of London's gastronomic hotspots. After all, gentlemen dine at their clubs, don't they? If not, they're most likely to be seen at *Wiltons*, 55 Jermyn St, SW1, T020-7629 9955, a wonderfully old-fashioned English restaurant for old-timers who enjoy the top-quality seafood and game. Dress smart. Similar in style, **Greens**, 36 Duke St, SW1, T020-7930 4566, has long been another of their favourite haunts, maybe when they were a little younger, serving up fresh fish and traditional British food in a congenial atmosphere.

More rakish and laid back, and virtually impossible to visit without a month's notice, is **Le Caprice**, Arlington House, Arlington St, SW1, T020-7629 2239, tucked away behind the Ritz. Looking like a London version of Rick's bar, it's a kind of hamburger joint as it might have been in the 40s, and has proved enduringly popular with wealthy people who don't want to show off but know what they want. Worth trying to eat here just for the experience.

The conspicuous consumers are more likely to be found on St James's St, at places like **@venue**, 7/9 St James's St, SW1, T020-7321 2111, where the huge glass frontage only narrowly denies punters a view of the Conservative party's favourite club, the Carlton. The spacious minimalist design easily soaks up the buzz of bankers young and old wolfing down schooldays, nostalgia food like '@venue fish fingers', at about £12 the least expensive main course. The pre- and post-theatre menus are particularly good value though.

Next door, **L'Oranger**, 5 St James's St, SW1, T020-7839 3774 (closed Sun), does very fine set-price southern French food in a much more reserved atmosphere. Further up the hill, **Che**, 23 St James's St, SW1, T020-7747 9380, is a funky bar restaurant of the moment doing modern European dishes upstairs briskly and well in a large, light room with a corporate atmosphere.

Nearer Piccadilly, food critics have raved about **Petrus**, 33 St James's St, SW1, T020-7930 4272, sometimes negatively about its high-handed service, but the imaginative menu confidently aims to join the ranks of the gastronomic elite. Finally, Conran's atmospheric overhaul of **Quaglino's**, 16 Bury St, SW1, T020-7930 6767, has proved to be one of his most successful and reasonably priced brasserie-style ventures. Even a drink or light meal at the bar has a sense of occasion thanks to the efficient staff, late opening hours (until 0100) and the glamour of the dramatically lit subterranean interior.

Mid-range The Trocadero can be a nightmare at any time, and it's home to two theme restaurants at the bottom of this bracket in both price and character: **Planet Hollywood**, T020-72871000, and the **Rainforest Café**, T020-7434 3111. The latter is more expensive, but then it comes complete with laughable animatronic animals and jungle soundtrack (tropical, not musical). Both might appeal to hardened post-modern ironists. A better idea is to make for the mother of all theme restaurants, that long-playing homage to all things rock 'n' roll, **The Hard Rock Café**, 150 Old Park Lane, W1, T020-7629 0382. It's less expensive and the burgers and Tex-Mex menu superlative. There's always a queue at the door because there's no booking, but it's worth the wait.

On a completely different note, two of the several Italian restuarants in St James's are special. **Al Duca**, 4-5 Duke of York St, SW1, T020-7839 3090, is a trendy hangout where Milan meets New York in the glass and wood décor and the modern Italian menu. More Neopolitan and old-style, **Il Viccolo**, 3-4 Crown Passage, SW1, T020-7839 3960 (Closed weekends), is a traditional, low-key restaurant tucked away near Pall Mall doing all the reliable staples of Italian country cooking.

On the lower ground floor of *Waterstone's* bookshop, 203 Piccadilly, is the **Red Room**, T020-7851 2464, an attractive and chic restaurant run by Searcey's Corrigan, who are also responsible for the brasserie at the Barbican, the new National Portrait Gallery restaurant, Lindsay House and the catering at the Royal Opera House. A 2-course set menu of modern British food costs £15.50. On the fifth floor, the **Studio Lounge** is an excellent, fairly expensive bar and brasserie with great views south towards Parliament and the London Eye.

Cheap

In the splendid art deco setting of the old Barclays bank on the corner of Piccadilly and Arlington St, *China House*, 160 Piccadilly, W1, T020-7499 6996, has great columns, chandeliers, and fairly good Chinese food at about £15 a head including drink. Reasonable value in the shadow of the Ritz. The ground floor café at *Mokaris*, 61 Jermyn St, SW1, T020-7495 5909, is a particularly good-value Italian restaurant, bar and café, while *Chubbie's*, 10 Crown Passage, SW1, T020-7839 3513, is a busy, popular caff serving up generous portions of English and Italian comfort food for under £5 during the day. Another cheap caff is the *New Piccadilly*, on Denman St, just off Shaftesbury Ave and a stone's throw from Piccadilly Circus. Setting foot in here is like visiting the 1950s, though it's recent listing in *Time Out* has meant an increasing number of art students and trendy tourists.

**Five of the best:
West End cocktail bars**

- *Duke's Hotel*, St James's.
- *Scotts*, Mount Street, Mayfair.
- *Detroit*, Earlham Street, Covent Garden.
- *Lobby Bar*, in the One Aldwych hotel, Strand.
- *Mondo*, Greek Street, Soho.

Cafés & sandwich bars
The regular supply of office workers ensures that sandwich bars are two a penny in St James's & Piccadilly

There are *Prêt à Mangers* at 163 Piccadilly, 41-42 Piccadilly, 21 Crown Passage, and on St James's St. *EAT*, Duke of York St, serves up delicious and different fresh soups every day, as well as good breads. The two Italians at the *Ideal Sandwich Bar,* Crown Passage, next to *Il Viccolo* restaurant (see above) are well known in the area for their toasted ciabattas and friendly service. The *Aroma* café in St James's Churchyard off Jermyn St and Piccadilly is also a good bet but can become very busy. Going upmarket, *Richoux Coffee Co*, 171 Piccadilly, T020-7629 4991, does excellent- value snacks in an elegant, clean and continental setting bang on Piccadilly. *The ICA Café*, The Mall, SW1, T020-7930 8619 (£1.50 day membership required), offers imaginative meals, several vegetarian, that are exceptional value at about £2.50 each.

Pubs & bars
▶▶ Go to page 422 for entertainment & nightlife

The Red Lion, 23 Crown Passage, SW1, T020-7930 4141, is a bog-standard British boozer that seems to have landed in St James's from some remote provincial outpost a long time ago, and the area would be much poorer without its reassuring cosiness, as welcoming to dogs and old men as suits and bohos. There's another *Red Lion*, at 2 Duke of York St, T020-7930 2030, a Heritage inn, with well-preserved Victorian mirrors and bar, and a more upmarket office clientele. *The Three Crowns*, tucked away in Babmaes St, is somewhere between the two in its olde-worlde style and custom, and does decent enough sausages and mash for about £5. *Chequers*, 16 Duke St, SW1, T020-7930 4007, is altogether more clubby and traditional, wood-pannelled and pumps very good beer.

Most of the expensive restaurants listed above also have smart bars that don't insist you buy a meal. *Che*, 23 St James's St, SW1, T020-7747 9380, with its sunken cigar club at the back and ground-floor bar stands out. It's a popular rendezvous for boozy businessmen but nothing like as bad as that makes it sound. *The ICA Bar*, The Mall, SW1, T020-7930 2402. £1.50 day membership required, open Mon until 2300, Tue-Sat until 0100, Sun until 2230. A lively late-night hangout for the arts brigade.

Shopping

The westside of Piccadilly Circus is dominated by the massive *Tower Records*, 1 Piccadilly Circus, T020-7439 2500, open until 2400 Mon-Sat, 1200-1800 Sun, in the Norman Shaw building that once housed Swan and Edgar's. Four floors packed with an independent selection of CDs, DVDs, Videos and a few LPs. There's also a large branch of *HMV* in the Trocadero, 18 Coventry St, W1, T020-7439 0447. Open until 2400 Mon-Sat, 1100-1800

Sun. On the south side is *Lillywhites*, 24-36 Lower Regent St, SW1, T020-7930 3181: Open until 2000 Mon-Fri, 1000-1900 Sat, 1100-1700 Sun. One of the largest and most famous sports shops in Europe with five floors carrying all the big brands.

Heading west on Piccadilly, the shops go upmarket, especially in the arcades, relying on the custom of tourists as well as city slickers, upper-crust gents and their wives from the Shires. The old English tailors *Cordings*, at 19 Piccadilly, are friendly, reliable and remarkably affordable.

The Piccadilly gent's favourite bookshop is likely to be *Hatchard's*, 187 Piccadilly, W1, T020-7439 9921, open 0930-1830 Mon-Sat, 1200-1800 Sun, now owned by the same company as Waterstone's, but retaining an independent choice of titles along with its old-fashioned woody and winding layout. There's also a *Books Etc*, at 23-26 Piccadilly, W1, T020-7437 7478, with a Starbucks café on the first floor.

The unmissable bookshop round here is *Waterstone's*, 203 Piccadilly, T020-7851 2400. Open 1000-2300 Mon-Sat, 1200-1800 Sun. The largest bookstore in Europe, this conversion of the old Simpson's store is already looking a bit tatty (the toilets are in urgent need of attention) but it's a bright, inspiring place to wander around, with either a café, restaurant or bar to take the book of your choice. On the lower-ground floor, the *News Café* is a good meeting place, next door to the *Red Room* restaurant (see Eating and drinking above).

Regular literary & celebrity events are also held here, T020-7851 2463

Further along Piccadilly, most people can't resist popping into *Fortnum and Mason*, 181 Piccadilly, W1, T020-7734 8040, open 1000-1830 Mon-Sat www.fortnumandmason.co.uk, even just for a glimpse of its theatrical way with shelf-stacking. Most famous for its own-label tea and fabulous food hall, it also sells traditional menswear, as well as china and cookware, and antiques on the fourth floor. On the same floor, *St James's Restaurant* is the place for full English teas while the *Patio* restaurant on the mezzanine at the back of the ground floor has a less formal atmosphere and a champagne and oyster bar.

On St James's St, three shops are tourist attractions in themselves: *Berry Brothers and Rudd*, 3 St James's St, SW1, T020-7396 9600, is an old-fashioned fine wine and spirit merchant with a 19th-century interior. *John Lobb*, 9 St James's St, SW1, T020-7930 3664, are bespoke bootmakers extraordinaire, where the cobblers can be seen at work, while *James Lock & Co*, 6 St James's St, SW1, T020-7930 8874, are hatmakers and milliners to Royalty. A wall cabinet displays the exact shape of various famous heads, including Chaplin's and Edward VII'. *D R Harris and Co*, 29 St James's St, SW1, T020-7930 3915, are pharmacists to the Queen Mother.

Jermyn St is world famous for its shirtmakers: every Piccadilly and City gent has his favourite, from *Turnbull and Asser*, *Harvey and Hudson* to *Charles Tyrrhwit*. Also on the street though are *Floris*, 89 Jermyn St, SW1, T020-7930 2885, an exclusive perfumier, and *Paxton Whitfield*, at 93 Jermyn St, W1, T020-7930 0259, one of the city's finest cheesemongers.

•••

Directory

Internet cafés *The Trocadero is also home to an Internet Café, T020-7437 3704.*
Sports *Not much in the area, unless you want to splash out at Champneys, 21a Piccadilly, W1, T020-7255 8000,*

www.champneys.com Attached to Le Meridien Piccadilly, a day programme here cost from £110 per person 0900-1700, including use of the swimming pool, health spa and beauty clinic.

Transport

Buses **Along Piccadilly westbound**:
No 8 and 38 to Victoria.
No 9 to Hammersmith via Knightsbridge and Ken High St.
No 14 to Putney via Knightsbridge, South Ken and Fulham.
No 19 to Battersea Bridge via Knightsbridge, Sloane Square and Chelsea.
No 22 to Putney via Knightsbridge, Sloane Square, Chelsea and Fulham.

Along Piccadilly eastbound:
No 8 to Shoreditch via Mayfair, Oxford Circus, Holborn, Bank, Liverpool St.
No 9 to Aldwych via Trafalgar Square.
No 14 to Tottenham Court Rd.
No 19 to Finsbury Park via Bloomsbury, Islington and Highbury.
No 38 to Islington via Bloomsbury.

Taxis Plenty along Piccadilly, in St James's on Duke St and King St, and usually along Pall Mall and The Mall. Piccadilly Circus itself not a good place to hail a cab.

Tubes Piccadilly Circus tube station (Piccadilly and Baekrloo lines) itself is an engineering feat worthy of the capital's hub, its circular layout providing well-signposted exits to every corner of the Circus. There's also an LT Travel Information office here. Green Park tube (Piccadilly, Victoria and Jubilee lines) is halfway down Piccadilly, with Hyde Park Corner (Piccadilly line) at the opposite end to Piccadilly Circus. St James's Park tube station tube (District and Circle lines) is on the far side of the park from here, a longish walk from St James's and Piccadilly, but quite close to Buckingham Palace.

Oxford Street and Marble Arch

⊖ *From east to west: Tottenham Court Rd, Oxford Circus, Bond St, Marble Arch*

Oxford Street brings out the worst in everyone. London's longest, ugliest and most popular shopping street always gets people going: snobs scoff at its shoddy mass-market consumerism, perhaps lamenting the days when the street was furnished with water troughs for their horses; fashion victims complain about its lack of real style or sartorial savvy; day-tripping bargain hunters moan about the heaving crowds of their fellow punters; and office workers push briskly along it without looking where they're going. Everyone objects to the pickpockets, bagsnatchers and con-artists busily dodging the CCTV. But still they keep on coming, in impossible numbers at least three times a year, for the winter and summer sales and for the Christmas season, revelling in the capital's glorified High Street.

It's extraordinary what a single-minded thoroughfare it can be, the one place in town that makes shoppers of us all because there's simply not much else to do. West of Oxford Circus, the great department stores look south to Mayfair, lined up on the north side of the street guarding their heavily scented entrance halls. East of Oxford Circus, inspired by Soho, the fly-by-night bargain-basement warehouses noisily compete in their pricing and the volume of their pumping in-store bass. There's nothing for it but to go with the flow, stay cool, hang loose, and keep an eye on your bag.

Shop till you drop

The Sales are a well-established retail festival every January and July. Oxford Street is guaranteed to be even more crazy during these months. In the weeks running up to Christmas, shopping hours are extended and the street puts on a high-tech light show. A celebrity switches on the lights sometime in the third week of November and brings traffic to a standstill. The crowds are often too busy to notice as they're shepherded across the major junctions by police vans with loudhailers. Retail therapy turned retail kill or cure.

History

Oxford Street lies along the route of a Roman Road that linked Hampshire with Suffolk, and, along with Piccadilly, it became one of the main roads out of the city. The River Tyburn flowed south across it and fields lined its way. From the 14th century until the 18th the road remained undeveloped, but throughout this time it was also the last journey for condemned prisoners. They would be drawn in a cart from Newgate Prison in the City, past St Giles's, where they would be offered the 'cup of charity', their last drink of ale, and on to the Tyburn Tree, a triangular gallows capable of taking 21 people at a time. The rope was attached and the cart drawn away, leaving the victim dangling – relatives would often run to pull at the body to try to ensure a swifter and less painful death.

Henry VIII legalized the sale of bodies (particularly murderers) to anatomists for dissection. Many were bought, but sales often ended in fights and riots over ownership of the body. Relatives naturally wanted a decent burial for their loved one, or to try resuscitation (it occasionally worked), while body-snatchers lurked in the graveyard further west in Bayswater (Laurence Sterne's body was snatched from here for dissection in 1768). Many people clamoured to touch the body, since it was believed to hold special powers. The disorder did little for the decorum of the area, and after the growth of building along the street, the gallows was removed to Newgate in 1783.

The Earl of Oxford had bought land north of the Street, thereby lending his name to what was popularly known as Tyburn Way, and in the 1760s building began in earnest. It became a place of entertainment. Tiger-baiting could be seen in Mr Broughton's amphitheatre, while the Pantheon (finally replaced by Marks & Spencer in 1937) supported a magnificent rotunda and hosted masquerades, fêtes and concerts.

In 1851 the Marble Arch, which had briefly served as an entrance to Buckingham Palace, was moved to its current site, although it wasn't islanded until 1908. It was only towards the end of the 19th century, however, that Oxford Street became such a shopping mecca. DH Evans and John Lewis (with smaller outlets than at present) moved here in the 1860s and 70s, but it was the Wisconsin merchant, Harry Gordon Selfridge, who demonstrated what a department store could be (John Logie Baird gave the first public demonstration of television here). The huge block of Selfridges was begun in 1907, with ionic columns lining its façade, (the original plans had included a massive tower), and the crowds have been flocking here ever since.

The West End

Hotels in the area

A The Berkshire
B Cumberland
C The Ivanhoe Suites
▸▸ Go to page 443

Sights

'Don't stop, shop!' could be Oxford Street's strapline, but then there's not much worth seeing here anyway. Emerging from Tottenham Court Road tube station at the east end of the street brings you out beneath the unmistakeable honeycomb of the Centrepoint tower. From here Tottenham Court Road heads busily north, Charing Cross Road twists south and New Oxford Street runs east. Walking west, past *The Tottenham*, the only pub on Oxford Street and ripe for refurbishment, you have to squeeze along the street's busiest, scruffiest and most second-rate stretch. Hanway Street, just up on the right, a curious little alley of private drinking clubs, second-hand record shops and Spanish bars and restaurants, doubles back to Tottenham Court Road as if it lacked the courage of its northward convictions.

Apart from a few good shops and the Plaza Shopping Centre (best avoided, along with all the £1-a-slice pizza merchants), there's nothing remarkable until Oxford Circus. Any of the roads off left lead into Soho; those to the right into Fitzrovia. **Regent Hall**, 275 Oxford St, W1, T020-7629 2766, is one of the few remaining buildings from when the street was built. It's now a West End church for the Salvation Army, thoroughly cleaned up and refurbished, with a bookshop and non-smoking café doing good-value (for the area) snacks and sandwiches (open Monday-Saturday 0930-1630).

Oxford Circus is a horrendously busy crossroads, although pedestrianized Argyll Street, off to the left just before it, packed with pubs, snack bars and restaurants, is a good shortcut into West Soho avoiding Regent Street. Beyond Oxford Circus, Oxford Street begins to acquire the dignity the capital's High Street deserves.

Further on to the left, **Dering Street** is sealed off by a pedestrianized area boasting a rare public convenience. This little street has become an exciting enclave for some of the city's leading dealers in contemporary art. Since the mid-70s *Anthony d'Offay* has been expanding into spaces at numbers 9, 23 and 24, T020-7499 4100, although he will be moving in 2001 to Haunch of Venison Yard, off Bond Street, into a large new space designed by Norman Foster. *Anthony Reynolds*, at 5 Dering Street, W1, T020-7491 0621, has been dealing in international contemporary art in all media here for almost as long, while *Annely Juda*, at 23 Dering Street, T020-7629 7578, deals mainly in abstract early 20th-century art and a few upcoming artists. *Anne Faggionato*, 4th Floor, 20 Dering Street, T020-7493 6732, is the most recent arrival. There's also a pleasantly ordinary pub, *The Duke of York*. The presence of these artworld impresarios is perhaps explained by their proximity to the silly money of New Bond Street, the next street off to the left.

Back on Oxford Street, a short way up on the right-hand side, opposite Bond Street tube, is Stratford Place. The grand classical building at the end is **Stratford House**, built in the 1770s, and once the home of the Earl of Derby, Secretary of War for the last years of the First World War. It is now the Oriental Club, a private club founded by members of the East India Company in the mid-19th century.

Apart from the great early 20th-century Ionic block of **Selfridges**, a sight in itself, the last sight Oxford Street has to offer is **Marble Arch**. Designed by John Nash in 1827 to stand in front of Buckingham Palace, it wasn't quite grand enough and was moved to this site 25 years later and eventually stranded in the middle of a hectic roundabout. Nearby, on Sundays,

Only senior Royals & the King's Troop Royal Horse Artillery are allowed through the arch

Five of the best:
West End cafés

- *Monmouth Coffee House*, Monmouth Street, Covent Garden.
- *Coffee Republic*, South Molton Street, Mayfair.
- *Mokaris*, Jermyn Street, St James's.
- *Carluccio's*, St Christopher's Place, off Oxford Street.
- *Bar Italia*, Frith Street, Soho.

Speaker's Corner has been providing a spot for any budding orator to let off steam since the middle of the 19th century. Nowadays the soap boxes are dominated by religious extremists and speakers with more passion than eloquence, but some draw surprisingly large and attentive crowds.

Eating and drinking

Oxford St is not about sitting down and eating, unless you count the department store restaurants. The only place within spitting distance that can be recommended is *Rasa W1*, 6 Dering St, W1, T020-7629 1346, an excellent Keralan restaurant. It's not particularly cheap, but some truly superb south Indian vegetarian dishes are served up in a strictly non-smoking and cheerful environment.

You're better off looking for something to eat in Soho, Mayfair, Marylebone or Fitzrovia

Borders Café, 2nd floor, 203 Oxford St, W1, T020-7292 1600, open Mon-Sat 0800-2230, Sun 1200-1730, is a licensed café in the bookshop that makes a useful haven from the frantic street outside which can be observed from above through large plate-glass windows. *Nanis*, 12 Winsley St, W1, T020-7255 1928, open Mon-Fri 0530-1730, Sat 0800-1700, is a long-established, bright and cheerful Italian sandwich bar and snack stop that opens very early in the morning and represents good value for the area. There are others at 36 Albemarle St, W1, T020-7493 0821, and 8-10 Wigmore St, W1, T020-7580 7936.

Cafés & sandwich bars

Otherwise head for St James's St, Barrett St and St Christopher's Place. The *Café Crêperie*, 26 St James's St, has outside tables and is reasonable value. *Giovanni*, 18 James's St, W1, T020-7493 7362, is open daily 1200-2330 for cheap, filling Italian food, and also has tables outside. In pedestrianized Barrett St, *Cranks*, 23 Barrett St, W1, T020-7495 1340, is a branch of the healthy eating salad bar with a basement seating area, while *Carluccio's*, 3-5 Barrett St, St Christopher's Place, W1, is a brand new outpost of the exceptionally stylish Italian deli and café. Expensive but worth it.

Coffee and sandwich bar chains continue to proliferate around here: they include *Aroma*, West One Centre, Oxford St, W1, T020-7495 6945; *Caffe Uno*, 28 Binney St, W1, T020-7499 9312; *Prêt à Manger*, 54-56 Oxford St, W1, T020-7636 5750, and at 556 Oxford St, W1, T020-7723 9004; and *Starbucks* in *Books Etc*, 421 Oxford St, W1, T020-7491 0466.

Again, Oxford St doesn't really do pubs and bars. Just off it though, the *Bar Madrid* and the *Zoo Bar*, 4 Winsley St, are open till 0300 every night. They do good-value cocktails and have a lively buzz. *The Woodstock*, 11 Woodstock St, W1, T020-7408 2008, is an ordinary pub where you can often find a seat, even at lunchtimes. The atmosphere is pleasant and food perfectly reasonable. *Bradley's Spanish Bar*, 42-44 Hanway St, W1, T020-7636 0359, open Mon-Sat until 2300, tapas until 2200, is a tiny place, a media boho favourite, with a basement dive bar and excellent jukebox on the ground floor.

Pubs & bars
▶▶ Go to page 423 for entertainment & nightlife

Shopping

Late closing for most of Oxford St is on Thu, usually at 2000. Otherwise they tend to shut up shop between 1800 & 1900

A shopping expedition is really the only reason to spend much time on Oxford St. Even so, apart from the department stores, there are surprisingly few shops with any distinctive character. Many of them are familiar High Street chainstore branches, and not necessarily the best-value branches at that, although here size is everything. With the department stores, it can be worth getting a store card for certain discounts, and privileges during the sales. Identification and proof of address are required but the benefits are usually immediate. For ease of reference, this section lists some of the more special or interesting shops as you head west from Tottenham Court Rd towards Marble Arch. Addresses with even numbers are on the right, odd numbers on the left.

Tottenham Court Rd to Oxford Circus

The *Virgin Megastore*, 14-16 Oxford St, W1, T020-7631 1234, sets the tone for this stretch of the street with four loud floors selling every multimedia music format you could wish for, as well as miniscooters, merchandising and computer games. Over the road is a small branch of *Waterstone's*, 19-23 Oxford St, W1, T020-7434 9759, focusing on best-selling fiction and non-fiction. *Morgan*, 7 Oxford St, W1, T020-7437 2768, is a branch of the UK chain specialising in zippy clothes for younger women. Their flagship store is further down at 393 Oxford St, W1, T020-7499 4101. Similar is *Jane Norman*, 262 Oxford St, W1, T020-7499 7454, one of three branches on the street. *Mash*, 73 Oxford St, W1, T020-7434 9609 is worth a look for its discounted designer labels.

The World of Football, 119-121 Oxford St, W1, T020-7287 5088, has a self-explanatory name: lots of team strips, tracksuits, balls, trainers and boots. *Muji*, 187 Oxford St, W1, T020-7437 7503, do a full range of excellent functionally designed Japanese lifestyle products, from furnishings and household goods, including kitchenware, through health and beauty to stationery. *HMV*, 150 Oxford St, W1, T020-7631 3423, the first of the two HMV music megastores on the street, marginally more hip than *Virgin* and easier to find your way around.

London's first book megastore, *Borders Books Music and Café*, 203-207 Oxford St, W1, T020-7292 1600, open Mon-Sat until 2300 and on Sun until 1800, holds a huge stock of books and music, and there's a decent café on the second floor with big windows overlooking the street. The regular special events at this branch tend towards the more middlebrow celebrity appearances, as opposed to the literary occasions at the Charing Cross Rd branch, which doesn't stock music.

JJB Sports, 301-309 Oxford St, W1, T020-7409 2619, is a sportswear superstore carrying the lastest lines from just about every big name except Fila for some reason. *Top Shop/Top Man*, 214 Oxford St, W1, T020-7636 7700, must be one of the largest high-street fashion stores in the world. *Jigsaw*, 9 Argyll St, W1, T020-7437 5750, do staple everyday wear for men and women about town, and their sales are always slightly later than everyone else's. *Tesco Metro*, open 24 hrs, until 2200 Sat, at 311 Oxford St, is a very useful central London branch of the UK supermarket. Grab a picnic and head for the park before you part with any more cash, or carry on down the street to explore the department stores.

From Oxford Circus to Marble Arch

Niketown London, 236 Oxford St, W1, T020-7612 0800, open Mon-Wed 1000-1900, Thu 1000-2100, Fri and Sat 1000-2000, Sun 1200-1800, landed on Oxford Circus in Jul 1999, a high-tech temple to all things Nike, the only one in the UK. In the 'launch area', a portentous inscription reads: 'To all athletes and the dreams they chase, we dedicate Niketown London'. Beyond, a multimedia 'core' claims to offer an 'in-depth look at athletes and product'. It's an introduction to the surreal presentation on three spacious floors of some heavily branded sportswear and accessories, all protected by four miked-up bouncers on the door. Whatever you may think of the Nike philosophy, the branding here is loud and aggressive.

Another sign of things to come perhaps, *Gadgetshop.com*, 272-274 Oxford St, T020-7493 8098, is the biggest outlet of the European multi-channel gifts-with-a-difference retailer. A shrine to the concept of clicks and mortar.

From a different century entirely is *Bonds of Oxford Street*, 330 Oxford St, W1, T020-7493 1025, a resolutely old-fashioned store packed with every possible accessory for smokers of pipes and cigarettes. Not far off Oxford St to the north, *Waterstone's*, 28 Margaret St, W1, T020-7580 2812, is another small branch of the bookshop chain.

This is where the department stores begin, starting with one of the most straightforward and dependable outfits in the country. The favourite of the middle classes, *John Lewis*, 278-306 Oxford St, W1, T020-7629 7711, has long been proudly claiming to be 'never knowingly undersold': if you find something here on sale for less elsewhere, they'll refund the difference. What really marks out the store though is the stake that all the staff have in the company. Service here is always polite, knowledgeable and as helpful as possible in making choices between their solid array of consumer durables. Next up, *DH Evans*, once a venerable favourite with the older generation, is being renamed *House of Fraser*, T020-7529 4700, after its owners, and given a revamp. *Debenhams*, 334-348 Oxford St, W1, T020-7408 4444, is nothing special but very reliable, especially for designer bargains. The restaurant is very reasonably priced but has the atmosphere of a motorway service station canteen. At the end of their main sales, the Blue Cross sales reduce prices even further.

Above and around Bond St tube station is the *West One Shopping Centre*, 383 Oxford St, W1, T020-7629 3929, a bustling home for the likes of *Tie Rack*, the *Sock Shop*, *Holland and Barrett* the wholefood shop, a *Prêt* sandwich bar, and *Lego Kidswear*. Opposite the tube is another *HMV* music megastore, T020-7514 3600. Further up on the right, James's St heads into Marylebone, lined with cafés and outside seating, including a *Stockpot* and a *Café Rouge*.

Just off here is St Christopher's Place, a quaint little bit of New Bond St that has slipped north of Oxford St and made itself marginally more accessible. It has a slightly precious, Parisian air, as do some of the shops, but it's a pleasant place to stop for a coffee. *Buckle My Shoe*, 19 St Christopher's Place, W1, T020-7935 5589, stock designer shoes for babies and children by Nick and Lulu Rayne; *Jane and Dada*, 20 St Christopher's Place, W1, T020-7486 0977, do everyday designerwear for women aged 30 plus; there's another branch of *Mulberry*, 11 Gees Court, W1, T020-7493 2546, the upper-crust accessory shop; *Droopy and Brown's*, 16-17 St Christopher's Place, W1, T020-7486 6458, specialize in spectacular occasional wear by Susan Kramer, patronized by the likes of Honor Blackman; and *Under Two Flags*, 4 St Christopher's Place, W1, T020-7935 6934, do collectable model toy soldiers.

Back on Oxford St, on the corner of Duke St, *The Body Shop*, 374 Oxford St, W1, T020- 7409 7868, is the busiest branch in the world of the very successful cruelty-free cosmetics and bodycare company.

Across the way is the Queen of Oxford St's department stores, *Selfridges*, 400 Oxford St, W1, T020-7629 1234. Nothing like as pretentious as Harrods, Selfridges does just as good a job of creating another grander and more leisurely world behind its heavy glass doors, and its customer services are legendary. On the ground floor, beyond the inevitable perfumery (in pole position because it makes more money per square foot than any other department), you'll find fashion accessories, wines and spirits, jewellery, toiletries, a cigar shop and menswear. The *Spirit Café* is next to the popular Selfridges Spirit range for young women. At the back, beyond the *Brass Rail Café* specialising in salt beef, and the fully licensed *Balcony Wine Bar*, the food hall is an extraordinary gastrodome of fresh and potted delicacies, including an oyster bar. A pint of Guinness and a dozen Irish oysters will set you back about £20. The first floor is given over to fashionable menswear concessions. The second and third floors are for womenswear. Interiors are on the fourth floor and Beauty on the fifth. The lower ground floor stocks leisure and audio-visual goods, alongside the fresh juice bar *Café Twin Peaks* and a *Yo Sushi!* concession. All in all, even if you might not want to fulfill its founder's boast that you can 'spend the day at the Selfridges', there's more than enough here for an entertaining few hours.

Opposite *Selfridges* is a branch of ***Books etc***, 421 Oxford St, T020-7495 5850, and a bit further along is the flagship store of the recently beleaguered ***Marks & Spencer***, 458 Oxford St, W1, T020-7935 7954. Declining profits have led to some bizarre advertising initiatives and, more damagingly, the abandonment of some of their traditional suppliers, but M&S still sets a nationwide benchmark for affordable high-quality clothes and food. Just beyond it and almost as venerable is ***The Clarks Shop***, 476 Oxford St, W1, T020-7629 9609, a chain that has been keeping British children well shod since 1825. Further up on Marble Arch, ***Bliss Chemist***, 5-6 Marble Arch W1, T020-7723 6116, is a late-night pharmacy open until midnight throughout the year.

Transport

Buses *These buses all run east of Oxford Circus; for buses west of Oxford Circus see under Mayfair*

No 7 to Russell Square, British Museum, Oxford Circus, Marble Arch, Paddington and Ladbroke Grove.

No 8 to Victoria, Mayfair, Oxford Circus, Holborn, Bank, Liverpool St and Shoreditch.

No 10 to Hammersmith, Ken High St, Knightsbridge, Marble Arch, Oxford Circus, Tottenham Court Rd, Euston and King's Cross.

No 25 to Oxford Circus, Holborn abd Bank (Mon-Fri) or Tower of London (Sat, Sun).

No 55 to Oxford Circus, Bloomsbury, Old Street, Shoreditch and Hackney.

No 73 to Victoria, Marble Arch, Oxford Circus, Tottenham Court Rd, Euston, King's Cross, Islington and Stoke Newington.

No 176 to Oxford Circus, Tottenham Court Rd station, Trafalgar Square, Aldwych, Waterloo, Elephant, Camberwell and Dulwich.

Taxis Cab ranks outside John Lewis, and in Market Court, Rathbone Place, Vere St, Wells St, west of Orchard St and in Winsley St. Usually plenty on Oxford St itself, which is restricted to buses and taxis 0700-1900 Mon-Sat; cars can only cross it during those hours.

Tubes Oxford Circus (Central and Victoria lines); Tottenham Court Rd (Central and Northern lines).

Directory

Internet cafés *easyEverything Internet Café, opposite Bond St tube.*

Sport *Centrepoint Snooker, beneath Centrepoint tower in Tottenham Court Rd tube station subway, is open 1100-0600 daily. 7 snooker tables, 5 American pool and 6 English pool tables. £3 entrance; snooker tables £5.90 per hr, pool tables*

£4.30 per hr, first come first served. Bar and food. T020-240 6886.

Useful Addresses *Oxford Street Association, T020-7629 2738, will give details of trading hours, Christmas lights, parking, and try to answer any other enquiries about the area.*

Central London

4

Central London

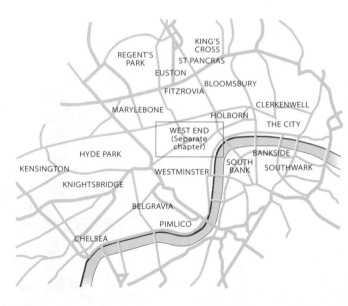

Westminster and Whitehall

*The seat of central government power in the Kingdom is an administrative bee-hive and one of the few parts of London that achieves any architectural cohesion. Parliament Square, especially viewed from the Broad Sanctuary by Westminster Abbey, manages to present a stirring picture of common purpose with its array of skybound Gothic towers. And Whitehall too makes a decent stab at Venetian grandeur as it connects Parliament with Trafalgar Square. Although the borough of Westminster encompasses most of the West End, to Brits the name really only refers to this relatively small area in the immediate vicinity of the **Houses of Parliament**. And even though there are easily enough places to see and things to do around here to occupy at least a whole day, the impression is very much one of being kept at arm's length. Even the river hardly gets a look in.*

Here there's unlikely to be much sense of involvement for the curious visitor. Apart from the obvious security considerations, that's understandable. After all, the battalions of politicos and civil servants, generally prematurely bald young men and smart foxy chicks, who scurry about at lunchtime and fill the area's pubs on the dot of five, have been running the country all day. Nightlife is non-existent. In the evenings the place feels like a quiet provincial town. Surprisingly though, plenty of people do live here, especially in the streets beyond Westminster Abbey between Millbank and Victoria Street, which are really the only place to look for a drink in an interesting pub or decent meal day or night.

⊖ *Charing Cross or Embankment tube for the top of Whitehall nearest Trafalgar Square. Westminster tube for Big Ben & Parliament Square, & St James's tube for Victoria St, the Abbey & the streets beyond*

Central London

History

As the Tyburn flows into the Thames, it forks to create an island of marshland. It was here on Thorney Island (Isle of Brambles) that in the eighth century King Offa founded a Benedictine monastery, the West Minster, precursor to the Abbey that now graces the site. The Danes subsequently sacked the area, and it wasn't until Edward the Confessor's reign in the 11th century that the site was re-established. While the new church was under construction, Edward opted to move his royal residence from the City to the banks of the river here in Westminster in order to supervise its construction. This move proved momentous for the political geography of London – it signalled the separation of the seat of royal power from the commercial centre of the land. The Abbey was consecrated at Christmas 1065, a few weeks before Edward's death. Nothing remains of the palace that Edward built, but Westminster Hall, which still displays its 14th-century hammerbeam roof, was part of William II's further development of the palace.

By 1265 the site further north up Whitehall was occupied by lands belonging to the Abbey of Abingdon to the west, with York Place, the Archbishop of York's London residence, sweeping down to the river to the east. The Tudors and Stuarts in the 16th and 17th centuries cemented the grandeur and power-base of the area. Wolsey developed York Place into a palace fit for a king (his wine cellar still exists under the modern

• •

Hotels in the area

B *Hilton London St Ermin's*
B *Sanctuary House Hotel*
➡ *Go to page 443*

Five of the best: sights in Central London

- *Tate Modern*, Bankside.
- *British Museum*, Bloomsbury.
- *Sir John Soane Museum*, Holborn.
- *Wallace Collection*, Marylebone.
- *Serpentine Gallery*, Kensington Gardens.

Ministry of Defence) and following the fall of the cardinal in 1530 Henry VIII took over the residence. He developed the newly named Whitehall Palace further, building extensively the other side of Whitehall alongside what became St James's Park. A tilt-yard (now Horse Guards), cockpit, bowling green and tennis courts were linked to Wolsey's palace by the magnificent Holbein and King's Gate that spanned Whitehall. James further developed the site, describing Elizabeth I's palace as an "old, rotten, slight-builded shed". All that remains of Inigo Jones's palatial vision, (and much of it was never more than a vision) is the Palladian Banqueting House, immortalized as the site of Charles I's execution.

Meanwhile, the area was swiftly becoming one of the busiest areas beyond the City walls. There were respectable lodgings available for the country gentlemen who came to attend court, and Flemish milliners and stalls selling hot pies, ale and porpoise tongues lined Whitehall. Westminster Hall provided cover for an odd mix of law courts (the King's Bench) on one side, and bookstalls on the other (William Caxton had set up the first printing press in a shop in the Abbey precincts). Nevertheless, crime and poverty were rife. Thieves and pickpockets roamed the area, attracted by the wealthy residents and visitors and the escape route presented by the Sanctuary tower just north of the Abbey. Slums sat within a stone's throw of the palace – Parliament Square was particularly squalid, and, due to the area's marshy origins, the people were frequently visited by plagues.

The growth of St James's as another royal residence merely reinforced Whitehall's role as the centre of political life. William III, newly arrived from Holland, chose Kensington over Whitehall as his residence on account of his asthma, and in 1698 a careless laundry-woman's error caused a fire to burn down the palace. Westminster, however, remained the administrative centre of Government, and under the Hanoverians residential houses sprung up to house the growing force of bureaucrats. Queen Anne's Gate (which dates from about 1704), (Lord) North Street, Smith Square and the cul-de-sac Downing Street remain to this day, the latter built on the site of the Axe, a brewhouse that once belonged to the Abbey of Abingdon. In 1834 the whole landscape changed with a fire that razed the hotchpotch Palace of Westminster to the ground. The colossal Gothic edifice that sits there now was the creation of Charles Barry, although the Commons itself did burn down in 1941 when hit by a German bomb (it was reconstructed).

As Britain's Empire spread so did the organs of state around Whitehall. The Treasury, Foreign Office, and War Office are all Victorian creations, the Ministry of Defence and Portcullis House are much more recent. The Downing Street façade, while retaining its simple street entrance, hides a network of 160 rooms linked to the Cabinet Office that looks onto Whitehall. Indeed, Westminster and Whitehall hide a series of subterranean offices built in anticipation of attack, most notably the 'Hole in the Ground' under Storey's Gate, several acres of offices protected by 17 ft of concrete. Political tentacles engulf the area – the Methodist's Central Hall hosted the inaugural meeting of the United Nations, while many of the area's residences,

Central London

restaurants and pubs are permanently linked up to Parliament so MPs can mix business with pleasure without missing crucial votes.

Sights

Westminster tube station brings you up right at the foot of **Big Ben** on the western end of **Westminster Bridge**. The first bridge here was opened in 1750 and anyone caught attempting to graffiti it faced the death penalty. Wordsworth stood on it at dawn and later recollected his emotions on the view in tranquility: 'Ne'er saw I, never felt, a calm so deep!'

Not much chance of that, even at dawn, on the cast-iron bridge of today that replaced Wordsworth's in 1862, but the view's still not bad at all, now including the full circle of the London Eye. The bridge's pavements are always busy, in winter with the hotly contested pitches for roast chestnut and caramelized peanut sellers. First thing in the morning though (or shortly after lunch during the week once the coach parties have headed off for St Paul's) is the best time to visit Westminster's main attraction, the Abbey.

Around Westminster Abbey

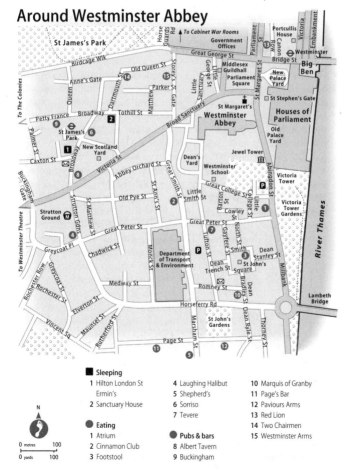

Sleeping
1 Hilton London St Ermin's
2 Sanctuary House

Eating
1 Atrium
2 Cinnamon Club
3 Footstool

4 Laughing Halibut
5 Shepherd's
6 Sorriso
7 Tevere

Pubs & bars
8 Albert Tavern
9 Buckingham

10 Marquis of Granby
11 Page's Bar
12 Paviours Arms
13 Red Lion
14 Two Chairmen
15 Westminster Arms

Westminster Abbey

Buses 3, 11, 12, 24, 53, 77a, 88, 159 & 211 all pass Westminster Abbey

A surprisingly small church for one of such enormous significance in the Anglican faith and British state (especially for its monarchy), Westminster Abbey's charm lies in its age. Sadly it has inevitably become a well-managed tourist trap. Heaven help any poor unsuspecting soul who wanders in without a ticket through any door other than the official visitors' entrance at the north transept (the one nearest Parliament Square). They'll be pounced upon by one of the Abbey's ever-vigilant vergers. That said, despite the milling crowds clutching the fairly patronizing audio guide and bossy 'free' floorplans, it remains a sacred building and anyone wishing to pray here (or join in a service on Sunday when the Abbey is closed to tourists) is allowed to do so free of charge. And there's also plenty worth seeing for the money.

One of the better approaches to the exterior is from St James's Park tube, a short walk down Broadway and Tothill, to the west front with its twin Hawksmoor towers of 1745, the most recent additions to what from here is clearly a very tall and thin old building. Walking clockwise round to the visitors' entrance, it's easy to understand how the Abbey's architecture could be described as 'the perfect governmental report on French Gothic': it does look like a tight and proper place, lacking the majesty of some other cathedrals in England or France and all the more appropriate for that, especially in comparison to the flamboyant neo-Gothic of the Houses of Parliament across the way.

Once inside it's another story: the length and especially the height (over 100ft) of the Nave are awe-inspiring. On the tourist route round from the north entrance, this impressive view is left until the end, the tour beginning in the oldest part of the main building, the central Crossing built in the 13th century. Visitors then turn sharp right to skirt the Sanctuary of the High Altar (where sovereigns are crowned) and the founder St Edward the Confessor's Chapel, past the tombs of Edward I and Henry III, to look at the **Coronation Chair**. Made to order for the 'Hammer of the Scots', Edward I, and used to crown every English monarch except three since 1308, the old wooden chair's most obvious feature now is the empty space below the seat purpose-built for the Stone of Destiny. The sandstone coronation block of Scottish monarchs since the ninth century is now back home in its native land and on display in Edinburgh Castle. Beyond is **Henry VII's Chapel** (or Lady Chapel), dating from the early 16th century, an extraordinary medieval pageant of flags, stalls, and tombs below a wonderful vaulted stone roof of cobweb intricacy. On either side of this chapel are the hushed tombs of Elizabeth I and Mary Queen of Scots.

Heading back towards the Crossing, the tour passes **Poet's Corner**, decorated with sculptures and monuments to Shakespeare, Chaucer and other poets and actors, as well as scientists, architects, historians and other worthies. A memorial here is the highest posthumous honour that Queen and country can bestow.

These three less busy rooms are well worth the small extra charge

Then it's out into the fresh air of the Cloisters of the 11th-century monastery, past the Chapter House, Pyx Chamber and Museum. In the octagonal **Chapter House**, where the House of Commons sat from the mid-14th-16th centuries, the medieval wall paintings of the Last Judgement and the Apocalypse, and remarkable tiled floor, decorated with griffins, lions, and mythical beasts, have a faded splendour. The dark little **Pyx Chamber** was the monastery's strong room and is the oldest building on site. And the

Central London

museum in the monks' Common Room contains some weird Royal funeral effigies from the Middle Ages as well as a more recent and peculiar effigy of the Duke of Buckingham. He died of tuberculosis in Rome in 1735 aged 19 and his waxwork image lies dressed up in his peers robes, wearing his own wig, in a glass case scratched with 19th-century graffiti.

The **Little Cloisters** are reached through an old whitewashed stone tunnel off the main Cloisters, giving a striking view of the Victoria Tower of the Houses of Parliament rearing up above a small fountain enclosed by the quiet stone arches. After time spent in the peace of the **College Garden** beyond (where concerts are sometimes given at lunchtimes on Thursdays in July and August), the busy tour route back in the main cloisters may seem like a distant memory. It returns though into the Abbey at the 14th-century part of that great Nave near the tombs of the Unknown Soldier and Sir Winston Churchill and ends outside the west front by the Abbey Bookshop.

From Tue to Thu, the Little Cloisters & College Garden are also well worth seeking out

■ *Open Mon-Fri 0930-1645 (last admission 1545), Sat 0930-1445 (last admission 1345). Admission £5; £3 concession; £2 under-16s; under-11's free with adult. Sun services 1000 (Matins), 1115 (Sung Eucharist), 1500 (Evensong), 1745 (Organ recital), 1830 (Evening service). Weekday services 0730 (Matins, 0920 Sat and Bank Holidays), 0800 (Holy Communion), 1230 (Holy Communion, except Sat), 1700 (Evensong, 1500 Sat). Chapter House, Pyx Chamber and Museum open summer 1000-1730 daily. Main Cloister open same hours as Abbey; admission free (from Dean's Yard). Little Cloister and College Garden open Tue-Thu summer 1030-1800, winter 1030-1600, admission free. T020-7222 5152; tours T020-7222 7110.*

Around Westminster Abbey

The early 16th-century Church of St Margaret's stands next to the Abbey to the north on Parliament Square. The House of Commons' local place of worship and a popular venue for society weddings, it was founded by the Abbey's monks in the late 11th century as a refuge from the crowds. The church's east window depicting the Crucifixion is famously one of the most beautiful arrays of pre-Reformation stained glass in London while the 19th-century west window celebrates the life of Sir Walter Raleigh, the Elizabethan courtier who helped found Virginia, introduced the potato to Europe and was buried in the Chancel here after his execution for treason. The modern stained-glass window in the south aisle was designed by the John Piper in the 60s. ■ *Open 0930-1630 Mon-Fri; Sun service 1100. Admission free. T020-7222 5152.*

Church of St Margaret's

The small archway by the Abbey's west front leads into **Dean's Yard**, the large quadrangle from which the cloisters and College Garden of the Abbey can be accessed and also the front entrance of **Westminster School**, one of the country's oldest and most prestigious public (ie fee-paying) schools. Tours of some of its Elizabethan buildings are available by arrangement during the school holidays. ■ *Westminster School, Little Dean's Yard, SW1. T020-7963 1000.*

The gate at the far corner of Dean's Yard gives onto **Tufton Street** at its meeting with the old ragstone wall of Great College Street, near Church House, the administrative centre of the Church of England. Look out for the sumptuous window display of clerical garb in the old shopfront of *J Wippell & Co* at 11 Tufton Street.

Central London

Around Smith Square
Labour HQ is now in Millbank Tower, a short way off

The quiet streets between here and Millbank though are the place to explore the secluded heart of British political life and make the perfect introduction to the pomp and circumstance of the Houses of Parliament. Many are occupied by wealthy MPs and former ministers because their centre is Smith Square, still home to the Conservative Central Office and once also the Labour party's HQ.

It comes as something of a shock on entering the square to be confronted by the massive Baroque shape of **St John's Hall** in the middle. Completed in 1728 it was much mocked a century later by the Victorians, including Dickens who said it looked like 'some petrified monster, frightful and gigantic, on its back with its legs in the air'. In fact the design had long been attributed to the short-tempered Queen Anne kicking a four-legged footstool over to demonstrate how she wanted the new church to look. Repeatedly gutted by fire, it was deconsecrated after the Second World War and has become one of the city's best classical music concert halls, with superb acoustics and its own resident Academy of Ancient Music.

The atmospheric *Footstool Restaurant* in the crypt (T020-7222 2779; open Mon-Fri 1000-1700 or until half hour after concerts start, and also open one hour before concerts start on Saturday, Sunday or Bank Holidays) is managed by Digby Trout, also responsible for the well-prepared and fairly reasonably priced modern European food at many other major London sights like the British Museum, Science Museum, Royal Court Theatre and Dulwich Picture Gallery. ■ *St John's Hall, Smith Square, SW1, T020-7222 1061, www.sjss.org.uk Tickets £8-£20.*

Victoria Tower Gardens is the most pleasant riverside spot around here

On the north side of Smith Square, the parallel 18th-century terraces of Gayfere Street and North Street are worth comparing, Gayfere Street clearly designed for the tradesfolk catering for the wealthier inhabitants of North Street. Both lead onto Great Peter Street where a right turn heads for Millbank and the **Victoria Tower Gardens**. Monuments in the small triangular park include a copy of Rodin's *Six Burghers of Calais*, a Gothic drinking fountain celebrating the abolition of slavery in the Empire, and a statue of the campaigner for votes for women, suffragette Emmeline Pankhurst.

Jewel Tower

Opposite the gardens, on Abingdon Street over the road from the Houses of Parliament and often overlooked, stands the little Jewel Tower, one of the last vestiges of the medieval Palace of Westminster. Surrounded by a dry moat, and emphatically not where the crown jewels are kept, this was a fortified wardrobe for Edward III built in 1365 and now contains a small exhibition on Parliament Past and Present along with a few other interesting things, including, in the ground floor shop, a rusted Rhineland sword of about 800 AD dug up in Victoria Tower Gardens.

Up the narrow winding stair, the exhibition displays some Speakers robes, contemporary china caricatures of prime ministers Gladstone and Disraeli, amid a series of explanatory wall texts. A 45-minute video in the top room tries to explain what MPs and Parliament do today. Also on display are a stack of the 19th-century Board of Trade's working standards. From 1869 to 1935 the Jewel Tower's thick walls and constant temperature suited its use as the nationwide centre for the accurate calibration of weights and measures. The brass barrels for converting gills, pints, and gallons into pecks, bushels and chaldrons were in use until 1962. A few niggardly comments in the visitors' book complain about the entrance fee though.

■ *Open summer 1000-1800; Oct 1000-1800 (last admission 1730) or dusk if earlier; winter 1000-1600 (last admission 1530). Admission £1.50, concession £1.10, 80p under-16s. T020-7222 2219.*

Houses of Parliament

The exhibition in the Jewel Tower just might stoke up an appetite to see Parliament doing its thing over the road in the **Palace of Westminster**, better known as the Houses of Parliament. The government of England has met on this spot since the reign of Edward III, when the King and his court of barons and bishops would meet in St Stephen's Chapel. The chapel and surrounding palace were almost completely razed to the ground by fire in 1834, resulting in the building of the golden Gothic glory in use today.

Its most famous feature is **Big Ben**, the clock tower overlooking Westminster Bridge. Remarkably accurate for such a big timepiece, the clock strikes the hour on the 13-ton bell that gives the tower its name, and which can be heard up to 4 ½ miles away, and sounds the quarters on four smaller bells to a tune from Handel's *Messiah*. Looking at the building from Parliament Square, the House of Commons is on the left and the House of Lords on the right.

The recently retired guide, who took visitors to the top and back, is reckoned to have climbed the equivalent of 76 Mount Everests

The oldest part of the building though is **Westminster Hall**, which survived the fire, behind the statue of the victor in the Civil War, Lord Protector Oliver Cromwell, standing proudly with the British lion at his feet. For about 25 years after his death though, the southern gable of the Hall was adorned with his head until, in 1686, it was blown off in a storm and hidden away. The ancient interior of the Hall with its great hammerbeam roof and the beautifully decorated **St Stephen's Crypt** can only be seen on a guided tour.

When Parliament is in session the public are admitted (after a thorough security check) to the 'Strangers' Galleries' of either House through St Stephen's Gate, just beyond Cromwell's statue. The queue for the Commons is on the left and the Lords on the right. Anyone is welcome to wait in line although whether or not you make it inside depends on the business of the day. If any debate of national interest is going on, the chances are slight. It's usually a less time-consuming process after 1700.

Parliament in session is indicated by a light on Big Ben and a Union Jack flying from the Victoria Tower

Generally it's easier and quicker gaining access to the **House of Lords**, a very grand and gilded debating chamber with its benches of red morocco. In front of the thrones is the woolsack, a cushioned ottoman for the land's senior judge the Lord Chancellor. By contrast, the **House of Commons** seems very small and business-like, its green leather benches looking quite tatty. The Government sit to the Speaker's right and the Opposition to his left with the front benches reserved for Cabinet Ministers and ex-Ministers.

Apart from during Prime Minister's Question Time on Wednesdays at 1500, which can only be seen on application to your MP or embassy, both houses are often half-empty or half-asleep. For the first time guided historical tours of both houses were available in 2000 during August and September and sold out well in advance. It's likely that the experiment will be repeated every summer. Check with the Information lines.

■ *Parliament usually in session mid-Oct to Christmas, Jan to Easter, Jun and Jul: Mon 1430-2000, Tue 0900-1300, 1430-2200, Wed & Thu 1430-2200 approximately. Commons Information Line T020-7219 4272; Lords Information Line T020-7219 3107; www.parliament.uk*

Central London

Parliament Square

Anyone genuinely interested in seeing the sharp end of the law in action can sit in on a case at the **Middlesex Guildhall Crown Courts** on the west side of Parliament Square, seven criminal courts usually in session from Monday to Friday 1030-1300, 1400-1600. Parliament Square was laid out by Sir Charles Barry, the designer of the Palace of Westminster, and since becoming the world's first roundabout in 1926 has gradually been dotted with worthy statuary, most prominently **Winston Churchill** looking sturdy and combative, and also Abraham Lincoln, just risen to his feet from his chair to hold forth on democracy. The simplest way of identifying all the different buildings around the square is to take a look at the Jubilee Walkway information board on the corner of the square nearest Great George Street.

Cabinet War Rooms

Admission is free with a ticket for the Imperial War Museum (see page 262)

More on Churchill and his achievement can be found at the Cabinet War Rooms, round the corner up Horse Guards Road on the right, at the foot of the Clive Steps on King Charles Street. During the Blitz these underground rooms in the only steel framed building in Whitehall became the nerve centre of Churchill's morale-boosting war effort. In the claustrophobic cabinet war room itself the U-shaped table laden with ashtrays encircles three hot seats for the Chiefs of staff of army, air force and navy. A sufferer from depression himself, which he called the 'black dog', Churchill propped a personal note against their water decanter: 'Please understand there is no depression in this house and we are not interested in the possibilities of defeat: they do not exist.'

Most of the rooms are off one long gloomy corridor, including his tiny bedroom, the cramped typing pool, the map room, and his office hotline to the US president, all echoing with ringing telephones and the sound of his famous speeches. Also on display is the original map used to hang the Iron Curtain at Yalta. The entertaining audio guide (included in the ticket price and taking about an hour and a half) features personal memories of the people who worked here, like the trainee typist tested by the great man's cigar-chewing speech impediment. Overall the place remains a testament to the dogged forbearance of a charismatic leader and his government with their backs against the wall.

■ *Open 1000-1800 winter; 0930-1800 summer. Admission £5.40, concession £4.10, unemployed £2.80, under-16s free. T020-7930 6961.*

From outside the Cabinet War Rooms, **St James's Park** (see page 125) stretches dreamily off into the distance, the start of an almost unbroken tract of green from here to **Kensington Palace**, a fact that has been officially recognized by the circular **Diana Princess of Wales Memorial Walk** that can be joined here. The seven-mile route through St James's Park, Green Park, Hyde Park and Kensington Gardens is marked with 90 rose-emblem plaques in the ground and was formally opened on 30 June 2000, the day before the 39th anniversary of Diana's birth. For more information: T020-7298 2000. Halfway up Birdcage Walk on the left is Queen Anne's Gate, a rare survival from the early 18th century, and number two is the United Kingdom Office of the European Parliament.

Whitehall

Details of Foreign Office visits on www.fco.gov.uk

Back by Westminster tube, on the left **Portcullis House** contains brand new and very expensive offices for MPs opposite the Houses of Parliament, the latest in the series of palatial government buildings that make up Whitehall. With its black ventilation stacks and deferential mock-Gothic design it makes interesting comparison with the huge Edwardian block on the corner of Parliament Square and Parliament Street. These 'New Government Offices' of 1898 now house some departments of the Treasury. A short way up Parliament Street on the left, through the triple arch of King Charles Street, is the Foreign and Commonwealth Office, SW1, T020-7270 1500, which occasionally arranges guided tours round its old building.

In the middle of the road, where Parliament Street becomes Whitehall, stands the **Cenotaph**, a simple block of Portland Stone designed rapidly by Lutyens for the peace celebrations in July 1919, it has become the focus for national remembrance of the dead of the two World Wars, where a service is held annually on the Sunday nearest November 11, the date of the Armistice in 1918.

Just further down on the left, in **Downing Street**, beyond the notorious gates installed by Margaret Thatcher in the 80s, number 10 is the deceptively small-looking home and offices of the Prime Minister, recognizable from the policeman standing outside. Next door, number 11 is the Chancellor of the Exchequer's home and offices.

Central London

Whitehall

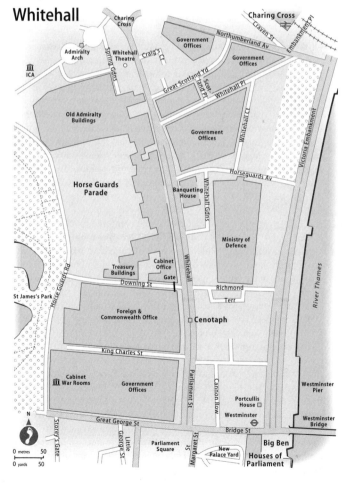

Central London

 Colourful events

Trooping the Colour *takes place on the third or second Saturday in June. Write in with SAE for up to three tickets for the day itself – two rehearsals on the Saturdays before are unrestricted – to Brigade Major, HQ Household Division, Horseguards, Whitehall, London, SW1A 2AX, T020-7414 2479. £7.50 for rehearsals, £15 for the main event. Parade starts at 1100 and lasts for an hour.*

RHS London Flower Shows *are held over two days, usually weekends, most months of the year (in January, February, March, April, June, September, October, November and December). Horticultural Halls, Greycoat Street, Westminster, London, SW1 Tickets T0870-906 3721; information T020-7649 1885. Admission £5 first day, £3 second day.www.rhs.org.uk*

Whitehall then continues its wide progress up to Trafalgar Square, lined with the offices of the Cabinet and the Treasury, and the Scottish Office. Opposite stands the massive **Ministry of Defence** (MOD), towering over a little statue of Sir Water Raleigh and big statues of Field Marshalls Montgomery (of Alamein) and Slim. The front entrance of the MOD on Horse Guards Avenue is flanked by enormous stone women representing Earth and Water.

On the corner of Horse Guards Avenue and Whitehall stands the last survivor from the original Whitehall Palace, Inigo Jones's **Banqueting House**. Completed in 1622, the building is the only Government property on Whitehall that welcomes uninvited visitors (although it, too, occasionally closes for private receptions). A visit includes an introductory 15-minute historical video in the cellars where James I used to drown his sorrows, followed by a 20-minute audio guide to the splendidly proportioned Banqueting Hall itself. Apart from its historical associations, the main attraction is the ceiling, decorated with nine canvasses by Rubens including the extraordinary Apotheosis of James I, aka Union Jack, in the middle, complete with a couple of mirror-table trolleys to save admirers from cricked necks. ■ *Open 1000-1700 Mon-Sat. Admission £3.80. T020-7930 4179.*

The main purpose of the guard seems to be to entertain tourists and stop people driving or bicycling through the arch without a special ivory pass from her Maj

Across the road another Palladian edifice built a century later, **Horse Guards**, is the HQ of the Household Division. The **Changing of the Queen's Life Guard** takes place here Monday-Saturday 1100, Sunday 1000, with the guard parading dismounted at 1600 daily, amid a strong smell of horse dung. The guard is drawn from the squadrons of the Household Cavalry stationed at Hyde Park Barracks, alternating daily between Life Guards (red tunics and white helmet plumes) and the Blues and Royals (blue tunics and red plumes). When the Queen is in London, the guard is commanded by an officer with standard and a trumpeter on a grey horse. When she's not, by an NCO without standard or trumpeter, inspected by an officer at 1600.

The parade ground itself is romantically lit at night by gas lamps

It's worth walking through to have a look at the **Parade Ground** facing St James's Park. From here the Duke of York's column on the Mall is often confused by visitors with Nelson's in Trafalgar Square to disorientating effect. On the right, the Old Admiralty Buildings stand next to the bomb-proof ivy-clad Citadel with its overgrown grass roof supposed to make aerial spotters think it a part of the park. On the left of the arch is the Chinese dragon mortar given in gratitude by the Spanish for the Duke of Wellington's relief of the siege of Salamanca by the French. It was ridiculed when it was erected.

Eating and drinking

Shepherd's, Marsham Court, Marsham St, part of the Langham Group founded by Michael Caine although now wholly owned by Peter Langham, is a dignified and very British place for the enjoyment of game in season, fish and the company of suits at supper and tourists having a treat. Otherwise fine dining options in Westminster are limited.

Expensive
● on map, page 141

Apart from the *Footstool* in the crypt of St John's, Smith Square (see page 144), one new arrival may herald the start of a new trend in the area. *The Cinnamon Club*, The Old Westminster Library, Great Smith St, SW1, T020-7517 9898, in the process of being created at the time of writing, will be a smart 200-seat Indian restaurant in the shell of the old library opposite Little Smith St. No doubt it will attract a flurry of interest when it opens.

The Atrium, 4 Millbank, T020-7233 0033, has been around for years, very popular with powerbrokers at lunchtime and quieter types in the evenings, reasonably priced (a bowl of pasta for about £8) modern Italian restaurant in the middle of a huge office block, which as the name suggests provides an outdoor dining area indoors. *Sorriso*, 10a The Broadway, SW1, T020-7222 3338 (closed weekends) is reached down a strange free-standing spiral staircase in the shadow of New Scotland Yard leading down to an air-conditioned cellar where there's a well-regarded and roomy ristorante Italiano.

Mid-range

Strutton Ground is lined with sandwich shops and cafés catering for the local office workers, many only open Mon-Fri. Here there's a *Bagel Express* and also *The Laughing Halibut*, Strutton Ground, T020-7799 2844 (open 1115-2000), for some perfectly decent fish and chips to eat in or take away. One of the most characterful places in the area though must be the *Tevere Restaurant*, open 1130-1500, a pannelled corner café seemingly unchanged since the 50s, an excellent venue for the likes of double poached eggs on toast for £1.80 or Italian and basic British hot meals for about £7.

Cheap

Government pen-pushers get thirsty, and they keep a variety of oases very lively. Their favourites are the Victorian splendour of the *Red Lion*, 48 Parliament St, SW1, T020-7930 5826, or the *Albert Tavern*, 52 Victoria St, SW1, T020-7222 5577, all creamy walls and etched glass; the smokey confines of the *The Colonies*, Wilfred St, SW1, T020-7834 1407; and for Tory MPs, the *Marquis of Granby*, 41 Romney St, SW1, T020- 7227 0941 (closed Sat & Sun), the closest watering hole to Conservative HQ.

Nearby are two genuine oddities: *Page's Bar*, 75 Page St, SW1, T020-7834 6791, www.pagesbar.co.uk, is an unlikely video music bar with a pool table run by Star Trek fans, also doing reasonable food; and the *Paviours Arms*, Page St, SW1, T020-7834 2150, is an original art deco pub, complete with 30s fittings. The buzzing red neon above the door gives way to the hum of its widely mixed clientele.

Nearer Parliament Square, the *Westminster Arms*, 9 Storeys Gate, SW1, T020-7222 8520, has tables outside and is fairly expensive but the wood-pannelled *Storeys Winebar* in the basement is a cosy and usually convivial spot. The *Two Chairmen*, 39 Dartmouth St, SW1, T020-7222 8694, near St James's Park is worth seeking out for its location in Queen Anne's Gate but not much else. Similarly the *Buckingham*, 62 Petty France, SW1, T020-7222 3386, close to the Passport Office, is a Young's pub opposite the barracks of the Scots Guards, that like many of the pubs in the area, looks grand on the outside but is not that special within.

Pubs & bars
▶▶ Go to page 423
for entertainment
& nightlife

Shopping

Strutton Ground Street market is best on Fris but has become rather tired, now peddling tacky consumer durables or not-so-durables to the local office workers. The *Abbey Bookshop* outside the west front of the Abbey is good for souvenirs, while *The*

This is not the place to come on a shopping expedition

Central London

Parliamentary Bookshop, 12 Bridge St, SW1, T020-7219 3890, is the very dry official bookshop of the House of Commons. No scurrilous political biographies here.

Transport

Buses

Usually plenty of taxis along Whitehall & around Parliament Square

Along Whitehall:

No 3 from Oxford Circus to Brixton via Piccadilly Circus, Trafalagar Square, Lambeth Bridge and Kennington.

No 11 from Fulham Broadway to Liverpool St via Chelsea, Sloane Square, Victoria, Trafalgar Square, Strand, Aldwych, Fleet St, St Paul's and Bank.

No 12 from Notting Hill Gate to Dulwich via Marble Arch, Oxford Circus, Piccadilly Circus, Trafalgar Square, Elephant, and Camberwell.

No 24 from Hampstead Heath to Pimlico, via Camden Town, Warren St, Leicester Square, Trafalgar Square and Victoria.

No 53 from Oxford Circus to Woolwich, via Piccadilly Circus, Trafalgar Square, Elephant, New Cross, Deptford and Blackheath.

No 77a from Aldwych to Wandsworth, via Trafalgar Square, Millbank, Tate Britain, Vauxhall Bridge and Clapham Junction.

No 88 from Oxford Circus to Clapham Common via Piccadilly Circus, Trafalgar Square, Tate Britain, Vauxhall and Stockwell.

No 159 from Marble Arch to Brixton via Oxford Circus, Piccadilly Circus, Trafalgar Square, Westminster Bridge and Kennington.

Over Westminster Bridge:

No 211 from Waterloo to Hammermsith, via Victoria, Sloane Square, Chelsea and Fulham Broadway.

River transport

Owing to extreme tidal conditions, always check sailing times before travelling

River boats from Westminster Pier to the Tower with *City Cruises*, T020-7930 9033, every 20 mins from 1020-2100 in summer, £4.60, takes 30 mins. From Westminster Pier to Greenwich, every 30 minutes, 1030-1700, takes an hour, return £7.60, single £6.30. Also to Kew, Richmond and Hampton court; £10 single, £14 return, children £4 and £7. Westminster Passenger Service Association, T020-7930 2062.

Tubes

Charing Cross (Northern and Bakerloo lines) or Embankment (District, Circle, Northern and Bakerloo lines). Westminster (District, Circle and Jubilee lines) for Big Ben and Parliament Square, and St James's Park (District, Circle and Jubilee lines) for Victoria St, the Abbey and the streets beyond.

Victoria, Belgravia and Pimlico

🔵 *Nearest tube stations are Victoria, Pimlico & Vauxhall; also St James's Park for the top end of Victoria St*

The grandeur of Belgravia's Eaton Square continues the line of Chelsea's King's Road up to the back door of Buckingham Palace, crossed before it gets there by the Belgrave Road striding up through Pimlico from the river to end in some style at Belgrave Square. Both seem to be doing their best to bypass and ignore the chaotic junction of Victoria and Grosvenor Gardens. Instead, one of central London's most bustling travel hubs has to make do with the lacklustre Vauxhall Bridge Road for company and is left to find its own short and unassuming way to Westminster down Victoria Street.

Little-loved Victoria hardly inspires much loyalty in Londoners – certainly there was never any chance that the local Catholic cathedral would take its name – but everyone knows it's there. In fact the scrum round the train and coach stations does much to enliven the almost deserted splendour of Belgravia – the poshest address in town – and Pimlico, its proper little neighbour. Meanwhile, down by the river on Millbank, the heavy classical portico of **Tate Britain** *belies the energy and imagination within, its collection of contemporary and British art still reeling from the excitement of coming into much more space to play downstream on Bankside. The old gallery is bravely managing to keep its head above the tide of attention turning towards the new arrival.*

History

While Westminster had created its own community outside of the City, the land beyond was largely left to pasture. In the 17th century, a large field stretched west behind Buckingham House. Criss-crossed by paths, earning it the name Five Fields, sheep and donkeys grazed on the treeless expanse that was to become Belgravia. A bridge over the Westbourne River became known as Bloody Bridge on account of the highwaymen who swooped here, and it was a favoured duelling spot. Ebury Farm, an estate of 430 acres, spread out across Pimlico and the swamps and creeks of Victoria, although the Reverend James Palmer's village of alms houses sat south of modern Victoria Street, and an annual fair, bull-baiting and a pleasure garden occupied the current site of Westminster Cathedral nearby.

Over the river, Vauxhall, named after Fulkes Hall, a house built there in the 13th century, was a mere village. It wasn't until the 18th century, and notably in the wake of George III's move to Buckingham House (later Buckingham Palace) in 1762, that the area began to show life. New Spring Gardens in Vauxhall and Ranelagh Gardens in Chelsea drew the crowds at the weekends. These "pretty contrived" plantations held firework displays and orchestral performances in among the rotundas, grottoes, statues and pavilions. In 1749 an orchestra played to a crowd of 12,000 in New Spring Gardens, and in 1786, 61,000 attended a fancy-dress party, although Horace Walpole argued that Ranelagh "has totally beat Vauxhall". Nearby, the Chelsea Bun House would attract queues of 50,000 on Good Fridays, a ridiculous claim, no doubt, but clearly popular.

Five Fields, now a patchwork of market gardens, still drew people to shoot duck and to watch bull-baiting and cock-fighting. Lanesborough House became a hospital, the Grosvenor Canal (some of it ran under the current Victoria Station) opened in 1725, and a row of houses in Grosvenor Place emerged to accommodate the royal household. When the Grosvenor estate, the owners of the land, came to an agreement with developer Thomas Cubitt in the early 19th century, building began in earnest.

The stuccoed houses of Belgravia drew the nobles from Mayfair, with Belgrave Square (the bricks were made on site from its own damp clay)

• •

Hotels in the area

AL *The Berkeley Hotel*
AL *The Lanesborough*
AL *Halkin Hotel*
B *Tophams*
B *Lime Tree Hotel*
C *Collin House*
C *The Blair Victoria Hotel*
C *The Victoria Inn*
C *Winchester Hotel*
D *Enrico Hotel*
E *Oak House*
➤➤ **Go to page 443**

Central London

Central London

Victoria, Belgravia & Pimlico

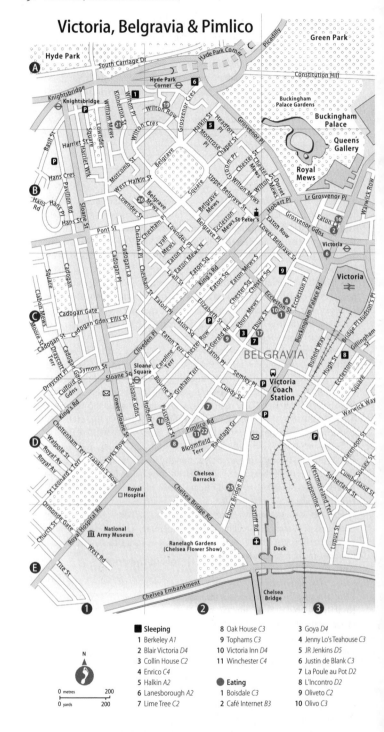

N

0 metres 200
0 yards 200

Central London

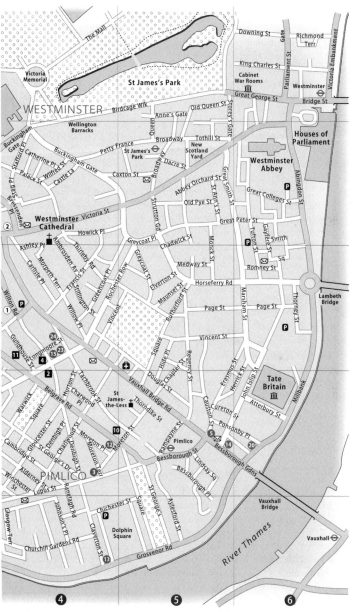

St James's Park

WESTMINSTER

Victoria Memorial

The Mall

Downing St
Richmond Terr.
King Charles St
Cabinet War Rooms
Westminster
Gate
Parliament St
Victoria Embankment
Great George St
Bridge St

Wellington Barracks
Birdcage Wlk
Anne's Gate
Old Queen St
Storey's Gate
Houses of Parliament

Buckingham Gate
Petty France
Broadway
Queen Anne's Gate
Tothill St
New Scotland Yard
Great George St

Buckingham Gate
St James's Park
Broadway
Dacre St
Westminster Abbey
Abingdon St

Caxton St
Palace St
Castle La
Stafford Pl
Catherine Pl
Wilfred St
Buckingham Gate
Abbey Orchard St
St Ann's St
Great Smith St
Great Colleges St

Westminster Cathedral
Victoria St
Old Pye St
Strutton Gd
Great Peter St

Ashley Pl
Howick Pl
Greycoat Pl
Chadwick St
Monck St
Great Peter St
Gayfere St
Smith Sq
Romney St

Morpeth Terr.
Ambrosden Av
Thirleby Rd
Francis St
Greycoat St
Medway St
Turton St

Carlisle Pl
Rochester Row
Elverton St
Horseferry Rd
Lambeth Bridge

Wilton Rd
Willow Pl
Vincent St
Maunsel St
Rutherford St
Page St
Marsham St
Page St
Thorney St

Guildhouse St
Longmoore St
Hide Pl
Square
Vincent St

Warwick Square
Belgrave Rd
Tachbrook St
Charwood Pl
Vauxhall Bridge Rd
Douglas St
Chapter St
Regency St
Erasmus St
Herrick St
John Islip St
Tate Britain
Millbank

St James-the-Less
Thorndike St
Cureton St
Atterbury St

Gloucester St
St George's Dr
Denbigh St
Moreton Pl
Moreton St
Rampayne St
Pimlico
Ponsonby Pl
Bessborough St

Cambridge St
Alderney St
Denbigh St
Charwood St
Moreton Terr.
Bessborough St
Lindsay Sq
Bessborough Gdns

Winchester St
Glasgow Terr.
Lupus St
Ranelagh Rd
Johnson's Pl
Chichester St
St George's Square
Aylesford St
Bessborough Pl

PIMLICO
Churchill Gardens Rd
Claverton St
Dolphin Square
Grosvenor Rd
Vauxhall Bridge
River Thames
Vauxhall

11	Peter's Café *D2*	● **Pubs & bars**	24	Pimlico Wine Vaults *C4*
12	Pizza Express *D4*	17 Ebury Winebar *C2*	25	Rising Sun *D2*
13	Pomegranates *E4*	18 Fox & Hounds *D2*	26	Star Tavern *B1*
14	Relish, the Sandwich	19 Grenadier *A2*		
	Shop *D5*	20 Morpeth Arms *D6*	○ **Entertainment**	
15	Seafresh Fish *C4*	21 Nag's Head *A1*	1	Apollo Victoria *C4*
16	Space Café *B3*	22 Orange Brewery *D2*	2	Victoria Palace Theatre *B4*
		23 Page *C4*		

the gleaming torch for new fashionable addresses. Cubitt then turned his attention to Pimlico (probably named after a local drink), the poorer relation to Belgravia, uprooting agricultural leaseholders to create a grid of stuccoed Italianate houses around Warwick and Eccleston squares. On its eastern riverbank lay the Millbank Penitentiary. Inmates in this star-shaped prison awaited transportation or referral, although many died in the scurvy and cholera that flourished in its marshy setting. At the turn of the century it was replaced with the Tate Gallery.

Victoria grew in the 1840's and 50s, most significantly with Victoria Street cutting through the slums in 1851, and the opening of the railway station in 1862. Victoria Station served most of the channel ports, so most troops left for the carnage of the First World War from this terminus. The building of Vauxhall Bridge Road in 1816 signalled the stirrings of Vauxhall, which grew steadily through the century as Lambeth and Kennington expanded. In more recent years, Belgravia and Pimlico have become popular among diplomatic and commercial concerns, while much of Victoria has been rebuilt. At the turn of the last century it was remarkable for holding some of London's earliest mansion blocks, and although some still survive, Victoria Street, for example, is now lined with post Second World War edifices.

Sights

Victoria Station is one of Central London's transport hubs, often extremely crowded. Quieter approaches can be made from Pimlico tube for Tate Britain

Pretty well everyone visiting London finds themselves in Victoria sooner or later, even though its status as the gateway to the continent has diminished since the opening of the Eurostar terminal in Waterloo. Even so, the combined impact of the trains serving Gatwick, Brighton and the southeast, and the National Express Coach station on Buckingham Palace Road still creates considerable foot pressure in the area. But most don't hang about here much. It's not hard to see why, with other more enticing parts of the city being so close at hand.

Westminster Cathedral

Buses 11, 24 & 211

The one sight worth a special trip is Westminster Cathedral on Victoria Street, the senior Catholic church in London. A vast edifice of stripy red brick and grey stone in a Byzantine style, the building was begun in 1895. The first worshippers passed through its doors in 1903 but the place wasn't consecrated for another seven years, church law forbidding the ceremony until the fabric of the building was complete. The echoing interior is still being decorated bit by bit, eventually to be lined throughout with the extremely expensive marble and mosaic that the architect JF Bentley envisaged. Currently it reaches about a third of the way up the columns marching down the widest nave in England.

The cathedral's most famous decorations are on the walls, the elegant stone reliefs by Eric Gill depicting the 14 Stations of the Cross. Gill also carved the statues of Saints Thomas More and John Fisher in the St George's Chapel. From Thursdays to Sundays, it's also possible to take the lift up the 273-ft campanile (or St Edward's Tower) for some broad views across central London.

■ *Open 0700-1900 Mon-Fri, Sun, 0800-1900 Sat. Audio guide. Campanile open Thu-Sun 0900-1700, admission £2, £1. Sun services: 0700, 0800, 0900, 1030, solemn sung mass 1200, 1730 and 1900. Mon-Fri sung mass 1730, Sat sung mass 1030, vigil mass 1800. T020-7798 9055.*

Around Pimlico

Victoria Street continues its unprepossessing way down to Parliament Square while, even less inspiring, from Victoria Station Vauxhall Bridge Road makes a busy and featureless beeline for the river. A little way down on the right though it's met by Warwick Way, the main shopping street in Pimlico with several interesting shops and some good places to eat. Tachbrook Street on the left hosts a rather forlorn local fruit n'veg street market overlooked by more tempting shops. After a short distance Warwick Way crosses the wide stuccoed pomp of Belgrave Road and cuts between Eccleston and Warwick Squares. These two grand squares are the heart of Pimlico, both with beautiful gardens for the use of keyholders only. The residential streets around here are a pleasant enough place to explore even though the uniformity of their creamy whiteness can be disorientating.

Belgrave Road runs parallel to Vauxhall Bridge Road down towards Pimlico tube. Between the two, off Moreton Street, stands the remarkable **Church of St-James-the-Less**, an amazing Victorian flight of fancy in red brick and grey slate fenced in with some impressive cast-iron work and more recently by a competition-winning 70s council estate. ■ *Open 1200-1500 Mon-Fri; Sun services: 0930 communion, also 1100, 1700 & 1915. T020-7630 6282, www.sjtl.org*

Central London

Tate Britain

A five-minute walk from Pimlico tube, past Paolozzi's strange industrial sculpture, and left off Vauxhall Bridge Road just before the bridge, leads onto Millbank and the area's main attraction, Tate Britain. The home of the national collection of British and modern art may have dramatically expanded into Tate Modern on Bankside, but this is only the latest and most impressive of a series of expansions – not least in Liverpool and Cornwall – since it opened on this site in 1897. The extra space on Bankside has prompted a rethink of the gallery's remit here and now it is nominally dedicated to British art both ancient and contemporary. In fact the boundaries between the collections on display in the two places are blurred: several continental or American works are still quite likely to be found here.

The location of specific works can be discovered on the gallery's website, www.tate.org.uk Buses 2, 36, 77a & 185

To coincide with the opening of Tate Modern, the sets of rooms here were also given four simple broad themes, replacing the original chronological arrangement, and each room given a more specific topic like City Life, War or The Land. At the time of writing, it looks like the four themes – Artists and Models, Literature and Fantasy, Home and Abroad, and Public and Private – will remain, although there are moves afoot to return to a more historical approach within these categories. There is every chance that the displays will include works by the visionary **William Blake**, the satirist **William Hogarth**, and the **Pre-Raphaelites**, among others.

Tate Britain remains the best place in the country to admire the work of arguably its greatest artist, **JMW Turner**, in the Clore Gallery to the right of the Millbank entrance. These purpose-built rooms opened in 1987 display the entire development of Turner's remarkable skill in handling the drama of natural scenes, atmosphere and the effects of light. From *Snow Storm: Hannibal and his Army Crossing the Alps*, painted in 1812, through his first brush with Mediterranean light on his regular visits to Italy, to *Snow Storm: Steam Boat off a Harbour's Mouth*, in 1842, the magic of his work hardly ever fails to delight.

Clore Gallery One room is also dedicated to the great landscape painter John Constable

Duveen
sculpture
galleries

Straight ahead from the front entrance are the information desks beneath the Rotunda, and directly beyond these the Duveen sculpture galleries, monumental meditative spaces for works like **Epstein**'s *The Visitation*, or **Richard Deacon**'s *For Those Who Have Ears*. To the left of these the themes are Public and Private, currently given over to displays of portraits and the work of **Joshua Reynolds**, and Literature and Fantasy, **Rossetti** and works relevant to the major special exhibition on **Blake**.

Beyond and to the right of the information desks, before reaching the Clore Gallery, Home and Abroad focuses on War, The Land, and the sculptor **Barbara Hepworth**, while Artists and Models features the Nude, Painters in Focus and the work of **Howard Hodgkin**.

As well as providing more space for British art down the centuries, the new layout is also meant to provide more room for the country's contemporary art scene, one of its key events being the award and exhibition of the Turner Prize each November. Recent winners have been **Wolfgang Tillmans**'s photographs, **Steve McQueen**'s dead-pan videos, and **Chris Ofili**'s elephant-dung paintings. In October 2001 the gallery hopes to open its Centenary Development of new galleries in the opposite wing to those already devoted to the regular special exhibitions. Downstairs in the basement the fairly expensive high-class à la carte restaurant is usually very busy and there's also a lively café.

■ *Open 1000-1750 daily. Admission free. Special exhibitions £8, £5 concession. Audio guide, guided tours, gallery talks, lectures and events. Café open 1030-1730 daily. Tate Restaurant (T020-7887 8825) open 1200-1500 Mon-Sat, 1200-1600 Sun. T020-7887 8000/8008.*

Turning right and right again out of the gallery's front entrance, Atterbury Street leads past the gloomy and disused Royal Army Medical College and Millbank Barracks, onto John Islip Street, a grand tree-lined avenue named after the great medieval Abbot of Westminster, and back onto Vauxhall Bridge Road. Turning left, Millbank rushes round to Lambeth Bridge and the Houses of Parliament. Directly opposite the gallery though, usually hidden by lines of tourist coaches, there's a small riverside terrace adorned with **Henry Moore**'s *Locking Pieces* and a view of Terry Farrell's high-tech ziggurat for the secret service MI6 on the south bank of the river by Vauxhall Bridge.

Belgravia

Beautiful Belgravia: Mistresses, Murderers, Musicians are walking tours conducted by local historian Liz Keay: T020- 7235 2591

North of Victoria Station, over Buckingham Palace Road, stretch the stately white-stuccoed squares and terraces of Belgravia, named after a small village on one of the Grosvenor family's country estates. Its centre is **Belgrave Square**, now almost entirely occupied by embassies and consulates, although many of the residences in the surrounding streets, and especially **Eaton Square**, still represent the pinnacle to which every self-respecting social climber aspires. That leaves little room around here for the general public to enjoy themselves much, other than by wondering what kind of baroque powerplays might be being acted out behind all the closed doors, although the area does boast some exceptional old-fashioned public houses and at least three of London's most luxurious hotels. Elizabeth Street is the main shopping drag while to the west of Belgrave Square, Chesham Place and Pont Street slide seamlessly via Cadogan Place into Knightsbridge. On Upper Belgrave

Street is **St Peter's Church**, an impressive neoclassical edifice redecorated internally during the 80s in an elegant way after a disastrous fire.

Eating and drinking

Apart from the restaurants in the *Halkin* and *Berkeley* hotels (see page 443), gourmet dining experiences are surprisingly thin on the ground in Belgravia. Almost as surprising though, *Boisdale*, 15 Eccleston St, SW1, T020-7730 6922, is one of London's very few specifically Scottish restaurants (although with a French twist) and its old-school whisky and cigar room at the back beyond the courtyard is a treat. Recently it has also opened up another small bar, christened the *Macdonald Bar*, open Mon-Sat until 0100, at the back of the main green, red and tartan restaurant. The whole creaking complex can become impossibly busy with shirt-sleeved bonhommie but then again it is a cheerful place.

In Pimlico, *Pomegranates*, 94 Grosvenor Rd, SW1, T020-7828 6560, is rather similar in style, even more clubby and old-fashioned, with an excellent wine list to accompany its rich, accomplished and eclectic fare. Both are at the lower end of this price bracket. Very different and more expensive than either, *L'Incontro*, 87 Pimlico Rd, SW1, T020-7730 6327, is for the refined appreciation of some modern Italian cuisine in a sleek environment.

Expensive
● *on map, page 152*

Very close to Victoria Station, *Justin de Blank*, 50-52 Buckingham Palace Rd, SW1, T020-7828 4111, is a busy modern bar and brasserie that specializes in good wines and organic food delivered in a brisk French manner.

A swish spot in Belgravia for some top-class and reasonably priced pizzas and pastas is *Oliveto*, 49 Elizabeth St, SW1, T020-7730 0074, and for a wider variety of Sardinian dishes, its more grown-up sibling *Olivo*, 21 Eccleston St, SW1, T020-7730 2505, (closed for lunch at weekends).

In Pimlico, a Spanish tapas bar and restaurant that's very popular with locals (and usually needs to be booked) is *Goya*, 32 Lupus St, SW1, T020-7976 5309. Ask for a table upstairs if possible.

Mid-range

Since 1995 it has come as some relief to find *Jenny Lo's Teahouse*, 14 Eccleston St, SW1, T020-7823 6331, open Mon-Fri 1130-1500, 1800-2200, Sat 1200-1500, 1800-1000, an excellent Chinese noodle bar (eat in or takeaway) run by the daughter of celebrity chef Ken Lo. Marginally more expensive than some elsewhere that have followed in its wake, the quality of the ingredients and fine vegetarian options keep it a cut above.

In Pimlico, the *Pizza Express*, 48 Moreton St, SW1, T020-7592 9488, is a perfectly good example of its type, while the *Seafresh Fish Restaurant*, 80 Wilton Rd, SW1, T020-7828 0747 is a typically no-nonsense and unfussy haven for some good quality fish and chips to eat in or take-away. Further west and cast in a similar mould, *Peter's Café*, 59 Pimlico Rd, SW1, T020-7730 5991, (open until 2200) is the cabbie's favourite local for its large platefuls of comfort food at sensible prices.

Cheap
It's hard to find an acceptable inexpensive meal in Belgravia

Near Victoria Station, the *Space Café*, 20 Buckingham Palace Rd, SW1, T020-7630 5020, usually does have space to sit down and its light meals are not astronomical in price despite the wacky intergalactic décor (next door is the *Café Internet*, see page 158).

Near Tate Britain, *JR Jenkins Café*, 10a Vauxhall Bridge Rd, SW1, T020-7821 8849 (closes 1530, Mon-Fri only) is an excellent and tiny bog-standard café for full-sized hot meals and teas, while *Relish, the Sandwich Shop*, 8 John Islip St, T020-7828 0628 (closes 1530, Mon-Fri only) make very good fresh sandwiches much appreciated by local office workers.

Cafés & sandwich bars

Central London

Pubs & bars
As station pubs go, the Weatherspoons in Victoria Station isn't too bad, but for places with more character the best destination is Belgravia

Three pubs tucked away in Belgravia stand out for their traditional atmosphere, interesting clientele and affable bar staff. The *Star Tavern*, 6 Belgrave Mews West, SW1, T020-7235 3019, is a rewarding find, a cosy wood-panelled place for some reasonable food, through an arch in its own little mews. Further north, *The Grenadier*, 18 Wilton Row, SW1, T020-7235 3074, is similar but with honest-to-goodness old-soldiering associations and often understandably overcrowded. *The Nag's Head*, 53 Kinnerton St, SW1, T020-7235 1135, is a freehouse with excellent beers, the largest and most rambling of the threesome.

Further west, the *Ebury Winebar*, 139 Ebury St, SW1, T020-7730 5447, is another old-fashioned place but with exceptional food. Despite being more of a modern European restaurant than a wine bar, a convivial atmosphere is allowed to prevail among drinkers of fine wines at the bar.

Two pubs owned by London brewers Young's are also worth the walk: *The Rising Sun*, 46 Ebury Bridge Rd, T020-7730 4088, and nearer Chelsea, the *Fox and Hounds*, 29 Passmore St, T020-7730 6367. The *Orange Brewery*, 37-39 Pimlico Rd, SW1, T020-7730 5984, does indeed brew its own beer, popular with local Sloanes but not usually at their most off-putting.

▶▶ *Go to page 424 for entertainment & nightlife*

In Pimlico, the once over-popular Slug and Lettuce has become *The Page*, 11 Warwick Way, SW1, T020-7834 3313, doing Thai food upstairs and rapidly attracting a loud and lively bunch downstairs. Much more genteel and more mature, the *Pimlico Wine Vaults*, 12-22 Upper Tachbrook St, T020-7233 5801, take their wine seriously and stock some top-quality clarets. Near Tate Britain, the *Morpeth Arms*, 58 Millbank, SW1, T020-7834 6442, is quite touristy but has some outside seating on pleasant Ponsonby Place.

Shopping

Warwick Way and especially **Tachbrook St**, with its food market and curious little shops, are likely to be the most fertile ground for a successful shopping trip in the area. The market, which closes around 1630, and doesn't operate on Sun, mainly sells fruit and veg to locals although occasionally other stalls turn up.

Interesting shops on the street include the *Wilton Cycle and Wireless Co*, 28 Upper Tachbrook St, SW1, T020-7834 1367, not for bikes or radios but for every conceivable type of Hornby trainset and several other model manufacturers. *Ivano's Deli*, 38 Tachbrook St, T020-7630 6977, is the place to assemble a fine southern Italian picnic from a variety of his specialities and excellent-value takeaway snacks. The patisserie at the *Bonne Bouche*, 40 Tachbrook St, T020-7630 1626, can provide some delicious French cakes.

On Upper Tachbrook St, on the other side of Warwick Way, *Cornucopia*, 12 Upper Tachbrook St, SW1, T020-7828 5752, do second-hand classic clothes from past eras at

Directory

Internet cafés *Café Internet, 22-24 Buckingham Palace Rd, SW1, Near Victoria Station, T020-7233 5786. A congenial place to go online over some simple snacks.*

Sports *Queen Mother Sports Centre, 323 Vauxhall Bridge Rd, SW1, T020-7630 5522. Opening hours 0630-1000 Mon-Fri; Sat, Sun 0800-2000. Large council-run swimming pool £2.35 a session. Also Courtney's gym, with squash, basketball,* *badminton, martial arts, and scuba diving.*

Tourist Information *Victoria Station Forecourt, SW1. Open: Easter-31 May, Mon-Sat 0800-2000, Sun 0800-1800; 1 Jun-30 Sep, Mon-Sat 0800-2100, Sun 0800-1800; 1 Oct-Easter, daily 0800-1800.*

Travel agents *Near Victoria station are the offices of USIT Campus Travel, 52 Grosvenor Gardens, SW1, T0870-2401 010, for cheap flights and holidays.*

bargain prices, while the **Rippon Cheese Stores**, 26 Upper Tachbrook St, SW1, T020-7931 0628, have a pungent and mouthwatering array of produce from all over Europe, including Scotland and Ireland. A short walk away, the **Pimlico Bookshop**, 48a Moreton St, T020-7233 6103 (only open Fri, Sat during winter), has a very select range of antique and second-hand titles.

In Belgravia, Elizabeth, Eccleston and Ebury streets are the best destinations for a more expensive jaunt. On Elizabeth St, there's the flagship store of American fashion designer **Ben de Lisi**, 40 Elizabeth St, SW1, T020-7730 2994; rare sweets at **The Chocolate Society**, 36 Elizabeth St, SW1, T020-7259 9222; and fine wine and cheese at **Jeroboams**, 51 Elizabeth St, SW1, T020-7823 5623.

Transport

From Victoria Station:

No 8 to Bethnal Green via Hyde Park Corner, Mayfair, Oxford Circus, Holborn, Bank and Liverpool St.

No 16 to Maida Vale via Hyde Park Corner, Marble Arch and Edgware Rd.

No 38 to Islington via Hyde Park Corner, Piccadilly Circus and Bloomsbury (for British Museum).

No 52 to Ladbroke Grove via Hyde Park Corner, Knightsbridge, Kensington and Notting Hill.

No 73 to Stoke Newington via Hyde Park Corner, Marble Arch, Oxford Circus, Euston, King's Cross, and Islington.

No 82 to North Finchley via Marble Arch, Baker St, Swiss Cottage, Golders Green and Finchley Central.

No C1 to Kensington High St via Sloane Square, Brompton Rd (Harrods), South Kensington, and Earls Court.

No 507 to Waterloo, via Lambeth Bridge (not Sat, Sun or evenings)

Along Belgrave Rd:

No 24 from Hampstead Heath to Pimlico via Victoria, Westminster, Trafalgar Square, Leicester Square, Warren St, and Camden Town.

Along Vauxhall Bridge Rd:

No 2 to Vauxhall, Stockwell and Brixton.

Along Millbank:

No 77a from Aldwych to Wandsworth via Trafalgar Square, Westminster, Vauxhall Bridge and Clapham Junction.

Cadogan (Chelsea Embankment) to Blackfriars via Westminster Mon-Fri every 30 mins from 0700 till 1000, returning from 1615 till 1945, with **Thames Speed Ferry Company** (T020-7731 7671).

Refreshment rank on Lupus St, Pimilico, and plenty on Warwick Way and Belgrave Rd.

Victoria for Gatwick Express and trains to Battersea, south London suburbs, Brighton and the southeast.

Victoria (District, Circle and Victoria lines), Pimlico (for Tate Britain; Victoria line) and Vauxhall (Victoria line). Also St James's Park (District and Circle lines) for the top end of Victoria St.

Buses
National buses leave from Victoria Station

River transport

Taxis

Trains

Tubes

Central London

Knightsbridge, South Kensington and Hyde Park

⊖ Hyde Park Corner tube for Hyde Park; Knightsbridge tube for Harrods & Sloane St; South Kensington tube for the museums, Fulham Rd & Chelsea; also Gloucester Rd

Like Mayfair and neighbouring Belgravia, Knightsbridge is one of the wealthiest areas in central London. In South Kensington next door the average per capita income is at least £40,000 a year. Favoured by cosmopolitan jetsetters, wayward little rich girls and anyone dressed up and on the pull, the multicultural cake mixed here has a noticeable Middle Eastern, Far Eastern and American flavour with some distinct French, Italian and Polish ingredients.

Knightsbridge especially is pretty much the impersonal and exclusive playground of silly-moneyed over-50s, with fashion labels, deluxe hotels, expensive restaurants and private clubs to match. The three tremendous exceptions, the icing, marzipan and middle of the cake, are the great museums: the **Victoria and Albert** *(V&A),* **Natural History***, and* **Science museums** *each deserve at least a day of anyone and everyone's time. In the near future it's likely that all three will be free of charge. Each of them has long been bending over backwards to make their vast collections as accessible and rewarding as possible, but although such a short distance apart, the temptation to 'do' all three in one visit should definitely be resisted. Even two could prove too rich a treat. To the south, Chelsea merges seamlessly with South Ken via Brompton and the Fulham Road. At the top of Exhibition Road, protecting the area from Bayswater to the north, the delightful green acres of* **Kensington Gardens** *and* **Hyde Park** *harbour grand or whimsical memorials and the world-famous little* **Serpentine Gallery***.*

History

In the Middle Ages the road from Piccadilly ran through a small village called Knightsbridge on the route to the village of Kensington. To the north, three manors occupied the land up to the Tyburn Way (Oxford Street) and stretching west of the Tyburn Lane (Park Lane). The River Westbourne flowed south across the land, with a crossing at the Knight's Bridge (it may have been King's Bridge), and deer, boar and wild bulls roamed the woods and pasture.

At the Dissolution of the Monasteries, Henry VIII sold two of the manors, but kept Hyde as a hunting ground. Knightsbridge boasted several taverns (Elizabeth I frequently stopped at the *Fox & Bull* en route to

Hotels in the area

AL *Blakes*
AL *Mandarin Oriental Hyde Park Hotel*
A *Basil Street Hotel*
A *Franklin Hotel*
A *The Gore*
A *Pelham Hotel*
B *The Gallery Hotel*
B *Aster House*
B *Five Sumner Place*
B *Number Sixteen*
B *Diplomat*
B *The Regency*
B *Holiday Serviced Apartments*
E *Albert Hotel*
E *Linstead Hall*
⟩⟩ *Go to page 443*

Central London

How to act like a Londoner on the tube

After the incredibly annoying London Underground tannoy warning of 'Mind the Gap', which is repeated ad nauseum by equally annoying tourists, should be added, " and do not, under any circumstances, talk to, or even look at, the natives".

Visitors please take note: that broadsheet newspaper is not for reading. It is the London tube traveller's shield against the outside world. London can be a tough place, full of highly undesirable and dangerous people, and those precious few millimetres of newsprint is all that stands between the London commuter and the

excrutiating pain and social embarrassment of human interaction with a perfect stranger in a crowded place.

So, please, dear visitor, be sensitive. Do not engage your neighbour in conversation – even if it's to tell them their hair's on fire – and do not attempt to read their newspaper. This can result in a severe bout of tut-tutting or, worse still, a filthy look. Just head straight for the nearest seat, open your copy of the Financial Times, and ignore everything and everyone around you – especially if it's someone asking if this tube stops at Buckingham Palace.

visiting her chief adviser Lord Burleigh in Brompton Hall), while Kensington further west had grown around the church founded in the 12th century, now St Mary Abbots. Market gardens and nurseries surrounded Knightsbridge, most notably the Brompton Park Nursery that flourished in the 18th century.

When William of Orange opted for Nottingham House, later Kensington Palace, as his main residence (he moved from Westminster on account of his asthma), Rotten Row, the *route du roi* from Kensington to St James's, became the first illuminated road in England when 300 oil lamps were hung from the trees lining the route.

In 1730 work began in the park. The Westbourne was dammed to create the Serpentine, the Broad Walk was laid out, and the Round Pond was created as a centrepiece in formal gardens. The gardens were largely closed to the public until George III took up residence in Buckingham Palace in the 1760s, when they were open to the respectably dressed. The Serpentine, although carrying much of the local area's sewage, was a popular swimming and boating venue and a grand fair in 1814 celebrated the triumph of Trafalgar by re-enacting the battle on the lake. A large enclosure, the Ring, hosted carriage racing.

But the park's high point, and the spark for the growth and development of Knightsbridge and South Kensington, was the **Great Exhibition** of 1851. The brainchild of Victoria's beloved Prince Albert, this display of national confidence was housed in a magnificent Crystal Palace. It was such a success (in just five months, six million visitors enjoyed the 19,000 exhibits and refreshments supplied by Messrs Schweppe), that the whole glass construction was transplanted to Sydenham, where it enjoyed continued popularity until it burnt down in 1936.

Although the likes of Onslow Square and Gardens, Pelham Crescent and Thurloe Place had all emerged before the 1850s, and hospitals such as the Royal Marsden and the Brompton reflected the area's reputation as being "remarkable for the salubrity of its air", it was the profits from the Great Exhibition that transformed South Kensington. The area was still largely market gardens and nurseries, with the occasional modest mansions, such as Gore House, Brompton Hall, Cromwell House and Gloucester Lodge, but the whole area was bought and transformed into a mix of museums, academic institutes and Italianate stuccoed terraces for the well-to-do.

Central London

Queen's Gate, Cromwell Road, and Exhibition Road framed a centre of learning in the High Victorian tradition, with the Natural History Museum and Victoria & Albert Museums among the most architecturally resplendent. The Royal Albert Hall, home to Sir Henry Wood's Promenade Concerts, held all kinds of events, from the Shakespeare Ball in 1911 attended by 80 visiting royals, to Oswald Moseley's fascist rallies or a psychic's public attempt to reunite Conan Doyle with 10,000 of his admirers one week after the author's

Knightsbridge & South Kensington

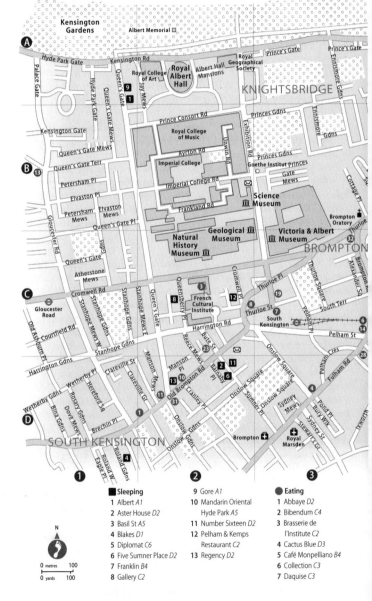

Sleeping
1 Albert *A1*
2 Aster House *D2*
3 Basil St *A5*
4 Blakes *D1*
5 Diplomat *C6*
6 Five Sumner Place *D2*
7 Franklin *B4*
8 Gallery *C2*
9 Gore *A1*
10 Mandarin Oriental Hyde Park *A5*
11 Number Sixteen *D2*
12 Pelham & Kemps Restaurant *C2*
13 Regency *D2*

Eating
1 Abbaye *D2*
2 Bibendum *C4*
3 Brasserie de l'Institute *C2*
4 Cactus Blue *D3*
5 Café Monpelliano *B4*
6 Collection *C3*
7 Daquise *C3*

death. The Albert Memorial overlooking the site testifies to Prince Albert's influence in these massive changes.

The last century's rebuilding has for the most part reflected the wealth of its residents – the Harrods store was rebuilt in 1905, and Knightsbridge now boasts many of London's smartest shops – while South Kensington continues to be 'Musuemland', with the Lycee Charles de Gaulle and the French Cultural Institute in Queensberry Place lending a Gallic air to the area.

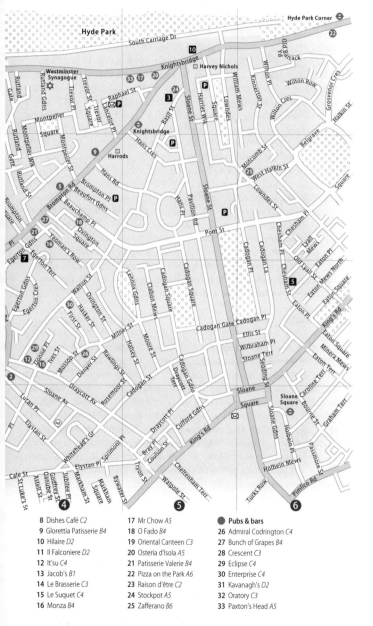

Central London

8 Dishes Café *C2*
9 Gloretia Patisserie *B4*
10 Hilaire *D2*
11 Il Falconiere *D2*
12 It'su *C4*
13 Jacob's *B1*
14 Le Brasserie *C3*
15 Le Suquet *C4*
16 Monza *B4*

17 Mr Chow *A5*
18 O Fado *B4*
19 Oriental Canteen *C3*
20 Osteria d'Isola *A5*
21 Patisserie Valerie *B4*
22 Pizza on the Park *A6*
23 Raison d'être *C2*
24 Stockpot *A5*
25 Zafferano *B6*

● **Pubs & bars**
26 Admiral Codrington *C4*
27 Bunch of Grapes *B4*
28 Crescent *C3*
29 Eclipse *C4*
30 Enterprise *C4*
31 Kavanagh's *D2*
32 Oratory *C3*
33 Paxton's Head *A5*

Sights

Hyde Park

The road called Knightsbridge begins at Hyde Park Corner, where Apsley Gate, Decimus Burton's classical screen, provides the most impressive entrance to the park. Just beyond is a colossal statue of Achilles erected in honour of the Duke of Wellington, like the plan of Hyde Park Corner itself. Parallel to Knightsbridge, the soft horse-riding track of **Rotten Row** heads west, once the site of the Great Exhibition's Crystal Palace. To the north along **Park Lane** stand huge hotels, car showrooms and mansion blocks hidden behind the trees.

The wide open stretch of grass between here and the Serpentine often seems deserted, even in summer, except during the regular open-air concerts, demonstrations and Royal occasions. Near the public toilets and Lookout Environmental Centre in the middle there's a funny push-button drinking fountain sculpture celebrating the 1979 International Year of the Child when 180,000 children from all over the UK were invited to a party here. A little further on, a tiny information centre selling official guidebooks and postcards can be found in the grand Old Police House.

From here the Meadow and the Dell roll down to the shore of the **Serpentine Lake**, a good place to hire a boat (but not to swim), in summer on the opposite bank at the *Lido* (T020-7298 2100), the more attractive of the two café-restaurants in the park. The *Lido* can be reached across the bridge that divides the Serpentine from the Long Water and hence Hyde Park from Kensington Gardens. The path in Hyde Park along the north side of the Long Water, past the **Henry Moore Arch**, ends up among the fish ponds and fountains of the Italian Gardens at Lancaster Gate. Look out here for the classical arch known as **Queen Anne's Alcove**, designed by Wren.

Kensington Gardens

Over the Long Bridge though, towards the *Lido*, is Kensington Gardens' prize asset, the **Serpentine Gallery**, a little square 1930s tea pavilion with a lantern and golden ball on the top. Outside are a semi-circle of stone benches by Ian Hamilton Finlay, inscribed with different translations of some evocative lines from Virgil. Inside, the quiet gallery was completely refurbished in 1998, confirming a reputation steadily acquired since its opening in 1970 for being one of London's most exciting small spaces for international contemporary art, charmingly at odds with its dinky situation. Recent exhibitions have included work by American artist Louise Bourgeois, Gillian Wearing, and Damien Hirst. ■ *Open daily 1000-1800, admission free. T020-7402 6075, www.serpentinegallery.org.uk*

Tree-filled Kensington Gardens spread out behind the gallery, criss-crossed with signposted paths leading to the Round Pond, the Peter Pan statue beside Long Water, and the Broad Walk in front of Kensington Palace. The latest suggested route is the seven-mile **Diana Princess of Wales Memorial Walk** through four of central London's Royal parks. ■ *For more information T020-7298 2000, or call into the Old Police House information centre.*

Albert Hall Beyond the gallery on the right looms the Gothic spire and canopy of the Albert Memorial, designed by Sir Gilbert Scott and finished in 1872. On closer inspection a 14-ft gilded bronze statue of Prince Albert can be found keeping his finger in the place where he's just left off reading the catalogue of his Great Exhibition. Much against his own wishes, Victoria's far-from-pompous consort is surrounded by an excess of ardently imperialist statuary and fancy stonework recently renovated at huge expense. Across the road is his much more fitting memorial, the great domed oval of the Royal Albert Hall. Queen Victoria unexpectedly christened the building as she laid the foundation stone in 1867, six years after Albert's death, and she was still too overcome with emotion to attend the opening four years later.

To the right of the Albert Hall is the **Royal College of Art** (T020-7590 4444) one of the city's most prestigious and accomplished art schools, mounting regular exhibitions of student's work. Left of the Hall, on the corner of Exhibition Road, is the **Royal Geographical Society** (open Monday-Friday 0930-1730; T020-7591 3000) adorned with sculptures of Shackleton and Livingstone, two of the explorers that the Society dispatched in its heyday. Off Exhibition Road are **Imperial College** and the **Royal College of Music** (see page 424) and also **The Polish Institute and Skiorski Museum**, 20 Princes Gate, a very traditional military memorabilia museum in memory of the Polish forces that fought in the Second World War. ■ *Open Mon-Fri 1000-1600, admission free, T020-7589 9249*. Nearby, the *Polish Hearth Club*, at 55 Princes Gate, T020-7589 4635, is a smart Polish restaurant. Next up on Exhibition Road is the first of the area's main events.

Around Albert Hall

Central London

Science Museum

The Science Museum prides itself on being one of the most forward-thinking, interactive and accessible museums in the country, a claim that has recently been enhanced with the opening of the new Wellcome Wing: four floors dedicated to displaying cutting-edge science and technology incorporating an Imax cinema and the first Virtual Voyage simulator in Europe. With origins similar to the V&A's, the emphasis here has always been on education. One of the best things about the Science Museum is that guidebooks or guided tours are hardly necessary: most of the exhibits either speak for themselves or are thoroughly labelled.

Buses 14, 70 & 74

Strictly speaking it's more a museum of technology or applied science than science itself, with the wonders of technology artfully employed to make their own story entertaining. The Post Office at the main entrance sets the everyday tone, where the Barclays cashpoint and Bureau de Change could almost be exhibits in themselves, next to the enormous wheels and landing gear of an Airbus. The museum is more open plan than most, its six long floors divided by broad themes and subjects rather than rooms, and with more than enough absorbing activities to keep children amused for hours.

In the basement is Launch Pad, a very popular hands-on gallery of educational scientific games

Immediately beyond the high-tech ticket desks and the Information Point on the ground floor, the pioneers of the Industrial Revolution are celebrated in *Power* and *Synopsis*, beautifully engineered steam engines alongside a reconstruction of James Watt's workshop and Foucault's Pendulum demonstrating that the earth spins on its axis. Leaping into the 20th century, the **Space Gallery** features a replica of the Apollo 11 lunar lander and explores rocket science in general.

★ **Five of the best: for kids**

- *Science Museum*, Knightsbridge.
- *Natural History Museum*, Knightsbridge.
- *London Zoo*, Regent's Park.
- *Tate Modern*, Bankside.
- *IMAX cinema*, Waterloo.

See-through glass lifts glide up and down from here between all floors. The main body of the ground floor is then taken up with *Making the Modern World*, a series of important 'firsts' from 1750 to 2000. These include: Puffing Billy from 1815; the oldest surviving steam engine in the world, Stephenson's Rocket; the streamlined powerboat Miss England from 1929; aircraft like the Lockheed 10A Electra hanging from the ceiling; a stack of Beetle Volkswagens on the wall; the Apollo 10 Command Module; and a copy of the spiral model for DNA. At the far end glows the weird blue light of the new Wellcome Wing.

The space age Deep Blue Café with its spooky underlit tabletops provides a spot to one side where the future can be discussed over coffee & rotisserie chicken

The **Wellcome Wing** brings the museum bang up to date with the latest advances in digital technology and biomedical science. On the ground floor, along with the gigantic **Imax Cinema** and a theme-park ride to Mars in the **Virtual Voyage Simulator**, the slickly designed displays of *Antenna* include Rapid Exhibitions based on scientific news changing weekly; features covering specific issues in more depth, changing every six months; and Newsflash, a digital information system on hot topics updated hourly. Twelve *Talking Points* are also dotted around, like the disturbing pc-powered euthanasia machine legalized in Australia's Northern Territory between 1995 ad 1997.

Three overhanging floors then take the debate upstairs: on the first, largest and most interesting, *Who am I?* looks at the Human Animal and what separates us from other species; charts the Family Tree growing in our genes; tests individuals with computers psychologically and physically in Identity Parade; and more radically, involves visitors in on-going research projects in Live Science. *Digitopolis* on the second floor is divided into five 'warps' exploring the impact of digital technology on our daily lives. The third floor encourages playful discussion with some specially designed computerized board games called *In Future* that seem rather temperamental.

If time is limited, don't miss the third floor of the main museum

On the **third floor** is the Gallery of Flight including Amy Johnson's Gipsy Moth, other antique and modern aircraft, and the Flight Lab of interactive exhibits and models exploring how we get airborne, as well as Health Matters, a newish high-tech gallery dedicated to advances in modern medicine.

On the **first floor**, *Time Measurement* includes almost 1,000 different historic timepieces of all types, while *Food for Thought* looks at the social history and science of food and how we've arrived at the supermarket (Sainsbury's to be precise).

The **second floor** is the most technical, including displays on computing, nuclear physics, chemistry and printing, as well as an extraordinary collection of model ships. The **top two floors** are dedicated to medical and veterinary history, art and science.

■ *Open 1000-1800 daily. Admission £7.95, £4.95 students, children, OAPs and unemployed free and various other prices for combinations of Imax and Virtual Voyage (£3.50 extra) or all the South Ken museums. Free after 1630 daily. Screenings in Imax Cinema (£12.50 including museum, £6.75 after 1630): at 1045 (Sat, Sun only), 1145, 1245, 1345, 1445, 1545, 1645 daily. Free 20-min*

Central London

guided tours on the hour every hour, as well as one 50-min tour of the whole museum usually at 1400. T020-7942 4455; booking and information T0870-8704868; www.sciencemuseum.org.uk

Natural History Museum

Behind the Science Museum, on Cromwell Road, stands the extraordinary old orange and blue terracotta building of the Natural History Museum. Until 1963 part of the British Museum, and since then also gobbling up the Geological Museum, this is a serious academic research institution that has become seriously fun-packed. Divided into Life Galleries and Earth Galleries, it tells the history of our animated planet with a not entirely successful combination of venerable artefacts and playschool attractions. Occasionally it feels as if the museum had been entrusted to an over-excited and over-budget biology teacher. Even so, it never disappoints children, and adults are sure to learn something about the natural world whether they want to or not.

Buses 14, 70 & 74

Greeting visitors in the impressive central hall behind the majestic main entrance on Cromwell Road is the famous skeletal cast of the large herbivorous dinosaur Diplodocus. Beyond, Waterhouse Way (named after the designer of the spectacular building) is the main spine of the **Life Galleries**. The front entrance of the **Earth Galleries** is on Exhibition Road down from the Science Museum.

The whole building has a fundamentally serious point, effectively made, about the threat that humanity currently poses to the balance of nature

Left and left again on Waterhouse Way leads to the main **Dinosaur Exhibition**, its animatronic models inevitably suffering comparison to Spielberg's special effects, although the most recent, enormously popular 10 ft T-Rex terrifies the kids. The exhibition as a whole raises questions. Nearby are the **Mammal Galleries**, including the giant model of a blue whale and the skeleton of a woolly mammoth. Upstairs are rooms full of stuffed animals demonstrating biodiversity and a model of natural history's totem thinker, Charles Darwin in his study, as well as a collection minerals and meteorites. A right turn on Waterhouse Way passes **Creepy Crawlies** and a very worthy **Ecology Exhibition** with a weird balloon-filled 'leaf factory' demonstrating photosynthesis.

Approaching the Earth Galleries from Life Gallery 50 unfortunately dissipates the initial impact of this more cogent and satisfying half of the museum: an escalator ride through the earth's core, best reached through the Exhibition Road entrance. At the top, there's the opportunity to experience the Kyoto earthquake in a Japanese supermarket, appreciate the span of geological time by touching a 3,850 million-year-old rock from Greenland, and ogle at some beautiful gemstones while exploring three floors of interactive questionnaires, touch-screen tellies and illuminated information panels.

The escalator ride through the earth's core, is best reached through the Exhibition Rd entrance

■ *Open Mon-Sat 1000-1750, Sun 1100-1750; free after 1630 Mon to Fri, and after 1700 Sat, Sun. Last admission is at 1730. Admission £7.50, concession £3.50, {**check prices**}OAPs free, children under 16 free (children under 12 must be accompanied by an adult). Season tickets including access to the Victoria and Albert Museum and the Science Museum: adult £29, joint adult £49.50, concessions £16. T020-7942 5000, www.nhm.ac.uk*

Victoria and Albert Museum

*The Victoria &
Albert Museum
is better known
as the V&A
Buses 14, 70 & 74*

The Victoria and Albert Museum is one of the world's greatest museums. Sur-prisingly, considering its grand façade on Cromwell Road, it wears that great-ness lightly. Originally called the Museum of Manufactures, and then the South Kensington Museum, it was founded in 1857 with the intention of edu-cating the populace in the appreciation of decorative art and design by exhib-iting superb examples of what could be achieved in that field: the object lesson equivalent to the exemplary lives held up for emulation at the National Por-trait Gallery (see page 64).

Never a narrowly nationalistic enterprise, its remarkable collection was gath-ered like the British Museum's from all corners of the globe. The overall impres-sion it makes though is much more human and domestic than the British Museum, despite its equally astonishing scale. Many of the objects on display around its seven-miles-worth of galleries would once have decorated or been in everyday use in people's homes – very wealthy and powerful people's homes for the most part – as well as in magnificent places of worship. And most are noth-ing like as ancient and remote as the antiquities in the BM. On making first acquaintance with the V&A, instead of trying to see as much as possible with a limited amount of time, a better bet is simply to wander slowly around in the certain knowledge that you'll find a rewarding number of amazing things.

Broadly speaking the galleries are arranged on six different levels either by area and/or period of origin or by type of material and/or object. At the front entrance and ticket desks, beneath the impressive dome of the Central Hall, a small army of staff attempt to orientate visitors with a formidable combina-tion of ground plans, audioguides, leaflets and polite concern.

*Ground floor:
Level A*

Immediately inside the front door, staircases lead down on the right to **19th-century Europe and America**, and on the left to **Europe from 1600 to 1800**: illuminated books, medieval ship-shaped salt cellars, stained glass, wooden carvings, renaissance ceramics, silverware, tapestries, dinner plates, and furniture among a horde of other things. Straight ahead on the ground floor (Level A) leads into **The Medieval Treasury**: early artefacts such as the carved ivory Veroli Casket made in 11th-century Constantino-ple the 12th-century Eltenburg Reliquary, the Gloucester Candlestick cast in molten coins, a spiralling contortion of men and monsters decorating its medieval shaft, or velvet priest's robes woven with silk and silver thread. Beyond is the **Pirelli Garden**, a lovely open-air sculpture court giving onto rooms full of graceful Renaissance sculptures from Italy. Behind these are the **Morris, Poynter and Gamble Rooms**, the V&A's original 19th-century refreshment rooms: William Morris's leafy-branched Green Dining Room, James Gamble's golden-arched and ceramic-tiled central room and Edward Poynter's Grill Room or Dutch Kitchen. The rooms were in use until the Second World War.

*One of the museum's
most popular exhibits
is Tippoo's tiger*

To the left of the information desks are rooms dedicated to the Arts of the Islamic World, India, the Dress Collection and the Raphael Gallery. Carpets, crystal decanters, brass basins, and an extraordinary tiled fireplace grace the Islamic Gallery; The **Nehru Gallery of Indian Art** displays sculptures based on temple dances, Mughal miniatures and jades, painted cotton coverlets, turban jewels, the golden throne of Maharaja Ranjit Singh, and Tippoo's tiger. One of the museum's most popular exhibits, this strange model of a tiger attacking a redcoat, complete with an internal organ to provide sound effects,

Central London

Events at the V&A

As well as undertaking conservation and research, the V&A also organizes an excellent range of events, often including special Friday night late openings, garden parties and concerts. General introductory tours leave the Cromwell Road entrance at 1030, 1130, 1330, and 1430 (also at 1630 on Wednesdays), lasting about an hour, while in-depth tours of specific areas of the museum leave at 1230 and 1530. Gallery talks by experts on individual galleries take place at 1300 daily.

was commissioned by Tipu Sultan, ruler of Mysore and scourge of the British East India Company until his defeat at Seringapatam in 1799.

In the **Raphael Gallery** on the left are the great Renaissance artist's paper cartoons – or preliminary designs – for the Sistine Chapel tapestries depicting the lives of St Peter and St Paul. Opposite is another of the museum's favourite attractions, the **Dress Collection** from 1600 to the present: the extremity and vagaries of fashion down the ages conclusively prove that the contemporary catwalk is no more bizarre than it's ever been. In the circular room above is a selection of the museum's collection of historic musical instruments.

To the right of the information desks are Chinese, Japanese and Korean art, plaster casts and the Canon Photography Gallery. Among the wealth of exhibits dating from 3000 BC to the present in the **TT Tsui Gallery of Chinese Art** are earthenware sculptures, beautiful bodhisattvas, and the lacquer throne of Emperor Chien Lung. Next door, in the **Toshiba Gallery of Japanese Art**, are lacquer screens, silk kimonos, and ceremonial swords. On the left the monumental **Cast Courts** contain full-size plaster casts of European architecture and sculpture including Trajan's Column (in two halves) and Michelangelo's David. Beyond, the **Canon Photography Gallery** mounts regular themed exhibitions on issues in photography and retrospectives of great photographers' work.

Between the ground and first floors, on Lower B, up the staircase immediately to left and right of the front entrance, are the **British Galleries**. At the time of writing these 15 rooms are being transformed by a £31 million project due for completion in November 2001. The history of British design from 1500 to 1900 will be told chronologically with the help of four themes: *Style*, *Who Led Taste?*, *What Was New?* and *Fashionable Living*, featuring big names like Robert Adam, Thomas Chippendale and William Morris along with the Great Bed of Ware, the Melville Bed, James II's wedding togs and furniture by Charles Rennie Mackintosh.

Level Lower B

On the first floor (Level B) are the Ironwork Galleries, the Jewellery Gallery, the Silver Gallery, Tapestries and the 20th-Century Gallery. The **Jewellery Gallery**, its precious exhibits dating from 2000BC to the present day, includes the Armada Jewel given by Queen Elizabeth I to her favourite vice-chamberlain; the finest **Tapestries** are the Devonshire Hunting Tapestries, wool-woven in the early 1400s, portraying the medieval chase both sporting and amorous. The intriguing **20th-Century Gallery** exhibits modern landmarks in design and applied art: a Bauhaus table lamp, mass-produced Eames furniture, Kandinsky's book of painted music *Klänge*, and the work of contemporary potters.

1st Floor: Level B

Central London

2nd floor: On the second floor (Level C), the **Glass Gallery** displays a sparkling array of
Level C glass dating back 4000 years, one highlight being the Luck of Edenhall, a beautiful Syrian beaker that has managed to avoid being broken since it was brought back from the Crusades.

3rd floor: On the third Floor (Level D), the **Ceramics Gallery** displays the most comprehensive collection of pottery in the world, including a very rare Medici porcelain bottle which was Europe's first attempt to copy the Chinese potters, and a vase by Picasso.

Henry Cole The Henry Cole Wing, named after the museum's first director, is devoted to
Wing the largest single collection of the great landscape painter **John Constable**'s oils and watercolours, donated by his daughter, as well as **Rodin** sculptures (both on level 6); marvellous 16th-century portrait miniatures by **Nicholas Hilliard** (level 4); the **European Ornament Gallery**; and the **Frank Lloyd Wright Gallery**.

■ *Open 1000 Mon, Tue, Thu-Sun 1000-1745, Wed 1000-2200. Admission £5, free for concessions and after 1630 daily.T020-7938 8500 (South Kensington Museums), T020-7942 2000, recorded information T020-7942 2528, recorded information for special exhibitions T020-7942 2530; www.vam.ac.uk*

Brompton Next door to the V&A, on Thurloe Place, stands the Brompton Oratory, the
Oratory most flamboyant Catholic church in London, built in 1884 and a very English take on the Italian and French church builders. With its marbles, candles and 17th-century statuary, it provides a grand and peaceful haven off the busy Brompton Road. ■ *Open 0630-2000 daily. Admission free. T020-7808 0900.*

Passing Harrod's (see Shopping below) on the right, near Knightsbridge tube is Basil Street, one of the best little secret streets in Knightsbridge linking the area's topping shopping attractions, **Harrods** and **Harvey Nichols**.

Eating and drinking

Expensive Of the many celebrity Italian restaurants, *Zafferano*, 15 Lowndes St, SW1, T020-7235
The fashionable 5800, is easily the best value (it only just scrapes into this bracket), not at all intimidat-
super-rich of ing and worth every penny. It's often fully booked though. Another less family-style
Knightsbridge and and much more chic destination might be *Osteria d'Isola*, 145 Knightsbridge, SW1,
South Ken are spoilt T020-7838 1044, a vast designer eaterie for fine and expensive Italian food upstairs and
for choice when they less formal dining and drinking downstairs. For poseurs with less style but more balls,
want to dine out on *The Collection*, 264 Brompton Rd, SW3, T020-7225 1212, is a DJ-driven music bar and
the town but most restaurant approached by a corridor catwalk, the sort of place where Posh might have
stick to a few tried and met Becks, choosing confidently from the global menu. It's the low-rise equivalent of
tested favourites the *Fifth Floor*, Harvey Nichols, 109-125 Knightsbridge, SW1, T020-7235 5250 (closed Sun nights), the penthouse joint atop London's most fashionable department store adored by fans of *Sex and the City* enjoying the light, bright atmosphere and each other as much as the global menu.

Much more restrained and mature is *Hilaire*, 68 Old Brompton Rd, SW7, T020-7584 8993, opposite *Christie's*, a distinctive blend of well-moneyed Home county and the Mediterranean combining for exquisite French dinners, perfect for taking Granny and little Freddy to on their best behaviour. Still happening after all these years is *Bibendum*, 81 Fulham Rd, SW3, T020-7581 5817, Conran's great big gastrodome above a stylish oyster and champagne bar, on the first floor of the old Michelin building.

One of the most delightful restaurants in this bracket is *La Brasserie*, 272 Brompton Rd, SW3, T020-7581 3089, a proper Parisian all-day nosherie that shows up some of its chain competitors, best for an evening rendezvous at the bar or a sit down with your shopping for a late brunch or high tea. *Le Suquet*, 104 Draycott Av, SW3, T020-7581 1785, is an intimate French seafood restaurant.

Mid-range
● *on map, page 162*

Near South Ken tube, another reliable option with a sense of occasion is *Kemps*, in *The Pelham Hotel*, 15 Cromwell Pl, SW1, T020-7589 8288, for some good modern British food in a genteel environment. *Monza*, 6 Yeoman's Row, SW3, T020-7591 0210, has a casual and home-baked Italian atmosphere that belies the quality of the food.

For top-quality Chinese cuisine, *Mr Chow*, 151 Knightsbridge, SW1, T020-7589 7347, is something of a Knightsbridge institution, making no concession to passing fashions in its interior design but sticking to the delivery of highly accomplished recipes from Beijing. Younger and more upbeat, *It'su*, 118 Draycott Av, SW3, T020-7584 5522, is one of the most fashionable conveyor belt sushi operations in London.

O Fado, 45-50 Beauchamp Pl, SW3, T020-7589 3002, is an old Portuguese restaurant with bags of character, never afraid to let the joint start jumping to live music. On the Fulham Rd, *Cactus Blue*, 86 Fulham Rd, SW3, T020-7823 7858, is a beautifully designed and hip New Mexican place where the surprisingly wide-ranging menu rarely disappoints.

Central London

More difficult to find is an inexpensive treat in this area, although the cafés below are all of a superior standard. The one charming place that tourists and Londoners agree can't be bettered is the *Daquise*, 20 Thurloe St, SW7, T020-7589 6117, a perennially fading but stubborn survivor, a Polish restaurant that sums up the spirit of old South Ken.

Cheap

The other long-standing old-timer is *Stockpot*, 6 Basil St, SW3, T020-7589 8627, beloved for its no-nonsense approach to basic hot meals. The *Oriental Canteen*, 2a Exhibition Rd, SW7, T020-7581 8831, does good noodle soups and rice dishes in an even more basic and no-nonsense atmosphere, a favourite with the local Cantonese.

The Pizza on the Park, 11 Knightsbridge, SW5, T020-7235 5273, is one of the better branches of Pizza Express with live jazz (£10-18) downstairs every night. *Abbaye*, 102 Old Brompton Rd, SW7, T020-7373 2403, is a Belgian beer and mussel bar that you wouldn't necessarily guess was owned by the Café Rouge chain.

For a traditional family-style Italian meal at a leisurely pace, *Il Falconiere*, 84 Old Brompton Rd, SW7, T020-7589 2401, is a bargain. *Brasserie de l'Institut* in The French Institute, 17 Queensbury Place, SW7, T020-7838 2144, also do very good-value set lunches. *Jacob's*, 20 Gloucester Rd, SW7, T020-7581 9292, is a quirky little Armenian 'wysiwyg' restaurant (ie, you can't understand the menu): order food direct from the display trolleys.

Top of the fashion pack has to be the *Fifth Floor Café*, Harvey Nichols, Knightsbridge, T020-7235 5000 (see above), not cheap but then that's not the point. Another busy, bustling Knightsbridge Italian institution is *Café Monpelliano*, 144 Brompton Rd, SW3, T020-7225 2926. *Raison d'être*, 18 Bute St, SW7, T020-7584 5008, is its charming French equivalent and it does excellent coffee.

Cafés & sandwich bars

The *Glorietta Patisserie*, 128 Brompton Rd, SW3, T020-7589 4750, is a sweet little Viennese cake shop opposite Harrods. A little further down is another fine branch of the delicious and sophisticated *Patisserie Valerie*, 215 Brompton Rd, SW3, T020-7823 9971. Much cheaper than any of them is the tiny and colourful two-level *Dishes Café*, 23 Cromwell Place, SW7, T020-7584 8839, next to South Ken tube, for gourmet sandwiches, jacket potatoes and hot meals.

Pubs & bars
Neither Knightsbridge nor South Ken really go in for pub life.
▶▶ *Go to page 424 for entertainment & nightlife*

Many of the area's old locals have been converted into restaurants or private houses, leaving the remainder to the tourists and language students. However, there are some notable exceptions such as the Edwardian splendour of the **Paxton's Head**, 153 Knightsbridge, SW1, T020-7589 6627, or the Victorian cosiness of the **Bunch of Grapes**, 207 Brompton Rd, SW3, T020-7589 4944.

One pub that has remained very popular with locals, despite refurbishment, is the **Admiral Codrington**, 17 Mossop St, SW3, T020-7581 0005, confidently crossing the divide between pub and bar. Nearby, **The Enterprise**, 35 Walton St, SW3, T020-7584 3148, has been turned into a swanky gastrobar with a considerable reputation for the quality of its expensive food. **The Eclipse**, 113 Walton St, SW3, T020-7581 0123, is a newish cocktail bar that may prove to have caught the pulse of the area with its combination of understated beige interior and enthusiastic staff. Then again, most of the area's smart restaurants (see above) offer drinking experiences of a similar style.

A little more grown-up than either is the **Oratory**, 232 Brompton Rd, SW3, T020-7584 3493, an unpretentious winebar in an old building with seats outside and amazing toilets located in the bowels of the Brompton Oratory itself, very convenient for the V&A. **The Crescent**, 99 Fulham Rd, SW3, T020-7225 2244, is a little designer surprise, also with fine wines, wonderful bar snacks and room upstairs. **Kavanagh's**, 109-118 Queen's Gate, is a lively Irish pub with live music.

Shopping

Lots of people go to Knightsbridge and South Ken solely for the shops, and very brave they are too. The chances are slim of escaping from an expedition down Sloane St, the Brompton Rd, Beauchamp Place, Walton St or Draycott Ave without being forced to phone an independent financial adviser.

Top of the heap of course is **Harrods**, 87-135 Brompton Rd, SW1, T020-7730 1234, www.harrods.com, open Mon-Sat 1000-1900. The smartest and most famous department store in the city, possibly the world, now blessed with a mawkish shrine to the owner's son Dodi Fayed and his girlfriend Diana. Dodge the gawpers and head boldly into what is undoubtedly one of the most lavish and disorientating temples to retail sales in the world, not just for its palatial food hall but for any kind of consumer durable. Many staff have perfected the exquisite supercilious tone of voice that the immortal sit-com enquiry 'Are you being served?' really deserves. Their stock is still admirable too but considering the mark-up is generally better left on the peg or shelf where it always looks as if it belongs. Service goes out of the window during the Sales every Jan and Jul, when the initial scrum beggars belief.

Knightsbridge's shrine to haute couture is **Harvey Nichols**, 109-125 Knightsbridge, SW1, T020-7235 5000, www.harveynichols.com Open Mon, Tue, Sat 1000-1900 on Wed, Thu, Fri til 2000, Sun 1200-1800. Harvey Nicks for short to the darlings that would simply die if this department store closed down. It too has unseemly Sales every Jan and Jul, and the store's ardent devotees have also been memorably satirised in the TV sit-com 'Absolutely Fabulous'.

Generally speaking the high fashion outlets and designer jewellery concerns around here are less concentrated but even more numerous than in Mayfair. On Sloane St can be found the likes of Chanel, Dior, D&G, Armani, Gucci, Hermes, Valentino and Starewski. Marginally more affordable and youth-orientated than these are the two **Joseph**, 16 Sloane St, SW1, T020-7235 1991, and 26 Sloane St, SW1, T020- 7235 5470. Its more casual *Essentials* range is at 315 Brompton Rd, SW3, T020-7225 3335.

Harrods' Hall of Fame

Harrods is hard to miss: well-signposted at Knightsbridge tube, its famous terracotta building, picked out like a fairground at night, has dominated the Brompton Road for almost a hundred years. Founded half a century earlier by Charles Harrod, his small perfume and cosmetics store became the largest general shop in the world, boasting the first escalator in London and employing thousands of staff. Its seven floors remain a sumptuous five-star shopping experience, featuring the marble chiller cabinets of the legendary Food Halls, acres of designerwear and an alarmingly tidy toy shop.

Since the 1980s though it has become almost as famous for the notoriety of its current owner, Mohammed Al Fayed. A controversial character who loves the limelight, he has stamped his personality all over the store, sadly all the more so since the death of his son Dodi with Princess Diana. Whatever they may be looking to purchase upstairs, most visitors don't want to miss the Diana and Dodi Memorial in the basement at the foot of one of the Egyptian escalators. Portrait photos of the tragic pair are sentimentally enshrined on a sort of funereal ivy-bedecked wishing-well, a fairly second-rate exhibition of the window dresser's art sandwiched between the Harrods marketing shop and the lost property department. Its most macabre feature is an actual wine glass supposedly in use on that fateful night at the Paris Ritz. As everybody knows, the couple were killed in a car accident pursued by paparazzi, making it all the more ironic that this is the only part of the whole store were photography is permitted.

Central London

In fact Brompton Rd is generally accessible to fashion victims under 35. Here is *The Library*, 268 Brompton Rd, SW3, T020-7589 6569, kind of Issy Miyake meets gay combat gear; and then *Issy Miyake*, 270 Brompton Rd, SW1, T020-7581 3760, for the more sombre classic lines than the colourful range at 52 Conduit St, T020-7851 4620.

Also on Brompton Rd: *Whistles*, 303 Brompton Rd, SW3, T020-7823 9134, for own-label and left-field women's designerwear; *Betty Jackson*, 311 Brompton Rd, SW3, T020-7589 7884, for wearable designs 'aimed at 20-60-year-old' women; the flagship store of *Emporio Armani*, 191 Brompton Rd, SW3, T020-7823 8818; and also *Formes*, 313 Brompton Rd, SW3, T020-7584 3337, with their French clothes for pregnant women and *Caramel Baby and Child*, 291 Brompton Rd, SW3, T020-7589 7001, minimalist designer baby and kidswear and accessories.

Beauchamp Place (pronounced Beecham) is also lined with upmarket boutiques, including the world-famous women's lingerie designer *Janet Reger*, 2 Beauchamp Place, SW3, T020-7584 9360.

Where the Brompton Rd becomes the Fulham Rd, heading south for the King's Rd are Sloane Ave and Draycott Ave, the home of outlets for *Paul Smith*, 84-86 Sloane Ave, SW3, T020-7589 9139; *Kenzo*, 70 Sloane Ave, SW3, T020-7255 1960; *Gallery Gautier*, 171 Draycott Ave, SW3, T020-7584 4648; and originals by *Betsey Johnson*, 106 Draycott Ave, SW3, T020-7591 0005, very feminine dresses, cute cardigans and matching skirts.

On the Fulham Rd designer jewellery and furnishings tend to take over from fashion, at places like the *Conran Shop*, Michelin House, 81 Fulham Rd, SW3, T020-7589 7401; *Oggetti*, 135 & 143 Fulham Rd, SW3, T020-7581 8088, for stylish household goods that partly explain why Brits take jobs in Milan; and also *Divertimenti*, 139-141 Fulham Rd, SW3, T020-7581 8065, a chain specializing in groovy kitchenware.

Near South Ken tube the shops diversify a little, with interesting one-offs like *Tridias*, 25 Bute St, SW7, T020-7584 2330, for wooden toys, some by independent toymakers; *Red Herring*, 6 Old Brompton Rd, SW7, T020-7581 0299, for funky footwear; *Bookthrift*, 22

Thurloe St, SW7, T020-7589 2916, next to the *Daquise*, for remaindered books on art and art history; *EK Wilson and Sons*, 87 Old Brompton Rd, SW7, T020- 7589 0046, an old-style hardware and ironmongery shop; and next door, the South Ken branch of fine art and antique auctioneers *Christies*, 85 Old Brompton Rd, SW7, T020-7581 7611.

Transport

Buses

No 2 from along Park Lane to Brixton via Victoria, Vauxhall and Stockwell.

No 9 between Aldwych and Hammersmith via Strand, Trafalgar Square, Piccadilly Circus, Hyde Park Corner, and Kensington.

No 10 from Kensington and Knightsbridge to Euston and King's Cross via Hyde Park Corner, Marble Arch and Oxford Circus.

No 14 between Tottenham Court road station and Putney via Piccadilly Circus, Hyde Park Corner, South Kensington and Fulham Broadway.

No 16 between Victoria and Kilburn via Hyde Park Corner, Marble Arch, Edgware Rd and Maida Vale.

No 19 between Battersea and Finsbury Park via Chelsea, Sloane Square, Hyde Park Corner, Piccadilly Circus, Bloomsbury, Islington and Highbury.

No 22 between Piccadilly Circus and Putney via Hyde Park Corner, Sloane Square, Chelsea and Fulham.

No 36 between Queen's Park and Lewisham via Paddington, Marble Arch, Hyde Park Corner, Victoria, Vauxhall, Oval, Camberwell, Peckham and New Cross.

No 49 between Shepherd's Bush and Clapham Junction via Kensington, South Kensington, Chelsea and Battersea, 74 between Baker St and Putney via Marble Arch, Hyde Park Corner, Knightsbridge, South Kensington, Earl's Court, and Fulham Cross.

No 52 from Victoria to Notting Hill Gate and Ladbroke Grove via Hyde Park Corner, Knightsbridge and Kensington.

No 73 between Victoria and Stoke Newington via Hyde Park Corner, Marble Arch, Oxford Circus, Tottenham Court Rd station, Euston, King's Cross, and Islington.

No 74 between Baker St and Putney via Marble Arch, Hyde Park Corner, Knightsbridge, South Kensington, Earl's Court, and Fulham Cross.

No 82 between Victoria and Finchley via Marble Arch, Baker St, Swiss Cottage, and Golders Green.

No 137 between Oxford Circus and Clapham Common via Marble Arch, Hyde Park Corner, Knightsbridge, Sloane Square, Chelsea Bridge, and Battersea Park.

No 345 between South Kensington and Peckham via Battersea, Clapham Junction, Clapham, Stockwell, Brixton and Camberwell.

No C1 between Victoria and Kensington High St via Sloane Square, Brompton Rd (Harrods), South Kensington, and Earl's Court.

Taxis

There are always plenty of taxis in the area, especially along Brompton Rd and around South Kensington.

Tubes

Hyde Park Corner (Piccadilly line) for Hyde Park. Knightsbridge (Piccadilly line) for Harrods & Sloane St. South Kensington (District, Circel and Piccadilly lines) for the museums, Fulham Rd & Chelsea. Also Gloucester Rd (District, Circle and Piccadilly lines).

Chelsea

*It's easy to see why Hillary and Bill Clinton named their daughter Chelsea: the name has a pleasant sound and a familiar ring in certain social circles. As far as London is concerned, it means a very comfortable part of town with an impeccable bohemian pedigree, occasionally displaying bursts of street cred. Its High Street, the **King's Road**, became one of the pivots of 'swinging London' in the 1960s and outraged middle England again a decade later by spawning the Sex Pistols, the shock troops of punk rock.*

*Nowadays much quieter and more expensive, freighted with designer boutiques and the sleek Chelsea boys and babes they attract, the well-heeled King's Road treads its well-worn path between the Fulham Road and the river, threading its way through a district characterized by smart residential squares and quaint cobbled mews. The most interesting streets to explore lie on its south side, towards the river, along Royal Hospital Road and the Chelsea Embankment up to the Albert Bridge. Apart from the Royal Hospital itself, very grand almshouses from another era for retired soldiers, this pretty area conceals the peaceful delights of the **Chelsea Physic Garden**, the pickled Victoriana of **Carlyle's House** and some very genteel pubs. Further down the King's Road, around the World's End, Chelsea loosens up a little to become fertile browsing ground for offbeat fashions and better-value restaurants.*

⊖ *Sloane Square tube and then bus or walk for the King's Rd. Fulham Broadway for the lower reaches of the King's Rd. South Kensington for the Fulham Rd. Nearest train station is Victoria*

Central London

History

Chelsea, or 'chelchythe', Isle of Shingles, was cut off from the spread of London by marshy fields and creeks around modern Victoria Station. The Domesday book describes it as a village in Middlesex, but when Chelsea Bridge was built in the 1850s workers uncovered Roman and British weapons and bones suggesting that a battle was fought hereabouts. Under the Tudors and Stuarts, it became known as the 'Village of Palaces' – HenryVIII built Chelsea Manor House, the Earl of Shrewsbury and Duke of Norfolk moved here, as did Sir Thomas More. At Beaufort House More welcomed distinguished visitors such as Erasmus and Holbein, and is said to have flogged heretics against trees in the substantial orchard.

All Saints church sat down by the river, so by the late 17th century a number of isolated houses were scattered across arable fields and pasture, orchards, gardens and riverside meadows. Chelsea Common provided grazing land and also held a gravel pit. The King's Highway (modern Fulham Road), notorious for its footpads, sped carriages to Portsmouth, while Charles II would use his private road (modern King's Road) to travel to Hampton Court. In 1687 Sir Christopher Wren built Chelsea Royal Hospital for veteran soldiers – Wellington lay in state here in 1852 and two people died in the crush – and the Physic Garden was set up by the Apothecaries Company. It exhibited the country's first rock garden and the first greenhouse, and sent cotton seed to America.

In the reign of Queen Anne town houses appeared in Cheyne Walk and Cheyne Row, while Sloane Square and Sloane Street took shape in the 1770s and 1780s, but by 1801 the population was still only 12,000. By 1901, however, it had risen almost eightfold.

• •

Hotels in the area

B *The Claverley*
C *Nell Gwynne House Apartments*
E *Oakley Hotel*
➤➤ *Go to page 445*

Chelsea

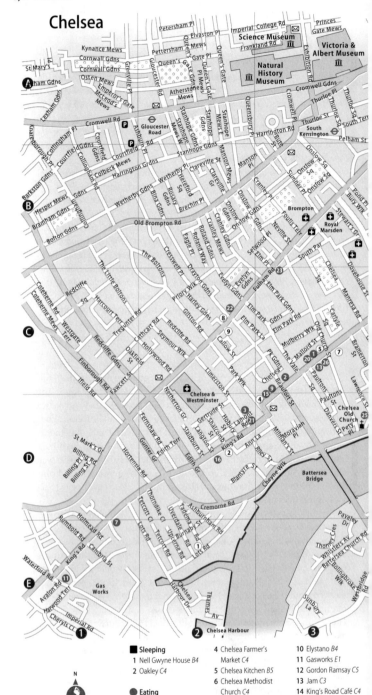

Central London

0 metres 200
0 yards 200

Central London

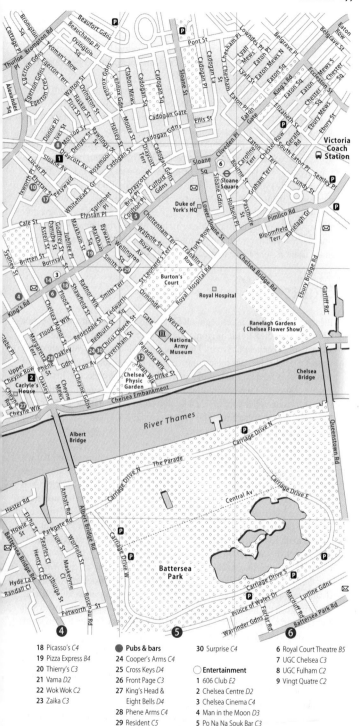

18 Picasso's *C4*
19 Pizza Express *B4*
20 Thierry's *C3*
21 Vama *D2*
22 Wok Wok *C2*
23 Zaika *C3*

● **Pubs & bars**
24 Cooper's Arms *C4*
25 Cross Keys *D4*
26 Front Page *C3*
27 King's Head & Eight Bells *D4*
28 Phene Arms *C4*
29 Resident *C5*
30 Surprise *C4*

○ **Entertainment**
1 606 Club *E2*
2 Chelsea Centre *D2*
3 Chelsea Cinema *C4*
4 Man in the Moon *D3*
5 Po Na Na Souk Bar *C3*

6 Royal Court Theatre *B5*
7 UGC Chelsea *C3*
8 UGC Fulham *C2*
9 Vingt Quatre *C2*

The area developed a reputation for its artistic community – the formation of the Chelsea Arts Club emerged from regular meetings of the likes of Whistler and Sickert in the *Six Bells* on the King's Road. George Eliot died in number 4 Cheyne Walk, and JMW Turner lived out his life under the pseudonym of Admiral or 'Puggy' Booth at number 119.

The 1830s saw Carlyle Square built over market gardens and Paulton Square emerge, The Boltons went up in the 1850s and Cadogan Gardens in the 1890s. Cremorne Gardens, meanwhile, became a popular venue. As with other pleasure gardens, it held a banqueting hall, grottoes and bowers, and hosted a bizarre collection of events, from the re-enactment of the storming of the fort in Sebastopol to Madame Genevieve crossing the Thames from here on a tightrope. By the 1880s, however, it was considered a "nursery of every kind of vice".

By the early 1900s, the site still held market gardens, (in 1977 a large council development known as World's End swallowed up the area), and Sloane Avenue was laid out in the 1920s. The football stadium was built in 1905 next to Brompton Cemetery, and the Michelin building on the Fulham Road produced tyres until it went the way of much of the rest of Chelsea and was turned into a fashion store and restaurant in the 1980s.

Sights

Belgravia ends and Chelsea begins at **Sloane Square**, quite an attractive spot spoilt by the endless traffic but romantic at night when the fairy lights are twinkling in the branches of its trees. The Square and Sloane Street, heading north up to Knightsbridge, take their names from Sir Hans Sloane, whose 'cabinet of curiosities' formed the nucleus of the British Museum's collection in the 18th century, but since then have more famously given their names to a particular breed of young upper-middle-class English society: 'Sloane Rangers' turn up their shirt collars, wear pearls and live according to a regimented set of social rules in Fulham and Parsons Green.

Punk's other main contenders, The Clash, grew up around Ladbroke Grove, in the shadow of the Westway

Lower Sloane Street heads south towards Chelsea Bridge, but it was the **King's Road**, the real spine of Chelsea, that became famous in the 1970s for what is now a much rarer breed: punks, and their arch enemies, the hippies. The King's Road weaves southwest for a mile before jinking sharp left and then right at the Moravian burial ground and *Man in the Moon* pub, and then carrying on down past the World's End to Fulham. Near this kink, at number 430, Malcolm Maclaren and Vivienne Westwood set up the shop called *Sex* that gave its name in 1976 to their brainchild, punk rock's most notorious band, the **Sex Pistols**. Recently celebrated in Julian Temple's film *The Filth and the Fury*, they briefly became the epicentre of one of rock's most anarchic, disaffected and influential new departures. Nowadays anarchy is hardly uppermost in the minds of the road's well-groomed shoppers. Number 430 King's Road has become the *World's End Shop*, a pricey outlet for Vivienne Westwood's wacky and ground-breaking designerwear.

Royal Hospital The Chelsea Flower Show takes place in the grounds every May

Almost any left turn off the King's Road shortly after Sloane Square passes through small Georgian streets, squares and mews towards Royal Hospital Road and the river. Here lives another of Chelsea's rare breeds, the **Chelsea Pensioners**, easily recognizable in their smart navy blue uniforms and peaked caps or in summer and on special occasions, their scarlet tunics and tri-cornered caps.

Flower power

*Organized by the Royal Horticultural Society, the **Chelsea Flower Show** is the country's most prestigious celebration of the art of gardening, taking place in the grounds of the Royal Hospital every year in the last week of May. The public are normally only admitted to the spectacular displays of model gardens, flower arrangements and trade stands on the last Thursday and Friday of the week. Open 0800-2000, T0870-9063781 or First Call T01293-433956. Admission £10-£27 depending on the time of day.*

Since 1689, about 400 veteran soldiers have been accommodated in the Royal Hospital and the building designed for them by Wren seems hardly to have changed. Its three splendid neoclassical courtyards still possess a stirring and solemn dignity. Visitors are allowed a look into the central one, with its statue of Charles II in a toga by Grinling Gibbons, as well as the wood-panelled Great Hall, containing an impressive portrait by Verrio of that dissipated monarch on horseback, and the Chapel, adorned with some French eagle standards captured at Waterloo. The Hospital's museum has just undergone a major refit, modernizing the telling of the pensioners' 300-year history.

■ *Museum, Chapel and Hall open 1000-1200, 1400-1600 Mon-Sat, 1400-1600 Sun. Admission free. T020-7730 5282.*

Appropriately enough, the National Army Museum is next door, difficult to miss thanks to the tracked armoured ambulance parked outside. Established here in 1971, the museum is an efficient public relations exercise as well as an important academic resource. 'The Modern Army', exhibiting many of the latest military gizmos in use today, is the most recent addition to the displays on the history of the British army since the reign of Henry VII, told through uniforms, memorabilia and antique oddities such as the skeleton of Napoleon's horse and a scale model of the Battle of Waterloo complete with flashing lights and cottonwool smoke. In fact, far from being triumphalist, the sobering impression made by the series of darkened rooms is that organized armed conflict has been a necessary even if occasionally glamorous evil down the ages. Another new exhibition is dedicated to the South African army before independence.

National Army Museum

■ *Open 1000-1730 daily. Admission free. T020-7730 0717.*

A little further down Royal Hospital Road, Swan Walk on the left leads to the entrance (No 66) of one of the area's most enchanting places, the Chelsea Physic Garden. This walled garden is at least as old as the Royal Hospital and still plays an important role in botanical research, hence the restricted opening hours. One concession to its increasing popularity is the special snowdrop openings on two Sundays in early February.

Chelsea Physic Garden

Apart from the riverside location, the garden's attraction lies in its small scale and the care that has clearly been lavished on the wide variety of rare and interesting plants within its walls. Here, as well as the world's first rockery and some very old trees and shrubs, are borders and flowerbeds neatly divided up and laid out according to their occupants' classification and taste for light or shade. Along with the flowers and vegetables in the greenhouses, these are just some of the plants that have given us painkillers, contraceptives and expensive perfumes. A statue of 1723 commemorates Sir Hans Sloane who bought the garden around that time and gave it to the Society of Apothecaries 'so that apprentices may better distinguish good and useful plants from those that bear resemblance to them and yet are hurtful'.

■ *Open 1 Apr-28 Oct, 1200-1700 Wed, 1400-1800 Sun (as well as daily throughout the Chelsea Flower Show and Chelsea Festival). Admission £4, £2 under-16s. T020-7352 5646.*

Chelsea Embankment & Cheyne Walk
Other notable Cheyne Walk residents were novelist Henry James & Dracula's creator, Bram Stoker

Royal Hosptial Road emerges onto the **Chelsea Embankment** at a point on the river where, at very low tide, it's sometimes possible to make out the remains of Mercian King Offa's embankment, constructed well over 1200 years ago, and also the cobbles and pilings of the old Chelsea wharves. From here **Cheyne Walk** (pronounced 'chainey') heads west, once the home of the Pre-Raphaelite brotherhood led by Dante Gabriel Rossetti and more recently the chosen address of the Rolling Stones at their peak. Among the houseboats usually moored along this stretch look out for an unusual private conversion of a Second World War Motor Torpedo Boat.

Carlyle's House
Beyond the **Albert Bridge**, built in 1873 and prettily lit at night, at No 24 Cheyne Row off to the right, can be found Carlyle's House, where the 'awesome sage of Chelsea', the historian and writer Thomas Carlyle and his spirited wife Jane lived from 1834. Bought by popular public subscription in the late 19th century the house is now run by the National Trust and has been kept much as it was during the couple's tempestuous cohabitation. From 1866 Carlyle lived on here alone after Jane's untimely death from a heart attack brought on by an accident involving a close friend's dog in Hyde Park. Even though his florid works are little read these days, his writing room at the top of the house, the cosy parlour, kitchen and the little back garden are all highly evocative of middle-class Victorian domesticity and mores.

■ *Open Apr-Oct 1100-1700 Wed-Sun. Admission £3.50, £1.75 concession. T020-7532 7087.*

Around the corner in **Glebe Place**, No 51 has long been supposed to be the oldest house in Chelsea, believed to have been a hunting lodge built for Henry VIII, although some doubt has been cast on whether it actually was. It's worth seeing though even if just for the extraordinary Art Deco house next door. Nearby, on Lawrence Street, where Chelsea China was once made, the novelists Henry Fielding and Tobias Smollett lived in Monmouth House.

Back on Cheyne Walk, **Chelsea Old Church** (■ *Open Monday-Friday 1200-1600, all day Sunday; T020-7352 5627*) is aptly named, dating from the early 14th century, although so badly bombed during the war that only parts of the original remain, including the More Chapel, rededicated by Thomas 'Man for all Seasons' More, the Catholic martyr, in 1528. On the site of his old house, **Crosby Hall** in Danvers Street is a 15th-century merchant's hall (now a private house) relocated here in 1908 from Bishopsgate in the City where Richard III is supposed to have plotted the murder of the princes in the Tower.

At the end of the Cheyne Walk, after it has moved onto the Chelsea Embankment and passed Battersea Bridge, Lots Road leads off on the left to **Chelsea Harbour**, ultra desirable condos for the very rich with a landmark tower topped by a ball that rises and falls with the tide.

Central London

Five of the best: cheap eats

- *King's Road Café*, King's Rd, Chelsea
- *Mary Ward Centre*, Queen Square, Holborn
- *Tas*, The Cut, South Bank
- *Jenny Lo's Teahouse*, Eccleston St, Victoria
- *Paolina*, King's Cross Rd, King's Cross

Eating and drinking

The most celebrated gourmet and Michelin-starred restaurant in Chelsea is the place that was once the *Tante Claire*, now rechristened **Gordon Ramsay**, 68 Royal Hospital Rd, SW3, T020-7352 4441, and run by the famously bad-tempered celebrity chef and named after himself.

Expensive
● on map, page 176

Less expensive, Terence Conran's **Bluebird**, 350 King's Rd, SW3, T020-7559 1000, is also an experience, a successful conversion of an old garage into a café with outside seating, a food market, and upstairs, a large and bustling restaurant doing reliable seafood and modern European dishes. Glamour-pusses, jetsetters and flashy businessmen have long enjoyed basking in the brisk Italian atmosphere at **Daphne's**, 112 Draycott Avenue, SW3, T020-7584 6883.

Well beyond the World's End, quite near Fulham Broadway, is the deeply eccentric **Gasworks**, 85 Waterford Rd, SW6, T020-7736 3830, a local institution where both food and wine come at set prices (£12 main course, £4 pudding and starters, £10 wine) and are served up in someone's house. **Chutney Mary**, 535 King's Rd, SW10, T020-7351 3113 is a top-quality Indian restaurant in grand surroundings, just off Lots Rd. **Vama**, 438 King's Rd, SW10, T020-7351 4118, another less expensive and less formal modern Indian restaurant, specializes in food from the northwestern frontier, on the corner of Limerston St.

Mid-range
Most of the less pricey options on the King's Rd are beyond the World's End

Nearer Sloane Square, between the King's Rd and the Fulham Rd, **Pellicano**, 19 Elystan St, SW3, T020-7589 3718, is a minimalist place to enjoy some very good modern Italian food with a Sardinian accent. On the same street, the **Elystano Restaurant**, 25-27 Elystan St, SW3, T020-7584 5248, is another good modern Italian restaurant popular with the locals. **Thierry's**, 342 King's Rd, SW3, T020-7352 3365, has been around for years, a thoroughly cosy and welcoming venue for some classic French recipes.

For a louder party atmosphere, **The Big Easy**, 332-334 Kings Rd, SW3, T020-7352 4071, tries to imitate an American BarbQ diner and Crabshack. Whether or not it succeeds, it remains very popular.

On the Fulham Rd, **Zaika**, 257 Fulham Rd, SW3, T020-7351 7823 is a sumptuously decorated Indian restaurant that is justifiably more expensive than many.

Most of the cheaper options are on the King's Rd itself. Nearest to Sloane Square is **The Chelsea Kitchen**, 98 King's Rd, SW3, T020-7589 1330, once a branch of the Stockpot chain and still doing basic meals at rock-bottom prices for this part of London. **Piccasso's**, 127 King's Rd, SW3, T020-7352 4921, part of the Dino's chain, has also long been a King's Rd institution, more expensive but with a lively atmosphere in which to enjoy Italian and British staples. The Chelsea branch of **Pizza Express**, 152 King's Rd, SW3, T020-7351 5031, occupies one of the King's Rd's grandest old buildings, **The Pheasantry**, an impressive setting for their reliable pizzas. Good fresh soups can also be found in the basement of the **Chelsea Farmer's Market** on Sydney St.

Cheap
There are surprising number of decent places in Chelsea where it's possible to eat a full meal (usually of Italian food) for not much more than a tenner

Perhaps the best bet for lunch though is the **Kings Road Café** (T020-7351 6645; open 10-1730 daily), in the branch of *Habitat*, 208 King's Rd, where the ingredients of the mainly Italian dishes are usually absolutely fresh. A little further down, **Buona Sera at The Jam**, 289 King's Rd, SW3, T020-7352 8827, has signature bunk-bed-style tables for fairly cheap and very cheerful platefuls of Italian food (just before *Bluebird* on the opposite side of the street).

Nearer the World's End, **Ed's Easy Diner**, 362 King's Rd, SW3, T020-7352 1952, do big, satisfying burgers in a buzzy atmosphere. Round the corner, the **Chelsea Bun**, 9a

Central London

Limerston St, SW10, T020-7352 3635, is another Chelsea institution, almost but not quite as popular as its 19th-century namesake, offering over 200 different straightforward meals like pasta or filled baked potatoes.

Two more expensive options for supper include the ***Ristorante La Bersagliera***, 372 King's Rd, SW3, T020-7352 5993, a traditional Italian doing fine pizza and pasta, and on the Fulham Rd, ***Wok Wok***, 140 Fulham Rd, SW10, T020-7370 5355, a smallish branch of the modern Chinese chain where standards are high and the atmosphere lively.

Cafés   Coffee and sandwich chains proliferate on the King's Rd, but near the World's End, ***Mona Lisa***, 417 King's Rd, SW1, T020-7376 5447, is a very friendly one-off, run by Italians (surprise, surprise) doing good-value hot meals and snacks. The best-value freshly made sandwiches on the King's Rd can be found in the café of the ***Chelsea Methodist Church***, 155a King's Rd, SW3, T020-7352 9305, next door to the Old Town Hall opposite *Habitat*, available 1000-1400 Mon-Fri.

Pubs & bars   The loudest and busiest drinking establishments are on the King's Rd, at places like the
Chelsea thrives on its   ***Chelsea Potter***, but it's the genial popularity of those tucked away in the side streets
pub life and it shows   that marks the area out as ideal territory for an enjoyable crawl. A good start might be
in their quality   ***The Resident***, Smith St, SW3, T020-7730 7721, a quiet haven 30 seconds off the King's Rd doing decent pub food with a clientele that represents a reassuring cross-section of locals and workers from beyond the borough. Round the corner is ***The Surprise***, 6 Christchurch Terr, T020-7349 1821, a roomy place with bare floorboards, large tables and pleasant atmosphere. Nearby, ***The Cooper's Arms***, 87 Flood St, SW3, T020-7376 3120, is a Young's pub boasting good newspapers, a stuffed bear and more big tables. Then there's ***The Phene Arms***, 9 Phene St, T020-7352 3294, which has long been a favourite with the area's gilded youth, a cosy old-fashioned two-bar affair with outside seating and a good but quite expensive menu.

▶▶ *Go to page 424*
for entertainment
& nightlife   Down by the river, with a great view of the Albert Bridge, the ***King's Head and Eight Bells***, 50 Cheyne Walk (at the junction with Cheyne Row), SW3, T020-7352 1820, is on the tourist coach trail but that doesn't detract from the quality of the real ales or the location. Heading back inland, the ***Cross Keys***, 1 Lawrence St, SW3, T020-7349 9111, has a real fire. Some may find the décor over-designed (done by the same people as *Beach Blanket Babylon* in Notting Hill) but it's good for a lively drink. Nip down Justice Walk and turn right to find ***The Front Page***, Old Church St, SW1, T020-7352 0648, on the left, a popular 'youngish-person's-pub' just off the King's Rd.

Shopping

Standing on the gateway to the King's Rd in Sloane Square, ***Peter Jones*** (T020-7730 3434) is the area's major department store (a branch of John Lewis), and the favoured repository of wedding present lists for the Sloaney set. Heading down the King's Rd, most of the big-name clothes and fashion shops are lined up on the stretch before the Old Town Hall, where a change in emphasis towards interior design, antiques and homewares is marked by the branch of the furniture shop ***Heal's***, 234 King's Rd, SW3, T020-7349 8411, the gateway to an area that is increasingly being branded 'Little Chelsea'.

In 'Big' Chelsea then, shops worth investigating might include ***Ted Baker Woman***, 75/77 King's Rd, SW3, T020-7351 6764, for the casual urban menswear brand's designs for women; the inimitable ***R Soles***, 109a King's Rd, SW3, T020-7351 5520, for their way-out selection of cowboy boots and 'western' footwear; or ***Daisy and Tom***, 181 King's Rd, T020-7352 5000, stocking tasteful toys and clothes for little Jeremies and Lucindas.

Beyond Heal's, *After Noah*, 261 King's Rd, SW3, T020-7351 2610, are specialists in contemporary and vintage 'furniture and furniment', bric a brac and objets d'art largely inspired by the arts and crafts movement. *The Corridor*, 309a King's Rd, SW3, T020-7351 0772, is Jane Arden's well-respected shop for nearly-new designer womenswear. Nearer the World's End, *KMK Designs*, 319 King's Rd, SW3, T020-7352 7710, stock some interesting jewellery while *Rococo Chocolates*, 321 King's Rd, SW3, T020-7352 5857, make their own amazing 'artisan' bars, and also stock delights by Valrhona.

The *World's End Shop*, 430 Kings Rd, SW10, T020-7352 6551, the turquoise number with the clock going backwards, once Vivienne Westwood's shop *Sex* is still hers, now stocking a wide variety of her designer clothes. Other designer outlets in the area include *Patrick Cox*, 129 Sloane St, SW1, T020-7730 8886, for ultra chic footwear for men and women, and *Agnes B's* womenswear shop at 111 Fulham Rd, SW3, T020-7225 3477. An exception to all the clothes shops is the *Books Bought Bookshop*, 357 King's Rd, SW3, T020-7352 9376, with a good stock of mainly second-hand biographies and humanities titles.

The World's End is dominated by restaurants & arty clothes shops

Transport

Around Sloane Square and along the King's Road:
No11 from Liverpool St to Fulham Broadway via Bank, St Pauls, Fleet St, Aldwych, Strand, Trafalgar Square, Westminster, and Victoria.
No 19 from Finsbury Park to Battersea via Highbury, Islington, Bloomsbury, Piccadilly Circus, Hyde Park Corner and Knightsbridge.
No 22 from Piccadilly Circus to Putney Common via Hyde Park Corner, Knightsbridge, and Fulham.
No 211 from Waterloo to Hammersmith via Westminster, Victoria, and Fulham Broadway.

Buses

Along Sydney St:
No 49 from Shepherd's Bush to Clapham Junction via Kensington, South Kensington, and Battersea.

Along Lower Sloane St:
No 137 from Oxford Circus to Streatham via Marble Arch, Hyde Park Corner, Knightsbridge, Chelsea Bridge, Battersea Park and Clapham Common.

Along the Fulham Rd:
No 14 from Tottenham Court Rd to Putney via Piccadilly Circus, Hyde Park Corner, Knightsbridge, South Kensington, and Fulham Broadway.
No 345 from South Kensington to Brixton via Battersea, Clapham Junction, Clapham and Stockwell.

Directory

Libraries *The Chelsea Library, in the Old Town Hall, SW3, T020-7352 6056. Open 1000-2000, Monday, Tuesday, Thursday, 1000-1300 Wednesday, 1000-1700 Friday, Saturday. has a good reference section and is an excellent source of local information.*

Sports *Chelsea Sports Centre, Manor St (next door to the Old Town Hall), T020-7352 6985. Swimming pool (£2.70), gym, classes. Open 0700-2130* **Chelsea Football Club**, *Stamford Bridge, Fulham Rd, SW6, T020-7385 5545, near Fulham Broadway tube.*

Central London

Along Royal Hospital Rd:
No 239 from Victoria to Clapham Junction via Battersea Bridge, Vicarage Crescent and Grant Rd (not Sun).

River transport Cadogan (Chelsea Embankment) to Blackfriars via Westminster Mon-Fri every 30 mins from 0700 till 1000, returning from 1615 till 1945, with *Thames Speed Ferry Company* (T020-7731 7671). Chelsea Harbour to Embankment Mon-Fri with *Riverside Launches*. Passengers must pre-book (T020-7352 5888).

Taxis Refreshment ranks on Chelsea Embankment and on Pont St, but usually plenty of cabs on the King's Rd itself.

Tubes Sloane Square (District and Circle lines) for the top end of the King's Rd. Fulham Broadway (District line) for the lower end. South Kensington (District, Circle and Piccadilly lines) for the Fulham Rd.

Marylebone and Regent's Park

⊖ *Bond St for Marylebone Lane & the Wallace Collection. Baker St for Madame Tussaud's. Oxford Circus for Portland Place & Regent's Park or Great Portland St tube for the Park. Camden Town for the Zoo & Regent's Park*

A discreet Georgian and Victorian backwater just to the north of the busiest street in the West End, much to its own surprise Marylebone has recently become almost fashionable. Marylebone Lane twists up from Oxford Street, an old-timer defying the regular gridiron of severe streets like Wigmore, Wimpole and Harley, and broadens out to become Marylebone High Street, still refusing to follow a straight path up to the traffic jam on the massive Marylebone Road.

*Over the last decade, the High Street has been steadily colonized by upmarket fashion boutiques and a few gourmet restaurants, while Marylebone's hidden treasure, the **Wallace Collection** of 18th-century French paintings in Hertford House, has had a centennial overhaul courtesy of the National Lottery Heritage Fund. Along with the Wigmore Hall, one of London's most endearing venues for chamber music and song, the Wallace Collection continues to conjure the ghost of 19th-century and Edwardian London. In many of the streets and mews around, it doesn't take much imagination to hear the clatter of carriage wheels carrying Sherlock Holmes back to his Baker Street home after his latest adventure.*

*The crowds imitating the traffic as they queue outside **Madame Tussaud's** might have been a familiar sight to him, although it's difficult to say what he would have made of the story of space exploration at the revamped Planetarium. Certainly he would still recognize much of **Regent's Park**, just to the north, still the most delightful place in central London to escape the crush of the West End. And if hell has become other people, here's the chance to get close to some of the protected wildlife in **London Zoo**.*

Hotels in the area

A *Langham Hilton*
C *Hart House Hotel*
C *Hallam Hotel*
C *Georgian House Hotel*
E *International Students House*
E *Carr Saunders Hall*
E *Indian Student YMCA*

▸▸ **Go to page 445**

History

Marylebone, sitting north of the Tyburn Road was until the 18th century a series of fields and isolated houses. In 1066 the western part was the Manor of Lileston (Lisson) and the Manor of Tyburn owned the land to the east. In the 14th century parishioners moved their church from near the Tyburn gallows – "the lurking place of cut-throats" – to alongside the river Tybourne, hence the name 'St Mary-by-the-bourne'. Henry VIII appropriated both manors, and sold much of the land to, among others, the Portman and Portland estates. He did, however, keep the northern part of the Tyburn Manor lands for his hunting pursuits, enclosing Marylebone Park (later Regent's Park) with a ditch, rampart and fence to ensure good sport, and converting Marylebone Manor into a hunting lodge.

A survey of 1649 reported over 16,000 trees, including oak, ash, elm, whitehorn and maple, but by 1800, thousands of trees had been felled to be replaced by small holdings that supplied London with dairy products and hay. Meanwhile, housing had grown north from Oxford Street. The two estates, Portland slightly ahead of Portman, built up the east and west respectively with streets named after members of their family or their country estates – Henrietta, Margaret, Harley, Holles, Wigmore, Wimpole. Cavendish Square, built in 1717, started the boom. St Peter, Vere Street, and the Oxford Market (meat, fish and vegetables) were built to support and encourage a growing community.

By the 1770s, a suburban development had grown up around Cavendish Square. Great Portland Street, Portland Place, and Baker Street ran north-south, while Wigmore and New (now Marylebone) Road ran east-west. Marylebone Gardens attracted gamblers and sharpers to its dog- and cock-fights, its bear and bull baitings, and to the human equivalent, boxing.

Later in the century, activities were more refined, with assembly rooms built for balls and concerts, and the discovery of medicinal waters providing for a spa. Indeed, the attraction of the *rus in urbe* ('the Country in the City') was growing. Sheep were imported to graze in Cavendish Square, and the likes of Portman Square were carefully landscaped.

The new vogue was not lost on the architect, John Nash, who developed the idea in his great project for his patron, The Regent's Park. This estate was to be the epitome of the *rus in urbe*, the "attraction of open space, free air and the scenery of Nature" as Nash put it. Surrounding the park, he planned grand stuccoed terraces, a scattering of some 56 villas, and a further residence for the Prince Regent. By 1828, when the building was largely done, the reality was somewhat scaled down, (only eight villas were built), but the effect was still magnificent.

To the northwest, market gardens and dairy farms gave way to increasing development along Wellington Street towards St John's Wood and the border with Hampstead, and building continued throughout the century such that when Marylebone Station opened in 1899, the Great Central Railway carved out 70 acres of picturesque suburbs. The area suffered heavy bombing in the middle of the last century – at least 300 bombs hit Regent's Park, which had been taken over for military encampments – and since then the properties have steadily been taken over as business premises.

Central London

Marylebone & Regent's Park

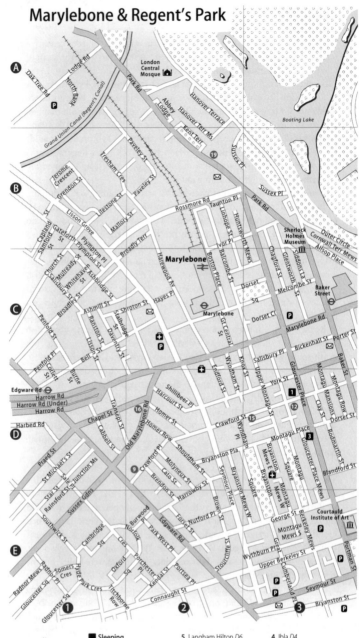

N

0 metres 100
0 yards 100

■ Sleeping
1 Georgian House *D3*
2 Hallam *D6*
3 Hart House *D3*
4 International Students'
   House *C6*

5 Langham Hilton *D6*

● Eating
1 De Gustibus *D4*
2 Golden Eagle *D4*
3 Golden Hind *D4*

4 Ibla *D4*
5 ITS *E5*
6 Kerala *E6*
7 Orrery *C5*
8 Patisserie Valerie *D4*
9 Patogh *D2*

Central London

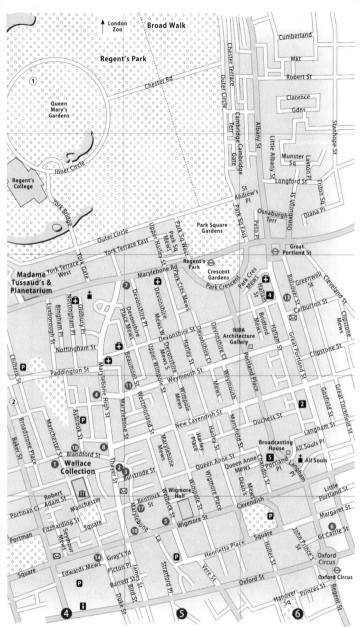

Broad Walk

↑ London Zoo

Regent's Park

Cumberland

Mkt

Robert St

Chester Rd

Clarence

Gdns

①
Queen Mary's Gardens

Regent's College

Inner Circle

York Bridge

Munster Sq

Longford St

St Andrew's Pl

Osnaburgh Terr

Diana Pl

Outer Circle

York Terrace East

Park Square Gardens

Regent's Park

Crescent Gardens

Great Portland St

York Terrace West

Madame Tussaud's & Planetarium

Marylebone Rd

Park Cres Mews

Park Crescent

Park Cres Mews

⑦

Devonshire Pl Mews

✝

RIBA Architecture Gallery

Nottingham St

⑦

Paddington St

⑦

New Cavendish St

Duchess St

Langham St

②

⑪

Wallace Collection

①

Blandford St

⑧

Bulstrode St

⑱

②③

Broadcasting House

⑤

All Souls Pl

All Souls

Wigmore Hall

⑰

⑤

Wigmore St

Little Portland St

Margaret St

⑥
Gt Castle St

⑤

Henrietta Place

Oxford Circus

Oxford Circus

⑭

Gray's Yd

Picton Pl

Edwards Mews

Barrett St

Oxford St

Hanover Sq

⑥

④

ℹ

⑤

Princes St

---

10 Purple Sage *E5*
11 Quiet Revolution *D5*
12 Thai West *D3*
13 Villandry *C6*
14 Wagamama *E4*

● Pubs & bars
15 Atlantis *D3*
16 Chapel *D2*
17 O'Conor Don *E5*
18 William Wallace *D4*
19 Windsor Castle *B2*

○ Entertainment
1 Open-Air Theatre *A3*
2 Screen on Baker Street *D3*

Sights

Marylebone Lane or James Street, both best reached by crossing Oxford Street from Bond Street tube, provide the most charming routes into deepest Marylebone. The winding path of Marylebone Lane, as its name suggests, is still just about recognizably the old village main street, before it turns into the grander breadth of modern-day Marylebone High Street. James Street (and parallel St Christopher's Place, see page 135) is lined with pleasant enough cafés. Both cross the wide progress of Wigmore Street as it rises from the gentle valley of the hidden river Tybourne.

Wallace Collection

Buses 2, 13, 30, 74, 82, 113, 139, 189 & 274

Over Wigmore Street and left up Hinde Street leads into the relative quiet of Manchester Square, dominated on its north side by the Georgian mansion of Hertford House, home of the Wallace Collection and a Marylebone must-see. In 2000 the Collection celebrated the centenary of its opening with the completion of architect Rick Mather's glass roof over the central courtyard of the old house, creating a sculpture garden and room for a smart French restaurant (*Café Bagatelle*, T020-7563 9505, open same hours as the Collection), as well as the redevelopment of the basement to provide a library, lecture theatre and three new galleries.

That said, the peculiar pleasure of a visit here has not been diminished: as well as the masterpieces on the walls – some of which are superb, including **Hals**' *The Laughing Cavalier*, **Rembrandt**'s portrait of his son Titus, **Velazquez**'s *Lady with a Fan* and **Delacroix**'s *Execution of the Doge Marino Faliero* – the best thing about the Wallace Collection remains the way that is has preserved intact the particular tastes, in fine art, furniture, and, more bizarrely, medieval armour and weaponry, of a succession of 18th- and 19th-century grandees, the Marquess of Hertford and their illegitimate heir Sir Richard Wallace.

The house & its extraordinary collection of 18th-century French paintings were bequeathed to the nation in 1897 by Lady Wallace

The most inspiring purpose-built gallery (**Gallery 22**) is at the back of the house on the first floor, reached by a sweeping staircase with a spectacular early 18th-century French balustrade. Turning right at the top of the stairs takes you through the room that was once Lady Wallace's boudoir – now hung with paintings from the 18th-century 'cult of sensibility' and home to a pair of Boulard chairs intended for Louis XVI's card room at Fontainebleau – and then a series of rooms displaying more pre- and post-Revolutionary French furniture and art.

The beautiful **great gallery** lies at the end, full of remarkable 17th-century European masterpieces, by the likes of Titian, Rubens, Poussin, and Van Dyck, all vying for space with the famous works mentioned above.

Continuing clockwise round the house are galleries devoted to Dutch and Flemish paintings, and just before arriving back on the landing, a gallery with six mid-to-late 18th-century views of Venice, two by Canaletto and four by Guardi, above a Riesener roll-top desk from 1769.

Back on the ground floor by the front entrance, **Gallery 5** (and the Hallway) was restored in 1995 to its former glory as the front state room and decorated with portraits of types like George IV as the Prince of Wales who would have visited the house in its heyday. Beyond it, going anti-clockwise round the courtyard, are galleries reflecting Sir Richard Wallace's enthusiasm for strange medieval and baroque objets d'art. Next are rooms packed full of a staggering array of renaissance and medieval European and 200-year-old Oriental weapons and armour, including a pair of jousting gauntlets from the middle ages inscribed 'amor'.

■ *Open 1000-1700 Mon-Sat, 1400-1700 Sun. Admission free (£3 donation requested). Restaurant and bookshop. T020-7935 0687, www.the-wallace-collection.org.uk Buses: 2, 13, 30, 74, 82, 113, 139, 189, 274.*

Turning right down Wigmore Street leads through Cavendish Square – from where Harley Street and all its very expensive private medical practices head dead straight north – to Langham Place and John Nash's round **Church of All Souls**, designed with its pointy spire in 1822 to provide a suitable conclusion to the march of his Regent Street forced to wiggle west north of Oxford Circus by an obstinate landowner called Langham.

Central London

Behind, at the start of Portland Place's stately drive up to Regent's Park, stands Broadcasting House, the heart of the BBC since 1932 and a place of mainly sentimental value. The **BBC Experience** here involves a guided tour of the building, telling the story of the Beeb's more than 75 years of broadcasting, and includes an opportunity to present the weather and visionmix a scene from their most popular soap opera, *Eastenders*. Fun for kids perhaps, neither the tour or hands-on displays are up to the standard that the Museum of the Moving Image achieved on the South Bank. ■ *First tour 1000 (Mon 1100), last tour 1630 (Sun 1630) until 1800. Admission £7.50, £6.50 under-16s. T0870-6030304.*

Broadcasting House
Most of the BBC's activity is nowadays concentrated further west in White City, where backstage tours are available to over-16s

Further up Portland Place, at No 66, is the RIBA Architecture Gallery. The gallery's Florence Hall was refitted and redeveloped in the autumn of 2000 and is now a large, airy and inviting space for exhibitions of architectural competitions, new projects, and architectural subjects of more general interest. ■ *Open 1000-1800 Mon-Fri, 1000-1700 Sat; bookshop and café. Ticket line, T020-7307 3792, programme details on T020-7307 3770, www.architecture.com*

RIBA Architecture Gallery

Regent's Park

Portland Place ends up in Nash's beautiful **Park Crescent**, the perfect introduction to his masterpiece, Regent's Park itself. The highlights of the park today are London Zoo (see below), the rose gardens, rockeries and Open-Air Theatre in Queen Mary's Gardens, and the Boating Lake, but the scale of its rolling, carefully planned layout makes the whole place a joy to explore.

From Park Crescent and Regent's Park tube, the Broad Walk begins within the Outer Circle, continuing the line of Portland Place straight up to Gloucester Green near Camden Town. About a third of the way up the Walk, beyond the lovely Avenue Gardens and the English Gardens, Chester Road cuts across it, left into the Inner Circle and Queen Mary's Gardens. Here there's a small ornamental lake, set among alpine rockeries and a cascade, as well as extraordinary rose gardens at their best in June although flowering well into the autumn.

In summer, the Chester Gate Lodge, off Chester Road, serves drinks & snacks in a little cottage, the oldest building in the park

The **Open-Air Theatre** stages enchanting plays during the summer (see page 425) and the *Park Café* (T020-7935 5729) is the largest of the park's 10 refreshment points, a self-service canteen with plenty of outside seating. During winter, only this one and the *Broadwalk Park Café*, a strange little chalet further north, are open.

Behind Queen Mary's Gardens lies the **Boating Lake**, and further round, the Boathouse for the hire of rowing boats and electric launches. The lake abounds in wild and domesticated waterfowl, the number of herons a good sign of healthy fish stocks, and it's an officially recognized inland bird observatory. There's an identification board near the stage door of the Open-Air Theatre. Near the northeastern arm of the lake, by the Children's Boating Lake, can be seen the distinctive domes of the London Central Mosque at Hanover Gate.

Back on the east side of the park, the Broad Walk continues past Cumberland Green and alongside the fence of London Zoo, a stretch recognizable as the place that Richard E Grant's failed-actor Withnail gazes mournfully at the pacing wolves as he quotes Hamlet at the end of *Withnail and I*. The Walk finally crosses the Outer Circle again (left here leads to the front entrance of the Zoo) and after crossing over the Regent's Canal hits Prince Albert Road. Further on, Primrose Hill provides an excellent viewpoint over London.

■ *Open 0500 until dusk daily. Boating on main lake from Apr-Sep, rowing and electric launches, information from Boathouse, T020-7486 4759. Also Children's Boating Lake: rowing, canoeing and pedalos (see also directory box on page 194). Information Office, The Store Yard, Inner Circle. T020-7486 7905.*

London Zoo

London Zoo is best reached either by a walk through the park, or by the waterbus service along the Regent's Canal from Camden Lock or Little Venice Nearest tube: Camden Town; bus 274

The zoo first opened to the public in 1828 and rapidly became a fashionable freak show. Monkeys, kangaroos, zebras and emus were some of the animals that people flocked to gawp at and prod. Mercifully all that's changed, and the top priorities now for the Zoololgical Society of London's gardens are research and conservation. As well as nurturing a particularly important collection of Golden Lion Tamarin monkeys, of which only about 500 are believed still to exist in the wild, all the animals have been given more space, and those not threatened with extinction or especially unsuited to confinement have been sent elsewhere. While this may lead to some disappointment for children – Bear Mountain is now home to only a couple of reclusive bears and there are no large hippos, polar bears or pandas – it makes a visit here much less harrowing for animal lovers.

Over 35 acres of winding paths, tunnels and bridges, the zoo still manages to care for an extraordinary variety of animals, from dwarf mongeese and pigmy marmosets, looking like a cross between a chimp and a small bird, to black rhinos, gorillas and Asian elephants, lions, tigers and Mexican red-knee spiders. Highlights of a day here include feeding the penguins at 1430, and at the same time on Fridays only, the snakes, and elephant bathtime at 1530. Every day at 1700 visitors can meet the one-eared giraffe called Achilles. Like the rest of his kind, he can never lie down because of the blood pressure in his brain.

Many of the buildings and enclosures are interesting in themselves, from the clapperboard aquarium to the graceful shape of the penguin pool and the soaring cage of Snowdon's aviary. The Web of Life Biodiversity Centre was opened in 1999, constructed to the latest high-tech energy-saving design, home to over 100 different species including a giant clam, giant anteaters and jellyfish. The Fountain Court in the middle of the zoo has a decent self-service restaurant, good-value cone ice creams in the *Fountain Café* and in summer, an open-air barbecue.

■ *Open daily 1000-1730 summer, 1000-1600 winter. £10 adults, £7 under-16s, £8.50 concession. T020-7722 3333, www.londonzoo.co.uk, or www.zsl.org Buses 274.*

Sherlock Holmes Museum

Leaving Regent's Park from the opposite corner to the Zoo, at Clarence Gate, leads onto Baker Street. Just down from here, the Sherlock Holmes Museum, is actually at 239 Baker Street, but has battled it out with the Post Office and Abbey National Building Society at 221 to claim the sleuth's fictional address. A passable reconstruction of his Georgian townhouse on four levels as described in the books, the place pleases fans but may seem expensive to the merely curious. ■ *Open 0930-1800 daily. Admission £6. T020-7935 8866.*

Look out for the statue of Sherlock Holmes outside Baker St tube station

Central London

Opposite it, the **Sherlock Holmes Memorabila Shop**, 230 Baker Street, NW1, T020-7486 1426, features the set from the TV series (admission £1.50) and sells videos, deerstalkers, Inverness Harris Tweed capes (£400) and Meerschaum pipes among other things.

The Planetarium

Left onto the Marylebone Road at Baker Street tube and it's impossible to miss the dome of the London Planetarium and next door, Madame Tussaud's. The Planetarium was finally updated in 2000: the show is now shorter (20 minutes) and much more sci-fi. Movie music and projections onto the darkened roof of the dome whizz through the history of the cosmos and make some attempt to explain astronomy. The refurbished exhibition on discovering the universe, including a full scale model of a moon rover, has been made more interactive. Even so, it's probably still only worth seeing if visiting the much more famous attraction next door.

■ *Open 1030-1700 first show summer 1030 daily, winter weekends 1030, weekdays 1230. Not bookable in advance. Admission £6.75, £4.65 for under-16s, £5.30 OAPs, not recommended for under-5s. T0870-400 3000. See below for combined entry tickets with Madam Tussauds.*

Madame Tussaud's

The popularity of Madame Tussaud's continues unabated, a surefire hit with tourists since shortly after the French Revolution when the aristocratic French woman exhibited the waxwork portraits of some of her friends who had lost their heads. In those days it may have been understandable, when people had little chance to see what the rich and famous looked like. Nowadays it's more baffling.

To avoid the queues, either book at least an hour in advance, or go first thing in the morning or in the afternoon after 1400 during the week, or at weekends after 1330

The latest stars to join the array of notables cast in wax – the likenesses are fairly hit and miss: some look as if they might just turn round and shake your hand, others look like waxwork dummies – are the likes of *Carry On* filmstar-turned-soap queen Barbara Windsor, the footballer David Beckham, supervamp Liz Hurley and actor Robert Carlyle, joining screen superstars like Sean Connery, Morgan Freeman and Samuel L Jackson. In the Grand Hall, monarchs and politicians rub shoulders, while the Chamber of Horrors remains the most crowded of the rooms, a gruesome celebration of goriness in very dubious taste that children adore. Finally, the Spirit of London dark ride speeds comically through London's history in five minutes, concluding appropriately with the lascivious comedian Benny Hill.

The whole moderately entertaining visit should take about an hour and a half, after which the unfamiliarity of strangers' faces on the streets comes as a real relief.

■ *Open 1000-1730 Mon-Fri, 0930-1730 Sat & Sun. 1000-1630 bookable in 30 min timeslots. Booking fee £1 per ticket. Admission to Tussaud's only: £11.95, £8.45 under-16s, under-5s free. Combined entry with The Planetarium: £14.45, £9.95 under-16s, £11.65 OAPs. T0870-400 3000, www.madam-tussauds.com*

Eating and drinking

Expensive

Marylebone has yet to become a destination for diners in the evenings, although at lunchtimes the hordes of office workers in the area raise demand

The best destination for a smart meal out in Marylebone is *The Orrery*, 55 Marylebone High St, W1, T020-7616 8000, one of the smaller and more recent additions to Terence Conran's gastronomic empire, complete with all his trademark designer trimmings and serving the freshest modern European food in a swish atmosphere. Another marginally less expensive option on the High St is *Ibla*, 89 Marylebone High St, W1, T020-7224 3799, a fine modern Milanese restaurant in the rooms vacated by *Villandry*, that belie the superb quality of their French way with the freshest ingredients. *Villandry* now occupies minimalist premises further east at 170 Great Portland St, W1, T020-7631 3131. Otherwise the restaurants in Mayfair are probably are better bet.

Mid-range
● *on map, page 186*

Purple Sage, 90 Wigmore St, W1, T020-7486 1912, is a laid-back place doing modern British cuisine, with set menus focusing on game and fish in season alongside Italian staples. The Irish restaurant above the *O'Conor Don* on Marylebone Lane (see Pubs below) is also understandably popular with lunching suits.

Cheap

The Golden Hind, 73 Marylebone Lane, W1, T020-7486 3644, is an old-school eat-in or takeaway fish and chip shop done up in a timeless style but perhaps more expensive than you might expect. The *Golden Eagle*, 59 Marylebone Lane, T020-7935 3228, does scrummy Biggles sausages at lunchtimes. Nearby is *Wagamama*, 101a Wigmore St, T020-7409 0111, a branch of the popular Japanese canteen famous for its queues at lunchtimes but always worth the wait.

Further east on Wigmore St, *ITS*, 60 Wigmore St, W1, T020-7224 3484, is a good branch of the reliable chain of pasta cafés. *Kerala*, 15 Great Castle St, W1, T020-7580 2125, is a busy south Indian restaurant near Oxford Circus.

Nearer Baker St, *Thai West*, 10 Crawford St, W1, T020-7224 1367, is a stylish basement Thai doing good-value set meals with a lively Thai tapas bar upstairs.

Nearer the Edgware Rd, unfussy and unlicensed (BYOB) Persian food can be enjoyed at *Patogh*, 8 Crawford Place, W1, T020-7262 4015.

Cafés & sandwich bars

On Marylebone High St, the unmissable destination is *Patisserie Valerie*, 105 Marylebone High St, T020-7935 6240, an excellent outpost of the patisserie française, less arty but more sophisticated than the one in Soho. Nearby, for a simple but expertly constructed sandwich made from a wide choice of breads, head for *De Gustibus*, 53 Blandford St, W1, T020-7486 6608, smaller than their new one in Borough, non-smoking but with a few tables outside. The *Quiet Revolution*, 62 Weymouth St, W1, T020-7487 5683, specialize in 100 % organic soups and delicious stews for about £5 to eat in or take away.

Five of the best: outdoor eating

★

- *Park Café*, Regent's Park.
- *The Founder's Arms*, Bankside.
- *Ball's Brothers*, Cheapside, City.
- *The Lido*, Hyde Park.
- *Blue Bird*, King's Road, Chelsea.

The *O'Conor Don*, 88 Marylebone Lane, W1, T020-7935 9311, is an Irish original, tatty and informal, and serving good food at the bar all day and in the restaurant upstairs for lunch and supper. The *William Wallace*, 31 Aybrook St, W1, T020-7487 4937, is its Scottish equivalent, although more of a standard boozer it does pull some exceptional pints from north of the border like Deuchar's IPA, relatively hard to find in London. *The Dover Castle*, 43 Weymouth Mews, W1, T020-7580 4412, is a fine and cheery Samuel Smith's pub hidden away in a small mews off Portland Place.

Nearer Regent's Park, the *Windsor Castle*, 98 Park Rd, NW1, T020-7723 9262, is a grand and busy old place with a pool table. More hip than any of these, nearer Baker St, is *Atlantis*, 114-117 Crawford St, W1, T020-7224 2878, a submarine music and cocktail bar in a basement decorated with an aquatic theme. In the far west of Marylebone, nearer Edgware, *The Chapel*, 48 Chapel St, NW1, T020-7402 9220, is a large gastropub popular with local office workers.

Pubs & bars

Marylebone is not blessed with the most exciting places to drink in London, but makes up for that with some very good pubs

Central London

▶▶ *Go to page 425 for entertainment & nightlife*

Shopping

The High St in particular is still going steadily upmarket. A little further afield in Lisson Grove, Church St is also well worth exploring for a less expensive and more offbeat expedition.

Quirky shops on Marylebone Lane include *Button Queen*, 19 Marylebone Lane, W1, T020-7935 1505, stocking a huge variety of old and modern buttons, buckles and cufflinks made from buttons, and *Biggles Gourmet Sausages*, 66 Marylebone Lane, W1, T020-7224 5937, making a wide range of superb full-meat sausages and nothing else.

Heading down the High St from the Marylebone Rd, signs of its prosperity are the presence of the *Conran Shop*, 55 Marylebone High St, T020-7723 2223, full of designer accessories and furnishings, *Agnes B*, 40-41 Marylebone High St, T020-7935 5556 and her neat fashions for women, and the newly expanded shop of *Shaker*, 72-73 Marylebone High St, W1, T020-7935 9461, the puritan-chic furniture, gifts and home-accessory designers.

A little further down are *Daunt's Books for Travellers*, 83 Marylebone High St, W1, T020-7224 2295, one of London's most charming travel bookshops, its galleried space stacked with just about every conceivable new title to do with travel as well as carrying an excellent stock of second-hand. On Wigmore St, *Talking Books*, 11 Wigmore St, W1, T020-7491 4117, is probably the largest stockist in Europe of talking books, cassettes and CDs, mostly in English but a few in French.

Marylebone Lane and High St are the main shopping streets in Marylebone itself

Further west, *Field and Trek*, 105 Baker St, W1, T020-7224 0049, was the first and largest branch in London of the expert mountaineering and hill walking chain. Northwest of the Marylebone Rd, in Lisson Grove, Church St has one of London's lesser-known but still lively fruit 'n' veg and clothes markets, at its best on Saturdays. *Alfie's Antique*

Market, 13-25 Church St, NW8, T020-7723 6066 (open Tue-Sat), is a rambling place with countless stalls and everything under the sun on sale at reasonable prices. Nearby, the *Gallery of Antique Costume and Textiles*, 2 Church St, NW8, T020-7723 9981, stocks yards and yards of antique cloth of a very high quality.

Transport

Bicycle *Wheelie Serious*, 63 George St, Marylebone, W1, T020-7487 3233 do bicycle hire (£10 a day), as well as selling and repairing two-wheelers.

Buses **Down Baker St southbound**:
No 2 to Brixton via Marble Arch, Victoria, Vauxhall and Stockwell.
No 13 to Aldwych, via Oxford Circus, Piccadilly Circus, and Trafalgar Square.
No 74 to Putney via Marble Arch, Hyde Park Corner, Knightsbridge, South Ken, Earl's Court, and Fulham Cross.
No 82 to Victoria via Marble Arch.
No 139 to Trafalgar Square via Oxford Circus and Piccadilly Circus.

Up Gloucester Place northbound:
No 13 to Golders Green, via Park Rd and Swiss Cottage.
No 30 to Hackney via Euston, King's Cross, Islington, and Highbury.
No 82 to Finchley via Park Rd, Swiss Cottage and Golders Green.
No 139 to West Hampstead via Lisson Grove.
No 274 to Angel Islington via Park Rd, The Zoo, Camden Town, Agar Grove and Caledonian Rd.

Along Portland Place:
No 135 and **C2** to Camden Town.

Along Marylebone Road:
No 27 to Chiswickr via Camden Town, Paddington, Notting Hill Gate, Kensington High St and Hammersmith.
No 30 to Marble Arch.

Canal transport London Waterbus Company service daily from Little Venice to Camden Lock, leaving *Full information:* The Zoo to Camden Lock hourly 1035-1635, last trip one-way 1735, to Little Venice *T020-7482 2660* hourly 1015-1615, last trip 1750 (summer timetable). Journey either way takes about 15 mins, £1.50, £2.50 round trips 40 mins. Winter timetable: hourly 1100-1600 Sat, Sun only. No need to book, pay on the boat.

Directory

Sports Seymour Leisure Centre, Seymour Place, W1, T020-7723 8019, bookings T020-7724 5057, www.courtneys.co.uk Open 0700-2000 Mon-Tue, Fri Sat, 0700-2100; Wed, Thu; 0800-2000 Sun. £2.15 a session. Large and well-appointed public swimming pool and leisure centre. **Regent's Park Tennis Centre**, York Bridge, NW1, T020-7486 4216. 12 courts newly resurfaced. Non-members £9 an hour, open throughout the year 0800 until dusk daily throughout the year.
Regent's Park Golf and Tennis School, Outer Circle, Regent's Park, NW1, T020-7724 0643. Golf lessons on driving range, non-members £25 for half an hour, Tennis £30 for 30 mins, throughout the year, open 0800-2100.

Central London

Plenty along Marylebone Rd, southbound down Baker St and on Wigmore St.   Taxis

Marylebone Station serves suburban Buckinghamshire and the Chilterns.   Trains

Bond St (Central and Jubilee lines). Baker St (Bakerloo, Hammersmith & City, Metropoli- Tubes
tan, Circle and Jubilee). Great Portland St (Hammersmith & City, Metropolitan and Circle). Camden Town (Northern line).

Euston, St Pancras and King's Cross

At street level London's rail gateway to England and the North hardly seems to be plugged into the big city at all. Somehow the area gets the worst of all worlds, sandwiched between more attractive parts of town like Regent's Park, Blooms-bury, Clerkenwell, Islington and Camden. It's cut off by the constant traffic on the huge Euston Road rushing through east-west, only stopping at the lights to let more traffic skoot north-south.

⊖ *King's Cross
St Pancras tube;
Euston tube;
Euston Square;
Warren St*

Central London

King's Cross especially has developed a bad reputation for prostitution, drugs and street crime. Most people hurry through on the Underground without even sur-facing. That said, the whole place may well soon be transformed by the arrival of the Eurostar terminal at St Pancras and this long-neglected and rundown district gets the break it deserves. Even the unlovely Euston Road has cleaned up its act in recent years. The opening of the state-of-the-art **British Library** *here represented the first bold public statement of government confidence in an area that now looks set to boom. Meanwhile on Friday and Saturday nights the Scala and the marshalling yards north of the stations are still a Mecca for clubbers, injecting a welcome dose of wide-eyed and healthy nightlife into one of the city's most desolate backyards.*

History

Until the development of the New Road (modern Marylebone, Euston and Pentonville Roads) in the mid-18th century, the area north of Bloomsbury and Fitzrovia was largely fields, with the River Fleet running alongside an ancient track (modern Pancras Road) up to Old St Pancras Church. There was a small village called Battle Bridge, but none of the settlement or manored estates to be found in neighbouring Marylebone.

The furthest north most people ventured was to visit St Chad's Well at the top of the Gray's Inn Road for its medicinal waters, or to seek sanctuary in the smallpox hospital located at King's Cross. Nursery gardens grew in modern Euston Square, while cattle were driven along the New Road on their way to Smithfield Market. But the laying of the road, and the arrival of the Regent's Canal in 1820 further north sparked a hotchpotch of development.

Somers Town began to grow from 1786, but remained an isolated sub-urb and later suffered at the hands of the railways. Much of the area became an industrial suburb fed by

• •

Hotels in the area

B *Shaw Park Plaza*

C *Euston Travel Inn Capital*

D *The Carlton Hotel*

E-F *Ashlee House*

E-F *The Generator.*

▸ **Go to page 446**

Euston, St Pancras & King's Cross

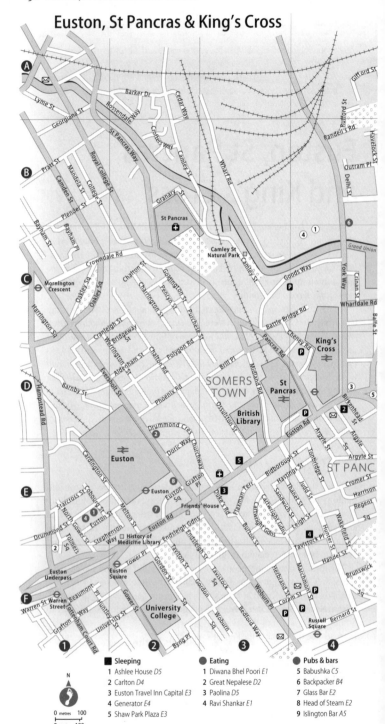

N

0 metres 100
0 yards 100

■ Sleeping	● Eating	● Pubs & bars
1 Ashlee House *D5*	1 Diwana Bhel Poori *E1*	5 Babushka *C5*
2 Carlton *D4*	2 Great Nepalese *D2*	6 Backpacker *B4*
3 Euston Travel Inn Capital *E3*	3 Paolina *D5*	7 Glass Bar *E2*
4 Generator *E4*	4 Ravi Shankar *E1*	8 Head of Steam *E2*
5 Shaw Park Plaza *E3*		9 Islington Bar *A5*

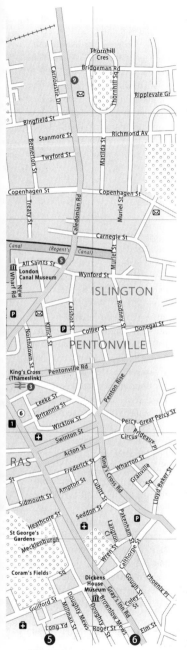

○ **Entertainment**
1 Bagley's Studios *C4*
2 Camden People's Theatre *F1*
3 Courtyard Theatre *D4*
4 Cross *C4*
5 Scala *D4*
6 Water Rats *D5*

the canal. Gasworks, timber and building trades, factories and workshops dotted the wasteland and brick fields, and St Pancras developed a reputation for furniture and piano manufacturing businesses. Agar Town, a shanty town dubbed 'Ague Town' whose stench Dickens claimed "is enough to knock down a bullock", grew up almost overnight in 1851 on fields that later became the site of St Pancras Station.

The Fig Mead scheme, the Duke of Bedford's attempt to develop a model middle-class suburb on land now occupied by Mornington Crescent, was also felled by the railway. The Duke's interest in the area, however, didn't extend to establishing links with his Bloomsbury estate. With the development of Seymour Street and Caledonian Road, and the dark courts and backyard industries springing up on Chalton and Ossulton Streets, he blocked off Seymour Street with gates in order to preserve the superior tone of Bloomsbury.

The advent of the railways ensured that when Nash built Albany Street on the eastern edge of Regent's Park it was to serve as a boundary between the wealthier west and the inferior east. **Euston Station** was the first railway station (1838), where an enormous Doric arch welcomed travellers into a magnificent great hall. Railway carriages would be drawn up the hill to Camden on a winch, and on their return ran downhill under the control of a brakeman. As was to become the fashion, the Adelaide and Victoria Hotels partially covered the grand screen of the station, but the structure's demolition for its current building in 1963 lost London one of its more dramatic architecural sights.

King's Cross, an altogether plainer affair, was built in the 1850s, but **St Pancras** (1863-72) earned the critics approval. "It stands without rival for palatial beauty, comfort and convenience" wrote one Victorian admirer, although the architect himself observed that the Midland Grand Hotel that was built around the train shed was "possibly too good for its purpose". Development continued to be patchy throughout the 20th century. **The Friends' House**, headquarters for the Quakers, was built in 1927, the St Pancras (now Camden) Town Hall in 1937 – it's flown the Red Flag in its time – and the new **British Library** opened to the public in 1998. In 1924 the vicar of St Mary's Somers Town observed: "Overcrowding and poverty are here being used by the Devil in order to steal from the children of God the health and happiness which are their right". Housing estates and blocks of flats were built between Euston and St Pancras, and warehouses and factories still share space with the railways.

Sights

King's Cross & the Euston Rd are not obvious destinations for a sightseeing trip, but both have enough places of interest to wile away more than a couple of hours

During daylight hours the streets behind King's Cross Station can even be an atmospheric and rewarding place to explore; after dark though they become central London's red-light district. King's Cross Station forecourt itself is still not a good place to linger, next to a fraught and chaotic road junction that has long been so depressing that everyone keeps hoping it will be 'regenerated' in the near future.

Across Pancras Road to the west is the magnificent red-brick neo-Gothic palace of **St Pancras Station**, formerly the Midland Grand Hotel. Its architect, Sir George Gilbert Scott, had hoped to build something similar in Whitehall but later wrote that he 'was glad to be able to erect one building in that style in London'. And most people passing the place today are glad that he was too, not least because its optimistic spirit now looks rather forlorn and ridiculous since being left to stand empty for several decades. Things really are set to change here though with the opening of the St Pancras Channel Tunnel rail terminal for Eurostar, even though that's now not expected until at least 2005.

A walk up Pancras Road between the two stations passes cobbled Cheney Road on the right, a generic 'East End' film location. At its northern end Goods Way comes in from York Way beneath spooky blackened railway arches. Sadly the old iron gasholders that have long made a dramatic contribution to the skyline here are due to be dismantled in July 2001 to make way for the Channel Tunnel rail link.

Their brooding presence will certainly be missed by the peaceful haven that can be found just up the road at the **Camley Street Natural Park**, near the junction with Goods Way, a sweet little community nature reserve run by the London Wildlife Trust. A place to watch dragonflies, herons, and even the occasional kingfisher in late autumn, these two wildflower acres beside the canal with their quiet reed-whispering pools are an unexpected inner city oasis. ■ *Open Mon-Thu 0900-1700, Sat 1100-1700, Sun 1000-1600. Admission free. T020-7833 2311.*

Another small local initiative can be found by continuing up Goods Way and crossing York Way to the **London Canal Museum**, at 12-13 New Wharf Road, N1. The museum tells the story of the Regent's Canal and the boats that worked it, especially those that supplied the ice house which the museum has preserved. Moored in the canal alongside is a renovated 1940s' tugboat. ■ *Open Tue-Sun 1000-1630. Admission £2.50, £1.25 concession. T020-7713 0836.*

Back by St Pancras Station over Midland Road, at 96 Euston Rd, NW1, stands the British Library, which has had its problems. Way over budget and a decade behind schedule, the building was finally completed in 1997 to the usual chorus of dismay and disapproval.

British Library
The British Library is the best reason to visit the Euston Rd on purpose on foot

Whatever people have made of the exterior, with its straight lines of plain red brick and dark green trim offset by its splendid Victorian neighbour, the interior has provoked few complaints. Cool acres of white stone and careful attention to details, such as the handrails, the spacing of the steps and the diffusion of light, all combine to make the building a joy to use. Anyone engaged in research can apply for free membership to gain access to the reading rooms and some 18 million volumes, as well as maps, manuscripts, the national sound archive and the newspaper library in Colindale, while the two permanent exhibitions (that can be seen without a pass) are well worth a visit in themselves.

The **Treasures Gallery** is a beautiful and carefully explained display of precious books and manuscripts: the illuminated Lindisfarne Gospel from around 700AD; a copy of the Magna Carta of 1215 – the document that laid the foundations for Parliamentary democracy; the Sherborne Missal – the only painted book in England to have survived the Reformation; Shakespeare's First Folio from 1623; and the manuscripts of great authors such as Jane Austen, Thomas Hardy, Charles Dickens and Lewis Carrol.

The library also has a good restaurant & two cafés

In **The Workshop** there are regular demos of bookbinding, caligraphy and printing, a reconstruction of a 15th-century illuminator's workshop and an exhibition on the history of recorded sound. Another space is reserved for special temporary exhibitions generally of a high standard.

■ *Open 0900-1800 Mon, Wed, Thu, Fri; 0930-2000 Tue; 0930-1700 Sat; 1100-1700 Sun. Admission free. T020-7412 7332, www.bl.uk*

A walk down Judd Street opposite the Library leads to Brunswick Square and **Coram's Fields** where Captain Thomas Coram persuaded the gentry to build a hospital for destitute children in the middle of the 18th century. A great friend of Hogarth, who did a very sympathetic portrait of him and persuaded other artists such as Reynolds and Gainsborough to contribute paintings, and of Handel, whose organ recitals made the hospital's chapel popular with the likes of Dickens, Coram's Foundation still exists in Berkhamsted.

The art collection hangs in an exact replica of the old Court Room at **The Foundling Museum**, 40 Brunswick Square, WC1, T020-7841 3600. (Closed from end of April 2001 for a two-year refurbishment.) St George's Gardens to the north of the children's playground in Coram's Fields are a delightful place for a picnic and a good starting point for an exploration of this often overlooked corner of Bloomsbury.

Back on the Euston Road, at No 173, is **The Friends' House**, the Quaker centre where there's a small exhibition on Thomas Penn and the slave trade abolitionists. ■ *Open 1000-1700 Mon-Fri. Sun meetings at 1100. T020-7663 1000.*

Beyond Euston Station, on the same side of the road, the **Two10 Gallery**, 210 Euston Road, puts on interesting exhibitions on current issues in medicine. ■ *Open 0900-1800 Mon-Fri. Admission free.* It's part of the Wellcome Trust, 183 Euston Road, NW1 (information line, T020-7611 7211), which is currently refurbishing its award-winning museum on biodmedical reasearch, although it's still possible to visit the **History of Medicine Library**. ■ *Open*

Central London

Mon, Wed, Fri 0945-1715, Tue, Thu 0945-1915, Sat 0945-1300. Admission free. Personal ID required for first visit which must be made Mon-Fri 0900-1700. www.wellcome.ac.uk/library

Eating and drinking

Cheap Not a hot destination for gourmets, King's Cross is surrounded by fast-food joints and dodgy cafés. Euston doesn't fare much better, although behind the station Drummond St is a famous destination for fans of bargain vegetarian south Indian food. *Ravi Shankar*, 133-135 Drummond St, NW1, T020-7388 6458, is the most mellow and comfortable, while the *Diwana Bhel Poori House*, 121 Drummond St, NW1, T020-7387 5556, is very basic and also unlicensed, so diners can bring their own booze.

On the other side of the station the *Great Nepalese*, 48 Eversholt St, NW1, T020-7388 6737, is a quirky little restaurant, probably the only one in London specializing entirely in Nepalese dishes, really quite different from Indian food, especially their famous starter, momo, thin pastry-based snacks that started life as street food but here have been raised to greater heights.

Cafés & Again, the area is packed with places catering badly for the passing trade. Exceptions are
sandwich bars the cafés in the British Library and also *Paolina*, 181 King's Cross Road, WC1, T020-7278 8176, a BYOB Thai café that is a reliable bargain, only open for lunch and supper.

Pubs & bars An exception near Euston Station is the *Head of Steam*, 1 Eversholt St, NW1, T020-7383
Many of the pubs 3359, www.headofsteam.com, part of a select nationwide chain that regularly stocks a
in the area are wide variety of excellent real ales, and where the train memorabilia adds charm to the
best avoided. convivial atmosphere, not solely appreciated by trainspotters.
▶▶ *Go to page 425* Another one-off right outside Euston Station is the women-only *Glass Bar*, a private
for entertainment members (mainly lesbian) club that welcomes any member of the fairer sex into the
& nightlife Tardis-like interior of one of the monumental windowless gatehouses of the old station. T020-7387 6184. Open 1700-late. www.glassbar.ndo.co.uk

Three bars near King's Cross are very popular for pre-club warm-ups: *Babushka*, 125 Caledonian Rd, N1, T020-7837 1924, with its strange stylish furniture and reasonable restaurant; and further up the Caledonian Rd, the *Islington Bar*, 342 Caledonian Rd, N1, T020-7609 4917, open until 2400 Mon-Thu, until 0200 Fri, Sat £3, a way-out and wild venue for DJ-driven dance nights. Even more crazy is the *Backpacker*, 126 York Way, N1, T020-7278 8318. Open Fri & Sat 1900-0200, Sun 1530-2300, with its sawdust floor, clinical 'shots chair', very loud music and bumper bargain all-you-can-drink offers, dedicated to drunkeness in the way only Australians do well.

Shopping

Not much in the area, although *Laurence Corner*, 62-64 Hampstead Rd, NW1, T020-7813 1010, boasts the strange combination of an Army surplus store and camping corner, with fancy dress hire at the back. A theatrical period costume costs £38 for a week. Nearby, at 151 Drummond St, *Delta of Venus*, T020-387 3037, is a shrine to pop culture of the 60s and 70s and great place for cheap retro clothing. It specializes in 60s and 70s and mid-80s second-hand clothes, pop and glamour, records and CDs. Open Mon-Sat 1000-1800. Next door, *Planet Bazaar*, 147 Drummond St, NW1, T020-7387 8326, does 60 and 70s furniture, lighting, telephones, mirrors and artwork.

Central London

Transport

Along Euston Rd:

No 10 between Hammersmith and Archway via Kensington, Knightsbridge, Hyde Park Corner, Marble Arch, Oxford Circus, Euston, King's Cross, York Way and Tufnell Park.
No 18 from Euston to Baker St Station.
No 30 between Marble Arch and Hackney via Baker St, Euston, King's Cross, Islington, Highbury, and Dalston.
No 73 between Victoria and Stoke Newington via Hyde Park Corner, Marble Arch, Oxford Circus, Euston, King's Cross, Islington and Newington Green.
No 91 between Trafalgar Square and Crouch End via Aldwych, Kingsway, Euston, King's Cross, Caledonian Rd and Holloway.

Along Pancras Rd:

No 46 between King's Cross and Kensal Rise via Kentish Town, Hampstead Heath, Rosslyn Hill, Hampstead Station, Fitzjohn's Avenue, Swiss Cottage, St John's Wood, Warwick Avenue and West Kilburn.
No 214 between Liverpool St and Highgate via Moorgate, City Rd, Islington, King's Cross, Camden Town, Kentish Town and Parliament Hill Fields.

Along Eversholt St:

No 168 between Hampstead Heath and Elephant, via Haverstock Hill, Chalk Farm, Camden Town, Euston, Kingsway, Aldwych and Waterloo.
No 253 between Euston and Aldgate via Mornington Crescent, Camden Town, Holloway, Finsbury Park, Manor House, Stamford Hill, Hackney, Cambridge Heath and Bethnal Green.

There are usually plenty of taxis outside Euston & King's Cross & along Euston Rd.

King's Cross for Scotland (east coast), North of England and north London suburbs. **St Pancras** for north west London suburbs. **King's Cross Thameslink** for Brighton, the City, south and northeastern suburbs, and also for London Luton Airport. **Euston** for Scotland (west coast), North of England and Midlands, northwest London suburbs.

King's Cross St Pancras (Piccadilly, Northern, Victoria, Circle, Hammersmith & City and Metropolitan lines). Euston (Northern and Victoria lines), Euston Square (Hammersmith & City, Metropolitan and Circle lines) and Warren St (Northern and Victoria lines).

Buses

Taxis

Trains

Tubes

Central London

Bloomsbury and Fitzrovia

*Bloomsbury is the academic heart of London, the home of the acronym, full of august institutions better known as SOAS, UCL, RADA and ULU than by their full names, most of them part of the sprawling University of London. North of High Holborn, south of the Euston Road and west of Judd Street, its long straight streets of Georgian and Victorian brick can be gloomy in winter, but in bright sunshine the area's severe little squares with their flower- and tree-filled gardens are a delight. Then again it's no coincidence that this is also the place to find three of the city's most rewarding museums, all free, and each defying expectations in their different ways: the revitalized and monumental **British Museum** obviously, but also the serene and quiet beauty of the Chinese ceramics in the **Percival***

⊖ *Tottenham Court Rd tube for southwest Bloomsbury, including the British Museum. Russell Square tube for eastern Bloomsbury. Goodge St tube for Fitzrovia & Warren St for northern Fitzrovia*

David Foundation and the intriguing collection of ancient Egyptian artefacts in the *Petrie Museum*.

The student population ensures that the area is packed with reasonable places to eat and sleep, surrounded by lively pubs and excellent bookshops. To the west, over Tottenham Court Road, that ugly northbound arm of Oxford Street, Fitzrovia is the name that has been given to the blocks south of Fitzroy Square from here to Portland Place. Something like an upmarket version of Soho, on Charlotte Street and Goodge Street, it even achieves some of its southern neighbour's media buzz.

History

Bloomsbury and Fitzrovia have long acted as magnets for London's intellectual and medical communities. Hospitals and university buildings dominate the area, scattered in and around Georgian squares and modern developments. Once upon a time though it was a series of fields, interspersed with buildings such as Tottenham Court (on modern Grafton Way), and tributaries from the River Fleet crossing its eastern edge. By the early 18th century, there was still little by way of suburban developments, although the Republic and then the Restoration had seen the building of a few grand residences. Southampton House, (whose gardens lay along modern Southampton Row), Montague House (later the British Museum) and Thanet House sat alongside each other on modern Great Russell Street, but the view north was still over pasture and meadows to the villages of Hampstead and Highgate on the distant hills.

In the 1660s The Earl of Southampton, in a shrewd series of deals worthy of any modern property tycoon, began to develop the area. He built a square (now Bloomsbury Square) south of his house, in the process launching a new style for town houses. These narrow-fronted terraces, four stories high with accommodation for the servants in the loft and their workspace in the basement, were so celebrated that foreign Princes were brought to see it. (The square drew more visitors in the 1960s when the country's deepest car park was excavated under the gardens – seven levels fed by a twin helix of ramps devised to avoid damaging the plane trees' roots.) Other streets were laid, particularly Queen Square, where George III was to stay with his doctor, Dr Willis, while suffering the tempests of his illness, and Great Ormond Street, where the Hospital for Sick Children was to open in the 1850s.

The area's association with sick children had begun 100 years earlier with Thomas Coram's Foundling Hospital for the care of sick infants. It sat, isolated, near Coram Fields, and its work was aided by fundraising by Hogarth and Handel, an act repeated in 1929 by JM Barrie when he bequeathed the copyright for *Peter Pan* to the Great Ormond Street Hospital. Over the Tottenham Court Road, the Middlesex Hospital emerged on a site next to a pond on Windmill Street, and Goodge Street, laid out in Crab Tree Field in the 1740s, followed the emergence of

Hotels in the area

A Charlotte Street Hotel
A myHotel
B Blooms
B Hotel Russell
B Academy
C The Crescent Hotel
C Harlingford
C Mentone Hotel
C Morgan
C St Margaret
D The Jesmond
▸▸ *Go to page 446*

Berners, Newman and Hanway Streets 20 years earlier. When the estate passed to the Dukes of Bedford in the 18th century, development began in earnest.

From 1775 when work began on Bedford Square, through to the late 1820s, terraces and squares spread northwards up to New Road (modern Euston Road). Six hundred houses were built on the Foundling Hospital estate, Brunswick, Mecklenburgh and Russell Squares were laid out, and Thomas Cubbitt, the architect behind Belgravia and Pimlico, set to on Gordon and Woburn Squares which were still forming by the 1860s. (Some were protected as private enclaves by gates, which were only removed in 1893.)

The University of London, from small beginnings in 1836, stamped its mark on the area in 1932 with Senate House, a "bleak, blank, hideous" (Max Beerbohm) creation that was the model for the Ministry of Truth in Orwell's *1984*, having been the real Ministry of Information during the Second World War.

Throughout this period, Bloomsbury and Fitzrovia (the term is a 1930s creation) were popular with lawyers, (for its proximity to the Inns of Court) but also among London's most lively artistic, literary, and intellectual community. William Morris, Charles Dickens, Charles Darwin and later WB Yeats and GB Shaw all lived hereabouts, while the British Museum's Reading Room witnessed Karl Marx and Lenin poring over books. The Bloomsbury Group, (which included Virginia Woolf, EM Forster and Roger Fry) formed in the belief that an appreciation of art and beauty are essential to progress, earned much public disapproval and scorn through their openly risqué behaviour (love triangles and lesbianism, for instance).

A slightly later generation – Dylan Thomas, Augustus John, as well as the nation's hangman, Albert Pierrepoint – frequented the pubs of Fitzrovia in the 1940s, most notably the Fitzroy Tavern.

After some damage during both wars (a Zeppelin bomb exploded in Queen Square in 1915) development continued, with Brunswick Square and the British Telecom Tower both examples of 1960s modernization, and the artists moved to Soho. The area's medical traditions have remained. With no less than eight hospitals, the area's reputation for being 'very healthful' is well founded.

Sights

British Museum

Most people visit Bloomsbury for the British Museum. With its new slogan 'illuminating world cultures', it now comes closer to that ideal in spectacular style. Anyone who's been before but not recently and expects to find this venerable institution untouched by the modern age is in for a big surprise. Architect Norman Foster's redevelopment of the central Great Court, opened in December 2000, has turned the museum's long-hidden central quadrangle into the largest covered square in Europe, rechristened the Elizabeth II Great Court.

Buses 1, 8, 10, 19, 24, 25, 29, 38, 55, 59, 68, 73, 91, 98, 134, 168, 188 & 242

A beautiful canopy made up of a latticework of 3312 unique panes of glass now wraps itself around the dome of the round Reading Room, free-standing once again at the heart of the museum. From beneath the grand old front portico on Great Russell Street little seems that different. Through the tall front doors though, visitors pass to startling effect straight into a vast creamy space to be

There are late openings for the major galleries on Thu & Fri

Central London

confronted by the Reading Room, freshly clad in white stone like a huge post box in the middle of the indoor square. The four classical porticos on each side have also been revealed again, the southern one causing some controversy because of the use of French limestone, less expensive than the Portland stone of the originals. Even so the overall impression of light and space the new design creates is generous and magnificent. And the museum is now much more accessible to London's working population, with longer opening hours.

Bloomsbury & Fitzrovia

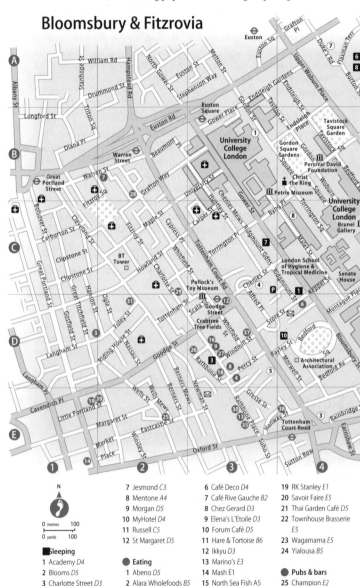

0 metres 100
0 yards 100

■ Sleeping
1 Academy *D4*
2 Blooms *D5*
3 Charlotte Street *D3*
4 Crescent *A5*
5 Generator *A5*
6 Harlingford *A4*
7 Jesmond *C3*
8 Mentone *A4*
9 Morgan *D5*
10 MyHotel *D4*
11 Russell *C5*
12 St Margaret *D5*

● Eating
1 Abeno *D5*
2 Alara Wholefoods *B5*
3 Back to Basics *D1*
4 Bam Bou *D3*
5 Bar Centrale *B5*
6 Café Deco *D4*
7 Café Rive Gauche *B2*
8 Chez Gerard *D3*
9 Elena's L'Etoile *D3*
10 Forum Café *D5*
11 Hare & Tortoise *B6*
12 Ikkyu *D3*
13 Marino's *E3*
14 Mash *E1*
15 North Sea Fish *A5*
16 Pied à Terre *D3*
17 Pizza Express *D5*
18 Rasa Samudra *D3*
19 RK Stanley *E1*
20 Savoir Faire *E5*
21 Thai Garden Café *D5*
22 Townhouse Brasserie *E5*
23 Wagamama *E5*
24 Yialousa *B5*

● Pubs & bars
25 Champion *E2*
26 Duke of York *D3*
27 Fitzroy Tavern *D3*
28 Grafton Arms *B2*

On entering the Great Court from the south, the information desk is on the left and the box office for special exhibitions and audio guides on the right, the places to pick up floorplans and get your bearings. Within the square itself there are now two cafés, two shops and, up the wide staircases round the outside of the reading room, a temporary exhibition area and a restaurant. Twelve sculptures are set around the place at ground level making up the Great Court Concourse Gallery, introducing the museum's collections: currently the likes of an Easter Island statue, an Anglo-Saxon cross-shaft, two Egyptian obelisks and, in another new departure from the norm, a piece by contemporary sculptor Anish Kapoor.

The Great Court
The Great Court's restaurant, shops & gallery are open in the evenings throughout the week (see details below)

Reading Room

Central London

Straight ahead as you enter is the little door into the Reading Room. Designed by Robert Smirke in 1823, the Round Reading Room was first opened in 1857 and its original colour scheme of light blue, cream and gold leaf has now been restored. A host of famous (mainly male) thinkers, writers, politicians and idlers have studied, mused or snoozed beneath the lofty dome at one of the 35 long tables fanning out from the central enquiry desk.

Once the pride of the British Library (now in new premises at St Pancras) and only for the use of card-holders, anyone can now soak up the room's resonant atmosphere and imagine the likes of Marx (presumed to have sat near row L), Lenin, Shaw, Carlyle, Elgar or Yeats hunched over their books. The reopening as the British Museum Reading Room includes: an exhibition on the Reading Room's history, with sample books by famous and infamous readers; the use of the Paul Hamlyn Library of reference books relevant to the museum's collection, and of colour and black and white photocopiers (coin or smart card); and the Walter and Leonore Annenberg Centre, 50 computer terminals comprising COMPASS (Collections Multimedia Public Access System) where you can plan a visit to the museum, take a virtual tour, find information on artefacts, or print out images (with smart cards, £2 from Central Enquiry Desk).

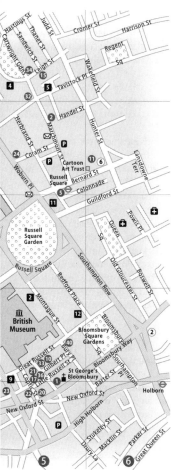

29 Jamie's *C2*
30 Jerusalem *E3*
31 King & Queen *D2*
32 Lord John Russell *A5*
33 Museum Tavern *D5*
34 Norfolk Arms *A5*
35 Office *E3*
36 Plough *D5*
37 Rising Sun *D3*
38 Sevilla Mia *E4*
39 Social *E2*
40 Truckles of Pied Bull Yard *D5*

○ **Entertainment**
1 Bloomsbury Theatre *B3*
2 Cochrane Theatre *D6*
3 Dominion Theatre *E4*
4 Drill Hall *C3*
5 Odeon Tottenham Court Rd *D3*
6 Renoir *B6*
7 The Place *A4*
8 ULU *C4*

Around the museum

A first visit to the British Museum galleries themselves is likely to both inspire and bewilder. That said, the new developments mean that the arrangement of several million objects from all over the world of every shape, size, and age laid out for inspection in over 90 rooms now seems much more straightforward.

The sheer range & variety of exhibits on display often provokes the observation that there's not much that's British in this museum at all

The main part of the museum is on the ground floor in the **west wing**, through the left-hand wall of the Great Court after entering from the main southern entrance. The galleries stretching the length of this wing are devoted to Ancient Egyptian sculpture, the Ancient Near East (including art from the palaces of Nimrud and Nineveh, and Assyrian sculpture), and Ancient Greece (including the sculptures from the Parthenon, the Nereid Monument and the Mausoleum of Halikarnassos). These collections also spill downstairs onto the lower floors of this wing.

On the right-hand side of the Great Court is the **east wing**, once the wonderful old King's Library, now a temporary exhibition space, likely to be devoted to the ethnographic collection that used to be in the Museum of Mankind.

Straight ahead past the Reading Room leads into the **north wing**, another temporary exhibition space and rooms devoted to artefacts from China, Southeast Asia, India and the Americas, with the African collection newly housed on the lower floors.

On the **upper floors**, above the galleries in the west wing – best reached up the south stairs on the left just before entering the Great Court from the front entrance – are more objects from Ancient Greece and also from the Roman Empire. Straight ahead at the top of these stairs leads into the rooms in the east wing devoted to Europe from the middle ages to modern times. Beyond these, on the upper floors of the east wing, can be found Roman Britain, Prehistory, and more monuments and treasures from the Ancient Near East which continue round into the north wing, also home to the museum's extraordinary collection of early Egyptian funerary objects – including mummies – as well as the Korean and Japanese collections.

It would be quite impossible to see everything in one day: apart from the guided and audio tours, it's well worth finding out from the Information desk when and where the free 50-minute 'EyeOpener' Gallery Talks are taking place (the first usually at about 1100 and the last at about 1500). Every day many of the museum's main areas are covered, with enthusiastic and well-informed volunteers describing the contents of a particular room in fascinating detail.

Main floor (Rooms 1-35)

In the west wing (on the left through the Great Court) among the sculptures from Egypt stands the **Rosetta Stone**, in Room 4, discovered by Napoleon's troops on the banks of the Nile. The three types of script on the block, each describing the same decree passed by priests gathered at Memphis, enabled the decoding of Egyptian hieroglyphs in the mid-19th century. In Rooms 6-10 look out for the fifth-century BC Assyrian relief of Ashurbanipal's garden party from the Palace of Nineveh, with the head of the defeated Elamite Teumann hanging from a tree.

The sculptures of the Parthenon, aka the **Elgin Marbles** (in Room 18), are fragments from a fifth-century BC processional frieze that decorated the temple on the Acropolis in Athens dedicated to Athena. Two-thirds of it have survived, just over half of it looked after by the British Museum. Far from being 'stolen', they were bought off Lord Elgin by the British Government for

considerably less than he himself had paid to have them removed and preserved after receiving permission to do so from occupying Turkish forces in
the early 1800s. A free audio guide in the room tells the full story.

The **Nereid Monument** (in Room 17) is a spectacular Ionic burial tomb
dating from 390BC from Xanthos in Turkey, featuring three sea nymphs in
extraordinary graceful robes. In Room 22 the carved column from the **Temple of Artemis at Ephesus**, which was one of the seven wonders of the ancient
world, shows the figures of Hermes, Thanatos and a woman who is likely to be
either Iphigenia, Alcestis or Eurydice. In Room 21, more fragments from one
of the wonders of the world include a 9-ft high statue and a frieze depicting the
Greeks at war with the Amazons, both from **The Mausoleum of
Helikarnassos** that once stood in modern-day Bodrum.

British Museum - main floor

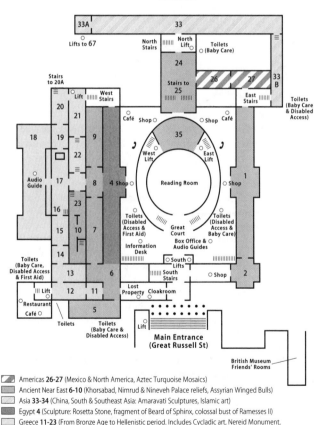

Americas 26-27 (Mexico & North America, Aztec Turquoise Mosaics)
Ancient Near East 6-10 (Khorsabad, Nimrud & Nineveh Palace reliefs, Assyrian Winged Bulls)
Asia 33-34 (China, South & Southeast Asia: Amaravati Sculptures, Islamic art)
Egypt 4 (Sculpture: Rosetta Stone, fragment of Beard of Sphinx, colossal bust of Ramesses II)
Greece 11-23 (From Bronze Age to Hellenistic period. Includes Cycladic art, Nereid Monument,
Parthenon Sculptures, Mausoleum of Helikarnassos)
Temporary exhibitions 1-2, 5, 24, 35
Sculpture (Great Court Concourse Gallery, Hoa Hakananai'a, Easter Island statue)

Central London

British Museum - lower floors

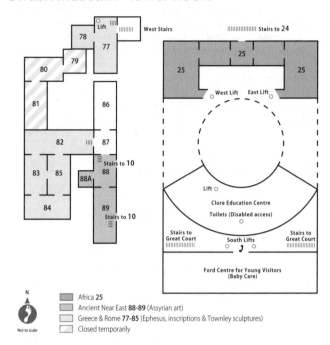

Africa **25**

Ancient Near East **88-89** (Assyrian art)

Greece & Rome **77-85** (Ephesus, inscriptions & Townley sculptures)

Closed temporarily

In the north wing (straight ahead), in Rooms 33-34, the **Amaravati sculptures** come from a Buddhist stupa in Andhra Pradesh, southeastern India, including carved slabs portraying the birth and life of Prince Siddartha.

Upper floors
(Rooms 36-73,
90-94)

In the southeast wing (double back on yourself up the stairs in the south entrance) highlights of the **European rooms** (40-48) include the Sutton Hoo Ship Burial (Room 41), an amazing Anglo-Saxon Royal grave hoard of ornate shoulder clasps, drinking bowls, and cauldrons, as well as a shield, sword and helmet. Discovered in Suffolk in 1939, the entire find was generously given to the museum by the landowner Mrs Edith Pretty. Next door in Room 42 are the Lewis chess men, part of four sets of chess pieces of mysterious origin carved from walrus tusks, dating from the 12th century and found on the wild and remote Outer Hebridean island of Lewis.

In Room 49, for **Romano-British finds**, it should still be possible to see one of the oldest representations in the world of the face of Christ, set into the roundel of a mosaic from Hinton St Mary in Dorset. Round in the east wing on this level, Room 50 is full of prehistoric British artefacts, and the home of **Lindow Man**, aka 'Pete Marsh' after the peat that preserved his body for almost two millennia. Sliced in half by a bog-cutting machine in Cheshire in 1984, these freeze-dried remains of a 25-year-old sacrificial or murder victim from the first century AD look as if they had been buried last year. Look out too for the Sweet Track, a section of neolithic pre-fab wooden plank walk from the Somerset Levels, dated about 3807 BC, that could be erected in the course of a day across marshy ground over a distance of about two miles.

The rest of the east wing (Rooms 53-59) contains objects from the ancient near east that include the **Oxus Treasure**, the most imporant single collection of Ancient Persian (5th-4th century BC) gold and silverwork in the world. Continuing round into the north wing, (above the Montague Place entrance), in Rooms 60-66, highlights include an astonishing array of Egyptian funerary archaeological finds – mummies, masks, sarcophagi and 'canopic' boxes and jars for preserving the internal organs of the deceased.

In Room 56, there's an extraordinary collection of objects from the ancient Mesopotamian city of Ur, including the '**Ram in the Thicket**', an 18-inch furniture support from around 2600 BC in the shape of a goat made from lapis

British Museum - upper floors

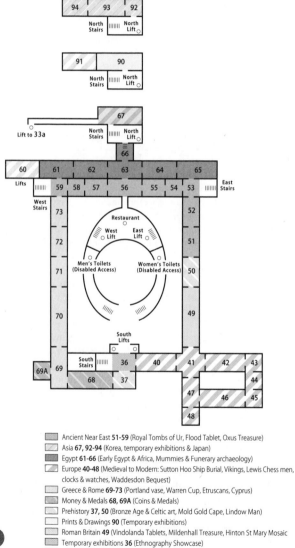

Ancient Near East **51-59** (Royal Tombs of Ur, Flood Tablet, Oxus Treasure)
Asia **67, 92-94** (Korea, temporary exhibitions & Japan)
Egypt **61-66** (Early Egypt & Africa, Mummies & Funerary archaeology)
Europe **40-48** (Medieval to Modern: Sutton Hoo Ship Burial, Vikings, Lewis Chess men, clocks & watches, Waddesdon Bequest)
Greece & Rome **69-73** (Portland vase, Warren Cup, Etruscans, Cyprus)
Money & Medals **68, 69A** (Coins & Medals)
Prehistory **37, 50** (Bronze Age & Celtic art, Mold Gold Cape, Lindow Man)
Prints & Drawings **90** (Temporary exhibitions)
Roman Britain **49** (Vindolanda Tablets, Mildenhall Treasure, Hinton St Mary Mosaic
Temporary exhibitions **36** (Ethnography Showcase)
Closed temporarily

N

Not to scale

lazuli, white shell and gold leaf, and the 'Royal Standard of Ur', a box decorated with the first known pictures of wheeled transport.

The upper floors of the west wing, (Rooms 69-73) contain more exhibits from Greece and Rome, including the beautiful deep-blue Portland vase (Room 70), from the first century AD, invisibly mended many times since, and an inspiration to British potters since it came into the possession of the Dukes of Portland in 1785.

■ *Museum Open 1000-1730 Sat-Wed, 1000-2030 Thu, Fri (late view of main floor galleries, Egypt and Ancient Near East galleries only). Admission free (donations appreciated); prices of temporary exhibitions vary. T020-7323 8000; disabled information T020-7636 7384; minicom T020-7323 8920. Great Court Open 0900-2100 Mon-Wed, 0900-2300 Thu-Sat, 0900-1800 Sun. Reading Room, T020-7323 8162, www.thebritishmuseum.ac.uk Guided tours: Highlights tour (90 mins) £7, £4 concession 1030, 1300 Mon-Sat, 1230, 1330, 1430, 1600 Sun; Focus tour (60 mins) at 1515 Mon-Sat, 1630 Sun, £5, £3 concession. EyeOpener gallery talks, free.*

Around Bloomsbury

Turning right out of the back entrance of the British Museum on Montague Street leads into **Russell Square**, the largest, most famous and least prepossessing of Bloomsbury's famous squares. The scruffy gardens in the middle are home to some battered looking trees and a basic outdoor café.

In the northwest corner of the square, on Thornhaugh Street, **The Brunei Gallery** is a newish exhibition space for London University's School of Oriental and African Studies (SOAS), putting on four temporary exhibitions a year of African and Asian art or anything else to do with those continents. Downstairs there's a plainly decorated commercial café. ■*Open Mon-Fri 1000-1700, free. T020-7898 4915.*

In the northeastern corner, Woburn Place heads confidently up to the Euston Road. Just before it reaches it, Woburn Walk is a quaint pedestrianized street dating from the early 19th century, with two good second-hand bookshops (see Shopping, page 215) and several cafés.

Russell Square tube is actually on Bernard St, opposite the Brunswick Shopping Centre

The Brunswick Shopping Centre, on Bernard Street, is the home of the excellent **Renoir Cinema** (see page 426) and also the **Cartoon Art Trust**, 7 Brunswick Centre, WC1, T020-7278 7172, which mounts regular (usually free) exhibitions of the work of great cartoonists and caricaturists as well as running classes and lectures on the subject. From the southeastern corner of the square, Southampton Row is regularly solid with traffic down to its junction with Bloomsbury Way near Holborn tube.

The airy classical interior of St George's is an enchanting place to hear a free lunchtime concert in summer

Hidden away in the angle of these two big roads, **Bloomsbury Square** has the distinction of being London's first and the gardens above the underground car park are a pleasant enough place to take a picnic. On Bloomsbury Way itself, **St George's Bloomsbury**, is an interesting church designed by Nicholas Hawksmoor, its stepped steeple modelled on the Mausoleum of Halicarnassus (see British Museum above) and surmounted with an unusual statue of George I in a Roman toga. ■ *Open Mon-Fri 0930-1730, Sun 0900-1700. T020-7405 3044.*

Much better if wanting to explore Bloomsbury though is to turn left out of the back entrance of the British Museum on Montague Street (or right and then right again out of the front entrance) and make for **Bedford Square**, the least altered of the squares and one that gives the best idea of how many of them would have looked in their heyday.

The leafy gardens are private and locked (unless you happen to meet a friendly keyholder), but the **Architectural Association** on the north side at Nos 34-36 (T020-7636 0974) welcomes visitors. Energetic and avant-garde, as well as training architects, the Association puts on thought-provoking exhibitions about contemporary architecture and has a select bookshop and licensed café doing good food at lunchtimes which becomes a pleasant enough bar in the early evenings.

The dark-brick Georgian terraces of **Gower Street** head north from the square's west side, home to the refurbished **Royal Academy of Dramatic Art** and also a substantial percentage of Bloomsbury's temporary population in a succession of grim-looking guesthouse hotels. A little way up on the right on Keppel Street, the **London School of Hygiene and Tropical Medicine** is decorated with the names of pioneers in the ongoing fight against infectious diseases alongside stone carvings of some of the bugs that have been blamed for them. Keppel Street also affords the most disturbing view of Senate House, on Malet Street, the austere administrative offices and library of the University of London.

A walk northwards up Malet Street takes you past the back door of RADA (Royal Academy of Dramatic Art), and the front entrance of its theatre, past Birkbeck College for extramural studies and mature students, and at the junction with Torrington Place, brings you to the University of London Union (ULU) which hosts cheap and cheerful club nights with occasional live bands on the up (see page 426).

Directly opposite Waterstone's bookshop on Torrington Street, in Malet Place, the Petrie Museum of Egyptian Archaeology is a hidden gem, bound to delight anyone whose appetite for all things Ancient Egyptian has been whetted by the British Museum. Donated by Sir Flinders Petrie to University College London (UCL) in 1933, this old-fashioned academic museum is a glass-cased treasure trove of amulets, beads, ornaments, instruments and decorative art. The museum's quiet rooms contain a huge variety of things strongly evocative of how lives were led in the Nile valley (and corpses interred), from the dawn of time through to more recent history. The collection ranges from the oldest dress in the world (2800 BC), discovered in 1977 amongst a pile of rags excavated by Petrie in 1912, down to weird things that might have helped Cleopatra with her make-up. Cat lovers should check out the small Langton Collection of miniature cat figures, donated by N&B Langton, authors of *The Cat in Ancient Egypt*.

Petrie Museum of Egyptian Archaeology *Part of the beauty of the collection is its intimacy*

■ *Open Tue-Fri 1300-1700, Sat 1000-1300. Admission free (donations appreciated). T020-7679 2000 (Ext 2884).*

Round the corner in Byng Place, the **Church of Christ the King** is a neo-Gothic masterpiece designed for a Catholic sect in 1853. Now used by the University of London, its side chapel is open for prayer, the rest of the church usually closed to visitors although there are lunchtime organ recitals at 1310 on the first Friday of every month. The church stands on the southwestern corner of **Gordon Square**, once the centre of literary Bloomsbury, as its numerous blue plaques testify, and still the square with the most attractive public gardens, its winding paths and borders home to a surprising variety of wildlife, including hedgehogs and, sadly increasingly rare, sparrows.

Percival David Foundation of Chinese Art

In the southeastern corner of Gordon Square (No 53), the Percival David Foundation of Chinese Art consists of a series of quiet, serene rooms containing a large collection of exquisite Chinese ceramics from the 10th-18th centuries. Ming, Qing, Song and Tang vases, dishes, pots, incense burners and water droppers, many of the items were previously owned by Chinese emperors. The cumulative effect of such an absorbing wealth of fine detail is memorable.

■ *Open Mon-Fri 1030-1700. Admission free (donations appreciated); under-14s must be accompanied by an adult. T020-7387 3909.*

Around Fitzrovia

Heading back west again and crossing over Gower Street, Torrington Place hits the middle of **Tottenham Court Road** just above Goodge Street Station at one of the most appealing stretches of this otherwise characterless north-bound thoroughfare. Left from here begins the succession of competing cut-price computer and hi-fi shops for which the Tottenham Court Road has become famous. Goodge Street is a busy shopping street, one of the gateways to Fitzrovia. There's not much in the way of 'sights' as such in Fitzrovia, but the area's tight network of streets and alleyways makes for rewarding browsing.

A little way down it on the right, at No 1 Scala Street, **Pollock's Toy Museum** looks like it belongs in another century, a quaint little place packed with olde-worlde toys, most famously the carboard cut-out theatres last made by Benjamin Pollock in Hoxton. The museum features a reconstruction of his shop and some of his original creations. The shop beneath the museum sells the modern equivalents and other new-old toys. ■ *Open Mon-Fri 1000-1800 Sat 1000-1700. Admission £3; child £1.50. T020-7636 3452.*

Further on to the left, **Crabtree Tree Fields** is a sweet little park just off the old mews of Colville Place, a popular lunchspot with office workers in the summer. Charlotte Street heads north-south close by, Fitzrovia's main artery, leading northwards to the **Fitzroy Square**. Originally planned by the Adams brothers, No 29 was the home of both GB Shaw and Virginia Woolf (at different times). Nearby, the British Telecom Tower is Fitzrovia's most prominent landmark, reminiscent of the space race. The revolving restaurant at the top has sadly been closed to the public since a bombscare in the 70s.

Eating and drinking

Expensive
● *on map, page 204*

Bloomsbury's largely academic and student population don't really encourage gourmet dining options whereas Fitzrovia's advertising execs and their clients certainly do. *Bam-Bou*, 1 Percy St, W1, T020-7323 9130, is the latest of their favourite places, a modern Southeast Asian restaurant with an airy wooden interior and high-style quotient.

Much more traditional in atmosphere, *Pied-à-terre*, 34 Charlotte St, W1, T020-7636 1178 (closed Sun), is a small Michelin-starred French restaurant expert at nouvelle cuisine.

More traditionally French in both its menu and clientele is *Elena's L'Etoile*, 30 Charlotte St, W1, T020-7636 1496 (closed Sat lunch and Sun). *Chez Gerard*, 8 Charlotte St, W1, T020-7636 4975, was the first of the Gallic chain, and one of the smaller and more intimate, doing a reliable menu of French classics, at a price.

Mash, 19-21 Great Portland St, W1, T020-7637 5555 is a media favourite, a 90's take on the 70s in the own-brew bar (open until 0100 Mon-Sat) and good food in the busy restaurant upstairs until 2300. *Rasa Samudra*, 5 Charlotte St, W1, T020-7637 0222 (closed Sun), is the latest and most laid-back branch of the excellent and expanding Rasa chain, distinguished from the others by doing seafood alongside the famously fragrant vegetarian south Indian dishes and having a smoking section. *Back To Basics*, 21a Foley St, W1, T020-7436 2181 (closed Sat, Sun), is another good destination for seafood, a cheerful restaurant at the lower end of this bracket.

Mid-range *Fitzrovia is also the best place to head for in this price bracket*

Museum St is a good destination for an inexpensive meal, at somewhere like the *Thai Garden Café*, 32 Museum St, WC1, T020-7323 1494, where you can bring your own wine, and as well as the Thai food also enjoy spectacular cakes in the takeaway shop out front. On the same street, *Abeno*, 47 Museum St, WC1, T020-7405 3211 is a newish Japanese restaurant doing teppanyaki and okonomiyaki (little stuffed doughballs fried at the table).

Cheap *Here Bloomsbury comes into its own*

Nearby, on Coptic St, there's a splendid tiled branched of the reliable *Pizza Express* chain and also the *Townhouse Brasserie*, 24 Coptic St, WC1, T020-7636 2731, slightly more expensive, a smart French restaurant with tables outside and an interesting menu that includes light meals and good-value fixed-price options. *Savoir faire*, 42 New Oxford St, WC1, T020-7436 0707, is more old-fashioned and intimate, doing an excellent 3-course lunch for about £7, and a 3-course dinner for about £13, friendly service and very good value.

Wagamama, 4 Streatham St, WC1, T020-7323 9223, is the brightly lit Japanese basement canteen that has been wowing trendy diners for some time with its brusque efficiency and the quality of its noodle soups. Queues still form regularly for lunch and supper.

On the other side of Bloomsbury, near Russell Square, the *Yialousa Greek Taverna*, 18 Woburn Place, WC1, T020-7837 4748, is a long-established favourite with the locals. The *North Sea Fish Restaurant*, 7-8 Leigh St, WC1, T020-7387 5892, do top-quality sit-down fish and chips in a timeless style at lunch and dinner. Next door there's a take-away chippie.

The *Hare and Tortoise*, 15-17 Brunswick Shopping Centre, Brunswick Square, WC1, T020-7278 4945, is a spacious and very cheap non-smoking Japanese dumpling and noodle bar.

In Fitzrovia, *RK Stanley*, 6 Little Portland St, W1, T020-7462 0099 (open until 2400 Mon-Sat), are very good purveyors of fine sausages and real ale in a stylish modern British take on American diner-style eating and drinking. *Ikkyu*, 67a Tottenham Court Rd, W1, T020-7636 9280, is another good basic and inexpensive Japanese restaurant.

The *Forum Café*, 62 Great Russell St, WC1, T020-7404 1878, is right opposite the British Museum, doing a wide variety of high-quality sandwiches, salads and hot snacks. A little further afield, *Cafe Deco* 43 Store St, WC1, T020-7323 4501, has an interesting range of Italian sandwiches and home-made pasta. Near Russell Square tube, the *Bar Centrale*, 4 Bernard St, WC1, T020-7278 5249, is a very popular 70s-style Italian café/sandwich shop, with a restaurant next door, doing a wide range of fillings and breads.

Cafés & sandwich bars *Museum St is a reliable destination for coffee & sandwiches, although the cafés along here can get very busy at lunchtime*

On Marchmont St, *Alara Wholefoods*, 58-60 Marchmont St, WC1, T020-7837 1172, do very good-value hot vegetarian and organic meals to take away or eat outside. *Patisserie*

Central London

Deux Amis, 63 Judd St, WC1,T020-7383 7029, is a good place for tempting cakes and baguettes with tables outdoors.

See also internet cafés in Directory box on page 216

In Fitzrovia, the *Café Rive Gauche*, 20-21 Warren St, W1, T020-7387 8232, opens early in the morning during the week (closed weekends), a sweet little French place for good salads and light meals. *Marino's*, 31 Rathbone Place, W1, T020-7636 8965, is an excellent down-to-earth and cheerful Italian café, if a bit smoky, doing great platefuls of inexpensive comfort food.

Pubs & bars

No surprise that Bloomsbury's large student population keeps a wide variety of pubs doing very good business

Near the British Museum, the *Plough*, 27 Museum St, WC1, T020-7636 7964, is larger and often less packed than the famous *Museum Tavern* at the end of the street. It too has a refurbished Victorian interior and serves reasonable food throughout the day. More popular with suits than students, *Truckles of Pied Bull Yard*, Off Bury Place, WC1, T020-7404 5338, is a good wine bar (part of the Davy's chain) hidden away in its own little courtyard among a clutch of expensive art shops. It has a cosy basement as well as tables outside in summer. On bustling little Marchmont St, the *Lord John Russell*, is a pleasant one-roomed local with a wooden interior and benches outside, a favourite with students and their tutors. Nearby, the *Norfolk Arms*, Leigh St, is often quieter, with no special beers but a fine Victorian ceiling.

More vibrant drinking can be found in several bars, many of them late-night, scattered around Fitzrovia

Jamies, 74 Charlotte St, W1, T020-7636 7556, is a fashionable wine bar on two levels popular with the local media set. *Jerusalem* 33-34 Rathbone Place, W1, T020-7255 1120. Open Mon-Thu 1200-0200, Fri 1200-0300, Sat 1900-0300 (admission charged after 2230; Mon-Thu admission £3, Fri, Sat £6. A roomy basement bar with great solid tables and vaguely dungeon-like atmosphere. Despite its size, it often gets loud and busy.

Nearby, and catering for a younger crowd, *Office*, 3-5 Rathbone Place, W1, T020-7636 1598 (open Mon-Fri 1200-0300, Sat 2130-0400; admission charged Wed £2 after 2230, Thu £5 after 2230, Fri £4 after 2230, Sat £5 after 2130, £7 after 2200 and £9 after 2300) is another large basement bar, funkily lit and always jumping late in the week. *The Social*, 5 Little Portland St, W1, T020-7636 4992 (open Mon-Sat 1200-2400, Sun 1700-2300) is an industrialized music bar serving food upstairs, hardcore sounds and demon cocktails in the basement, popular with twenty-somethings on pre-club warm-ups. Very different in style, *Sevilla Mia*, 22 Hanway St, W1, T020-7637 3756, (open Mon-Sat 1900-0100, Sun 1900-2400) is a scruffy, cosy little basement tapas bar that often has live Spanish guitar music.

▶▶ Go to page 426 for entertainment & nightlife

Good old-style pubs in Fitzrovia include the beautifully decorated *Champion*, 12-13 Wells St, W1, T020-7323 1228, its tiled and stained-glass interior an antique homage to winning sportsmen of all kinds. The *King & Queen*, 1 Foley St, W1, T020-7636 5619, is a resolutely unreconstructed old boozer with friendly bar staff behind Middlesex Hospital. The *Grafton Arms*, Grafton Way, W1, T020-7387 7923 specializes in first-class real ales and has a tiny little roof terrace, popular with students and local office workers during the summer.

The *Duke of York*, 47 Rathbone St, W1, T020-7636 7065, is a cosy little Greene King pub on the corner of the chi-chi shopping mews of Charlotte Place. The *Fitzroy Tavern*, 16 Charlotte St, W1, T020-7580 3714, rests happily on its reputation as the haunt of literary drinkers in the 50s, although since its refurbishment it has lost some of its soul. Similar in style is the *Rising Sun*, 46 Tottenham Court Rd, W1, T020-7636 6530. The *One Tun*, 58 Goodge St, W1, T020-7209 0559, is a lively Young's pub with a well-established clientele of local office workers. *Flutes Wine Bar and Brasserie*, 61 Goodge St, W1, T020-7636 0177, is a good and unashamedly retro wine bar.

Shopping

The main seller of new books in the area is **Waterstone's**, 82 Gower St, WC1, T020-7636 1577 (open until 2000 Mon-Fri, unitl 1900 Sat, 1100-1700 Sun), the university bookshop, formerly *Dillons*, with a wide range of academic titles and a good second-hand section too. Great Russell St and Museum Street are home to several good specialist, second-hand and antiquarian bookshops: **Arthur Probsthain Oriental & African Bookseller**, 41 Great Russell St, WC1, T020-7636 1096, caters comprehensively for the graduates and students of SOAS, the School of Oriental and African Studies. **Robert Frew**, 106 Great Russell St, WC1, T020-7580 2311, is an antiquarian bookshop specializing in travel, illustrated books and library sets.

Books
Like the Charing Cross Rd, when it comes to shopping Bloomsbury means books, mainly antiquarian, out of print, second-hand & remaindered

Central London

The **Museum Bookshop**, 36 Great Russell St, WC1, T020-7580 4086, is a charming and scruffy establishment, stocking new and out-of-print books, with archaeology, ancient history, and conservation as strong points, but definitely not to be confused with the new **British Museum Shop** on Bloomsbury St (the place to pick up museum souvenirs without going into the place). Also on Bloomsbury St, **Unsworths**, 12 Bloomsbury St, WC1, T020-7436 9836 (open until 2000 Mon-Sat) is very popular with students for second-hand and remaindered humanities titles, while **Bookmarks**, 1 Bloomsbury St, WC1, T020-7637 1848, specializes in new socialist material.

Gosh!, 39 Great Russell St, WC1, T020-7636 1011 (open till 1900 Thu, Fri) do comics and cartoons with a gallery in the basement. **Forbidden Planet**, 71 New Oxford St, WC1, T020-7836 4179 (also open until 1900 Thu, Fri) is similar but much larger and more geared to science fiction and horror, also selling videos, games and CDs. The **Cinema Bookshop**, 13-14 Great Russell St WC1, T020-7637 0206, has a vast range of new and out-of-print books on the movies, while the **Atlantis Bookshop**, 49a Museum St, WC1, T020-7405 2120, stocks any and every esoteric and occult title, embracing mysticism, mythology and folklore, both new and second-hand. **Words Etcetera**, 37 Museum St, WC1, T020-7404 9428, rent their shelves out to a variety of different second-hand booksellers and always turn up surprises.

A little further afield, **The Bloomsbury Bookshop**, 12 Bury Place, WC1, T020-7404 7433, is a mostly second-hand academic bookshop, specializing in history and economics. Nearby, **Skoob**, 15 Sicilian Ave, WC1, T020-7404 3063, is one of the largest second-hand bookshops in London, very popular with students both buying and selling their books. On the other side of Bloomsbury, **LCL International Booksellers**, 104 Judd St, WC1, T020-7837 0486, have a wide range of foreign language books. **Judd Books**, 82 Marchmont St WC1, T020-7387 5333, have lots of low-price second-hand academic titles, especially on philosophy, architecture, and film, while **Gay's the Word**, 66 Marchmont St, WC1, T020-7278 7654, is one of London's premier gay and lesbian bookshops.

Further up on picturesque Woburn Walk, **Book Art and Architecture**, 12 Woburn Walk, WC1, T020-7387 5006, do a good selection of second-hand and rare books mainly on the subjects their name suggests.

In Fitzrovia, **Samuel French's Theatre Bookshop**, 52 Fitzroy St, W1, T020-7387 9373, is the destination par excellence for theatrical bibliophiles, and stocks just about every new play in print.

Other than books, **James Smith & Sons**, 53 New Oxford St, WC1, T020-7836 4731, is one of the best places in London to buy a good umbrella, or a walking- shooting- or sword-stick, with a long-established and extraordinary range of the things on display. For furniture, gifts and accessories with a certain flair, **Heals**, 196 Tottenham Court Rd, W1, T020-7636 1666 (open until 2000 Thu) is usually a good but fairly expensive bet.

Miscellaneous

Central London

Transport

Buses **Northbound up Tottenham Court Rd**:
No 10 to Euston and King's Cross.
No 24 to Hampstead Heath via Camden Town.
No 29 to Finsbury Park via Camden Town and Holloway.
No 73 to Stoke Newington via Euston, King's Cross, and Islington.
No 134 to Camden Town.

Southbound down Gower St:
No 10 to Hammersmith, via Oxford Circus, Marble Arch, Hyde Park Corner and Knightsbridge.
No 24 to Pimlico via Leicester Square, Trafalgar Square, Westminster and Victoria.
No 29 to Trafalgar Square.
No 73 to Victoria via Oxford Circus, Marble Arch and Hyde Park Corner.

Along Great Russell St:
No 7 from Russell Square to Ladbroke Grove via British Museum, Oxford Circus, Marble Arch and Paddington.

Eastbound on Bloomsbury Way:
No 1 to Aldwych via Holborn.
No 8 to Bethnal Green via Holborn, Bank and Liverpool St.
No 19 and **38** to Islington.
No 55 to Shoreditch via Old Street.
No 242 to Shoreditch via Holborn, Bank and Liverpool St.

On Woburn Place, Russell Square and Southampton Row:
No 59 and **68** to Waterloo.
No 91 to Crouch End via Kingsway, King's Cross, Caledonian Rd, and Holloway.
No 168 to Hampstead Heath via Kingsway, Euston, Camden Town and Chalk Farm.

Taxis Taxi on the rank on north side of Russell Square, also usually plenty outside British Museum on Great Russell St.

Tubes Tottenham Court Rd (Central and Northern lines) for the British Museum. Russell Square (Piccadilly line). Goodge St (Northern line) and Warren St (Northern and Victoria lines).

Directory

***Internet cafés** Global talk, 68 Marchmont Street, WC1, T020-7278 6723. Open Monday-Friday 0900-2300 Saturday/Sunday 0930-2300. Cybergate 3 Leigh Street, WC1, T020-7387 381. Open Monday-Saturday 0900-2100, Sunday 1200-1700. **Cyberia Cyber Café**, 39 Whitfield Street, W1, T020-7681 4200. Open Monday-Friday 1000-2100, Saturday 1100-1900, Sun 1200-1800, was one of London's first, and occasionally offers free internet access.*

***Sport** YMCA Health and Fitness Centre, 112 Great Russell Street, WC1, T020-7343 1700. £37 a week associate membership, swimming pool, gym and sauna. **University of London Students Union**, open until 1900, associate membership, £15 a year associate membership, gym, pool, sports hall, squash court, three bars; The Venue, Bar 101, and the Duck and Dive.*

Holborn and Clerkenwell

East of the West End and west of the City, Holborn falls between two stools, long colonized by lawyers, the press and intermediaries of all kinds. Twenty years ago though the media and its journos moved out east to Wapping and Docklands and the buzz of the latest news being churned on Fleet Street has died down. Without the newspapers to leave the lump, the district is now dominated by the atmosphere of the ancient Inns of Court, neat and officious places founded on discretion and class-ridden legal traditions: don't be caught pronouncing the silent L – for litigation – in Holborn. It's pronounced Ho-bon. That said, the quiet lawns, secret alleyways and collegiate architecture of the barristers' stamping grounds are peaceful havens for outsiders to explore, and Lincoln's Inn Fields houses two of the city's most unusual museums, the **Hunterian Museum of the Royal College of Surgeons** *and the spellbinding curiosity of Georgian architect* **Sir John Soane's home**.

Over the same period Clerkenwell, on the other hand, northeast of the City and Holborn beyond the Gray's Inn Road, has become one of the most vibrant and creative parts of London, the fashionable home of design consultancies, independent media groups and sassy restaurants. Although it's beginning to look as though the party might already be over, with some tenants feeling the pinch of City property prices, the old streets north of **Smithfield Market** *are still a top place to paint the town red.*

Holborn or Chancery Lane tubes for Lincoln's Inn Fields; Temple tube (closed Sun) for Fleet St; Farringdon or Barbican tube for Clerkenwell

Central London

History

At the end of the 14th century, Holborn and Clerkenwell were still separated by fields, with the 'Holebourne', a tributary of the River Fleet, running across it. The track running east carried carts of wool, corn, cheese and wood, and ended at the Holborn Bar, where tolls were exacted and rogues and lepers refused entry to the City. A hamlet had grown up around the Bar, and further west there were the inns of court, Lincoln's Inn, and Gray's Inn. The latter included a windmill, dovecots and lakes and occupied the site of the manor house of Purpoole alongside the ancient road to the north, now Gray's Inn Road.

Clerkenwell.org, 53 Clerkenwell Close, EC1 T020-7251 6311, is a local history information point & outlet for local crafts

There was little else but fields to the west until St Giles-in-the-Fields. Clerkenwell, situated just outside the city walls and set in meadowlands rich in springs, was a hamlet that evolved to serve the two 12th-century monastic foundations, St Mary's Nunnery (the Clerk's well supplied the nunnery) and the Priory of St John of Jerusalem. Closer to the City walls lay Charterhouse, a Carthusian monastery built on burial ground set aside for victims of the Black Death, and a ten-acre field surrounded by ponds and trees.

'Smoothfield' (later Smithfield) was well known for its horse market (although other livestock were also traded), and, for over 700 years, as the venue for the annual Bartholomew Fair until it was suspended in 1855 for rowdiness and debauchery. It also served as a medieval sports field where archery, wrestling, athletics, jousting and royal tournaments could be seen.

Following the Reformation, and the redistribution of monastic lands, a 'better qualitie' of resident arrived in the several mansions erected by the nobility. When General Monck rode down the Gray's Inn Road into the City to proclaim the Restoration of

• •

Hotels in the area

A-B *The Rookery*

▸▸ **Go to page 447**

Charles II, it also signalled a change of gear in Clerkenwell's development. Since the court was now settling further west, and its acolytes followed suit, so the great houses were sold on to merchants and craftsmen. Town houses sprang up in modern Britton Street, and 'a little towne', Hatton Garden, was built alongside the Bishop of Ely's London palace. Gardens opened up, spurred on by the area's 'medicinal waters'. English Grotto, Merlin's Cave, London Spa (behind modern Exmouth market) and Sadler's Wells drew enthusiastic crowds through much of the 18th century, while Mohocks (gangs of aristocratic thugs) roamed around Snow Hill looking for old ladies to sieze and roll down the hill in a barrel.

Artisans and craftsmen, many foreign, moved in, as the area earned a reputation for its jewellers (particularly in Hatton Gardens) and watchmakers. The good waters attracted brewers (Whitbread) and gin distillers such as Gordon's and Booth's. During the 19th century, as the local population rocketed, so both Holborn and Clerkenwell earned notoriety for their slums. The Fleet River was a virtual sewer, Smithfield Market continued to trade in live animals (blood and entrails ran in the gutters, and stray cattle took refuge in houses and shops), and once pleasant streets saw urban squalor for the first time.

Despite the large slum clearances that made way for the Clerkenwell and Farringdon Roads, Holborn Circus and Viaduct, and later the Metropolitan Railway, the area still presented a horrifying spectacle for the Prince of Wales when he visited in 1884. The poverty ensured it became a lively centre of radicalism. In the Gordon Riots of 1780 a mob attacked and set alight Clerkenwell's two prisons and Orator Hunt launched his assault on the Tower from Spa Fields (1816). Clerkenwell Green has launched many a subversive act, whether Chartist meetings in the mid-1800s, the Socialists setting off to Trafalgar Square on Bloody Sunday in 1887, or Lenin producing several editions of *Iskra* from what is now the Marx Memorial Library. The last century, however, has seen a gradual change in fortunes. Businesses have moved back into Holborn after the area suffered severe bombing in the Second World War, and Clerkenwell has more recently become a fashionable residential district, while still supporting a cottage industry of craftsmen.

Sights

Around Holborn

North of the river four busy main routes through Holborn connect the West End with the City: the Victoria Embankment, Fleet Street, High Holborn and Theobald's Road.

Inns of Court
The warren of streets around the four venerable Inns of Court are a peculiar place to explore, still very much alive but also pickled in the aspic of legal tradition

The Victoria Embankment sweeps round to Blackfriars Bridge from the riverside frontage of Somerset House, passing Temple tube and the old gardens of the **Inner and Middle Temple Inns of Courts**. These ancient alleyways and courtyards stuffed with lawyers' offices and barristers hustling about their business take their name from the crusading Knights Templar, the Inner Temple being the one nearest the City, the Outer Temple long gone.

The Templars built their distinctive little round church here in 1185, the most important of the nine in the UK and the only one in London. Like the others dotted about the country, the design of **Temple Church** was based on the Church of the Holy Sepulchre in Jerusalem. Only one doorway from 1285 is original, the building having been badly damaged in the Second World War, but its mixture of Romanesque and Gothic, already much tinkered with by Wren and Decimus Burton in the 18th century, was beautifully restored in the early 1960s.

Located in the Inner Temple, the Church is shared with the **Middle Temple** (T020-7427 4800), which boasts a magnificent old wooden Hall dating from 1573. Thanks to its great hammerbeam roof, crested screens of oak and a high table hewn from one solid trunk donated by Queen Elizabeth I, it's not that difficult to picture the first ever performance of *Twelfth Night* that was staged here with Shakespeare himself quite probably taking part. The little table was supposedly made from the timbers of Francis Drake's globe-trotting ship the *Golden Hind* replicated on Bankside.

■ *Temple Church open Wed-Sun 1100-1600. T020-7797 8241 for guided morning tours (£10) that include Inner Temple Hall. Middle Temple open 1000-1200, 1500-1600 Mon-Fri. Admission free. Hall T020-7797 7768.*

Above the Inner Temple Gate opposite Chancery Lane, at 17 Fleet Street, is another period piece from roughly the same era, **Prince Henry's Room**, so named because it was used by lawyers acting on behalf of James I's oldest son. Oak pannelled with its fine moulded plaster ceiling dating from 1610, it narrowly escaped the Great Fire of 1666. On display are some artefacts relating to the room's history and the diarist of the Great Fire, Samuel Pepys. ■ *Open 1100-1400 Mon-Sat, admission free. T020-7936 4004.*

Fleet Street was once the main artery of the 'fourth estate', when it was lined with publishing houses, newspaper offices and printing works, and its pubs and restaurants were packed with journalists scratching a living. Since computerization and Rupert Murdoch gave the chop to the print unions by moving *The Times*, *The Sun* and their Sunday counterparts to Wapping, the street has become much like any other main road around here.

On the other side of Chancery Lane though, the **Church of St Dunstan in the West** is easily recognized by its strange clock, apparently the first in London with minute marks, featuring a pair of muscle-bound gong-beaters said to represent Gog and Magog. The clock was installed in 1671 in gratitude for the church being spared the flames. ■ *Open 1000-1600 Tue, 1400-1800 Sat, 0900-1500 Sun. T020-7242 6027.*

On the right of the church through a heavy iron gate into the forecourt stand the statues of King Lud and his children (the pre-Roman rulers of London) and of Queen Elizabeth I, all originally from the Ludgate demolished like other City gates in 1760. Towards the bottom of the street, near the old smoked-glass Art Deco building of the Express (now in Southwark), there's a fine view of St Paul's standing on the top of Ludgate Hill.

Just to the north of Fleet Street, at 17 Gough Square, can be found the home from 1748-59 of one of the street's most fearsome, productive and engaging characters, 'Dictionary' Johnson, aka Ursa Major to his friends. Dr Johnson's House sensibly does not attempt a full period reconstruction of the chaotic squalor in which the awesome man of letters and his six amenuenses compiled his great dictionary. Instead this is a fine place to browse around, with plenty to read and a facsimile of the big book itself, particularly influential in its use of literary precedents but also famous for its sense of humour, defining lexicographer as 'a compiler of dictionaries, a harmless drudge'. The work went on in the top room of the narrow house and all four floors have been furnished in an

Fleet Street & around

Dr Johnson's House

Central London

Holborn & Clerkenwell

Central London

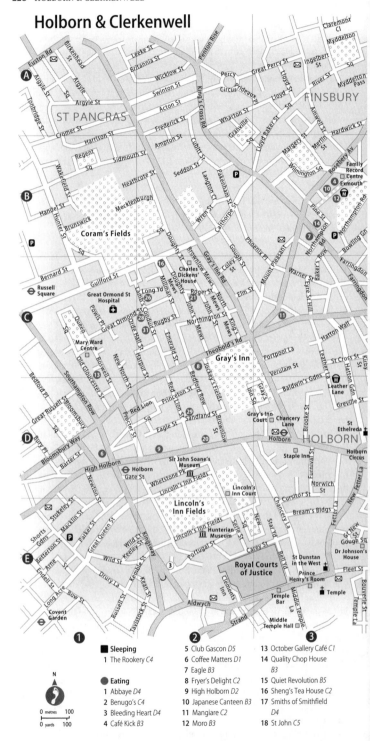

■ Sleeping	**5** Club Gascon *D5*
1 The Rookery *C4*	**6** Coffee Matters *D1*
	7 Eagle *B3*
● Eating	**8** Fryer's Delight *C2*
1 Abbaye *D4*	**9** High Holborn *D2*
2 Benugo's *C4*	**10** Japanese Canteen *B3*
3 Bleeding Heart *D4*	**11** Mangiare *C2*
4 Café Kick *B3*	**12** Moro *B3*

13 October Gallery Café *C1*
14 Quality Chop House *B3*
15 Quiet Revolution *B5*
16 Sheng's Tea House *C2*
17 Smiths of Smithfield *D4*
18 St John *C5*

N

0 metres　100
0 yards　100

Central London

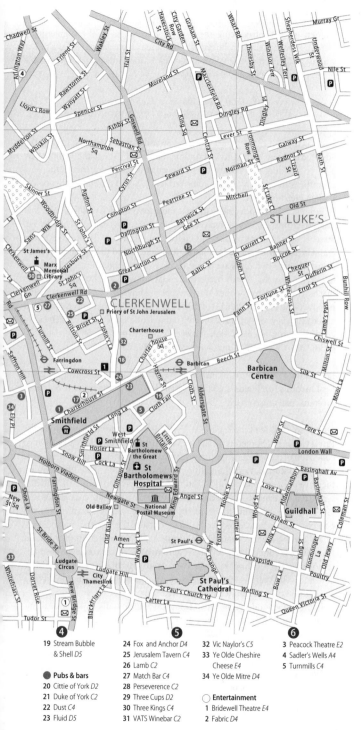

appropriate style with displays on a variety of Johnsonia, the one on his women friends introducing the original blue-stocking, the frighteningly learned Elizabeth Carter who could speak seven languages, as well as a rather whimsical 25-minute video drama-doc of Johnson showing his indefatigable biographer Boswell round the house.

■ *Open winter 1100-1700 (last admission 1645); summer 1100-1730 (last admission 1715). Admission £4, concession £3. T020-7353 3745.*

Back at the top of the street near the Strand stands a bronze griffin, the adopted emblem of the City of London, marking the site of the Temple Bar, a Wren building that controlled and eventually fatally restricted the flow of traffic into the City. It was removed in 1878 and rebuilt at Theobald's Park in Hertfordshire.

From here it's impossible to mistake the great red-brick Gothic edifice that holds the **Royal Courts of Justice**. Designed by aspiring cathedral builder GE Street, it was completed in 1882, its high moral, religious and national purpose emphasized with statues of Solomon, Jesus and Alfred the Great. This High Court is where civil cases are heard: divorces, bankruptcy hearings, building disputes, tribunals, custody battles and endless others, as well as criminal cases that have been referred to the Court of Appeal. Through the front entrance, the massive Great Hall (where a list of current cases is posted; the curious can ask an usher what they're about) is a suitably intimidating space, hardly much enlivened by a funny little exhibition of lawyers' regalia to one side. ■ *Open Mon-Fri 0930-1200, 1300-1630. Admission free. T020-7947 6000.*

Behind the Royal Courts of Justice, between Kingsway and Chancery Lane, lies **Lincoln's Inn Fields**, the largest square in London and home to two of its most unusual museums.

Hunterian Museum of the Royal College of Surgeons
It's well worth going on the guided tour to have the signficance of the specimens explained

On the south side of the square, at 35-43, is the Hunterian Museum of the Royal College of Surgeons. In the 18th century John Hunter amassed a huge collection of pathological specimens, human and animal, in the course of his anatomical studies. With the addition of thousands more in the 19th century, the museum once held a world-beating variety of pickled body parts and dissected animal exhibits. Badly damaged during the war, quite enough has survived for the museum to be pretty disturbing, neatly organized in the deceptive calm of a galleried library. No doubt with the right training the specimens can be seen as beautiful and important. No collection of this kind would be permitted today of course, although the recent row over hospitals removing organs without relatives' consent suggests that Hunter's attitude is alive and well. Apart from the more ghoulish attractions, the museum holds a famous portrait of a rhinoceros by George Stubbs.

In the same building, the **Odontological Museum** displays a large number of old teeth, including some gathered on the battlefield of Waterloo and others strung together on a necklace brought back from the Congo by Stanley the explorer, as well as some gruesome dental instruments.

■ *Open Mon-Fri 1000-1700. Tours 1400 on Wed lasting about 1 hr. Admission free. T020-7869 6560.*

On the opposite side of the square, at Nos 12-14 Lincoln's Inn Fields, Sir John Soane's Museum is unique, a remarkable memorial to the imagination of one of Georgian London's greatest architects, and today one of the city's most extraordinary sights. Most famous for designing the Bank of England, Sir John Soane left his treasured project of a lifetime to the nation on his death in 1837. The eight or so rooms in No 13 that can now be seen are a purpose-built showcase for his highly idiosyncratic and eclectic collection of antiquities, artworks and objets d'art, as well as being a successful and much admired manipulation of architectural space. At its most atmospheric (although often also most crowded) during the late openings on the first Tuesday of every month (candlelit in winter), an hour spent here is usually enough to persuade most people that they need to come again with more time.

Unmissable are: the rooms specially constructed for Hogarth's series of paintings, *The Rake's Progress* (from inherited wealth to the madhouse) and *The Election* (a satire on political ambition); the hieroglyphic sarcophagus of Pharaoh Seti I from around 1200BC; the bogus monk's parlour; the breakfast room; and the comparatively airy drawing room on the first floor with Soane's answer to Nash's ideas on urban planning. The museum also holds regular temporary exhibitions on other great architects.

■ *Open Tue-Sat 1000-1700, first Tue of month also 1800-2100 by candlelight in winter. Admission free. Guided tour on Sat at 1430, £3, concessions free. T020-7405 2107, www.soane.org*

Lincoln's Inn Court itself, although closed to the public, can be seen through its gates from the square. A very pleasant way to enjoy its collegiate gardens however is to take in one of the open-air Shakespeare productions that are usually stage there in the summer. On Chancery Lane, the Inn's Tudor gatehouse was where Oliver Cromwell lodged as a young law student.
■ *T020- 7405 6360.*

A few steps to the east towards Chancery Lane tube, **Staple Inn**, one of the nine Inns of Chancery and now occupied by the Institute of Actuaries, is a remarkable refurbished survival of a tudor courtyard; again, it too was severely blitzed but has since been renovated.

At the foot of Gray's Inn Road, High Holborn and its massive office blocks become plain Holborn before reaching Holborn Circus. On the left beyond the Gray's Inn Road, **Leather Lane Market** runs north, one of London's better street markets (see Shopping below). Parallel to Leather Lane, **Hatton Garden** has long been the centre of London's diamond trade, which partly explains the market's wide variety of customers.

Nearby the little Gothic **Church of St Etheldreda**, Ely Place, EC1, is the only Catholic church to have survived from the reign of Edward I. The 'Strawberry Fayre' held here on a day in mid to late June is a charity street party in Ely Place commemorating the old episcopal palace's famous strawberry fields.
■ *Open 0730-1830 daily. T020-7405 1061.*

In the angle of Gray's Inn Road and Holborn lies Gray's Inn Court itself, founded in the 14th century but badly damaged during the Second World War. Most famously associated with its 16th-century treasurer, the great natural philosopher Francis Bacon, its now much renovated Hall was where Shakespeare's Comedy of Errors was first performed. A walk through these hushed courtyards and their expansive gardens can lead appropriately enough up to Charles Dickens, the novelist who memorably described the

Sir John Soane's Museum
There are far too many surprising effects & curious or beautiful things to take in or understand on a single visit

Central London

Lincoln's Inn Court

Gray's Inn Court

punishing effect of the law's interminable delays in *Bleak House*. ■ *The walks are open in summer 1230-1400 Mon-Fri. T020-7458 7800.*

Charles Dickens' House
Charles Dickens' House, 48 Doughty Street, WC1, is a smart four-storey Georgian terraced house where Dickens lived for two years while writing *Oliver Twist* and *Nicholas Nickleby*, between 1837 and 1839. The drawing room, wash house and wine cellar have been recreated as they were in his day, with the drawing room in particular using much of his original furniture; indeed all the rooms are packed with Dickens memorabilia sure to delight fans of the troubled storyteller.

As well as manuscripts of his works on display, and lots of Dickensia for sale in the shop, a half-hour video runs through the high and low points of Dickens' life, while in June and July on Wednesdays at 1930, 'The Sparkler of Albion' is a two-hour theatre show doing much the same but with more gusto (£12.50). ■ *Open Mon-Sat 1000-1700. Admission £4, £3 concession. T020-7405 2127 .*

> **Five of the best: funky loos**
>
> • *Stream*, Long Lane, Clerkenwell.
> • *Prism*, Leadenhall Street, City.
> • *The Oratory*, Brompton Road, South Kensington.
> • *Bam-Bou*, Percy Street, Fitzrovia.
> • *Wine Wharf*, Stoney Street, Bankside.

A short walk left along Guilford Street from here leads to Guilford Place at the top of **Lamb's Conduit Street**, a quiet pedestrianized street with its original gas lamps still in place and several pubs and shops of real character. The conduit was a dam in one of the tributaries of the Fleet river in Elizabethan times, hence the elegant statue of the water carrier in Guilford Place.

There's an excellent-value vegetarian café in the Mary Ward Centre; open Mon-Thu 0930-2100, Fri 0930-2030, Sat 0930-1600
West of the street lies Bloomsbury, and beyond Great Ormond St Hospital for Children, the peaceful haven of Queen Square, home to several other specialist hospitals. Here also is the **Mary Ward Centre**, Queen Square, T020-7831 7711, named after the best-selling 19th-century novelist known as Mrs Humphrey Ward, who in 1899 founded the first school for physically handicapped children in England. Evening classes and various courses now take place in its fine red-brick, black-and-white tiled building.

Clerkenwell

Clerkenwell is one of the more exciting parts of London to wander around, not simply because of the clutch of new shops, restaurants, clubs and bars that have opened up here in the last decade, but also because it's an old part of town still visibly in a state of fashionable flux.

Smithfield Market
A good place to start is in the south of the area around Smithfield Market, London's meat distribution centre. Unlike the other wholesale fish and fruit and veg markets at Billingsgate and Covent Garden, the market has managed to cling on to its ancient site in the city centre. Especially late at night and at dawn, when the area round about is partying hard or fast asleep, the comings and goings of huge articulated and refrigerated lorries unloading endless fresh carcasses into its grand late 19th-century building can take on a surreal quality.

Blood and guts

The blood and entrails of the livestock slaughtered in Smithfield ran in the streets' gutters, and rogue bulls sought sanctuary in the houses and shops around – hence the phrase 'bull in a china shop'.

But it wasn't only animals who were butchered at Smithfield Market. Until the gallows moved west to Tyburn (modern Marble Arch), this was also a place of execution. Burnings, roastings and boilings were visited on witches and heretics in front of enthusiastic crowds, and Wat Tyler, leader of the Peasants' Revolt of 1381, was stabbed here before being beheaded in front of St Bartholomew's Hospital.

Just to the northeast of the market is **Charterhouse Square**, named after the Tudor manor house on its north side. The Charterhouse is a set of beautiful 16th-century almshouses on the site of a 14th-century Carthusian monastery which later became a top public school that moved out to Surrey in the 19th century. It's long been the Anglican church's venerable equivalent of the Royal Hospital at Chelsea, providing peaceful accommodation for gentleman pensioners. ■ *Open for guided tours Apr-Jul, Wed 1415, £3, otherwise by appointment. T020-7253 9503.*

The Charterhouse The tour includes the gardens, medieval buildings & 17th-century chapel as well as the manor house

Central London

Nearby in West Smithfield is the oldest parish church in London, **St Bartholomew the Great**. Not much of the 12th-century priory church remains, but the Norman nave has featured in several major films including *Shakespeare in Love, The End of the Affair, Jude* and *Robin Hood Prince of Thieves*. ■ *Open 0830-1600 Mon-Fri, 1030-1330 Sat, 1400-1700 Sun. T020-7606 5171.*

In the 12th century, St John Street was already the main road north from Smithfield Market to the Angel Islington. Its wiggling pack-pony trail is now Clerkenwell's most happening street at night. Just off to its west, tucked away down St John's Lane, stands the early 16th-century gatehouse of the **Priory of St John of Jerusalem**, the impressive remains of the medieval home of the Knights Hospitaller. In the 19th century the place was taken over by the Order of St John, a Victorian chivalric society that founded the St John's Ambulance Brigade which provides voluntary ambulances and first aid at a huge number of public events around the country.

The **Museum of the Order of St John** in the gatehouse has a small exhibition divided between the stories of the Order and its Brigade and the armour of the Knights Hospitaller. ■ *Open 1000-1630 Mon-Sat. Admission free. Guided tours (£4 lasting about 1 ½ hrs) Tue, Fri, Sat 1100, 1430, include the Church and Crypt. T020-7253 6644.*

A left turn at the end of St John's Lane onto the Clerkenwell Road leads to Clerkenwell Green. Here the classical poise of the late 18th-century **Church of St James** (T020-7251 1190; open 1000-1800 Monday-Friday, Sunday service 1100) contributes to the charming atmosphere of one of the area's most subversive corners, a centre for its artisan associations with several interesting crafts designers and the place to find the **Marx Memorial Library**, at 37a Clerkenwell Green, EC1.

Built as a Welsh Charity School in the early 18th century, in 1933 it became a members lending library of socialist literature in honour of the great economist, having been the offices from 1892-1922 of the radical Twentieth

Five of the best: caffeine kicks

- *Café Kick*, Exmouth Market, Clerkenwell.
- *Raison d'être*, Bute Street, South Kensington.
- *Café Rive Gauche*, Warren Street, Fitzrovia.
- *Coffee Matters*, Southampton Row, Holborn.
- *Konditor and Cook*, The Cut, Waterloo.

Century Press supported by William Morris. Marx is even reckoned to have taken coffee on the Green, still not a bad idea today. The lending library is available to members upstairs and anyone is welcome to have a look around the ground floor. ■ *Open Mon 1300-1800, Tue-Thu 1300-2000, Sat 1000-1300. Admission free. T020-7251 4706.*

Clerkenwell Green joins up with Farringdon Lane, where at No 16 the lid of the Clerk's Well that gives the area its name can be seen through a window. Closer inspections can be arranged through Finsbury Lending Library (T020-7527 7960).

Farringdon Lane joins the traffic-choked Farringdon Road opposite the offices of the Guardian newspaper which so much enjoys and contributes to the left-wing vogue of the area. At the top of the hill, where Farringdon Road meets Rosebery Avenue, is **Exmouth Market**, a pedestrianized old street where the market had died on its feet before being revitalized by a wave of hip eateries and boutiques.

At the end of the street, at 1 Myddelton Street, EC1, the **Family Record Centre** is the branch of the Public Records Office where births, deaths, marriages and adoptions can be traced as far back as July 1837. On the first floor there's an exhibition on the first national census taken in the 19th century, and anyone is welcome to browse the indexes for documents (facsimiles available) on their friends, family or ancestors. ■ *Open Mon, Wed, Fri, 0900-1700, Tue 1000-1900, Thu 0900-1900, Sat 0930-1700. Admission free. T020-8392 5300.*

Eating and drinking

Expensive **In Holborn**, the latest venue for some widely acclaimed haute cuisine is *High Holborn*, 95-96 High Holborn, WC1, T020-7404 3338 (closed weekends, like most of Holborn), a modern French restaurant with funky and colourful décor and a lively bar downstairs. The *Bleeding Heart Bistro and Restaurant*, Bleeding Heart Yard, off Greville St, EC1, T020-7242 2056 (closed weekends) is a bustling old-fashioned place for some superior French and Kiwi cooking.

In Clerkenwell, *Club Gascon*, 57 West Smithfield, EC1, T020-7796 0600, specializes in the regional produce of Gascony, foie gras of course, exquisite (and expensive) gastronomic delights served plate by plate in a gentle, slightly fey and appreciative atmosphere. *Moro*, 34-36 Exmouth Market, EC1, T020-7833 8336, is a large modern Spanish restaurant that has been wowing the area's hipsters, shakers and movers for some time with its artful way with super fresh ingredients. It's been so successful that one of its main suppliers, *Brindisa Spanish Food Importers*, have opened up a deli next door.

Mid-range
For discerning carnivores, Clerkenwell is a top destination

Especially good is *St John*, 26 St John St, T020-7251 0848, where offal and freshly baked bread are served up in a stark old smokery celebrating 'nose to tail' eating. Nearby, **Smiths of Smithfield**, 67-77 Charterhouse St, EC1, T020-7236 6666 www.smithsofsmithfield.co.uk, is another meat-market restaurant, a loud busy place playing club music with different tones on each of its four levels.

Meat again further up the Farringdon Rd near Exmouth Market, *The Quality Chop House*, 92-94 Farringdon Rd, T020-7837 5093, is a long-standing cod-working-class diner doing very good (but quite expensive) basic British fare, including fish and chips. Over the road, *The Eagle*, 159 Farringdon Rd, T020-7837 1353, was one of the first pubs to go gastro, cooking up excellent modern European food right behind the bar. Back in Smithfield, but for fish surprisingly, *Stream Bubble and Shell*, 50-52 Long Lane, EC1, T020-7796 0070, is a champagne, Guinness, oyster and lobster bar that's very good value and often very busy, with wacky toilets. More traditional, *Abbaye*, 55 Charterhouse St, EC1, T020-7253 1612, is a Belgian beer and mussel bar run efficiently and well by the Dome chain.

Cheap

In Exmouth Market, the *Japanese Canteen*, 21 Exmouth Market, EC1, T020-7833 3521, is a busy branch of the basic Japanese chain. In Holborn, just round the corner from the Dickens' House Museum, *Sheng's Tea House*, 68 Millman St, WC1, T020-7405 3697, is a cheerful Chinese, while *Mangiare*, 4-6 Theobald's Rd, WC1, T020-7831 9268, do excellent fresh pizza slices. *The Fryer's Delight*, 19 Theobald's Rd, WC1, T020-7405 4114, is a traditional fish and chip shop beloved by cabbies. In summer, the secret garden of the *October Gallery Café*, 24 Old Gloucester St, T020-7242 7367, comes into its own at lunchtimes.

Cafés & sandwich bars

In Holborn, *Coffee Matters*, 4 Southhampton Row, WC1, T020-7242 9090, specialize in Fair Trade coffee, organic yoghurt, and delicious salads.

In Clerkenwell, *Café Kick*, 43 Exmouth Market, EC1, T020-7837 8077, is as much a bar as a café, a shrine to table football that does a huge variety of different coffees and decent food. A little further afield, *The Quiet Revolution*, 49 Old St, T020-7253 5556, is a very popular organic soup café. *Benugo's Sandwich and Juice Bar*, T020-7253 3499, on the junction of St John St and Clerkenwell Rd, is a hip joint for healthy drinks and good breads.

Pubs & bars
It doesn't come as much of a surprise that Holborn has plenty of antique drinking holes

In Holborn The famous three are: the *Cittie of York*, 22 High Holborn, WC1, T020-7242 7670, with its extra long bar, cubby holes for lawyers and crude wallpaintings of famous tipplers; the warren of historic wooden rooms at *Ye Olde Cheshire Cheese*, 145 Fleet St, EC4, T020-7353 6170; and the last word in cosy and quaint, *Ye Olde Mitre Tavern*, Ely Court, Ely Place, EC1, T020-7405 4751, tucked away up a tiny alleyway. All three are old-hands at serving crowds of boozy office workers and tourists.

A quieter and in many ways more satisfying destination is Lamb's Conduit St, starting with *The Three Cups*, 21 Sandland St, WC1, T020-7831 4302, a very pleasant old-school Young's pub with tables outside in summer. Even more local and also inimitable, *VATS Winebar*, 51 Lamb's Conduit St, WC1, T020-7242 8963 is genially stuck in the 50s with a loyal troupe of affable middle-aged bon viveurs. A little further up, *The Perseverance*, 63 Lamb's Conduit St, WC1, T020-7405 8278, is a proper London freehouse popular with a younger crowd and a new restaurant upstairs. Last on the street is *The Lamb*, 94 Lamb's Conduit St, WC1, T020-7405 0713, a cosy old-timer that hasn't changed in years and keeps a loyal and mixed crowd of fans happily in their pints of Young's Special. Near the Dickens' House Museum, the *Duke of York*, 7 Roger St, WC1, T020-7242 7230, does good real ales, has tables outside and serves up scrummy but expensive food.

In Clerkenwell, three pubs are especially well worth seeking out: the scruffy wood-pannelled Georgian charm of *The Jerusalem Tavern*, 55 Britton St, T0200-7490 4281, the sole London outlet for St Peter's Ale from Bungay in Suffolk; the colourful old pâpiér mached interior of Clerkenwell Green's local, *The Three Kings*, 7 Clerkenwell

▶▶ *Go to page 426 for entertainment & nightlife*

Central London

Close, EC1, T020-7253 0483, and near Smithfield Market, the Victorian correctness of the *Fox and Anchor*, 115 Charterhouse St, EC1, T020-7253 4838, for very full breakfasts served up to meat market porters from 0700.

It's the bars rather than the pubs that lead the way in Clerkenwell, most staying open at least until midnight, and many until later on Fri & Sat

Fairly typical is *Dust*, 27 Clerkenwell Rd, EC1, T020-7490 5120, open until 0200 Fri, Sat, midnight on Thu, a music bar with bare wooden floorboards, basic furnishings, loud music and hip drinks. A touch more sophisticated, *Match Bar*, 45-47 Clerkenwell Rd, T020-7450 4002, does excellent food and cocktails in a sleek and happy atmosphere. More old-style, the restaurant and bar at loud and cheerful *Vic Naylor's*, 38-40 St John St, EC1, T020-7608 2181, open until midnight Mon-Thu, till 0100 Fri & Sat, was used as the location for Sting's bar in Guy Ritchie's hit movie *Lock, Stock and Two Smoking Barrels*. More alcoholoic hip replacement at *Fluid*, 40 Charterhouse St, EC1, T020-7253 3444.

Shopping

Not much reason for a shopping trip to Holborn, other than *Blacks* 10/11 Holborn, T020-7401 5681, for outdoor activity gear. **Leather Lane Market** though is worth the scrum: Cockney barrowboys selling all sorts of quality and tat lord it over a curious mixture of customers, very busy at midday, and good for bargain clothes for women.

In Clerkenwell, apart from *Simply Sausages*, 421 Central Markets, on the corner of Charterhouse and Farringdon Rd, SW1, T020-7329 3227, and their superb bangers, the name of the game is arts and crafts. The *Clerkenwell Green Association*, Pennybank Chambers, 33-35 St John's Square, EC1, T020-7251 0276, represent and provide space for craftworkers, stage exhibitions of their work and can point the curious towards the likes of Lesley Craze or Hazel Faithfull. *Malapa*, 41 Clerkenwell Rd, T020-7490 5229, is a bargain sale shop for designer womenswear by the likes of Tristan Webber, Dai Rees, Mulligan, Maria Chen, and Preen, as well their own label.

Exmouth Market is the best spot for fashion though, with T-shirt supremos *Antoni and Alison*, at 43 Rosebery Ave, T020-7833 2002, and *North 2*, 31 Exmouth Market, T020-7837 5822, doing men and women's designer clothes by Kenzo, Geoffrey West shoes, and an emphasis on the cutting edge. *Space EC1*, 25 Exmouth Market, T020-7837 1344, stock an inspired range of gifts, from bags and cushions to mugs.

Transport

Buses **Along Kingsway and Southampton Row**:
No 1 to Canada Water via Holborn Station, Aldwych, Waterloo, Elephant, South Bermondsey and Surrey Quays.
No 59 to Brixton via Russell Square, Aldwych, Waterloo and Kennington.
No 68 to Waterloo via Aldwych.
No 91 to Crouch End via Aldwych, Euston, King's Cross, Caledonian Rd and Holloway.
No 171 from Holborn Station to Waterloo.
No 188 to Greenwich via Aldwych, Waterloo, Elephant, Bermondsey, Canada Water, Surrey Quays and Deptford.

Along Fleet St:
No 11 to Fulham Broadway via Bank, St Paul's, Aldwych, Strand, Trafalgar Square, Westminster, Victoria, Sloane Square and Chelsea.
No 15 to Tower of London via Marble Arch, Oxford Circus, Piccadilly Circus, Trafalagar Square, Aldwych, St Paul's and Cannon St.
No 26 to Shoreditch via Aldwych, St Paul's, Bank and Liverpool St.

No 76 to Stoke Newington via Waterloo, Aldwych, Ludgate Circus, St Paul's, Mansion House, Bank, Moorgate, Old Street Station, Hoxton and Dalston.
No 341 to Islington via Grays Inn Rd.

Along High Holborn:
No 8 to Bethnal Green via Bank and Liverpool St.
No 45 to Brixton via Gray's Inn Rd, Holborn Circus, Blackfriars, Elephant and Camberwell.

Along Holborn:
No 242 to Hackney via Bank, Liverpool St, Shoreditch and Dalston.

Along Theobald's Rd:
No 19 to Battersea via Bloomsbury, Piccadilly Circus, Hyde Park Corner, Knightsbridge, Sloane Square, and Chelsea.
No 38 to Islington.
No 55 to Old St and Shoreditch.
No 98 from Holborn Station to Willesden via Oxford Circus, Marble Arch, Edgware Rd and Kilburn.

Plenty along High Holborn, Theobald's Rd, Farringdon Rd and Clerkenwell Rd.   Taxis

Blackfriars and City Thameslink for King's Cross, London Bridge, Waterloo East, north   Trains
and south London suburbs, Gatwick Airport and Brighton.

Holborn (Central and Piccadilly lines) or Chancery Lane (Central line) for Lincoln's Inn   Tubes
Fields. Temple District and Circle lines; closed Sun) for Fleet St. Farringdon or Barbican
(Hammersmith & City, Metropolitan and Circle lines) for Clerkenwell.

Central London (side margin)

The City

The City is where London began, and judging from the harried look of its working population, it ain't over yet. Nowhere is the contrast stronger between weekday and weekend, or even between lunch and supper. During the week thousands storm into the Square Mile to deal with billions of other people's money, fortunes are made or broken with a few megabytes in massive offices, and then come Saturday it all might never have happened: the place is left to the coach parties and tourists, a gigantic modern ghost town sprinkled with empty little churches.

    The grand exception is **St Paul's Cathedral**, its great stone interior always echoing with sightseers or worshippers, its dome one of the most beautiful, symbolic landmarks in London and a spectacular view point. Some idea of what has being going down as well as up all around its prime position over the centuries can be discovered at the excellent **Museum of London**, while next door the **Barbican Centre** provides another cultural oasis for live performances of a consistently high standard. Like Wren's churches though, all three seem sadly and oddly isolated from their local situation: with its guilds, livery companies and all-powerful Corporation, its banks, brokers and beadles, its secrecy and greed, the City has become a formidable but characterless money market and global betting shop.

⊖ St Paul's tube for the Cathedral, or Museum of London & the west end of the City. Also Barbican tube for the Museum of London. Bank or Monument tube for the rest of the City

History

The Square Mile has always been the pulsating business end of London, around which the rest of the city has grown. Although Celtic settlements dotted the banks of the Thames, Roman Londinium, occupying a smaller area than the later medieval City, was the first substantial settlement here. Following Boudicca's destruction of the city in AD 61 it was fortified by a wall three miles long, 8 ft thick and up to 20 ft high. The commercial heart was a giant basilica on Cornhill, public baths lay by formidable city gates (recalled in the current names Ludgate, Newgate, Bishopsgate and Aldgate) and a fort was erected near Cripplegate.

The richer merchants built villas along the eastern banks of the Walbrook, and the Thames shoreline was lined with jetties and wharves laden with goods. A wooden bridge spanned the Thames to a small settlement that became Southwark. Tacitus, in about AD 67, described Londinium as 'a celebrated centre of commerce', and towards the end of Roman rule in 410, it boasted a population of at least 50,000.

There is no record of City life until the seventh century, when the Christian King of Kent, Sebert, founded St Paul's, and built a palace at Aldermanbury that served successive Saxon kings until Edward the Confessor moved to Westminster in 1060 to supervise the building of the Abbey. Following the sacking of the city by the Danes, King Alfred re-established the trading prowess of London, and when another Viking invasion saw Canute take the throne in the early 11th century, London replaced Alfred's Winchester as the capital of England.

The Norman invasion brought further consolidation of the City's political and economic status. The White Tower was built just outside the city walls, and a couple of further forts within the city itself, Baynard's Castle and Montichet's Tower, served to control the Saxon subjects as much as to defend the city. Medieval London flourished, despite the fact that two thirds of its people died painfully during the Black Death of 1347-48.

London's independence was granted in a charter from King John, entitling the City to elect its own Mayor who was answerable to none but the sovereign. Guilds (or later the City Livery Companies) formed to represent their member's interests, and built fine halls in which to meet. Mercers, Grocers, Drapers, Fishmongers, Ironmongers, Clothworkers… there were 80 of them in all and they governed the city from the Guildhall, a legacy of Mayor Richard 'Dick' Whittington.

London Bridge was rebuilt in stone, a ditch was dug around the city, and the markets flourished. Poultry could be found at Leadenhall; fish, corn and salt at Billingsgate; old clothes on Petticoat Lane; while Bread (John Milton was born here) Milk, and Wood Streets speak for themselves. Lombard Street was where one sought financial expertise, the Lombards having arrived from Italy following the expulsion of the Jews in 1290, who had themselves occupied the area around Old Jewry (Cromwell welcomed them back in the 17th century).

Market gardens and orchards spread out by the north wall. Violence was rife. Cheapside, the largest market, witnessed bloody battles between the Skinners and the Fishmongers, and an explosion of xenophobia against foreign merchants in 1517.

Hotels in the area

AL *Great Eastern Hotel*
AL *The King's Wardrobe*
E *YHA City of London*
E *Barbican YMCA*
E *London City YMCA*
▸▸ *Go to page 447*

The companies of guilds were always at each others throats, sometimes literally, especially the spicers and the pepperers, or the tailors and the drapers. Religious houses dotted the landscape – Austin friars, Crossed (Crutched) Friars, Dominicans at Blackfriars (the site of Baynard's Castle).

By the 16th century, the city was overcrowded, and the hamlets beyond the gates and Bars (Temple, Holborn and others) began to grow. Henry VIII freed up a good deal of building land within the City with the Dissolution of the Monasteries, and London's central position in European trade was aided by the Royal Exchange, built as a meeting place for City merchants. Stock companies such as the Levant Company emerged to benefit from Britain's expansion to the New World and the East. But once again, in 1665-66, the City and its residents were virtually destroyed by two apocalyptic events.

The Great Plague was brought by Norwegian brown rats, but its rapid spread was aided by the close, cramped, overhanging houses and filthy streets (Houndsditch is so called because it's where the dead dogs were thrown). The close, wooden housing also meant that, following a hot, dry summer and aided by an easterly wind, the **Great Fire** swept through the streets for four days, destroying four-fifths of the City. Despite rebuilding plans of grand design being submitted by the likes of Sir Christopher Wren, the merchants couldn't afford to wait, so the rebuilding followed the medieval street plan, but this time using stone and brick.

Wren's **St Paul's** emerged as intended – a Protestant rival to the Catholic St Peter's in Rome – and he supervised a further 51 churches erected within the City. The Bank of England was founded to finance war with France, and the Mansion House to house the Mayor. The Roman Wall and old city gates were demolished, the houses and shops lining the bridge were removed and in 1769 Blackfriars became the first new bridge out of the City since the first London Bridge built by the Romans. Nevertheless, slums also emerged, like those around Smithfield (see page 224).

With the Industrial Revolution the City changed rapidly. A new system of sewers was built following cholera epidemics in the 1830s and 40s; new roads and surfaces were laid to accommodate the Omnibus Company; railways ploughed into Cannon Street, Liverpool Street and Blackfriars; and the first underground (the Metropolitan Line) was opened in 1863. Edwardian and modern structures continued to rise up in the course of the last century – *The Daily Telegraph* and *Daily Express* moved to Fleet Street, and Leadenhall and Bishopsgate saw several office blocks in the 1920s.

Further upheaval was caused following the Second World War, when the City was heavily bombed. Twenty of the City's churches and 18 of its livery halls were destroyed, and while the subsequent rebuilding has not always been of great architectural merit there are some notable exceptions, such as the Lloyd's Building in 1986. The 1970's Barbican estate, reviled by some, is now the only residential centre in the Square Mile (the residential population is only about 5,000, although over 250,000 commute in every weekday). The City is now almost exclusively home to financial institutions, with more foreign banks than any other city in the world, and as such is seen as the economic pillar of the state, as the IRA chose to demonstrate by bombing the Baltic Exchange in 1992.

Central London

Sights

The City proper begins in the west at the site of the old Temple Bar on Fleet Street (see page 219). Fleet Street heads down into the valley of the Fleet River at Fetter Lane, near Ludgate Circus providing one of the most impressive approaches (especially at night) to what is undoubtedly the City's most spectacular sight, St Paul's Cathedral.

St Bride's Church

Close to Ludgate Circus though is another Wren masterpiece, St Bride's Church, known as the 'Cathedral of Fleet Street', and one of the finest specimens of the Italian style in England. With its wonderful wedding cake spire, it's believed that here the 6th-century Irish St Bridget (who shares her feast day with Brigit, the Celtic goddess of fertility) founded a church near the holy Bride Well. The church is also the burial place of the printer Wynkyn de Worde, the apprentice to Caxton who set up shop on Shoe Lane establishing Fleet Street's traditional trade. The excavated crypt exposed by bombing in the Blitz houses a small museum on the street's associations with the press.

■ *Open 0900-1600 Mon-Fri and Sun services 1100, 1830. T020-7427 0133.*

St Paul's Cathedral

Buses 4, 11, 15, 17, 23, 26, 76, 100 & 172

Standing proud at the top of Ludgate Hill is St Paul's Cathedral. At least the fifth church on the site, it was started in 1675, taking about 35 years to complete and was paid for with taxes raised on coal and wine coming into the Port of London. Hemmed in on all sides over the centuries, Wren's relatively colossal church still inspires awe and wonder.

The current redevelopment of Paternoster Square hopes to open up new views of the place, reflecting its Portland stone in plate-glass office blocks, while the Millennium Bridge now provides a neat approach from the riverside and Tate Modern. Wren had originally hoped to build a church in the form of a Greek cross, but this plan, and his desire to top it with a dome rather than a steeple, were vetoed. Instead he settled on the more traditional Latin cross for the ground plan, and then carried on the building work in such secrecy that no one could complain before his vision, including the dome, was substantially in place. The final result is a kind of mini version of St Peter's in Rome, much less flamboyantly decorated, and one of the most successful Classical interpretations of Gothic in the world.

Twenty-two wide steps lead up to the West Front, looking down Ludgate Hill, with its double portico containing a bas-relief depicting the conversion of the tax-collector Paul. At the apex stands St Paul himself, the patron saint of the City of London, with St Peter on his right and St James on his left, flanked by the two belltowers, each topped with a decorative pineapple. The southern clock tower is home to the 17-ton Great Paul, the biggest bell in Britain, used to announce the start of services. The clock itself strikes the hours on three other bells, the largest of which was cast in the reign of Edward I and is traditionally tolled for two hours on the death of a monarch. Behind is the Great Dome, invisibly supported with reinforced concrete and a chain of steel after it was discovered that Wren's builders had skimped on the use of solid stone for the supporting columns.

Central London

Inside, the massive nave of the Cathedral is wonderfully vast and bare. In fact most of the decoration was only added in the late 19th and early 20th centuries, and not very well at that. It's definitely well worth climbing up the long, gentle, wide wooden spiral staircase to the **Whispering Gallery**, around the base of the inner dome, decorated with statues of Early Church Fathers and painted scenes from the life of St Paul. People press their ears to the wall here hoping to catch what their friends are whispering on the other side. Unfortunately the hubbub from far below often drowns out the famous effect.

Unlike Westminster Abbey, there's room in the Cathedral for visitors not to be so strictly regimented in what they see

Several steep and narrow flights of stone steps with regular resting places then lead up to the **Stone Gallery** outside, where the views through the balustrade are quite spectacular. In order to look west from here though it's necessary to brave the extraordinary series of vertiginous cast-iron spiral stairways heading up to the **Golden Gallery**. The tremendous wrap-around open-air views from the cramped little balcony up here easily rival those from the London Eye. And they're not even from the very top of the building. Further flights of wooden steps closed to the public lead up to a viewing platform for about 10 people inside the ball beneath the Cross. Descending via those westward vistas from the Stone Gallery provides an opportunity to appreciate the dome's threefold construction and see the hollow brick cone between the inner and outer domes that supports the Orb and Cross.

During the summer, the crowds can be avoided by arriving first thing in the morning during the week

Back in the main body of the Cathedral, unmissable sights include the **choir** gorgeously carved by Grinling Gibbons; **Henry Moore's sculpture** of Mother and Child in the north choir aisle; the copy of Holman Hunt's *The Light of the World* in the north transept; a small display on the firewatch that saved the building during the Blitz; and the **American Memorial Chapel** at the very east end of the church in the apse, consecrated to the memory of over 28,000 US servicemen based in Britain who died in the Second World War.

Downstairs, 'the largest crypt in Europe' contains the OBE Chapel, monuments to Wellington, Nelson and many others, and more interestingly, Wren's original models for the Cathedral and the Treasury of the Diocese of London. There's also a shop, expensive café and a restaurant.

■ *Open 0830-1600 Mon-Sat, admission £5 including Cathedral Crypt and Galleries, £2.50 under-16s. Guided tours 1100, 1130, 1330, 1400 Mon-Sat £2.50, £2 concessions & under-16s. Audio guide £3.50. Organ recitals 1700 Sun, free. T020-7236 4128, www.stpauls.co.uk Buses: 4, 11, 15, 17, 23, 26, 76, 100, 172.*

Around St Paul's

South of St Paul's Churchyard, beyond the *City Information Centre* (■ *Open 0930-1700 Mon-Fri, 0930-1200 Sat, T020- 7332 1456*), the streets around Carter Lane have kept much of their medieval layout, leading down to the 17th-century **Apothecaries Hall**, Blackfriars Lane, EC4 (*T020-7236 1180; open for group tours of 10-25 people, £3 each*), and the plain brick church of **St Andrew by the Wardrobe**, the last that Wren built in the City.

Nearby is the beautiful 17th-century home of the **College of Arms**, 130 Queen Victoria St, EC4, the place to find out whether a family is qualified to carry a heraldic coat of arms. Three kings of arms (Garter, Clarenceux, and Norroy), six heralds, and four pursuivants regulate the bearing of arms and trace pedigrees. Visitors can see the Court of the Earl Marshal (always the

Duke of Norfolk), who organizes most of the state ceremonies involving the monarchy, and evening tours are given by arrangement. ■*Open Mon-Fri 1000-1600. T020-7248 2762.*

Old Bailey   West of St Paul's, on Newgate Street, stands the Old Bailey, or Central Criminal Court, topped by its copper dome and famous statue of Justice balancing a sword and a pair of scales, on the site of the notoriously brutal Newgate

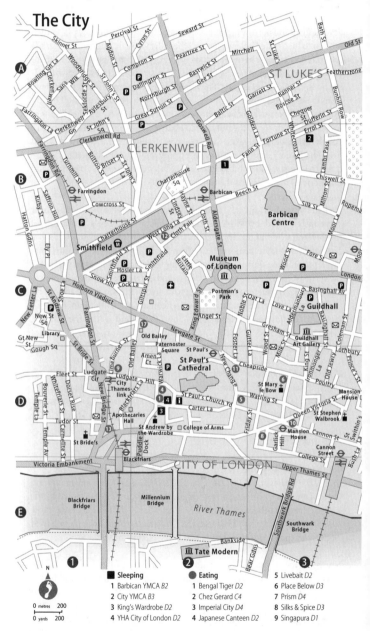

The City

■ Sleeping	● Eating	5 Livebait *D2*
1 Barbican YMCA *B2*	1 Bengal Tiger *D2*	6 Place Below *D3*
2 City YMCA *B3*	2 Chez Gerard *C4*	7 Prism *D4*
3 King's Wardrobe *D2*	3 Imperial City *D4*	8 Silks & Spice *D3*
4 YHA City of London *D2*	4 Japanese Canteen *D2*	9 Singapura *D1*

0 metres 200
0 yards 200

Prison. The prison was finally pulled down in 1902 after countless people had literally rotted away there, forcing the judges to stop their noses with scented posies. Much of the front of the new building used stones from the old prison. Nowadays the famous British justice system, tarnished in the recent past by a series of flawed convictions in the fight against terrorism, can be seen in action from the public galleries of 18 modern courtrooms. ■ *Open 1030-1300, 1400-1630 Mon-Fri. T020-7248 3277.*

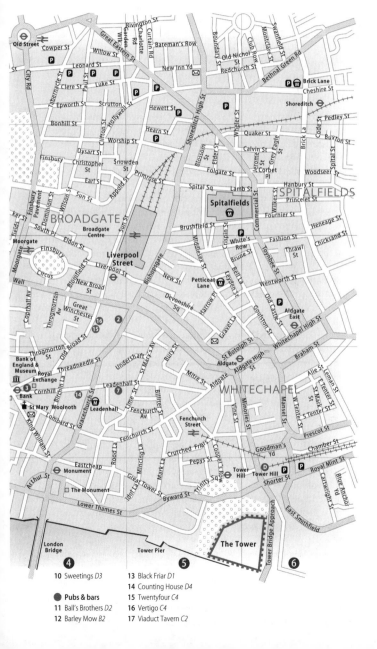

10 Sweetings *D3*

13 Black Friar *D1*
14 Counting House *D4*

● **Pubs & bars**
11 Ball's Brothers *D2*
12 Barley Mow *B2*

15 Twentyfour *C4*
16 Vertigo *C4*
17 Viaduct Tavern *C2*

Postman's Park North of St Paul's, beyond Paternoster Square, King Edward Street heads past the old General Post Office into Little Britain. On the right is the tiny Postman's Park, behind the church of St Botolph's-without-Aldersgate, where the wall of Commeration of Heroic Sacrifice overlooks a fountain and fish pond in the garden where the founder of Methodism John Wesley once preached. China memorials describe the heroic deeds, such as 'PC Percy Edwin Cook who voluntarily descended high tension chamber at Kensington to rescue two workmen overcome by poisonous gas, 7 October 1927', or 'Mary Rogers, Stewardess of the Stella, self-sacrificed by giving up her lifebelt and voluntarily going down with sinking ship, March 30 1899', or 'Edmund Emery of 272 King's Rd Chelsea who leapt from a steamboat to rescue a child and was drowned July 31 1874'.

Museum of London

This is one of London's liveliest museums Just round the corner, at 150 London Wall, bang in the middle of a busy roundabout on the site of a Roman fort, is the excellent, purpose-built Museum of London. Opened in 1976, it has a refreshing visual approach to the social history of the city, illustrating the daily lives led here down the ages with a combination of genuine artefacts, reconstructions and canny design.

On the first level, after the temporary exhibition galleries, the museum plunges back into prehistory with mock-ups of how the landscape may have looked way back when, complete with an atmospheric soundtrack enhancing the appreciation of a variety of Iron Age objects, many dredged up from the river. It really gets into its stride with Roman London though, featuring a reconstruction of a wealthy Roman's house and the museum's most exciting recent addition: a cache of 43 gold coins dating from AD 65-170 discovered in the autumn of 2000 buried in a hole in the floor of Plantation House, just off Eastcheap. Many are in almost mint condition, the Emperors' profiles still remarkably vivid. Eight of these coins could have bought a boy slave, or maybe about 23 acres of Kentish woodland.

The Dark Age and Saxon galleries are inevitably quite scant in artefacts, but the Medieval and Tudor galleries beyond make up the deficit with carvings, astonishing jewellery, armour and more coins set amid excellent scale models of how a few important buildings may have looked before that defining event, the disastrous Great Fire. This apocalyptic conflagration is described by extracts from Pepys' diary commenting on a rather tame diorama of the City skyline.

Downstairs the story of the city's rebuilding, expansion and growth continues around the Garden court and the sumptuously decorated Lord Mayor's Coach, still used annually for the Lord Mayor's Show. The late Stuart and 18th-century London galleries include a reconstructed late 17th-century room, the door of a cell from Newgate Prison, and some gorgeous dresses. In the 19th-century and Imperial Capital galleries the contrast between the city's architectural grandeur and the prevailing squalor becomes acute. A beautiful art deco lift from Selfridges is the highlight of transition into the early 20th century, the Second World War and London Now room.

■ *Open Mon-Sat 1000-1750, Sun 1200-1750, admission £5 (valid for one year), £3 concession, free after 1630. Café open Mon-Sat 1000-1730, Sun 1130-1730. T020-7600 3699, events T020-7814 5777, www.museumoflondon.org.uk*

Barbican Centre Close by the Museum between Aldersgate and London Wall rears the immense, famously disorientating and surprisingly popular 70s housing complex called the Barbican, one of the City's very few residential enclaves. Somewhere in here it's usually an enjoyable challenge looking for the Barbican Centre, with its vibrant galleries, cinemas, music halls and theatres. Be sure to allow plenty of 'ticket time'.

The **Barbican Art Gallery**, on Level 3 of the Barbican Centre, mounts a wide variety of exhibitions, usually lasting two or three months, with a reputation for taking interesting angles on all kinds of different aspects of art and design: centenary celebrations, fine art retrospectives, furniture making and jewellery as well as much more. ■ *Open 1000-1800 Mon, Tue, Thu-Sat; 1000-2000 Wed; 1200-1800 Sun. Admission around £7; £4 under-16s. T020- 7638 8891; enquiries T020-7638 4141.*

Just southeast of the Barbican off Gresham Street is the City of London's town The Guildhall
hall, the Guildhall, the 500-year-old home of the city council aka the Corporation of London. The fully restored 15th-century Great Hall with its bizarre cod-Indian façade is festooned with flags and arms of the 12 major livery companies. Above the gallery at the west end stand the statues of Gog and Magog, replacing the 14-ft versions carved in 1708 that were destroyed in the Blitz. Wickerwork models of these two characters were traditionally carried in the Lord Mayor's procession.

According to legend Gog and Magog were more accustomed to doing the carrying themselves as porters at the royal palace of the mythical English King Brute, the captive and sole survivors of his triumph over their sibling giants, all bastard offspring of some demons and the 33 husband-murdering daughters of the Emperor Diocletian. Now they look down each year on the keynote Prime Minister's speech at the Lord Mayor's Banquet, held in the hall on the Monday after his annual Show. The crypt below contains a forest of columns and a spectacular vaulted ceiling.

■ *Open Mon-Fri 0930-1700. Admission free. Details on tours of the crypt from the Remembrances department, T020-7332 1460. General enquiries, T020-7606 3030.*

Next door in Guildhall Yard, the Guildhall Art Gallery opened the doors of its Guildhall Art
smart new purpose-built accommodation in November 1999, having been Gallery
delayed for 10 years by the discovery of a Roman amphitheatre beneath the site. Carefully excavated, the remains will one day be open to the public. Meanwhile a circle in the Yard marks the projected outline of the theatre. The Gallery displays the Corporation's large collection of art in fine style, mainly 19th-century portraits and paintings and some of topographical interest.

■ *Open Mon-Sat 1000-1700 (last admission 1630), Sun 1200-1600 (last admission 1545). Admission £2.50, £1 under-18s, free all day Fri, and after 1530 Mon-Sat). T020-7332 1632; recorded information T020-7332 3700.*

In the neck of the yard, just before Gresham Street, No 1 Guildhall Yard Buildings was once the **Irish Chamber** that was used by the Irish Society, an independent charity that still administers the sizeable revenue from the City's Northern Irish estates in Londonderry and Coleraine, a legacy of the 17th-century 'Ulster plantations'. All the money raised by the Society must by statute be spent in the province.

Central London

Opposite is **St Lawrence Jewry**, founded in the 12th century and topped with a gridiron weathervane, a reminder that the Saint's martyrdom involved being roasted alive. Only the walls and tower of this neo-classical Wren church were left standing after the Second World War. Fully rebuilt and now rather soulless, it's the Corporation's grand official place of worship and also the official church of the New Zealand Society. ■*Open Mon-Fri 0700-1300. T020-7600 9478.*

Guildhall Library & Clockmakers' Museum

In the Guildhall's modern west wing is the Library and the Clockmakers' Museum. The oldest collection of its kind in the world, the chief attraction of this museum run by the Clockmakers' Company is the overall aesthetic appeal of the hundreds of ancient watches and grandfather clocks on display. Individual timepieces of interest include Harrison's chronometer, made famous by Dava Sobel's *Longitude*, which first allowed navigators to calculate their distance east or west from the meridian; a clock in the shape of a skull that supposedly belonged to Mary Queen of Scots; and the first watch to reach the summit of Everest, on the wrist of Sir Edmund Hillary in 1953. In the same building there's the extensive public reference library on London history and a small bookshop specializing in the city.

■ *Open Mon-Sat 0930-1700; Clockmakers' Museum open 0930-1630 Mon-Fri (often closed Mon morning, and may soon be closed for a 9-month overhaul) Admission free. T020-7332 1868.*

Gresham Street runs eastwards from here down to the corner of Lothbury and Prince's Street which leads past the 19th-century Grocers' (or Pepperers') Hall to where seven roads converge at Bank. If anywhere can really claim to be the hub of the City of London, this is it. The hectic junction is dominated by the Bank of England, the Royal Exchange and Mansion House, three neoclassical monuments to the City's former Imperial power.

Bank of England Museum

The only time the public are allowed into the high-security vaults of the Bank itself is on the Open House day each year in late Sep

The Bank of England occupies the entire north side between Prince's Street, Lothbury, Threadneedle Street (hence its nickname 'the old lady of Threadneedle Street') and Bartholomew Lane where visitors are welcomed free of charge into the museum. The centrepiece is a reconstruction of Sir John Soane's original stock office, with six other rooms telling the history of the Bank since 1694 entertainingly enough, including a couple of real gold bars and a pyramid of replicas. There's also the opportunity to chance your arm with a three-minute spot of simulated foreign exchange trading. Here the Great Motivator gets all the respect it deserves.

■ *Open 1000-1700 Mon-Fri. Admission free. T020-7601 5545.*

Opposite is the **Royal Exchange**, opened in 1844 after fire destroyed the replacement for Sir Thomas Gresham's Elizabethan trading hall, itself lost in the Great Fire. Unfortunately the building's famous ambulatory and frescoes are closed to the public. The **Church of St Mary Woolnoth** on the corner of Lombard Street and King William Street, was rebuilt by Hawksmoor for Queen Anne and boasts one of the architect's most beautiful interiors. ■*Open 0930-1630 Mon-Fri. T020-7626 9701.*

King William Street leads down to Monument tube at the north end of London Bridge. **The Monument**, is a 320-year-old column designed by Wren to commemorate the Great Fire, with 311 steps up a steep spiral stairway that takes 13 turns to reach a height that equals the distance from the base of the column to the place in Pudding Lane where the fire started. Breathless but not breathtaking riverside views from the top. ■ *Open 1000-1740 daily. Admission £1.50, 50p under-16s. T020-7626 2717.*

Across the way from the Royal Exchange stands the offical residence of the Lord Mayor, the **Mansion House**, which can only be seen by groups giving at least two months notice. Constructed in the 1740s with the money from fines levied on Nonconformists, its Corinthian portico conceals a lavish Egyptian Hall, but the place really comes into its own at the Lord Mayor's show. ■ *Open by appointment only; T020-7626 2500, www.cityoflondon.gov.uk*

A little further down the street the **Church of St Stephen Walbrook**, 39 Walbrook, T020-7283 4444, was Wren's rehearsal for St Paul's. Badly damaged in the Second World War, the property developer Peter Palumbo paid for its restoration, including an altar by Henry Moore that was nicknamed 'the Camembert'.

Poultry and Cheapside head back to St Paul's from here, passing the **Church of St Mary-le-Bow**, on Cheapside, famous for the Bow Bells that confer true Cockney status on anyone born within earshot. Rebuilt by Wren in the 1670s, it was destroyed in the Blitz, but its beautiful spire was restored in the 50s. ■ *Open 0630-1730 Mon-Thu, 0630-1600 Fri. T020-7248 5139.*

Heading east from Bank Cornhill leads up to Gracechurch Street. Tucked away to the left off Gracechurch Street is the **Leadenhall Market**, a superb Victorian cast-iron covered market. Not really a street market any more, it now houses some fine food shops and cafés that are always packed at lunchtimes. North and east from here towards Liverpool Street the City really means business. Beyond the gleaming Lloyd's building and the former Nat West tower, behind Liverpool Street Station, stands the enormous new Broadgate Centre. In its massive scale, snappy shops and American confidence it makes interesting comparison with the quaint old Leadenhall Market.

Eating and drinking

Although expense-account dining is one of the City's favourite pastimes there are surprisingly few excellent gourmet restaurants in the Square Mile. The emphasis in most restaurants in this bracket tends to be firmly on the powerbroking rather than the food. One reliable new option is Conran's *Aurora*, T020-7618 7000, on the ground floor of the *Great Eastern Hotel* at Liverpool St Station, and similar in its prices and modern European cooking to the *Orrery* in Marylebone.

Expensive
● *on map, page 234*

Prism, 147 Leadenhall St, EC3, T020-7256 3888, is the latest venture from Harvey Nichol's in the City, where accomplished brasserie-style food can be enjoyed in chic designer surroundings. *Imperial City*, Royal Exchange, Cornhill, EC3, T020-7626 3437 (closes at 2130), is a Cantonese restaurant in a very grand vaulted room beneath the old Royal Exchange. *Silks and Spice*, Temple Court, 11 Queen Victoria St, EC4, T020- 7248 7878, is a pricey and sophisticated Thai restaurant, while *Singapura*, 1 Limeburner Lane, EC4, T020-7329 1133, www.singapura-restaurants.co.uk, run the gamut of Malay, Indonesian, Thai and Singaporean recipes in a busy and friendly atmosphere.

The French brasserie food at *Chez Gerard Bishopsgate*, 64 Bishopsgate, EC2, T020-7588 1200, has rarely been known to disappoint, and the same can be said of the seafood at the same chain's *Livebait St Paul's*, 1 Watling St, EC4, T020-7213 0540.

Mid-range
Almost every restaurant apart from Pizza Express is closed on Sat and Sun when the only signs of life are usually to be found around Liverpool St Station

Central London

Taxi driver

Cabbie, cabbie, wherefore art thou cabbie? Repositories of all wisdom - social, political and personal - proud possessors of The Knowledge - a mental map gathered on scooter of all the major streets in London - knights of the road, and never there when you need one.

The problem is that there are simply not enough black cabs to go round. Only about 20,000 drivers cover the Greater London area, most working one of three shifts, meaning that at any one time there are only about 7,000 on the streets. So how do you track down these rare beasts? They favour the wealthier areas where passing custom is most likely to flag them down on

a whim: in the West End along Piccadilly (eastbound only), Pall Mall (westbound), in Mayfair, South Ken and Knightsbridge, and in Covent Garden or the City. Many gather at railway stations - mysteriously never quite enough to meet demand - and also at the big hotels. Drivers here may be evasive towards non-residents for fear of losing the hotel's airport run.

Unfortunately the shortage of licensed cabs leaves room for illegal and uninsured drivers to take advantage of hapless West Enders late at night: Oxford Street, the Charing Cross Road and Tottenham Court Road are the most notorious spots for these potentially lethal lifts home.

Cheap Bargain vegetarian breakfasts and lunches can be found at *The Place Below*, St Mary-le-Bow, Cheapside, EC2, T020-7329 0789 (open 0730-1430 Mon-Fri), in the crypt of the church on Cheapside. *Sweetings*, 39 Queen Victoria St, T020-7248 3062 (open 1130-1500 Mon-Fri), is a City institution, a very down-to-earth fish restaurant.

Bengal Tiger, 62-66 Carter Lane, EC4, T020-7248 6361, www.bengaltiger.co.uk (open Mon-Fri 1130-2330), is a hip and modern tiger-print Indian restaurant and bar, while round the corner the *Japanese Canteen*, Ludgate Broadway, T020-7329 3555 (1130-2000 Mon-Fri), is a small branch of the excellent noodle bar chain.

Reliable savoury Italian flatbreads can be had at *Pizza Express*, 125 Alban Gate, London Wall, T020-7600 8880 (open 1130-2300 Mon-Fri, 1200-2100 Sat, 1200-2000 Sun), beneath Chase Manhattan Bank, and also at their new branch nearer Finsbury Circus, 150 London Wall Buildings.

Pubs & bars
Many of the pubs & bars are closed at the weekend & some close early during the week.
▶▶ *Go to page 427 for entertainment & nightlife*

There's no shortage of drinking establishments in the City but some can become pretty obnoxious once the suits are well in their cups. Famous for its extraordinary carved interior and outdoor drinking area near Blackfriars Bridge is the *Black Friar*, 74 Queen Victoria St, EC4, T020-7236 5474 (open Sat 1200-1500). Near Smithfield, *The Barley Mow*, 50 Long Lane, EC1, T020-7606 6591 (open 1100-2300 Mon-Fri) is a surprisingly laid-back Hogshead pub pulling some good real ales.

For some quiet Victorian splendour close to the Old Bailey, make for the *Viaduct Tavern*, 126 Newgate St, EC1, T020-7606 8476, open Mon-Fri 1100-2300, Sat 1200-1500, although the beers are nothing special.

Fine wines and a genteel atmosphere as well as outside seating with views of St Paul's are the strong points of *Ball's Brothers*, 6-8 Cheapside, EC2, T020-7248 2708 (open 1130-2130 Mon-Fri). Another pub with exceptionally grand décor is the *Counting House*, 50 Cornhill, EC3, T020-7283 7123 (open 1100-2300 Mon-Fri), a loud and busy Fuller's outfit in a former bank.

Near Liverpool St, the *George Bar*, Great Eastern Hotel, 40 Liverpool St, EC2, T020-7618 7400, www.terminus-restaurant.co.uk (open 1100-2300 Mon-Sat, 1200-2030 Sun), is worth knowing about for its food and the fact that it's open at weekends, but not much else, while the same could be said of the *Weatherspoon* pub in the station itself, Hamilton Hall, Liverpool St Station, T020-7247 3579; open 1100-2300 Mon-Sat, 1200-2030 Sun.

Three bars stand out for their style, location and expert way with cocktails: the basement bar at *Prism*, 147 Leadenhall St, EC3, T020-7256 3888 (open 1200-2300 Mon-Fri) has expensive bottled beers and is a sophisticated place to enjoy some top-quality bar snacks; *Twentyfour*, Level 24, Tower 42, 25 Old Broad St, EC2, T020-7877 2424 (1200-2300 Mon-Fri), with wide comfortable views over the City and elegant cocktails from half way up the old Nat West tower, but not at all cheap; and for even wider views from the top of the tower, *Vertigo*, Level 42, Tower 42, 25 Old Broad St, T020- 7877 7742 (1200-1500, 1700-2300 Mon-Fri), which does fine champagne and seafood, also at City prices.

It's not that difficult to find any number of rowdy expensive bars in the early evening during the week

Shopping

Walter Thurgood, 161 Salisbury House, EC2 (near London Wall), T020-7628 5437, look as if they have been selling pipes, cigars, cigarettes and tobaccos since the fashion took hold. *Thresher and Glenny*, 50 Gresham St, EC2, T020-7606 7451, are tailors and shirt-makers to City gents, with the oldest Royal warrant of them, and they also do shoes by Harry B Hart. Otherwise shops in the City specialize in computers, organisers, or sports-wear, like *Multisports*, 61 Cheapside, EC2, T020-7248 4917, and jewellery and silver-ware, like *Links of London*, 24 Lime St, EC3, T020-7623 3101, near Leadenhall Market, with its branches of *Jigsaw*, *Hobbs*, and various sandwich shops.

The City shops in the West End, but there are a couple of old-timers worth a look if you happen to be passing

Transport

Past St Paul's:
No 11 to Chelsea via via Bank, Fleet St, Aldwych, Strand, Trafalgar Square, Westminster, Victoria and Sloane Square.
No 15 to Marble Arch via Tower of London, Cannon St, Aldwych, Trafalgar Square, Piccadilly Circus and Oxford Circus.
No 26 to Shoreditch via Bank and Liverpool St.
No 76 to Stoke Newington via Ludgate Circus, Mansion House, Bank, Moorgate, Old Street, Hoxton and Dalston.

Buses

Through Bank:
No 8 to Bethnal Green via Liverpool St.
No 242 to Shoreditch via Holborn and Liverpool St.
No 133 to Brixton via Bank, London Bridge, Elephant and Kennington.

Past Liverpool St:
No 35 between Clapham Junction and Shoreditch via Clapham Common, Brixton, Camberwell, Elephant, London Bridge and Monument.
No 344 between Clapham Junction and Liverpool St via Battersea, Vauxhall, Lambeth, Elephant, Southwark Bridge and Monument.

Always lots around Liverpool St Station and along Bishopsgate, Cheapside, Cannon St Station and Bank.

Taxis

Directory

Sports **Broadgate Ice Rink**, *Broadgate Circus, Eldon St, EC2, T020-7505 4068. Mon-Fri 1200-1430, 1530-1800, Fri also 1900-2200, Sat 1100-1300, 1400-1600 Sun 1100-1300, 1400-1600, 1700-1900, £7 adults, £4 under-16s. Open-air skating within the spectacular circle of the Broadgate Centre.* **Tourist information** *Corporation of London Information T020-7332 1456, St Paul's Churchyard, south side of the Cathedral.*

Central London

Trains   Cannon St for London Bridge and southeast; St Paul's City Thameslink for Blackfriars, Farringdon, King's Cross, London Bridge, Waterloo East, north and south London suburbs, and Brighton; Moorgate for Liverpool St; Liverpool St for Essex and north-eastern suburbs.

Tubes   St Paul's (Central line), Bank and also Monument (Central, Waterloo & City, DLR, Northern, Circle and District lines), Blackfriars, Mansion House, Cannon St (District and Circle lines), Moorgate (Northern line, Metropolitan, Circle and Hammersmith & City lines), Barbican (Metropolitan, Circle and Hammersmith & City lines), Liverpool St (Central line, and Metropolitan, Circle and Hammersmith & City lines)

Bankside and Southwark

⊖ Southwark or Blackfriars are the closest tubes to Tate Modern & the Globe. London Bridge train & tube stations are the closest to Southwark Cathedral & HMS Belfast

Over the last 10 years the south bank of the river between Blackfriars and Tower Bridge has been transformed. The conversion of the old Bankside Power Station into a world class modern art gallery at **Tate Modern** *is the latest and most spectacular confirmation of the area's new-found success, but it joins a wide variety of other attractions that are already well established. The most notable and unfortunate exception is the striking new* **Millennium Footbridge** *over the river to St Paul's, at time of writing yet to be cured of its wobble. An unforgettable walk downstream from the gallery passes* **Shakespeare's Globe***, the* **Golden Hinde***,* **Borough Market***,* **Southwark Cathedral** *and, beyond London Bridge, the* **Old Operating Theatre** *and* **HMS Belfast***. Further 'inland' to the south, Southwark and the Borough have rediscovered some of the energy that has always characterized their long history, with thriving markets, pubs, cafés and streetlife. That said, neither has entirely shaken off its reputation for being the gateway to south London's bandit country. The City's disreputable southern neighbours can be relied upon to continue throwing up surprises both pleasant and unpleasant.*

History

Sitting just over the river from the City, there has been a settlement at 'South Warke' since the Roman occupation. Archaeological evidence suggests a wooden bridge spanned the river (east of the current London Bridge), and a hamlet grew up around the bridgehead with two Roman roads (modern Newington Causeway and Old Kent Road) meeting in Borough High Street. A settlement survived the vacillations of Danish and Saxon rule (a church has existed on the site of Southwark Cathedral since the seventh century), such that by the end of the Middle Ages Southwark was the most significant community (after Westminster) outside of the City.

Far to the west, Lambeth Palace, London residence for the Archbishop of Canterbury, was surrounded by marsh, meadows and woodland, the Bishop of Winchester's house and lands stretched around Clink Street, and St Thomas' Hospital emerged in the grounds of the Augustinian monastery centered around St Saviour and St Mary Overie, now Southwark Cathedral. Indeed, partly because the area could escape the jurisdiction of the City, Southwark served a strange mix of people. Several prelates had their London residences here – the Bishops of Winchester and Rochester, the

Hotels in the area

B Mercure London City Bankside Hotel
C Holiday Inn Express
D Bankside House
F St Christopher's Inn Backpackers' Village
▸▸ **Go to page 447**

Abbots of Lewes and Battle on modern Tooley Street, and Bermondsey Abbey sat further to the east, but the area was also swimming in taverns and brothels.

Bankside, particularly, was the centre for the 'stewes', a series of brothels that were regulated by and provided revenue for successive Bishops of Winchester, earning the prostitutes the name 'Winchester Geese'. Taverns (and some breweries) lined the streets, such as the Tabard, where Chaucer's pilgrims met before starting on the road to Canterbury, and the Queen's Head was finally sold by a certain John Harvard to help found a university across the Atlantic.

In the 16th century, theatres (the Rose, Swan, Hope and, of course, the Globe) sat alongside bear-, bull-, dog- and cock-fighting and baiting pits – there were even gladiatorial contests in which men slashed at each other before baying crowds. Such dissipation warranted some sense of control, and over the years several prisons emerged in the area, notably Marshalsea and the Clink (hence the expression 'in the clink'), a presence oddly complimented by the sanctuary at St Saviour's that attracted fleeing criminals. The gatehouse to London Bridge (houses, stores and a chapel were built along it) displayed the boiled and tarred heads of criminals and traitors (William Wallace and Sir Thomas More among them), sometimes 30 at a time. An evening out in Southwark offered the lot – drink, sex and entertainment, with possible absolution or incarceration just down the track.

By the start of the 19th century wet docks had been excavated in Rotherhithe, wharves, warehouses and timber yards lined the river, while building had rapidly developed along Borough High Street, partly in the wake of a fire that swept Southwark in 1676. Elephant & Castle emerged as a coaching, and later tram, terminus, while the coaching inns of Borough High Street were the destination of the traffic from the southeast. Breweries, tanneries, foundries, glassmakers and print machinery manufacturers provided the local small industry, while the fruit and veg market that first appeared in the 13th century continued to thrive.

Over the next hundred years the population more than trebled to over 200,000. Blackfriars (1769) and Southwark (1819) bridges encouraged expansion, as did a new London Bridge further upstream (1831) and the arrival of a railway terminal nearby, but the area became suffused with slums and lodging houses for ex-convicts. Guy's Hospital continued to expand, but St Thomas' moved to Lambeth. The market sought a new site, and towards the end of the century a new nave at St Saviour's helped create Southwark Cathedral. Hay's Wharf continued to invite river traffic, and pioneered cold storage for butter and cheese from New Zealand. More recently, the railway's growth has cut swathes through the area, but the reconstruction of the Globe and the conversion of Bankside Power Station into a modern art gallery maintains Southwark's traditional association with entertainment.

Sights

Tate Modern

Heading east along the south bank of the river, the Queen's Walk passes beneath Blackfriars Bridge and enters Bankside. And there stands Tate Modern, one of the most spectacular and popular new additions to London in years. Opened in May 2000, the converted Bankside Power Station now houses the Tate's collection of international modern art from 1900 to the present. An extraordinary great solid box of brick with a single free-standing

Buses 45, 63, 100, 381

Central London

square chimney front centre, the power station was designed by Sir Giles Gilbert Scott to be a striking landmark, responding architecturally to its position across the river from St Paul's Cathedral. The building was begun in 1937 but didn't start generating electricity until 1963. Decommissioned in 1986, it was left desolate and empty for a decade. Swiss architects Herzog and de Meuron were finally appointed to adapt the building to its new role. Typically, the praise for their work has not been entirely unqualified but the hype surrounding the project as a whole now seems to be completely justified.

The main entrance is not where you might expect, on the river front beneath the chimney

The main entrance is through the west, right-hand side of the building (turn right, away from the river, just beyond the riverside pub the Founder's Arms). A wide sloping ramp of brick leads down into the immense Turbine Hall, an astonishing space for artworks on a grand scale. In here, towering up through seven storeys on the north side of the building facing the river, linked by

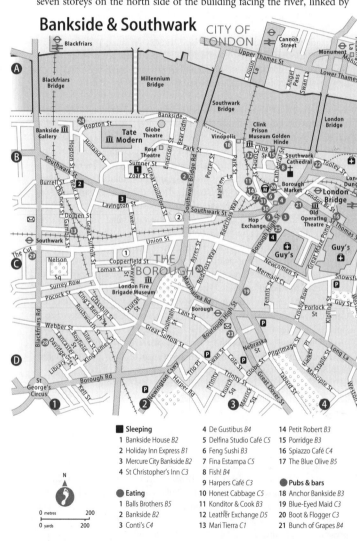

Bankside & Southwark

N

| 0 metres | 200 |
| 0 yards | 200 |

■ Sleeping
1 Bankside House *B2*
2 Holiday Inn Express *B1*
3 Mercure City Bankside *B2*
4 St Christopher's Inn *C3*

● Eating
1 Balls Brothers *B5*
2 Bankside *B2*
3 Conti's *C4*
4 De Gustibus *B4*
5 Delfina Studio Café *C5*
6 Feng Sushi *B3*
7 Fina Estampa *C5*
8 Fish! *B4*
9 Harpers Café *C3*
10 Honest Cabbage *C5*
11 Konditor & Cook *B3*
12 Leather Exchange *D5*
13 Mari Tierra *C1*
14 Petit Robert *B3*
15 Porridge *B3*
16 Spiazzo Café *C4*
17 The Blue Olive *B5*

● Pubs & bars
18 Anchor Bankside *B3*
19 Blue-Eyed Maid *C3*
20 Boot & Flogger *C3*
21 Bunch of Grapes *B4*

central escalators and stairways, are the galleries themselves, standing proud as illuminated boxes of light.

In a much-publicized break with traditional historical and chronological hangings, the collection is permanently arranged around four themes suggested by the four genres of fine art laid down by the French Academy in the 17th century: Still Life, Landscape, the Nude and History.

On level 3, Still Life/Object/Real Life covers the contents of the 14 exhibition spaces on the east side of the building, while Landscape/Matter/Environment covers those on the west side. **Level 4** is taken up with temporary exhibitions (admission charged), while **on level 5**, the Nude/Action/Body galleries are on the east side, and History/Memory/Society on the west. Under these headings the galleries are devoted to selections from the collection that are changed every six months or so, arranged as monographs to single artists, currently such as Bruce Nauman, Joseph Beuys, and Stanley Spencer, or under themes like *The Intelligent Object*, *Inner Worlds* and *Transfiguration*. The method is designed to ensure that the gallery as a whole can respond to changing currents in contemporary art as well as commenting on how the traditional subjects of artistic activity have been interpreted throughout the modern era.

Central London

At the time of writing, the *Subversive Objects* room in the **Still Life wing** was proving very popular, displaying a variety of peculiar and disturbing works questioning the familiar: Dali's lobster telephone, Sarah Lucas' *Bunny gets snookered, No 7* – a weird stuffed thing in stockings slumped on a chair – and Cathy de Monchaux's erotic *Erase* – a large bolt padded with velvet and poppered denim. Further on, Peter Fischli and David Weiss's installation meticulously recreates in styrofoam a gallery under construction, a kind of three-dimensional trompe l'oeil.

On the other side of the building, in the **Landscape section**, the early 20th-century surrealist Max Ernst's *Celibes* – a haunting image of a kind of boiler with an elephant's trunk – could be found in *Inner Worlds*. In a room called *Landscape Encoded*, young contemporary artist Leila Curtis's *United Kingdom 1999* mixes up Ordnance Survey maps on the outline of England and Scotland: London becomes Aberdeen and Dundee, Loch Ness cuts a deep channel south west from King's Lynn and Edinburgh gets marked up as Stockton-on-Tees and Middlesbrough.

Up on level 5, in the **Nude/Action/Body galleries**, is artist Sam Taylor-Wood's *Brontosaurus*, her friend John is captured on video dancing naked in slow-mo, set incongruously to Samuel Barber's elegiac Adagio from Oliver Stone's *Platoon*. Observing the effect on people passing through can be as entertaining as the piece is moving.

Website: Because of the mission and layout of the gallery, it's impossible to say exactly
www.tate.org/modern what can be seen or heard where and when, but a visit to the website in the **Clore Study Room on level 1** enables the location of specific works or of artists room by room. The collection (which even in this vast building cannot be permanently on display in its entirety) contains examples of work by most of the big names of 20th-century art, from Duchamp, Matisse and Picasso through to Bacon, Beuys and Warhol, whose pieces are likely to be found in striking juxtaposition to those of lesser-known or more contemporary artists.

Gallery tours From the Turbine Hall information desk and also on level 3, **hand-held audio tours** (£1) in several languages are available, including the **Collection Tour**, with illuminating commentaries by artists and curators explaining the galleries' themes (each room also has an explanatory panel), specific works and artists, and the **Director's Tour**, a personal highlights tour recorded by Lars Nittve, the director of the gallery. Free audio points are also available in some of the rooms and **free guided tours** leave from level 2 at 1030, 1130, 1430, and 1530, from near Damien Hirst's *Forms without life* – a clinical MDF cabinet full of exotic pristine seashells – and the Starr Auditorium, which incorporates a cinema showing free films throughout the day and special seasons by art directors in the evenings.

Overall, the gallery's popularity is the strongest testament to its success in making modern art accessible: each of the rooms provokes different atmospheres, but few the hushed reverence traditionally associated with art galleries. The place has an industrial impersonality, and yet comfortable armchairs and sofas overlook the Turbine Hall on several of the levels; on level 4, the espresso bar has an outside terrace, while the Reading Points on level 5 provide another chill-out zone with great views and some relevant reading matter. And then there are the views: the East Room on level 7 hosts special events and gives impressive panoramic view over the thatched circular roof of the Globe Theatre towards the City. Eventually the power station's central chimney will also become an observation tower, with two lifts taking visitors up 93 m for a 360°-degree view of London. Friends of the Tate (annual membership £36) can use the members tearoom and terrace on level 6, a considerable privilege when the gallery is at its busiest. Of the three shops, the one on the ground floor is the largest, those at the north entrance and on level 4 the quietest, each stocking stacks of Tate merchandising (including desk tidies, shoulder bags, umbrellas and rainjackets), postcards and books on modern art.

■ *Open Sun-Thu 1000-1800; Fri & Sat 1000-2200. Admission free (charges for special exhibitions). T020-7887 8000; ticket bookings T020-7887 8888; information T020-7887 8008.*

Around the Tate Modern

Back by the river, those with healthy bank balances inspired to own a piece of contemporary art for themselves might want to look into *Purdey Hicks*, 65 Hopton Street, SE1, T020-7401 9229. For traditionalists, or for anyone who paints, the *Bankside Gallery*, 48 Hopton Street, SE1, T020-7928

Five of the best: views of London ★

- *Tate Modern*, Bankside.
- *St Paul's Cathedral*, City.
- *Vertigo*, Tower 42, City.
- *Westminster Cathedral*, Victoria.
- *Broad Sanctuary*, Westminster.

7521 (admission £3.50, £2 concession) is the answer, the home of the *Royal Watercolour Society* and the *Royal Society of Painter-Printmakers*, it also has a shop selling artists' materials. Next door there's a useful newsagent, sweet shop and tobacconist at 50 Hopton Street.

Opposite Tate Modern, the new **Millennium Bridge** – a footbridge designed by architect Norman Foster with the sculptor Anthony Caro and engineered by Ove Arup – arcs gracefully over the river to St Paul's. Unfortunately when it opened in the summer of 2000 its experimental design caused an alarming wobble. Some thought it an exciting feature of the new crossing – the London Evening Standard even launched a campaign to 'Save the Wobble' – but safety concerns prevailed and the engineers were called back to limit the swaying of the bridge under the heavy foot pressure it's expected to have to bear.

A short walk downstream brings you to Bankside pier and Shakespeare's Globe Theatre. The brainchild of American film-maker Sam Wanamaker, who sadly didn't live to see its completion, this sweet little open-air Elizabethan playhouse – Shakespeare's 'wooden O' – reconstructed using original techniques and materials, has been an enormous success: under the inspired directorship of Mark Rylance, its summer season of four productions played in rep, some in period dress, often sells out well in advance. It's typical of the new spirit of Bankside that the view of the sky through the thatched roof from the hard benches now frames the purple light box on the top of Tate Modern's chimney. The theatre's balustraded balconies and gorgeously decorated stage can be viewed throughout the year on guided tours and there's also a bookshop, restaurant and café with river views.

Globe Theatre *Cheap standing room for 'groundlings' is usually available in the yard*

■ *Open May-Sep, 0900-1200 daily; Oct-Apr, 1000-1700 daily. Admission £7.50; £5 child; £6 concession. T020-7902 1500, www.shakespeares-globe.org*

From the Globe east to Southwark Cathedral

The actual original site of the Globe was a short walk from here, visible from Park Street outside the backdoor of the offices of the Financial Times beneath Southwark Bridge. An information panel and preservation area mark the spot.

On the way, you can visit the site of another Elizabethan theatre, the Rose, at 56 Park Street, SE1, where the foundations, in the process of being preserved, are marked out with illuminated light pads, and there's a 20-minute video on the history of the site and the area.

Rose Theatre

■ *Open winter 1200-1700 daily (last entry 1630), 1000-1700 in summer. Admission £3; £2 under-16s; £2.50 concession; £1 off with Globe ticket. T020-7593 0026, www.rosetheatre.org.uk*

London Fire Brigade Museum

Further away from the river, at 94a Southwark Bridge Road, SE1, and likely to be mainly of interest to aficionados, the London Fire Brigade Museum explains the history of firefighting in the capital since 1666, the year of the Great Fire. It includes some original fire engines among the exhibits and a temporary exhibition space covering different aspects of blaze-busting down the ages in detail.

■ *Entry by advance booking only for 2 hour guided tours at 1030, 1230, 1430, Mon-Fri. Admission £3, £2 child and concession (under-7s free). T020-7587 2894.*

Vinopolis, City of Wine

Next door Majestic Wine sell the stuff at bargain prices by the box

Continuing the walk along the riverbank towards London Bridge takes you past the historic and frequently overcrowded *Anchor* pub and into one of the most evocative and distinctive parts of Bankside, hidden away beneath giant road and railway arches. On the corner here, at 1 Bank End, is another new attraction, Vinopolis, City of Wine, an expensive, gimmicky and fairly superficial celebration of all things vinificatory, including tellies on Vespa windshields telling the story of Italian wine and airline seats doing the same for Australian wine growing. A visit should at least succeed in giving you a thirst for the stuff itself though, and the ticket price includes five free tastings.

■ *Open Tue-Fri 1000-1730 (last entry 1530). Late nights (not in Dec) Sat-Mon from 1000 (last entry 1800). Admission £11.50; £5 child; £10.50 OAPs; £1 discount if booked in advance. T0870-4444 777; wine tastings T020-7940 8322; www.vinopolis.co.uk*

Clink Prison Museum

Just round the corner, at 1 Clink Street, beneath the arch of the railway, the Clink Prison Museum is a small exhibition, with wall displays of a standard familiar from junior school classrooms, in a blackened breeze-block building on the site of the old jail that provides the excuse for the museum. Some of the torture instruments are moderately interesting.

■ *Open 1000-1800 daily. Admission £4; £3 child and concession. T020-7378 1558, www.clink.co.uk*

Golden Hinde

Anyone with children & more time should consider one of the very popular overnight stays, provided complete with period food, activities, dress & bedding (£30 per person)

Just down the road, past an extraordinary ruined rose window surviving from the Bishop of Winchester's 16th-century palace, demolished in the civil war, is another excellent reconstruction of a thing in wood from the Elizabethan era, the Golden Hinde, at St Mary Overie Dock in Cathedral Street. It's an exact replica of the type of square-rigged galleon in which Sir Francis Drake sailed around the world from 1577 to 1580. Launched in 1973, it spent two decades circumnavigating the world before docking here and becoming an educational museum. Self-guided tours of the little ship's five decks can be made during the day, or tours complete with entertaining costumed 'crew' can be booked.

■ *Open 1000-1700 daily (phone to check for weekends). Admission £2.50; £1.75 child; £2.10 concession. Guided group tours bookable in advance £3, child £2.25, concession £2.60. Bookings and information T020-7403 0123, www.goldenhinde.co.uk*

Borough Market

Borough Market, next to Southwark Cathedral, is an early morning wholesale fruit 'n' veg market throughout the week, under threat from Railtrack looking to widen their viaduct in two years time. On Fridays and especially on Saturdays, the traders are joined later in the day by a wide variety of specialist food retailers. Many are small producers of rare food mainly from Britain: look out for some excellent potted shrimps from Morecambe Bay, home-produced garlic, blueberries and rare breeds of meat. **Brindisa Ltd**, T020-7403 6932, are specialist importers of Spanish delicacies. A wide variety of breads are also the hot new thing here.

Round the corner, in Montague Close, is Southwark Cathedral, a beautiful place of worship dating back to the seventh century. It may be small in comparison to other cathedrals in the country, but its place in the heart of a crowded inner-city community makes it distinctive. Both the new London Bridge and the railway nearly ploughed straight over it. The tower was completed in the late 17th century, still standing over the fourth nave that was constructed for the church in the late 19th century, and refurbishment still continues.

Southwark Cathedral

Inside, notable monuments include the tomb of John Gower, a friend of Chaucer's and like him one of the fathers of English poetry; a monument to Shakespeare, the cathedral having been his parish church and the supposed burial place of his brother Edmund; and a rare wooden effigy of an unknown 13th-century knight. In the north transept, which dates from the same era, a chapel has been dedicated to John Harvard, founder of the American university, who was baptised here in 1607. The retro-choir, the oldest part of the cathedral, behind the high altar and its 16th-century great screen, is currently being restored. It should still be possible to see the Nonesuch Chest, a beautiful wooden box given to the church in 1588 for the safe-keeping of parish records. ■ *Open 0900-1800 daily (closing times vary on religious holidays). Three services each day throughout the week. Admission free (donations appreciated). T020-7367 6700, www.dswark.org*

A new visitor centre and refectory should be open by the time you read this

Nestling beneath the cathedral, Borough Market is a wholesale fruit 'n' veg market that has probably been trading near this spot since the Middle Ages and certainly on this spot since the middle of the 18th century. Nowadays it shelters beneath a great cast-iron Victorian canopy but like other old buildings around here is under threat from the proposed widening of the railway viaduct above. The market itself caters mainly to the restaurant trade and other fruit 'n' veg stallholders, and is at its busiest at dawn, although there are some interesting one-offs.

Borough market
See also shopping, on page 253

From the market, steps lead up onto London Bridge. Built 1967-72, this is the third stone bridge called London Bridge to have crossed the river near this point. The first, a little further downstream, stood for over 600 years, crowded with houses, a chapel in the middle, and almost damming the river with its 19 arches. For several centuries it was the only bridge in London, and Southwark's position at its southern end, beyond the jurisdiction of the City fathers, was responsible for the area's importance to trade, as well as its heavy drinking, gambling, prostitution and lawlessness. The approach from the south dominated by the famous drawbridge and gate adorned with an array of traitors' heads pickled in tar and stuck on stakes, a tradition that

London Bridge
The second bridge, built 1823-31, was sold & rebuilt in Lake Havasu City, Arizona

Central London

continued up to the 17th century, including in its time those of the Scottish freedom fighter William Wallace, the rebel Jack Cade, and the Catholic martyr Thomas More.

South from London Bridge

For more information on the Hop Exchange, contact the Peer Group, T020- 7940 8900

South of the bridge, Borough High Street rushes towards Elephant and Castle. Just down here on the right, at the junction with Southwark Street, stands **The Hop Exchange**, 24 Southwark St, once the biggest and busiest of all the exchanges in the area, trading in brewer's hops from the fields of Kent for most of the 19th century. Its central courtyard surounded by cast-iron galleries is a unique survival from the era. Now run as office space for about 20 small businesses, the doorman is usually happy to let visitors have a quick look inside.

Old Operating Theatre, Museum & Herb Garret

Heading east down St Thomas Street, there's an even more extraordinary survival from the 19th century at no 9a. The Old Operating Theatre, Museum and Herb Garret is a remarkably well-preserved surgeons' demonstration theatre dating from 1822, discovered in the roof-space of St Thomas' Church in 1957. A narrow and steep winding staircase leads up to the theatre and museum, both highly evocative and atmospheric reminders of the advances that have been made in medicine over the last 150 years. Centre stage in the little U-shaped attic lined with tiers of standing stalls for students and spectators, the battered operating table stands above a sawdust box that stopped the blood dripping through the floorboards into the church below.

The herb garret next door was used by the apothecary to store and cure herbs in medicinal compounds and there's a chance to try your own hand at pill making. The museum displays surgical instruments for amputation, bleeding, cupping and scarification as well as pickled specimens of the results: lungs, brains, hips, etc and an exhibition on medieval monastic health care. Special events, talks and demonstrations (thankfully not of the period) are included in admission price. Not for the faint-hearted, over-sensitive or infirm, but genuinely educational and entertaining.

■ *Open 1000-1600 Tue-Sun, most Mon (phone to check). Admission: £3.25; £2.25 concession; £1.60 child. T020-7955 4791.*

East from London Bridge

London Dungeon
Very small saucepan lids (kids) may find this too scary

Not far away, at 28-34 Tooley Street, the blood and guts theme continues, but in a much less authentic way, at the London Dungeon. Waxwork animatronic models, reconstructed instruments of torture, and sensationalist light effects on a variety of 'dark rides' are intended to scare the living daylights out of visitors. Themes include the Jack the Ripper Experience, Judgement Day and most recently, the Great Fire of London. Children enjoy it, judging from the attraction's enduring popularity, but adults are likely to be less impressed.
■ *Open Oct-Mar, 1000-1730 (last admission 1630) daily; Apr-Sep 1000-2000 (last admission 1730) daily (late night openings Jul & Aug). Admission £10.95; £6.95 child; £9.50 concession. T020-7403 7221, www.thedungeons.com*

Winston Churchill's Britain at War Experience

On the same street, at No 64-66, Winston Churchill's Britain at War Experience is another, less high-tech tourist attraction, probably also worth avoiding unless with children. It does at least treat history with more respect, including a mock-up underground station, exhibitions on women at war, bomb disposal and the home front, and a Blitz experience, sadly not much more effective than the (less expensive) one at the Imperial War Museum. If the Second World War is your thing, remember that *HMS Belfast* is moored only a short walk away.

■ *Open Apr-Sep 1000-1730 daily; Oct-Mar 1000-1630 daily. Admission £5.95; £2.95 child; £3.95 concession. T020-7403 3171, www.britainatwar.co.uk*

After a visit to either of these, the fresh air by the river will come as a relief. **Hay's Galleria** is quite an impressive shopping mall, with some decent restaurants and bars catering chiefly to the local office population.

From here it's difficult to miss the great grey bulk of *HMS Belfast*, the Second World War cruiser now permanently moored opposite the Tower of London, at Morgan's Lane, Tooley Street, in the care of the Imperial War Museum. Launched in 1938, it saw active service protecting the Arctic convoys to Russia, at the D-Day landings, and even supported the UN in Korea, before being retired in 1965. Anyone yearning to impersonate Jack Hawkins should certainly visit the bridge. The cramped conditions on its eight decks, including the massive engine room, make for quite an exhausting visit, likely to take at least an hour and a half, especially if accompanied by children, who find the ship much easier to get around. Most of the rooms are clearly marked up with informative wall panels about the difficulties and dangers of life on board and there are regular temporary exhibitions on particular aspects of the ship's history.   *Open Mar-Oct 1000-1800 daily (last entry 1715); Nov-Feb 1000-1700 daily (last entry 1615). Admission £5; £3.80 concession; under-16s free. T020-7940 6328, www.hmsbelfast.org.uk*

HMS Belfast

Central London

Eating and drinking

The *Tate Cafés* on levels 2 and 7 of the Tate Modern (T020-7401 5020) are open throughout the week for lunch (expect to queue) and in the evenings on Fri and Sat, last orders at 2130 but open until 2300, both offering excellent brasserie-style modern European food, sandwiches and snacks. Tables cannot be reserved, so it's best to arrive not much later than 1830 to guarantee a window seat in the evenings. The one on level 7 has the extraordinary views and a full wine list, while the one on level 2 is bigger, has more buzz and a smoking area. Both are at the lower end of this price bracket.

Mid-range
● *on map, page 244*

One of the best branches of the rapidly expanding absolutely fresh fish chain, also at the lower end of this price bracket, is located in a spacious glass and metal pavilion in Borough Market: *fish!*, Cathedral St, SE1, T020-7234 3333 (closed Sun evenings) is very busy at lunchtimes and quieter in the evenings, the place for piscivores who know how they want them, with a choice of simple sauces.

Nearby, *Petit Robert*, 3 Park St, SE1, T020-7357 7003 (closed Sun) is much more traditional, a popular and intimate little French provincial restaurant. The new *Bankside Restaurant*, 32 Southwark Bridge Rd, entrance on Sumner St, SE1, T020-7633 0011, is a large modern international restaurant, 170 covers, zippily designed by Dalziel and Pow, with art on the walls. Cheaper food in the brasserie, away from the corporate atmosphere at lunchtimes.

Further downstream, *Balls Brothers*, in Hay's Galleria, Tooley St, SE1, T020-7407 4301, is a new-old-fashioned wine bar doing decent food, also majoring on fish, popular with local office workers, and they run the free Pétanque Terrain in the middle of the Galleria open in the summer if you feel like imitating old Frenchmen.

Away from the river, and much more gastronomically ambitious (and also more expensive) is the **Delfina Studio Café**, 50 Bermondsey St, SE1, T020-7357 0244, open for lunch only, closed weekends. The name belies the quality of the food but declares the place's affiliation to one of the first of the wave of fashionable galleries still opening up in Bermondsey. Booking is advisable for some imaginative modern British dishes using top-quality ingredients.

Cheap Tucked away off Union St, a short walk from Tate Modern, **Mar i Terra**, Gambia St, T020-7928 7628, open 1200-233, closed Sun, is a very good authentic Catalan tapas bar and restaurant. The food is great value and prepared from the finest ingredients direct from Spain, served up in a very jolly atmosphere.

Near Borough Market, **Feng Sushi**, 13 Stoney St, SE1, T020-7407 8744, www.fengsushi.co.uk, does maki Sushi cut rolls, tempura, and feng sushi selections, eat in or take away, and boasts stylish and exotic oriental décor. The **Southwark Cathedral** refectory has had a major overhaul and offers an excellent home-made menu and good sandwiches during the day.

On the other side of Borough High St, **The Blue Olive**, 56-58 Tooley St, SE1, T020-7407 6001 (closed Sun) is a reliable Italian bar and restaurant, with a cheaper menu of contemporary Italian snacks at the bar. On the same road, **Fina Estampa**, 150 Tooley St, SE1, T020-7403 1342 (closed Sun), is probably the UK's only specifically Peruvian restaurant with a healthy emphasis on seafood and live music on Mon.

Not far away down Bermondsey St, **The Honest Cabbage**, 99 Bermondsey St, SE1, T020-7234 0080, is the sister restaurant to the *Honest Goose* in the Cut at Waterloo, doshing up wholesome, warm-hearted fare under a variety of simple headings.

Further afield in Bermondsey, **The Leather Exchange** wine bar and restaurant in the Leather Market is a good upmarket wine bar and brasserie with an affordable menu.

Cafés & sandwich bars Just off Borough High St, **Spiazzo Café**, Unit 3, 21/27 St Thomas St, SE1, T020-7403 6996, is a reliable Italian café/sandwich bar, with home-made pasta and fresh baguettes, popular with workers at Guy's Hospital opposite. If that's too busy, **Harpers Café**, 3 Southwark St, SE1, T020-7407 9666, is another Italian café, on a prominent corner site with lots of seating and good-value hot meals and sandwiches. Near the *Golden Hinde*, in the same road as the Clink, **Porridge**, Pickford's Wharf, T020-7407 3400, is a basic place that does very cheap pasta dishes.

For sandwiches, **De Gustibus**, on Borough High St, T020-7407 3625, opposite London Bridge tube, is the place to go for high-quality sandwiches, featuring a choice of 19 varieties of bread, also hot food and soups. **Conti's**, 53 Borough High St, SE1, T020-7407 2002, and 53-57 Southwark Bridge Rd, SE1, T020-7234 0218, is more straightforward and less expensive, offering a full range of well-filled sandwiches.

Next to Borough Market, **Konditor and Cook**, 10 Stoney St, SE1, T020-7407 5100, is the local branch of the exceptional Waterloo outfit, the home of luxury cakes, sandwiches, biscuits, teas and top-notch natural ingredients. On Bermondsey St, **Roses Café** is a highly recommended caff that serves up very good fish fresh from Borough Market on Fri.

Pubs & bars
▶▶ Go to page 428 for entertainment & nightlife
On the corner of the Cut and Blackfriars Rd, **The Ring**, 72 Blackfriars Rd, SE1, T020-7928 2589, is a straightforward boozer distinctive for being decked out with tributes to the area's boxing history. Further down this busy main road, **Mbibe**, 173 Blackfriars Rd, SE1, T020-7928 3693, is a funky modern bar/restaurant with DJs on Fri and Sat and decently priced British food.

For a glass of exceptionally good wine at lunchtime or early evening, local office workers favour **The Boot and Flogger**, Redcross Way, T020-7407 1116 (closed Sat, Sun) hidden away off Union St. Leather armchairs and woody furnishings give it the appreciative atmosphere of a gentleman's club.

Late-night drinking

Late drinking options in the area tend to be rowdy but fun, including the thumping disco delights of **St Christopher's Inn** *and for an older, more mixed crowd,* **The Dover** *Castle, Great Dover St, T020-7357 8881, open Monday-Wednesday until 0100, and until 0200 with DJs on Friday and Saturday.*

On the river, the **Founders Arms**, 52 Hopton St, SE1, T020-7928 1899, is an excellent Young's pub that must be laughing all the way to the bank since the opening of Tate Modern. That said, its combination of large riverside terrace with outside seating and efficient, friendly service of decent food all day and everyday deserves to be a success.

Further downstream, the historic **Anchor Bankside**, 34 Park St, SE1, T020-7407 1577, is almost too famous for its own good, a much older, very busy warren of rooms, very touristy and also with a riverside terrace tucked beneath the railway line into Cannon St.

Central London

The **Wheatsheaf**, 6 Stoney St, SE1, currently under threat from the widening of the viaduct, is an unreconstructed working men's pub with decent food at lunchtime and bags of character. **The Market Porter**, 9 Stoney St, SE1, T020-7407 2495, is another masculine kind of place, pumping excellent real ales in a dark woody atmosphere and opening to thirsty market traders at 0600 in the morning on weekdays. **The Southwark Tavern**, on the corner of Stoney St and Southwark St, opens at 0630 on weekdays. Nearby, **The Globe**, 8 Bedale St, T020-7407 0043, is a scruffy, good-natured pub with a pool table and a bunch of affable regulars. Utterly different, the **Wine Wharf**, Stoney St, SE1, T020-7940 8335, www.vinopolis.co.uk, is part of the Vinopolis complex with a vast selection of excellent wines, no beers or spirits and a decent enough, reasonably priced tapas menu, sandwiches and hot specials to be enjoyed in a tasteful brick, wood and steel interior.

Away from the river, several pubs near Borough Market are exceptional

Two pubs on Borough High St are worth mentioning: most famously, the **George Inn**, 77 Borough High St, SE1, T020-7407 2056, is London's last remaining coaching inn, its galleried design the inspiration for Elizabethan theatres, and now a convivial low-ceilinged series of rooms much enjoyed by both local office workers and tourists. Further down the street, the **Blue Eyed Maid**, 173 Borough High St, SE1, T020-7378 8259, is typical of the 'new' Borough, a brasserie-cum-pub with tables outside and clean, good-looking modern interior.

Near the Old Operating Theatre, on St Thomas St, the **Bunch of Grapes**, 2 St Thomas St, SE1, T020-7403 2070, is a fine Young's pub with wooden floors and pews, popular at lunchtimes but not excessively so. A much more wacky alternative is **Cynthia's Cyberbar**, 4 Tooley St, SE1, T020-7403 6777, www.cynbar.co.uk, decorated in a sci-fi style and home to two cocktail-mixing robots.

Shopping

Close by Tate Modern, **Marcus Campbell Art Books**, 43 Holland St, SE1, T020-7261 0111, www.marcuscampbell.demon.co.uk, is a well-stocked bookshop that sells new, second-hand, rare and out-of-print books on all aspects of art and stays open late on Saturdays. Near Borough Market is **Neal's Yard Dairy**, 6 Park St, SE1, T020-7645 3550, are open throughout the week providing a comprehensive range of cheeses from around the British Isles. On the walkway between London Bridge Station and London Bridge itself, **Odden's Cameras**, London Bridge Walk, SE1, T020-7407 6833, are reliable retailers and repairers of new and second-hand cameras, stocking a wide range of different films.

Surprisingly perhaps, with such a variety of places to see and things to do in the area, shopping is not really a strongpoint, but there are some special exceptions

Further south but well worth the trek early on a Fri morning is **Bermondsey Market**, T020-7351 5353, in Bermondsey Square. A professional antiques market that gets going as early as 0330 in the morning and winds down around mid-morning, this is the place to find an astonishing array of Victorian furniture, jewellery, kitchenware and oddments. Not necessarily cheap, it's the most authentic of London's antiques markets, decidedly not a haven for tacky bric-a-brac.

Nearby, up Long Lane and off Weston St, in the Leathermarket is the **London Glassblowing Workshop**, 7 The Leathermarket, SE1, T020-7403 2800, open 1000-1700 Mon-Fri, a workshop and gallery, occasionally open at weekends, where glassblowers can be seen at work and which hold exhibitions of their own and others' work.

Transport

Bicycle **On Your Bike**, 52-54 Tooley St, SE1, T020-7378 6669, is a good stop for bikes and cycle gear.

Buses

Best places to catch a cab are London Bridge Station & Borough High St or Blackfriars Bridge

Over Blackfriars Bridge:
No 45 northwards to King's Cross via Holborn; and southwards to Streatham via Elephant, Camberwell and Brixton.
No 63 northwards to King's Cross via Farringdon; and southwards to Crystal Palace via Elephant, Old Kent Rd, and Peckham.

Over Southwark Bridge:
No 344 northwards to Liverpool St Station; andsouthwards to Clapham Junction, via Southwark, Elephant, Vauxhall and Battersea

Over London Bridge:
No 35 northwards to Shoreditch via Liverpool St; and southwards to Clapham Junction via Elephant, Camberwell and Brixton.
No 47 northwards toShoreditch via Liverpool St; and southwards to Catford , Canada Water, Surrey Quays, Deptford and Lewisham.
No 133 northwards to Liverpool St via Bank; and southwards to Tooting via Elephant, and Brixton.

River transport From Westminster to St Katharine's via London Bridge City and South Bank Festival daily every 40 mins with **Crown River Cruises** (T020-7936 2033); £5.80 adult return

Directory

Internet Internet: Backspace Internet Providers, Winchester Wharf, Clink St, T020-7234 0804.
Laundry The Launderette, 78-80 Redcross Way. **Quality Dry Cleaners**, 131 Southwark Bridge Rd, T020-7407 4680.
Scarpa Dry Cleaners and Shoe Repairs, Unit 3 Hays Galleria, Tooley St, SE1, T020-7357 8792. Open 0800-1800 Mon-Fri
Tours and tourist information Tourist Office, London Bridge, T020-403 8299. Open Easter-Oct Mon-Sat 1000-1800, Sun 1030-1730, Nov-Easter Mon-Sat 1000-1600, 1100-1600.

The **Pool of London and Southwark Heritage Centre**, 12a Lower Ground Floor, Hays Galleria, Tooley St, SE1, T020-7357 9294.
Southwark Information Centre, 6 Tooley St, T020-7403 8299, with Portland stone needle at 19 degrees, 19 m high
South Bank Events 'from Vauxhall Bridge to St Saviour's Dock': www.London-SE1.co.uk
Bankside Walks: meet at Bankside pier (opposite the Globe), bookings: T01689 838410.

(hop-on, hop-off service, ticket valid all day). To and from Savoy Pier and Canary Wharf. For information, **Collins River Enterprises** T020-7237 9538.

London Bridge for Waterloo, Charing Cross and SE London, suburbs and Kent; Cannon Street, Blackfriars. **Trains**

London Bridge (Northern and Jubilee lines), Southwark (Jubilee line), Borough (Northern line), Blackfriars (Circle and District line), Tower Hill (Circle and District lines, DLR), Monument (Central, Northern, Waterloo and City, District and Circle lines, DLR). **Tubes**

South Bank and Waterloo

*Londoners have finally rediscoverered their river and the South Bank is booming. And it's about time too. As architecture critic Ian Nairn noted back in the 60s, the area is 'a real skeleton key. London is bent around the Thames: however much the north bank might wish to forget it, the south holds the centre of gravity.' That's never been more true than now. On the map, this is the centre of the city. A crow flying from Westminster Abbey to St Paul's Cathedral would have to dodge the vast white frame of the **London Eye**, cast its shadow over the concrete slabs of the largest arts complex in Europe, and swoop past the red neon-lit noughts and crosses of the Oxo tower.*

*The 18th-century obelisk in St George's Circus, Lambeth, records the fact that this is the only spot exactly one mile from Westminster, Fleet Street (once the home of 'the fourth estate'), and the City. Even so, it comes as some surprise that the riverside walk marketed as the **Millennium Mile**, from County Hall to London Bridge, has become a must for every visitor with more than a day to spend. Only 10 years ago the faceless grey blocks of the **South Bank Centre** and the **National Theatre** were accused of being a dirty, graffiti-stained and inaccessible ghetto for culture vultures. Nowadays, especially on sunny summer weekends, the riverside teems with people from all over the world enjoying breezy traffic-free views of the Thames.*

Nearest tubes for most of the sights here are Westminster (then cross the river) or Waterloo

History

With the exception of the Archbishop of Canterbury's London residence at Lambeth Palace, which first appeared in the 13th century, marshland and fields covered much of this area until the early years of the 18th century. St George's Fields, a large open space between Lambeth and Southwark, drew crowds through the centuries, either for Sunday leisure, or as a place of execution. As late as 1780 it was the gathering point for the Protestant Association before they embarked on their protest that became the Gordon Riots.

Following the building of Westminster and Blackfriars bridges in the mid-18th century, modern Blackfriars Road and Westminster Bridge Road saw ribbon development along their length, meeting at an obelisk at St George's Circus. Once the marshy land was drained, one Charles Bascom built Belvedere House on the reclaimed land, eventually turning its grounds into a pleasure garden, one of many that emerged in the area over the next century.

Hotels in the area

AL-A *London Marriot County Hall Hotel*
C *Days Inn*
D *London Country Hall Travel Inn Capital*
D *The Mad Hatter*
D *Wellington Inn.*
▸▸ Go to page 447

★ **Five of the best: things to do on the South Bank**

- The concert halls, galleries, bars and bookshop of the *South Bank Centre*.
- *The Imperial War Museum*, a unique cultural institution.
- A free lunchtime concert and low-price matinee at the *Royal National Theatre*.
- Exploring the little craft shops and cafés of *Gabriel's Wharf*.
- A rare classic at the *National Film Theatre*.

Wharves and light industry sprang up (timber yards lined the curve of the Thames), the largest concerns being the Lambeth waterworks and Coade's Artificial Stone Manufactory which used a secret mixture of terracotta, quartz and other materials to produce a revolutionary hard-wearing 'stone'. In 1837 the material was used for the figurehead on top of the Lion Brewery that replaced the waterworks. The lion now stands in pride of place at the southern end of Westminster Bridge, alongside St Thomas' Hospital from Southwark which, when it first moved here in 1871, was a magnificent Victorian edifice, a worthy companion to the Palace of Westminster opposite. It was here that Florence Nightingale introduced her radical overhaul of nursing training that raised its status as a profession.

During the First World War, County Hall was erected as the seat of London's local government, and during the Second World War, the old Waterloo Bridge was replaced by the beautiful five-span reinforced concrete one of today. Designed by Sir Giles Gilbert Scott, it was nicknamed 'the women's bridge' after the women that helped build it when the war caused a shortage of manpower.

But it wasn't until after the Second World War that the area really came into its own, with the Festival of Britain in 1951. Mooted two years earlier by the Labour government as a morale booster after the war, the Festival included a Dome of Discovery, a Ferris Wheel (precursors of the Dome in Greenwich and the London Eye), and most importantly, the construction of the Royal Festival Hall. Other concert halls and the Hayward Gallery were added in the 60s, followed by the National Theatre, the National Film Theatre and the BFI's IMAX cinema.

With the opening in 1993 of the Eurostar terminal, designed by Nicholas Grimshaw, the seal was set on the strategic importance of the South Bank and Waterloo. Development continues apace: future projects include new footbridges along both sides of the Hungerford Railway Bridge, ambitious plans for Jubilee Gardens and improved access to the area from Waterloo Bridge.

Sights

The riverside itself is still best approached from the north, from Westminster or Embankment tube stations, or over Waterloo Bridge, simply because of the magnificent view

The promenade between Westminster and Blackfriars bridges has become central London's multicultural playground. Crowds wander down from the Eye and County Hall, past the Royal Festival Hall and the Royal National Theatre, towards Tate Modern and the Millennium Bridge on Bankside. In some ways the most typical, central spot is the open-air second-hand book market sheltering beneath the arches of Waterloo Bridge. It does brisk business, surrounded by buskers, skateboarders and coffee-drinkers perusing their programmes in the National Film Theatre's café. Overhead, the graceful sweep of the bridge provides the best approach to the area from the north and Covent Garden, famously offering the finest view of the city to be found at road level.

As you emerge from the main entrance of Waterloo Station, you're greeted by the great glass cylinder of the British Film Institute's latest venture, a pur-pose-built **IMAX Cinema**. Standing in the middle of the roundabout at the southern end of Waterloo Bridge, the building swept away Waterloo's notori-ous 'cardboard city', the squalid semi-permanent home of countless down-and-outs in the pedestrian area beneath the road known as 'the bull-ring'. The exterior of the building is an extraordinary blow-up of a Howard Hodgkin painting (see also page 428).

South Bank & Waterloo

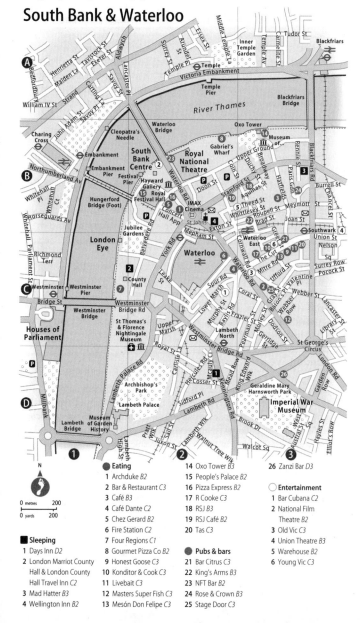

Central London

Central London

Local action keeping the riverside alive

That the riverside around the Oxo Tower is even accessible to visitors is thanks largely to the concerted efforts of a small group of local residents who resisted the big property developers in the 70s and early 80s. Oxo Tower Wharf itself, which at that time was reduced to producing the extended tubular eggs for the middle of pork pies, was to be demolished and replaced with a skyscraper hotel and 20-storey office block designed by Richard Rogers. As had happened in Covent Garden a few years earlier, an action group was formed to protect the interests of residents, proposing instead a new park, a riverside walkway, room for shops, and most importantly, affordable housing. Remarkably enough, the success of their proposals can now be appreciated today.

The campaign lasted seven years, including two public inquiries, the second of which granted planning permission to both the community and the office developers. Ownership of the land then became the key issue. Thankfully the Greater London Council stepped in to support a small not-for-profit organization set up by local community groups. Eight plots of wasteland and warehousing were bought around Coin Street. Most remarkable of all, Coin Street Community Builders, as the organization was called, is still going strong. They are now responsible for Gabriel's Wharf, Bernie Spain Gardens, named after Bernadette Spain, one of the members of the original action group, the Oxo Tower development, including the Bargehouse and Museum of..., and the Coin Street Festival. Plans for the future include the Thames Lido, an Olympic-sized swimming pool floating on the river, and a River Thames Discovery Centre in the Barge- house. It's heartening that these projects are being proposed and managed by people living here by the river. The Coin Street Information Centre (see page 261) is a good place to find out more about their story.

Jubilee Gardens

Left out of the station, down York Road and right towards the river, Jubilee Gardens is a small riverside park laid out in 1977 in celebration of the 25th year of the Queen's reign. Plans are afoot to redevelop it as the headquarters of the British Film Institute, incorporating a new National Film Theatre At present it provides plenty of room for the queues forming up at the most popular sky-ride in town.

London Eye

Buses: 12, 26, 53, 59, 68, 76, 159, 168, 176, 188, 211

The British Airways London Eye is also known as the Millennium Wheel, even though it wasn't quite ready in time for the big night. The vast spoked white wheel beside Westminster Bridge has already become one of the most welcome additions to the London skyline in years. Well over 100 m in diameter, the larg-est structure of its kind in the world, it's visible from unexpected places all around the city. There's no denying its novelty value, or even perhaps its beauty.

The half-hour 'flight' in one of its surprisingly roomy glass 'capsules', mov-ing at a quarter-metre a second, provides superb 25-mile views over the city, and is neither vertiginous nor at all boring. On a clear day you can see all of London and beyond, including Guildford Cathedral, Windsor Castle and the river flowing out into the North Sea. If the weather is less fine, and there's no banking on it if you've booked in advance (or even stood in the queue for an hour), you're at least guaranteed the peculiar sensation of looking down on the top of Big Ben and overlooking Nelson on his column. The wheel has received permission to remain in its prime site on the Thames until 2005, when its future will be reconsidered.

■ *Open daily Apr-Oct 0900-2200, Nov-Mar 1000-1800. £7.95 (advance booking system). T0870-5000600, www.ba-londoneye.com Westminster or Embankment tube and cross river, or Waterloo tube.*

Built just before the First World War for the London County Council, the fate of this magisterial building, which became the seat of the left-wing Greater London Council (GLC), is one of London's odder ironies. Since the GLC's abolition by Margaret Thatcher in the mid-80s, London's town hall has been thrown open to the people by its Japanese owners as a hotch-potch leisure and tourist development. It now houses the London Aquarium, a Macdonalds, the Premier League Football Hall of Fame, a Namco videogame arcade, a 24-hour health club, and a Chinese restaurant, as well as a five-star Marriot Hotel and a budget Travel Inn. Ken Livingstone, leader of the GLC in 1986, might have difficulty finding his way around it. As the newly elected Mayor of London, he and his Greater London Assembly will eventually be housed in brand new purpose-built offices, which resemble a giant gherkin, near Tower Bridge.

County Hall
The ticket hall for the Eye is in County Hall

Central London

The London Aquarium was opened to great acclaim in the late 1990s, thanks in part to the wackiness of the idea of lots of exotic fish swimming about so close to the humble Thames. That said, its success is largely deserved: you descend through three darkened floors of aquaria cunningly designed around two huge tanks, Atlantic and Pacific, home to small sharks, stingrays and conger eels among others. The favourite attractions for children of all ages are the open-top 'touch pools' downstairs: a rock pool alive with crabs and anemones, and the beach pool full of thornback rays. Not as prickly as their name suggests, these personable rays seem to enjoy performing aquabatic feats and allow themselves to be stroked and petted. On the way out, there's a display on the threat mankind's activities pose to the marine environment.

London Aquarium

■ *Open daily 1000-1800 (last admission 1700). Admission £8, £5 under-16s. T020-7967 8000, www.londonaquarium.co.uk*

The FA Premier League Hall of Fame is the most recent attraction to join the line-up at County Hall. A celebration of the success of the FA Premier League brandname, soccer fans can discover the history of the 'beautiful game' in the Hall of Legends, gawp at waxworks of star players in the Hall of Fame, and appreciate their own contribution to the game's success in the Hall of Fans. The Club Shop, stocking Premier League club shirts and footballing souvenirs, is also open to non-visitors.

FA Premier League Hall of Fame

■ *Open daily 1000-1800; last admission 1700. Admission £7.95, £4.50 concession. T020-7928 1800.*

The South Bank Centre

Downstream from County Hall and Jubilee Gardens, just beyond the Hungerford railway and footbridge, stands the South Bank Centre (SBC). The largest arts complex of its kind in Europe, it grew up around the **Royal Festival Hall**, the centrepiece of the Festival of Britain. Apart from the main concert hall, the Grade I listed building also houses an exhibition space, a good bookshop, the Poetry Library, and the high-class People's Palace restaurant. Nearby, connected by concrete terraces overlooking the river, are more concert halls, the Purcell Room and Queen Elizabeth Hall (see page 428), as well as the cutting-edge Hayward Gallery.

Buses 26, 59, 68, 76, 168, 176, 188

All change at Jubilee Gardens

The small park next to County Hall has not had a particulary happy life since it was laid out in celebration of the Queen's silver jubilee in 1977. For much of the 90s it was a construction site, first for the extension to the Jubilee tube line and then for the Millennium Wheel. Now it looks as though it will finally be taking a turn for the better, albeit after another stretch of time as a building site. The South Bank Centre and British Film Institute's proposals for the park involve doubling its size, providing access from the new footbridges alongside the Hungerford Railway Bridge, and turning it into the grassy roof for a concert hall, the Museum of the Moving Image and the National Film Theatre. The first phase of the development, which is already underway, is the complete refurbishment of the Royal Festival Hall. The second phase will create a gentle slope up from the riverside to a three-storey arts and shopping complex on Belvedere Road. Architect Rick Mather, recently responsible for making over the National Maritime Museum and the Wallace Collection, has come up with a masterplan that will provide superb views of the river as well as space for a supermarket, carpark, shops and restaurants. It is to be hoped that work on this transformation will have begun by the time the Gardens are celebrating their own jubilee in 2002.

Hayward Gallery The Hayward Gallery was opened in 1968 and is now one of the few remaining examples of 'brutalist' architecture in London. It will probably survive the planned alterations to the South Bank Centre. The cantilever tower of neon tubes on its roof, a kinetic sculpture controlled by the windspeed, has become a familiar, very 70s landmark. This is the place to come for major state-subsidised temporary exhibitions of contemporary art. They tend to focus on four main areas: single artists, historical themes or artistic movements, other cultures, and contemporary art. It will be interesting to see how its curatorial policy will respond to the recent opening of the massive Tate Modern gallery downriver on Bankside.

■ *Open Mon, Thu-Sun 1000-1800, Tue, Wed 1000-2000. Admission £6 approximately. T020-7928 3144, www.sbc.org.uk*

Also managed by SBC, but beneath the arches of Hungerford Bridge, **Feliks Topolski, Memoir of the Century**, is one artist's highly idiosyncratic take on his travels around the world throughout the 20th century. Opened in 1984, the comic and nightmarish quality of the late Feliks Topolski's disturbing, atmospheric walk-in installation makes it one of the South Bank's more peculiar institutions. ■ *Open Mon-Sat 1700-2000, free.*

National Film Theatre Next up on the riverside, beneath the arches of Waterloo Bridge, is the National Film Theatre (T020-7928 3535). Its restaurant and bar have become one of chattering London's favourite meeting places. Major relocation of the cinema to Jubilee Gardens is planned in the near future, although it will hopefully still be possible to take some refreshment, and shelter from the weather, beneath the bridge. The fabulous Museum of the Moving Image is unfortunately already closed until 2003, as part of these new developments projected by the British Film Institute. Selected parts of the exhibition on the history of cinema and television will be touring the country until then.

Central London

Next door is the **Royal National Theatre**. The foundation stone was laid for the Festival in 1951, but architect Denys Lasdun's terraced concrete ziggurat didn't open until 1976, the new home for the National Theatre Company. Its grey blocks suit its position next to Waterloo Bridge, although Lasdun apparently hoped they would turn interesting shades of green once lichen and algae had bloomed on the textured walls. Air pollution has so far put paid to the desired effect. Recent developments have created Theatre Square, an open-air performance space for street entertainers and occasional showcase events.

Continuing downriver, past the National Theatre, beyond the offices of IBM and the distinctive black and white stack of the London Weekend Television tower, Gabriel's Wharf is a quirky little riverside area. Another initiative of the Coin Street Community Builders (see page 258), this small square with its pavilion in the middle, craft shops and restaurants, looks slightly twee but is full of surprises, not the least of which is its popularity. Busy with weekend shoppers and afterwork drinkers and diners, a village atmosphere has been conjured out of nothing. Unfortunately plans are afoot to redevelop the site, which was always intended to be temporary, one explanation perhaps for its charm. Next door are Bernie Spain Gardens, named after the campaigning founder of Coin Street Action Group in the 1970s, before you arrive at the Community Builders proudest achievement, the redeveloped Oxo Tower Wharf. **Gabriel's Wharf**

The Oxo tower became a trademark landmark in the 1920s when the famous stock cube manufacturers got round local advertising regulations by putting a light inside their logo on top of their warehouse. The distinctive noughts and cross are now picked out in red neon, shining out above the successful redevelopment. The striking redesign by Lifschutz Davidson turned it into affordable flats for locals, with showcase applied art workshops on the second floor and a swish bar, brasserie and restaurant run by the stylish Knightsbridge store Harvey Nichols at the top (see Eating and drinking below). The views of the river, the City and St Paul's from here are superb, although unfortunately the bar and brasserie can't allow seating outside if there's the slightest wind. **Oxo Tower** *Nearest tube is Southwark*

The Museum of… (T020-7401 2255) is an interesting temporary exhibition space dedicated to exploring the idea of museums themselves. Plans are afoot to establish a permanent Museum of the River Thames here.

Beyond Blackfriars Bridge lies Bankside, a stretch of the riverside that has already begun to rival the South Bank for new developments and attractions (see page 242).

Lambeth and Waterloo

Staying with the river, heading upstream from County Hall along the Albert Embankment is as good a place to start an exploration of Lambeth as any, behind St Thomas' Hospital, providing the most-photographed view of the Houses of Parliament across the water.

A short walk 'inland', south of the river, takes you away from the mainstream into a district that still retains a strong sense of its own identity. This is Lambeth, childhood home of Charlie Chaplin, site of the 'Lambeth Walk' from *Me and My Girl*, and also the largest, most mixed-up borough in London. Taking a stroll around its northern part always throws up surprises among the wide boulevards and avenues feeding traffic into the heart of town.

Florence Nightingale Museum

The Florence Nightingale Museum is located in St Thomas' Hospital, at 2 Lambeth Palace Road, where the 'lady with the lamp' opened the world's first nursing school in 1860. The Hospital had recently relocated to its present site in order to be nearer the new Waterloo Station. The small exhibition includes a 20-minute video on her life and displays explaining her experiences in the Crimean War, her influence in the British Army and the primitive hospital conditions of her era. A fuller understanding of her life and times is provided by the 20-minute tours daily at 1400 and 1500.

■ *Open 1000-1600 Mon-Fri, 1130-1600 Sat & Sun. Admission £4.80, £3.60 concession. T020-7620 0374 .*

Museum of Garden History
The museum includes a reconstruction of a 17th-century knot garden in the little churchyard & a decent café

At the southern end of Lambeth Bridge, at St Mary-at-Lambeth on Lambeth Palace Road, the Museum of Garden History is a small display in a converted church on the history of gardening. A quirky enough place, it's not really aimed at amateurs, appealling mainly to real horticultural historians, honouring the great Elizabethan and Jacobean gardeners, the Tradescants. Their original collection of exotic animals and plants was inveigled out of the family by Elias Ashmole, founder of the Ashmolean in Oxford. It included the pineapple, hence the exotic fruit's presence on Lambeth Bridge over the road. There's a memorial to Ashmole in the church, which was restored in the 19th century, although the tower is 14th-century, while in the graveyard you'll find the tomb of John Tradescant, next to that of Captain Bligh of the mutinous *Bounty*.

■ *Open Feb-Dec , Sun-Fri 1030-1700 . Admission free. T020-7261 1891.*

The museum stands next door to the gate of **Lambeth Palace**, the London home of Archbishops of Canterbury since the early 13th century. It experimented with opening to the public in 2000, although may not do so again. The Library in the 17th-century Great Hall is viewable by appointment; group bookings only, T020-7898 1200.

Over the road, at 1 Lambeth High Street, is the **Museum of the Royal Pharmaceutical Society**, the place to explore the history of Western medicine's increasing reliance on drug treatment. On three floors in the HQ of the UK pharmacists regulating body, you can wonder at the complexity of the cataloguing in an early 20th-century pharmacy, gaze at antique pestles and mortars, ponder theories of kill or cure and gasp at the extraordinary compounds that patients have swallowed down the ages.

■ *Open by appointment only 0900-1700 Mon-Fri. Admission Free. T020-7735 9141, Ext 354.*

Imperial War Museum
Nearest tube is Lambeth North

Heading away from the river down Lambeth Road brings you to The Imperial War Museum, founded in 1917 to record the British Empire's involvement in the First World War. Since then it has dedicated itself to the history and consequences of all 20th-century warfare. Just before the Second World War it was relocated from its original site in Crystal Palace to be housed appropriately enough in the 19th-century lunatic asylum known as Bedlam, the Bethlem Royal Hospital. Its grounds now include the Tibetan Peace Garden, opened by the Dalai Llama in 1999, symbolizing understanding between cultures. The bronze cast of the Kalachakra Mandala, associated with world peace, is a good object of contemplation in juxtaposition with the grand entrance to the museum, guarded by a pair of the largest naval guns ever built.

Central London

On the ground floor you'll find an even more fearsome collection of military hardware, all quiet, cleaned up and cut away for easy viewing: tanks, mini-subs, aeroplanes and more peculiar equipment like the little observer's pod that was dangled beneath zeppelins hidden in the clouds. Downstairs the museum expertly explains and illustrates its horrific subject matter without over-exploiting its dubious entertainment value. A reconstructed First World War trench, 'The Trench Experience', is genuinely unpleasant, although thankfully nothing like as awful as the original must have been. 'The Blitz Experience' is more dramatic, but oddly less effective. These two are part of walk-through static displays explaining a mass of memorabilia, backed up by informative touch tellies explaining the historical contexts and some harrowing films. A large new exhibition on the Holocaust, opened in June 2000, puts the whole bloody business in perspective. A visit to the museum, however brief, is likely to be memorable and sobering.

Depending on your sensibilities, you may only be able to cope with a couple of hours here

■ *Open daily 1000-1800. Admission £5.20, free after 1630. T020-7416 5000, www.iwm.org.uk*

Central London

Eating and drinking

The smartest restaurant in the area is still the ***Oxo Tower Restaurant***, 8th Floor, Oxo Tower Wharf, Barge House St, SE1, T020-7803 3888. It's a busy, costly, corporate favourite run by Harvey Nichol's Fifth-Floor team doing excellent modern European food with the best views on the river from just beneath the Oxo Tower. ***The People's Palace***, Level 3, Royal Festival Hall, SE1, T020-7928 9999, F020-7928 2355, also has superb views onto the river through the huge plate-glass windows of the Festival Hall. Solicitous staff serve upmarket French food in the spacious Soviet-style dining room.

Expensive
● *on map, page 257*

The best seafood can be found at ***Livebait***, 41-45 The Cut, SE1, T020-7928 7211, F020-7928 2279, with its two cheerful, dark green and white-tiled rooms in full view of the busy kitchen. ***RSJ***, 13a Coin St, T020-7928 4554, is a very good French restaurant tucked away off Stamford St. Ask for a table upstairs if available, where the atmosphere is more romantic. ***Chez Gerard***, 9 Belvedere Rd, T020-7202 8470, is a brand new basement branch of the successful chain behind the Festival Hall.

More casual, but with a varied and interesting global menu, is the restaurant part of ***The Fire Station***, 150 Waterloo Rd, SE1, T020-7620 2226. Service can be erratic, and the large bar area at the front sometimes gets very loud, but the reliable food is excellent value. A reasonable alternative if you want somewhere quieter might be the ***Bar and Restaurant***, 131 Waterloo Rd, T020-7928 5086, a slightly smarter outfit just behind the Old Vic Theatre.

Mid-range

For some high-quality tapas in a very lively atmosphere (tables are bookable before 0830, it's always packed after that), complete with live Spanish guitar, try ***Mesón Don Felipe***, The Cut, T020-7928 3237. ***Four Regions***, County Hall, SE1, T020-7928 0988, is a relatively expensive but unusually grand Chinese restaurant with tremendous views of floodlit Big Ben.

Probably the best value is the newish Turkish restaurant ***Tas***, 33 The Cut, SE1, T020-7928 1444. Fixed-price mezes, decent main courses, friendly staff and cheerful, modern décor set *Tas* apart. Also on The Cut, the ***Honest Goose***, 61 The Cut, SE1, T020- 7261 1221, concentrates on a simple, reasonably priced, global menu that changes twice daily.

Cheap
There are plenty of options for inexpensive meals in the area

For pizza, try the ***Gourmet Pizza Company***, Gabriel's Wharf, 56 Upper Ground, SE1, T020-7928 3188, which is right on the river, or there's the reliable formula offered by ***Pizza Express***, 9 Belvedere Rd, SE1, T020-928 4091, in their new place behind the Festival

Central London

Hall. Nearby, a little more expensive, but the place to go for great sausages and a lively atmosphere is the bar/restaurant *The Archduke*, (under the arches), Concert Hall Approach, South Bank, SE1, T020-7928 9370. For top-quality fish and chips, possibly the best in London, go to *Masters Super Fish*, 191 Waterloo Rd, T020-7928 6924. For traditional pie and mash and eels, head for *R Cooke*, 84 The Cut, SE1, T020-7928 5931.

Cafés & sandwich bars There are lots of cafés and sandwich bars catering for the local office workers, the best of which is the new non-smoking *RSJ Café* on the corner of Stamford St and Cornwall Rd, T020-7928 5225. One of the best traditional 'greasy spoons' in London, doing the like of ham, egg and chips at bargain prices, is somewhere simply called *Cafe*, 4-5 Hatfields, but it closes early in the afternoon and doesn't open at weekends. *Café Dante*, 6 Baylis Rd, SE1, T020-7928 5225, is a traditional Italian café doing enormous platefuls of comfort food in a smoky atmosphere at very reasonable prices.

At the opposite end of the spectrum, the *Konditor and Cook* café next to the Young Vic Theatre on The Cut is a stylish place for patisserie and people-watching. Their *Bespoke Bakery and Fine Food Shop*, at 22 Cornwall Rd, SE1, T020-7261 0456, make some of London's most superb pastries and cakes as well as sandwiches and soup. *Delirium*, 19 Lower Marsh, T020-7928 4700, is a gourmet sandwich bar, while *Coopers Natural Foods*, 17 Lower Marsh, SE1, T020-7261 9314, has a good coffeeshop and does homeopathic medicines as well as a wide range of wholefoods.

Pubs & bars *The King's Arms*, Roupell St, with its wooden public bar, upholstered saloon, and *For an area of* strange 'conservatory' at the back, stands out. It pulls a good pint, is very lively and *town that combines* does standard pub food. *The Stage Door* in Webber St, behind the Old Vic, is more *some of the best* quirky, a 'pop memorabilia pub' decorated with shrines to the Beatles and others, run *aspects of traditional* by Australians and offering huge inexpensive burgers. *Zanzi Bar* is another one-off, *& modern London,* right next to the Imperial War Museum, with its exotic, plant-filled variation on a tradi-*there are surprisingly* tional pub interior and straightforward pub grub. The bars in the area are generally a *few good, old-* better bet, including *The Fire Station* (see above) on Waterloo Rd, a busy, scruffy bar *fashioned pubs.* that brews its own beer and is useful for meeting people coming off trains at Waterloo. ▶▶ *Go to page 428* The *NFT bar* is another good rendezvous, with its long tables in the shelter of Waterloo *for entertainment* Bridge. On The Cut, *Bar Citrus* is a new place that has already become very popular. *& nightlife*

Shopping

Lower Marsh Street Market is all that remains that of the huge New Cut market that once stretched all the way to Blackfriars Rd along The Cut. At its best on a Fri, the stalls are mostly laden with cheap new goods, with a couple of second-hand clothes dealers and fruit and veg at the Westminster Bridge Rd end. Behind the market though are some interesting shops, like *Twice the Siren*, 28 Lower Marsh, T020-7261 0025, for Caroline Scott's colourful, casual designerwear, *Radio Days*, 87 Lower Marsh, T020-7928 0800, excellent beatnik second-hand shop stuffed with collectables, vintage clothing and accessories, and *Gramex*, 25 Lower Marsh, SE1, T020-7401 3839, open 1230-1800 Tue-Sat, offering wide range of second-hand classical CDs and LPs complete with guarantees.

Ian Allan Books, 45/46 Lower Marsh, SE1, T020-7401 2100, www.ianallanpub. co.uk, is the London outlet for the 'world's leading transport publisher', the shop also stocks model railways of all shapes and sizes. Two more specialist bookshops are military buffs *ISO Publications*, 137 Westminster Bridge Rd, SE1, T020-7261 9588, and the international political bookshop with communist leanings, *Pathfinder Bookshop*, 47 The Cut, SE1, T020-7401 2409. Run by volunteers, it's only open 1730-1930 Tue-Thu, 1600-1900 Fri, Sat 1000-1700. Also on The Cut, *Farey and Sons* are very good traditional shoemenders and also keycutters.

Transport

Evans Cycles, 77-81 The Cut, SE1, T020-7928 4785, F7928 7735. Reliable repairers.   **Bicycles**
Mountain bikes are sold at their other shop nearby, 111-115 Waterloo Rd.

Going over Westminster Bridge: **Buses**
No 12 for Trafalgar Square, Piccadilly Circus, Oxford Circus and Notting Hill.
No 159 for Trafalgar Square, Piccadilly Circus, Oxford Circus and Brixton.
No 211 for Waterloo, Sloane Square, Chelsea and Hammersmith.

Going over Waterloo Bridge:
No 1 for Tottenham Court Rd.
No 26 for the City and Liverpool St.
No 59 for Bloomsbury and Euston.
No 68 for Euston.
No 76 for the City and northeast London.
No 168 for Euston, Camden Town and Hampstead Heath.
No 171 for Holborn and Camberwell.
No 176 for Trafalgar Square and Oxford Circus.
No 188 for Russell Square and North Greenwich.
No 341 for Islington.

Going over Blackfriars Bridge:
No 45 for King's Cross and Brixton.
No 63 for King's Cross.
No 100 for the City and Wapping.

The Millennium Wheel Pier Boats will probably still go to Greenwich (details   **River transport**
unknown at time of writing).
   The Festival Pier (between Hungerford and Waterloo bridges): circular
cruises via Westminster, Festival Pier, London Bridge, St Katharine's Dock, summer
season only, Sat, Sun 3 Apr -28 May, 4 Sep-29 Oct leaving Festival Pier at 1105, then
every 40 mins until 1705. Peak summer season, 29 May-3 Sep, daily service, leaving
Festival Pier at 1105, then every 30 minutes until 1805. The full circle £5.80, part circle,
eg Festival Pier-London Bridge £4.20. Contact *Crown River Cruises*, T020-7936 2033.

Directory

Communications Main *Post Offices* at
52 Blackfriars Rd, SE1 8NN, 57 Waterloo Rd
SE1 8UB, and 125/131 Westminster Bridge
Rd, SE1 7HJ.
Laundry Red and White Laundries, 59
The Cut. *Lower Marsh Dry Cleaners*, 13
Lower Marsh, SE1 T020 7928 9301
Medical Services St Thomas's Hospital, 2
Lambeth Palace Rd, SE1 T020 7928 9292
Places of worship St Georges RC
Cathedral, St George's Rd, SE1. *St John's*
Waterloo, Waterloo Rd.
Sports Wellingtons Health Club, 101
Lower Marsh, SE1 T020 401 8616 Open

700-2100 Mon-Fri, 900-1600 Sat,
1000-1600 Sun. Day membership £10.
Fully equipped gym, aeorobic classes and
a steamroom. *The Club* at County Hall,
Open daily 24 hrs, jacuzzi, sauna,
steamroom, 25-m swimmingpool, gym,
aerobic classes, karate, yoga. £12.50 for
the day, extra for classes. Under-16s
allowed in pool only from 1000-1200,
1400-1700. Bar with views of the river.
Useful addresses During the day a good
source of local information is the *Coin St
Information Centre*, Oxo Tower Wharf,
SE1 T020 7401 2255

Taxis   There are taxi ranks on Waterloo Rd, at Waterloo Station and on Westminster Bridge. All the bridges are usually good places to find an empty cab.

Trains Visitors travelling by train from the continent arrive beneath the spectacular snaking canopy of Waterloo International. It stands alongside Waterloo mainline station, the terminus for trains to the southwestern suburbs and southwest England. Those heading for the City use the Waterloo and City tube line, popularly known as 'the Drain'. The opening of the Jubilee line extension has finally ensured that this major point of entry is now much better connected to the rest of London.

Tubes   Waterloo (Northern, Bakerloo, Jubilee, Waterloo and City lines), Southwark (Jubilee line), Lambeth North (Bakerloo line).

East London

5

East London

East End

*The East End has long been forced to make the best of a bad lot. North and east of the wealth in the City of London, there's little room here for complacency about cheery cockneys weathering the worst of it with their colourful rhyming slang and robust attitude to a fair deal. In particular, many parts of East London have always had a nasty track record when it comes to race relations. Resentment still festers all too easily here, of strangers, of the government and of change. That said, the small area round Shoreditch, Spitalfields and Whitechapel has changed considerably in recent years, now attracting a large number of outsiders and boasting the most vibrant nightlife in the city beyond Soho. The spectacular boom in late-night clubs, bars and restaurants here has made the area one of the most exciting afterwork destinations in town later in the week. On Sunday mornings, the markets on **Brick Lane**, **Columbia Road** and **Petticoat Lane** continue to thrive. Daytime during the week the area's working-class history is still keenly apparent, although the one attraction in the East End that should definitely not be missed is the antique splendour of the **Geffrye Museum**, providing a peaceful and unlikely insight into well-to-do domestic interiors down the ages.*

Old St tube for Hoxton & Shoreditch; Aldgate East for Whitechapel & Brick Lane

East London

History

The East End has over the centuries earned a reputation as 'the dark continent beyond Aldgate', for as the City has expanded east, the cockney's 'sturdy optimism' has been an essential attitude for survival in the poverty and squalor that has plagued the area. But this was a problem that reached its peak in the 1800s – up until the 17th century, development in the East End was sporadic.

Spitalfields was a mass of sprawling monastic lands, bricks were manufactured in kilns in fields along Brick Lane, and the village of Bethnal Green huddled around modern Bethnal Green Gardens, with mansions nearby for the likes of the Bishop of London. Hackney presented a similar scene, with nobles', merchants' and academics' mansions (Sutton House still survives; the Astronomer Royal, Edmund Halley, lived in Haggerston) dotting the pleasant open countryside around a sprawling village. In Mile End, the common land was a popular recreation and meeting place (in 1381 the peasants met Richard II here to demand an end to serfdom), although by 1600, cottages and enclosures had arrived.

A milling industry built up around the River Lea, where grain from Hertfordshire was unloaded around a bow-shaped stone bridge – Bow was busy enough to earn its own chapel as early as 1311. Whitechapel, close to the City, had begun to grow in the 14th century (a chapel was built here in 1338), around the road east to Essex. Trades considered to be a nuisance were expelled by the City, so the likes of metalwork moved out to Whitechapel (the Bell Foundry moved here from Houndsditch in 1583).

Although there were wealthy residents in the area during this time, they moved west as cottages, alleys, and yards spread during the 17th century. Huguenot refugees arrived in huge numbers after 1685, boosting the weaving industry in Spitalfields and Bethnal Green, and establishing a chapel in Fournier Street. Sephardic

Hotels in the area

B *Holiday Inn Express London-City*
C *City Hotel*
F *Tent City Hackney*
▸▸ *Go to page 448*

Popney rhyming slang

Fancy a Britney Spears? And then maybe a Sinead O'Connor afterwards on the way home from the tube station? No, this is not some bizarre new karaoke game, but an updated version of the world famous cockney rhyming slang. Londoners are now using pop stars' names to substitute the old favourites, such as dog and bone (phone), apples and pears (stairs) and saucepan lids (kids).

Some of the best (and cleanest) include: Barry White – fright; Ricky Martin – side parting; Tina Turner – nice little earner; Ronan Keating – central heating; Slim Shady – old lady; Jarvis Cocker – off your rocker; Thom Yorke – leg of pork; Mel C – cup of tea. And Posh and Becks? We'll leave you to work that out for yourselves!

For a full list, check out www.music365.com

Jews set up around the modern Leman Road, and bought land for a burial ground in Brady Street. Wealthy silk merchants moved into Fournier Street, and by 1724 there were 'close-built and well inhabited' houses from Spitalfields to Brick Lane.

Whitechapel High Street was lined by coaching inns, choked with cattle, sheep and tradesmen with their carts, but when the London Hospital moved to its current site in 1750, fields still spread east. Mile End New Town grew as an expansion of Spitalfields, housing labourers for the dyehouse, metalworks, refineries and the Truman Brewery. Nevertheless, it still had its more pleasant open areas, and Captain Cook ('discoverer' of Australia) lived here in the 1760s.

By the middle of the 18th century, Bethnal Green had a population of 15,000 (weavers, mariners and manufacturers), but market gardens still spread out on its eastern side. Hackney was still largely rural until the 19th century, when the plight of the East End slums attracted attention. Cholera was a recurrent problem (there was no public drainage), juvenile thieves prowled the maze of alleys, and 'purefinders' would collect dog-shit (used to dress leather) rather than face the workhouse.

The Whitechapel murders, committed by Jack the Ripper against local prostitutes, gave the area national coverage. The East End was variously described as 'an evil plexus of slums that hide human, creeping things', or 'ancient, dirty and degraded', with slum districts such as Jago notorious for their crime and poverty. Such deprivation couldn't go unnoticed, not least among the Victorian philanthropists and clergy. Several initiatives were introduced. Slum clearances made way for the likes of Commercial Street and Bethnal Green Road, and educational colleges such as the People's Palace, Toynbee Hall (Arnold Toynbee would tell East Enders that "we have sinned against you grievously") and Oxford House emerged in the 1880s. Both The Salvation Army and Dr Barnardo's were first established in Mile End, and George Peabody built his first artisan dwellings on Commercial Street in 1864.

Towards the turn of the century, a large influx of Jewish refugees from Eastern Europe ensured that the one time Huguenot Chapel on Fournier Street became a synagogue. When the fascist Oswald Moseley planned a march through the East End in 1936, radicals and residents barricaded Cable Street to prevent its progress. They clashed with the police, and Moseley was persuaded to cancel the march. A week later, however, all the Jewish shops along Mile End Road were smashed, and a year later the fascist candidate earned 23% in the local election. Since the Second World War, when the East End suffered extensive destruction, the Georgian and Victorian terraces have been

Art attack

Many of the artists themselves may have been forced out by rising rents, but their influence remains in the variety of important galleries dotted around east London. Along with the fine public space at the Whitechapel Art Gallery, the commercial galleries here are broadly more adventurous than their West End counterparts. One that still bestrides the contemporary art scene like a colossus, with a foot in both hemispheres, is **White Cube²**, 48 Hoxton Square, N1, T020-7930 5373. Jay Jopling's space has imparted snappy cult cachet to the otherwise slightly dubious charm of Hoxton Square, and has recently joined by the prestigious premises of Victoria Miro, at 16 Wharf Road, N1, T020-7336 8109. Vibrant galleries worth checking out deeper in the East End are **Modern Art**, 73 Redchurch Street, E2, T020-7739 2081, **Interim Art**, 21 Herald Street, E2, T020-7254 9607 and **The Approach Gallery**, 47 Approach Road, E2, T020-8983 3878. At the latter it's possible to combine a pint and a good meal in the pub below, before or after appreciating the latest developments upstairs.

East London

replaced with municipal housing estates. Refugees from Bangladesh are among the latest arrivals in the area, and the Fournier Street Synagogue is now the Jamme Masjid Mosque.

Sights

Old Street, Hoxton and Shoreditch

Old Street tube surfaces on a large and unfriendly roundabout that spins traffic around just north of the City. From this frantic crossroads Old Street itself runs west back to Clerkenwell and east into Shoreditch, while the City Road heads south to the Square Mile and Moorgate, and northwest to the Angel Islington.

To the right on the southbound arm of the City Road lies the non-conformist burial ground of **Bunhill Fields**, aka 'the cemetery of Puritan England' and the last resting place of many of London's dissenters and freethinkers. The shady graveyard contains memorials to John 'Pilgrim's Progress' Bunyan, Cromwell's son-in-law General Fleetwood, Daniel Defoe and William Blake. Also buried here is Susannah Wesley, the mother of John Wesley, the founder of Methodism who lived across the road.

John Wesley's House now a museum, is next door to the chapel that he had built in 1778, known today as the Cathedral of World Methodism. Wesley lived in the fine 18th-century house for the last 11 years of his life, and it has been restored to look as it might have done in his day. The museum in the atmospheric crypt of the chapel contains an extensive collection of Methodist memorabilia, including a moving portrait of the great preacher on his death bed. ■ *Museum of Methodism and John Wesley's House, 49 City Rd, EC1, T020- 7253 2262. Open 1000-1600 Mon-Sat, 1200-1400 Sun. Admission £4, £2 concession and under-16s, Sundays free.*

Next to Bunhill Fields stands **Armoury House**, the little castle of the Honour-able Artillery Company. It's the grand 19th-century home of an organization that claims to be the oldest military unit in Britain, dating back to a fraternity

East London

Shoreditch

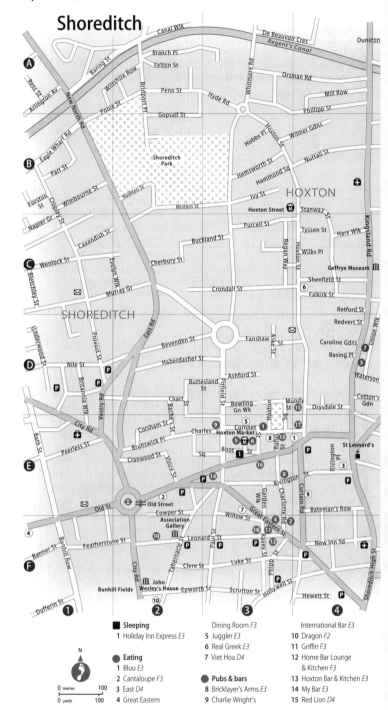

Sleeping
1 Holiday Inn Express *E3*

Eating
1 Bluu *E3*
2 Cantaloupe *F3*
3 East *D4*
4 Great Eastern

Dining Room *F3*
5 Juggler *E3*
6 Real Greek *E3*
7 Viet Hoa *D4*

Pubs & bars
8 Bricklayer's Arms *E3*
9 Charlie Wright's

International Bar *E3*
10 Dragon *F2*
11 Griffin *F3*
12 Home Bar Lounge
   & Kitchen *F3*
13 Hoxton Bar & Kitchen *E3*
14 My Bar *E3*
15 Red Lion *D4*

N

0 metres 100
0 yards 100

East London

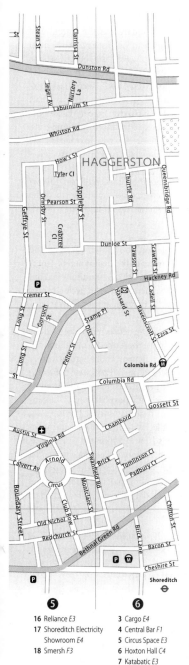

of crossbowmen who were granted a charter by Henry VIII. The HAC still performs ceremonial duties around London and takes part in the Lord Mayor's Show.

Left off the City Road before Armoury House down **Leonard Street** leads into the heart of an area dubbed 'Sosho' (south Shoreditch) by estate agents keen to expand an arty district's fashionable cachet. Little to show for it yet in fact, although the amount of building work and number of late bars and restaurants still opening up suggests the place may soon become more vibrant than Shoreditch itself. Look out here for **Space**, on Leonard Street, a sleek new contemporary art gallery, and the **Association Gallery**, 81 Leonard Street, EC2, T020-7739 6669, a contemporary photography space that was one of the first kids on the block.

Leonard Street meets the massive Great Eastern Street at its junction with northbound Curtain Road, the name a reminder that it was on this spot that the first playhouse in London was opened by James Burbage in 1576. Called simply 'The Theatre', it was dismantled 22 years later and its timbers used to construct the original Globe Theatre on Bankside. Memorials to many of Shakespeare's contemporaries, including James Burbage, can be found in the restored 18th-century **Church of St Leonard's**, in the centre of Shoreditch nearby. A whipping post and village stocks can also be found in the churchyard. Next door to the church, the Clerk's House, 118 Shoreditch High Street, fared less badly in the Blitz than many and is the oldest house in the area, dating from 1735. For some time it was home to a second-hand bookshop that sadly now only trades on the web, at www.ibooknet.co.uk

At the top end of Curtain Road, at its junction with Old Street, Hoxton Street continues north. On the left, **Hoxton Square** was the epicentre of Shoreditch's rebirth as the most happening place in the East End. Apart from the bright lights of the new *Lux cinema* and *Hoax gallery*, the square itself is a gloomy little spot but then that adds to its offbeat appeal. Art dealer Jay Jopling opened a second tiny space here called *White Cube²*. By contrast **Hoxton Market** next door has had a thorough makeover, now a smart pedestrianized area, and not to be confused with **Hoxton Street Market** further up the eponymous street on Saturdays, one of the most welcoming and laid-back of London's local street markets. Halfway down is Hoxton Hall, the last surviving Victorian music hall with a fashionable programming policy.

Northbound, Shoreditch High Street becomes the Kingsland Road, following the course of the Roman road, Ermine Street, dead straight north all the way through Dalston, Stoke Newington, Stamford Hill and out towards Cambridgeshire.

Geffrye Museum
Most of the furniture & fittings in each are original, the atmosphere in a few enhanced by music of the time

On the right a few hundred yards up from St Leonard's church, on Kingsland Road, are the peaceful 18th-century almshouses of the Ironmongers' Company that have housed the Geffrye Museum since 1913. A beautifully laid out history of furniture and interior design is told here, a series of period rooms along the front of the old building decorated as they might have been at various times between 1600 and the late Victorian age.

Apart from the aesthetic value of the décor, the details reminiscent of the social history of the different eras – for example the stuffed armadillo in the 17th-century room a reminder of the time's excitement about natural history – make the museum much more than a dry lecture on different ways to furnish a small room. Capitalizing on the TV-driven enthusiasm for home decorating, the museum was recently extended to include a purpose-built 20th-century gallery, with four rooms dating from the Edwardian era, the 1930s, 1960s, and a fairly flash 1990s loft conversion complete with bottle of balsamic vinegar beside the cooker, and Nigella Lawson's *How to Eat* on the coffee table. The extension also includes a good-value non-smoking café, a shop and a wacky wooden spiral staircase leading down to a temporary exhibition space for contemporary design. At the back of the building, plots have been divided up into a series of period 'garden rooms', including a lovely walled herb garden, open in the summer only.

■ *Open Tue-Sat 1000-1700, Sun 1200-1700. Admission free. T020 -7739 9893; recorded information T020-7739 8543; www.geffrye-museum.org.uk*

Spitalfields, Brick Lane and Bethnal Green

Spitalfields Market

Southbound Shoreditch High Street heads into the City via Bishopsgate. Off to the left just before Liverpool Street Station stands the green cast-iron and brick spectacle of the old Spitalfields Market. The wholesale fruit 'n' veg market here was closed down in 1992, and since then the building has been the subject of local concern about its future, a campaign being rallied under the acronym SMUT. It now looks as if half will inevitably soon be replaced by a new development, while the Victorian eastern part will be preserved. Catch the ramshackle whole while you can, at its best during the Farmers' and Crafts Market on Sundays.

Also on Sundays, many of the streets south of here are taken up by the huge Petticoat Lane and infamous Petticoat Lane Market. Masses of new leather jackets, fake Market desinger labels and gold jewellery among other goods of questionable provenance are flogged here with serious enthusiasm. Although there's always the chance of discovering an exception, the average quality of the merchandise is low. Then again many of the punters look as though they have come for the event itself and have no intention of parting with much cash anyway.

Back behind Spitalfields Market, on Commercial Street, rears the huge Christ Church Hawksmoor creation of Christ Church Spitalfields. The full restoration of the Spitalfields exterior of this striking local landmark was completed in late 2000, although the vast interior will not be receiving attention until mid-2003. Every year the Spitalfields Festival of Music take place here in June and during the two weeks before Christmas. For information T020-7377 0287, with concerts of mainly baroque music, as well as some by new composers.

■ *Open lunchtimes 1300-1500 Mon-Fri (until Oct 2001) and for Sun services. T020-7247 7202.*

Beyond the church the mid-18th-century streets like Fournier and Princelet running towards the aptly named Brick Lane are some of the most atmospheric and evocative in London. Still gaslit at night, the old brick terraces adapted for weavers have not yet been over-restored, while a few have been converted into galleries and shops. Most are still private homes in various states of genteel dilapidation or refined refurbishment.

The desire to slip back into the past was taken to an artistic extreme by the late Dennis Severs' Dennis Severs, who ran an eccentric 'living museum' nearby at his home, No House 18 Folgate Street. His life's work, a painstaking recreation of period décor from the mid-18th century to early 20th can now be explored on 'The Experience', where visitors are encouraged to reassess their attitudes to their own thoughts and feelings about past, present and future in the mysterious light of Dennis Severs' obsessive attention to detail. Certainly one of the oddest visitor attractions in London, the current caretakers discourage anyone not prepared to enter into the spirit of their friend's vision.

■ *'The Experience' on first Sun of month 1400-1700 (£7) and the Mon after 1200-1400 (£5), and 'Silent Night' by candlelight every Mon evening (£10) or by appointment. T020-7247 4013, www.dennissevershouse.co.uk*

Running roughly parallel to Commerical Street, Brick Lane is the main artery Brick Lane of 'Bangla Town', famous for its Bengali and Bangladeshi curry houses and warehouses, and also for the extraordinary market held at its top end every Sunday morning (see Shopping below). Hard-working and impoverished, the long narrow street is currently undergoing controversial proposals for major regeneration. The area was recently attacked by a lone racist with a nail bomb and has witnessed violent confrontations between the young Asian and white population. By and large the Balti houses still manage to draw people in and the old Truman Brewery building has been successfully converted into the fashionable *Vibe Bar* as well as a cutting-edge performance and contemporary art space. At the bottom end, Osborn Street comes out near Aldgate East tube and Whitechapel.

East London

East London

East End

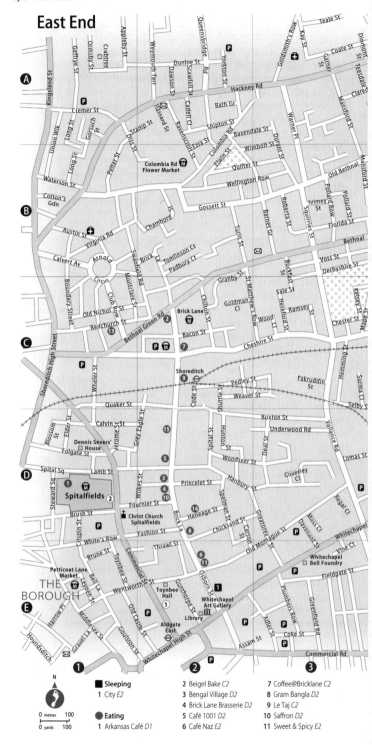

Sleeping
1 City *E2*

Eating
1 Arkansas Café *D1*

2 Beigel Bake *C2*
3 Bengal Village *D2*
4 Brick Lane Brasserie *D2*
5 Café 1001 *D2*
6 Café Naz *E2*

7 Coffee@Bricklane *C2*
8 Gram Bangla *D2*
9 Le Taj *C2*
10 Saffron *D2*
11 Sweet & Spicy *E2*

N

0 metres 100
0 yards 100

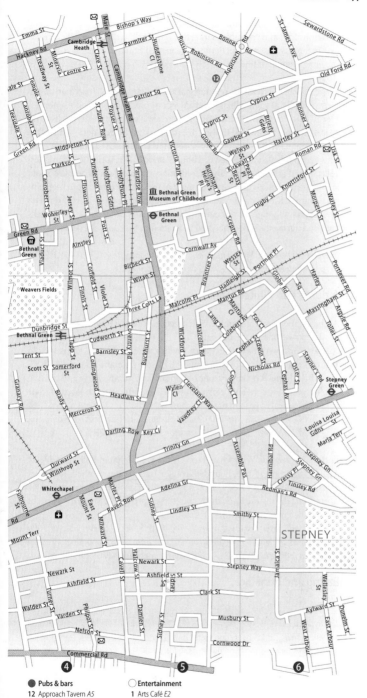

East London

● **Pubs & bars**
12 Approach Tavern *A5*
13 Owl & Pussycat *C1*
14 Pride of Spitalfields *D2*
15 Vibe Bar *D2*

○ **Entertainment**
1 Arts Café *E2*
2 Spitz *D1*

To the north Brick Lane hits Bethnal Green Road. The hard-bitten and tenacious fruit and vegetable market that sets up shop on this street every day except Sunday, just north of Bethnal Green itself, could reasonably claim to be the heart of the East End.

Bethnal Green Museum of Childhood
The museum is next to Bethnal Green tube station

There may be no room for sentiment at the Bethanl Green Road market, but plenty nearby at the Bethnal Green Museum of Childhood, on Cambridge Heath Road. Part of the Victorians' urban renewal scheme, it was established as a local museum for the East End in 1872 (the building a direct descendant of the Great Exhibition of 1851) and only became the Museum of Childhood in 1974. This delightful offshoot of the V&A houses an extensive, superior and priceless collection of antique doll's houses, old puppets, model trains and just about anything else that has been manufactured in the last few centuries to keep nippers amused. Kids today are less likely than adults to be particulary taken with the displays, although the museum organizes a variety of special events at weekends and during the school holidays in an attempt to redress the balance.

■ *Open 1000-1745 Mon-Thu, Sat, Sun. Admission free. T020-8983 5200. Recorded information T020-8980 2415, www.vam.ac.uk*

Aldgate and Whitechapel

At the southern end of Commercial Street, Aldgate is a frantic road junction on the site of one of the old gates into the City, its name a corruption of All-gate (or open to all). Next door to Aldgate East tube station is the old **Whitechapel Library**, 77 Whitechapel High Street, E1, and also, at No 80-82, the **Whitechapel Art Gallery**, one of London's most innovative and exciting public spaces for contemporary art, opened in 1901. Its art nouveau façade belies the radical edge to many of its shows.

■ *Art Gallery open 1100-1700 Tue, Thu-Sun; 1100-2000 Wed. Admission free. T020-7522 7888; recorded information T020-7522 7878.*

Further up towards Whitechapel tube is the **Whitechapel Bell Foundry**, at 32-34 Whitechapel Road. Founded in 1570, the firm has cast bells for Westminster Abbey since 1583. The premises are too small and dangerous to be operational during the tour which nonetheless provides a fascinating insight into an ancient manufacturing process.

■ *A small foyer display is open during office hours, and every Sat at 1000 guided tours are give by appointment (£7; no under-16s), usually booked up months in advance. T020-7247 2599, www.whitechapelbellfoundry.co.uk*

Eating and drinking

Mid-range
● *on maps, pages 272 & 276. Hoxton & Shoreditch are the best place to look for a good meal in this bracket*

The restaurant here that has had just about every food critic reaching for superlatives is *The Real Greek*, 15 Hoxton Market, T020-7739 8212, bright blue on the outside and mellow yellow within, a very successful pub conversion where Greek staples reach new culinary heights. The two-course menu for about £14 is good value, while mezes and small dishes are about £8.

Less casual and with a louder City buzz is the *Great Eastern Dining Room*, 54-56 Great Eastern St, EC2, T020-7613 4545, where decent modern Italian dishes are rustled up at speed next to a busy bar which is open until 0100.

The Cantaloupe, 35-42 Charlotte Rd, EC2, T020-7613 4411, was one of the first restaurant-bar combinations to establish Shoreditch's reputation as a hip destination for a dinner out and it continues to provide good-value modern European food in a surprisingly intimate dining area raised above a heaving bar.

In Hoxton Square itself, *Bluu*, 1 Hoxton Square, N1, T020-7613 2793, www.bluu.co.uk do a good Cal-Ital menu in comfortably fashion-conscious surroundings in the building that was once the ground-breaking *Blue Note* club.

Five of the best: cheap eats in the East End

· *Viet Hoa Café*, Kingsland Road, Shoreditch.
· *Gram Bangla*, Brick Lane, Spitalfields.
· *Café 1001*, Brick Lane, Spitalfields.
· *Beigel Bake*, Brick Lane, Bethnal Green.
· *The Juggler*, Hoxton Market, Hoxton.

The sheer number of options on Brick Lane itself is bewildering and competition is fierce. One reliabe old-timer, slightly more expensive than most but worth the extra spend, is *Le Taj*, 134 Brick Lane, E1, T020-7247 4210. In the thick of the scrum around Hanbury St, the clean modern décor of the *Brick Lane Brasserie*, 67 Brick Lane, E1, T020-7377 8072, caters for more modish tastes while *Café Naz*, 46-48 Brick Lane, E1, T020-7247 0234, was one of the first to take the traditional curry house in a more contemporary direction.

Two others stand out for the quality of their service and kitchens, the *Bengal Village*, 75 Brick Lane, E1, T020-7366 4868, and *Saffron*, 53 Brick Lane, E1, T020-7247 2633. And if you don't want curry, the best bets are the cafés or bars listed below.

Cheap
Brick Lane is still the best destination in the East End for an inexpensive meal as long as you fancy a curry

In Shoreditch, excellent Vietnamese food can be found at the *Viet Hoa Café*, 70-72 Kingsland Rd, E2, T020-7729 8293, and if that's too busy, next door is *East*, 58 Kingsland Rd, E2, T020-7729 5544, where an extensive Chinese and Vietnamese menu is served up in expansive and smart surroundings.

For lunch in Spitalfields Market, meat-eaters make for the *Arkansas Café*, Unit 12, Old Spitalfields Market, E1, T020-7377 6999 (closed Sat), an inimitable American barbecue shack that's excellent value.

On Brick Lane, *Gram Bangla*, 68 Brick Lane, E1, T020-7377 6116, is a clean, basic café specializing in fish and curries from Sylhet, while *Sweet and Spicy*, 40 Brick Lane, E1, T020-7247 1081 (closes 2230), is also very cheap and popular with locals. Both are BYOB.

Further up, *Café 1001*, Dray Walk, 91 Brick Lane, E1, T020-7247 9679, is a funky sandwich bar in fashionable Dray Walk, the place for jacket potatoes and excellent coffee, although *Coffee@brick lane*, 154 Brick Lane, E1, T020-7247 6735, is the best place for a damn fine brew, a hip joint on the corner of Cheshire St. Open 0800-2000 daily.

At the top of the road, the Brick Lane *Beigel Bake*, 159 Brick Lane, E1, T020-7729 0616, has long been doshing out well-filled beigels to all and sundry 24-hours.

In Hoxton Market, *The Juggler*, 5 Hoxton Market, N1, T020-7729 7292 (open until 1830), is a stylish café attached to the Shoreditch Art Gallery.

Cafés & sandwich bars

City workers, tourists and trendies flock into Shoreditch at the end of each week to enjoy any number of stylish music bars confidently blurring the difference between diners and drinkers. Most have kitchens attached serving up fairly reasonably priced food either at the bar or in separate rooms.

Pubs & bars
▶▶ *Go to page 430 for entertainment & nightlife*

In Hoxton, the *Shoreditch Electricity Showrooms*, 39a Hoxton St, N1, T020-7739 6934, have set the tone for the area, with battered sofas and rickety tables offset by sparse designer décor and witty touches like the idyllic Alpine scene on one wall.

More of a dive and a more serious music bar is the *Hoxton Bar and Kitchen*, 2 Hoxton Square, T020-7613 0709, a bricky, low-lit cavern next door to the Lux Cineman. Round the corner is the pub that has found most favour with young local artists, the

East London

★ Five of the best: late-night DJ bars in the East End

- **Sosho Match**, Tabernacle Street, Shoreditch.
- **The Dragon**, Leonard Street, Shoreditch.
- **Mother Bar**, Old Street, Shoreditch.
- **Herbal**, Kingsland Road, Shoreditch.
- **Vibe Bar**, Truman Brewery, Brick Lane

scruffy little DJ-driven **Red Lion**, Hoxton St, N1, pulling a superior pint of Guinness.

On Old St, one promising new arrival is **My bar**, 302 Old St, EC2, T020-7739 7311, with bar billiards, a piano and light meals, as well as an outside seating area, and DJ-driven sounds at weekends. Two more traditional pubs with upstairs dining rooms and a warm welcome around here include **The Reliance**, 336 Old St, EC1, T020-7729 6888, www.thereliance. co.uk, and for a slightly younger crowd, the raucous delights of the **Bricklayers Arms**, 60 Charlotte St, T020-7739 5245. **Charlie Wright's International Bar**, 45 Pitfield St, N1, T020-7490 8345, is a legendary latenight spot owned by a formidable weightlifter that attracts a lively mix of locals and visitors.

In Sosho, the most typical of the new wave of designer drinking and eating venues is **Home Bar Lounge and Kitchen**, 100 Leonard St, T020-7684 8618, www.homebar.co.uk, with its smartish restaurant upstairs and laid-back, surprisingly large lounge bar downstairs. Across the road is **The Griffin**, 93 Leonard St, EC2, T020-7739 6719, an ordinary freehouse pub with a pool table that makes a refreshing alternative to some of the area's more self-conscious designer excesses, serving up very reasonably priced pub grub. Unmarked on the same street nearer the City Rd, **The Dragon**, 5 Leonard St, EC2, T020-7490 7110, is a wacky pub conversion with thumping house music on the ground floor and a chill-out zone in the basement, more popular with afterwork drinkers than its tatty bohemian atmosphere might suggest. Equally hard to locate and generally much less busy is the strange red-painted vodka divebar **Smersh**, 5 Ravey St, T0961-869876, a cramped music bar with a coffee bar on the ground floor. Also in Shoreditch is **Herbal**, 12-14 Kingsland Rd, T020 7613 4462. It's nothing but a green door on the outside, but inside two floors, one DJ-driven and both usually open until 0200 most nights. Admission charged Fri and Sat.

Around Brick Lane, the most happening destination is still the **Vibe Bar**, Truman Brewery, 95 Brick Lane, T020-7377 2899, with four free internet terminals, a large courtyard drinking area, sofas, big tables and the latest dance tracks. Much more of a locals' local and something of a Brick Lane institution is the **Pride of Spitalfields**, 3 Heneage St, E1, T020-7247 8933, a friendly boozer that has become popular with an arty crowd. Another old-fashioned pub, marooned beyond the Bethnal Green Rd, **The Owl and the Pussycat**, 34 Redchurch St, E2, T020-7613 3628, attracts a more mature crowd of local characters, with a pool table and décor paying tribute to the artist and writer of nonsense verse, Edward Lear. In Bethnal Green, **The Approach Tavern**, 47 Approach Rd, E2, T020-8980 2321, combines an art gallery with a characterful old boozer and serves good food.

Shopping

The best way to fully appreciate the character of the East End is to pay a visit to its markets. Easily the most vital and varied is the **Brick Lane Market** on Sunday mornings. The action takes place north of Buxton St and south of Bethnal Green, with traders arriving as early 0500 to grab a pitch. Cheshire St is one of the best spots to look for retro clothing and furniture, while second-hand toys, bikes, books and a whole lot of other bargains and junk clutter the pounds off Sclater St and the stalls along Brick Lane itself. Cygnet St is where the patter-merchants can be heard winding up their audience to purchasing-pitch for a variety of cut-price consumer durables. Things become even more desperate on the Bethnal Green Rd.

Very different in atmosphere is the *Columbia Road Flower Market*, a little to the north, also on Sunday mornings, where wholesale flower traders and florists fill a polite Victorian terrace with a magnificent array of blooms and bushes, a weekly flower fest that is quite a sight in itself.

The rest of the week, look out for warehouse shops like *Beyond Retro*, 110-112 Cheshire St, E2, T020-7613 3636, www.beyondretro.com, a huge jumble of second-hand clothes from the 60s and 70s.

The Truman Brewery lets out large amounts of space to retails like *Eatmyhandbagbitch*, 6 Dray Walk, T020-7375 3100, stacked full of 20th-century vintage furniture and lighting, www.eatmyhandbagbitch.co.uk, while a little further afield, *Story Space Ltd*, 4 Wilkes St, Spitalfields, E1, T020-7377 0313, is an unusual craft and art gallery-shop in an old weaver's house. Anyone who thinks the British are prudish should visit *Sh!*, 39 Coronet St, N1, T020-7613 5458, www.sh-womenstore.com, open 1000-2000, a bright and cheerful shop selling erotic playthings for women like dildos and furry handcuffs. Male browsers here have to be accompanied by a woman.

Transport

East London

Through Shoreditch: Buses

No 26 between Waterloo and Hackney Wick via Aldwych, St Paul's, Bank, Liverpool St, Shoreditch and Hackney Wick.

No 35 between Clapham Junction and Shoreditch via Clapham Common, Brixton, Camberwell, Elephant, London Bridge, Monument and Liverpool St.

No 47 between Catford Garage and Shoreditch via Lewisham, Deptford, Surrey Quays, Canada Water, Jamaica Rd, London Bridge, Monument and Liverpool St.

No 48 between London Bridge Station, and Walthamstow Central via Monument, Liverpool St, Shoreditch, Cambridge Heath, Hackney and Clapton.

No 55 between Oxford Circus and Leyton Green via Tottenham Court Rd Station, Bloomsbury, Old St, Shoreditch, Cambridge Heath and Hackney.

No 78 between Shoreditch and Peckham Rye via Liverpool St, Aldgate, Tower Bridge, and Bermondsey.

No 149 between Ponders End and London Bridge via Edmonton, Tottenham, Stamford Hill, Stoke Newington, Dalston, Shoreditch, Liverpool St and Monument.

No 242 between Tottenham Court Rd tube station and Homerton Hospital via Holborn, Bank, Liverpool St, Shoreditch, Dalston, Hackney and Clapton Park.

Along Whitechapel Rd:

No 25 between Oxford Circus, Holborn, and Bank (Mon-Fri) or Tower of London (Sat, Sun) and Ilford via Aldgate, Bow, Stratford, Forest Gate and Manor Park.

No 253 between Aldgate and Euston via Bethnal Green, Cambridge Heath, Hackney, Clapton, Stamford Hill, Manor House, Finsbury Park, Holloway, Camden Town, and Mornington Crescent.

Along Commercial Rd:

No 15 between Blackwall DLR and Paddington via Poplar, Limehouse, Aldgate, Tower of London, Cannon St, St Paul's, Aldwych, Trafalgar Square, Piccadilly Circus, Oxford Circus and Marble Arch.

● ●

Directory

Sports West Ham United, *Boleyn Ground, Green St, E13, T020-8548 2700 Upton Park.*

Through Spitalfields:
No 8 between Victoria and Bow Church via Hyde Park Corner, Mayfair, Oxford Circus, Holborn, Bank, Liverpool St, Bethnal Green and Old Ford.

Taxis   Hoxton Car Services, freephone T0800-6343939, or T020-7729 3939.

Trains   Liverpool St for northeastern suburbs, Cambridgeshire and Essex. Stratford for Docklands Light Railway and eastern suburbs.

Tubes   Liverpool St (Circle, Central, Metropolitan, Hammersmith and City lines), Aldgate (Metropolitan line), Aldgate East (District, Hammersmith and City lines), Whitechapel (District, East London, Hammersmith and City lines), Shoreditch (East London line: peak hours and Sunday mornings only), Bethnal Green (Central line), Stepney Green (District, Metropolitan lines), Mile End (Central, District, Metropolitan lines), Stratford (Central, Jubilee lines).

The Tower and around

⊖ *Tower Hill tube or Tower Gateway DLR*

Londoners traditionally dislike the **Tower of London**. *After all, it wasn't built to protect them 900 years ago, but to subdue them, a role it played until the mid-19th century when it was freshly fortified against the Chartist rioters. Nowadays many have their revenge by either ignoring the place or dismissing it as a tourist trap. In fact it's less a trap than a treat, making an enormous effort to elucidate its wealth of historical associations and bring the old buildings to life for their two and a half million or so visitors each year. Inevitably the gate pressure means that the castle and its grim story come across a bit like a sanitized medieval theme park, but the central place it occupies in the Royal heritage and history of Britain and its capital is impossible to deny.*

It may be no coincidence that the Tower has ended up lonely and isolated, wide busy roads cutting it off from the City if not from the river. The entertaining neo-Gothic extravagance of Tower Bridge keeps it company though, leading over to **Shad Thames** *and* **Butler's Wharf**, *another of Sir Terence Conran's gastrodomes and home to two highly individual museums, the* **Design Museum** *and the* **Bramah Tea and Coffee Museum**. *Across the water, north of the river again, St Katherine's Dock is not quite the fashionable playground of the super-rich that it would like to be, more a tranquil and rather chi-chi waterside development. Downstream, Wapping introduces Docklands.*

History

In 1076, William the Conqueror commissioned a certain Gundulf to build him a stone keep in the eastern wall of the City. Fifteen feet deep at the base, with four floors rising to 90 feet high, the White Tower has been besieged and attacked several times in its long history, but never captured. It was designed to secure the Norman hold on the crown of England. Steps, which could be removed, rose to the only entrance on the south side, 15 feet above ground level. The ground floor held the stores (and later the infamous dungeons), the first floor was for soldiers and servants, the next the

Hotels in the area

B *Novotel London Tower Bridge*
E *Butler's Wharf Residence.*
➼ *Go to page 448*

nobility, banqueting hall and St John's Chapel, and the top floor provided the royal bedrooms and council chamber.

Used as a royal residence until the beginning of the 17th century, it has been constantly added to by successive monarchs, but has always served as a garrison, armoury, jewel house and, even, a museum. Since 1235, when the Holy Roman Emperor gave Henry III three leopards, the Tower held a menagerie that was open to the public. A polar bear and elephant followed (gifts from Louis IX), until in 1609 an inventory listed 11 lions, three eagles, two mountain cats, two leopards, two owls, a jackal and, briefly, a bear, which having killed a small child, was torn apart by baiting dogs.

James I staged animal fights (such as lions against mastiffs), but when the number of species had grown to over 50 in 1835, and a lion attacked some members of the garrison, the collection was moved to the recently opened zoo in Regent's Park.

Under Charles II the public were invited to peer at the inmates in the dungeons and watch new arrivals pass through Traitor's Gate. Executions at the Tower were either conducted outside the walls on Tower Hill, or in the relative privacy of Tower Green – like beheading, a privilege granted only to a distinguished few. The list of those executed here is impressive – Anne Boleyn, Catherine Howard and Lady Jane Grey share the accolade with countless heretics, rebels, traitors and in the case of the Princes in the Tower, victims of regicide. Prior to their expulsion from the country in 1290, 600 Jews were held in St John's Chapel – 267 were subsequently executed for coin clipping, and several of the crowd died when a stand collapsed at what turned out to be the last beheading in England in 1747. The Tower served as a prison until well into the 20th century – Rudolph Hess was held here for four days during the Second World War.

Other than a few hamlets in service to the Tower (hence Tower Hamlets), the area around the Tower was largely fields until the 16th century. To the north, the Minories, an abbey of nuns, was taken over by Henry VIII and replaced by a mansion, an armoury and workhouses. Until the late 19th century, it was noted for its gunsmiths. To the east, the Foundation of St Katharine, located at a creek, gave shelter to many foreigners refused entry to the city. A hospital, brewery and glassworks emerged until the whole area was cleared for St Katharine's Dock in 1828. Nearby a ghetto of up to 10,000 freed or abandoned slaves settled over the course of the 18th century.

Further east, wharves and boatyards emerged, and with it a settlement called Wapping-in-the-Wose that was hemmed in from the north by the Wapping marshes until it was drained in the 16th century. It became a popular place of entertainment for sailors (in 1750 there were 36 taverns on Wapping High Street, and many of the more squalid brothels), but in the 19th century warehouses replaced the "alleys of small tenements and cottages". Execution Dock, the graveyard of pirates, still saw corpses chained to the riverbank and pecked by passing birds. Tower Bridge, the first bridge down river from London Bridge, opened in 1894. During the 20th century St Katharine's Dock became a coveted residential and office area, sited around a marina developed by Taylor Woodrow. Wapping, having suffered badly from the Blitz, witnessed industrial disputes following the arrival of News International (publishers of *The Sun* and *The Times* newspapers), but has been redeveloped with flats, gardens and offices.

East London

The Tower & around

East London

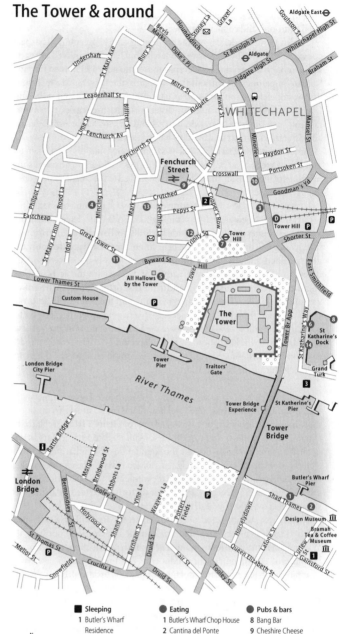

The Tower & around map labels:

Aldgate East, Goulston St, Gravel La, Storey La, Houndsditch, Bevis Marks, Duke's Pl, St Botolph St, Aldgate, Whitechapel High St, Braham St, Undershaft, St Mary Axe, Bury St, Mitre St, Aldgate High St, Leadenhall St, Jewry St, Mansel St, Billiter St, Lime St, Fenchurch Av, Fenchurch St, Aldgate, WHITECHAPEL, Vine St, Minories, Haydon St, Fenchurch Street, Friars, Crosswall, Portsoken St, Philpot La, Rood La, Mincing La, Mark La, Crutched, Pepys St, Cooper's Row, Goodman's Yd, Eastcheap, Seething La, Trinity Sq, Tower Hill, Great Tower St, Shorter St, St Mary at Hill, Idol La, Byward St, Tower Hill, East Smithfield, Lower Thames St, All Hallows by the Tower, Tower Hill, Custom House, The Tower, Tower Br App, St Katharine's Way, St Katharine's Dock, Tower Pier, Traitors' Gate, Grand Turk, London Bridge City Pier, River Thames, St Katharine's Pier, Tower Bridge Experience, Tower Bridge, Battle Bridge La, Morgans La, Braidwood St, Abbots La, Weaver's La, Butler's Wharf Pier, London Bridge, Bermondsey, Tooley St, Vine La, Shad Thames, Design Museum, Holyrood St, Shand St, Barnham St, Druid St, Potters Fields, Horselydown, Lafone St, Bramah Tea & Coffee Museum, Queen Elizabeth St, Curlew St, Gainsford St, Mellor St, St Thomas St, Crucifix La, Fair St, Druid St, Tooley St, Snowfields

N

| 0 metres | 100 |
| 0 yards | 100 |

■ **Sleeping**
1 Butler's Wharf Residence
2 Novotel London Tower Bridge
3 Thistle Tower

● **Eating**
1 Butler's Wharf Chop House
2 Cantina del Ponte
3 India Raj
4 Poons in the City
5 Vestry
6 Vineyard
7 Wine Library

● **Pubs & bars**
8 Bang Bar
9 Cheshire Cheese
10 Fine Line
11 Hung, drawn & quartered
12 Liberty Bounds
13 Ship
14 Tsunami

Sights

The Tower of London

Outside Tower Hill tube a viewing platform overlooks The Tower of London, a classic photo-opportunity for an overall picture of the layout of the fortification and its many towers, with Tower Bridge and the river in the background. In the middle stands the original fortress, the White Tower, one of the first, largest and most complete Norman keeps in the country, surrounded at a respectful distance by smaller buildings erected over the last 900 years, all protected by the 13th-century inner wall and ten towers added by Henry III. His son Edward I had the whole lot ringed with an impressive outer curtain wall and moat which was drained in the mid-19th century. The main public entrance and ticket office is round to the right, near the river in the western corner.

With some justification, the Tower claims to be several tourist attractions in one and for clarity's sake divides itself into seven colour-coded areas, each taking a suggested 20 or 30 minutes to see: the Western Entrance and Water Lane, the Medieval Palace, the Wall Walk, the Crown Jewels, Tower Green, the White Tower, and the Fusiliers' Museum.

Western Entrance & Water Lane

Passing through the **Middle Tower** and over a stone bridge across the moat, chances are you'll be greeted by one of the castle's most celebrated and engaging features, a Beefeater. More properly known as Yeoman Warders, these genial old coves in their quaint uniforms display an allegiance to the Queen and the Tower that no museum attendant could hope to match, all eager to beard visitors with tall tales of their home's grisly past.

One of them delights in the title of Ravenmaster, charged with feeding the Tower's seven flesh-eating feathered friends: Hardey, Cedric, Gywlum, Munin, Hugine, Odin and Thor. The big black birds patrol four territories around the White Tower and can't fly away because their wings have been clipped, stacking the odds on the truth of the legend that the Tower and its monarch will collapse should they choose to leave.

Beneath the Byward Tower in the outer wall, the **Bell Tower** on the inner wall was where Elizabeth was imprisoned by Bloody Mary, and from here Water Lane runs between the two walls to the river entrance at **Traitor's Gate**, part of Edward I's extension of the castle, replacing the water gate of the Bloody Tower in the inner wall.

Medieval Palace & White Tower

Beyond lies the Medieval Palace, including the Wakefield Tower, done up as it might have been in the reign of Edward I and enlivened by costumed guides. The Lanthorn Tower further on is the starting point for the entertaining Yeoman Warder guided tours.

A small gate leads through the inner wall to a souvenir shop and café and the main event, the White Tower. Up its wooden outside staircase and narrow winding stair, the most extraordinary place in here comes first: the small **Chapel of St John the Evangelist**. With its heavy round columns, tiny arched windows and surrounding gallery, the Chapel conjures up the Middle Ages more surely than any of the reconstructed rooms elsewhere. The bare Norman stonework adds to the ancient atmosphere, although apparently it would once have been brightly painted. A leap back into the 21st century is then made next door with a three-dimensional virtual tour of the Tower's construction projected onto the wall.

East London

Downstairs, the other floors are given over to exhibitions from the Royal Armouries, displaying fully armoured cavalry, muskets and pistols, and the Spanish Armoury, with breastplates, wooden model horses, canons and the axeman's chopping block.

Crown Jewels Behind the White Tower, the **Waterloo Barracks** contain the Jewel House, its entrance hall lined with the crested pews of English monarchs down the ages, although strangely there only seems to be room for two more. Roped crowd-controllers then wind through several large, loud projected videos of Queen Elizabeth II's coronation and other royal ceremonies and displays of maces, bugles, and swords. Finally, through a pair of massive metal doors glitter the glass-encased crown jewels themselves, flanked by two slow travelators that can be ridden as often as the crowds permit. The right-hand travelator affords a view of the legendary Koh-i-Noor diamond set in the crown of Queen Elizabeth the Queen Mother. The Imperial State Crown contains more than 3000 precious gems, with the oblong diamond Star of Africa beneath its encrusted cross, while in the head of the Sceptre sits the largest top-quality cut diamond in the world, the second Star of Africa, estimated to be worth a cool £350 million.

On emerging behind the barracks, the Martin Tower is the end of the Wall Walk along the Tower Bridge side of the castle from the Salt Tower. The Martin Tower also contains a small exhibition on the history and making of the crowns and their jewels.

Tower Green West of the Waterloo Barracks lies Tower Green, site of the scaffold where the privileged were executed away from the crowds on Tower Hill. Most of its victims are buried in the crypt of the adjacent Tudor Chapel of St Peter ad Vincula, of which the historian Macaulay wrote that "there is no sadder spot on earth". Behind the chapel, but closed to the public, Devereux Tower is the most strongly fortified of all the towers on the inner wall, facing the City to the northwest and named after its prisoner Robert Devereux, Earl of Essex, the popular hero and favourite of Elizabeth I who was forced to order him beheaded here. The first floor of the Beauchamp Tower on the west side contains the engraved signatures of many other noble prisoners.

The south side of the green is overlooked by the **Queen's House**, traditionally the Lieutenant's lodgings, where Guy Fawkes was tortured and from which Lord Nithsdale, a supporter of the Old Pretender, escaped in drag in 1716. Next door is the **Bloody Tower**, where the rooms have been decorated as they might have looked during the days and nights of its most famous prisoner, Sir Walter Raleigh. The room above is supposedly where the child Princes were murdered, and also where Sir Thomas Overbury was slowly poisoned to death with sweetmeats sent in by the Countess of Somerset.

By applying in writing at least two months in advance, the public are admitted free to the seven-minute Ceremony of the Keys at 2200 every night (atmospherically floodlit in winter), when the Tower is locked and the keys handed over to the Governor. The Chief Warder cries 'God preserve Queen Elizabeth' and the Guard responds 'Amen' followed by the sounding of the Last Post.

■ *Open Mar-Oct 0900-1700 Mon-Sat; 1000-1700 Sun; Nov-Feb 1000-1600 Mon, Sun; 0900-1600 Tue-Sat. Admission £11 (various combined, group and family prices, phone for details). Yeoman Warder tours (60 mins) every 30 mins from 0925, (Sun, Mon from 1000), last tour 1430. Meeting point: Lanthorn*

East London

Tower. Illustrated talks: Prisoners and Punishment (35 mins) 1130, 1415; Hidden Life of the Tower (35 mins) 1015; Illustrated talk and tour: Attack the Tower! (45 mins) 1215, 1500. Medieval Palace costumed guide presentations on life at the court of Edward I (35 mins) 1000-1630. Audioguide 'Prisoners of the Tower' (50 mins, £2 deposit required). T020-7709 0765, www.hrp.org.uk

Around Tower Hill

Back beside Tower Hill tube, to the east stands one of the best-preserved and most impressive parts of the Roman wall that once encircled Londinium and ran down to the river protecting the White Tower. West of the tube is Trinity Square, the site of the Tower Hill scaffold, and local street names like Seething Lane and Savage Gardens are a reminder of the crowds that liked to watch the hangman at work. Trinity House (closed to the public) on the north side of the square is the headquarters of the organization founded in 1515 that maintains the automated lighthouses dotted round the coast of the UK. Next door are the enormous former headquarters of the Port of London Authority.

East London

Across the road, on Byward Street, more Roman remains can be found in the crypt of the church of **All Hallows by the Tower** including a beautifully preserved tesellated Roman pavement, the floor of a domestic house, as well as an interesting model of the extent of Roman London. On the ground floor, the Saxon arch exposed by the the Second World War bombing is also worth a look, proof that there has been a church on this site for at least 1300 years. Famous names associated with this venerable place of worship include William Penn, Lancelot Andrewes, Albert Schweitzer and the founder of the charity born of the the First World War trenches, Toc H, the Rev Philip Clayton. The diarist Samuel Pepys watched London go up in smoke from the church tower.

A new restaurant opened in 2001 as part of the church's ongoing restoration appeal (see Eating below)

■ *Open Mon-Fri 0900-1645, Sat, Sun 1000-1700; Crypt Open Mon-Sat 1100-1600. T020- 7481 2928.*

Tower Bridge

Traffic rushes constantly along Byward Street and Tower Hill from here, round the Tower of London to Tower Bridge, best approached during the day from the riverside. London's most famous bridge was first opened in 1894, and until the completion of the Dartford Crossing remained the only bridge downstream of London Bridge.

It now houses the **Tower Bridge Experience**, run by the Corporation of London, capitalizing on people's natural curiosity about this strange Victorian building, the views and the antique heavy engineering involved in raising the massive bascules. This is an impressive free show when it happens, a few hundred times a year. The 1½ hour semi-guided 'Experience' takes visitors up the four storeys of the north tower, via displays including animatronic storytellers and illuminated information boxes, to 'A View from the Bridge' on the covered walkway between the towers. After descending the south tower, perhaps the most genuinely interesting parts of the museum are the steam engines in the basement.

Half a century ago the bridge needed to be raised and lowered at least 15 times a day

■ *Open daily Apr-Oct 1000-1830, Nov-Mar 0930-1800 (last entry 1 hr 15 mins before closing). Admission £6.25, £4.25 concession and under-16s,* under-5s free. T020-7403 3761; recorded information T020-7940 3985; bridge lift recorded information line T020-7940 3984, www.towerbridge.org.uk

St Katharine's Dock

The Pool of London Tourist Zone continues along the north bank into St Katharine's Dock, an expensive marina full of flashy yachts and some charming old Thames barges. In the middle stands the Ivory House, where shameful quantities of tusks were once unloaded and stored, now adapted into a smart waterside shopping arcade.

One of the dock's more engaging attractions is the **Grand Turk**, a replica 18th-century three-masted Man o' War, constructed in Turkey in 1997 for Queen's Waterman Michael Turk, a must-see for fans of Horatio Hornblower having starred as 'Indefatigable' in the TV series. Although adapted for film-making, with higher ceilings and wider doorways than strictly authentic, this fully operational floating film set is also the workplace of an enthusiastic crew of fitter-uppers who are happy to explain the ship's finer points and expand about life on board then and now.

■ *Open daily Sep-Mar 1030-1530, Apr-Aug 1030-1730. Admission £4, £2 under-16s, OAPs £3. T020-8546 2434, www.turks.co.uk*

Other sights around the dock include the old swing bridges and lock gates designed to cope with the Thames' 10-metre tides, the dockmaster's house, and the views of Tower Bridge. For information on berthing your boat here, contact St Katharine's Haven, T020-7264 5312.

On the south bank of the river across Tower Bridge, to the west is the location of the new headquarters of the Greater London Assemby, near HMS Belfast and Bankside.

Design Museum

The museum's famous Blueprint Café has excellent river views

To the east the riverside walk continues along Shad Thames past Butler's Wharf to the Design Museum. Housed in a cunningly converted white-clad 50s banana warehouse, since 1989 the museum has made a stylish stab at illustrating and describing the designs we meet with every day, but might not know as such, with a permanent collection and review gallery on the second floor. It explains how and why mass production has affected the use and appearance of chairs, cars, radios and just about anything else that needs a blueprint. Currently the displays are undergoing a major refit to allow much more exhibition space. On the first floor, temporary displays of innovative contemporary design are mounted three times a year.

■ *Open 1130-1800 daily (last entry 1730). Admission £5.50, £4 child & concession, students £4.50. T020-7403 6933, www.designmuseum.org*

Bramah Tea & Coffee Museum

Almost next door is the Bramah Tea & Coffee Museum, an intriguing one-man crusade against the tea-bag, at 1 and 4 Maguire Street, on the corner of Gainsford Street. Edward Bramah has amassed an extraordinary collection of teapots and coffee machines, pressing them entertainingly into service on his mission to remind the British how they used to enjoy their tea: by taking the time to warm the pot, allowing the delicate leaves to infuse, and avoiding skimmed milk. Proudly claiming to be two museums for the price of one, with coffee in the next door building, both also provide an entertaining insight into the history of the tea trade, involving the Opium Wars with China, the racing clipper ships and the Russian samovar, as well as the local history of the area.

East London

Open 1000-1800 daily (last tour 1730 Nov-Mar). Admission: £4; £3 child & concession. T020-7378 0222, www.bramahmuseum.co.uk

Further east on the north bank of the river, Wapping High Street makes a good introduction to Docklands, with its vast converted wharehouses, old south-facing riverside pubs and surreal views of the gleaming Canary Wharf development. Unfortunately, apart from a few oases, it remains deserted and forlorn at night.

Eating and drinking

Near the Tower of London, *Poons in the City*, 2 Minster Pavement, Minster Court, Mincing Lane, EC3, T020-7626 0126 (open Mon-Fri 1100-2230), is a smart branch of the reliable Chinese chain. For lunch, brunch or high tea, a good bet is the new *Vestry Restaurant*, All Hallows by the Tower, EC3, T020-7488 4933, open 0930-1730 Mon-Sat, 1230-1730 Sun, where a variety of well-made dishes majoring on fish are served up in an airy glass room with tables outside (starters about £5, mains £12).

Mid-range
● *on map, page 284*

East London

On Shad Thames, the three just-about-affordable Conran restaurants each in their own way reward holding out for a window seat with river views. The first, most expensive and with the best vantage point overlooking the river is the *Blue Print Café* in the Design Museum, Shad Thames, SE1, T020-7378 7031, for some inspired modern British cuisine. The *Cantina del Ponte*, Butler's Wharf, Shad Thames, SE1, T020-7403 5403, is less pricey, playing delicious variations on Italian peasant cooking, while the *Butler's Wharf Chop House*, Butler's Wharf Building, 36e Shad Thames, SE1, T020-7403 3403, has an excellent view of Tower Bridge illuminated at night and specializes in some thoroughly well-sourced, home-grown British recipes. *Café Spice Namaste*, 16 Prescot St, E1, T020-7488 9242, does superior Indian cuisine in a colourful and loud great big warehouse conversion.

Close to the Tower, the *Wine Library*, 43 Trinity Square, EC3, T020-7481 0415 (open lunch Mon-Fri 1130-1400, evening Tue-Fri 1730-2000) is an oenophile's delight, a well-stock cellar where a £10 cheese and cold buffet lunch can be enjoyed with a bottle of good-value wine selected from the racks around. *The India Raj*, 105a Minories, EC3, T020-7481 1022 (open Thu, Fri until midnight, closed weekends), is a busy and reasonably priced little Tandoori restaurant under the railway.

Cheap

Slightly further afield, *The Vineyard*, International House, 1 St Katharine's Way, E1, T020-7480 6680, part of the Davy's chain, do reliable British fare and decent wines in a sawdust-strewn basement.

In Wapping, *Il Bordello*, 75-81 Wapping High St, E1, T020-7481 9950, is a well-known superior pizzeria with a lively atmosphere.

The nearest decent pub to the Tower of London and All Hallows is the appropriately named *Hung Drawn and Quartered*, 26/27 Great Tower St, EC3, T020-7626 6123, a Fuller's pub with many of its Edwardian fittings intact. *The Liberty Bounds*, 15 Trinity Square, EC3, is the local Weatherspoon operation, a huge multi-level boozer with all the usual JD hallmarks: cheap beer, a reasonable and basic menu, no-smoking area and no music. Deeper into the City, *The Ship*, 3 Hart St (off Mark Lane), EC3, T020-7481 1871, is a tiny little local pub with a spectacular frontage and considerably more character. The *Cheshire Cheese*, 48 Crutched Friars, EC3, T020-7265 5141, is larger, beneath the railway and a decidedly no-nonsense City pub. More sophisticated but not quite as convivial drinking can be found at the *Samuel Pepys Bar* in the *Novotel*, or at *The Fine Line*, 124-127 Minories, EC3.

Pubs & bars

Near Tower Bridge, *Tsunami*, St Katharine's Way, E1, T020-7488 3482, is a stylish Pacific-influenced cocktail bar and restaurant with a sleek interior and surprisingly good value for money. In St Katharine's Dock nearby, *The Bang Bar*, above the Aquarium fish restaurant, Ivory House, St Katharine's Dock, E1, T020-7480 7781, is one of this quiet area's louder and more lively venues for some well-mixed cocktails and designer lagers.

In Wapping, the most famous (and touristy) but charming of the riverside pubs is the *Prospect of Whitby*, 57 Wapping Wall, E1, T020-7481 1095, a short walk from the tube. If that's too busy for its good, the *Town of Ramsgate*, 62 Wapping High St, E1, T020-7264 0001, is a reliable local alternative with as much history but not quite as old-fashioned.

Transport

Buses **No 15** Between Poplar and Paddington via Limehouse, Aldgate, Tower of London, Cannon St, St Paul's, Aldwych, Trafalgar Square, Piccadilly Circus, Oxford Circus and Marble Arch.
No 25 Between Tower of London (Sat, Sun only) or Oxford Circus, Holborn and Bank (Mon-Fri) and Ilford via Aldgate, Bow, Stratford, Forest Gate and Manor Park.
No 42 Between Liverpool St and Denmark Hill via Aldgate, Tower Bridge, Old Kent Rd, Albany Rd and Camberwell Green.
No D1 Between County Hall and Harbour Exchange via Waterloo, London Bridge, Tower Hill (eastbound) or Aldgate (westbound), Wapping, Marsh Wall, and South Quay.

River transport River boats from Westminster Pier to the Tower with *City Cruises*, T020-7930 9033, every 20 mins from 1020-2100 in summer, £4.60, takes 30 mins. From Westminster Pier to Greenwich, every 30 minutes, 1030-1700, takes an hour, return £7.60, single £6.30. Embankment Pier to Greenwich via Tower Millenium and St Katherine's, daily every 30 mins, with *Catamaran Cruises* (T020-7987 1185).

Taxis Usually plenty near Tower Hill, heading up Minories or over Tower Bridge. Also outside the Thistle Tower Hotel in St Katharine's Dock.

Trains Fenchurch St for Limehouse, West Ham, Barking, Tilbury, Southend and the south Essex coast. Tower Gateway Docklands Light Railway.

Tubes Tower Hill (District and Circle lines) and Tower Gateway (DLR).

Docklands

➲ *The purpose-built driverless Docklands Light Railway (DLR) is easily the most efficient way of reaching the area. Alternatively, there is a fast riverboat commuter service morning and evenings from the West End & the City. Nearest tubes: Shadwell (East London line) & Canary Wharf*

'*Just a short hop from the overcrowded centre of the City on the Docklands Light Railway (DLR).' At least that was the guiding principle of the London Docklands Development Corporation (LDDC) set up in 1981 to regenerate the abandoned docks on the Isle of Dogs. Ah, the docklands … such a romantic sound to the name, with its promise of the open seas, adventure and precious goods from far and wide coming and going within this wide meander of the Thames. Twenty years on, the result is a pristine and ultimately bland extension to the teeming money-driven office life of the City of London. Slowly, resident streetlife and visitors are following in the wake of the workers, although at weekends the area is still pretty much a watery desert. Where once the masts of tall ships dominated the skyline, the massive obelisk of **Canary Wharf** now towers over gleaming office* *blocks and swish apartments, winking across lots of landlocked riverwater. Even so, the peculiar history of the place makes it an intriguing destination and the views from Island Gardens are compensation enough for the architectural eyesores. From September 2001 the* **Museum of Docklands** *hopes to entice more visitors into the area. Now fully linked up by rail to Greenwich and beyond just south of the river, there should be plenty of life in the Isle of Dogs yet. Further north, Limehouse has remained truer to its East End roots.*

History

London's water trade meant busy quays and wharves lining the bank from London Bridge to east of the Tower. Remnants of Roman quays have been found near Customs House, but the first wet dock was built at Blackwall in the early 16th century. Although places such as Billingsgate, the Tower, and Wapping offered further unloading space, most ships anchored in the river itself and unloaded their cargo onto lighters. River traffic was therefore busy, plentiful and chaotic, and to ensure that smuggling was kept to a minimum, Elizabeth ordered that goods should be unloaded at only the 'legal quays' between London Bridge and the Tower.

Although some quays existed beyond Wapping, by the 17th century there was still little development inland. The fields of Limehouse held lime kilns producing thin tile-like bricks, and were a popular residential area among distinguished Elizabethan explorers and seafarers. Shadwell was a hamlet with a tide mill where a few wealthy families had also settled. The Isle of Dogs, probably so-called because the royal kennels resided here, was marshland until the 13th century, and thereafter was barely populated until the 18th century, despite its windmills and cornfields.

The 1700s saw a burgeoning in the river's activity. Limehouse became London's foremost shipbuilding centre – Hawksmoor's fine church to St Anne was erected to serve a growing population – and in Shadwell ropemakers, tanners and brewers mixed with the regular turnover of seamen, watermen and lightermen. London's trade increased fivefold, and with it the need for an overhaul of the docks.

In the first decade of the 1800s, and then steadily over the next hundred years or more, huge docks were built along the north bank. East of Wapping were the London Dock for coffee, cocoa, fruit and wine, the West India for rum and hardwood, and later the Royal Victoria and Royal Albert Docks, where the warehouses were "filled to overflowing with interminable stores of every kind of foreign and colonial products", while to the west of Wapping was St Katharine's for sugar and rum. Cubitt Town on the Isle of Dogs was built to house the workers in the nearby shipyards and factories.

Predictably, slum areas soon developed. Shadwell was said to have "homes and workshops [that] will not bear description" and Limehouse grew a reputation for its brothels, gambling and opium dens, the latter aided by a sizeable Chinese population that had grown here in the 1890s, but which later gravitated to Soho as the docks' fortunes declined.

Following severe damage caused by regular raids during the Second World War, the docks mustered a brief revival, but by the 1960s

East London

Hotels in the area

A *The Four Season's Hotel, Canary Wharf*
B *The International Hotel*
D *Ibis, Isle of Dogs*
D *Travelodge Docklands*
E *Urban Learning Foundation*
E *Rotherhithe Youth Hostel*
▸▸ *Go to page 448*

Docklands

East London

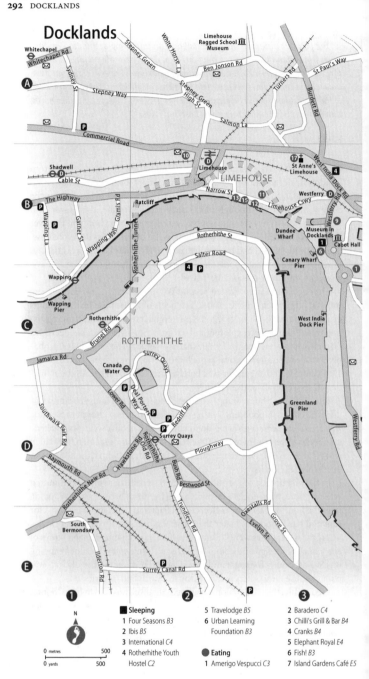

Whitechapel
Whitechapel Rd
Stepney Green
White Horse Rd
Limehouse Ragged School Museum
Ben Jonson Rd
Turners Rd
St Paul's Way

Stepney Way
Sydney St
Stepney Green High St
Salmon La
Burdett Rd

Commercial Road
Shadwell
Cable St
10
Limehouse
LIMEHOUSE
St Anne's Limehouse
17
West India Dock Rd
4

The Highway
Ratcliff
Narrow St
13 15
11
12
Limehouse Cswy
Westferry
Westferry Rd
9

Wapping La
Garnet St
Wapping Wall
Glamis Rd
Rotherhithe St
Rotherhithe Tunnel
Dundee Wharf
Museum in Docklands
1
6
Cabot Hall

Wapping
Salter Road
4
Canary Wharf Pier
1

Wapping Pier
Rotherhithe
ROTHERHITHE
West India Dock Pier

Jamaica Rd
Brunel Rd
Canada Water
Surrey Quays
Lower Rd
Deal Porters Way
Redriff Rd
Greenland Pier

Southwark Park Rd
Hawkstone Rd
Rotherhithe Old Rd
Surrey Quays
Ploughway
Westferry Rd

Raymouth Rd
Rotherhithe New Rd
Bush Rd
Bestwood St
Oxestalls Rd
Evelyn St
Grove St

South Bermondsey
Trundleys Rd

Ilderton Rd
Surrey Canal Rd

N

0 metres 500
0 yards 500

■ **Sleeping**
1 Four Seasons *B3*
2 Ibis *B5*
3 International *C4*
4 Rotherhithe Youth Hostel *C2*
5 Travelodge *B5*
6 Urban Learning Foundation *B3*

● **Eating**
1 Amerigo Vespucci *C3*
2 Baradero *C4*
3 Chilli's Grill & Bar *B4*
4 Cranks *B4*
5 Elephant Royal *E4*
6 Fish! *B3*
7 Island Gardens Café *E5*

East London

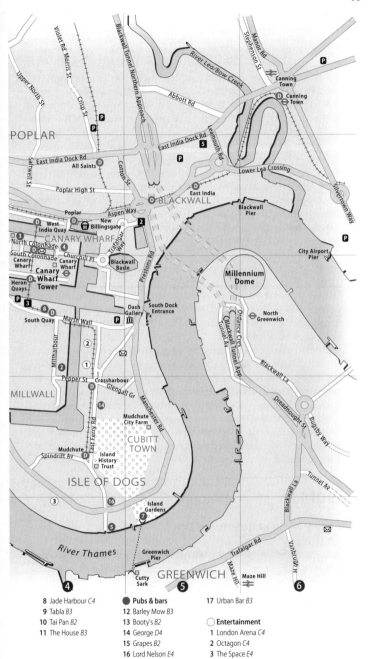

8 Jade Harbour *C4*	● **Pubs & bars**	17 Urban Bar *B3*
9 Tabla *B3*	12 Barley Mow *B3*	
10 Tai Pan *B2*	13 Booty's *B2*	○ **Entertainment**
11 The House *B3*	14 George *D4*	1 London Arena *C4*
	15 Grapes *B2*	2 Octagon *C4*
	16 Lord Nelson *E4*	3 The Space *E4*

Hollywood's moving stars

There appears to be no end to Hollywood's blossoming love affair with London. Robert de Niro, star of Taxi Driver and Meet the Parents, is only the latest in a long line of movie stars who have upped and left Los Angeles to tread the boards in the West End. The list of actors who have chosen to live and work on this side of the pond includes Kathleen Turner, Daryl Hannah, Nicole Kidman, Jessica Lange, Macauley Culkin, Kevin Spacey and Donald Sutherland. Earlier this year, de Niro was reported to have bought a penthouse in an exclusive new development in Docklands – London's so-called `Little Hollywood' – and is set to take a part in Yasmina Reza's smash hit play, Art. Another big name to hit the West End soon is Calista Flockhart, star of the hit TV series, Ally McBeal.

So why are all these big names coming over here? Well, it certainly ain't the money. Nicole Kidman took a role in the Donmar Warehouse production of The Blue Room for a mere £250 a week, and Kathleen Turner made only around £200,000 for revealing all as Mrs Robinson in a 19-week run of The Graduate. Maybe, then, it's the anonymity. Nicole Kidman's ex-hubbie, Tom Cruise, quickly found that his fame counted for little amongst the capital's terminally unimpressed population when he went to rent a movie at his local Blockbusters video store and was asked to produce some form of ID.

business was in decline. Competition from Rotterdam hurt a dwindling industry as the Empire was dismantled, and the huge modern ships needed deeper water in which to dock.

By 1980, most of the docks were undergoing some form of development, the most high profile of which was the office tower at Canary Wharf, at 500 m, the tallest building in Britain. Developers were encouraged by favourable tax breaks, but limited public investment in the transport links meant the Docklands Light Railway and Jubilee extension have been slow to finish, and the early 1990s recession left investors struggling with empty premises. Docklands is currently undergoing a new lease of life, but the waters are now part of a landscape of offices and expensive apartments, and rarely see any significant river traffic at all.

Sights

Canary Wharf and the Isle of Dogs

Canary Wharf tube station on the Jubilee line is a modern architectural wonder in itself

Arriving on the DLR at Canary Wharf, or emerging from Norman Foster's fairly awe-inspiring new station for the Jubilee line, it's impossible to miss the **Canary Wharf Tower**, 1 Canada Square, E14, the beacon at the heart of Docklands. Fear of a terrorist attack means no public access to Europe's second tallest building, but standing at the bottom of Cesar Pelli's tower looking up is just as daunting.

Cabot Square is the best place for taxis

On the other side of the tube, in Cabot Square, after several years of cultural dearth, signs of normal human existence are beginning to sprout. The Square boasts an impressive array of high street shops, whilst **Cabot Hall**, Cabot Place West, E14, T020-7481 2783, is starting to host some serious music events and theatre.

A little to the north, the new **Museum in Docklands**, Warehouse No 1, West
India Quay, Hertsmere Rd, E14, T020-7515 1162, takes the themes of River,
Port and People to tell the story of the area from salty seafarers via desolation
to corporate hospitality. The full history of Docklands will be covered in
depth at this outpost of the Museum of London, and it is to be hoped that it
will capture some of the area's exciting past. *The museum opens in Sep 2001*

A little to the south, **The Dash Gallery**, Jack Dash House, 2 Lawn House
Close, Marsh Wall, E14, T020-7364 5031, is a purpose-built circular arts gal-
lery and part of the emerging Docklands cultural scene. Recent events include
Shaffique Uddin and the Daily Mirror Photographer of the Year.

Beyond the Enterprise Business Park and the London Arena on Millwall
Inner Dock, a strange anomaly in the area is the **Mudchute City Farm**, Pier
Street, E14, Britain's largest city farm. Always a big hit with the kids, its location also offers a superb view back up the Isle of Dogs to Canary Wharf, and
also away up the Thames to the City. ■ *Open 1000-1600 Admission free but
donations appreciated. T020-7515 5901.*

Over the playing fields from here, the **Island History Trust**, 197 East Ferry
Road, E14, hold at least 5,000 photos depicting the Isle of Dogs in the 20th
century. Along with the new museum, a visit here is a must to fully appreciate
the changes, good and bad, the area has undergone in recent times. ■ *Open
Tue, Wed 1330-1630. Admission free. T020-7987 6041.*

Nestling at the tip of the Isle of Dogs, **Island Gardens** is a small park that
makes an ideal place to sit and admire the glorious view of maritime Greenwich and the Cutty Sark. Look over your shoulder, and you're back in the 21st
century with a bang, Canary Wharf still oddly close though more than a mile
away. From Island Gardens, the Greenwich foot tunnel, constructed in 1902
for the West India dockers, sneaks under the river and back in time.

Limehouse and Poplar

North of the Isle of Dogs, smacking more of the East End than the river or the
sea, Narrow Street, Limehouse's sleepy main thoroughfare, gives an idea of
what Docklands could yet become. The old has been renovated and preserved
in splendid riverside warehouses and pubs (see below), while the newer flats
and houses, more sensitively designed than the space pods around Canary
Wharf, are beginning to weather and mellow into their surroundings.

St Anne's, Limehouse, 3 Colt Street, E14, Hawksmoor's grand creation, with
its leaning framework and eroding pyramid in the churchyard, is a reminder
of the area's former importance and gives a glimpse of an older, more ramshackle Limehouse. Built in 1714, it also boasts London's second highest
clock tower after Big Ben. ■ *Open 1400-1600. Mon-Fri, 1400-1700 Sat, and
1430-1730 Sun.*

A walk up the Grand Union Canal from the station is **Limehouse Ragged
School Museum**, 46-50 Copperfield Road, E3, a tiny but charming social his-
tory of Limehouse told through the eyes of Barnardos children from 1880 to
1900. With Canary Wharf just minutes by foot, it all seems so far away.
■ *Open 1000-1700 Wed, Thu, and 1400-1700 on the first Sun of each month.
T020-8980 6405.*

East London

North Woolwich

Further east beside the City Airport and the riverside Royal Victoria Gardens, the **North Woolwich Old Station Museum**, Pier Road, E16, is a train buff's Mecca paying tribute to the defunct London and North Eastern Railway. Take a flask of weak lemon drink, an anorak and a packed lunch. ■ *Open Jan-Nov 1300-1700 Sat, Sun and school holidays. Admission free. T020-7474 7244.*

Eating and drinking

Expensive
● on map, page 292

The Quadrato Restaurant, *Four Seasons Hotel*, 46 Westferry Circus, E14, T020-7510 1999, is Docklands' only truly world-class restaurant, with Milanese chef Marco Bax serving up international delicacies from an open-plan kitchen amid the diners. Accountability right before the customer's eyes: Mrs Thatcher would have been proud.

Mid-range

Tabla, The Dockmaster's House, West India Dock Gate, Hertsmere Rd, E14, T020-7345 0345, closes Sat lunch and Sun, is a smart Indian restaurant in a historic Georgian house. Excellently spiced and very good value food, even if more expensive than the average, its menu is based around fish fresh from Billingsgate (the salmon samosas are superb).

The Canary Wharf Complex contains all the usual quality chains like *Pizza Express* and *Browns*, but a short walk away the area contains a few hidden gems. *The House*, 27 Ropemaker's Field, Narrow St, E14, T020-7538 3818, is a bastion of modern British food in a bastion of old British architecture. Sample venison sausages, pheasant and the like in a solitary London townhouse amid the dark glass and concrete. *Tai Pan*, 665 Commercial Rd, T020-7791 0118, is an honest family-run Cantonese, oyster sauce et al. *The Elephant Royal*, Locke Wharf, Ferry Rd, E14, T020-7987 7999, is a modern Oriental at a gorgeous location on the river opposite Greenwich with a cocktail bar that's lively at weekends. Set meal for one comprises 6 courses for £24. *Amerigo Vespucci*, 25 MacKenzie Walk, E14, T020-7513 0288, does above-average Italian Cuisine for the English palate. Decent wine list.

Cheap

Fish!, Hanover House, 33 Westferry Circus, E14. Fresh fish in airy surroundings. Pleasant and great value at lunch time. No reported cases of food poisoning suggests the fare is not caught by one of the fishermen on the wharf at the rear. *Baradero*, Turnberry Quay off Pepper St, E14, is a good-value tapas bar in a quiet shopping precinct. *Jade Harbour*, Marsh Wall, E14, T020-7987 0771. Despite looking like an executive car park this place serves up no-nonsense Chinese tucker, a stone's throw from Canary Wharf. Roast Duck for £6.

Cafés &
sandwich bars

Cranks Concourse Level, Cabot Place East, E14, T020-7519 1616, is a sparkling branch of the popular and long-established vegetarian chain. *Chili's Grill and Bar*, Floor 2, Cabot Place, E14, T020-7363 5678. This is hardly nouvelle cuisine, but a decent enough bet for meat and two stodge. The *Island Gardens Café*, Island Gardens, E14, T020-7515 4532. Overlooking the Royal Naval College at Greenwich this is a garden shed with a view. Standard snacks like chilli and baked potatoes for around £4. Also worth checking out is the café at the Space Arts Centre (see page 431).

Pubs & bars
▶▶ *Go to page 431 for entertainment & nightlife*

The Grapes, 76 Narrow St, E14, T020-7987 4396. Allegedly an inspiration for Dickens' *Our Mutual Friend*, this oak-panelled boozer has seen centuries of satisfied drinkers gaze out onto the Thames. When it gets overcrowded it's worth trying *Booty's* 92a Narrow St, E14, T020-7987 8343, or *The Barley Mow*, 44 Narrow St, E14, T020-7265 8931, for similar riverside vistas without the history and attendant tourists.

East London

The Urban Bar, 27 Three Colt St, T020-7537 1601, is a refreshing blast of Soho chic in an area where most water-holes have the atmosphere of an airport departure lounge after an IKEA makeover. A leopard-skin exterior and very low sofas inside ensure a funky crowd at weekends. Nice food too. *The Lord Nelson*, 1 Manchester Rd, E14, T020-7987 1976, is a quiet, relaxed family pub, ideal for a refreshing pint if you've just popped through the tunnel from Greenwich. *The George*, 114 Glengall Rd, E14, T020- 7987 2954, is a rare historic boozer next to the DLR at Crossharbour. Real ales, quiet conversation and definitely no cocktails. Apparently the back of the building contains an area consecrated to a covert masonic lodge.

Shopping

Cabot Place is the only place in Docklands for standard high street shops. A decent array of stores, especially clothing for professionals are on offer, such as *Phase Eight*, T020-7513 0808, and *Austin Reed*, T020-7513 0146. Overall you'll being doing well to find anything out of the ordinary, but a few of the more interesting places to look are **Pepper Street**, a pleasant pedestrian precinct by the water with clothes, jewellery and boutiques amongst the grocer's stores. *New Billingsgate Market*, Trafalgar Way, E14. London's 900-year-old fish market is now at modern new premises just off the A13 behind Canary Wharf. Get there early, it shuts at 0830. Near All Saints DLR, *Chrisp Street Market*, E14 (Tue, Thu, Sat) is a pleasant but unremarkable local market featuring food, clothes and bric-a-brac.

Docklands is not exactly a shopper's paradise

East London

Transport

No 15 Between Poplar and Paddington via Limehouse, Aldgate, Tower of London, Cannon St, St Paul's, Aldwych, Trafalgar Square, Piccadilly Circus, Oxford Circus and Marble Arch.

Buses

No 277 Between Highbury & Islington and Canary Wharf via Mildmay Park, Dalston, Hackney, Victoria Park, Mile End and Limehouse.

No D3 Between London Chest Hospital and Isle of Dogs District Centre via Bethnal Green, Wapping, Limehouse, Canary Wharf, Millwall Dock, Mudchute and Cubitt Town.

No D6 Between Hackney Central and Isle of Dogs District Centre via Cambridge Heath, Bethnal Green, Limehouse, Poplar, Blackwall DLR and Prestons Rd.

No D7 Between Mile End Station and Poplar via Limehouse, Canary Wharf and South Quay.

No D8 Between Stratford and Isle of Dogs District Centre via Bow, Devons Rd, Poplar, South and South Quay.

Directory

Sports *Docklands Sailing and Watersports Centre*, Millwall Dock, Westferry Road, E14, T020-7537 2626. Open 0930-1130 Mon-Fri, 0930-1700 Sat and Sun. Dragon boat racing, sailing, rowing, canoeing. *Docklands Watersports Club*, Gate 14, King George V Dock, Woolwich Manor Way, E16, T020- 7511 7000. Jet-skiing. *F1 City Racing*, 199 Connaught Bridge, Royal Victoria, E16, T020-7476 5678. Open-air go-karting. *London Arena*, Limeharbour, E14, T020- 7538 8880. If it's spectator sport you're after then major London ice hockey and basket ball teams play their home games here.

Tourist information Tower Hamlets Information T020-7364 4970. Mainly for local residents. *Toureast* T020-7531 1996.

River transport
Information from
Collins River
Enterprises,
T020-7237 9538

From **Savoy Pier to Canary Wharf** via Blackfriars Pier, London Bridge City Pier, and St Katharine's Pier at 0705, 0747, 0815, 0845. From **Canary Wharf to Savoy Pier** via St Katharine's Pier, London Bridge City Pier, and Blackfriars Pier at 1905, 1945, 2015, 2045. High-speed commuter service about £4 return, pay on the boat.

Tubes & trains

DLR to Bank, Shadwell, Limehouse, West Ferry, Poplar, West India Quay, Canary Wharf, Heron Quays, South Quay, Crossharbour & London Arena, Mudchute, Island Gardens. Also Canary Wharf (Jubilee line) and Limehouse train station into Fenchurch St and south Essex coast.

East London

North London

North London

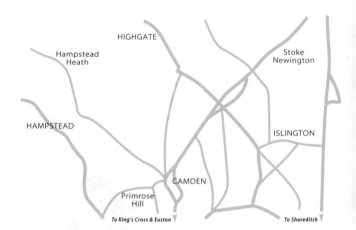

Hampstead and Highgate

Hampstead is a London high point. An affluent town astride the hills to the north, it competes in both elevation, social status and antique authenticity with the neighbouring hilltop village of Highgate. Although no longer the liberal, bohemian enclaves they once were, both remain strongly associated with their literary and cultural heritage. Blue plaques adorn many of the beautifully preserved Georgian and Victorian buildings, some of which are open to the public, while their labyrinth of narrow lanes and leafy picturesque streets are a joy to explore. Virginia Woolf, Andrew Marvell, Wordsworth, Coleridge, Dickens, DH Lawrence, John Constable, Gerard Manley Hopkins and Sigmund Freud are just a few of the greats who have settled here.

Both places are also deservedly famous for the 800 or so acres of rolling grassland, meadows and woodland of **Hampstead Heath** *that divides them. There's a distinctive 'villagey' feel to the area, passionately protected by the locals who have even persuaded the resident 'McDonalds' to abandon its usual garish branding. Hampstead's two cinemas and clutch of theatres cater for the well-to-do artistic community that has long been at home here, while more recently it has also been adopted by a younger handful of celebrities and fashionable emigrants from West London. Highgate is often seen as the poor relation, but its famous cemetery and village atmosphere make it a rewarding destination on the more attractive eastern side of the Heath.*

Nearest tubes: Hampstead, Belsize Park, Highgate. Highgate is best reached by bus (see page 310), as the tube is some way down the hill from the village near the Queen's Wood

History

Hampstead and Highgate, with commanding views over the Thames valley, have long been popular sites for human settlement. Tribes lived here in prehistoric times (they left a barrow on Parliament Hill), and the Roman road to St Albans ran across the heath through woodland brimming with deer, boars, wild cattle and wolves. By medieval times, the land was in the possession of the church.

Highgate grew around the gate to the Bishop of London's Hornsey Estate, and the Abbot of Westminster came to the heath to escape (unsuccessfully) the Black Death. Hampstead regularly featured as a place of refuge, with Londoner's fleeing to its hillsides from real or imagined catastrophes – in 1524 to escape the predicted great floods, in the 1660s from the Great Plague and the Great Fire, and in 1736 for the end of the world.

When in 1700 its spring water was being sold in London's taverns, Hampstead's reputation for health and safety was confirmed. The village boomed – new lodging houses and taverns were built, bun and teashops lined the High Street, and Keats and Byron were part of a distinguished political and literary world. William Blake (who was imprisoned for debt following a well-intentioned attempt to establish a hospital for orphaned children in Highgate), was not so taken by the village, describing a "journey to Hampstead without due consideration" as "only for a soldier of Satan to perform".

Hotels in the area

B Forte Posthouse
B The Sandringham Hotel
C The House Hotel
C The Langorf Hotel and Self Catering Apartments
D La Gaffe
E Belsize
F Hampstead Heath Youth Hostel
▸▸ *Go to page 448*

Hampstead

North London

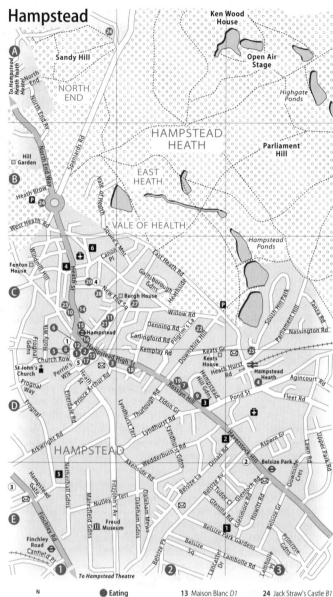

N

0 metres 200
0 yards 200

● Eating
1 Bagel St *D1*
2 Café Bianco *D1*
3 Coffee Cup *D1*
4 Cucina *D3*
5 Dim T Café *D1*
6 Dome *C1*
7 Giraffe *D2*
8 Gresslins *D1*
9 House on Rosslyn Hill *D2*
10 Jin Kichi *C1*
11 Le Cage Imaginaire *C1*
12 Louis Patisserie *C1*

13 Maison Blanc *D1*
14 Maxwells *C1*
15 Pizza Express *D1*
16 Toast *C1*
17 Villa Bianca *D1*
18 Zen W3 *D2*

● Pubs & bars
19 Bar Room Bar *D2*
20 Duke of Hamilton *C1*
21 Flask *C1*
22 Freemasons Arms *C2*
23 Holly Bush *C1*

24 Jack Straw's Castle *B1*
25 Magdala *D3*
26 Spaniards Inn *A1*
27 Wells *C2*
28 Ye Olde White Bear *C1*

○ Entertainment
1 Everyman *C1*
2 Screen on the Hill *D3*
3 Finchley Road Warner Village *E1*
4 New End Theatre *C1*
5 Pentameters *D1*

■ Sleeping
1 Belsize *E3*
2 Forte Posthouse *D3*
3 House *D2*
4 La Gaffe *C1*
5 Langorf *E1*
6 Sandringham *C1*

He may have had a point. Until it was drained in 1777, the Vale of Health was a malarial swamp, known as Hatches Bottom. Highgate, on the other hand, was "a most pleasant dwelling", and also popular.

Aristocrats built huge piles (Arundel, Cromwell, Fitzroy and Lauderdale houses), merchants erected elegant townhouses, and morris-dancing and fairs were held on

Five of the best: North London sights

- *Fenton House*, Windmill Hill, Hampstead.
- *2 Willow Road*, Hampstead.
- *Highgate Cemetery*, Highgate.
- *Camden Lock Market*, Camden.
- *Primrose Hill*, Camden.

the green. Nevertheless, development was slow and by 1835, Hampstead was still little more than a large village. The Caen Wood (later Kenwood) Estate sprawled to the north, beyond the isolated Vale of Health and Church Row was a genteel "avenue of Dutch red-faced houses" with St John's church at the end.

A footpath over the fields and past the ponds led to Highgate, a smaller village radiating from the church. It was soon to open the cemetery which became a tourist attraction initially for its architecture and views over London, and latterly also for its residents (Karl Marx and Tom Sawyer, the last of the bare-fisted fighters whose funeral in 1865 drew 100,000 mourners). Urban expansion arrived in the 1880s, but the villages' "august respectability" remained. Highgate's grand houses became convalescence homes, and Hampstead drew more and more literary and political figures: over the years, Katherine Mansfield and Ramsay MacDonald, DH Lawrence and Harold Wilson, Mohammed Jinnah and Rabindranath Tagore. Sigmund Freud spent his last years in Hampstead, adding another element to its reputation. In the 1960s Doris Lessing described Hampstead as a world of "political intellectuals, reformers, therapists, feminists", a situation not wholly unrecognizable today.

Sights

From Hampstead tube, Heath Street heads sharply uphill towards Hampstead Heath, an oasis of uncultivated land where it is easy to forget the urban mayhem as one wanders leafy avenues, open fields and shaded woods. Divided roughly into **West Heath** and **East Heath**, West Heath stretches down towards Golders Green, while East Heath comprises the main body of the heath reaching towards Highgate. West Heath is notorious for its gay cruising scene but is also home to the lovely **Hill Garden**, which has a magical landscaped walkway through the woods. East Heath is more traversable, with walks to suit all ages. An especially good one is to **Kenwood House** near Highgate (see below) which is best begun from the avenue at the end of Well Walk and then through Kenwood Woods (between 30 minutes and an hour).

Spectacular views of London can be found from the top of Parliament Hill, which is also a great place to fly kites. At the bottom of the hill, near the running track, is an Italian family-run café serving hot dishes and light snacks. There are three swimming ponds; mixed, ladies and men's, as well as an open-air swimming pool (■ *Open 0700 till dusk daily, free admission; T020-7485 4491*). Die-hard aficionados swim here all year round, cracking the ice in winter for their daily dips. In the 18th century, the water in Hampstead was declared medicinal and a Spa and Bathhouse were built in Well Walk where there is still a fountain for drinking from. The Vale of Health is a secret cluster of highly derirable houses on the fringes of the Heath.

Hampstead Heath
For details of local street festivals, see the local paper 'The Ham & High'

North London

Around Hampstead

Burgh House
This genteel Queen Anne house on New End Square, NW3, was saved from the developers by local support. It now contains a small museum of local Hampstead history as well as changing exhibitions with a local flavour. Evening concerts and talks by famous residents are also often given here. The buttery in the basement serves light meals when the house is open.

■ *Open 1100-1700 Wed–Sun. Free. T020-7431 0144.*

Keats House
At Wentworth Place, Keats Grove, NW3, is the little Regency house and garden where Keats penned his most famous poem, *Ode to a Nightingale*, under a plum tree while staying there in 1819. The house was saved and opened to the public in the 1920s largely thanks to the poet's American fans, and since being taken over by the Corporation of London in 1997 is undergoing an extensive and ongoing five-year refurbishment. Rooms display various items of Keats memorabilia, manuscripts and letters while in the garden a mulberry tree survives from the romantic's day.

■ *Closed until 1 May 2001 but normally open Apr-Oct 1200-1700 Tue-Sun; Nov-Mar 1200-1600 Tue-Sun. Admission £3, £1.50 concession, under-16s free but donations gratefully accepted. T020-7435 2062.*

Fenton House
This late 17-century Merchant residence, at Windmill Hill, Hampstead Grove, NW3, is a beautiful example of the smart houses once typical of Hampstead, containing a collection of early keyboard instruments (concerts sometimes given) and porcelain with a lovely walled flower garden to stroll around and relax in.

■ *Open Mar–Oct, phone to check. Free admission. T020-7435 3471.*

2 Willow Road
This is a very fine example of modern domestic architecture designed and lived in by Erno Goldfinger from 1939, complete with artwork by Moore, Max Ernst, and Bridget Riley. Call for tour details, which include illuminating explanations of the architect's methods and rationale.

■ *Open Apr-Oct, 1200–1600. Admission by guided tour only every 45 mins. Admission £4.30. T020-7435 6166.*

The Freud Museum
At 20 Maresfield Gardens, NW3, is the Arts and Crafts house where the great psychoanalyst spent the last years of his life. The house has been preserved for posterity, now including a reconstruction of his study and consulting room, complete with the famous couch, and a surprising number of classical antiquities testifying to Freud's passionate interest in the ancient world. Upstairs there's a gallery devoted to exhibitions with some relevance to the great shrink as well as a display centred around his wife's handloom and work on child therapy.

■ *Open Wed-Sun 1200-1700. Admission £4, £2 concession. T020-7435 2002.*

St John's Churchyard
St John's Church, in Church Row, is the site of Constable's tomb. The churchyard offers a shady retreat if in need of relief from too much shopping or walking, with a peaceful secluded view over London. Church Row itself is one of the most beautiful avenues of elegant Georgian houses in the area, once home to the likes of HG Wells, and it remains a good spot for some nostalgic time travelling.

Around Highgate

Highgate Hill runs up from Archway and becomes the High Street of the old village. A left turn into South Grove leads to the top of the steep slope of Swain's Lane which runs downhill between Highgate Cemetery and Waterlow Park.

Highgate Cemetery

Highgate Cemetery, most famous for being the burial place of **Karl Marx**, in the more modern eastern part of the cemetery; on its western side is also one of London's most extraordinary and atmospheric burial grounds. The western part is the most overgrown and now carefully protected by a society of friends who offer informative guided tours taking in the remarkable Egyptian catacombs, famous graves, monuments and an abundance of wild flowers. Both parts are sometimes closed to the public during funerals.

■ *Eastern cemetery open 1000-1600 Mon-Fri, 1100-1600 Sat, Sun. Western cemetery Oct-Feb Sat, Sun tours at 1100, 1200, 1300, 1400, 1500, Mar-Oct weekdays also at 1200, 1400, 1600; tours cost £3. T020-8340 1834.*

Waterlow Park

Waterlow Park is one of the most attractive of north London's green spaces, with wooded walks, ponds and splendid views of London, something which the local borough is considering capitalizing upon with a controversial observation tower and restaurant development. In a secluded corner of the park stands **Lauderdale House**, a mid-17th century house that stages regular concerts, art exhibitions and theatre shows.

■ *Open Tue-Sun 1100-1600. T020-8348 8716.*

Kenwood House

The Brew House café & restaurant attached to the house offers delicious breakfasts, lunches & teas in the old coach house as well as outside in a peaceful walled garden

Highgate High Street ends at the top of the hill near the *Gatehouse* pub, from where Hampstead Lane leads round the north side of Hampstead Heath to Kenwood House. This 17th-century mansion renovated in 1760 by the architect Robert Adam, stands in the middle of the Heath in a glorious sweep of landscaped grounds, looking down on a wide lake. The house is open free to the public and holds a permanent display of European Art, bequeathed by its last owner, Lord Iveagh Guinness, including Gainsboroughs, Reynolds, Vermeers and van Dycks, as well as mounting temporary exhibitions (admission charged) on a variety themes.

The gardens and grounds are delightful, especially in May when the explosion of colour from the rhododendron blossoms rivals a Las Vegas chorus line. Sculptures by the likes of Henry Moore and Barbara Hepworth are dotted around the park. In the summer months there are delightful open-air concerts in the Kenwood Bowl to on one side of the lake. Paid entrance guarantees a view of the orchestra but anyone can bring a picnic and settle on the meadow to enjoy the sound of the string drifting across the lawns on a summer's evening, often finishing up with a firework display.

■ *Open daily 1000-1800 Apr-Sep; 1000-1700 Mar & Oct; 1000-1600 Nov-Feb. Free admission. T020-8348 1286.*

Eating and drinking

Mid-range

● *on maps, pages 302 & 306*

In Hampstead *Toast*, 50 Hampstead High St, NW3, T020-7431 2244, is an achingly hip restaurant and bar right above the tube station, with a brasserie and 'fine dining' menu featuring a mixture of modern British and Mediterranean dishes with an emphasis on fish. The fashionable set have already descended, including celebrities like the

Gallagher brothers (at least till Noel left the Big Smoke for pastures new) and others who don't baulk at the Mayfair tariff.

ZenW3, 83 Hampstead High St, NW3, T020-7794 7863, is the north London outpost of the Zen group and as such offers reliable, delicately presented Chinese food in a spacious restaurant that's also popular with local celebs. Another good option is the modern fusion-food at *Gresslins*, 13 Heath St, NW3, T020-7794 8386, which also has a strong oriental bias.

Highgate & Hampstead Heath

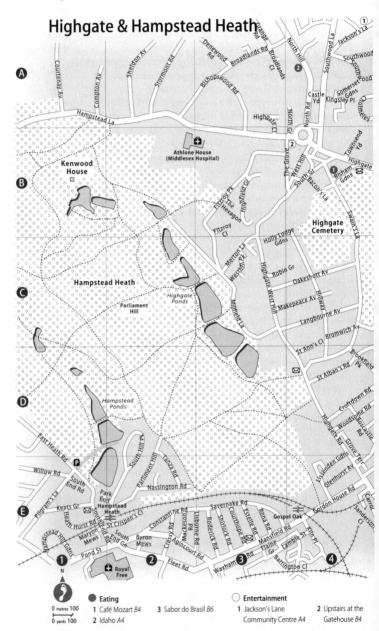

Eating
1 Café Mozart *B4*
2 Idaho *A4*
3 Sabor do Brasil *B6*

Entertainment
1 Jackson's Lane Community Centre *A4*
2 Upstairs at the Gatehouse *B4*

The most esteemed Japanese restaurant in Hampstead could well be the *Jin Kichi*, 73 Heath St, NW3, T020-7794 6158, always busy with a varied and lively crowd. The walls here are decorated with autographs and praise for the place from famous customers that have dropped in for some reasonably priced delicacies, although all the tempting little treats inevitably add up.

Villa Bianca, 1 Perrins Court, NW3, T020-7435 3131, is a long-established Italian restaurant with a small outside terrace for al fresco dining in the summer months. *Le* Cage Imaginaire, 16 Flask Walk, NW3, T020-7794 6674, is an intimate cosy French restaurant tucked away in a little lane off the High St.

South of the Heath, *Cucina,* 45a South End Green, NW3, T020-7435 7814, has a delicatessen out front selling delicious breads, salads and cakes with a Modern European menu served up behind in bright designer-styled surrounds. Understandably very popular with locals.

In Highgate, *Idaho*, 13 North Hill, T020-8341 6633, is a new hip and modern American eaterie that has had good reviews.

In Hampstead *Dim T café*, 3 Heath St, NW3, T020-7435 0024, is a trendy dim sum café-style restaurant serving a variety of noodle-based dishes and changing specials, its bright and cheerful design with Mao-emblazoned cushions encouraging a laid-back atmosphere. *Base,* 71 Hampstead High St, NW3, T020-7431 2224, offers a Mediterranean menu of a high standard in a tastefully decorated small dining room. At the front there is more of a deli/sandwich bar operation with outside pavement seating.

Cheap

Giraffe, 46 Rosslyn Hill, NW3, T020-7435 0348, is a cheerful brasserie, kid friendly café/restaurant which serves great breakfasts, fresh juices and an interesting mix of dishes for lunch and dinner canteen style - long communal tables with a few intimate tables for 2-4 people.

Nearby, *The House on Rosslyn Hill,* 34 Rosslyn Hill, NW3, T020-7435 8037, is always packed with a young vibrant crowd. The alarmingly relaxed staff keep the regulars happy, and outside heaters allow a cosmopolitan vibe to flourish on the pavement tables long after the warmer months have passed. It does a fairly standard brasserie menu with good sized portions.

North London

Hampstead's *Pizza Express*, 70 Heath St, NW3, T020-7433 1600, is an unusually cosy, sofa-decked branch of the chain serving up the usual range of pizzas, while *Maxwells*, 76 Heath St, NW3, T020-7433 1600, is the local branch of the long-established American-style diner serving up hamburgers, salads and shakes in a cavern of a restaurant decked out with US memorabilia, popular with families and a young teenage crowd.

In Highgate, *Sabor do Brasil,* 36 Highgate Hill, N19, T020-7263 9066, is run by an Englishman and his flamboyant Brasilian wife, a place that's a real pleasure to visit and where you get a warm welcome. A la carte and buffet at £10 is recommended as it gives you a sample of the main Brasilian staples.

Cafés & sandwich bars **In Hampstead** A distinctly Hampstead atmosphere prevails at the *Louis Patisserie*, 32 Heath St, NW3, T020-7435 9908, Hungarian tea rooms where delicious cakes and patisseries are served in a genteel olde worlde style in elegant surroundings, at a price. *The Coffee Cup*, 74 Hampstead High St, NW3, T020-7435 7565, is another Hampstead institution that has staved off numerous threats of closure thanks to tireless petitions from local residents. The loyalty of its eccentric local clientele must be due more to nostalgia than the particularly good quality of the food or drink, although they do a mean hot chocolate. A people-watcher's haven with a good view of the High Street poseurs from within its dark rather gloomy interior, or from the seats outside.

Maison Blanc, 62 Hampstead High St, NW3, T020-7431 8338, is a superior French patisserie selling cakes, breads, sandwiches, quiches and an array of tempting confectionery with a tiny seating area. *Café Bianco*, 12 Perrins Court, NW3, T020-7431 0363, do generously filled sandwiches in a tiny café with tables outside on a pleasant pedestrian walkway between the High St and Heath St and also claim to do the best breakfasts in town. *Bagel St*, Oriel Place, NW3, T020-7431 6709, have a wide variety of assorted fillings for their bagels and do decent coffees and teas.

On Heath St there's a spacious branch of *The Dome*, 58-62 Heath St, NW3, T020-7431 0399, with friendly staff serving light lunches and café staples as well as offering a kids menu. In the evening it's popular with more of a bar crowd.

In Highgate, *Café Mozart* in Swains Lane do great cakes although the staff could do with a spell at charm school, while near the tube in Queens' Wood the excellent *Oshobasho* café does decent veggie food and has a pleasant outside seating area.

Pubs & bars
▶▶ *Go to page 431 for entertainment & nightlife*
In Hampstead itself, one of the most popular drinking places for a young crowd is the *Bar Room Bar*, 48 Rosslyn Hill, NW3, T020-7431 8802. It's a busy hangout that also does coffees, bar snacks and light lunches, with exhibitions by local artists and photographers on the walls. And then there's *Toast,* 50 Hampstead High St, NW3, T020-7431 2244 (see above), the fashionable new members' bar which operates a door policy after 1800 and aspires towards exclusivity but often admits anyone suitably dressed up. Oriental style bar snacks are available here.

A more rounded impression of Hampstead life can be found in its pubs. *The Holly Bush*, 22 Holly Mount, NW3, T020-7435 2892, is a timeless old pub, much beloved by locals and visitors alike and beautifully maintained, in its own little square, perched above Heath St. It can best be reached on foot up a flight of stone steps between 73 and 75 Heath St opposite the tube.

Other old peculiars hidden away in the backstreets include *The Flask*, 14 Flask Walk, NW3, T020-7435 4580, a characterful pub with a strong local flavour, and *The Wells*, Well Walk, NW3, T020-7794 2806, which has a lively atmosphere – especially on football nights. Outside tables make it especially popular in the summer when it is crammed with young upper-middle-class revellers and post-Heath walkers.

Next door to the little New End Theatre, *The Duke of Hamilton*, New End, NW3, caters to the pre- and post-show audience in a more sedate atmosphere while at the bottom of New End *Ye Olde White Bear*, New End, NW3, T020-7435 3758, is a small and friendly old-fashioned establishment with a few tables outside on a narrow pavement strip and some superior pub grub. Food is also the strong point at the *Magdala*, 2a South Hill Park, NW3, T020-7435 2503, down near South End green, where an old pub has been revamped with stripped pine and boasts an accomplished kitchen.

Also near the Heath, *The Freemasons' Arms*, Downshire Hill, NW3, T020-7433 6811, is large and impersonal, but its huge garden comes into its own in the summer after a walk on the Heath. Pretty much the same is true of *Jack Straw's Castle*, Whitestone Pond, NW3, a vast clapperboard pub between East and West Heath next to Whitestone Pond with plenty of outside seating.

The most famous and characterful of this tourist threesome is the *Spaniard's Inn*, NW3, a landmark highwayman's pub perched on the edge of West Heath near Kenwood, with little dark rooms and a large beer garden.

In Highgate, the warren of rooms and heated front garden at another pub also called the *Flask*, 77 Highgate West Hill, N6, T020-8340 7260, overflows with a lively crowd every weekend.

Shopping

The two main thoroughfares in Hampstead (the High St and Heath St) are lined with familiar stores and brand names. More interesting is **Flask Walk**, a small pedestrian alley off Hampstead High St. (near the tube station) which preserves a quaint, timeless feel in all the shop fronts and has a wonderful second-hand book shop, *Keith Fawkes*, which is stuffed with books and infused with the aroma of musty pages. Opposite is *Villa Fern*, established around 30 years ago, which sells freshly ground coffees and a variety of interesting grocery gift items including a nostalgic selection of old-fashioned sweets still served out of glass jars. Further up is *Verde*, a haven of natural plant-based therapeutic and beauty products for men, women and children.

Continuing down Flask Walk all the way to the bottom, you come to Well Walk. On the corner is the *Well Walk Pottery*, which sells imaginative pottery and stained-glass items made by the owner who also runs short and long courses in both arts.

Back on Hampstead High Street, at the weekend, there is a *Community Market* in the hall near the post office which sells locally produced crafts as well as antiques and bric-a-brac. Tea and coffee, home-made cakes and snacks available. Designer clothes can be found at *Linea* in Perrins Court. There are also a couple of second-hand designer clothes shops on the High St. Ethnic imports can be purchased at colossal expense at *David Wainwrights* on Rosslyn Hill. Modern artefacts for home, etc at *Ruth Aram shop* on Heath St.

Directory

Sports **Swiss Cottage Sports Centre**, Winchester Rd, NW3. T020-7974 6490. Public Sports Complex with two swimming pools, gym, badminton, sunbeds, etc. **Springfield Leisure**, 81 Belsize Park Gardens, NW3, T020-7483 6800. Private Health Club but offers daily membership at £15 or weekly at £30 to use facilities of gym, small swimming pool, sauna, steam and classes.

North London

Transport

Buses **For Hampstead and Highgate**:

No 24 between Pimlico (for Tate Britain) and Hampstead Heath (South End Green) via Victoria, Westminster, Trafalgar Square, Leicester Square, Warren St, and Camden Town.

No 46 between Kensal Rise and King's Cross via West Kilburn, Warwick Ave, St John's Wood, Swiss Cottage, Fitzjohn's Ave, Hampstead, Rosslyn Hill, Hampstead Heath and Kentish Town.

No 168 between Hampstead Heath and Waterloo via Haverstock Hill, Chalk Farm, Camden Town, Eversholt St, Euston, Kingsway and Aldwych.

No 268 between Golders Green and Finchley Rd via Hampstead, Rosslyn Hill, Belsize Ave and Swiss Cottage.

No 210 between Finsbury Park and Golders Green via Stroud Green, Hornsey Rise, Archway Station, Highgate Village, Kenwood and Hampstead Heath.

No 214 between Highgate Village and Liverpool St via Parliament Hill Fields, Kentish Town, Camden Town, King's Cross, Islington, City Rd and Moorgate.

No 271 between Highgate Village and Moorgate (Liverpool St on Sat, Sun) via Archway, Holloway, Highbury, Essex Road Station, Hoxton and Old St Station.

No C2 between Parliament Hill Fields and Oxford Circus via Kentish Town, Camden Town, and Great Portland St.

No C11 from Archway Station to Hampstead Heath via Parliament Hill Fields.

Taxis Usually plenty on Hampstead High St and down Rosslyn Hill, Highgate.

Trains Nearest train stations Hampstead Heath (North London Link) and Gospel Oak (North London line).

Tubes Hampstead and Belsize Park (Northern line; Edgeware branch) and Highgate (Northern line; High Barnet/Mill Hill East branch).

Camden

Camden Town tube, although it becomes one-way into the area on Sat & Sun: no way out of the mayhem except from Chalk Farm or Mornington Crescent tubes, or by very slow bus. Alternatively, there's Camden Rd Station on the North London Link

*North of Euston, St Pancras and King's Cross, Camden is the spigot around which north London spins. And a strange mixed-up place it is too, with its music, markets and self-aware media-savvy, its dirt, hard drinking and organic juice bars. The scruffy High Street teems with grungy indie kids, stylish bohos, raving drunks and bright young tourists, during summer becoming impassable every weekend thanks to the crowds cramming into the markets. Meanwhile the Chalk Farm Road carries the High Street on northwest past the genteel slopes of **Primrose Hill**, a chi chi celebrity hideout, towards the social heights of Hampstead. Kentish Town Road wobbles up to Tufnell Park, Archway and Highgate village, while the ugly great Camden Road makes a brisk beeline northeast through Holloway to Finsbury Park and Seven Sisters.*

*The **markets** are obviously Camden Town's main attraction, the city's weekly street festival, but the dubious charm of the area lies in the messy and animated job it makes of tying up all north London's loose ends before they head into the centre of the city. It manages this with a formidable combination of loud music, Irish accents, plenty of booze and late opening hours. Take your courage in both hands and go with the flow.*

History

When the canons of St Paul's visited their manor at 'Cantelowes' in the 11th century, the nearby Primrose Hill was brimming with stags, bucks, boars and wild bulls, but Elizabeth I cleared it for meadowland and the abundance of primroses that subsequently grew here probably accounts for the hill's name. Cows grazed on the fine pastureland to the east around the manor, where the heavy clay soil prevented the sinking of wells or effective drainage. As a result, it wasn't until the end of the 18th century when the First Earl of Camden leased land for 1,400 houses that Camden Town began to show any signs of life. In the same year, 1791, the Veterinary College on College Street was the country's first training college in the field.

In 1804, however, little more than Camden itself was built up, and rural lanes criss-crossed hedged-in fields. Thomas Cubitt lent some time to building here before turning his attention to Belgravia in the 1820s, and Morningside Crescent went up in 1821. But it was the arrival of the Regent's Canal in the 1820s, and the railways after 1830 that sparked speedier changes.

Coal Wharves and small industry sprang up along the canal, and a huge depot was built for the railway. For a while, carriages were hauled up and down the Camden Incline to Euston by cable, having been uncoupled at the depot, and used the Round House for turning. A tunnel was drilled through Primrose Hill to link up with Chalk Farm. Businesses moved in, and the area gained a reputation for manufacturing musical, astronomical and scientific instruments. Dickens, who lived briefly as a child in Bayham Street, observed in *Dombey & Son*: "Everywhere were bridges that led nowhere; Babel towers of chimney…, temporary wooden houses and ragged tenements".

In 1846, riots broke out between Irish and English navvies. Nevertheless, when Miss Frances Buss set up her school for girls in 1851 (later Camden School for Girls), despite finding the limits of their general knowledge to be "beyond belief", the area was still "thickly inhabited by professional men".

In time, the professionals moved out, and the new householders turned to renting out rooms to lodgers. The area earned a reputation as a haven for artists and writers that it retains to this day, most notably the Fitzroy Group (now known as the Camden Town Group), formed in 1911 by Walter Sickert from rented studios around Mornington Crescent. In the 1950s Dylan and Caitlin Thomas used to have rows in their caravan parked in a friend's garden (neighbours used to gather to listen), while Primrose Hill is currently home to writers such as Martin Amis, Alan Bennett and Ian McEwen. A Greek Cypriot community settled here after the Second World War, during which a huge anti-aircraft battery sat on Primrose Hill.

Camden went down in the world in the 1960s, but its bohemian reputation earned it a revival that has seen a return of the professionals to the restored Victorian terraces while the media and music industry continue to mythologize its new-found status.

Hotels in the area

A London Marriot Regent's Park
A Thistle Euston
C The Camden Lock Hotel
D Ibis
D-E YHA St Pancras International
▸▸ **Go to page 449**

North London

Sights

Camden Market

The reason most people come to Camden in the first place, the 'market' (although markets would be more accurate), has ballooned from lowly beginnings into a series of stalls occupying any vacant space on the High Street between Camden Town tube and Camden Lock every Saturday and Sunday. Camden Market and the Electric Ballroom (both on the High Street) and the High Street itself, with its outsize shop signs, are a pop kids' Mecca, awash with cheap leather jackets, brashly sloganed T-Shirts and hectic drinking holes.

In recent years though, **Camden Lock Market**, on Camden Lock Place, off Chalk Farm Road, with its array of more interesting clothes, jewellery, books and handicraft, and **Stables Market** (off Chalk Farm Road at the junction with Hartland Road, T020-7485 5511), with its furniture and bric a brac, have provided satisfying browsing for those who do not wish to dress as if it were still 1966. The **Canal Market** runs off Chalk Farm Road, just over the bridge from the High Street on the right, with a mish-mash of stalls inside and out. If none of these tickle your fancy you can always plump for plain old fruit 'n' veg at the market on **Inverness Street.**

■ *Camden Market open 0900-1730 Thu–Sun; T020-7938 4343. Electric Ballroom open 0900-1730 Sun; T020-7485 9006. Camden Lock Market open 1000-1800 Sat, indoor stalls Tue–Sat; T020- 7284 2084.*

Camden Lock By the High Road stand many of the original Grand Union buildings alongside the huge new Suffolk Wharf shop, restaurant and office development under construction. Walk along the towpath for a minute and you'll see the kind of mix of old and new, rich and poor, public and private that London specializes in. Ridiculously expensive waterside condos back onto dilapidated railway bridges, and the area's gentrification doesn't stop the odd shopping trolley disfiguring the canal. From here, **The London Riverboat Company** operates trips regular via the Zoo as far as Little Venice.

The Round House
See also page 432
On Chalk Farm Road is The Round House. Stephenson's goods engine turntable house has enjoyed a colourful history, especially as a radical socialist performance venue in the 1960s under the directorship of Arnold Wesker. Now its cavernous interior plays host to a mixed bag of performance events.

All Saint's Greek Orthodox Cathedral On the corner of Camden Street and Pratt Street stands the imposing All Saint's Greek Orthodox Cathedral, a reminder of one of Camden's first immigrant communities. This charming grand and ornate church was built in 1822 by Inwood and son who also designed the St Pancras New Church. It was taken over by the Greek Orthodox community in 1948, appropriately enough since its design displays the influence of the young Inwood's travels in Greece.
■ *Open 1000-1700 daily, Sun service 0930-1300; T020-7485 2149.*

TV-am Building & Sainsbury's Terry Farrell's TV-am Building in Hanley Crescent and Nicholas Grimshaw's **Sainsbury's Supermarket** on Camden Road, pay testimony to the influx of the modern, artistic and influential in the past few decades. The latter is certainly groundbreaking, is it a second-division football stadium or a grocery store? Judge for yourself.

A bit of rough

Camden Town has long had an attraction for artists and bohemian types, due to its rough and ready image and the availability of cheap housing and spacious commercial premises. The reason Camden was cheap was the large Irish immigrant population, who had something of an undesirable reputation for drunk and disorderly behaviour. The old saying, 'Camden Town for the rough lie down' is a reference to their supposed habit of sleeping in the streets after the pubs closed and the fighting stopped.

This museum, at 129 Albert Street, is a relatively recent addition to the area, with an interesting display on the history of Judaism in Britain and London, including a video and extraordinary treasures from the Nazi-bombed Great Synagogue such as a 16th-century Arc of the Covenant.

The Jewish Museum
There's another branch of the museum on Finchley Rd

■ *Open Mon, Thu & Sun 1000-1600. Admission £3. T020-7284 1997.*

This small exhibition, in The Royal Veterinary College, on Royal College Street, charts the history of the college from its inception in 1791, the first of its kind in the world, including a stuffed two-headed cow. You probably wouldn't want some of the implements on display here used on your beloved pooch.

The Veterinary Museum

■ *Open 0900-1700 Mon-Fri by appointment. T020-7468 5162.*

A few minutes walk from the High Street, or best reached directly over the railway bridge from Chalk Farm tube, the pretty village here could hardly be more different from its raving eastern neighbour. The hill itself affords magnificent vistas over central London and Essex and Kent beyond. The London Eye in the distance makes a striking addition to one of the city's greatest views, which was much marred in the 60s by a series of thoughtless housing projects.

Primrose Hill

North London

Eating and drinking

Near the High St itself, two old-timers still deliver the goods: the **Camden Brasserie**, 216 Camden High St, NW1, T020-7482 2114, has changed little since 1983, when it was one of the newly fashionable area's first brasserie-style eateries; a 3-course Frenchified meal with good wine can be had here for little over £20, in busy and convivial surroundings (needs to be booked Fri and Sat). The other, slightly more upmarket, is **Café Delancey**, 3 Delancey St, NW1, T020-7387 1985, with tables outside and inside the kind of place where just about anyone can feel at ease.

Mid-range
● *on map, page 314*

Further south, the **Trattoria Fiorentina**, 42 Camden High St, NW1, T020-7419 7163, nestles amid a string of identikit 'trendy' eateries at the scruffiest end of the High street, an oasis of independent-minded cuisine. The food is genuinely Florentine (yes, that does mean tripe and kidneys), down to the repro Botticellis on the wall.

Less expensive than any of these, **Cheng Du**, 9 Parkway, NW1, T020-7485 8058, do western versions of Oriental classics in modern, shrink-wrapped surroundings, while **Café Bintang**, Kentish Town Rd, NW1, T020-7428 9603, offers simple but excellent Malaysian, Thai and Indonesian cuisine in tiny, friendly, family-run premises. Lunchtimes often offer ridiculous give-aways (£5 for three courses).

Further north, **Mum's Kitchen**, 99a Kentish Town Rd, NW1, T020-7428 0820, is a one-woman Caribbean hothouse where the proprietor has been serving up quality jerk chicken for years.

The dining is generally more polite in deepest Primrose Hill

One of London's finest 'gastropubs', *The Engineer*, 65 Gloucester Ave, NW1, T020-7722 0950, is no exception. At lunchtime this labyrinthine establishment with its outside dining yard offers superior versions of global cuisine (check out the very meaty burgers). In the evenings the food is more adventurous, blending various Mediterranean styles. If fully booked, nearby is its chief competitor, *The Landsdowne*, is more of a pub than a restaurant although the food in the new upstairs dining room has been praised (see Pubs below).

North London

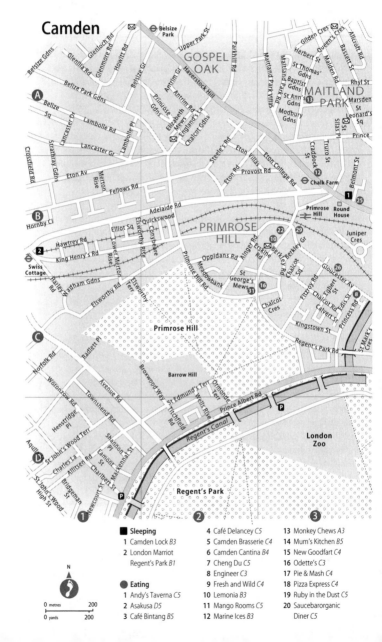

Camden

Sleeping
1 Camden Lock *B3*
2 London Marriot Regent's Park *B1*

Eating
1 Andy's Taverna *C5*
2 Asakusa *D5*
3 Café Bintang *B5*
4 Café Delancey *C5*
5 Camden Brasserie *C4*
6 Camden Cantina *B4*
7 Cheng Du *C5*
8 Engineer *C3*
9 Fresh and Wild *C4*
10 Lemonia *B3*
11 Mango Rooms *C5*
12 Marine Ices *B3*
13 Monkey Chews *A3*
14 Mum's Kitchen *B5*
15 New Goodfart *C4*
16 Odette's *C3*
17 Pie & Mash *C4*
18 Pizza Express *C4*
19 Ruby in the Dust *C5*
20 Saucebarorganic Diner *C5*

N

0 metres 200
0 yards 200

Odette's, 130 Regent's Park Rd, NW1, T020-7586 5486, is a locally patronized shrine to Modern British cookery with a decidedly superior winebar; it's the place to catch a glimpse of local celebs munching on game pie. *Lemonia*, 89 Regent's Park Rd, NW1, T020-7586 7454, also on Primrose Hill's charming main street, is a Greek version of an American diner offering an extensive range of Aegean classics in airy surroundings.

Further afield and considerably more offbeat, *Monkey Chews*, 2 Queen's Crescent, NW5, T020-7267 6406, is a bizarre mixture of arty pub, decent fish restaurant and music bar, worth seeking out for its independence of spirit.

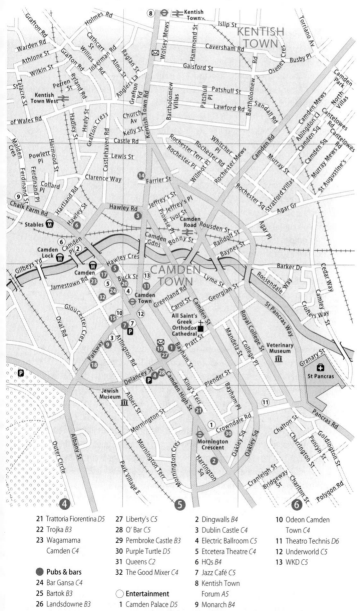

North London

21 Trattoria Fiorentina *D5*	27 Liberty's *C5*	2 Dingwalls *B4*	10 Odeon Camden Town *C4*
22 Trojka *B3*	28 O' Bar *C5*	3 Dublin Castle *C4*	11 Theatro Technis *D6*
23 Wagamama Camden *C4*	29 Pembroke Castle *B3*	4 Electric Ballroom *C5*	12 Underworld *C5*
	30 Purple Turtle *D5*	5 Etcetera Theatre *C4*	13 WKD *C5*
	31 Queens *C2*	6 HQs *B4*	
● Pubs & bars	32 The Good Mixer *C4*	7 Jazz Café *C5*	
24 Bar Gansa *C4*		8 Kentish Town Forum *A5*	
25 Bartok *B3*	○ Entertainment	9 Monarch *B4*	
26 Landsdowne *B3*	1 Camden Palace *D5*		

Cheap In the new Glass House development on Jamestown Rd, *Wagamama Camden*, 11 Jamestown Rd, NW1, T020-7428 0800, provides the kind of efficient Japanese canteen food that helped kick start the cuisine's reputation in London. Next door, *Pie and Mash* is a slightly more expensive modern British restaurant in equally transparent surroundings.

The *Mango Rooms*, 10 Kentish Town Rd, NW1, T020-7482 5065, are a super-cool venue for some traditional West Indian tucker, goat curry a speciality. *Andy's Taverna*, 81 Bayham St, NW1, T020-7485 9718, is a Greek Cypriot taverna with a jolly atmosphere and a fine way with its fresh ingredients. *Saucebarorganic Diner*, 214 Camden High St, NW1, T020-7482 0777, was an early-starter in the organic craze and with its 95% organic ingredients, can proudly claim to be one of the fertilizer-free aristocracy's favourite and most restrained hangouts.

Pizza Express, 85-87 Parkway, NW1, T020-7267 2600, may be about as original as going to a McDonald's, but this branch is still a cut above many of the local pizza and pasta providers. Further south, *Asakusa*, 256 Eversholt St, NW1, T020-7388 8533, does excellent Japanese fare and always needs to be booked at weekends, its low prices and lively atmosphere ensuring its continuing popularity.

Further north, *Marine Ices*, 8 Haverstock Hill, NW3, T020-7485 3132, is an utterly genuine Italian restaurant and ice-cream parlour that has been serving up the very best sweet and savoury dishes since 1946; a North London institution.

Cafés & sandwich bars **In Camden** *Fresh and Wild*, 49 Parkway, NW1, T020-7428 7575, is a very hip new organic diner and vegetarian juice bar, very popular with the local lunch crowd. The *New Goodfare Restaurant*, 26 Parkway, NW1, T020-7485 2230, could hardly be more different, a defiantly traditional café that serves up good, simple Italian and British snacks and light meals at low prices.

The *Camden Cantina*, 34 Chalk Farm Rd, T020-7267 2780, offers cheap and cheerful Tex-Mex in garish premises near Camden Lock, while *Ruby in the Dust*, 102 Camden High St, T020-7485 2744, is a superior brunch venue, Spanish themed but conceding to boorish Brits in the evenings.

In Primrose Hill, *Trojka,* 101 Regent's Park Rd, NW1, T020-7483 3765, is reasonable value and also worth checking out for being one of London's few Russian and Polish tea rooms.

Pubs & bars **In Camden** Many of the older pubs are better avoided later in the night, but thankfully there are plenty of alternatives. *The Good Mixer*, 30 Inverness St, NW1, T020-7916 7929, usually lives up to its name, originally a down-beat Irish boozer that gained international fame during the mid 1990s Britpop explosion. Those heady days are over, and now it's a quieter place selling souvenir T-shirts for Scandinavian indie-tourists and comfortably reminiscing about the glory days. Nearby, the Bar Gansa, 2 Inverness St, NW1, T020-7267 8909, is a self-consciously cool drinking-den still favoured by the young and beautiful, but not by those who want to talk over a quiet beer: the music in the evenings can be deafening, but then most of its patrons want to be seen, not heard. Further down the street is *Bar Vinyl*, 6 Inverness St, NW1, T020-7681 7898, one of the pioneers of the concept of DJ-driven drinking.

Camden boasts a bewildering range of drinking options. Every evening the whole place seems to be loudly drowning its sorrows with a vengeance

▶▶ *Go to page 432 for entertainment & nightlife*

More civilized, almost painfully so, is *Bartok*, 78-79 Chalk Farm Rd, NW1, T020-7916 0595, its thirty-something Ikea-style décor just about forgiveable because it specializes in modern classical music, a rare treat in Camden. A chilled place to sit back in the sofa and talk to friends. On the High Street itself, *Liberty's*, 100 Camden High St, NW1, T020-7485 4019, features the stripped wooden floors of modern Camden, but has retained just enough custom from its previous incarnation as an Irish boozer to provide a mixed and interesting crowd.

The *O'Bar*, 111-113 Camden High St, NW1, T020-7911 0667, is a good place to go with a large group at weekends and enjoy cheap and cheerful cocktail fun while *The*

Purple Turtle, 61/65 Crowndale Rd, NW1, T020-7383 4976, is an expansive joint that, like its nation-wide counterparts, caters for a boisterous crowd of students and other committed drinkers.

In Primrose Hill the *Pembroke Castle*, 150 Gloucester Ave, NW1, T020-7483 2927, is a large and relatively lively pub for the area, favoured by the younger locals. Further down the same street, the *Lansdowne*, 90 Gloucester Ave, NW1, T020-7483 0409, is a genteel gastropub that provides a welcome break from all the loud music and shouting on Camden High St. *Queens*, 49 Regent's Park Rd, NW1, T020-7586 0408, is a friendly Aussie-run corner pub on Primrose Hill's main street with a balcony giving onto the park and a thoroughly competent kitchen.

Five of the best: cheap eats in North London

★

· *Dim T Café*, Heath Street, Hampstead.
· *Mango Rooms*, Kentish Town Road, Camden.
· *Wagamama Camden*, Jamestown Road, Camden.
· *Afghan Kitchen*, Islington Green, Islington.
· *Gallipoli*, Upper Street, Islington.

Shopping

Camden Lock is choc-full of jewellers, antiques, boutiques and ethnocraft. Check out *Kaleido*, East Yard, open Tue-Sun, 1000-1800, for exciting modern jewellery among much of the prevailing tat. *Afghan, Persian and Turkman Rugs*, East Yard, T020-7482 4355, open Tue-Sun 1000-1800, has a better quality range than many of the stalls, whilst the *Blackgull Bookshop and Bindery*, East Yard, T020-8740 0713, open Tue-Sun 1000-1800, is an excellent place to pick up a cheap fictional or academic read.

It goes without saying that the markets are the thing here, but if you want to avoid the standard second-hand and cheap clothing stalls, it's best to head for Camden Lock

Stables Market, at the junction of Chalk Farm and Hartland Roads, open weekends, 0800-1800, meanwhile, offers an array of household accessories and furniture for those who like a bit of kitsch in their abode. And for those who like to dress accordingly, there is *FU Baby,* T020-7267 3346, open 1230-1830 Fri, 1030-1830 Sat, which specializes in spanking good Danish fetish gear.

Elsewhere, **in Primrose Hill**, *Anna*, 126 Regent's Park Rd, NW1, T020-7483 0411, caters for ladies who might consider Camden High Road a little beneath them with a limited but very stylish range of labels. *Sixteen 47*, 69 Gloucester Ave, NW1, T020-7483 4174, stock actress Dawn French's range for the larger lady. *Skate Attack,* 95 Highgate Road, NW5, T020-7485 0007, claims to be Europe's largest skating emporium stocking every conceivable set of wheels or blades you could want to put on your feet. *LA1*, 17 Chalk Farm Rd, NW1, T020-7267 2228, do designer labels for the young, beautiful and not too short of cash while *GB*, 61 Parkway, NW1, T020-7485 5354, walks the tightrope between cool and traditional, a well-established gentleman's clothier for every soon-to-be-dad in North London. *Rhythm Records*, 281 Camden High St, NW1, T020-7267 0123, stock possibly one of London's finest selections of independent music past and present. *Music & Video Exchange*, 229 Camden High St, T020-7267 1898, open daily 1000-2000, small branch of the Notting

Directory

Sports *Camden Town Sports Complex, 44 Crowndale Road, NW1. T020-73872037. Five-a-side soccer pitches. Kentish Town Sports Centre, Prince of Wales Road, NW5, T020-7267 9341.*

Swimming, gymnasium, aqua-fitness and sunbeds. Mornington Sports Centre, 142-50 Arlington Road, NW1, T020- 7207 3600. Badminton, basketball and five-a-side soccer.

North London

Hill-based store, good for vintage vinyl as well as cheap CDs and vids. **Walden Books**, 38 Harmood St, NW1, T020-7267 8146, is an excellent second-hand bookshop away from the crowds.

Transport

Buses **No 24** to Hampstead Heath.

No 27 between Chalk Farm and Chiswick via Camden Town, Marylebone Rd, Paddington, Notting Hill Gate, Kensington High St and Hammersmith.

No 29 between Trafalgar Square and Finsbury Park via Warren St, Camden Town and Holloway.

No 31 between Camden Town and Notting Hill Gate via Camden Lock, Chalk Farm, Swiss Cottage, Kilburn and Westbourne Park.

No 46 between King's Cross and Kensal Rise via Camden St, Kentish Town, Hampstead Heath, Rosslyn Hill, Hampstead, Fitzjohn's Avenue, Swiss Cottage, St John's Wood, Warwick Avenue and West Kilburn.

No 134 between Tottenham Court Rd and Finchley via Camden Town, Kentish Town, Archway, Highgate Station, Muswell Hill and Friern Barnet.

No 135 between Marble Arch and Archway via Oxford Circus, Great Portland St, Camden Town, and Kentish Town.

No 214 between Liverpool St and Highgate Village via Moorgate, City Rd, Islington, King's Cross, Camden Town, Kentish Town and Parliament Hill Fields.

No 253 between Euston and Aldgate via Mornington Crescent, Camden Town, Holloway, Finsbury Park, Manor House, Stamford Hill, Clapton, Hackney, Cambridge Heath and Bethnal Green.

No 274 between Islington (Angel) and Marble Arch via Caledonian Rd, Market Estate, Agar Grove, Camden Town, the Zoo and Baker St.

Taxis There are usually plenty of taxis along the High St

Tubes Camden Town (Northern line) is best for the market, and is also the closest station to London Zoo. Also Mornington Crescent (Northern line, Charing Cross branch) for the Roundhouse and southern end of Camden High St; and Chalk Farm (Northern line, Edgeware branch) for Primrose Hill

Islington

⊖ *Angel for the*
southern end of
Upper St; Highbury
& Islington for the
northern end

Sitting on a low hilltop northwest of the City and east of King's Cross, Islington now likes to think of itself – with some justification – as the left-wing Notting Hill of north London. Its transformation over the last 20 years into the fashionable stamping ground of the liberal middle classes has not always been entirely happy. It remains one of London's most socially deprived and densely populated boroughs, although either side of Upper Street, among the genteel Georgian and Victorian estates of Canonbury and Barnsbury – formerly home to Prime Minister Tony Blair – you'd hardly know it. More confident than ever since being credited with nurturing the political ideals of the current government, Islington rewards visitors not with its sights but with a welcoming attitude (although surprisingly few hotels or guesthouses), a wide array of ethnic restaurants, old pubs and fashionable bars, a thriving theatre and music scene, and two excellent small markets. The antique shops in **Camden Passage** *have long been a major attraction, while* **Chapel Market** *is a thriving local street market and increasingly hot nightspot.*

Friday and Saturday night excitement in Islington can be just as mad, bad and dangerous-to-know as anywhere in the West End – which is quite an achievement in itself.

History

Although it wasn't until the late 18th century that Islington began to show signs of developing as a suburb of London, a church has stood here since the 14th century. The manors of Barnsbury, Canonbury and Highbury lie to the north, set among fields and fine grazing meadows, where young bucks would come to the fields to practice archery. Henry VIII kept mistresses in Newington Green and hunted nearby, while elegant mansions with fine gardens and orchards dotted the landscape (Sir Walter Raleigh lived on Upper Street). Canonbury Tower stood proudly by the Priory, the manor house surrounded by rich dairy fields, and with Barnsbury Manor up on the hill.

Although Londoners took refuge in the fields around Islington during the turbulent years of the Great Plague and the Great Fire, it was only during the 18th century that it became popular. It earned a reputation for its duck shooting, cakes and cream (there were several dairies in the area), its tea-gardens and spa. Pleasant walks were taken to Canonbury at the weekend, or trips to see 'Bruising Peg', the female boxer, do battle at Mr Stokes' Amphitheatre. Further north, at the Highbury Barn, Willoughby's bowling green and tea-garden attracted large crowds. Closer to the city, Copenhagen House began as a ninepins and skittles venue, but turned to bulldog fights and bull-baiting when a certain Mr Tooth became the landlord. Proprietors of pleasure gardens employed Foot Guards to escort visitors back to London from the Angel Inn, where reputedly Thomas Paine penned some of the *Rights of Man*.

The developers followed the crowds. Upper Street was lined by houses by 1735, Colebrooke Row 30 years later, Liverpool Street grew from a short terrace after 1790s, and Canonbury Square and Compton Terrace around the turn of the 19th century. Landowners established brickfields on their estates. Developments along Liverpool Street into Barnsbury went up in the 1820s (Cubitt built Manchester Terrace), and the London Fever Hospital moved here in 1848. Canonbury displayed fine villas, and was earning a reputation as a pretty suburb.

Nevertheless, by the 1830s, all the roads out of Islington still opened onto fields, nurseries and market gardens. When the Regent's Canal ducked under Islington through a long tunnel, its arrival, and that of the railway, attracted some small industries, but smart shops still lined the High Street, and theatres and music halls, such as the Collin's, drew the crowds. The 'Leviathan' at Highbury Barns could boast the gymnast Leotard, the highwire artist Blondin, and the original Siamese Twins. Slums also developed and by the beginning of the 20th century, Barnsbury and Islington were declining in popularity. Absentee landlords and small tenancies meant the fabric decayed, and after it suffered severe damage during the the Second World War, many streets gave way to modern council housing estates. Islington regained popularity with the media and entertainment set in

Hotels in the area

B *Hilton London Islington*
C *Jurys London Inn*
D *Kandara Guest House*
D *Rose and Crown Pub and Guest House*
▸▸ **Go to page 449**

North London

Islington

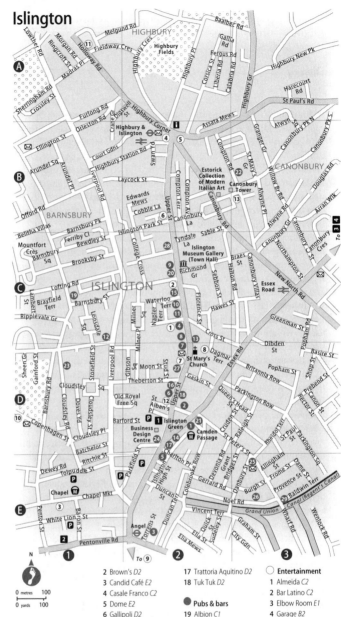

North London

N

0 metres 100
0 yards 100

■ **Sleeping**
1 Hilton London
  Islington D2
2 Jurys London Inn E1
3 Kandara Guest
  House C3
4 Rose & Crown C3

● **Eating**
1 Afghan Kitchen D2

2 Brown's D2
3 Candid Café E2
4 Casale Franco C2
5 Dome E2
6 Gallipoli D2
7 Gallipoli Again D2
8 Granita C2
9 La Piragua C2
10 La Porchetta C2
11 Le Mercury C2
12 Monitor C1
13 Pasha C2
14 Portofino D2
15 Rite Bite C2
16 Strada D2

17 Trattoria Aquitino D2
18 Tuk Tuk D2

● **Pubs & bars**
19 Albion C1
20 Bierodrome C2
21 Camden Head D2
22 Compton Arms B3
23 Crown D1
24 Cuba Libre D2
25 Duke of Cambridge E3
26 Island Queen E3
27 Matt & Matt D2
28 Medicine Bar C2
29 Narrow Boat E3

○ **Entertainment**
1 Almeida C2
2 Bar Latino C2
3 Elbow Room E1
4 Garage B2
5 Hen & Chickens B2
6 Hope B2
7 King's Head D2
8 Little Angel D2
9 Old Red Lion E2
10 Red Eye D1
11 Rocket A1
12 Screen on the
  Green D2
13 Tower Theatre B3

the 1960s, a desirability that remains intact in and around areas such as the Cloudesley Estate and Canonbury.

Sights

Angel tube deposits passengers on Upper Street, Islington's main drag, at the junction of St John Street coming all the way up from Clerkenwell, the City Road from Shoreditch, and the Pentonville Road coming up from King's Cross. **Crafts Council**, at 44 Pentonville Rd, N1, is a bookshop and library with regularly changing craft and design exhibitions. ■ *Tue-Sat 1100-1800, Sun 1400-1800. Admission free. T020-7278 7700.*

Take a right turn out of the tube station and Upper Street forks almost immediately where the toll gate of the Great North Road once stood. Liverpool Road heads off left, and Upper Street carries on for almost a mile to Highbury Corner and Highbury & Islington tube. Islington High Street is no more than a quaint pedestrianized stretch off Duncan Street.

Most of the action in Islington takes place on Upper St & the streets immediately around, including Chapel Market

On the right, just beyond the *Duke of York* pub, the little High Street ends up in Camden Passage, running parallel to Upper Street for a short distance, lined with enticing antique shops and restaurants and hosting a bric-a-brac market on Wednesdays (see Shopping on page 324). At the end, where the Essex Road meets Upper Street, **Islington Green** is a triangular garden that only really comes into its own at the Islington Festival when it often provides space for stalls and a fairground.

To the north of these gardens, on the site of the present *Waterstone's* bookshop, the **Collins Music Hall** was once one of London's most famous, where the likes of George Robey, Vesta Tilley and Marie Lloyd all made appearances. Plans are currently afoot to resurrect it. The statue on the junction commemorates Hugh Myddelton, a Welsh goldsmith who brought fresh water into the city with his construction of the New River in 1613.

On the other side of Upper Street stands the **Business Design Centre** (T020-7359 3535) on the site of the old Royal Agricultural Hall built in the mid-19th century. The enormous 'Aggie' became North London's most prestigious exhibition hall and Royal ballroom before winding up as a Royal Mail parcel office by 1971. Some of its former glory can still be appreciated from the Liverpool Road. The mock-crystal palace of the Business Design Centre now also holds huge trade fairs and art shows.

Further along Upper Street, the 18th-century tower of **St Mary's** survived the Second World War bombing and now stands opposite the crumbly old *King's Head Theatre Pub*, where Dan Crawford almost single-handedly established North London's booming fringe theatre scene in the 70s and still insists that his till tell its prices in pounds, shillings and pence.

Behind the church is the **Little Angel Puppet Theatre**, and on the left beyond the pub, the **Almeida**, London's most star-studded medium-scale theatre, is currently refurbishing its home, the old Islington Literary and Scientific Institute built in 1837.

Past Islington Town Hall on the right, home to the **Islington Museum Gallery** (T020-7354 9442), a small local museum, the imposing presence of Cubitt's **Union Chapel** dominates the east side of the street. Formerly a Congregational chapel containing a fragment of the rock on which the Pilgrim

North London

Fathers landed, it has been semi-converted into a performance venue for all manner of different events, including a flamenco club, theatre, art shows and music in its echoing auditorium and studio theatre. ■ *T020-7226 3750. Recorded information line T020-7226 1686.*

Opposite is the *Hope and Anchor* pub, one of the places that punk rock was born and still a thriving live indie music venue.

West of Upper Street stretch the polite terraces and squares of Barnsbury. One square worth a look, just off Barnsbury Street between Upper Street and the Liverpool Road, is the mid-19th-century **Milner Square**, described by architecture critic Ian Nairn as being "as near to expressing evil as a design can be". Certainly its long thin shape, soaring height, serried ranks of windows, and spindly columns can be seriously spooky at night.

Estorick Collection of Modern Italian Art East of Upper Street lies Canonbury, best appreciated by a visit to the Estorick Collection of Modern Italian Art, at 39 Canonbury Square (entrance on Canonbury Road), not least for a good opportunity to take a look inside a fine Georgian house and enjoy some good food from the café indoors or out. The intriguing permanent collection of Italian art here, featuring an especially strong selection of Futurist work, is often complemented by eye-catching contemporary exhibitions.

■ *Open Wed-Sat 1100-1800, Sun 1200-1700. Admission £3.50, £2.50 concession. T020-7704 9522, www.estorickcollection.com*

Nearby, **Canonbury Tower**, in Canonbury Place, is an Elizabethan building dating back to Roman times, supposedly on a site of considerable pagan significance. Famous tenants down the ages have included Sir Francis Bacon, Oliver Goldsmith and Washington Irving, and since 1952 the amateur Tavistock Rep theatre company have been staging plays in the little theatre.

A right turn into Willow Bridge Road from here leads down to Myddelton's New River and the *Marquess Tavern*, a Victorian real-ale pub.

The Essex Road leads on to Newington Green and eventually to **Stoke Newington**, where 18th-century Church Street is still recognizably a village high street. Daniel 'Robinson Crusoe' Defoe was educated here, and today the street is lined with a surprising number of good-value restaurants, shops and lively pubs, including the original south Indian vegetarian *Rasa* (now also in the West End), a popular Thai restaurants called *Yum Yums*, and the *Anglo-Anatolian*, a cosy Turkish barbecue restaurant.

Eating and drinking

Mid-range
● on map, page 320 Adventurous modern European cooking can be enjoyed in the once superhip minimalist décor of **Granita**, 127 Upper St, N1, T020-7226 3222, where it's now usually not too difficult reserving a table for mains like breast of Barbary duck, char-grilled red chard, ginger braised celery and orange vinaigrette, or roasted cod with yellow split-pea puree, broccoli and tartare sauce (each about £14).

Lola's, 359 Upper St, N1, T020-7359 1932, is above the smart Mall antiques arcade, doing an assured modern British and continental menu, from steak and chips to liver and chestnut squeak, in a very Islington atmosphere. Less expensive or exclusive than either of the above, **Casale Franco**, 134-137 Upper St, N1, T020-7226 8994, is a popular and bustling ristorante pizzeria tucked away behind a French rotisserie chicken joint.

Over the road, *Pasha*, 301 Upper St, N1, T020-7226 1454, does superior Turkish cuisine in a restrained and formal atmosphere and can be excellent value for money. *Browns*, 9 Islington Green, N1, T020-7226 2555 www.browns-restaurants.com, is a brand new branch of the English brasserie chain, an efficient and roomy diner in a kind of old-fashioned New York kind of a style. The *Ristorante Portofino*, 39 Camden Passage, T020-7226 0884, is a favourite with Italian ex-pats and locals alike.

Five of the best: outdoor drinking in North London

· *The Narrow Boat*, Noel Road, Islington.
· *The Duke of Cambridge*, St Peter's Street, Islington.
· *The Albion*, Thornhill Road, Islington.
· *Flask*, Highgate West Hill, Highgate.
· *The Engineer*, Gloucester Avenue, Camden.

In Stoke Newington, *Mesclun*, Stoke Newington Church St, T020-7249 5029, is a small Anglo-French restaurant that always requires booking at the weekends, such is its reputation.

The Afghan Kitchen, 35 Islington Green, N1, T020-7359 8019 (closed Sun, Mon), is a fine little place for some café-style Afghan home cooking, items such as Suhzi Gosht - Lamb with spinach, or Bonjan-e-Barani (aubergines with yoghurt), both for £5 and also some good value French wine.

Cheap
Islington abounds in relatively inexpensive places to eat, one reason no doubt for its popularity with the more penniless chattering classes

Le Mercury, 140a Upper St, N1, T020-7354 4088, is an Islington institution on the corner of Almeida St, a busy French restaurant where the low prices and busy atmosphere are more important than any kind of French food snobbery. Next door, *La Porchetta*, 141-142 Upper St, N1, T020-7288 2488, is a very popular new branch of the phenomenally successful Stroud Green pizzeria with a clean-cut, efficient and bright look.

Gallipoli, 102 Upper St, N1, T020-7359 0630, is a Turkish café-restaurant that has braved its unfortunate name to the extent that it has also opened *Gallipoli Again*, 120 Upper St, N1, T020- 7359 1578, both good-value venues for salads and some meaty Turkish staples, the former with tables outside, the latter more cosy. *Tuk Tuk*, 330 Upper St, N1, T020-7226 0837, is a funky little Thai café that understandably often becomes impossibly busy in the evenings while *La Piragua*, 176 Upper St, N1, T020-7364 2843, is a South American restaurant done up in vivid red with an attitude to match.

The branch of the sleek new modern Italian pizzeria chain *Strada*, 105-106 Upper St, N1, T020-7226 9742, doesn't accept reservations but offers a pager service to let diners know when a table is free (it's not always that packed out though) for the enjoyment of their wood-fired flatbreads. A much more traditional restaurant is the little *Trattoria Aquilino*, 31 Camden Passage, T020-7226 5454, where regulars and visitors alike are fussed over until they feel at home with the straightforward presentation of some hearty Italian staples.

On the Liverpool Rd, the *Monitor* café and bar, Liverpool Rd, N1, T020-7607 7710 (on corner of Richmond Av), does an assured Pacific rim and Mediterranean menu, with a few tables outside in summer and a cheerful atmosphere inside.

A little further afield, *Sariyer Balik, Chargrill Fish Restaurant*, 56 Green Lanes, Newington Green, N16, T020-7275 7681, is a tiny, very inexpensive and charming Turkish fresh fish restaurant.

Some seriously cheap Stokie restaurants include: *Baraka*, 1 Farleigh Rd, N16, T020-7254 1500, Turkish home cooking, vegetarians well catered for, cheap, BYO, open 7 days 1700-2300; *Halkevi*, part of the Kurdish Community Centre, Stoke Newington Rd, N16, very large and traditional restaurant, excellent Kurdish cuisine cooked on charcoal grill, lamb speciality, super cheap, BYO, open 7 days 0900-2200; *Solen*, 84 Stoke Newington High St, N16, Turkish charcoal grilled meats, cheap, BYO, open 7

North London

days 1700-2400; *Mangal,* 27 Stoke Newington Rd, N16, T020-7254 6999, Turkish, good quality, similar to above, also BYO, open 7 days, 1700-2300.

Cafés &
sandwich bars

Many of Islington's cheaper restaurants (such as *Gallipoli* and *Tuk Tuk*) double up as cafés all day, while the leader of the ubiquitous chain gang has to be the *Dôme*, 431 Upper St, N1, T020-7226 3414, one of the first and still a popular Upper St institution. The miniscule *Rite Bite*, 149 Upper St, T020-7226 7717, is a sweet and basic little café doing a cheap range of sandwiches and snacks on red-check tablecloths. More hip and happening, the *Candid Café*, 3 Torrens St, T020-7278 9368, is attached to an art events and theatre space, and does good sandwiches, Italian and Spanish meals and soups.

Pubs & bars
*At weekends, the
string of pubs & bars
on Upper St are most
people's reason for
being there; quite
a few stay open
after 2300.*

The more interesting and vibrant places tend to be a little way away from Angel tube, either on Upper St beyond the Business Design Centre or on Chapel Market. *Cuba Libre*, 72 Upper St, N1, T020-7354 9998, is a loud, cheery and late-night restaurant and bar with a vaguely Cuban theme. For the sounds of Ibiza, a pool table and cocktails, try *Matt&Matt*, 112 Upper St, N1, T020-7726 6035. *Bierodrome*, 173-174 Upper St, N1, T020-7226 5835, www.belgo-restaurants.com, is a much-hyped and seriously designer bar concept, part of the Belgo group, and regularly jumps until midnight throughout the week. One of the few regular old pubs worth checking out near Upper St is the *Camden Head*, Camden Walk, N1, T020-7359 0851, with a pleasant outside drinking area and almost unreconstructed Victorian interior. *The Medicine Bar*, 181 Upper St, N1, T020-7704 9536, becomes members only on Fri and Sat but its dark, scruffy and comfortable décor makes a refreshing change from some of Islington's other over-designed music bars.

▶▶ *Go to page 433
for entertainment
& nightlife*

Just about within walking distance of Upper St, several pubs rather than bars are particularly worth seeking out. *The Albion*, 10 Thornhill Rd, N1, T020-7607 7450, with its flower-bedecked frontage, benches outside and cosy country-pub interior is a favourite, very Barnsbury local. Nearby, *The Crown*, 116 Cloudesley Rd, T020-7837 7107, is a roomy and laid-back gastropub with slightly more youth appeal, open lunch and evenings.

Two of Islington's more characterful boozers are down by the Regent's Canal: the *Island Queen*, 87 Noel Rd, N1, T020-7704 7631, with its nautical décor, excellent little pool room and hot food at lunchtimes was once one of playwright Joe Orton's favourites; the *Narrow Boat*, 119 St Peter's St, N1, T020-7288 9821, is right on the waterside, and features a back bar true enough to the pub's name to make it feel as if it's afloat.

A pleasant walk can be taken back towards the Angel tube from here along the Regent's Canal towpath, past the City Rd Basin. The *Duke of Cambridge*, 30 St Peter's St, N1, T020-7359 3066, is an excellent quite expensive organic (even the wines and beers) gastropub that has become very popular with the locals, partly because of its outdoor drinking and dining opportunities in a quiet part of the area.

Also tucked away from the mayhem on Upper St is the *Compton Arms*, Compton Terr, T020-7359 6883, a country pub in the middle of Canonbury with a small and leafy back yard.

Shopping

*One of the best
reasons for a visit
to Islington are
its markets*

One of London's less well-known and still very busy old street markets is *Chapel Market*, open 0900-1600 Tue, Wed, Fri, Sat; 0900-1300 Thu, Sun. For well over a century stalls have lined this scruffy street laden with the fruit 'n' veg and comestibles of all kinds as well as a good deal of not very durable tat.

Altogether different in tone is *Camden Passage Market,* open Wed and Sat 0800-1600, an antiques and bric-a-brac market (second-hand book market Thu, farmers' market on Sun) in a covered area at the end of a street full of superior antique shops that make for intriguing browsing. Most of these shops are closed on Mon.

The Mall, 359 Upper St, T020-7351 5353, is an arcade with some of the smartest dealers in the area. Don't expect bargains, but plenty of unlikely discoveries. Nearby, the *Angel Bookshop*, 102 Islington High St, N1, T020-7226 2904, is an excellent little independent bookseller. *Bootle and King*, 23 Arlington Way, T020-7278 4497, is one of the area's few second-hand bookshops, specialising in genealogy, family history, and architecture, close to the Family Record Centre.

Apart from bars and restaurants, Upper St is packed with Estate Agents, jostling for space with some interesting gift, home furnishing and designerwear shops. *Segunda Mano*, 111 Upper St, N1, T020-7359 5284, stock a good range of used and new designer clothes. *After Noah*, 121 Upper St, N1, T020-7359 4281, is the North London branch of the King's Rd art nouveau and deco furniture shop. *The Hart Gallery*, 113 Upper St, N1, T020-7704 1131, sells just about affordable contemporary art for the living room. *Twenty Twenty One*, 274 Upper St, N1, T020-7288 1996, do contemporary furniture and glassware, as do *Aria*, 296 Upper St, N1, T020-7704 6333 www.aria-shop.co.uk, who also stock dinky gifts and accessories. *Diverse*, 286 Upper St, N1, T020-7359 0081, do designer streetwear for men, with their shop a little further down at 294 Upper St, N1, T020-7359 8877, stocking designer label womenswear. Both best visited in Jan or Jul. At 79 Upper St is *Reckless Records*, T020-7359 7105, which sells second-hand CDs and vinyl. It's mostly mainstream but has comprehensive soul and dance sections.

Less expensive options can be found on Cross St, such as *Clusaz*, 56 Cross St, N1, T020-7359 5596, for designer womenswear and accessories, shawls and handbags, while *High Society*, 46 Cross St, N1 T020-7226 6863, stocks a wide range of mid-market menswear. At the end of the street near the Essex Rd, *Theorem*, 4 Cross St, T020-7354 9713, is a funky hairdresser for all types of colouring and hair extensions. Next door is the extraordinary *Get Stuffed*, 105 Essex Rd, N1, T020-7226 1364, one of London's most famous taxidermists: pick up a stuffed chaffinch for £75, or a stuffed lion for £5000. The glass domes and display cases on sale are also unique.

Flashback, 61 Essex Rd, N1, T020-7354 9356, open Mon-Sat 1100-1800, stocks a huge selection of clothes from the 50s to the present, with the emphasis on the 70s. Lots of bargains to be had for keen-eyed browsers. Over the road at No 50 is their music outlet, which boasts an excellent collection of second-hand vinyl and CDs covering just about every type of music.

Fans of retro styles are well catered for in Islington

Out of Time, aka *Metro Retro*, 21 Canonbury Lane, N1, T020-7354 5755, has a wide array of domestic appliances, accessories and fittings dating from the 40s and 50s. *Cloud Cuckoo Land*, 6 Charlton Place, T020-7354 3141, stock fine vintage clothes for women, as do *Annie's Vintage Costume and Textiles*, 10 Camden Passage, T020-7359 0796. For a good range of retro basics, particularly for women, is *Ribbons and Taylor*, 157 Stoke Newington Church St, N16, T020-7254 4735, in the heart of trendy Stoke Newington.

A but further north, at 88 Stamford Hill, is the *Shoe Centre for Men*, T020-8806 1602, open Mon-Thu 0930-1800, Fri 0930-1600, Sun 1000-1530, which stocks classic men's shoes at knockdown prices. For cheap Clarks shoes try the *Clarks Factory Shop*,

Directory

Libraries *Central Reference Library, 2 Fieldway Crescent, N5, T020-7619 6932/Islington Council T020-7527 2000, www.islington.gov.uk*
Sports *Highbury Swimming Pool,*

T020-7704 2312. **Arsenal FC**, *Highbury Stadium, T020-7704 4000.* **Islington Tennis Centre**, *Market Rd, N7, T020-7700 1370.* **Sobell Leisure Centre**, *Hornsey Rd, N7, T020-7609 2166.*

at 67-83 Seven Sisters Rd (nearest tube Finsbury Park), T020-7281 9364, open Mon-Sat 0930-1730.

Some way out on the Holloway Rd, is *162*, at 162 Holloway Rd, open Mon-Sat 1000-1800, Sun 1100-1800, which is friendly, laid-back and also happens to be one of the cheapest places in London to get decent authentic retro clothing. Opposite, at 251 Holloway Rd, is *To be continued*, T020-7609 4796, open Mon-Fri 1000-1800, Sat 1030-1830, which is a bit more conventional but worth a visit, especially if you're after cheap ski jackets.

The Fantasy Centre, 157 Holloway Rd, N7, T020-7607 9433, is almost unique in London for its comprehensive stock of second-hand science fiction and fantasy books.

Transport

Buses **No 4** between Archway and Waterloo, via Dartmouth Park Hill, Tufnell Park Rd, Holloway, Finsbury Park, Highbury, Islington, Barbican, St Paul's, Fleet St, and Aldwych (Sun between Archway and Islington only).

No 19 between Finsbury Park and Battersea, via Highbury, Islington, Bloomsbury, Piccadilly Circus, Hyde Park Corner, Knightsbridge, Sloane Square, and Chelsea.

No 30 between Marble Arch and Hgihbury via Baker St, Euston, King's Cross and Islington.

No 38 between Victoria and Islingtonv ia Hyde Park Corner, Piccadilly Circus, Bloomsbury and Rosebery Ave.

No 73 between Victoria and Stoke Newington, via Hyde Park Corner, Marble Arch, Oxford Circus, Euston, King's Cross, Islington and Newington Green.

No 214 between Highgate Village and Liverpool St, via Parliament Hill Fields, Kentish Town, Camden Town, King's Cross, Islington, City Road, and Moorgate.

No 274 between Angel Islington and Marble Arch, via Caledonian Rd, Agar Grove, Camden Town, the Zoo and Baker St.

No 341 between County Hall and Newington Green via Waterloo, Aldwych, Fetter Lane, Gray's Inn Rd and Islington.

Taxis Usually plenty along Upper St and City Rd.

Trains Highbury and Islington, Canonbury (both North London Link).

Tubes Angel (Northern line, City branch) for the southern end of Upper St. Highbury & Islington (Victoria line) for the northern end.

West London

West London

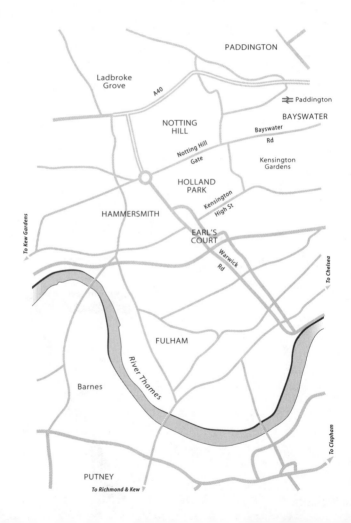

Notting Hill and Holland Park

*It's hard to say to what greater heights of fashionability Notting Hill can reach. Here TV presenters and popstars have sacrificed their lives; politicians have gambled their careers for houses; and Hollywood has made the movie. Notting Hill basks in celebrity status, even if sometimes for all the wrong reasons. One of London's original and now more successful gentrified multicultural districts, its sloping terraces may not be the most attractive in town but the fashionable types patrolling its boutiques, galleries, cafés and bars probably are. Most famously, once a year at the **Carnival** these spectacularly cool media darlings give way to the wildest and most uninhibited street party in Europe. Now an unfortunate victim of its own success, plans are afoot to reroute the full-on two-day festival of Afro-Caribbean and urban youth culture away from W11's narrow streets and into Hyde Park, a move that has already divided the community. The rest of the year, **Portobello Road Market** continues to pull in the punters every Saturday for its antiques, groovy second-hand clothes and bric-a-brac. Close by but a world apart, the houses on Campden Hill and around **Holland Park** are some of the most expensive and sought after in London, but the park itself is a delightful place to explore and one of the best approaches to the exotic splendours of **Leighton House**.*

Notting Hill Gate tube for Portobello Rd's southern end, Ladbroke Grove for its northern end. Either Holland Park or Notting Hill Gate tube for Holland Park

West London

History

The explosion in the development of Notting Hill and Holland Park took place in the 19th century. Until then, Notting Hill (and its northwestern extremities in Notting Dale) was largely farmland, with piggeries scattered across the fields, and Portobello and Notting Barns providing the main farm settlements. A hamlet had developed around the Kensington Gravel Pits at the northern end of Kensington Church Street, and a gate had been built to regulate the Uxbridge turnpike during the 18th century.

To the south, the hill now known as Holland Park was one of the four manors in the Kensington Estate, and from 1606 was crowned by the majestic Jacobean mansion of Cope's Castle, or Holland House. Further mansions were built, such as Campden House in 1612, and Aubrey House (over a medicinal spring) some 80 years later, while the surrounding fields supplied hay for the city. When the Parliamentarians confiscated Holland House during the Civil War, Cromwell is reputed to have taken his deaf son-in-law, General Ireton, into the fields so he could 'shout' tactics and still avoid being overheard.

Further south, the village of Kensington grew at the foot of the hill around St Mary Abbots, with nurseries and market gardens to the south. In the late 18th and early 19th century, Lady Holland hosted lavish parties (albeit with indifferent food apparently) for Whig politicians like Earl Grey, George Canning, Lord Palmerston, and even Talleyrand, as well as London aesthetes and writers like Lord Byron, William Wordsworth, Charles

Hotels in the area

A Portobello Hotel
A Westbourne Hotel
B The Abbey Court Hotel
B Holland Court
D London Visitor's Hotel
E YHA Holland House
▸▸ *Go to page 449*

West London

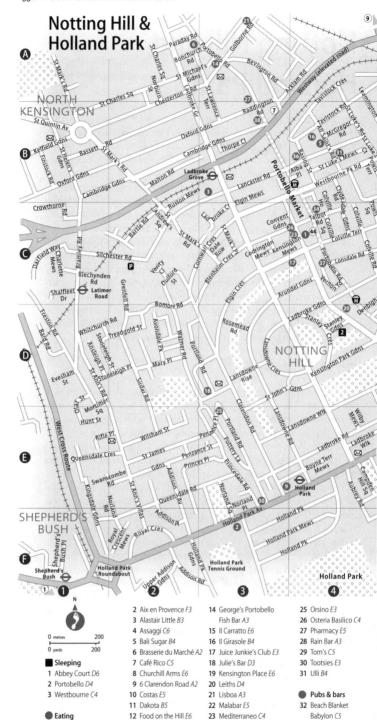

Notting Hill & Holland Park

Sleeping
1 Abbey Court *D6*
2 Portobello *D4*
3 Westbourne *C4*

Eating
1 192 *C4*
2 Aix en Provence *F3*
3 Alastair Little *B3*
4 Assaggi *C6*
5 Bali Sugar *B4*
6 Brasserie du Marché *A2*
7 Café Rico *C5*
8 Churchill Arms *E6*
9 6 Clarendon Road *A2*
10 Costas *E5*
11 Dakota *B5*
12 Food on the Hill *E6*
13 Geales *E6*
14 George's Portobello
   Fish Bar *A3*
15 Il Carratto *E6*
16 Il Girasole *B4*
17 Juice Junkie's Club *E3*
18 Julie's Bar *D3*
19 Kensington Place *E6*
20 Leiths *D4*
21 Lisboa *A3*
22 Malabar *E5*
23 Mediterraneo *C4*
24 New Cultural Revolution *E5*
25 Orsino *E3*
26 Osteria Basilico *C4*
27 Pharmacy *E5*
28 Rain Bar *A3*
29 Tom's *C5*
30 Tootsies *E3*
31 Ulli *B4*

Pubs & bars
32 Beach Blanket
   Babylon *C5*

West London

Dickens and Sir Walter Scott. In 1802 the Earl and his wife met Napoleon, and became his firm supporter thereafter – they sent him a fridge while he was in exile in Elba.

In the 19th century, however, the area was developed massively. Campden Hill was laid out to give access to grand lodges that had been built along its length – though Thorpe, Moray and Bedford have since been replaced by Holland Park Comprehensive School and the Queen Elizabeth College. Campden Hill Square emerged in the 1820s and 30s (JMW Turner used to frequently paint sunsets from beside a tree in the gardens), the Phillimore Estate began to build on their land to the west of St Mary Abbots, and land south of the Bayswater Road was sold for development in the 1860s, with building extending as far west as Holland Villas Road by the 1870s.

Further north, the Norland Estate (between Norland and Portland Roads) was under construction by the 1840s and the Ladbroke Estate, following the failure of the Hippodrome racecourse (commemorated in Hippodrome Place) in the 1830s, embarked on developing their land with paired villas set in picturesque crescents around St John's church. Chepstow and Pembridge Villas were up by the 1860s, and the Greek Cathedral of St Sophia emerged to cater for the growing Greek population in Bayswater. Later still, the wealthy began building grand residences in Holland Park – Lord Leighton's pile still features his magnificent Arab Hall, while 'Peacock House' on Addison Road, with its glorious tiled façade, was built for Sir Earnest Debenham in 1906.

But it wasn't simply a tale of grand mansions for grand personages. At the turn of the last century infant mortality in the northern estates of Notting Hill reached 50%, and the influx of West Indian immigrants in

The party's over?

Since 1966, the Notting Hill Carnival has been on the last weekend of August, on the Sunday and Bank Holiday Monday. Traditionally Sunday is a marginally quieter day for children, while Monday is the main event. What began as a small celebration of Afro-Caribbean culture has exploded into a full-blooded European carnival attracting millions from across the globe, taking place just about everywhere south of Kensal Rise, around Westbourne Park and Ladbroke Grove and north of Notting Hill tube. Thumping DJ-driven sound systems, spectacular floats and steel bands and several live music and performance stages jostle for position with countless food stalls, market traders, dancers and street performers, as well as impossible numbers of sightseers. Unfortunately several Carnivals of recent years have resulted in isolated incidents of violence and even murder, forcing local residents and the Greater London Assembly to reassess the future of the event. Many accuse the organizers of losing touch with the Carnival's community roots and allowing the weekend to become just another excuse for a massive Euro rave in unpoliceable circumstances. Some have suggested that the event be moved out of the area altogether.

Latest details on www.nottinghillcarnival.net.uk

the 1950's was met with racial intolerance that resulted in race riots in the 1958 when West Indian homes were systematically attacked around the Pembridge Road. The Westway, completed in 1970, cut a swathe over and through the area, but the Notting Hill Carnival, an annual celebration masterminded by the West Indian community that has grown to be the largest in Europe, now passes through streets lived in by wealthy residents in an increasingly desirable neighbourhood.

Sights

The relatively unprepossessing main road called **Notting Hill Gate** continues the westward thrust of Oxford Street and the Bayswater Road towards Holland Park Avenue. The tube station straddles the street at the point where Kensington Church Street dips south to High Street Kensington and Pembridge Road heads north to the Portobello Road, Ladbroke Grove and Westbourne Grove. Notting Hill itself is at the top of Ladbroke Grove, ringed with grand crescents and squares around the church of St John, but most of the action in the area day or night can be found either on the Gate or along Portobello. Near the tube are the area's cinemas and high street shops, while the Portobello Road gradually goes downmarket as it approaches the Westway flyover. This is the end to look for most of Notting Hill's more happening retailers and restaurants. Bear in mind that it's less of a walk from Ladbroke Grove tube.

Holland Park
The Orangerie & the Ice House are 2 small galleries in the park run by Leighton House, one of Holland Park's hidden gems

South of Notting Hill Gate to the west, the pretty white stuccoed terraces on the slopes of Campden Hill provide an attractive backdrop for a walk up to Holland Park. In the grounds of the former Holland House – this is the most charming and individual of central London's parks. From fine hilly woods to wide-open sports fields busy with the local dog walkers, joggers, nannies and babies – Holland Park has something for everyone. The walled exterior makes it feel like a private garden at the Holland Park entrance and yet once you've meandered through each different flowered garden, rose garden and the meditational Japanese garden, there are wooded walks, little duck ponds and sculpture trails as well as hidden adventure playgrounds and bustling coffee shops, ice-cream kiosks, resounding tennis courts and an open-air theatre beside the wide greensward sweep down to **Ken High Street**. The peacocks, the wild rabbits and squirrels complete the semi-rural idyll.

■ *Open dawn (0700) to dusk throughout the year.*

At 12 Holland Park Road, W14, Leighton House is an exquisite, pre-Edwardian, red-brick treat – despite being Victorian – with its extensive pre-Raphaelite collection of Millais, Burne-Jones and of course, Lord Leighton's own paintings. The private house was built between 1864-79 by the Royal Academy President – his salon conjours up the heady whirl of Arabian spice and Oscar Wilde salaciousness. The central fountain in the Arab Hall with its opulent gilt mosaic frieze and intricate Isnik tiles are a thrilling miniature Alhambra, despite now being run by the local council and as far from the magic of the Moors as leafy Holland Park can be.

Leighton House
Regular events including drawing classes, special exhibitions & classical concerts – with a strong emphasis on the arts & crafts & a few events for children

■ *Open 1100-1730 Mon, Wed-Sun. Admission free. T020-7602 3316, F020-7371 2467.*

Eating and drinking

On Notting Hill Gate itself, *The Pharmacy*, 150 Notting Hill Gate, W11, T020-7721 2442, is so hip that it needs bouncers to protect the stars arriving for some delicious, creative food in vast white Damien Hirst-designed surroundings. The other mega fashionable hangout is *Dakota*, 127 Ledbury Rd, W11, T020-7792 9191, which does a wonderful American-style brunch menu, but don't hassle the waiters because they just don't care.

Expensive
● *on map, page 330 & 334*

Leiths, 92 Kensington Park Rd, T020-7229 4481, is a more private, luxurious restaurant run by Pru Leith, one of the original haute cuisine gurus in England, and this is her flagship. Effortlessly delicious and romantic. *192*, 192 Kensington Park Rd, W11, T020-7229 0482, is definitely where every producer wants to make sure they're seen, preferably hobnobbing with the stars, at this easy, clubbable restaurant. Booking is essential and Sun lunch a popular hangover cure.

Kensington Place, 201 Kensington Church St, W8, T020-7727 3184, was Lady Diana's former favourite lunch spot, west of the Ivy. Its long windows and simple chic has never changed. Its contemporary European menu is reliable, delicious and more upmarket than 192. At *Assaggi*, 39 Chepstow Place, W2, T020-7792 5501, the chef is the toast of other London chefs. The finest Italian food in London – although the space isn't great – it's tucked away and not easy to find. Booking essential (months in advance).

In Holland Park, *The Belvedere*, Holland House, Holland Park, W8, T020-7602 1238, is a magical location in the heart of the park where diners look out after the public over the orangerie and the rose gardens and can stroll around the exhibitions, hear peacocks cry or the opera waft through the vast windows as they eat. *Orsino*, 119 Portland Rd, W11, T020-7221 3299, is a huge but hidden corner restaurant, a stylish Italian in the New York fashion – very chic.

Aix en Provence, 129 Holland Park Av, W11, T020-7221 5411, F020-7229 8516, is another stunning restaurant where the food is always excellent and the elegant dining room a favourite with visiting stars, the little walled garden making it even more romantic in the hot weather, popular with power lunchers, brunchers and late-night rendezvousers.

West London

West London

Mid-range **In Notting Hill Gate**, several restaurants south of the tube are worth seeking out. In this bracket the *Malabar*, 27 Uxbridge St, W8, T020-7727 8800, behind the Coronet cinema, is a chic Indian restaurant high on style, spice and price but an established local favourite that does a good-value buffet lunch on Suns.

Slightly off the beaten track, *Alastair Little*, 136a Lancaster Rd, W11, T020-7243 2220, is a very fine spin off of the ground-breaking chef's flagship Soho branch. The food is consistently inventive and fine and the set menu makes it an affordable date for funky media types. The *Rain Bar & Restaurant*, 303 Portobello Rd, W10, T020-8968 2001, does New Asian cuisine, typical of the new range of exotic 'world' chic.

6 Clarendon Road, at 6 Clarendon Rd (where else?) W11, T020-7727 3330, dinner only Tue-Sat, is upmarket but informal. Very simple and small – standard white walls

High St Kensington & Holland Park

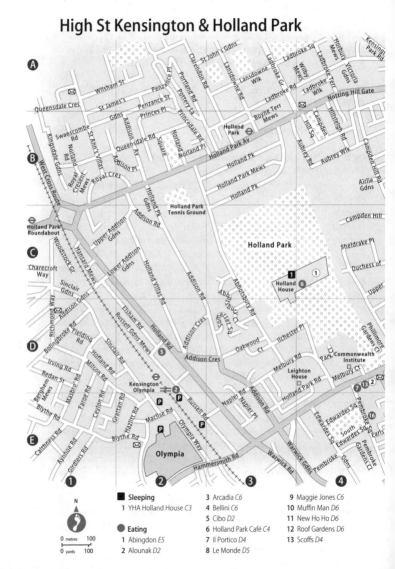

■ **Sleeping**	3 Arcadia *C6*	9 Maggie Jones *C6*
1 YHA Holland House *C3*	4 Bellini *C6*	10 Muffin Man *D6*
	5 Cibo *D2*	11 New Ho Ho *D6*
● **Eating**	6 Holland Park Café *C4*	12 Roof Gardens *D6*
1 Abingdon *E5*	7 Il Portico *D4*	13 Scoffs *D4*
2 Alounak *D2*	8 Le Monde *D5*	

N

0 metres 100
0 yards 100

and tablecloths – with an excellent wine list to accompany some fine euro-dining. On the same street, *San Sui*, Clarendon Rd, T020-7229 7136, is a little family-run Japanese restaurant recently refurbished. *Bali Sugar*, 33a All Saints Rd, W11, T020-7221 4477, was formerly the supercool Sugar Club, but its strange back garden and excellent global menu still make it a hip place to hang out.

In Holland Park, *Julie's Bar and Restaurant*, Holland Park Village, 137 Portland Rd, W11, T020-7229 8331 (restaurant), T020-7727 7985 (bar), is a 60s survivor, many-chambered and multifarious, a must for any visitor in one of the prettiest corners of the area. The food varies wildly but book in at different times and experience the difference between Sunday brunch, dinner and the everyday team. Off Holland Rd, *Cibo*, 3 Russell Gdns, W14, T020-7371 6271, is a fine Italian local, with big paintings on the walls and excellent lobster dishes on the tables.

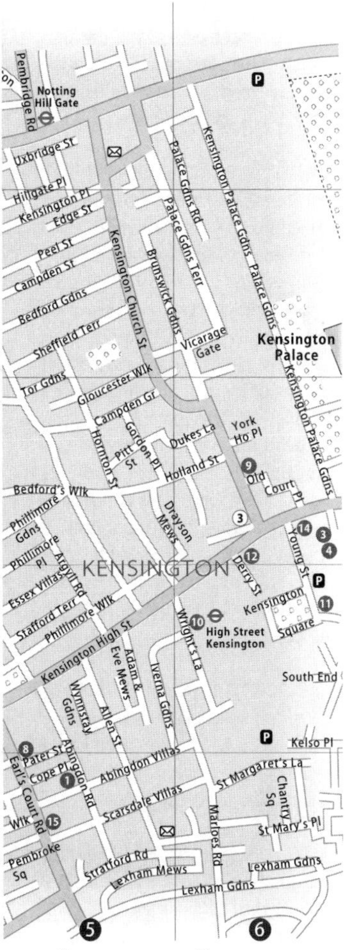

Hidden away behind Notting Hill tube are three popular old-timers: *Geales*, 2 Farmer St, W8, T020-7727 7528, is a delightful fish restaurant, a sort of old seaside stalwart; *Costas Grill*, 14 Hillgate St, W8, T020-7229 3794, is an inimitably cheap and cheery Greek taverna, also doing excellent fish dishes; and *Il Carratto Ristorante*, 20 Hillgate St, W8, T020-7229 9988, is a lively and reasonably priced Italian local.

Cheap

The New Cultural Revolution, 157-159 Notting Hill Gate, W11, T020-7313 9688, is a popular branch of the Chinese noodle bar chain. Further afield and more of a Portobello scene, *Ulli*, 16 All Saint's Rd, W11, T020-7727 7511, does a good mixture of Chinese, Malaysian and Thai food. For some surprisingly good Thai food at ridiculously cheap pub prices (£5-6 per main course), you can't beat the *Churchill Arms*, 119 Kensington Church St, W8, T020-7792 1246, open Mon-Sat 1200-1430, 1800-2130, Sun 1200-1430. The restaurant is through the back in the indoor 'beer garden' and you may have to wait for a table if you haven't booked.

The *Brasserie du Marché Café-Restaurant*, 349 Portobello Rd, W10, T020-8968 5828, is a Parisian corner spot at the northern end of Portobello Rd with an old-fashioned and tasty menu and good-value *prix fixe* lunch all week except Sat.

On Kensington Park Rd, and at the top of this bracket, are *Osteria Basilico*, 29 Kensington Park Rd, W11, T020-7727 9372, rated by many locals the best Italian pizza parlour in London – definitely

West London (sidebar)

● Pubs & bars	○ Entertainment
14 Bar Cuba *C6*	1 Holland Park Open-Air Theatre *C4*
15 Hansom Cab *E5*	2 Odeon Kensington *D4*
16 Scarsdale *E4*	3 St Mary Abbots *C6*

Five of the best: cheap eats in West London

- *Churchill Arms*, Kensington Church Street, Notting Hill.
- *New Cultural Revolution*, Notting Hill Gate, Notting Hill.
- *New Ho Ho*, Kensington Square, High Street Kensington.
- *Mandola*, Westbourne Grove, Bayswater.
- *206 Café*, Munster Road, Fulham.

needs booking (and try for a table upstairs), and *Mediterraneo*, 37 Kensington Park Rd, W11, T020-7792 3131, another Italian with less rustic décor and equally fine recipes.

Tootsies, Holland Park Av, W11, T020-7229 8567, is a West London hamburger chain, where the meat sandwiches are meaty, juicy, and fun for all the family. This branch is very friendly, does takeaways, and also real banana milkshakes.

Off Holland Rd, *Alounak*, 10 Russell Gdns, W14, T020-7603 7645, is like an Iranian caravan canteen that has put down roots. Its huge open oven provides endless hot pitta-type bread to wrap around fresh handfuls of mint and cheese. Dish of the day is always the best bet (usually a lamb stew). Persian food may not be for vegetarians but its BYOB – pile in with your own crate of red wine and soak up the souk.

Cafés & sandwich bars
The Golborne Rd at the northern end of the Portobello Rd is lined with excellent Portuguese cafés

In Notting Hill Top of the heap is *Lisboa*, 57 Golborne Rd, W10, T020-8968 5242. Rough and ready, it does the best '*galao*' and immediately whisks you off to Lisbon (the locals gossiping inside and out help the dream). If there's no spare corner, wander over to *Oporto* or further down – the whole street is rich in Portuguese groceries and bakers.

Near Notting Hill Gate, *Food on the Hill*, 1 Farmer St, W11, T020-7792 5226, open Mon-Sat (not evenings), is a wholefood, home-made lunchtime café doing very good soups and main dishes of the day. *Toms*, 226 Westbourne Grove, W11, T020-7221 8818, is Terence Conran's son's fashionable hit. The café is the place to sit and sip, the front shop the place to take out. Over the top in price but delicious in stock. High in local celebs: every other customer wearing jeans and shades is likely to be a star.

If that's too hectic, nearby *Café Rico*, 118 Westbourne Grove, W11, T020-792 2112, is an airy and delicious patisserie. *The Juice Junkies Club*, 13 Elgin Cres, W11, T020-7229 4871, is mega trendy hi-tech juice bar. Does specials and will concoct any combination you please – it should do for the price of the squeeze. *Il Girasole*, 78 Tavistock Rd, W11, T020-7243 8518, is an Italian coffee shop and takeaway that's very down to earth. Tables outside in the paved cul-de-sac make this a happy spot. *George's Portobello Fish Bar*, 329 Portobello Rd, W10, T020-8969 7895, was established in 1961 by George & Eve and remains the cleanest and most fun chippie in the locale.

In Holland Park, the *Holland Park Cafeteria*, T020-7602 2216, run by Mike and Yvonne is the local favourite, full of mums, tourists, dog-wakers and locals all rubbing shoulders in a little portocabin under the beautiful tiled arches in the ruins of the old Holland House. Take away or eat in (come rain or shine), it's dirt cheap and hits the spot (soups and main lunches as well as sandwiches and cakes to order).

Pubs & bars
Bars come & go like boy bands in Notting Hill

The Bed Bar, Portobello Rd, W10, T020-8969 4500, www.seriously.com, is the latest funky new bar to open up on the main strip – already 'seriously in' as it likes to claim. Less posing and more drinking goes on at *Ruby in the Dust Café*, Portobello Rd, W10, T020-8969 4626, a slinky, cool, dark branch of the chain so popular that it may be around for some time.

▶▶ Go to page 434 entertainment & nightlife

The First Floor, 186 Portobello Rd, W11, T020-7243 0072, and *The Market Bar*, 240a Portobello Rd, W11, T020-7229 6472, are both similarly suave, trendy all-day bars – with a high style quotient at night. Both serve decent fusion food. Beneath the *First Floor*, the *Ground Floor Bar*, 186 Portobello Rd, W11, T020-7243 8701 with its muted

West London

tones, sensible menu and huge glass windows on the corner has become a firm favourite with the local schmoozers.

Still in another league though is *The Pharmacy*, 150 Notting Hill Gate, W11, T020-7721 2442, for its expensive late-night cocktails amid cabinets full of pills and packets courtesy of Damien Hirst. Another long-player is *Beach Blanket Babylon*, 45 Ledbury Rd, W11, T020-7229 2907, a camp place always heaving with the pre-club scene. The restaurant's pricey but good, spread about in strange little nooks, serving surprisingly accomplished grub in opulent portions – great for brunch when the bar is quiet and the weird furniture holds sway – all wrought iron and vulgar vast cushions.

As well as designer bars, Notting Hill does a fine line in pub-restaurant conversions. Leading the herd is *The Cow*, 89 Westbourne Park Rd, W2, T020-7221 5400, Tom Conran's Oirish hit. As well as the posh separate restaurant upstairs, there's a cosy nook at the back, and summer or winter it's a local favourite because it has remained an old-fashioned if quite expensive pub.

Across the road is its rival, *The Westbourne*, 101 Westbourne Park Villas, W2, T020-7221 1332, busier and more sexy. This joint is just as popular, if less relaxing if you're without a posse. Most of the hip circuit may be knocking back cocktails and pretending to be quickly on the move, but hours later they're still there, as if standing about were an end in itself. Dress down but groovy. It's a bigger drinking hole and munch place than *The Cow* (Sun brunch is huge), but both are the perfect place to stroll after a foray along the market. In the long spring and summer evenings the big front benches can barely hold the revellers.

On Portobello Rd itself, the *Portobello Star*, Portobello Rd, T020-7229 8016, is a determinedly basic and un-souped-up local pub that makes a fine rendezvous for all and sundry. *The Hillgate*, 24 Hillgate St, W8, T020-7727 8543, is also a good eccentric local with tables outside beneath flowerbaskets and traditional panelled pub décor.

Further up Camdpen Hill, *The Windsor Castle*, 114 Campden Hill Rd, W8, T020-7243 9551, is very old and snug. The Tudor-style interior is a hit with old Etonians, while wintry mulled wines, panelled seating and nooks make it more authentic when autumn sets in. In summer the big walled garden has a char-grilled barbecue.

Shopping

Portobello Road and its market on Sat is the destination for antiques, fruit 'n' veg and all kinds of second-hand gear. Most of the superior antique stalls are at the top southern end of the street, giving way to food and clothes halfway down, before finishing up beneath the flyover with jumble stalls where many a bargain is likely to lurk. Also on Sat mornings, the Farmers' Market in Hillgate Village is a quirky event where the Hillbillies like to pretend they know their onions.

One of the most rewarding shopping areas in London, Notting Hill boasts an extraordinary array of independents & one-offs

Antique and bric-a-brac shops open throughout the week and those worth a look include *Bazar*, 82 Golborne Rd, W10, T020-8969 6262, for its French antique and period furniture – great for nestbuilding and original presents; *Nick Haywood*, 198 Westbourne Grove, W11, T020-727 8708, an original period lighting emporium, also good for household delights, antiques and special gifts – the best and one of the oldest on a strip of rococo boutiques; *MAC*, 86 Golborne Rd, W10, T020-8960 3736, a treasure trove of architectural and decorative antiques – many from France and the west country; and *David Wainwright*, 251 Portobello Rd, T020-7792 1988 who specializes in Oriental antiques and bric-a-brac, one of the best of the bunch.

Antiques

West London

Art   *Art4Fun*, 196 Kensington Park Rd, T020-7792 4567 (T020-8994 4800 information), www.art4fun.com (open daily) is an activity fun shop, paint-and-make centre, great for kiddies, hen parties and birthdays, £3.95 per person for all day, items from £1. Serves tea or bring a bottle of wine. *Apart*, 138 Portobello Rd, W11, T020-7229 6746, is one of the best new, just about affordable galleries – bringing eglitarian new art to the streets in a big friendly corner gallery. The idea is to introduce new artists to new patrons. Each canvas hangs on a rail and is constantly changing, the latest art school graduate can flog stuff here to the average browser. Seek out the new Warhol.

Books   *The Travel Bookshop*, 13-15 Blenheim Cresent, W11, T020-229 5260, is one of the best travel bookshops in the city, and yes, Hugh Grant was the manager here in the movie. Blenheim Crescent has a little chain of rival specialist bookshops – from gardening to *Books for Cooks*, 4 Blenheim Crescent, W11, T020-7221 1992, www.booksforcooks. com, offering shop-made lunches, coffee and cakes from the Test Kitchen, cookery demos and even cookery holidays in Tuscany, as well as a cornucopia of recipe reads.

   Simon Finch Rare Books, 61a Ledbury Rd, W11, T020-7792 3303, specialize in modern literature, photography, art and design – pretentious high design mostly. *Notting Hill Books*, 132 Palace Gardens Terrace, W8, T020-7727 5988 (closed Thu afternoons) do bargain paperbacks and discounted press edition hardbacks. Popular with everyone from bishops to backpackers, this little bookstore is well frequented and refuses credit cards. Notting Hill Gate may be slowly yielding to the mass-market high street chains but this place is typical of the area's wealth of second-hand and exchange stores ribboning the main road.

Fashion   *Emma Hope's Shoes*, 207 Westbourne Grove, W11, T020-7313 7493, are the shoes to buy when Cinderella is invited to the ball – individual, gorgeous and the fave of policewomen to princesses (may be best visited in the sales). *The Shirtsmith*, 38b Ledbury Rd, W11, T020-7229 3090, do fashionable ready-to-wear and made-to-measure, his and hers shirts. Simple, elegant and the most striking of this street's elite boutiques. For designer clothing, *Antoine at Lili*, 32 Uxbridge St, W8, T020-7792 9922, is a corner boutique with its spirited 'mode, Deco and cadeaux'. Big in Paris this is their first London branch. *The Cross*, 147 Portland Rd, W11, T020-7727 6760, stock very expensive, must-have designer womenswear, popular with the likes of Nicole Kidman. *Notting Hill Exchange*, 32 & 34 Pembridge Rd, W11, T020-7727 4805, open daily 1000-2000, bargain women's retro clothing at No 32, and similarly for the guys at No 34. *Skins*, 232 Portobello Rd, W11, T020-7221 4203, open Mon-Fri 1030-1800, Sat 1030-1830, great for 70s gear, and though prices have risen with the area's growing gentrification, there's still a bargain to be found.

Food & drink   For commendable comestibles, *Mr Christians Delicatessen*, 11 Elgin Cres, W11, T020-7229 0501, stocks a wide selection of fine foods from around the Med. On Sat – their breads, sandwiches and pastries spill onto the street stall outside, they are so popular – it saves the crowds pushing inside. *R Garcia & Son*, 248-250 Portobello Rd, W11, T020-7221 6119, Tue-Sat 0830-1800, is a excellent Spanish grocery – very authentic and comprehensive, deli and other combestibles.

   Holland Park Ave is a good spot to compile a pricey but very special picnic: smart off-licences in the area include *Nicolas*, 98 Holland Park Av, W11, T020-7727 5148, www.nicolas-wines.com, with free wine-tasting and bargain champagnes, chilled wines and special French waters and the usual spirits and cigar selections; the best and oldest French wine retailer. Next door, *Jeroboams*, 96 Holland Park Av, W11, T020-7727 9359 stock excellent cheeses, cider, charcuterie, oil and sandwiches. *Maison Blanc*, Holland Park Av, T020-72212494. The fine French bread and cake mini-chain finishes off any picnic (or you can stand and munch on the premises).

Authentic French fêtes demand they supply epiphany cakes and chocolate logs as if you're there. Nearby *Lidgates*, T020-7727 8243, is one of London's finest organic butchers. Much lauded with queues round the corner for Christmas turkeys – its prices reflect its upmarket appeal. *Speck*, 2 Holland Park Terr, in Portland Rd, T020- 7229 7005, is an excellent Italian deli – everything from lasagne to pickles. Expensive but worth the indulgence.

Five of the best: fashion shops

- *Emma Hope's Shoes*, Westbourne Grove, Notting Hill.
- *Graham and Green*, Elgin Crescent, Notting Hill.
- *Designer Bargains*, Kensington Church Street, High Street Kensington.
- *Orsini*, Earl's Court Road, High Street Kensington.
- *Skins*, Portobello Road, Notting Hill.

Jewellery

The Necklace Maker Workshop, 259 Portobello Rd, W11, T020-7792 3436, have an extraordinary array of exotic beads, jewellery and necklace-making equipment. Rare, antique, precious, enthnic beads, trinkets, fasteners and all the things you need to make your own jewellery. For designer furniture that needs to be seen to be believed, check out *Ogier*, 177 Westbourne Grove, W11, T020-7229 0783, ogier@dircon.co.uk, completely over-the-top in price and chic – the African moment meets the East Village.

Miscellaneous

Something of a Notting Hill institution is *Graham & Green*, 4, 7 & 10 Elgin Cres, W11, T020-7727 4594, a funky, chic series of shops has spread across both sides of the road. From fun, quirky toys, presents, and arty household nick-nacks to stationery, fabrics, clothes and jewellery – their stock is very influenced by the Big Apple and the Milan precincts. *"Turquoise Island"*, 222 Westbourne Grove, W11, T020-7727 3095, a famous tiled folly, is part clock, part toilet and mainly a flower stall – spilling out onto the pavement in this ultra fashionable corner. It's bold modern architecture won wide acclaim when it was created; the flowers are lovely, too.

Music & video

Video City, 117 Notting Hill Gate, W11, T020-7221 7029, "the best little video store in the world", they assure us – don't forget to ring and say you need it for an extra night for nothing, and they'll agree. The *Music & Video Exchange*, is another Notting Hill institution. Their sprawling chain of scruffy shops on Notting Hill Gate stock a vast selection of vinyl and CDs. For general rock, pop and modern jazz head for No 38; for classical go to No 36; and for blues, folk and trad jazz No 42. All branches are open daily 1000-2000.

Transport

Buses

No 7 from the British Museum to Ladbroke Grove via Tottenham Court Rd tube station, Oxford Circus, Marble Arch and Paddington.

No 12 between Notting Hill Gate and Dulwich via Bayswater Rd, Marble Arch, Oxford Circus, Piccadilly Circus, Trafalgar Square, Westminster, Elephant, Camberwell, and Peckham.

No 23 between Aldwych and Ladbroke Grove via Trafalgar Square, Piccadilly Circus, Oxford Circus, Marble Arch and Paddington.

No 27 to Chiswick from Notting Hill Gate via Kensington High St and Hammersmith.

No 28 from Notting Hill Gate to Wandsworth Bridge via Kensington High St and Fulham Broadway.

No 31 between Notting Hill Gate and Camden Town via Westbourne Park, Kilburn, Swiss Cottage, Chalk Farm and Camden Lock.

No 52 from Kensal Rise to Victoria via Ladbroke Grove, Notting Hill Gate, Kensington, Knightsbridge and Hyde Park Corner.

West London

No 70 from Ladbroke Grove to Kensington High St via Westbourne Grove, Queensway and Notting Hill Gate and (Mon-Sat only).

No 94 to Piccadilly Circus from Notting Hill Gate via Bayswater Rd, Marble Arch and Oxford Circus.

No 328 between Golders Green and Chelsea via West Hampstead, Kilburn, Westbourne Park, Notting Hill Gate, Kensington High St, and Earl's Court.

Taxis   Always plenty along Notting Hill Gate. Fewer down Portobello Rd, but usually a few on Ladbroke Grove.

Tubes   Notting Hill Gate tube for Portobello Rd's southern end, and Ladbroke Grove for the northern end. Either Holland Park or Notting Hill Gate tube for Holland Park. District and Circle lines for NottingHill Gate. Central line for Holland Park. Hammersmith and City line for Ladbroke Grove.

High Street Kensington and Earl's Court

⊖ *High St Kensington, Gloucester Rd & Earl's Court tubes*   *Sandwiched between the slopes of Holland Park and South Kensington, Kensington itself is a quieter, more residential and family-friendly continuation of Knightsbridge west of Museumland. North of High St Ken, as it's usually abbreviated, antiquey Kensington Church Street twists up to super-hip Notting Hill, while to the south, either side of the Earl's Court Road, peaceful squares and tall Victorian terraces contain some very expensive addresses indeed. The High Street once bustled with some of the buzz of the King's Road in Chelsea, but since the 80s it too has become considerably more wealthy and more staid, dominated now by chain stores and multinational clothing brands. To the east, in the west end of Kensington Gardens, stands the explanation for the persistence of the area's cachet, **Kensington Palace**, former home of Princess Diana and still the second most important Royal residence in London after Buckingham Palace. Some 20 splendid rooms here are open to the public throughout the year, housing the faintly ridiculous and genuinely priceless Royal Dress Collection. To the southwest, Earl's Court is the Kensingtons' embarrassing neighbour, a lively, dodgy and terminally unfashionable district long colonized by hard-partying Antipodeans and South Africans and more recently by the gay scene, most famous for its massive exhibition centre. The wide range of mid-price hotels boosts the transient population.*

History

Since at least the 12th century, the little hamlet of 'Chenesit' nestled at the foot of the hill, around a church that lay on the site of St Mary Abbots. It had grown little by the time William III moved into Nottingham House on the western edge of Hyde Park, and set Wren the task of transforming it into Kensington Palace. In the

Hotels in the area

A *The Royal Garden Hotel*
C *Maranton House Hotel*
C *Merlyn Court Hotel*
D *Albany Hotel*
D *The Burns Hotel*
D *Barkston Gardens Hotel*
E-D *Henley House Hotel*
F *The Court Hotel*
▸▸ *Go to page 450*

previous hundred years Holland House and Campden House had been built in extensive grounds overlooking Kensington, while Earl's Court remained as a hamlet of farms to the south. Meadowland, fruit gardens and nurseries lay in between, and although Kensington Square went up in 1685, it was still surrounded by fields some 30 years later.

During the 1700s, Kensington grew as society followed royalty to settle close to the court at Kensington Palace. Villas sprang up along the hillside north of the High Street, the Phillimore Estate sold their land for building, and by the early 19th century buildings extended as far Edwardes Square. There was such significant evening traffic between Kensington and Piccadilly that horse patrols were introduced to protect travellers from marauding highwaymen (George II himself was robbed, with 'much deference', within the grounds of Kensington Palace).

Kensington's population had risen eightfold in the 18th century to 8000, yet by 1901 it was some 175,000. Street after street spread west, swallowing up the market gardens and the hamlets of Earl's Court and Walham Green on the way towards Hammersmith and Fulham. Further impetus was provided by the arrival of the railways.

In the 1860s Earl's Court was still largely market gardens employing a significant Irish workforce for whom the Roman Catholic St Thomas' had been built in 1848. Nevertheless, a farm was cleared to make way for a station, and development grew in earnest from the 1880s. Spectacular arenas of entertainment emerged nearby. Olympia opened in 1884 and hosted the circus troupes of Bertram Mills and Barnum. The 'Paris Hippodrome' of 1886 displayed chariot racing and stag hunting. Further south the Earl's Court Pleasure Ground offered the Great Wheel and annual spectaculars such as 'Buffalo Bill's Wild West Show'.

When the Exhibition Hall was built on the site in 1937, however, it was soon in use as an internment camp. By then, Earl's Court tube station had been honoured as the first station to boast an escalator. Attempts to allay public anxiety extended to employing the one-legged 'Bumper' Harris to ride up and down the contraption throughout the opening day.

Houses were divided up into several lodgings or converted to hotels as the area gained a growing, but transient, population. In Kensington, Barker's continued to expand into new buildings (there were 400 staff as early as the 1880s), and the Georgian terraces in Kensington were largely replaced by flats in the 1930s.

As the century progressed Earl's Court earned the nickname 'Kangaroo Valley' as a largely young Australian community populated the bedsit jungle. Since the 1960s and 70s, Earl's Court has also drawn a gay community (Brompton Cemetery has long been a famed venue for trysts), while Kensington has retained some of the grandeur it first experienced in the 1700s.

Sights

High Street Kensington tube emerges via a shopping arcade onto Kensington High Street's western end. A right turn heads past Kensington Church Street, Barkers department store, and the Royal Garden Hotel to Kensington Palace and Gardens.

Queen Victoria's birthplace is one of the most significant and evocative of the Royal palaces, unfortunately all the more so since the death of Princess Diana,

Kensington
Palace

West London

who lived here after her separation from Prince Charles. Various Royals still have residences here, including the Queen's sister, Princess Margaret and Alice the Grand Duchess of Kent who will be 100 years old on Christmas Day 2001.

The Palace itself has been open to the public for at least a century, the 20 or so rooms on the one and a half hour audio-guided tour including the antique-stuffed King's State Apartments, William Kent's *trompe l'oeil* ceilings and staircases, a considerable selection of old master paintings from the Royal Collection in the Long Gallery and some fine views over the lakes and gardens. Also on display is the Royal Ceremonial Dress Collection, which now rather ghoulishly contains some of the dresses that Diana wore on state occasions, as well as the gilded pageantry of the 19th century. The Queen Victoria dress collection looks very restrained in comparison. As the Palace is keen to point out, everything that can be seen is the genuine article. What any of it really represents is more of a mystery.

■ *Open daily Nov-Feb 1000-1700 (last admission 1600), March-Oct 1000-1800 (last admission 1700). Admission £8.50, concession £6.70 including audio guide. T020-7937 9561, www.royal.gov.uk*

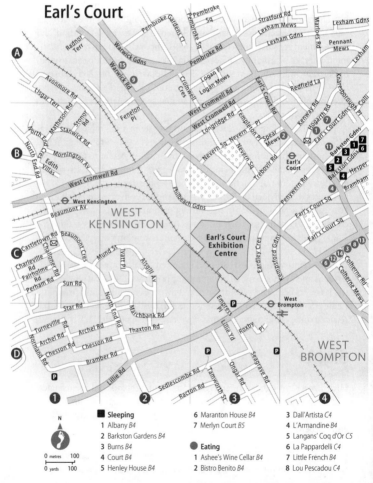

Earl's Court

N	
0 metres 100	
0 yards 100	

■ **Sleeping**	6 Maranton House *B4*	3 Dall'Artista *C4*
1 Albany *B4*	7 Merlyn Court *B5*	4 L'Armandine *B4*
2 Barkston Gardens *B4*		5 Langans' Coq d'Or *C5*
3 Burns *B4*	● **Eating**	6 La Pappardelli *C4*
4 Court *B4*	1 Ashee's Wine Cellar *B4*	7 Little French *B4*
5 Henley House *B4*	2 Bistro Benito *B4*	8 Lou Pescadou *C4*

Left out of the tube station leads down the main High Street shopping drag, a **Commonwealth** smaller version of Oxford Street, to the distinctive blue-green copper-roofed **Institute** Commonwealth Institute. This is a marvellous Empire-wide resource from library to conference/event centre – nestling at the bottom of Holland Park – that hasn't lost that 60s post-colonial passion for change. The display of its curious collection of tribal masterpieces is being refurbished until 2002, although the education department regularly organizes special events, adding up to a down-to-earth take on England out of Europe.

■ *Open Mon-Fri 0900-1700, T020-7603 4535, info@common-wealth.org.uk 'Commonwealth Resource Centre' (library) open Mon-Sat 1000-1600, T020-7603 4535, ext 210, F020-7603 2807, www.common-wealth.org.uk*

Opposite the Commonwealth Institute, the Earl's Court Road heads south towards the lower end of the King's Road and Chelsea, while Kensington High Street continues towards Hammersmith, passing the **Olympia Exhibition Centre**. Trade shows and exhibitions are staged here, as well as at the even bigger Earl's Court Exhibition Centre some way down Warwick Road, from the super popular 'Ideal Home Show' to the mega 'Boat Show' and the Royal Tournament.

West London

Eating and drinking

In Kensington *The Abingdon*, 54 **Expensive** Abingdon Rd, W8, T020-7937 3339, is ● *on maps,* another example of the rash of corner *pages 334 & 342* pubs which are no longer pubs but fancy brasserie/restaurants with fine wine lists. A light, airy, luxurious yet informal place. Locals choose to dine in the long bench-like conservatory. Booking essential, but high tables or bar seats serve expensive beers and snacks – less satisfying but unhurried (and cheaper).

Maggie Jones, 6 Old Court Place, Kensington Church St, W8, T020-7937 6462. Sister act to the marvellous Belgravia 'La Poule Au Pot' this is a more sombre Kensington hideaway. Always packed, it serves delicious French-influenced hearty fayre – especially recommended for a Sun lunch and then a stroll through the passage to the back entrance of Kensington Gardens to walk off the feast.

The Roof Gardens, 99 Kensington High St, T020-7937 7994, open 0900-1700, a new restaurant and floor, club, phone to check no function in progress to see the extraordinary and exotic

9 Moshsen *A2*
10 Mr Wing *C5*
11 Pin Petch *B4*
12 Troubador Café *C4*

● Pubs & bars
13 Balans West *C4*
14 Colherne *C4*
15 Warwick Arms *A2*

fully fledged roof garden itself. Next to Barkers, on the top of the old *Biba* building, the restaurant's a treat with the rich bitch eurotrash crowd.

In Earl's Court, just about the only fine dining option is *Langans' Coq d'Or*, 254-260 Old Brompton Rd, SW5, T020-7259 2599.

Mid-range **In Kensington** *Arcadia*, Kensington Court, 35 Kensington High St, W8, T020-7937 4294, is a rather wonderful crisp-clothed dining place in a little cobbled yard providing respite from the Ken High Street noise. It offers a fine gourmand Italian-French menu with a live parrot and individualistic décor. Next to Arcadia, is *Bellini*, 47 Kensington Court, W8, T020-7937 5520, much more trendy, with a long bar and cocktails, modern and unpretentious in a Soho kind of way.

In Earl's Court, at the lower end of this bracket, *Mr Wing*, 242 Old Brompton Rd, SW5, T020-7370 4450, open daily 1230-2400, all performances 2015-2345, £2 cover charge, a curious nightspot – a Chinese restaurant offering live jazz every Thu, Fri, Sat, tacky and fun. *Lou Pescadou*, 241 Old Brompton Rd, SW5, T020-7370 1057, is an excellent local seafood restaurant. Blue paint and white linen, fresh, French and real with 3-course weekday lunches for about £10.

Cheap **In Kensington** *Scoffs*, 267 Kensington High St, W8, T020-7602 6777, open 7 days. Italian trattoria and the cinema stalwart, the place to grab a cappuccino out of dining hours, or hungry bowl of pasta anytime all day or just before or after you've popcorned at the Odeon next door. Unchanged in decades because it works. *Il Portico*, 277 Kensington High St, W8, T020-7602 6262, is another classic Italian restaurant – as authentic and as old as its nextdoor neighbour *Scoffs* – but this is the white table-clothed, more expensive version and demands more time and a bit of luck with a table in order to savour the food.

As the string of Thai, Italian and other chain outlets come and go all along the shopping string of Ken High Street, *The Dome*, 35a/b Ken High St, W8 (inside Kensington Court) T020-7937 6655, remains as one of the best – in the summer it has quiet outside seats on the cobbles, its reliable *prix fixe* and brasserie menu lasts all day … and its staff are usually friendly to tourists and shoppers, too.

Tucked away in Kensington Square, *The New Ho Ho*, 9 Kensington Square, W8, T020-7937 4898, is a cheap (for the area) and basic little Chinese caff with an informal cheerfulness.

In Earl's Court, at *Ashee's Wine Cellar Bar*, 22 Hogarth Place, SW5, T020-7373 6180, oysters and Swiss cheese fondue seem to be the house speciality in an archetypical winebar vault in the area's cutest street. Next door, *The Little French Restaurant*, 18 Hogarth Place, SW5, T020-7370 0366, is romantic and very French – little white tables and fresh handwritten menu.

The *Pin Petch*, 4-12 Barkston Gdns, SW5, T020-7370 1371, is a reasonable Thai restaurant and takeaway, right next to all the hotels – very handy. *Moshsen*, 152 Warwick Rd, W14, T020-7603 9888, is a surprising find on the otherwise rather bleak Warwick Rd – an authentic friendly, open-ovened Persian treat.

Opposite the massive drive-in *Homebase*, just up from the bright 24-hr *Tesco*'s, equidistant from Olympia and Earl's Court Exhibition centre. *Dall'Artista*, 243 Old Brompton Rd, SW5, T020-7373 1659, is a friendly, cheap pizzeria-pasta place while *Equals Bar & Restaurant*, 233 Earl's Court Rd, SW5, T020-7370 6994, is continental in style, with trendy stainless steel décor. *Bistro Benito*, 166 Earl's Court Rd, SW5, T020-7373 6646, cucina Italiana, small, cheap, cheerful and traditional Italian find – open 7 days – has the pud trolley and the chequred tablecloths. *La Pappardella*, 253 Old Brompton Rd, SW5, T020-7373 7777, also open 7 days, is another, offering home-made pasta and tempting pizzas.

In Kensington Near Ken High St, *The Muffin Man*, 12 Wrights Lane, W8, T020-7937 6652, is an old-fashioned sit-down, doilly and teacup tearoom, round the corner from the tube. *Patisserie Française*, 27 Kensington Church St, W8, T020-7937 9574, like its Baywater sisters, is a reliable French gâteaux takeaway and sit-down – a slice of unchanged continental sipping. At the other end of the shopping strip, *Le Monde*, 56 Earl's Court Rd, W8, T020-7938 1206, is a fresh, all-window café – good for lunch – similar to all the coffee shops across London – but being a one-off has its own charm.

Cafés & sandwich bars

In Earl's Court, *L'Armandine*, Earl's Court Rd, SW5, T020-7244 0400, is a lively, authentic continental sandwich bar and lunch spot, but best of all is the inimitable *Troubadour Café*, 256 Old Brompton Rd, SW5, T020-7370 1434, a dark and atmospheric brasserie/bar/café open all day until late and with a small garden. A very individualistic place- a slice of Paris in an otherwise unprepossessing zone – with regular poetry events and classical music.

Bar Cuba, 11-13 Ken High St, W8, T020-7938 4137 (open until 0200 Mon-Sat), is great fun – running regular excellent Samba classes on Wed nights – a hugely popular Latin bar which downstairs offers one the tiniest, liveliest slice of honest raunch in London. Not remotely sleazy, a holiday atmosphere prevails.

Pubs & bars
▶▶ *Go to page 435 for entertainment & nightlife*

Hidden away in a lovely Georgian secret square is *The Scarsdale*, 23a Edwardes Square, W8, T020-7937 1811, right behind the cinema – like a lively seaside inn with proper tables outside for the summer and log fires for the winter, charming bar staff and all-day dining. Similar but without the benefit of the quiet location is *The Hansom Cab*, 84 Earl's Court Rd, T020-7793 4821, on the main road but also with good grub.

Nearer Earl's Court, *Balans West*, 239 Old Brompton Rd, SW5, T020-7244 8838, is the sister act to the one in Soho, a very hip corner spot where the locals and the gays love to cool their heels with some sexy cocktails. Nearby, *The Colherne*, 261 Old Brompton Rd, SW5, T020-7244 5951, is a big, dark, throbbing gay pub with a disco-lit pool table – you don't have to have a skinhead and a moustache here but it helps.

A little further afield, *The Warwick Arms*, 160 Warwick Rd, W14, T020-7603 3560, is a real find, a traditonal Irish pub with no frills but genuine warmth on the unfriendly Warwick Rd.

West London

Shopping

Kensington is not what it used to be – if you remember its 60s heyday then *Biba* was an ephemeral moment. Worse still, the indoor market stalls that gave the street some much-needed offbeat appeal have just been closed. For three decades these were the place to find antique clothing, avant garde high-fashion, punk and leatherwear, making Ken High Street the must-stop shop above tatty Camden.

Ken High Street no longer offers the unique, so much as a select trail of all the best high street chains from *Jigsaw* to *Zara*, from *Dixons* to *Office*. They're all here including a reasonably good department store: *Barkers*, 63 Ken High St, W8, T020-7937 5432, open Mon-Wed 1000-1900, Thu 1000-2000, Fri 1000-1900, Sat 0930-1900, Sun 1200-1800. Four floors, part of *House of Fraser*.

The only individual shops that hint at the old boutique style crawl up Kensington Church Rd, lead you up to Notting Hill and turn into a string of specialist fine antique shops ... or down the other end by the cinema there is the cluster at the top of the Earl's Court Rd. The long wide High St now boasts everything from *Safeways*, *M&S*, *Boots* to all the other late-night necessities near the tube station. There's also a mini mall in Barkers with Morgans, Karen Millen and other trendy clothing chain stores.

On Kensington Church St, *Amazon*, 1-22 Ken Church St, W8, is a hugely discounted designer and one-off label men and women's fashion retailer in three separate shops. Nearby, *Designer Bargains*, 29 Kensington Church St, T020-7795 6777, stock some excellent women's second-hand finds – from Gucci to Chanel, Jigsaw to Katherine Hamnett.

Alternatively, go bargain-hunting for vintage ladies clothing and pick some period wonders from the 20s to the 60s at the other end of the High at *Orsini*, 76 Earl's Court Rd, W8, T020-7937 2903, Tue-Sat 1200-1800 only, with a mass of classic prints and satin feathery shoes, frocks and suits; a real treat. Nearby is *Rassells Nursery*, 80 Earl's Court Rd, W8, T020-7937 0481, a pretty and comprehensive house & garden nursery with indoor and outdoor expertise – say it with flowers.

A new phenomenon in London is the nailbar *Scarlet*, 7 Kensington Church St, T020-7499 5898, with only 4 branches so far, where the pampering for the digits is dazzling. The *Non Stop Party Shop*, 214/216 Ken High St, T020-7937 7200, is full of party ideas and little gifts and an unlimited choice of personal printing and other miscellaneous services. The *Children Books Centre*, 237 Ken High St, T020-7937 7497, F020-7938 4968, www.childresnbookcentre.co.uk, is a superb kiddy specialist shop – always full of enthusiastic admirers – close by *Gap Kids*. *Cyclecare*, 54 Earl's Court Rd (next to the police station) T020-7460 0495, is one of those rare ordinary but very specialist bicycle sellers and menders, while *Barston & Barr*, 32 Earl's Court Rd, W8, T020-7937 6511, is a super fine and welcoming cheese shop – defying you not to try some.

The main purchase made here is clearly an international phone card

There's not a lot in Earl's Court really. Dotted along the main drag are the odd second-hand charity shop, a string of newsagents and travel agents and bakeries up and down the Earl's Court Rd. Gloucester Road has a *Waitrose* and a smaller version of *Partridges* (the fine specialty food shop on Sloane Street), otherwise the area lacks boutiques and only caters for snackers and news.

West London

Transport

Buses
There are always plenty of taxis along High St Ken & along the Old Brompton Rd

No 9 from Kensington to Trafalagar Square via Knightsbridge, Hyde Park Corner and Piccadilly Circus.

No 10 from Kensington to King's Cross via Knightsbridge, Hyde Park Corner, Marble Arch, Oxford Circus and Euston.

No 27 from Camden Town to Ken High St via Marylebone Rd, Paddington and Notting Hill Gate.

No 28 from Notting Hill Gate to Fulham Broadway via Ken High St.

No 49 to Kensington from Clapham Junction via Battersea, Chelsea and South Kensington.

No 52 from Kensington to Victoria via Hyde Park Corner.

• •

Directory

Libraries *Kensington Central Library & Town Hall Philimore Walk W8, T020-7937 2542. Behind Kensington High Street – the big borough-wide resource – all info from the usual multi-media lending facilites to jobs, arts, fashion and antique fairs in their portals.*

Sports *Soho Gyms, Earl's Court Gym, 254 Earl's Court Rd, T020-7370 1402. 'Urban fitness' very efficient and seemingly*

*very gay. **The Phillimore Club**, 45 Phillimore Walk, Kensington, W8, T020-7939 2882, www.phillimoreclub.com, "Quietly celebrating the privilege of being a woman", offering enzymatic sea mud wrap (30 mins at £24) to Ayurvedic Indian head and face massage (75 mins for £45). Mother and Daughter day (1½ hrs each £175). Bride to Be day (£265 for 5 hrs).*

No 328 from Westbourne Park to Chelsea via Notting Hill Gate, Ken High St and Earl's Court.

No C1 between Ken High St and Victoria via Earl's Court, South Kensington, Brompton Rd (Harrods) and Sloane Square.

No C3 between Earl's Court (*Tesco*) and Clapham Junction via Lots Rd, Chelsea Harbour, Sands End (*Sainsbury's*), Wandsworth Bridge and Plough Rd.

Kensington Olympia Station for Clapham Junction and Willesden; West Brompton. **Trains**

High St Ken (Circle and District lines), Gloucester Rd and Earl's Court (Circle, District and **Tubes** Piccadilly lines).

Bayswater, Paddington and Little Venice

From Marble Arch, the Edgware Road pushes busily plumb straight northwest towards Maida Vale, Kilburn and Cricklewood, while leafy Bayswater Road sidles along the northern edge of Hyde Park, taking the line of Oxford Street out west to Notting Hill. The wedge on the map between these two main roads is one of London's most contradictory areas. At its tip, Sussex Gardens isolates an exclusive enclave of stately mansions and expensive squares from the scruffy chaos around Paddington Station. Further north, beyond the Westway flyover and the rundown Harrow Road, the area called Little Venice overstates its case but is nevertheless a watery and genteel haven on the Grand Union Canal, its Paddington arm receiving a facelift. Meanwhile, west of Lancaster Gate, which is one of the most attractive entrances to Kensington Gardens via the Italian gardens, Bayswater is an almost uniform stretch of crumbling stucco and porticos labouring under the weight of a population continually on the move. Queensway is the tacky hub of the area, so glitzy and gawdy that it's really quite good, always buzzing with passing trade, while at its north end Westbourne Grove goes steadily upmarket as it approaches Notting Hill.

⊖ The revamped Paddington Station for tubes & trains greets the Heathrow Express. Queensway tube is at the main drag's southern end, near Hyde Park; Bayswater tube is halfway down

History

Followers of the Anglo-Saxon chieftain 'Padda' probably gave Paddington its name, as they settled around modern Paddington Green. The Edgware and Bayswater Roads were ancient Roman routes north and west respectively, but development was limited, not least because from the 14th century the Tyburn gallows (at modern Marble Arch) ensured 'Tyburnia' retained a notorious reputation. In Westbourne Park (the River Westbourne ran south through here) a farm existed until the mid-19th century, and there were reservoirs where Sussex and Talbot Squares now sit.

From the 15th century the Bayswater conduit supplied the city with water (Bayswater is named after Bayard's Spring, situated near

Hotels in the area

AL The Hempel
B Byron Hotel
C Fairways Hotel
C Lancaster Hall Hotel
D Border Hotel
E-F Dean Court Hotel
▸▸ **Go to page 450**

West London

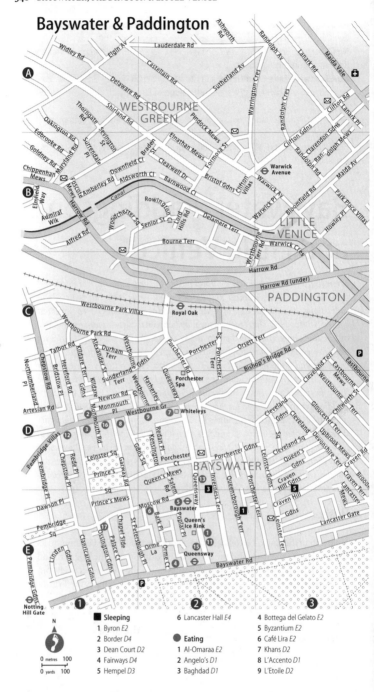

Bayswater & Paddington

0 metres 100
0 yards 100

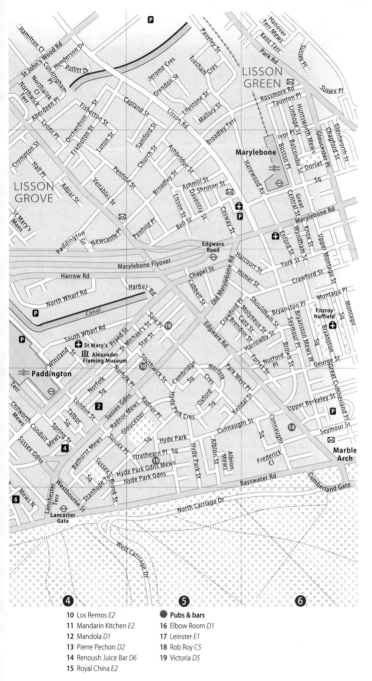

West London

10 Los Remos *E2*	● **Pubs & bars**
11 Mandarin Kitchen *E2*	16 Elbow Room *D1*
12 Mandola *D1*	17 Leinster *E1*
13 Pierre Pechon *D2*	18 Rob Roy *C5*
14 Renoush Juice Bar *D6*	19 Victoria *D5*
15 Royal China *E2*	

Queensway), but until it was diverted in 1834, the Westbourne became so polluted that the Serpentine, which it also fed, became a cesspit. Although the village of Paddington grew following an influx of Huguenots in the 18th century, and small farms and taverns (in which Shakespeare is reputed to have performed) lined the Edgware Road, it was the removal of the gallows in 1783 that enabled the settlement to expand.

A further impetus for development followed the opening in 1801 of a section of the Grand Junction Canal between Uxbridge and the Paddington Basin, and later the arrival of the railways. Expansion spread north and west – Tomlin's Town housed canal workers, and Connaught Place signalled plans to create a rival to Belgravia.

For a while, Bayswater did indeed become a much coveted address. Stuccoed mansions in Westbourne Terrace earned it the description as 'the finest street in London', Westbourne Grove became a popular shopping street, especially for fashionable drapers, and in the 1850s large houses went up in Lancaster Gate, Leinster and Princes squares. Military officers returned from India to settle here, as did a range of distinguished writers and entrepreneurs. WH Smith moved in to Sussex Square, Thomas Hardy wrote his (rejected) first novel, *The Poor Man and the Lady*, from Westbourne Park Villas, Aubrey Beardsley and Oscar Wilde lived in Palace Court, while later JM Barrie wrote *Peter Pan* while living on the corner of Bayswater Road and Leinster Terrace.

In the second half of the century expansion continued westwards: Notting Hill, Kensal Town and Queen's Park all grew through to the 1870s. Meanwhile, Paddington underwent its own transport revolution. Following the completion of the canal in 1801, a link to the Regent's Canal was built in 1820. A railway station was built in 1838, although the current station was designed by Isembard Kingdom Brunel a touch further east. Queen Victoria arrived at the original wooden station following her first railway journey, although perhaps the most internationally acclaimed arrival was that of a lost (and fictional) bear from Peru to launch a popular children's book series.

In 1861 horse-drawn trams were introduced on Bayswater Road, George Shillibeer's Omnibus ran from the Green to the City, and the new Metropolitan underground line arrived in 1863. Predictably, perhaps, the streets surrounding the canal and railway became slums, such that soon 'rags and riches eyed each other in Paddington'. St Mary's Hospital on Praed Street (where Sir Alexander Fleming discovered penicillin in 1929) and Paddington Green Children's Hospital (its building destroyed the last thatched house in London) catered for the growing population, a task made all the more important as more and more Victorian terraced streets turned to slums. Unscrupulous landlords such as Rachman exploited the squalid housing and the growing immigrant population in the 1950s (there is still a large Arab population along the Edgware Road), and the area became notorious for crime and prostitution. It is only just beginning to restore its reputation to that of its heyday in the mid-19th century.

Sights

Apart from delayed trains, there's not much to keep anyone for long in Paddington. If you happen to have time to kill in the area, then the **Alexander Fleming Museum**, in St Mary's Hospital, Praed Street, is worth a quick look. It contains the actual laboratory in which the great man accidentally discovered penicillin and hence invented antibiotics, a video on the history of his

West London

research and its wide-reaching benefits, and an exhibition on the history of the pills that were once hailed as cure-alls. Boffins like to joke that this celebration of the power of the petri dish is the one spot of 'culture' in the Paddington Basin. ■ *Open Mon-Thu 1000-1300. Admission £2 adults, £1 concessions. T020-7725 6528.*

Warwick Avenue and **Little Venice** are a short distance north of the station, but reached with difficulty from here because of the hectic road systems around the Marylebone flyover. It's easier, and certainly safer, to take the tube one stop to **Warwick Avenue**. Blomfield Road is the most attractive of the canalside streets of this quiet residential area. The best reason for a visit are the narrowboat trips up to the Zoo, Regent's Park and Camden Lock (see Canal transport, page 354).

On Bayswater Road, the strangest thing is the regular market of terrible paintings hung on the railings of Hyde Park every Sunday. For some bizarre reason these mostly amateurish daubings have recently become all the rage. Whatever, they make a good introduction to the fiercely unfashionable and cheesy main drag of Queensway heading up to Westbourne Grove. The **Queen's Ice Rink**, the shopping mall of **Whiteleys**, and the **Porchester Spa** nevertheless make an impressive trio of attractions along with any number of cheap restaurants and cafés.

Eating and drinking

Apart from the restaurant in the Hempel Hotel, the place to treat yourself is the *Royal China*, 13 Queensway, W2, T020-7221 2535, the glamorous and cavernous Chinese highspot of the area. It's like walking into a dark, 70s disco, where large round tables feed gangs of those who like their Peking Duck flown in fresh and the dim sum are legendary (filling and considerably less expensive than a full meal). Delicious and definitely worth travelling to find.

Expensive
● *on map, page 348*

Among the other Chinese restaurants on Queensway, the *Mandarin Kitchen*, 14-16 Queensway, W2, T020-7727 9012, is famous for its lobster noodles, which put it squarely in this price bracket. More simple and still pretty delicious food can also be had here for half the price. A little way off the beaten track, *L'Accento*, 16 Garway Rd, W2, T020-7243 2664, is a very fine and quiet modern Italian restaurant open for lunch and dinner only.

Mid-range

On Westbourne Grove itself, *Angelo's*, Westbourne Grove, W2, T020-7221 8843, is a Greek late-night institution with hard-drinking and dancing upstairs and a busy restaurant in the basement. Worth seeking out if you have the nibbles, feel like mingling and dancing and getting lively with the locals.

In Paddington, *Los Remos*, 38 Southwick St, W2, T020-7723 5056, is an old-fashioned Spanish restaurant and lively little basement tapas bar open all day until late, while Queensway and Westbourne Grove are classic destinations for a cheap meal out. Many are best avoided, but the Lebanese *Al-Omaraa*, 27 Queensway, W2, T020- 7221 8045, is the best of the cheap deals along this strip. Friendly with good prices and obliging service. *Hung To*, 51 Queensway, W2, T020-7727 5753, is a busy Chinese, full of locals tucking in and an authentic piece of Chinatown.

Cheap

On Wesbourne Grove, *Khans*, 13-15 Westbourne Grove, W2, T020-7727 5420. Open 1200-1500, 1800-1200 (Mon-Thu) 1200-2400 (Fri-Sun), is probably the biggest and most popular curry house in London. A must-have stop for the area – its bustle and cheapness make it London's answer to Paris' 'Chartier'. Don't count on friendliness from the busy staff – it's the speed with which the Delhi grub arrives that makes people rendezvous and return here for years.

For Arabic cuisine and a charcoal grill, head for **The Baghdad Restaurant**, 107 Westbourne Grove, W2, T020-7229 3048. Open daily 1700-2330 and also at lunchtimes during weekends, where charming service in a pretty tiled room offers the full range of Middle Eastern eats. Cleaner and brighter than the ubiquitous doner kebab fare that dominates the area.

A little further along, the **Mandola**, Westbourne Grove, W2, T020-7229 4734, is a local Sudanese favourite that has recently expanded into the next door room. BYOB (bring your own bottle) – and sit for hours over an authentic North African feast. Their mezze and the pot of the day is always reliable. The Sudanese coffee is an Arabian treat while the staff are as unaffectedly beautiful as ebony statues in their natural woven wraps. Best to book.

Cafés & sandwich bars On the Edgware Rd, the **Ranoush Juice Bar**, 43 Edgware Rd, W2, T020-7723 5929, www.ranoush.com (open until 0300), is an Arabian juice bar with impeccable style. **Pierre Pechon**, 127 Queensway, W2, T020-7229 0746, has been Queenway's foremost Patisserie Française since 1925. It's still a lively spot, good for hot coffees and all the usual comfort foods. Takeaway cakes and breads are perfect for Sun brunch.

L'Etoile, 73 Westbourne Grove, W2, T020-229 0380, is another popular French patisserie. **Byzantium**, 31 Moscow Rd, W2, T020-229 9367, is one of the best cafés in an area full of them. The food and cakes may not beat the French ones, but this fuggy backwater is the one where the locals stay and gossip and read their papers. The owner is so cheerful that your stay is welcome however little you sip. Open late. Nearby **Café Lira**, Moscow Rd, W2, T020-7727 5310, is a popular quiet little café – continental and stylish eats and cakes. Tables in and out – handy for doing laundry in the truly 'my beautiful laundrette' spot next door in the *Central Wash* at 91 Moscow Rd.

On the Bayswater Rd itself, **Bottega del Gelato**, 127 Bayswater Rd, W2, T020-7243 2443, do an astonishing array of delightful fresh home-made ice creams.

Pubs & bars
▶▶ Go to page 435 for entertainment & nightlife Most of the pubs in Bayswater are tourist traps, but the **Elbow Room**, 64 Westbourne Grove, W2, T020-7221 5211, www.elbrow-room co.uk, has perfected a popular and trendy 90s concept of making pool, lounge, groove and bar all come together. The coolest place to hang, shoot pool and have a meaty snack over a long, slow cocktail. The original one of a chain of three where the tables aren't green and the players only sport designer anoraks and Oasis haircuts.

A pub that also pulls in the locals with its recent refurbishment is the **Leinster**, 57 Ossington St, W2, T020-7243 9541, another opportunity to drown your sorrows while your smalls are spinning in the *Central Wash* launderette next door. No frills but the natives are friendly. Nearer Paddington, the **Victoria**, 10a Strathearn Place, W2, T020-7724 1191, is a posh old Victorian pub with a lovely upstairs bar, while the **Rob Roy** at 89 Sale Place, T020-7262 6403, is one of London's few Scottish boozers, the sister act to the *William Wallace* in Marylebone.

Shopping

Whiteleys was targeted by Hitler as his preferred HQ in London & German bombers were ordered to spare it during the Second World War

Bayswater is known for its central shopping mall **Whiteleys** which was once one of the first and most successful wonderful old department stores. Its founder was shot in his office by his bastard son who received widespread sympathy, resulting in his death sentence being commuted to hard labour. The transformation into major mall emphasizes its origins, retaining the original white stucco pillars and high inner arches. All the usual stores offer the shopper long hours and delights from *M&S* to *Jigsaw*. The central fountains with coloured lights and regular mini 'events' prove popular with the waiting dads and pushchairs. At night, the teenagers gather in the top floor bars and fake boulevards where the brasseries and bars spill onto the pavement, actually a vinyl extension of the escalator. The mini-multiplex cinema is the big draw – with all the latest Hollywood releases on show, as is the late-opening (on Fri and Sat) branch of **Tower Records** (T020-7229 4550).

The avenue of Queensway itself is a busy strip of cheap eateries – all the world's flavours are on offer – a well-known draw for oriental, Greek and Middle East muncheries as well as Häagan Dazs and other pastry shops. The cheap boutiques and shops are many – mainly brisk, pile-em-high, hi-fi, electronic and lugguage shops. You can find most things here – cheaper than Oxford St. There's even a *Millets*; great for a late-night panic buy before hitting the Paddington express to Heathrow or the moors.

Nickoldeon Video, 53 Queensway, W2, T020-229 1333. Open 7 days 1030-2230, is the best of the string of video stores (stocks the lot and is an independent). Everything at £1 only per night. Staff have the shifty, edgy look of Tarantino before he was famous. **Capital News**, Queensway, T020-7229 8007, open daily and very late, is the oldest and liveliest of the strip's newsagents – all the world's papers and magazines, telephone cards and sweeties – clearly a favourite gossip spot for all the locals from far-flung places. **Queensway Market**, 23-25 Queensway, open 1000-2200 daily, has a tattoo and piercing studio at **Skinflash**, T020-7243 2323, and around 80 stalls reminiscent of Kensington Market in its heyday but even more tacky and tasteless, above a leisure centre.

Nearer Notting Hill, **Archie**, 14 Moscow Rd, W2, T020-7229 2275, is an English, Continental, Middle Eastern deli, veg, groceries – a useful authentic corner shop (before you hit Hyde Park for a picnic) while next door the **Athenian Grocery**, 16a Moscow Rd, W2, T020-7229 6280, specializes in Greek Cypriot wines and foods with even more fruit and veg than their neighbour.

On Wesbourne Grove, **Planet Organic**, 42 Westbourne Grove, W2, T020-7221 7171, is the original large, and ludicrously expensive must-have organic supermarket. The mecca for the must-do betters. Full of Holland Park-Hoxton trustifarians and lonely merchant bankers seeking out a fly-free beetroot. Delicious if you want to prove your veggie cred. Anyone sensible supports the locals and picks out the best from the butchers and Portobello greengrocers for a fifth of the price.

Aero, 96 Westbourne Grove, W2, T020-7221 1950, do avant garde designer furniture for the home, office and desk. Good for presents and nick-nacks. **B2**, Westbourne Grove, W2, 24-hr shop is the most New York local; see and be scene in the middle of the night in this handy, former 7-11.

West London

Directory

Sports A treat in the area are the old Turkish and Russian steam baths and pools at the **Porchester Spa**, 225 Queensway, W2, T020-7792 3980, ladies only Tue, Thu, Fri 1000-2200 (last entry 2000), men only Mon, Wed, Sat 1000-2200 (last entry 2000), Sun women only 1000-1600, mixed couples 1600-2200 (last entry 2000). £18.95 non-members, £26.75 per couple (who are allowed re-entry thoru). Turkish, Russian steam rooms, cold plunge pool, jacuzzi, showers, therapy rooms and swimming pool. Café open daily 1100-1930. Towel and wrap provided, must bring own shower stuff and swimming costume.

Queen's Ice Bowl, 17 Queensway, W2, T020-7229 0172. The 50,000-ft ice rink is a real gem. It's always been there and it's got to be the best ice rink in London for being such fun. Since refurbishment it now also offers 12 lanes of fullsize tenpin bowling, 50 hi-tech video games, amusements, licensed bar and Wimpy restaurant.

Transport

Buses **No 6** between Kensal Rise and Aldwych via West Kilburn, Edgware Rd, Marble Arch, Oxford Circus, Piccadilly Circus and Trafalgar Square.

No 7 from the British Museum to Ladbroke Grove tube station via Tottenham Court Rd tube station, Oxford Circus, Marble Arch and Paddington.

No 12 from Bayswater Rd to Westminster via Marble Arch, Oxford Circus, Piccadilly Circus and Trafalgar Square.

No 23 between Liverpool St and Wesbourne Park via Bank, St Paul's (Mon-Fri only), Aldwych, Trafalgar Square, Piccadilly Circus, Oxford Circus and Marble Arch.

No 27 from Camden Town to Paddington via Marylebone Rd.

No 36 from Paddington to Peckham via Marble Arch, Hyde Park Corner, Victoria, Vauxhall, Oval and Camberwell.

No 46 between Kensal Rise and King's Cross via West Kilburn, Warwick Avenue tube station, St John's Wood, Swiss Cottage, Fitzjohn's Avenue, Hampstead Station, Rosslyn Hill, Hampstead Heath and Kentish Town.

No 94 from Bayswater Rd to Piccadilly Circus via Marble Arch and Oxford Circus.

No 70 from Ladbroke Grove through Westbourne Grove, Queensway and Notting Hill Gate to Kensington High St.

Canal transport
There's no need to book, pay on the boat

London Waterbus Company service daily **from Little Venice to Camden Lock**, leaving The Zoo to Camden Lock hourly 1035-1635, last trip one-way 1735, to Little Venice hourly 1015-1615, last trip 1750 (summer timetable). Journey either way takes about 15 mins and costs £1.50; £2.50 for round trips taking 40 mins. Winter timetable: hourly 1100-1600 Sat, Sun only. Full information, T020-7482 2660.

Taxis Plenty along the Bayswater Rd and around Paddington Station.

Trains Paddington for Heathrow (see page 33), western suburbs and the West of England.

Tubes Paddington (District, Circle, Hammersmith and City, and Bakerloo lines), Warwick Avenue (Bakerloo line), Lancaster Gate (Central line), Queensway (Central line), Bayswater (District and Circle lines), Royal Oak (Hammersmith and City line).

Fulham, Hammersmith and Putney

Fulham Broadway tube, Hammersmith & Putney Bridge tubes. Putney Bridge tube best for the river & Bishop's Palace. Parsons Green tube for the New King's Rd

*Beyond the glamour of Chelsea and the passing trade of Earl's Court, densely residential Fulham stretches steadily down to the river. Once a solidly working-class area, its regular terraces of little houses have long since become some of the most sought after in West London, where the idea of village London has become enshrined. Half the population apparently heads off at the weekends for the real thing in the country and regards the rest of London as 'up town'. Around Parsons Green and down by the river at the **Bishop's Palace**, this is Middle England in the big smoke. Apart from a small area around Fulham Broadway, the evenings are quiet in Fulham, but that's hardly the case in Hammersmith, a little further upstream. Here a couple of big music venues, the lively Riverside Studios and the innovative Lyric Theatre boost the cultural life of an area almost obliterated by massive roads and streaming or stationery*

West London

*traffic. Most visitors and locals escape to the riverside, where a popular prome-
nade lined with a variety of pubs does brisk business summer and winter. Across
the river, Barnes is a peaceful backwater, now blessed with its very own waterfowl sanctuary at the **Wetland Centre**, while a walk back downstream towards
Fulham takes in the little town of Putney.*

History

By the 14th century, small riverside settlements such as Fulham,
Hammersmith and Putney were common features along the banks of the
Thames. Further inland, isolated hamlets such as Parsons Green, Walham
Green and Earl's Court were surrounded by fields, market gardens and nurs-
eries. Fulham Palace, on the river's edge, was the residence for Bishops of
London from 704 to 1973, and it is thought that the huge moat (it was finally
filled in 1921) followed the line of a Roman defensive earthwork.

Putney, where there was also once a Roman settlement and maybe even a
bridge, was a riverside village concentrated on fishing and farming. Under the
Tudors, it became a popular site for Tudor mansions (Thomas Cromwell,
chief architect of the Dissolution of the Monasteries, lived here), and a
wooden bridge was built in 1729 (from which Mary Wollstonecraft threw
herself in an attempt to commit suicide) for the Fulham Road and the busy
coaching route to Portsmouth and the southwest.

By the 18th century, traffic was busy enough for highwaymen to patrol the
heath and several further houses had been built as merchants sought out purer
air than the City offered. Hurlingham House (it didn't turn to sports until the
mid-1860s, when pigeon shooting, skittles, croquet and polo were introduced), Brandenburgh House (with a theatre in the grounds), Chiswick and
Sandford Manor House were among the grander residences.

In Hammersmith the Lower Mall, Upper Mall (William Morris lived and
died here) and Hammersmith Terrace were fashionable riverside addresses,
commanding privileged views of the Thames Regatta, and London's first suspension bridge opened at Hammersmith in 1827. At Parson's Green the
grand houses surrounding the green were inhabited by 'Gentry and Persons
of Quality'. Walham Green, later to become part of Fulham Broadway,
housed a green, pond and whipping post, but was yet to earn a church.

Expansion continued sporadically until after the mid-19th century (both
Fulham and Hammersmith were still renowned for their spinach and strawberries in the 1840s) when the tide of expansion from Kensington finally swallowed up the area. Now a range of industries, from distilleries to mills to
boatyards was being established. The Fulham Hospital opened to serve the
workhouses, and Irish labourers drawn by the railways moved into cottages
set on boggy land around Brook Green. Shops opened along Putney High
Street, and the tentacles of housing spread into Fulham, such that it became 'a
portion of the outer fringe of the great city'.

Over the last century Fulham has become increasingly fashionable, while
Hammersmith has suffered somewhat from road building programmes such
as the flyover and Great West Road. Putney has endured little rebuilding since
the Victorian and Edwardian era, and retains its popularity as a smart residential retreat.

West London

Fulham & Putney

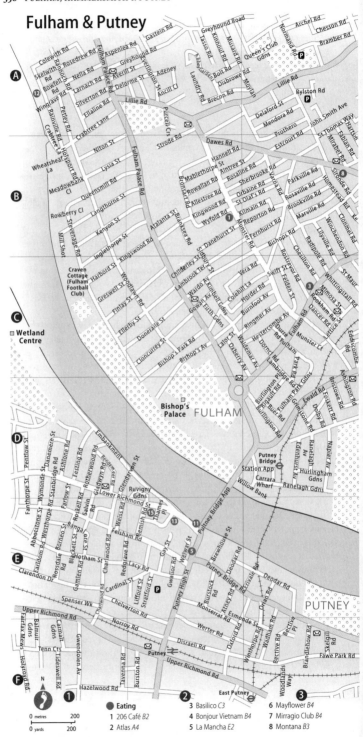

West London

● Eating
1 206 Café *B2*
2 Atlas *A4*

3 Basilico *C3*
4 Bonjour Vietnam *B4*
5 La Mancha *E2*

6 Mayflower *B4*
7 Mirragio Club *B4*
8 Montana *B3*

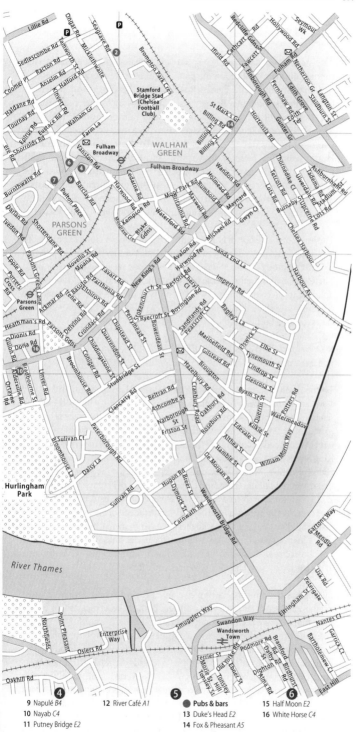

West London

Sights

Fulham is famous for its antique shops, especially along the Fulham Rd south of Fulham Broadway, while the New King's Rd boast a few just about affordable designer boutiques, superior off-licences & delicatessens

It's generally accepted that Chelsea ends and Fulham begins at the railway line running through West Brompton past Chelsea FC's Stamford Bridge football stadium, crossing first the Fulham Road and then the King's Road. Both roads head southwest for Putney Bridge roughly parallel to each other, but the difference between the two says a lot about Fulham's divided nature. The King's Road is the more polite, and its stretch as the New King's Road around Parsons Green is the most desirable part of the area. To the south on the river is the Hurlingham Club, a very exclusive private members' croquet and tennis club with beautiful gardens on the river bank. The Fulham Road on the other hand takes in Fulham Broadway, where the area's nightlife is concentrated, and then weaves for about a mile through row upon row of gentrified workers' cottages down to the river and Fulham's main visitor attraction: the Bishop's Palace.

Bishop's Palace The home of the Bishop of London until 1973, this doesn't look like much of a palace at all, but instead is a beautiful, early 16th-century diamond-patterned red-brick house with an 18th century bell-turret set in an attractive park. There's a small museum on the history of the area and guided tours of the building are given on Sundays twice a month in summer, once in winter. The riverside walk shaded with huge plane trees in Bishop's Park provides fine views towards Putney.

■ *Open Mar-Oct Wed-Sun 1400-1700, Nov-Feb Thu-Sun 1300-1600. Admission museum £1.50, guided tours £3, free under-16s. T020-7736 3233.*

Hammersmith To the northwest, up the Fulham Palace Road, Hammersmith and its arty associations have been badly mauled in the 20th century by road building schemes. First impressions on leaving the tube are that the place is one big roundabout. At the Hammersmith flyover the Cromwell Road becomes the Great West Road rushing out to Chiswick towards the M4 motorway. Scruffy King Street is the heart of the area, home to the Lyric Theatre and the Polish Cultural Centre. Most visitors quite sensibly head for the river though, and the strip of pubs lining Lower and Upper Malls west of Hammersmith Bridge.

A very pleasant walk leads all the way along the north bank of the river from here to pretty Chiswick Mall and beyond. Just to the east of the bridge are the **Riverside Studios** (see page 435), with their art gallery, cinema, theatre and TV studios. Closed to heavy traffic except buses, the bridge links Barnes to the rest of London. It crosses the river to the Wildfowl and Wetland's Trust Wetland Centre in the converted Barn Elms Water Works a mile to the south (see below).

Putney & Barnes Putney has the atmosphere of a riverside provincial town, while its quiet neighbour **Barnes** still feels like a village. Both make as pleasant an escape from traffic-choked central London as Hampstead in the north.

From Putney Bridge, a walk west along the south bank for about a mile along the Embankment, past Putney Boat House and the spooky old Harrod's repository looking across the river to Bishop's Park, leads eventually to the new **Wetland Centre** on Queen Elizabeth's Walk. Converted from four Victorian water-work reservoirs, the reed-filled ponds look surprisingly natural. After a look round the Discovery centre, with its AV displays on wetland habitats, visitors stroll around the perimeter of the 105-acre site, viewing the entire area and the waterbirds from a three-storey hide and also via hidden cameras dotted about the birds' feeding ground. ■ *Open daily summer 0930-1800 (last admission 1700), winter 0930-1700 (last admission 1600). Admission £6.75, under-16s £4. T020-8409 4400, www.wildfowlandwetlands.org.uk*

Eating and drinking

For some time now the celebrated TV chefs and cookery writers Ruth and Rosie have been wowing the 'new establishment' with their Tuscan recipes at the *River Café*, Thames Wharf, Rainville Rd, W6, T020-7381 8824. The restaurant was designed by Ruth's husband Richard Rogers, and it's airy and light, and so famous that it often needs to be booked a month in advance. The river views, if not perhaps the food, are better at *Putney Bridge*, The Embankment, SW15, T020-8780 1811, where very refined modern French food is served up in designer surroundings in a plum location.

Expensive
● *on map, page 356*

In Fulham, *Montana*, 125-129 Dawes Rd, SW6, T020-7385 9500, www.montana.plc.uk does southwestern American meat dishes in a mellow atmosphere created by low lighting and live jazz every night except Sun. Worth seeking out for the friendly service alone.

Close to the Riverside Studios, *The Gate*, 51 Queen Caroline St, W6, T020-8748 6932, is a rich and satisfying vegetarian treat in an old church building very popular with locals.

Mid-range

The Atlas, 16 Seagrave Rd, SW6, T020-7385 9129, is a vibrant and woody gastropub with an excellent daily changing Mediterranean menu, no bookings, tucked away behind the Earl's Court Exhibition Centre but reachable from Fulham Broadway.

Fulham Broadway itself provides a variety of options in this bracket, with the genuinely Italian and tiny little *Miraggio Club*, 510 Fulham Rd, SW6, T020-7384 3142, and also *Napulé*, 585 Fulham Rd, SW6, T020-7381 1122, www.book2eat.com, a very lively wood-fired pizzeria.

Opposite each other nearby are the superior Chinese cuisine at *Mayflower*, 488 Fulham Rd, SW6, T020-7386 0657, and the large, less formal, stack-em high Vietnamese *Zen Bonjour Vietnam*, 593-599 Fulham Rd, SW6, T020-7385 7603, www.bonjour-vietnam.co.uk, £14.50 per person for as much as you want to eat.

Some way from the action and considerably less expensive, very popular with BYOB Fulhamites, is the *206 Café*, 206 Munster Rd, SW6, a tiny Thai restaurant full of personality, not least that of its owner, Joy. At the southern end of the Fulham Rd, *Basilico*, 690 Fulham Rd, SW6, T020-7384 2633, www.basilico.freeserve.co.uk, is the place to look for top-quality but fairly expensive thin crust pizzas to eat in at tiny designer tables or to take away. *Nayab*, 309 New King's Rd, SW6, T020-7731 6993, in Parsons Green is an accomplished but not very cheap Punjabi restaurant that generally gets pretty busy around pub closing time.

In Putney, *La Mancha*, 32 Putney High St, SW15, T020-8780 1022, is a buzzing Spanish tapas bar and restaurant, a superior paella factory, open 7 days. Meanwhile in Hammersmith, *Lowiczanka*, 238-246 King St, W6, T020-8741 3225, is a friendly and traditional Polish café-restaurant on the first floor of the Polish Cultural Centre.

Cheap

In Fulham, the *Fox and Pheasant*, 1 Billing Rd, SW10, T020-7352 2943, is a straightforward old boozer near Chelsea FC that almost stands alone in the area against the tide of chain bars and ropey theme pubs. In Parsons Green, the *White Horse*, 1-3 Parsons Green, SW6, T020-7736 2115 (known by some as the 'Sloaney Pony'), is a heaving real ale pub right on the green with a small restaurant in the converted coach house at the back, the place to take the pulse of this increasingly wealthy area.

In Hammersmith, the friendliest and most cosy of the pubs on the strip along the river is the *Blue Anchor*, 13 Lower Mall, W6, T020-8748 5774. Further along, the most famous and often overcrowded is the *Dove*, 19 Upper Mall, W6, T020-8748 5405, while

Pubs & bars
There's a serious dearth of decent pubs or bars in Fulham.
▶▶ *Go to page 435 for entertainment & nightlife*

West London

the *Old Ship*, 25 Upper Mall, W6, T020-8748 2593, is the least pretentious and most family-friendly.

In Putney the best pub near (but not on) the river is the *Half Moon*, 93 Lower Richmond Rd, SW15, T020-8780 9383, where Young's ales are pumped amid antiques and bric-a-brac, and there's regular good live music. Overlooking the Thames, the *Duke's Head*, 8 Lower Richmond Rd, SW15, T020-8788 2552, is a huge party pub that does reasonable food at lunch and dinner. *The Putney Bridge*, Embankment, 2 Lower Richmond Rd, SW15, T020-8780 1811, also has river views, an expensive designer bar attached to the French restaurant (see above).

Transport

Buses **No 9** between Hammersmith and Trafalgar Square via Kensington, Knightsbridge, Hyde Park Corner and Piccadilly Circus.
No 10 between Hammersmith and King's Cross via Kensington, Knightsbridge, Hyde Park Corner, Marble Arch, Oxford Circus and Euston.
No 11 between Fulham Broadway and Liverpool St via Chelsea, Sloane Square, Victoria, Westminster, Trafalgar Square, Strand, Aldwych, Fleet St, St Paul's and Bank.
No 14 between Putney and Tottenham Court Rd tube station via Putney, Fulham Broadway, South Kensington, Knightsbridge, Hyde Park Corner and Piccadilly Circus.
No 28 between Notting Hill Gate and Fulham Broadway via Kensington High St.
No 33 from Hammersmith to Richmond via Barnes.
No 74 between Baker St and Putney via Marble Arch, Hyde Park Corner, Knightsbridge, South Kensington, Earl's Court, Lillie Rd and Fulham Cross.
No 190 between West Brompton and Richmond via Lillie Rd, Charing Cross Hospital, Hammersmith, Chiswick and Chiswick Bridge.
No 209 between Hammersmith and Mortlake via Barnes.
No 211 between Hammersmith and Waterloo via Fulham Broadway, Chelsea, Sloane Square, Victoria and Westminster.
No 283 from Barnes to Hammersmith.
No 295 between Hammersmith and Clapham Junction via Fulham Broadway.
No 391 between Fulham Broadway and Richmond via Hammermsith, Chiswick and Kew Gardens tube station.

River transport Summer only: Westminster to Hampton Court via Putney, Kew and Richmond at 1030, 1115 and 1200 taking 3½ hrs. Also from Westminster to Kew via Putney at 1015, 1100, 1400, 1430 taking 1½ hrs. Phone to check times and prices (about £12 Westminster-Hampton Court return). T020-7930 2062.

Taxis Usually plenty on the New King's Rd, around Hammersmith and crossing Putney Bridge.

Trains Putney or Barnes (from Clapham Junction, Victoria, Waterloo).

Tubes Fulham Broadway or Parsons Green (District line – Wimbledon branch), Putney Bridge or East Putney (District line – Wimbledon branch), Hammersmith (Piccadilly, Hammersmith and City lines, District line – Richmond, Ealing Broadway branches)

Directory

Internet cafés *E hello!, 645 Fulham Rd, SW6, T020-7736 2344, www.gohello.co.uk, is a clean new internet café with 36 terminals, open 0900-2400 daily, £1 for 15*

mins, with a good range of simple Cal-Ital snacks to enjoy as you surf.
Sports *Fulham FC, Craven Cottage, Stevenage Rd, SW6, T020-7893 8383.*

South London

8

South London

Brixton, Battersea and Clapham

In the long-established rivalry between north and south London, the south often comes off worst. It's not just that much of it is off the tube network (in fact the overland rail services are often quicker and more efficient anyway), or because the south is generally poorer (Dulwich boasts house prices to match Hampstead's, and Clapham is hardly less expensive than Camden), it's because the people that live here couldn't care less about the perceived second-class status of their local areas.

*Broader and more expansive than the north, the south is generally more at ease with itself. The stereotype of the 'sarf' London wideboy always on the make is just that: a stereotype probably dreamed up in some painfully socially aware north Londoner's cramped designer apartment. That said, the south's laid-back attitude can also translate into some of the city's wilder and more dangerous corners. The drug-fuelled 80s club craze was passionately embraced from the Elephant and Castle to Brixton and beyond. And much of the spirit of those years lives on in the vibrant pubs, bars and clubs of SW4, 8, 9 and 11. Apart from the **Dulwich Picture Gallery** and the **Horniman Museum**, south London does not boast many extraordinary sights. The best reason for taking a trip to Battersea, Brixton or Clapham is to enjoy some slices of 'real' London life: the clubs, venues, market and bars of multicultural Brixton; the restaurants, riverside park and cutting-edge live arts centre at Battersea; the wide common, cafés and pubs of Clapham and the quaint village atmosphere of Dulwich.*

Tube stations at Brixton, Clapham North, Clapham Common, Clapham South & Stockwell. Battersea is best reached by bus via Chelsea or by train from Victoria to Battersea Park or Clapham Junction, or by train from Waterloo to Clapham Junction

South London

History

Apart from developments closer to the City, such as Southwark, and along the river's bank such as Putney, little of South London had developed by 1800. The Falcon Brook ran between Clapham and Wandsworth Commons to spill into the Thames at Battersea, a virtual island in the marshland. The River Effra rose at Norwood, passed through Dulwich and Brixton to the Thames at Lambeth. Saxon settlements – Badric's Isle (Battersea), Osgod Clapha (Clapham), 'Dile-wisc' ('the meadow where dill grew', Dulwich), and Brixistane (Brixton) – grew up around the rivers, but they grew slowly over the ensuing centuries. Each settlement had a common for water, fuel, grazing livestock (there were still sheep on Clapham Common in 1903) and fairs and meetings, and further afield, undulating farmland spread to a caravan of gypsies living on the hill to the south.

In 1619 the College of God's Gift at Dulwich (Dulwich College) was founded by the new lord of the manor, Edward Alleyn, a Shakespearian actor and bear-baiter. Although the village remained a relative backwater for the rest of the century, the fashionable spa at Dulwich Wells, the school and the rural setting saw the village grow.

Hotels in the area

B *Windmill on the Common*
C *Lavender Guest House*
C *Beltwood*
C *Dudley Hotel*
D *Compass Travelodge Battersea*
D *Barclay Court Hotel*
D *Dufort Guest House*
D *The Abbeville*
▸▸ **Go to page 451**

South London

For much of the 17th century, Clapham remained a wild and marshy tract, whose common was patrolled by highwaymen such as Robert Forrestor (dressed in drag), and prostitutes (presumably not in drag). Following the exodus here to escape the Great Plague and Fire in the 1660s, however, the village grew so much that by 1690 there was a stagecoach service to Gracechurch Street in the City. Captain Cook is reputed to have lived in the imposing Georgian mansions on the north side, dubbing his balcony the 'quarterdeck', but the area is better known as the home to the Clapham Sect. The evangelical group, or 'The Saints', which included the MP William Wilberforce, were instrumental in the fight for the

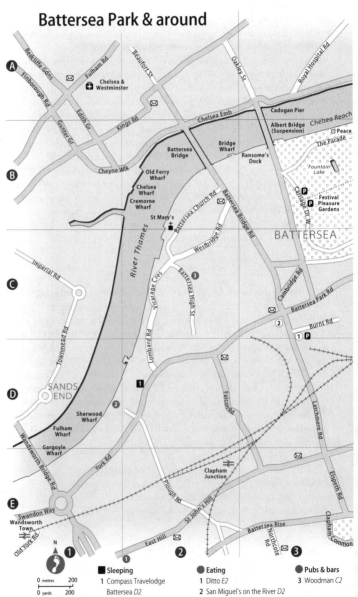

Battersea Park & around

■ **Sleeping**
1 Compass Travelodge
   Battersea D2

● **Eating**
1 Ditto E2
2 San Miguel's on the River D2

● **Pubs & bars**
3 Woodman C2

0 metres 200
0 yards 200

abolition of slavery. Their place of prayer was Holy Trinity Church, and their 'African Academy' gave a home to 25 black children brought from Jamaica.

Sparked by the railways, Brixton and Battersea grew in the 19th century. Clapham Junction opened in 1863, and candle, glucose and glove factories and gas works were established in Battersea (the Power Station wasn't built until 1937). Workers moved into cottages on the Shaftesbury Park estate and went drinking in the *Red House* tavern, singing in the music halls near Clapham Junction or pigeon-flying in Battersea Park where, after 1896, the new craze of bicycling took off.

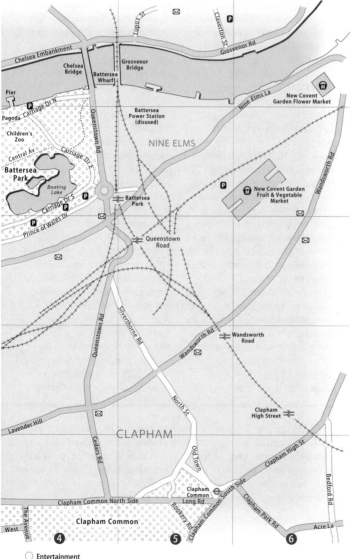

○ **Entertainment**
1 Latchmere Leisure Centre *C3*   2 The Grace Theatre,
                                        Latchmere Pub *C3*

Destination Dulwich

Okay, so it may not sound the most enticing of London's longer-haul destinations. Apart from its name – pronounced 'dullitch' – Dulwich's quaint village atmosphere has been enlivened by Tom and Nicole in happier times, and by Margaret Thatcher in retirement, and its little old Picture Gallery has received a glassy designer face-lift courtesy of superfashionable architect Rick Mather.

*The **Dulwich Picture Gallery** claims to be the first purpose-built public art gallery in the world, specially designed by Sir John Soane and opened to the public in 1817. A neo-classical temple to Old Masters, it stands in peaceful gardens next to the house of Edward Alleyn, Christopher Marlowe's flamboyant manager, on the site of the original Dulwich College (relocated in the 19th century to much grander premises nearby). Inside, beneath elegant arches and restored roof lanterns, and above some rare antique furniture, hangs a small treasury of English, Italian, Spanish, French and Dutch paintings from the 17th and 18th centuries – by the likes of **Gainsborough, Rembrandt, Van Dyck, Canaletto** and **Watteau**. (Dulwich Picture Gallery, T020-8693 5254, www.dulwichpicturegallery.org.uk open Tuesday-Friday 1000-1700, Saturday and Sunday 1000-1700. Admission £4, £3 concession, free on Fridays; extra charge for special exhibitions).*

*The problem is getting there. North Dulwich train station (three trians every hour from London Bridge) is a 10-minute walk through the village, while West Dulwich station (twice an hour from Victoria) is also a 10-minute walk away. Much easier, slower, and passing through the parts of London that most tourists never reach, is to take a ride on the top deck of the **No 12** from the West End. Hop aboard on Oxford Street, Regent Street, at Piccadilly Circus or Trafalgar Square, and about an hour later you'll be on Lordship Lane, a five-minute walk across Dulwich Park from the gallery. On the way, the bus rattles past some of the best and worst south London has to offer.*

Down Whitehall, past Parliament Square, Big Ben and the London Eye, the bus grinds beneath the snaking blue pipes and glass canopy of Waterloo International and then enters south London proper at Lambeth North. Other traffic melts away as the clapped-out old Routemaster shows a dangerous turn of speed approaching the obelisk in St George's Circus that marks an exact mile from the City, Fleet Street and Westminster.

*Next comes the Elephant and Castle, home to the Ministry of Sound and a strange multi-faceted silver box in the middle of one of the busiest road junctions in the city. Hard to find much reason to hop off here, although Pizzeria Castello at the top of the Walworth Road has an excellent reputation. Grim housing estates line the road on the left, before the bus shudders to a halt outside the **Cuming***

Electric Avenue in Brixton became one of the first electrically lit streets in the 1880s, as the market spread under the railway arches, and its houses converted to lodgings. After the Second World War, West Indian immigrants settled in Brixton, particularly in Somerleyton and Railton Roads. A generation later, economic decline and simmering racial tensions boiled up into riots against the police in 1981, 1985 and 1995.

Museum: 'The Health of the People is the Highest Law' reads the inscription on a building that houses a bizarre collection of objects from round the world gathered together by archeaologist Henry Cuming about a hundred years ago. His study has been reconstructed, including ranks of drawers that can be opened to reveal peculiar things from the anthropological Lovett collection of superstitious charms and totems. (Cuming Museum, 155 Walworth Road, SE17, T020-7701 1342, www. southwark.gov.uk Open Tuesday-Saturday 1000-1700, admission free).

Rumbling on past the lively East Street Market and Burgess Park on the left, with its multicultural gardens in the old Chumleigh Street Almshouses (T020-7525 1050), the bus pulls into Camberwell Green. Here the Red Star Bar is the funkiest of several in an area that is becoming more and more popular with nightlife party-goers. Past Southwark Town Hall, the South London Art Gallery and the Camberwell College of Art, the route then sways through Peckham. On the left the bright new Library has won architectural awards, famously 'the building with the beret', and has become the focus of some much needed investment in one of Southwark's most notorious districts.

Slow progress is made down Rye Lane, the unofficial High Street, packed with bargain-basement and fly-by-night shops, before reaching Peckham Rye, where **William Blake** conversed with angels and Muriel Spark set her seminal novel. Along the edge of the wide park, the bus then swings right at the Clockhouse Pub, a timely and convivial place, to fly up tree-lined Barry Road straight uphill towards the distant spire of the Christchurch United Reform – quite an experience in itself. At the top, on Lordship Lane, Eynella Road leads past Dulwich Library to the gates of the park where a right fork heads for the Gallery. Alternatively, catch a No 312 bus from Barry Road for the short hop to the **Horniman Museum**, one of the more eccentric museums in London and a lot of fun for kids. A new permanent exhibition on Africa opens here in May 2001, along with a refurbished aquarium and natural history gallery. The gardens give panoramic views over London and contain a small zoo of wallabies, turkeys, goats and guinea pigs while the museum's extensive collection of strange musical instruments will be on display again in new galleries come Autumn 2002. (100 London Road, SE23, T020-8699 1872, www.horniman.demon.co.uk Closed until 30 April 30 2001, then open 1030-1730 Monday-Saturday, 1400-1730 Sunday throughout. Admission free). Return via Forest Hill Station to London Bridge. Either way, as long as you've kept your wits about you, and the bus hasn't broken down, been diverted, or worse, been 'steamed' by local teenagers, you'll have seen south London in all its contradictory chaos, squalor and splendour.

South London

Sights

Battersea

Just south of Chelsea Bridge, **Battersea Power Station** is one of London's best-known modern landmarks, its four towers unmistakeable when approaching Battersea from the north. Closed in 1983, the shell remains as a testament to industrial modernization and increasing environmental awareness, though only as a result of long-standing indecision over what should happen to the site. The latest plans once again include a multi-use development involving shops, cinemas, and affordable homes.

Battersea Park
Sports facilities include an all-weather pitch (T020-8871 7535), tennis courts T020-8871 7542) & running track (T020-8871 7537)

Across the Queenstown Road, along the south bank of the river between the Chelsea and Albert bridges, lies Battersea Park, complete with adventure playgrounds, sports facilities (see below), a children's zoo, a beautiful boating lake, and modern art museum in the **Pump House** (T020-73500523). Queen Victoria's gift remains a focal point of the borough. The riverside **Peace Pagoda**, donated by Japanese monks in 1985, and the **Festival Gardens** are of special

South London

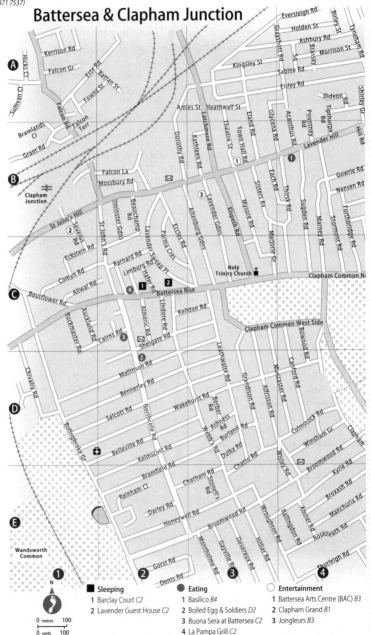

Battersea & Clapham Junction

Sleeping	Eating	Entertainment
1 Barclay Court *C2*	1 Basilico *B4*	1 Battersea Arts Centre (BAC) *B3*
2 Lavender Guest House *C2*	2 Boiled Egg & Soldiers *D2*	2 Clapham Grand *B1*
	3 Buona Sera at Battersea *C2*	3 Jongleurs *B3*
	4 La Pampa Grill *C2*	

0 metres 100
0 yards 100

N

interest. A major restoration project is currently underway, refurbishing the Victorian lakeside areas, sub-tropical gardens, rosery garden and the riverside promenade. The Festival Gardens, with their Italianate terrace, and the designer Russell Page's old English Flower Garden, laid out for the 1951 Festival of Britain, are also receiving attention. Work is due to be completed by early 2003.

■ *Open 0800-dusk. T020-8871 7530.*

A 20-minute walk west from the park is the riverside **St Mary's Church**, Battersea Church Road, SW11. Dating from 1775, this old church is where William Blake was married, and Turner sat to sketch the river from the vestry window. Turner's favourite chair is exhibited in the chancel. ■ *Jun-Sep Tue, Wed 1100-1500; all other times by appointment; T020-7228 9648.*

Clapham

Clapham Common is a picturesque stretch of commonly owned land which makes a pleasant walking ground at weekends when families and footballers are usually out in force. The long terrace of Georgian townhouses on the north side dates from around 1720 and includes the former residences of Captain Cook and Charles Barry (architect of the Houses of Parliament).

Holy Trinity Church, Clapham Common North Side, SW4, T020-7627 0941, was originally built in 1776 and partially rebuilt after The Second World War. Holy Trinity is the former headquarters of the zealously Anglican 'Clapham Sect' led by notable anti-slavery campaigner William Wilberforce. The fountain on the common donated by the local temperance society is an appropriately dry testament to their local influence.

Brixton

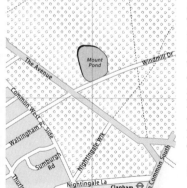

Electric Avenue was one of the first streets in London to be supplied with electricity, and is nowadays the pulsating centre of ethnic Brixton. Dingy and verging on the dilapidated, the energy which emanates

South London

from **Brixton Market** (see below) represents the heart of this lively multicultural town at its effervescent best.

Nearby is the **Black Cultural Archives**, 378 Coldharbour Lane, SW9. Frequent exhibitions and with an interesting shop, the Archives is a good information point on black issues and a mouthpiece for Brixton's strong Afro-Caribbean cultural awareness. ■ *Mon-Sat 1000-1900. Admission free. T020-7738 4591.*

Clapham

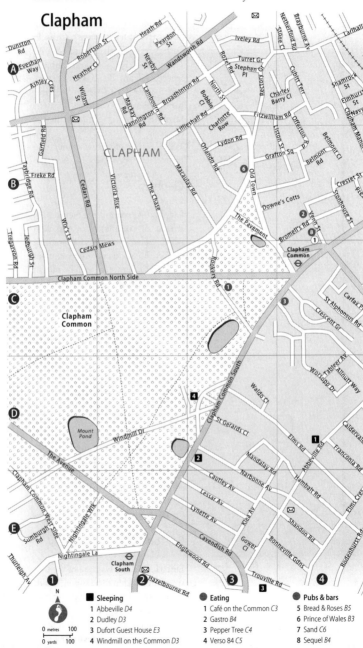

■ Sleeping
1 Abbeville *D4*
2 Dudley *D3*
3 Dufort Guest House *E3*
4 Windmill on the Common *D3*

● Eating
1 Café on the Common *C3*
2 Gastro *B4*
3 Pepper Tree *C4*
4 Verso 84 *C5*

● Pubs & bars
5 Bread & Roses *B5*
6 Prince of Wales *B3*
7 Sand *C6*
8 Sequel *B4*

0 metres 100
0 yards 100

Photofusion, 17a Electric Lane, SW9, have an extensive library of photos documenting contemporary British life with an emphasis on social issues. The facilities are for members only, but the galleries of regularly changing exhibitions are open to the public. Photofusion also holds film nights at the Ritzy Cinema (see page 436).

■ *Open Tue, Thu, Fri 1000-1800; Wed 1000-2000; Sat 1100-1700. Admission free; www.photofusion.org*

A short walk up Brixton Hill is the **Brixton Windmill**, Blenheim Gardens, a 19th-century windmill that's perhaps the last thing you'd expect to see in the down-trodden urban environs of South London. Ramshackle and forlorn, it diverts attention from the surrounding social decay and the dreadful prison next door; it's worth a visit for the juxtaposition alone.

East of here, on Dulwich Road, is **Brockwell Park**, with its lido (see page 376), hilltop café and walled lakeside garden giving wide views over London.

Eating and drinking

Situated in the trendy restaurant strip leading off Clapham Common, *La Pampa Grill*, 60 Battersea Rise, SW11, T020-7924 4774, is a living shrine to all things steak. Vibrant and atmospheric, it boasts a good list of Argentinean wines and 101 uses for sizzling red meat. A little further afield, towards Wandsworth, is *Ditto*, East Hill, SW18, T020-8877 0110, a lively modern European gallery-bar restaurant with a comfortable sofa area.

In Brixton, at *Helter Skelter*, 50 Atlantic Rd, SW9, T020-7274 8600, a wide variety of dishes cooked to perfection, combined with friendly staff and efficient service make this international restaurant a world-beater; Brixton's best, so booking is essential. In the market is the pizzeria *Eco*, 4 Market Row, Brixton Market, Electric Lane, SW9, T020-7738 3021 (and also at Clapham, 182 Clapham High St, SW4, T020-7978 1108), these are more pre-night-out kind of places than a secluded dinner venue, but this small chain provides decent pizza and pasta at a reasonable rate.

Back in Clapham, *Gastro*, 67 Venn St, SW4, T020-7627 0222, is indeed a rare

Mid-range
● *on maps, pages 364, 368, 370 & 372*

South London

Entertainment
1 Clapham Picture House *B4*
2 Upstairs at the Landor *B6*

breed – unabashedly Gallic yet wonderfully uncontrived. The prices verge on the expensive, though the French provincial food is generally of a very high standard and the lively atmosphere itself merits the extra cost.

Cheap **In Battersea**, *Buona Sera at Battersea*, 226 Northcote Rd, T020-7228 9925, do pizza, pasta and a full Italian country menu served up in an unfussy way at marble tables. Nothing fancy. *Basilico*, 175 Lavender Hill, SW11, T020-7924 4070, is another pizzeria, more expensive but decidedly upmarket flatbreads baked in wood-fired ovens. At *San Miguel's on the River*, Molasses House, Plantation Wharf, Battersea Reach, SW11, T020-7801 9696, though the menu is relatively ordinary, the tapas on offers are well presented and low in price. Panoramic views of the river add value and there's also a much more expensive restaurant menu for those who want to splash out.

Brixton

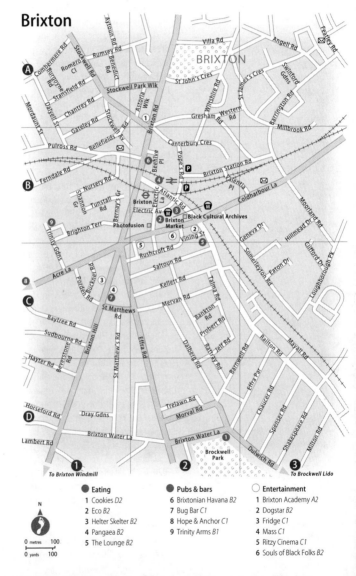

● Eating	● Pubs & bars	○ Entertainment
1 Cookies *D2*	6 Brixtonian Havana *B2*	1 Brixton Academy *A2*
2 Eco *B2*	7 Bug Bar *C1*	2 Dogstar *B2*
3 Helter Skelter *B2*	8 Hope & Anchor *C1*	3 Fridge *C1*
4 Pangaea *B2*	9 Trinity Arms *B1*	4 Mass *C1*
5 The Lounge *B2*		5 Ritzy Cinema *C1*
		6 Souls of Black Folks *B2*

In **Brixton**, *Pangaea*, 15 Atlantic Rd, SW9, T020-7737 6777, is more authentic than *Eco* and has lower prices, an Italian dinner destination par excellence. Colourful and friendly with a good range of pizzas, definitely worth a visit.

In **Clapham**, *Pepper Tree*, 19 Clapham Common Southside, SW4, T020-7622 1758, has long communal benches and tables ensuring an intimate experience in this busy Thai den. Bargain prices for some excellent Thai cooking. *Verso 84*, 84 Clapham Park Rd, SW4, T020-7720 1515, is a tremendous Neapolitan pizzeria with a delightfully laid-back atmosphere.

Five of the best: pubs in South London

★

- *Clockhouse*, Barry Road, Peckham.
- *Bread and Roses*, Clapham Manor Street, Clapham.
- *Hope and Anchor*, Acre Lane, Brixton.
- *Prince of Wales*, Clapham Old Town, Clapham.
- *Woodman*, Battersea High Street, Battersea.

In **Clapham**, *Café on the Common*, 2 Rookery Rd, SW4 (daily 1000-1800), T020-7498 0770, is a seemingly ramshackle café in the middle of Clapham Common serving amazingly good food, from standard café fare to almost gastronomic heights. There's precious little seating inside, so either wrap up warm or come on a summer's day and enjoy the scenery. *Boiled Egg & Soldiers*, 63 Northcote Rd, SW11 (Mon-Sat 0900-1800; Sun 1000-1700), T020-7223 4894, is a small family establishment offering spruced up traditional café fare. Kids abound unimpeded, so perhaps not the best place for a quiet snack, but otherwise a warm, clean and friendly local. And yes, boiled egg and soldiers are a speciality. Directly opposite is a more down-to-earth, good old greasy spoon where you can pile on the cholesterol while scanning the Sunday papers.

In **Brixton**, *The Lounge*, 88 Atlantic Rd, SW9 (Mon-Fri 0800-1800; Sat, Sun 0800-2200), T020-7733 5229, is small and laid back, with a wide and varied menu, newspapers and a couple of computers with net access for patrons' use. Don't get too comfortable though, because it's an easy place in which to lose the day. Not far away, *Cookies*, Brixton Water Lane, SW2 (daily 0900-1800), T020-7642 0380, is a relatively new addition to Brixton café culture, with a good selection of coffees and snacks, exhibitions, and plans are afoot to add a couple of internet terminals here too.

Cafés & sandwich bars

The Woodman, 60 Battersea High St, SW11, T020-7228 2968, is a fine creaking old-fashioned boozer with a cracking selection of ales, real and otherwise. Thankfully the food is not the usual bar-room stodge, the kitchen carrying off an interesting menu well. A place to sit back and watch the footy.

Although primarily a restaurant, at *Sequel*, 75 Venn St, SW4 (Mon-Fri 1700-2300; Sat 1100-1600, 1730-2300; Sun 1200-1730, 1800-2230), T020-7622 4222, next door to the Clapham Picture House, there's often room to sneak in for a shifty cocktail or two in this classy bar. Great for both a peaceful pre-movie concoction and pensive post-picture ruminations.

Sand, 156 Clapham Park Rd, SW4 (Mon-Fri 1700-0300; Sat 1200-0200; Sun 1200-0100), T020-7622 3022, is a curious but classy bar/restaurant with comfy sofas and softly lit intimate little booths. Good wine served by the glass and flashy cocktails at relatively decent prices combined with elegant décor.

Pick of the bunch though, *Bread and Roses*, 68 Clapham Manor St, SW4 (Mon-Sat 1100-2300; Sun 1200-10:30), T020-7498 1779, must be one of the finest pubs in the south, if not the whole of London. A Workers' Beer Company co-operative in the middle of bourgeois Clapham, it plays host to poetry, comedy and music, though it's best sampled on a Sunday when the Mwalimu Express, showcasing the music of a different African country each week, rolls into town with accompanying buffet.

Pubs & bars
▶▶ *Go to page 436 for entertainment & nightlife*

Clapham is packed with pubs & bars

South London

For an eccentric pint head for Clapham Old Town and seek out the *Prince of Wales*, 38 Clapham Old Town, SW4, a small low-lit snug full of bizarre bric-a-brac.

In Brixton, *Brixtonian Havana*, Beehive Place, SW9 (Tue, Wed 1200-0100; Thu-Sat 1200-0200), T020-7924 9262, is tucked away near the market, serving cracking cocktails (including the infamous 'Brixton Riot') and the largest range of rum this side of the Antilles. Its stylish mock-colonial interior can get a little too busy for its own good at weekends, but it's well worth investigating.

Camberwell, Brixton & Dulwich

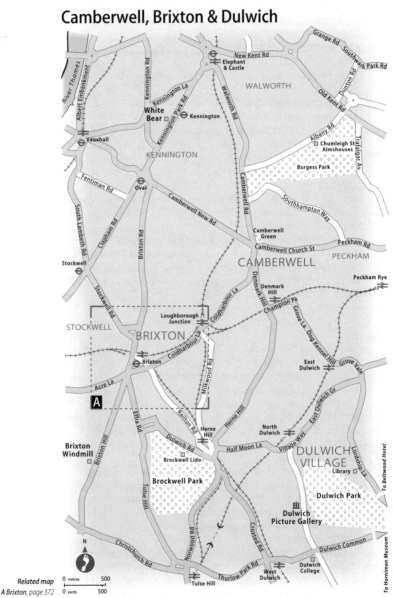

Related map
A Brixton, page 372

0 metres 500
0 yards 500

Beneath the massive church opposite the Town Hall and the Fridge Club lurks the *Bug Bar*, The Crypt, St Matthew's Church, SW2 (Mon-Wed 1900-0100; Thu 1900-0200; Fri, Sat 1900-0300; Sun 2000-0100), T020-7738 3184. The cavernous depths of St Matthew's crypt make a loud and lively starting point for a night on the town. The prevailing atmosphere is appropriately dance-driven and dangerous with seating provided by a few sofas and old oak pews, the only major downside being the admission charge after 2100 at weekends.

The *Hope and Anchor*, 123 Acre Lane, SW2 (Mon-Sat 1100-2300; Sun 1200-2230), T020-7274 1787, is a standard and friendly pub with large and elaborately ornamented garden and an non-age specific clientele. Good beer, warm atmosphere and the best roast dinner in Brixton. Nearby, tucked away in Trinity Gardens, *The Trinity Arms*, T020-7274 4544, is a cosy little local with a garden pulling fine pints of Young's.

Shopping

Brixton Market, Electric Ave, Pope's Road, Brixton Station Rd, SW9 (Mon, Tue, Thu-Sat 0800-1800; Wed 0800-1500) is a melting pot of Afro-Caribbean food, fresh fish, clothes, wigs, bric-a-brac, reggae and religion. A surprising and wide-eyed shopping trip is guaranteed, with the streets around good for second-hand clothing bargains. *Bookmongers*, 439 Coldharbour Lane, SW9 (Mon-Sat 1030-1830), T020-7738 4225, is a well-arranged and comprehensive second-hand bookshop, also selling remainders and slightly damaged new copies. *Souls of Black Folks*, 407 Coldharbour Lane, SW9 (Mon-Thu, Sun 1000-2300; Fri-Sat 1000-0200), T020-7738 4141, is an intriguing second-hand bookshop devoted solely to black issues. Worth visiting for the café cocooned amidst the bookshelves which hosts readings, comedy and other events.

In Clapham, *Change of Habit*, 65 Abbeville Rd, SW4 (Mon-Fri 1200-1800; Sat 1030-1730; Apr-end Aug, Sun 1000-1600), T020-8675 9474, is a dress agency offering a number of designer bargains.The *Old Post Office Bakery*, 74 Landor Rd, SW9, is a venerable organic bakery. Get there fast at lunchtime because its popularity is entirely justified.

In Battersea, the name of the *Hive Honey Shop*, 93 Northcote Rd, SW11 (Mon-Fri 1000-1700; Sat 1000-1800), T020-7924 6233, says it all – honey shampoo, soap, health products, herbal treatments, pots and tableware – as well as a living and working beehive.

Transport

From Clapham Common: Buses
No 37 to Putney via Clapham Junction and Wandsworth.
No 88 to Oxford Circus via Stockwell, Vauxhall, Tate Britian, Westminster, Trafalgar Square and Piccadilly Circus.
No 137 to Oxford Circus, via Battersea Park, Chelsea Bridge, Sloane Square, Knightsbridge, Hyde Park Corner and Marble Arch.
No 155 to Stockwell.
No 255 to Streatham.
No 355 to Brixton.
No 417 to Crystal Palace, via Streatham Hill.

From Brixton:
No 3 to Oxford Circus via Kennington, Lambeth Bridge, Westminster, Trafalgar Square and Piccadilly Circus.
No 37 to Putney, via Clapham Common, Clapham Junction and Wandsworth.
No 59 to Euston Kennington, Waterloo, Aldwych, Kingsway and Russell Square.
No 133 to Liverpool St via Kennington, Elephant, London Bridge and Bank .
No 159 to Marble Arch, via Westminster Bridge, Trafalgar Square and Oxford Circus.

South London

From Clapham Junction:
No 35 to Shoreditch, via Brixton, London Bridge, Monument, and Liverpool St.
No 39 to Putney Bridge, via Wandsworth, Southfields and Putney Heath.
No 49 to Shepherd's Bush, via Battersea, Chelsea, South Kensington, and Kensington.
No 77 to Tooting Broadway via Earlsfield.
No 156 to Wimbledon, via Wandsworth and Southfields.
No 295 between Ladbroke Grove and Clapham Junction.
No 319 between Sloane Square and Clapham Junction, via Chelsea and Battersea.
No 345 between South Kensington and Peckham, via Battersea, Clapham Junction, Clapham, Stockwell, Brixton and Camberwell.
No 344 to Liverpool St, via Battersea, Vauxhall, Southwark Bridge, and Monument.
No C3 between Clapham Junction and Earl's Court.

Taxis Notoriously difficult to find although Clapham and Battersea do get to see the occasional black cab. Only take a local minicab from a reputable office.

Trains Battersea Park, Queenstown Rd Battersea, Clapham Junction, Clapham High St, Brixton.

Tubes Brixton (Victoria line), Clapham North, Clapham Common and Clapham South (Northern line), Stockwell (Northern and Victoria lines). Battersea is best reached by bus via Chelsea or by train from Victoria to Battersea Park or Clapham Junction, or by train from Waterloo to Clapham Junction

Sports facilities

Latchmere Leisure Centre, Burns Rd, Battersea, SW11, T020-7207 8004. Swimming pool: Mon-Thu, Sun 0700-2130; Fri 0700-1800; Sat 0700-1930; £2.60 peak for adult non-members, £2.40 off-peak. Gym: Mon-Thu 0700-2230; Fri, Sun 0700-1000; Sat 0700-2000; £5.90 per session for non-members. Sports Hall also available for hire.
Brixton Recreation Centre, 27 Station Rd, SW9, T020-7926 9779. Saunas, swimming pool, indoor tennis and basketball, badminton and even an indoor bowling green.
Battersea Park, Albert Bridge Rd, SW11, T020-8871 7542. Tennis: weekdays 0800-2200; weekends 0800-2000; £4.70 per hour peak; £3.40 per hour off-peak (before 1800 on weekdays). Athletics: weekdays 0730-2200; weekends 0730-1930; £1.70 for adults.
Foster's Oval, Surrey County Cricket Club's home ground, T020-7582 7764.
Brockwell Lido, Brockwell Park, Dulwich, SE24. Open-air swimming summer only: 0645-1000, 1200-1900, early morning £1.50, all day £4. Yoga and meditation all

year. Poolside café. Theatre and art events. T020-274 3088.
Streatham Mega Bowl, 142 Streatham Hill, SW2, T020-8671 5021. Open 1000-2300, Sun, Mon, Tue-Sat 1000-0130. 36 bowling lanes, biggest in Europe, £4.75 adults, £3.75 under-16s per game including shoe hire. Burger King and two bars. Booking advisable for weekends.
Streatham Ice Rink, 386 Streatham High Rd, SW16, T020-8769 7771. Open 1930-2200 Mon-Fri, 2000-2300 Sat. £6.50 including skates, last ticket sold one hour before closing. Large old local rink with a basic café.
Catford Stadium, Ardenmore Rd, SE, T020-8690 8000. Greyhound racing every Thu at 1920 until after 1000.
Crystal Palace National Sports Centre, Leddrington Rd, Upper Norwood, SE19, T020-8778 0131. One of the largest sports centres in the UK with 50-m swimming pool, gym, tennis, squash, badminton, boxing events, running tracks. www.crystalpalace.co.uk Crystal Palace train station.

Up and down the river

9

Up and down the river

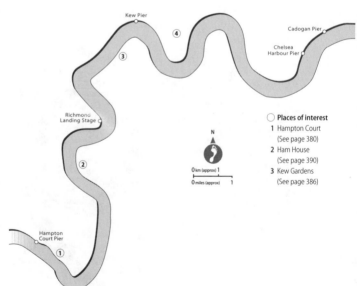

Kew Pier

④

③

Cadogan Pier

Chelsea
Harbour Pier

Richmond
Landing Stage

②

N

0 km (approx)   1
0 miles (approx)   1

Hampton
Court Pier

①

○ **Places of interest**
1 Hampton Court
   (See page 380)
2 Ham House
   (See page 390)
3 Kew Gardens
   (See page 386)

Up and down the river

Going with the flow from the 15th-century Royal palace at Hampton Court downstream to the Barrier, the river describes the course of the city's development from a unique perspective at the centre of things. Beyond Teddington Lock, the river's tidal limit, well-wooded banks give way to acres of parkland setting off the 17th and 18th century houses of the aristocracy at Ham, Marble Hill and Syon Park. Past the attractive old town of Richmond, and rounding the bend at the Royal Botanical Gardens, Kew, the Thames meanders through flowery and pros-perous Chiswick before hitting the urban environment proper at Hammersmith. On the south side here though Barnes still looks like a provincial village, just before the regular rows of old working class terraces in Fulham with their backs to the river and the huge 19th-century pile of the old Harrod's repository across the water. The Bishop's Palace looks south to Putney before the river weaves northwest past Chelsea to the north and Battersea to the south, with its park and power station, turning due north at Pimlico and Vauxhall for Westminster and Waterloo. Running east through the City and Southwark beneath London Bridge, past the Tower and through Tower Bridge, the river suddenly twists south beyond Bermondsey to wrap itself around the Isle of Dogs in full view of stately old Greenwich. Round the Dome and over the Blackwall tunnel, the Barrier finally comes into view, its shiny great steel studs pinning the river down near Woolwich before it flows on to the sea.

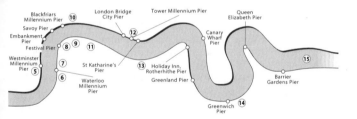

Up & down the river

Hampton Court and Windsor Castle

Hampton Court, in East Molesey, Surrey, is reached by boat from Westminster Pier or Richmond during the summer. Also reached by train from Waterloo. Trains go to Windsor from Waterloo or Paddington; coaches leave from Victoria

Hampton Court is the most beautiful and engaging of the Royal palaces in London. It set the standard for grand houses along the river and is best seen at sunset, when its mellow old red brick glows with warmth and the riverside gardens take on an other-worldly quality. Best reached by boat, which explains its situation, the Palace is also easily reached by train from central London. What particularly marks it out as a visitor attraction is the variety of history on display, from the late-medieval architecture of Henry VIII's court to the Georgian splendour of the Cumberland Suite. Sir Christopher Wren was asked to demolish the Tudor palace, but thankfully ended up simply extending it. The contrast between his classical wings with their formal gardens and the crumbly old buildings erected by Cardinal Wolsey illustrates 300 years of Royal history over a period when England was in the process of turning itself into a world power. Most of the interiors have been successfully restored to their original state. Nearby the seemingly endless expanse of Bushy park stretches north, while Thames Ditton is a sweet riverside village, one stop down the line. Apart from the Tower of London, the other famous Royal palace on the river is Windsor Castle. Also definitely a day trip, the Castle is still very much in use by the Queen who likes to spend her family Christmases here.

History

Until the 16th century, Hampton was little more than a small settlement in the bend of the river, although there is also evidence of a Bronze Age settlement in Bushy Park in among the roe-deer, boars and beavers that flourished in the woods around. In 1514, however, Henry VIII's adviser Cardinal Wolsey bought land between the hamlets of Hampton and Hampton Wick from the Order of St John of Jerusalem and set about building himself a palace of truly regal proportions. Some 500 staff served him in his 280 rooms until he fell out of favour for failing to secure a divorce for Henry VIII; in an attempt to win back his position he gave Hampton Court to Henry.

It soon became another of the monarchy's preferred residences, and over the next 200 years the Court flourished. Henry VIII enlarged and enriched it, adding the hammerbeam Great Hall, the Chapel Royal kitchens and both indoor and outdoor tennis courts. The boy-king Edward VI spent much of his time here before dying aged 16 at Greenwich Palace, while Elizabeth held banquets, masques, balls and plays, often to entertain one of her many suitors freshly arrived from the Continent. The enclosed parks either side of the Hampton Court Road offered plentiful sport, whether hunting stags or tilting or coursing. Even Protector Cromwell took up residence here during the Commonwealth, and although Charles II had to conduct considerable repair work, William and Mary extended the Palace further by commissioning Wren to build the State Apartments.

It was also a place of refuge – for Charles I fled here just before the start of the Civil War, for fashionable Londoners escaping the Great Plague, and for George I, unpopular and

Up & down the river

Hotels in the area

B *The Carlton Mitre Hotel*

C-B *Kingston Lodge Hotel*

» *Go to page 451*

homesick, who would hide away down here. Meanwhile, courtiers built fine houses nearby. The Old Court House and Prestbury House sat on the green, what are now known as Garrick's Villa and House along Hampton Court Road, and Orme, Barham, Old Grange and Grove houses in Hampton itself.

After the death of George II in 1760, the palace ceased to be used by reigning monarchs, but it wasn't until Victoria's reign that the Palace's treasures were opened to the public. Londoners would come to play in the grounds, get lost in the maze, or picnic under the chestnut blossom in Bushy Park. Hampton itself expanded towards New Hampton, but until the middle of the 20th century the area was still covered by up to 50 flourishing market gardens and nurseries.

During the First World War Bushy Park was home to Canadian troops, and in the Second, much of the park was taken over by American forces. Wire camouflage netting covered a military post of 400 huts, five office blocks and several of the ponds. Chestnut Avenue was used as an airstrip, and it was here that Eisenhower and his staff met for the initial planning stages of the D-Day landings.

Sights

Hampton Court Palace

Like the Tower of London, Hampton Court Palace is run by Historic Royal Palaces and bears some of that company's hallmarks: lively costumed tours, clarity in the signposting, and division into different themed areas of interest. Unlike the Tower though, the history of the Palace and its presentation to the public focuses mainly on two particular reigns: Henry VIII (1509-1547) and his many wives, and William and Mary (1689-1702) who until Mary's death in 1694 were unique in sharing the monarchy.

Six different routes around the interior take in Henry VIII's State Apartments, the Tudor Kitchens, the Wolsey Rooms and Renaissance Picture Gallery, the King's Apartments (William's), the Queen's State Apartments (Mary's) and the Georgian Rooms (decorated by George II – 1727-1760 – the last monarch to use the Palace).

The main entrance is at its west front via William III's **Trophy Gate** through the gatehouse built by Cardinal Wolsey. Originally two storeys higher, the gatehouse was found to be unstable in the late 17th century. Beyond, the **Base Court** is still much as Wolsey intended it, although Anne Boleyn's Gateway straight ahead was heavily restored in the 19th century.

The next courtyard is the **Clock Court**, the best place to orientate yourself and appreciate the conflicting range of styles and eras the palace presents. Above the gate on the western Tudor side is the **Astronomical Clock**, designed for Henry VIII in 1540 and showing the phases of the moon and the sun revolving around the earth. To the north is Henry's **Great Hall** and his State Apartments. To the south is Wren's colonnade leading to **William and Mary's State Apartments**. And to the east are the Cumberland Suite and Georgian rooms behind a façade displaying William Kent's attempt to imitate the Tudor style. Through the George II Gate on this side is Wren's **Fountain Court**.

Highlights of the Tudor Palace are Henry VIII's **State Apartments**, especially the **Great Hall**, with its massive hammerbeam roof, and the **Chapel Royal**,

Up & down the river

with an equally extraordinary ceiling. This is all that remains of the original chapel, although the 18th- and 19th-century interior is splendid too, some of it designed by Wren for Queen Anne.

Nearby are the **Tudor Kitchens**, set up as if in preparation for a late-medieval banquet. Only the cauldrons in the Great Kitchen are original, with its three enormous open fireplaces, although the other kitchenware is convincing repro. Round about are the Boiling House, the Spicery and Pastry House, Larders and Sculleries, the Fish Court and the Cellars. The best feature of the Wolsey Rooms is their superb linen-fold panelling, while the Renaissance Picture Gallery contains works by **Correggio**, **Cranach**, **Titian** and **Bruegel** from the Royal Collection.

The **King's Apartments**, built by Wren, are reached via a grand staircase painted by Antonio Verrio. After being severely damaged by fire in 1986, the apartments have been immaculately restored to how they would have looked in 1700. Passing through the Guard Chamber, Presence Chamber and Eating Room, the worst damage was sustained by the Privy Chamber, now hung with magnificent tapestries telling the story of the life of Abraham. The Little Bedchamber contains some priceless Chinese porcelain, while the Closet next door was William's study, featuring his writing desk and a 17th-century lavatory made for Charles II.

On the ground floor are more of the king's private apartments, including the beautifully panelled East Closet carved by **Grinling Gibbons**. Beyond the Orangery, paved with distinctive purple and grey Swedish limestone, the King's Private Dining Room has been laid as if for the third course of a small supper, overlooked by the *Hampton Court Beauties*, a painting by **Godfrey Kneller** of some of the ladies that attended on Queen Mary. The **Queen's State Apartments** seem considerably more 'modern' in appearance, their staircase designed by William Kent, while the playwright and architect Sir John Vanbrugh had a hand in the look of the Guard Chamber and Presence Chamber. The Queen's Drawing Room in the middle of the east front was designed by Wren to line up with the Long Canal in the gardens outside.

Highlights of the much more comfortable **Georgian Rooms**, several designed by William Kent, are Wolsey's Closet, for a taste of how the 19th century went about recreating Tudor interiors; the Communication Gallery hung with the *Windsor Beauties* by **Sir Peter Lely**, and portraying some of the women at the court of Charles II (although not his mistresses); and the Cartoon Gallery, with its copies of the Raphael cartoons in the V&A. The most exceptional original paintings in the Palace though are **Andrea Mantegna**'s series of nine on the triumphs of Julius Caesar, completed in about 1492 and acquired by Charles I in 1629. These can be found in the Lower Orangery in the South Gardens, in a setting designed to evoke their original home in the Palace of San Sebastiano in 1506.

The gardens

If weather permits, time should definitely be allowed for enjoyment of the Palace's beautiful gardens

The **Privy Garden**, in front of the King's State Apartments, has been restored to the way it may have looked in William's day, down to the original species known to have been planted then. The Great Vine was grown by Capability Brown in 1768 and claims to be the oldest in the world, still producing grapes, although it was outgrown by a cutting planted in the Royal Gardens at Windsor in 1775. In the gardens outside the East Front comical trembling topiary bushes line the Broad Walk down to the riverbank. To the north of the palace, the famous *Maze* is fun for all the family: stick to the right hand hedge on the way in and the left hand hedge on the way out if you don't want to be wandering around it all afternoon. Otherwise a visit to the Palace requires at least three hours.

■ *Open Oct 28-Mar 24 1015-1630 Mon, 0930-1630 Tue-Sun (last admission 1545), Mar 24-Oct 27 1015-1800 Mon, 0930-1800 Tue-Sun (last admission 1715). Admission £10.50, £7 under-16s, under 5s free, concession £8. Privy Garden only £2, £1.50 under-16s. Maze only £2.50, £1.50 under-16s. Self service cafeteria in the grounds and coffee shop in the Palace. T020-8781 9500, www.hrp.org.uk*

Beyond the Palace grounds to the north lies the expanse of Bushy Park, a royal demesne of over 1000 acres, home to over 300 deer, and putting on some spectacular floral displays: with its avenues of lime trees, in spring with carpets of daffodils; in May the flowering candles of the apparently endless Chestnut Avenue punctuated by Charles I's Diana Fountain, heading dead straight from the Palace up to Teddington. ■ *T020-8979 1586.*   Bushy Park

Windsor Castle

The other Royal Palace on the river, much further west and still very much in use, is Windsor Castle. Founded by William the Conqueror on a strategic sight affording far-reaching views and being within a day's march of the Tower of London, it ensured the dominance of the invading monarch over the western approaches to the city.

The public are admitted throughout the year (except on state occasions, phone first), to the State Apartments, including Charles II's apartments and the Waterloo Chamber, decorated with paintings from the Royal Collection by **van Dyck**, **Holbein**, **Rubens** and **Rembrandt** and some very fine furniture; the castles' precincts; and Henry VIII's gorgeous Gothic **St George's Chapel**, where ten sovereigns are buried (and where Edward and Sophie tied the knot).

Highlight of the State Apartments is St George's Hall, fully restored after the fire in 1992, where the Queen holds banquets and receptions. From April to June, the Changing of the Guard occurs here at 1100 Monday-Saturday. From July to March, the ceremony takes place on alternate days. The best vantage points are the Lower Ward of the Castle or outside on Windsor High Street. During winter (see below), the Semi State Rooms are also open, featuring some of the Castle's most splendid interiors.

One very popular curiosity is **Queen Mary's Doll's House**, the most famous of its kind in the world, a complete palace built to a scale of 1 in 12 by at least 1000 master craftsmen in the 1920s. All the little palace's fixtures and fittings are in full working order, including the bathrooms, lifts and electricity supply. Eton College and the riverside are within easy reach of the castle.

■ *Open Mar-Oct 0945-1715 (last admission 1600); Nov-Feb 0945-1615 (last admission 1500). Semi State Apartments open to 25 Mar 2001 and between 29 Sep 2001–24 Mar 2002. State Apartments closed 9-22 Jun. Admission for adults £11.00, over-60s £9.00, under-17s £5.50, family (2 adults, 2 under-17s) £27.50, under-5s free. Guided tours available of the restored areas not on the main public route including the Medieval Undercroft and Great Kitchen. One tour each morning and afternoon on Tue and Wed until 21 Mar 2001 and from 2 Oct 2001 to 20 Mar 2002. T01753-831118. For more information T01753-869898, windsorcastle@royalcollection.org.uk*

Up & down the river

Eating and drinking in Hampton Court

Mid-range
For a special occasion, the superior and fairly formal French cuisine at *Monsieur Max*, 133 High St, Hampton Hill, Middlesex, T020-8979 5546, needs booking well in advance but rarely disappoints.

Cheap
Within walking distance of the Palace, Bridge Rd is the best bet, with the *Chu Chin Chow*, Bridge Rd, T020-8979 5993, a pricey but highly recommended Chinese restaurant and the *Vecchia Roma*, Bridge Rd, T020-8941 5337, a traditional Italian. Right opposite the gate, *Blubeckers*, 3 Palace Gate, Hampton Court, Surrey, T020-8941 5959, is open for American-English lunches and supper, £4 starter, £10 mains, with an excellent-value early-evening happy hour. Further afield in Hampton Hill, *Café Society*, 92 High St, Hampton Hill, Middlesex, T020-8977 7691, is a good fish restaurant and coffee bar serving food all day (Sat, Sun 1200-1430, 1800-2130).

Pubs & bars
▶▶ *Go to page 437 for entertainment & nightlife*
In Hampton Court itself there are sadly no pubs on the river. *The Albion*, 34 Bridge Rd, East Molesey, Surrey, T020-8941 9421, is a friendly local with a comfortable atmosphere, while nearby *The Prince of Wales*, 23 Bridge Rd, East Molesey, Surrey, T020-8979 5561, does food all day and can get very busy Sun. Another option is to take the train back to Thames Ditton and stroll down Church Walk to the river. The *Fox on the River*, Queen's Rd, Thames Ditton, T020-8339 1110, does all-day food everyday right on the waterside opposite the Palace's east gardens. On Summer St, *The Crown* is the liveliest pub in the area, popular with a younger crowd, with a pool table and regular special events.

Transport

Buses
To Windsor from London, *Green Line* operates daily services from Victoria Coach Station, T0870-6087261 (from UK only).

River transport
From Westminster Pier (T020-7930 2062) up to 4 hrs to Hampton Court.

Trains
Waterloo to Hampton Court, about 30 mins, or to Kingston and then buses 111, 216, 411, 416, 451, 461, 513, 726, from Cromwell Rd bus station in Kingston. For Windsor Castle to Windsor from London Waterloo Station or London Paddington Station, T08457- 484950 (from UK only)

Tubes
Wimbledon tube (District line; Wimbledon branch), then Platform 8 for twice hourly Hampton Court train, or Richmond tube (District line; Richmond branch), then R68 bus to Hampton Court Palace.

Richmond and Kew

☻ *Best reached by boat (summer only) or train, both Richmond & Kew are also on the tube*
*A visit to Kew or Richmond from central London is likely take up a whole day, but with fine weather the two-hour riverboat or half-hour train journey will be well rewarded. The varying seasonal delights of the **Royal Botanical Gardens** at Kew are world famous, while the town of Richmond with its tree-lined riverside walk, views from the hill and rolling **deer park** are the most rural places within easy reach of the city. Here in the buckle of Surrey's stockbroker belt, the English dream of house and garden – rus in urbe – reaches its most complete expression. As well as the more obvious attractions such as Kew Gardens and Richmond Hill, many*

of the area's old mansions are also worth travelling to find, especially the early 17th-century **Ham House**, *just over the river by foot ferry from Marble Hill House, the Orleans House Gallery and Twickenham. Children love exploring the London Butterfly House and its strange insects in the grounds of stately* **Syon Park**. *Closer to London,* **Chiswick House** *and* **Hogarth's House** *make a fine 18th-century destination near the flower-filled riverside along Chiswick Mall.*

History

The old palace of Shene was a popular royal residence in the 14th century (it is said that Richard II entertained 10,000 guests here over the summer months), but by Henry VII's accession it was a relatively unspectacular manor house next to a hamlet of fishermen's cottages. When the house burnt down, however, Henry elected to build a palace on its site. Named Rychemond after his earldom in Yorkshire, the palace spawned craftsmen's cottages and taverns.

Pageants shared the green with grazing sheep, a spectacle that could be seen from a number of Elizabethan houses built nearby, and the hill was dotted with wealthy men's houses overlooking the Thames. Courtiers moved into Kew, either to serve Richmond Palace itself, or the various nobles and royalty established in houses around. The Dutch House (later to become Kew Palace) was built by a Dutch merchant, while Charles I enclosed the park with an eight mile wall taking common land and estates from his subjects in the process. There were grumbles, but the compensation was considered fair.

Towards the end of the 17th century, Richmond Wells opened in the grounds of Cadigan House on Richmond Hill. Such was the attraction of dancing in the summer season that the two sisters who lived opposite bought it in order to close it down. Further fine houses emerged, such as those on Maids of Honour Row, and Richmond's increasing popularity saw the introduction of public buildings such as the Theatre Royal or the Star & Garter Inn, 'more like the mansion of a noblemen' which held grand parties for grand guests.

But as Richmond Palace decayed, so the focus shifted to Kew. Frederick, Prince of Wales, built a pleasure garden here, his wife later set out a nine-acre botanical garden and in the 1770s Lancelot 'Capability' Brown laid out new grounds. The Isabella Plantation was enclosed within the park in 1831, and Queen Victoria lent Pembroke Lodge to the then Prime Minister, Lord John Russell – his grandson Bertrand Russell, the philosopher, must have done much of his early thinking here. The ferry to Twickenham had been replaced by a bridge in 1777, and a railway bridge was added in 1848, but the railway brought little in the way of industry or rapid development. Richmond remained a quiet, healthy and genteel suburb. Fishing was still a popular pastime, and the *Star & Garter*, now rebuilt and considered 'a great disfiguring wart or wen on the face of Richmond' served as a home for disabled soldiers during the First World War.

Virginia Woolf came here to recuperate from a mental breakdown. With her husband, she formed the Hogarth Press in their flat, from which TS Eliot's *The Wasteland* was first published. Electric trams reached Kew in 1901, inevitably drawing more residents; the area remains a much-favoured suburb, despite the heavy flow of people passing through to visit the The Royal Botanical Gardens.

Up & down the river

Hotels in the area

B *Richmond Gate Hotel*
B *Richmond Hill Hotel*
B *Richmond Inn Hotel*
C *Doughty Cottage*
C *Hobart Hall Hotel*
D *Chelwood House*
D *Mr and Mrs Leach*
▸▸ **Go to page 451**

Sights

Kew Gardens

In an area rich in parkland, gorgeous scenery, antique architecture and oodles of stereotypical English charm – somewhat disturbed by the airliners roaring overhead every two minutes into Heathrow – the Royal Botanical Gardens (Kew Gardens for short) are the jewel in the crown. Originally founded as a pleasure garden in the grounds of what became *Kew Palace* by Prince Frederick, the ill-fated heir to George II, in 1731, Kew has evolved into a 300-acre site containing more than 33,000 species grown in plantations, borders and glasshouses and is a world-renowned centre for horticultural research.

The first ports of call for most visitors are the **Palm House** and the **Princess of Wales Conservation Centre**. The former was the first and still most magnificent of the glasshouses, recently fully restored, and is tropical in both content and humidity, while a rather fine exotic aquarium lurks underneath. The latter houses ten different zones of computer-maintained climates, complete with wildlife as well as foliage, carnivorous and otherwise.

The **Temperate House** is awe-inspiring, if not in content at least in size. The most outstanding feature among the representatives of each of the world's continents is the *Chilean Wine Palm*, which now measures around 60 ft and is one of the largest indoor palms in the world. Just behind the Temperate House lies the rather self-explanatory **Evolution House**, though while the subject is fascinating, the hi-tech sound and light approach is patronizing.

Outside, the 18th-century gardens are an attraction in themselves. Originally designed in the 1760s, the later work of Capability Brown (possibly the greatest of British romantic landscapers) can be appreciated in the lake dominating the Syon Vista. Original features punctuate a wide expanse of flowerbeds and woodland: the **Orangery**, once a notable hothouse, is now a decent restaurant, though the **Pagoda**, at 163 ft, is the most noticeable and impressive thing in the gardens, despite the effects of age and erosion. A number of 18th-century neoclassical temples can be found near the Victoria Gate (now the main entrance), but be sure to explore the **Ruined Arch** with its artful dilapidation and scattered symbols of post Roman barbarism. For utter seclusion, check out **Queen Charlotte's Cottage** to the distant southwest, too far for the crowds to trek.

The palace remains closed to the public for now, though the seemingly never-ending renovation work will probably be completed by the end of 2001

Kew Palace is Britain's smallest Royal residence and only George III ever actually lived here, even then at the peak of his illness. The exterior is worth a quick view and a visit should be essential once its innards have been replaced. If nothing else, have a quick glance before exiting the gardens at the **Main Gate** which is still impressive despite being superceded in its original role by the Victoria Gate. To get the best out of Kew, visit in the summer and spend the day. It can be done in less, but it's all too gorgeous for a fleeting visit.

■ *Gardens open daily 0930-1615, last admission 1545. £5 for adults. T020-8940 1171, www.kew.org.uk*

Around Kew

Having exited the gardens via the Main Gate you step into the country idyll that is **Kew Green**. Surrounded by Georgian architecture and with a cricket pitch in the centre, nothing could be more quintessentially English. At the end of the Green, **St Anne's Church** dates from 1714 and is the secluded resting place of the painters Gainsborough and Zoffany, so secluded in fact that finding them takes some time and effort.

A former Victorian pumping station, the Kew Bridge Steam Museum, on Green Dragon Lane, is on the one hand a shrine to the steam engine, and on the other an examination of the history of London's water supply. At its best at weekends when a few of the engines are put through their paces, the emphasis is on interactivity and exploration, great fun whichever end of the spectrum fascinates you most. Essential viewing for those interested in the functions of the Roman toilet spoon. ■ *Open daily 1100-1700; weekdays £3 for adults; Weekends £4. T020-8568 4757.*

Kew Bridge Steam Museum

Opposite Kew Gardens, on the west bank of the river, Syon House is the grand art-stuffed home of the Dukes of Northumberland, with fine Capability Brown gardens, an adventure playground and in the grounds, the London Butterfly House. This, the oldest exhibition of its kind in the world, is a tropical indoor garden filled with fluttering butterflies and also, safely behind glass, scorpions, spiders, giant land snails and millipedes.
■ *Gardens open daily 1000-1730 or dusk. House open summer only 1100-1700 Wed, Thu, Sun and Bank Holidays. Admission gardens only £3, £2.50 concession. House and gardens £6.25, £5.25 concession. T020-8560 0881. London Butterfly House open 1000-1530; summer 1000-dusk. Admission £3.30, £2 children. T020-8560 7272; information on T020-8560 0378, www.butterflies.org.uk Nearest train station Syon Lane.*

Syon House

On Sat afternoons children can 'Meet the Minibeast'

Back downstream nearer the centre of London and Hammersmith, Chiswick House, on Burlington Lane, is less of an austere family seat and more of an aristocratic toy. Designed by owner-architect Lord Burlington to mimic the style of the archetypal Roman villa, the house, though surprisingly small, is decorated with fine interiors, paintings and furniture, while the sumptuously lavish Blue Velvet Room is a magnificent example of Romantic aristocratic decadence. The 18th-century classical ornamental gardens are a perfect foil to Burlington's masterpiece and a very pleasant place to take a summer stroll.
■ *Open Apr-Sep 1000-1800; Oct 1000-1800 or dusk if earlier; Nov-Mar, Wed-Sun 1000-1600; closed 1300-1400 every day; T020-8995 0508.*

Chiswick House

Beware the Kamikaze scooter-mounted progeny of debonair local residents

A touch confusing to hunt down (beware contradictory signposts), the 18th-century residence of painter William Hogarth lies just 50 yds from the frenetic Hogarth roundabout, on Hogarth Lane, and within a stone's throw of Chiswick House. The house and exhibition tell the story of the artist's life and work, with many of Hogarth's major works being on display, including the witty social criticism of *The Rake's Progress* and *The Harlot's Progress*. Not all of them are genuine, though copies are undoubtedly better than nothing at all.
■ *Nov-Mar, Tue-Fri 1300-1600, Sat and Sun 1300-1700; Apr-Oct, Tue-Fri 1300-1700, Sat and Sun 1300-1800; closed Jan. Admission free. T020-8994 6757.*

Hogarth's House

Up & down the river

Richmond

On exiting the tube/train station in Richmond, it is readily apparent that you are in the shopping centre of the borough. The road is lined on both sides of the street with high street branches (*Gap*, *Laura Ashley*, etc) which make up the staple of the average Richmond shopper. Richmond Hill itself is lined with expensive antique shops.

Richmond Park Europe's largest city park and a former Royal hunting ground dating from the 13th century, Richmond Park is a popular attraction due largely to its freely roaming deer and the historic attraction of the panorama over Surrey and

Up & down the river

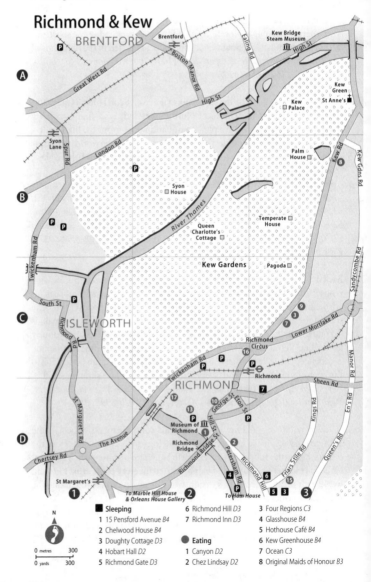

Richmond & Kew

■ **Sleeping**	6 Richmond Hill *D3*	3 Four Regions *C3*
1 15 Pensford Avenue *B4*	7 Richmond Inn *D3*	4 Glasshouse *B4*
2 Chelwood House *B4*		5 Hothouse Café *B4*
3 Doughty Cottage *D3*	● **Eating**	6 Kew Greenhouse *B4*
4 Hobart Hall *D2*	1 Canyon *D2*	7 Ocean *C3*
5 Richmond Gate *D3*	2 Chez Lindsay *D2*	8 Original Maids of Honour *B3*

London (especially from **King Henry VIII's Mound**, the highest point in the park). There is more than just this however: **Pembroke Lodge**, once the childhood home of Bertrand Russell and now an ornate tea-house, the bird sanctuary that is **Sidmouth Wood**, the beautifully landscaped **Isabella Plantation**, and the **White Lodge**, built on the command of George II though inhabited by Queen Caroline, his wife. ■ *Open Mar-Sep, 0700-dusk; Oct-Feb 0730-dusk. T020-8948 3209.*

As a former Royal resort, it would be easy for the **Museum of Richmond,** Old Town Hall, Whittaker Avenue, to focus on this aspect alone. To its credit, however, it charts the history of the area from prehistoric times to the present day

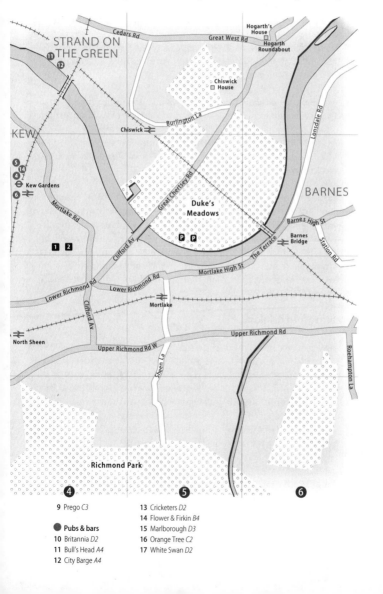

Up & down the river

Five of the best: views of the river

- *Island Gardens*, Docklands.
- *Waterloo Bridge*, South Bank.
- *The Embankment*, Putney.
- *Kew Gardens* across to Syon Park.
- *King Henry VIII's Mound*, Richmond Park.

with numerous exhibits to back it up and friendly and informed staff to boot. ■ *Open May-Oct, Tue-Sat 1100-1700; Sun 1300-1600; Nov-Apr, Tue-Sat 1100-1700. Admission £2 for adults. T020-8332 1141.*

North of the river, on Richmond Road in Twickenham, a rare survivor of the string of grand villas which once lined the Thames, **Marble Hill House** was built in the 1720s for Henrietta Howard, mistress of George II. Regally decorated and perfectly proportioned, this handsome Palladian mansion, refreshing in its authenticity, also possesses examples of early Georgian painting and furniture. ■ *Open Apr-Oct, daily 1000-1800; Nov-Mar, Wed-Sun 1000-1600. Admission £3 for adults; T020-8892 5115. Reached most easily from St Margaret's train station.*

Next door, the **Orleans House Gallery** is an intriguing early 18th-century octagonal building containing the Ionides Collection of local topographical pictures and mounting regular interesting temporary exhibitions. ■ *Open Tue-Sat 1300-1630, Sun 1400-1630, Summer Tue-Sat 1300-1730, Sun 1400-1730. Admission free. T020-8892 0221, www.richmond.gov.uk/depts/opps/leisure/arts/orleanshouse*

Maybe because of its slightly disjointed position away from the rest of Richmond's box of delights, but easily reached by the foot ferry from the end of Orleans Road, **Ham House** is often overlooked by visitors to the area. It's a shame really as it's also one of the most appealing of the local estates with original 17th-century artwork (including van Dyck) and furniture, the ornate extravagance of the Great Staircase, and an enchanting garden with statutory tea-room. ■ *Open Apr-Oct, Mon-Wed, Sat, Sun 1300-1700. Admission £5 for adults; T020-8940 1950.*

Eating and drinking

Mid-range
● on map, page 388

Classy décor and oodles of atmosphere give the superior Chinese restaurant *Four Regions*, 102-103 Kew Rd, Richmond, Surrey, T020-8940 9044, an edge over its rivals. The quality of the service and the food is very high, though unfortunately so is the price. Hugely popular nonetheless. *The Canyon*, Riverside, near Richmond Bridge, Richmond, Surrey, T020-8948 2944, is a white airy building with a picturesque riverside setting. It is a good, though fairly pricey, establishment with an unmistakably American (rib-eye steak and apple pie) theme. The prices could prove a touch restrictive, though that does tend to go with the area, and by and large you get what you pay for.

Sat neatly outside Kew Gardens tube station, *The Glasshouse*, 14 Station Parade, Kew, T020-8940 6777, has rapidly built itself a reputation for friendly service in a warm, intimate location with, perhaps above all, very good food and an extensive and varied European menu. The set meals offer very good value (dinner is around £25 for 3 courses) though the wine is more expensive. *Prego*, 106-108 Kew Rd, Richmond, T020-8948 8508, is well staffed and very stylish with an airy main section and a more intimate back area. The food is pleasant and the atmosphere is appealing, despite fairly high prices.

Up & down the river

An enclave of Northern France in leafy Richmond, *Chez Lindsay*, 11 Hill Rise, Richmond, T020-8948 7473, is true to its origins in both authentic haute cuisine and even more authentically aloof staff, although with a sizeable 3-course meal on offer for under £12 it would be difficult for even the staunchest Eurosceptic to reject its Gallic offerings. *Ocean*, 100 Kew Rd, Richmond, T020-8948 8008, is a stylish modern restaurant with a pleasant row of outdoor tables. The limited menu ensures that you are not spoiled for choice, though what there is offers a good mixture of modern and traditional tastes (from sushi to fish pie) at a reasonable price.

Cheap

Pembroke Lodge, Richmond Park, Richmond, is a pretty tea-room with outdoor seating on the crest of Richmond Hill, a good place to relax and enjoy the view. The *Hothouse Café*, 9 Station Approach, Kew, T020-8332 1923, is one of the better places to languish near the gardens, laid back and breezy with a mellow jazz soundtrack to soothe away your troubles. Along with a good variety of tea and coffee, the Hothouse boasts a decent menu and rapid service, especially popular at lunchtimes. Close by, on the main approach from Kew Gardens tube, *The Kew Greenhouse*, 1 Station Parade, Kew, T020-8940 0183, is a good place to study the native aspiring middle-class in their prime habitat. As floral as the name suggests, the conservatory and outdoor seating make it a prime summer spot. The *Original Maids of Honour*, 288 Kew Rd, Kew, is opposite Kew Gardens on the road leading off the Common, a teashop as English as its environs. It was here that Maid of Honour tarts were baked for Henry VIII and his household, and the present incumbents resolutely continue the tradition along with the other fineries of olde Englishe tea culture.

Cafés & sandwich bars

Chiswick House Café, Chiswick House, Burlington Lane, W4, is located bang next door to the house itself, one of the better stately home cafés with a decent snack menu and a wide selection of refreshments. Anything with Chiswick Gardens as a backdrop can't be all that bad.

Despite the odd chain-pub feature, *Flower and Firkin*, Station Parade, Kew, T020-8332 1162, is an honest-to-goodness and laid-back pub conveniently situated for a post/pre-wander pint having explored the expansive acres of Kew Gardens. Well partitioned with a conservatory backing onto the station platform, complete with sofas.

Pubs & bars
▶▶ *Go to page 437 for entertainment & nightlife*

On the north bank of the river over Kew Bridge, the cosy *Bull's Head*, 15 Strand on the Green, T020-8994 1204, and the *City Barge*, 27 Strand on the Green, T020-8994 2148, have sunny south-facing tables on the river.

In Richmond, the *Orange Tree*, 45 Kew Rd, Richmond, T020-8940 0944, is a pleasant if slightly sanitized pub across the way from the theatre with which it shares its name. Punters hoping for big screen football will be disappointed – this is a rugby only zone and the daytime clientele reflect this. A popular haunt for the pre-theatre crowd in the evening. *The Britannia*, 5 Brewers Lane, Richmond, T020-8940 1071, is tucked away snug and cosy between busy George St and Richmond Green. Its tiny size gives it much of its charm along with an open fire, ensuring a warm and friendly atmosphere. A good little hideaway. *The Marlborough*, 46 Friars Stile Rd, Richmond, T020-8940 0572, is a pretty pub perched on Richmond Hill, surprisingly intimate and secluded inside with good wine list, expansive garden and enchanting view over the Thames making it a very popular spot in summer.

Five of the best: riverside pubs

- *City Barge*, Strand on the Green, Kew.
- *White Swan*, Riverside, Twickenham .
- *Fox on the River*, Thames Ditton, Hampton Court.
- *Trafalgar Tavern*, Greenwich.
- *London Apprentice*, Isleworth, Richmond.

Up & down the river

Hidden among cottages, *The White Swan*, 26 Old Palace Lane, Richmond, T020-8892 2166, is a classic country boozer. Slightly off the beaten track and thus mostly populated by locals, it's worth the venture to avoid the crowds and have a peaceful pint or a bite of regular pub grub. The *Cricketers*, Maids of Honour Row, The Green, Richmond, T020-8940 4372, is named in honour of the bordering cricket pitch on the green, offering a decent selection of real ales and a (comparatively) reasonably priced menu of unspectacular pub fare. Conjures images of summer pints on the lawn.

In Isleworth, at 62 Church St, T020-8560 1915, a short walk along the river from Marble Hill House, the *London Apprentice* is a riverside pub popular with the rugby crowd but with a pleasant beer garden out front. Further upstream is the *White Swan*, Twickenham, T020-8892 2166, which has more character and overlooks the river at Eel Pie Island, which was a haven for hippy chicks and rockers in the 60s.

Transport

Buses **To Kew Gardens and Richmond**:
No 65 from Ealing Broadway, via South Ealing, Kew, Richmond and Petersham.
No 391 from Fulham Broadway, via West Kensington, Hammersmith, Turnham Green, Chiswick and Kew Gardens tube station.

For Chiswick House, Hogarth's House and Syon Park:
No 237 from Shepherd's Bush, via Goldhawk Rd, Turnham Green, Chiswick, Kew Bridge, Brentford and Isleworth
No 267 from Hammersmith, via Turnham Green, Chiswick, Kew Bridge, Brentford, Isleworth and Twickenham.

River transport Summer only: Westminster to Hampton Court via Putney, Kew and Richmond, leaving Westminster at 1030, 1115, and 1200 taking 3½ hrs. Also from Westminster to Kew via Putney at 1015, 1100, 1400, 1430 taking 1½ hrs. Phone to check times and prices (about £12 Westminster-Hampton Court return). T020-7930 2062.

Trains Kew Bridge, Chiswick, Richmond and St Margaret's (from Clapham Junction, Waterloo and Victoria).

Tubes Kew Gardens (District line), Gunnersbury (District line), Richmond (District line).

Directory

Sports *All England Lawn Tennis Club*, Church Road, Wimbledon SW19, T020-8944 1066. Site of the annual tennis championships and also of a new interactive museum on the game and its stars. *London Welsh RFC*, Old Deer Park, Kew Road, Richmond, Surrey (Information T0336-421744; Tickets: T020 8940 2368). *Harlequins RFC*, The Stoop Memorial Ground, Craneford Way, Twickenham (Information T020-8410 6000; Tickets T0870-8870230).

Greenwich

Greenwich has been attracting visitors for centuries. Initially a few were far from welcome, like the Danes who arrived and murdered the bishop in the 11th century. But about 1000 years later the town was the obvious focus for the nation's millennium celebrations. As well as being the home of Greenwich Mean Time, the area's ancient Royal and naval associations made it seem an appropriate spot to wave goodbye to the lost Empire of the 20th century and welcome in the era of 'New Britain'. Unfortunately the Millennium Dome and its contents got such bad press that far fewer than expected bothered to turn up. Its future hangs in the balance, but meanwhile the old town is still a favourite weekend destination for Londoners and very popular with visitors to the city. It's not hard to see why: a fairly short river trip from Westminster past many of London's most famous sights, Greenwich rewards the journey with a convenient cluster of top attractions, most especially the **National Maritime Museum***, but also the* **Royal Observatory***, Greenwich Park and the 18th-century grandeur of the* **Royal Naval College***. The town itself is also pleasant to explore, packed with antiques, artists and idiosyncratic Greenwich villagers. Nearby are the even quainter sloping streets of fashionable Blackheath, while downstream the dockyard and arsenal at Woolwich, along with the state-of-the-art 1930s house and medieval hall at* **Eltham Palace***, are revamped and offbeat attractions hidden away to the southeast.*

⦿ Best approached by boat for the views of the Cutty Sark, the Royal Naval College & Queen's House from the river; otherwise by the foot tunnel from Island Gardens or the DLR to Cutty Sark. Alternatively by overland train from Charing Cross or London Bridge

History

Greenwich, or 'green port' as the Saxons called it, only really emerged in the life of London in the 15th century when Humphrey, Duke of Gloucester and brother to King Henry V, built himself Bella Court, a grand residence on the riverside. Until then, Greenwich had seen the Danish Fleet anchor offshore in the 11th century, and there is evidence of a Roman settlement in what is now the park. But in early medieval times its manor was merely the sub-manor to Lewisham, with the Greenwich marshes spread out to the east.

Henry VII rebuilt the house, and it soon became popular with the Tudor monarchs, such that for a while under Henry VIII it became the political and diplomatic focal point for the country. He built a tiltyard and armouries, went hawking and hunting, and visited his warships anchored nearby. England's first masquerade was performed here in 1516, and it was at a May Day tournament that Anne Boleyn allegedly dropped a hanky as a signal to a lover. She was in the Tower the next day.

Later in the century Shakespeare is said to have performed in his plays here before Elizabeth I. James I walled in the park, and his wife, Anne of Denmark, commissioned Inigo Jones to build the Palladian Queen's House. When the Parliamentarians took control following the Civil War, having emptied it of much of its treasures (Charles I was an extensive art collector), it spent time as both a biscuit factory and a holding house for Dutch prisoners of war.

Following the Restoration, Charles II had designs on a new palace, but money and enthusiasm dried up, leaving only the west wing of the Naval Hospital, later the Royal Naval College. The parks were laid out though, inspired by the French designer, Le Notre, and in 1675 the Royal Observatory was built on the site of

Up & down the river

Hotels in the area

D *Ibis Hotel*

▸▸ *Go to page 452*

Humphrey's watchtower, an event that led, almost literally, to Greenwich's unique relationship with Father Time. Some 200 years later, at Washington in America, it was agreed that the Greenwich Meridian should define 0° longitude. The Royal Observatory's fine reputation (Edmond Halley was Astronomer Royal, and its Nautical Almanac of 1767 became the navigators bible the world over), earned it this special status.

Meanwhile, Greenwich as a settlement grew little. In the 18th century some grand houses were erected, such as the Ranger's House and Vanburgh's Castle, but by the mid-19th century it was more a venue for Londoners to visit on steamers, gigs and hackney-coaches. London's first railway line ran to Greenwich, a much-celebrated affair with orchestras at the stations. The population grew with the spread of the Docklands, music halls and theatres opened up, and Goddard's Eel and Pie House (only recently closed down) gained a sizeable reputation. In 1902, the Greenwich Foot Tunnel opened, giving the dockers

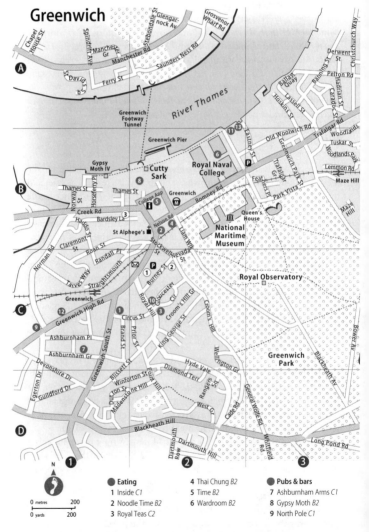

Greenwich

Up & down the river

0 metres   200
0 yards   200

● Eating		4 Thai Chung *B2*	● Pubs & bars
1 Inside *C1*		5 Time *B2*	7 Ashburnham Arms *C1*
2 Noodle Time *B2*		6 Wardroom *B2*	8 Gypsy Moth *B2*
3 Royal Teas *C2*			9 North Pole *C1*

easier access to the West India Docks, and by 1905 the houses stretched all the way south to Blackheath and Lewisham. The building of the Dome at the end of the 20th century may have been much ridiculed, but it has provided employment and hope of some much needed regeneration in the area.

Sights

Appropriately enough, visitors to Greenwich arriving by boat land right next to the Cutty Sark, moored at King William Walk, SE10. This is the only surviving tea clipper of the kind that raced around the world under sail for the Empire, laden with tea or opium and displaying a turn of speed that could cover about 350 miles in a day. Built in 1869 in Dumbarton, on the Clyde, and named after the skimpy nightie on a dancing witch admired by Tam O'Shanter in Burns'

Cutty Sark

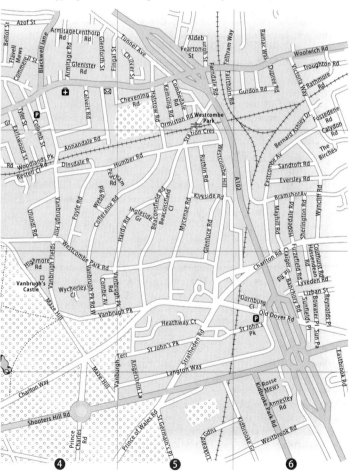

Up & down the river

poem, she made her last commercial voyage in 1922, and was dry-docked in Greenwich in 1954. Two decks can be explored, including the Captain's cabin, as well as a large collection of figureheads from other tall ships.

■ *Open daily 1000-1700 (last admission 1630). Admission £3.50, £2.50 concession. T020-8858 3445, www.cuttysark.org.uk*

Next door is **Gipsy Moth IV**, the 54-ft ketch that Sir Francis Chichester sailed single-handedly round the world in 1966-67, although forced to land in Sydney, denying him the non-stop record. No longer open to the public, the yacht is still worth a look, not least in the light of Ellen MacArthur's recent achievement. Close by is the distinctive domed entrance to the eerie Greenwich Foot tunnel under the Thames to the Isle of Dogs.

Heading inland, Greenwich Church Street leads up to the centre of the town which is dominated by **St Alphege's Church**, named after Greenwich's patron saint, the bishop murdered on this spot by the Danes in the 11th century. Hawksmoor designed its impressive exterior in 1712. ■ *Open 1000-1600 Mon-Sat, 1300-1600 Sun. T020-8858 6828.*

Royal Naval College

The Ward Room in the Undercroft is a smart new lunch place (see Eating and drinking below), & the Tilt Yard Café is in the Greenwich gateway furthest from the river

Greenwich High Road rounds the corner towards the train station and New Cross, while Romney Road leads off to the left past Greenwich market towards the main event, the National Maritime Museum (see below) on the right in Greenwich Park and the Royal Naval College on the left beside the water. Designed by Royal command not to obstruct the view from the river of the Queen's House at the centre of the museum, the College represents English architecture at its grandest and most formal. Three of the most celebrated 18th-century British architects had a hand in the design – Wren, Hawksmoor and Vanbrugh – and its twin domes and columns still make a stunning picture when seen from the water or from the hills of Greenwich Park.

Now part of Greenwich University, visitors can wander its great riverside quads and see the Painted Hall, beneath the southwestern cupola, an extraordinary and theatrical room, busy with murals beneath a magnificent ceiling, all painted by Thornhill over a period of 19 years. In the Undercroft beneath the hall, temporary exhibitions are displayed in Queen Mary's anteroom.

■ *Open daily 1000-1700 (last admission 1615), Admission £3, £2 concession. Free on Sun. T020-8269 4744, www.greenwichfoundation.org.uk*

Queen's House

The Queen's House, in Romney Road, SE10, was the first truly Renaissance house constructed in England, now standing bang in the middle of the National Maritime Museum. It has recently been fully refurbished, reopening in May 2001, and contains a portrait gallery of old sea captains and other salty types in an exhibition called 'Sea of Faces'. Nothing could diminish the beauty of the architecture: the Great Hall is a perfect cube, while the 'tulip staircase' named after the designs on its bannisters is beautiful too. Look out for **Canaletto**'s view of the Royal Hospital and Greenwich from the Isle of Dogs, little changed today.

■ *Open daily 1000-1700 (last admission 1630). Admission (including Maritime Museum) £7.50, concession £6, OAPs and under-16s. T020-8858 4422; information T020-8312 6565.*

Up & down the river

National Maritime Museum

A covered colonnade connects Queen's House on either side to the National Maritime Museum, with its three levels pretty much doing justice to their enthralling subject, the sea. In a bold move the museum was transformed in early 1999 by the completion of architect Rick Mather's extraordinary £21 million glass roof over the central Neptune Court, manufactured by the company that built the Eiffel Tower.

The National Maritime is one of the most engaging museums in London

The ground floor here contains a new exhibition on Maritime London, including the original façade of Lloyd's Coffee House and is divided into five themes: Shipping and Shipbuilding, Pageantry and Pleasure, Bridges and Buildings, Companies and Cargoes, and London Lives. The west wing covers Explorers, from the Vikings and Phoenicians to the Polar expeditions, one highlight being a fragment of Sir John Franklin's last message, written in 1847, on his way to his death searching for the Northwest Passage.

Ground floor

In the Neptune Court, an adjunct to these displays covers the history of underwater exploration and the discovery of the Titanic. 'Passengers' in the south wing looks at emigration, and life on board the great ocean liners, while 'Cargoes' in the east wing examines the rise of Rotterdam and containerization, in the light of the fact that nine times more trade now goes by ship than half a century ago. The display includes a huge map of the world's shipping lanes and a scale model of the brand new container port at Algeciras.

On the first floor (Level 2), the Upper Court, flooded with natural light from the glass roof, 'Future of the Sea' next to the café contains the Museum's brave attempt to explain the ecology of the sea, using a walk-in cube, sphere and tower, each focusing on different objects related to mankind's impact on the oceans and his attempts to understand them.

First floor

The east wing on this level is the picture gallery, hung with a selection from the Museum's vast collection of maritime paintings, from **Eric Ravilious**' *Submarine Dream* to **Whistler**'s *Black Lion Wharf*. Overlooking Greenwich Park, 'Trade and Empire' covers the touchy matter of the British Empire's global expansion across the billowing ocean wave, with displays on slavery, the missionaries and white settlement of the colonies. Among the objects providing ample food for thought here are the figurehead of HMS Seringapatam carved to represent Tipu Sultan, the Indian ruler defeated in 1798, and the Nordenfelt machine gun from 1890. Up the stairs the Seapower Gallery features a full-size replica of an A-class submarine's torpedo tube.

On Level 3, one of the Museum's most popular rooms is still the Nelson Gallery, containing plenty of memorabilia relating to the flawed hero, the man and the myth, including the blood-stained tourniquet for his wound and a computer animated Battle of Trafalgar. On the same level, two hands-on galleries for kids are The Bridge, where a ferry needs to be steered out of Dover and a Viking ship docked, and All Hands, with interactive exhibits on diving, gunnery and cargo handling. The south wing overlooking the park is given over to temporary exhibitions: until September 2001 'South' charts the story of the tragic race for the South Pole.

Level 3

■ *Open daily 1000-1700 (last admission 1630). Admission £7.50, concession £6, OAPs and under-16s. T020-8858 4422; recorded information T020-8312 6565, www.nmm.ac.uk*

Up & down the river

Dome alone

It was meant to be so different. A beacon of hope for a new millenium and proof that UK Plc could be like its continental cousins and successfully realise an ambitious large-scale public building project of its very own. But it all went pear-shaped right from the start. It didn't help that the editors of the main national newspapers – the heads of Britain's 'fourth estate' – were left standing outside in the freezing cold for two hours at Stratford tube station on Old Year's Eve. Someone would pay.

The Dome's fate was sealed before it even opened. It had always been a political football – if you'll pardon the cliché - with an ever-sceptical media as referee. The public became tired and increasingly cynical of the relentless spin and hype surrounding the contents of the "giant tent" and the projected visitor numbers. Meanwhile, building costs escalated and there were delays on the completion of the Jubilee line extension.

So bad was the press, it's a miracle anyone actually bothered to visit the thing. But visit they did – in modest numbers – and soon London was divided into two camps: the 'pros' and 'antis'. The 'pros'

consisted of those who were single-minded enough to pay a visit and not ashamed to admit they enjoyed themselves. The much larger 'anti' camp consisted of those who hadn't been but knew someone who had and who said it was a waste of money, and those who had been but were too "highbrow" to admit liking it.

The numbers continued to fall below expectations and calls continued to be made to chop off the heads of anyone even remotely linked to the whole messy affair. Enter Mister PY Gerbeau – or Gerbil as he became known – a former employee of Disneyland Paris who had been drafted in to rescue the Dome. This only added insult to injury and the press had a field day. A foreigner – and French to boot – brought in to spare the government's blushes? What was the world coming to? White van man was frothing at the mouth.

And so it closed. Now no one has a dome to go to. But the controversy rages on. Reputations have been tarnished to say the least, and The Dome's ability to embarrass the government shows no sign of abating.

Royal
Observatory

A steep walk up the hill through the park behind the Museum leads to the Royal Observatory. Most prominent of the buildings is **Flamsteed House** which looks and sounds like something out of Harry Potter but is in fact the 17th-century home of the Astronomer Royal. On its roof, the red Time Ball drops on the dot of one o'clock every day, put up in 1833 to give an exact time signal to the docks in the distance.

A visit to the Observatory starts in the **Meridian Courtyard**, where it's possible to straddle the dividing line between eastern and western hemispheres, and then takes in Flamsteed House, with its four reconstructed period rooms and Wren's Octagon Room for watching celestial events; the Harrison Gallery containing four of the revolutionary clocks that allowed sailors to find longitude accurately for the first time in 1735; the Meridian Building and the instruments used down the centuries to determine the meridian; and next door the Airy Transit Circle, the telescope that pinpointed the current meridian in 1851 and now the source of the green laser beamed exactly due north every evening. A spiral staircase then leads up to the large 28-inch telescope, housed in its distinctive dome and in use until 1957 examining the orbits of binary stars. Beyond is the **Altazimuth Pavilion**, named after a type of telescope that plotted the co-ordinates of a planet or star by measuring their altitude above the horizon and their azimuth, or position east along the horizon. The building now houses a photoheliograph used to look at an image of the sun projected onto a flat plate.

■ *Open daily 1000-1700 (last admission 1630). Admission £6, £4.80 concession. OAPs and under-16s free, www.rog.nmm.ac.uk Joint ticket with Museum £10.50, £8.40 concession. T020-8858 4422, information T020-8312 6565.*

Famous for its wide views over Docklands, the City, Tower Bridge and round to the London Eye and Big Ben, best appreciated from near the Observatory or from One Tree Hill, Greenwich Park is a relatively high rolling expanse of green, criss-crossed by tree-lined avenues embracing a lakeside flower garden, deer park and some Roman remains.

Greenwich Park

In fact it's surrounded on all sides by old buildings of considerable interest. **Crooms Hill** on the west is a sloping row of very fine Georgian houses leading up to the red-brick 18th-century Rangers House, on Chesterfield Walk (T020-8853 0035, www.english-heritage.co.uk), the home of the Suffolk collection of English 16th-18th-century portraits but closed until April 2002 for extensive refurbishment. Beyond Rangers House lies the Dell and the Blackheath Gate, the usual starting point for the London Marathon every April, and in the park's often-deserted eastern corner, woodland walks and another viewpoint. At the bottom of Maze Hill stands **Vanbrugh's Castle**, a mock-medieval folly, the first of its kind in the country, designed and lived in by Sir John Vanbrugh. On summer weekends, the park is always crowded with visitors and Londoners picnicking and taking the air.

Further south, the almost featureless expanse of Blackheath stretches down to Greenwich's smart little neighbour, **Blackheath Village**. Also unmistakable from most viewpoints in the park is the huge **Millennium Dome** in North Greenwich. At the time of writing, this great white elephantine structure has yet to find a new owner or purpose after failing to attract anything like the number of visitors anticipated.

■ *Open 0700-dusk daily. T020-8858 2608.*

Beyond Greenwich

Downriver past the Millennium Dome, at 1 Unity Way, SE18, and best viewed by boat, the **Thames Barrier** is the world's largest movable flood barrier, completed in 1982 after seven years under construction. An impressive sight in itself, with its rank of shining steel 'sails', the barrier has often been raised in emergencies. Alarmingly enough, it has already been suggested that even this formidable barrier will be incapable of preventing central London from flooding as a result of a surge tide within the next two decades.

The Visitor Centre on the southern bank explains the hydraulics that operate the massive paddles and also explains the threat the river presents. Ideally a visit should be timed to coincide with one of the monthly testings, phone for details.

■ *Visitor Centre open 1000-1500 daily. Admission (tickets from café) £1, 50p concession and children, 75p OAP. T020-8305 4188.*

A mile further downstream is Woolwich, a top destination for fans of gunnery being home to the Museum of Artillery, recently relocated to the old buildings of the Royal Arsenal, and open in May 2001 re-christened 'Firepower'. The new displays combine the collections of the Royal Artillery Regimental

Museum of Artillery
Woolwich Arsenal Station

Up & down the river

Museum, the Rotunda Museum and the Medal Collection, ranging from pieces of 14th-century ordinance to nuclear Lance missiles. The older museum in the Rotunda Gun remains open, featuring a cannon from the Mary Rose sunk in 1545, and a 12-pounder given to Queen Victoria by Louis Napoleon when she visited Paris in the 1850s. Outside there are howitzers as well as Chinese and Russian-made guns captured in the Gulf War, and a unique 18-inch British railway gun guarding the gate on Repository Road. Built in 1917 to defend the coast during the First World War, not actually fired until 1921.

■ *Open daily 1000-1700. Rotunda Museum open Mon-Fri 1300-1600. Admission free. T020-8316 5402, www.firepower.org.uk*

Eltham Palace Further to the southeast, Eltham Palace is the 1930s home of millionaire Stephen Courtauld which he had purpose-built around the Great Hall of a medieval palace. Most impressive is the entrance hall, a spectacular reception room for Virginia Courtauld's glamourous parties. Like the rest of the house, it has been lavishly restored to its art deco heyday, but some may be disappointed by the absence of original paintings. The garden has also recently been returned to its former glory.

■ *Open Wed, Thu, Fri, Sun 1000-1600. Admission £5.90, £4.40 concession. Summer open until 1800. Best reached from Charing Cross Station, taking either the Dartford line via Bexley Heath to Eltham, or Sidcup line to Mottingham, then a 15-min walk, or No 161 bus. Or take bus 286 from Greenwich beside Cutty Sark, about 20 mins. T020-8294 2548.*

Eating and drinking

Mid-range **In Greenwich** Most promising newcomer in this bracket is *The Wardroom*, Royal
● *on map, page 394* Naval College, SE10, T020-8269 4797 (closed on Sat), a lunchtime restaurant in the undercroft beneath the Painted Hall, with very high standards of service, fairly formal but friendly in a historic building. Another good bet is *Inside*, 19 Greenwich South St, T020-8265 5060, for its acclaimed modern European fusion food in an unpromising location, lively and fun. The Sun brunch here is good value for £8-9.

In Blackheath, *Chapter Two*, 43/45 Montpelier Vale, Blackheath Village, SE3, T020-8333 2666, do imaginative modern British food in comfortable surroundings.

Cheap At the top of this bracket, a funky place to enjoy a changing menu of modern European food with its finger on the pulse of young Greenwich is *Time*, 7a College Approach, SE10, T020-8305 9767. The small restaurant on a balcony overlooks the bar with its sofas, comfy chairs and art gallery in a converted church hall. Starters might be a warm asparagus salad for £5, or rib-eyed steak and spinach £12.95. Definitely needs booking Fri-Sun nights.

Best budget option though is *Noodle Time*, 10-11 Nelson Rd, SE10, T020-8293 5263, roomy, cheap and cheerful, where a generous bowl of noodles costs about £5. Open 7 days all day and evenings. If that's impossibly busy, next door is *Thai Chung*, 8 Nelson Rd, SE10, T020-8858 8588, also doing Thai food, noodles, pad thai and Ho Fun. Open all day until 2330.

Cafés & **In Greenwich** From the places that open up specifically at the weekends, *Royal Teas*,
sandwich bars 76 Royal Hill, SE10, T020-8691 7240, do excellent home-made meals, tea and coffee on a boutique lined strip that's popular with the local intelligentsia.

In Blackheath, the *Village Delicatessen*, 1/3 Tranquil Vale, SE3, T020-8852 2015, is a local deli and café with superb freshly baked bread.

In Greenwich Right on the dockfront near the Cutty Sark, and consequently usually heaving with tourists, is the *Gipsy Moth*, T020-8858 0786. Downstream, next to the Royal Naval College, the *Trafalgar Tavern*, Park Row, SE10, T020-8858 2437, is a large historic pub with river views, often loud and busy on Fri and Sat, but a traditional retreat serving reasonable grub at other times. Next door is its rival, *The Yacht*, 5 Crane St, SE10, T020-8858 0175, tucked down an alleyway, the cosy old back bar now spreading into a modern extension overlooking the river. No music and decent Theakston's Old Peculiar.

▶▶ *Go to page 438 for entertainment & nightlife*

Slightly off the beaten tourist track and much more popular with the locals is the *Ashburnham Arms*, 25 Ashburnham Grove, SE10, T020-8692 2007, off Greenwich South St. Good beer, bar billiards and a good-natured atmosphere. *The North Pole*, 131 Greenwich High Rd, SE10, T020-8855 3020, does very good breakfasts and has outside seating, while *The Wine Vaults*, 165 Greenwich High Rd, SE10, T020-8858 7204, may be part of the Davy's chain, but are nonetheless authentic cellars with loyal staff and reasonable food. Up on fashionable Royal Hill, *Richard I*, 52 Royal Hill, SE10, T020-8692 2996, is a good Young's pub with a beer garden, decent food lunchtimes and evenings and a largely appreciative local crowd.

In Blackheath, *Zerodegrees*, 29-31 Montpelier Vale, SE3, T020-8852 5619, is a trendy new microbrewery, light and modern, with an interesting menu and long winelist. *Cave Austin*, 79 Montpelier Vale, SE3, T020-8852 0492, is a typical Blackheath-style bar while *The Hare and Billet*, Hare and Billet Rd, SE3, T020-8852 2352 is a very busy and popular local on the heath.

Shopping

At weekends, *Greenwich Market*, T020-7639 8659, is no longer excellent for antiques, riddled as it is with a fair amount of tat, but the odd gem may show up. *The Village Market* on Stockwell St has the most jumble, junk and the odd rare record; *Greenwich High Rd Market* is where people flog their surplus consumer durables; while the *Church St Market* in the old covered market is full of craftsfolk peddling their handywork.

Greenwich is strong on antiques the rest of the week, a reliable and long-standing destination being *Spread Eagle Antiques*, 9 Nevada St, SE10, T020-8305 1666, and also *Spread Eagle Books*, 8 Nevada St, with a junk shop on Greenwich South St. *Halcyon Books*, 1 Greenwich South St, T020-8305 2675, is a large and rambling second-hand bookshop complete with small stools for weary browsers. *Marcet Books*, 4a Nelson Rd, T020-8853 5408, also do general second-hand books.

On the main drag, *Bullfrogs*, 22 Greenwich Church St, T020-8305 2404, specialize in urban unisex clubwear and casual clothes, shoes and sunglasses. Royal Hill is an increasingly fashionable strip of shops, typical outlets being *The Greenhouse*, 18 Royal Hill, SE10, T020-8305 1772, a well-respected garden shop, and *Cheeseboard*, 26 Royal Hill, Greenwich, SE10, T020-8305 0401, for award-winning cheeses, breads along with excellent service – an immaculate deli.

In Blackheath, *Hand Made Food*, 40 Tranquil Vale, SE3, T020-8297 9966, will deliver delicious modern-European meals to your door, as well as cheeses, pastas, salads and frozen ready-mades.

Up & down the river

Transport

Buses	**For Greenwich**:

For Greenwich:

No 177 between Thamesmead and Peckham via Crossway, Abbey Estate, Woolwich, Greenwich and New Cross.

No 188 between North Greenwich and Russell Square via Greenwich, Deptford, Surrey Quays, Canada Water, Bermondsey, Elephant, Waterloo, Aldwych and Kingsway.

No 199 between Elephant and Catford Garage via South Bermondsey, Surrey Quays, Pepys Estate, Deptford, Greenwich, Lewisham and Catford.

No 286 between Greenwich Church and Sidcup via Blackheath, Kidbrooke, Eltham, and Avery Hill.

River transport **From Greenwich Pier** (T020-8305 0300). Tours to Thames Barrier; Catamaran Cruises, T020-7987 1185; sightseeing cruises between Embankment, Tower and Greenwich.

Taxis Best for taxis is Greenwich High Rd.

Trains Cutty Sark or Greenwich DLR (from Canary Wharf), Greenwich or Maze Hill (from Charing Cross, London Bridge), Blackheath, Woolwich Arsenal.

Tubes North Greenwich (Jubilee line) for Millennium Dome.

Up & down the river

Entertainment and nightlife

10

Entertainment and nightlife

The London music scene

Contemporary music: rock, jazz, folk, roots, world

If London really is the most cosmopolitan city in Europe, it shows clearly in the bewildering array of live music it has to offer. As the population centre of Britain it is the obvious and essential stopping-off point for the world's largest musical acts, whilst its unrivalled position as the hub of the British music industry means that numerous aspiring artists gravitate towards its plethora of pubs and clubs to showcase their potential. Along with your everyday pub, club and stadium acts, London also boasts the Notting Hill Carnival comprising two days of loud (invariably reggae) music, parades and dancing, and even a touch of sun if you're lucky. The Carnival takes place annually on the Sunday and bank holiday Monday of the last weekend in August. Of course, such is the scale of the scene that there are a number of places where one can sample some of the untapped talent trying to impose itself on an often fickle listening public. Everyone has to start somewhere after all, and the briefest venture into the music history books reveals how many of the world's greatest and most revered music acts could first be seen peddling future hits to a half-hearted London pub audience.

For a picture of who is playing where and when, the best listings are to be found in *Time Out* magazine, London's entertainment bible, and the traditional music fan's weekly, the *New Musical Express* (NME). London's daily newspaper, the *Evening Standard*, also publishes the very handy 'Hot Tickets' as a supplement on Thursdays. Tickets range in cost, depending on the artist, from £2 to around £50 for the U2s of this world, and are almost always available directly from the individual venues. Stargreen Box Office near Oxford Circus, Ticketweb and the ubiquitous TicketMaster (see below) offer decent alternatives if you're not able to get there. Stargreen also prints an expansive free sheet listing of upcoming gigs. If worst comes to worst there are always ticket touts, though prices are hugely inflated and there's no guarantee that the ticket you buy will be genuine. Remember, these people are not there for your benefit. However you get in there, though, it's worth the effort. London has the best music the world has to offer. Pay the price, and you've got the world at your fingertips.

Where to buy tickets www.bigmouth.co.uk is the Uk's most comprehensive gig guide; & you can buy tickets on-line

Stargreen Box Office, 20-21a Argyll Street, Oxford Circus, W1, T020-7734 8932, www.stargreen.com *TicketMaster*, offices dotted around London, T020-7344 4444, www.ticketmaster.co.uk *Ticketweb*, T020-7771 2000, www.ticketweb.co.uk

The West End and Central London

Central London presents rich pickings for the discerning live music fanatic. Based on the outskirts of Soho, the **Astoria** is arguably the most eminent and varied venue, despite the lack of any aesthetic value whatsoever. It does suffer from the fact that a number of weekend gigs are cut short in preparation for the popular weekly G.A.Y. nights, though it does boast security which won't break your legs in order to 'discourage' an effervescent crowd. Next door to the Astoria sits the **Mean Fiddler**, having recently moved into the former Astoria 2 (LA2) from the wilds of Northwest London, presumably for reasons

Soho ▶▶ *Go to page 419 for a full list of music venues*

of accessibility. It's difficult to tell what plans, if any, Vince Power (impresario of the Mean Fiddler chain) has for his itinerant flagship, but in its previous home it housed anything from Rock to Soul. The venue itself is small, and while the view is by no means fantastic, good sound quality is assured.

The nearby **Borderline** is a club of the more intimate variety, and the bands are generally new and unheard of. It is, however, a very nice venue, and has its place in London music folklore as the stage where REM played in 1991 under the more than faintly ridiculous moniker of Bingo Handjob.

The mecca of the central jazz scene, **Ronnie Scott's** still boasts some of the finest jazz in the metropolis. A night out here isn't cheap, though the quality of the music remains strong and no visiting jazz enthusiast can seriously miss paying the place a visit. The **100 Club** is another name with a healthy record in the music annals having staged the birth of British punk in 1976. Things have slightly changed since then however, and the club is now more the home of *Take 5* than *God Save the Queen* as traditional jazz rules the roost. The odd obscure indie act does rear its head every now and then, but this is largely a testament to decent venue which doesn't take itself too seriously.

The **Blues Bar** also lives up to its name and can be found tucked away behind Carnaby Street.

Covent Garden
▶▶ *Go to page 421 for a full list of venues*

As with any area there are naturally places to avoid, though the main offenders are thankfully within spitting distance of each other in the bustle of Covent Garden. Despite its illustrious past, the **Rock Garden** peddles pretty generic and thoroughly unexciting rock and indie, all of which makes it slightly painful to recall that the Smiths played their monumental first London gig there. If you eat at the restaurant on the forecourt however, entry to the club is free. The **Roadhouse** meanwhile makes its trade by providing a platform for old former chart toppers and the odd middle-aged group belting out renditions of *Mustang Sally*. Nice. Covent Garden does have a saviour however. The **Africa Centre**, on first entry, resembles an ill-equipped youth club, though the bona fide African bands who can be found here most Fridays are absolutely top notch. Between the music, the lady selling cans of lager upstairs and the cosy bar (with draught) in the basement, the centre is an unmissable experience.

The **12 Bar Club** presents a fusion of country, folk and funk in intimate and friendly surroundings, and a bar extension and new restaurant out front can only enhance a club whose reputation has soared in recent years making it one of London's finest.

Bloomsbury
& Fitzrovia
▶▶ *Go to page 426 for full details*

Heading North, the **University of London Union** (**ULU** for short) offers quality indie stock to a predominantly student audience. As the name suggests its primary role is as a student bar. This, of course, means extremely cheap beer, so even if the bands disappoint the evening is never entirely wasted.

East London

▶▶ *Go to page 430 for a full list*

East London, like the South, is afflicted by a paucity of good live venues. It does however possess the new and increasingly prominent **London Arena**. Situated in the heart of the Docklands developments, the colossal Arena has started to play host to more and more of the better known bands (Marilyn Manson and Eminem most recently), fans of whom unfortunately fall victim to exorbitant ticket and concession prices in what is an acoustically barren cultural wasteland. Slightly more accessible (and a whole lot more fun) is

Entertainment & nightlife

Spitz which houses a restaurant and bar as well as live music. It is also notable for its free 'live classic jazz' shows every Friday night.

North London

The soulless, expensive and unatmospheric Wembley Arena apart, the live North London scene is largely centred around three areas – Camden Town, Kentish Town and Highbury and Islington. Though Wembley Stadium itself will be out of action for at least the next three years owing to a massive rebuilding programme, **Wembley Arena** continues to play host to the Britneys, Whitneys and Bon Jovis of the world. Whilst its capacity is an understandable attraction to those who do play there, the sound is flat and the building is lifeless, and it really does no favours for the fans who shell out often silly amounts of money for the privilege of attending. On a happier note, there are some very good medium-sized venues, though the strength of the North lies in the numerous pubs and small clubs which occupy the area around Camden and Kentish Town.

The Camden scene was especially potent throughout the early 80s and 90s when it gained its reputation as the hangout of the likes of Madness (who often played at the Dublin Castle), and then a decade later as the creative centre of the Britpop explosion, despite the fact that the instigators of the movement hailed from everywhere but. Britpop is now dead, but Camden has retained its reputation and is still a hotbed of fresh and undiscovered talent, though still mainly of the Indie variety.

Camden
▶▶ *Go to page 432 for a full list of venues*

The **Underworld** is one of the (comparatively) larger Camden venues, and its appearance fits its name. A string of dark and seemingly perpetual corridors eventually lead to a peculiarly proportioned underground room which houses its predominantly indie acts, and while it has character, a number of obstacles too often obscure the view. **Dingwalls**, despite its intimacy, is not predominantly a music venue. Tables and seating can prove obstructive and it is more at home hosting the Jongleurs comedy nights at the weekend. You can get very close to the performers though, who are more often than not largish indie bands.

The **Dublin Castle** is in many ways the epitome of the Camden pub scene. Dim and dingy, the Castle gives a platform to aspiring bands who all tend to churn out raucous indie rock. Admission is on the door and the back room is in no way large, so be prepared to be disappointed if one of the acts has conned all its mates into turning up. The **Monarch** tends to house slightly larger (again, predominantly indie) acts, though the defection of the weekly 'Barfly' live music nights from the defunct Camden Falcon does cater for the smaller bands.

Camden is not purely indie however. Despite its name, the **Jazz Café** presents an eclectic mix of world, funk and folk music, as well as its jazz staple, and the acts are always of a decent standard. It often pulls in the big names and the atmosphere is relaxed and enjoyable. Slightly awkward positioning of the bar can make it a hassle to gain refreshment while an act is on stage and the natter of the smug-looking VIPs around the balcony tables can be a touch off-putting, but these are minor quibbles to a fine venue providing first-rate entertainment.

Finally, for folk fans, there's the **Cecil Sharp House**. Undiluted and traditional, the Cecil Sharp is a leader in an otherwise under-represented field and involves nigh-on mandatory audience participation.

Entertainment & nightlife

Kentish Town.
▶▶ Go to page 432
for a full list of venues

The **Forum** is undoubtedly one of the best venues in London. Despite its size, the demarcation between the front and back of the hall makes for an intimate connection between band and audience, with the only disadvantage being possibly that there is no real place near the front to simply stand and watch. The bar facilities are excellent and should hunger get the better of you there is even a small food counter.

Similarly, the **Bull and Gate** is one of the city's top pub venues and regularly presents three bands at a time for a very modest sum. The chances of ever having heard of/hearing of any of them again is, of course, minimal, though it is a renowned haunt of the A&R industry.

Highbury
& Islington
▶▶ Go to page 433
for a full list of venues

The **Garage** on Highbury Corner, despite being an otherwise mediocre venue, appears especially adept at attracting strong line-ups from both sides of the Atlantic, with less renowned acts being exiled to the room upstairs. It does tend to be generally indie and rock orientated, but the occasional foray into jazz is not unheard of.

Complete with pews and pulpit, the **Union Chapel** is bizarrely as good as its name suggests, and while its relatively infrequent gigs generally favour no particular genre, it's a fairly safe bet that satanic-nazi-death metal is not especially welcome. Far easier to categorize is the small but perfectly formed **Hope and Anchor** pub which tends to stick to a tried and tested formula of bright and breezy indie pop and rock.

West London

▶▶ Go to page 434
for a full list

Dispensing with the aberration of **Earl's Court** (the owners and organizers should come to grips with the fact that it is an exhibition centre; to even try and pass it off as a music venue is, frankly, heresy), the West's trump card is the **Shepherd's Bush Empire**. The Empire bears a strong similarity to the Brixton Academy and the Forum not only in terms of exterior and décor but also in the strength and range of what's on. Criticisms are virtually non-existent, though watch for the over-zealous attendants in the gallery intent on stopping people smoking.

The **London Apollo**, though also large and theatre-esque, suffers from a decidedly middle-of-the-road line-up, so don't expect anything especially groundbreaking. Technically in Chelsea (see page 424), the **606 Club** has nightly jazz by purely local acts. Non-members can only drink by buying a largish meal, and entry at weekends can usually only be gained by non-members if they eat. Admission is free, though there is a 'music charge' of around £6 which is added to the bill. A night out is quite expensive, but the music is quality and the 606 is well worth the trip to Chelsea.

If you fancy breaking into a sweat and having some real fun however, check out the **Hammersmith and Fulham Irish Centre**. Hosting the full range of Irish musical merriment from ceilidhs to biggish trad bands, the centre constitutes a fine antidote to bad Irish theme pub induced nausea.

South London

Southeast
London
▶▶ Go to page 438
for entertainment
& nightlife

Southeast London has spawned some of the greatest music talent to have come out of the city – David Bowie was born in Bromley, the Rolling Stones grew up in the southeast and Dire Straits first came together there as a band. Strangely though, it lacks any really noteworthy venues. The **Blackheath Concert Halls** stage the occasional show – politico folk legend Billy Bragg and top saxophonist Courtney Pine have played there in recent times – though such performances are infrequent. The **Trafalgar** pub in Greenwich (see page 401) holds regular gigs for aspiring local acts (indie upstairs, jazz downstairs) and the **Amersham Arms** in New Cross (see page 401) hosts a number of student bands, mainly of the punk and indie variety, benefiting from its proximity to Goldsmith's College. It's also worth noting that the **South Bank Centre** (comprising the Royal Festival Hall, the Queen Elizabeth Hall and the Purcell Room) has begun to stage more and more contemporary gigs, most notably perhaps the annual Meltdown festival, the line-up for which in 2000 was chosen by Scott Walker (see page 428).

The southwest, conversely, boasts the mighty **Brixton Academy**. This old Victorian hall has a capacity which attracts the biggest of artists while not appearing over-large, and in any case it is invariably full. Much comment is made of the Academy's steeply sloping floor which, while ensuring a good view for all, has the disadvantage of making drunken dancing mildly perilous. For this reason, some of the big dance acts who occasionally play all-nighters prefer to level the floor artificially. It is, however, a fantastic venue and it was no surprise when it was picked out by Madonna as the stage for her 'secret' reintroduction to the world's audiences in 2000.

Southwest London
▶▶ Go to page 436 for a full list

The **Swan** pub in Stockwell is the most Irish place you'll find south of, well, Kilburn. Though it allows the odd rock act through its doors at weekends, you can guarantee semi-traditional Celtic stuff during the week along with a loud and lively atmosphere.

Classical and opera

One of the best places in Europe to hear excellent classical music, London boasts four world class orchestras and numerous notable ensembles. However, for many years, the city's esteemed classical music scene has been deeply troubled by financial difficulties. Still, as we enter the new century it is beginning to appear that the annual funding problems which have plagued classical music in London are beginning to ease. As new avenues of funding have opened up in the last few years many are beginning to feel a little optimism concerning the preservation of what is an otherwise healthy, vibrant and varied scene.

The **London Symphony Orchestra**, based at the notoriously difficult-to-find Barbican Centre (beware street signs pointing in opposite directions), is arguably the pick of the bunch, though it is closely followed by the **Philharmonia** and the **London Philharmonic Orchestra** (both resident at the Royal Festival Hall), as well as the itinerant and slightly weaker **Royal Philharmonic Orchestra**. In addition, there are a number of venues, large and small, which hold regular concerts by internationally renowned musicians, local artists and students. The **Barbican Centre** (see page 427), as well as housing the LSO, plays host to guest orchestras and is the domain for international acclaimed soloists and conductors, though the music is often safe and traditional.

The **South Bank Centre** (see page 428) is really three venues in one. The positively huge **Royal Festival Hall** holds large-scale symphonic orchestral and choral concerts, whilst the smaller **Queen Elizabeth Hall** and smaller still **Purcell Room** stick to chamber music, though the QEH can also stage opera.

Entertainment & nightlife

Concert dates for 2001

BBC Sir Henry Wood Promenade Concerts: 20 July-15 September; www.bbc.co.uk/proms
The BOC Covent Garden Festival: 14 May-3 June; www.cgf.co.uk

City of London Festival: 26 June-12 July; www.city-of-london-festival.org.uk
Spitalfields Festival: 4 June-22 June summer season, winter to be arranged; www.spitalfieldsfestival.org.uk

The **Royal Albert Hall** (see page 424) is home to the world-famous Sir Henry Wood Promenade Concerts (Proms for short), the annual classical feast running from July to September with music ranging from the well-loved to the new and cutting-edge. Seats can be booked in advance, but to truly sample the essence of the season try slumming it with one of the dirt-cheap Arena standing tickets.

Wigmore Hall (see page 425) is ornate, intimate, affordable, acoustically perfect and its concerts and recitals are of a high standard. Furthermore, the Wigmore celebrates its centenary in 2001 so expect a commemorative season of the highest calibre – check local listings for details. On the cheaper side of things, the **Royal College of Music** (see page 424) holds afternoon chamber concerts on term-time weekdays, most of which are free and open to the public. The standard is very high despite the musicians' amateur status, and well worth investigating. Look out also for some of the many festivals which take place throughout the year. The best and most interesting of these are the BOC Covent Garden Festival, the City of London Festival and the Spitalfields Festival.

Opera is best served in London by the **Royal Opera House** and the English National Opera at the **Coliseum** (see page 418). Despite the Royal Opera House's rather stuffy and conservative reputation, the old place appears to have loosened up a touch since its long-awaited refurbishment. Prices remain exorbitant (up to £115), though there are seats available in the gods for under £20. There is also a restaurant and bar in which to while away the day, and tours are available for the curious. The Coliseum, on the other hand, prides itself on being the antithesis to the ROH. Housing the English National Opera, its programme tends to be more ambitious, tickets are cheaper and the music is sung in English. In truth, both are of a high standard and the ROH has done much to regain its prestige after the public relations disasters of the last 10 years.

London club scene

London is without doubt the musical capital of Europe offering every conceivable form of music in its various bars, clubs and auditoriums. Whether it's dance clubs or live music you want, you'll never be short of options. Over the last decade live music and rock in particular have been taken over by dance music and nightclubs with clubbing now established as the preferred social activity for London's young people.

One of London's biggest and most famous nightclubs is **The Ministry Of Sound** (Gaunt Street, SE1), just south of the river Thames in London's Elephant & Castle district. The Ministry was Britain's first ever purpose-built

Entertainment & nightlife

'super club' and over its eight years in existence has built itself into a multinational business and the biggest dance brand name in the world. The club itself remains as popular as ever and features different styles of dance music on different nights of the week with Saturday nights usually reserved for a visiting big-name American DJ. There are almost always queues and it can be difficult to get into, so be warned.

For those not wanting to trek to South London there are now two more recently opened super clubs nearer the centre of town. **Home** was opened in 1998 by Darren Hughes, one of the partners in the famous Cream club, and is a multistorey club situated on Leicester Square. As well as dance floors, Home features a restaurant and private members' bar, with the club area attracting a young crowd and featuring many of the UK's leading DJs. The musical policy varies but is generally harder house music and trance. ▶▶ *Go to page 417*

London's most fashionable super club is without a doubt the purpose-built **Fabric** which opened two years ago in the super-cool Clerkenwell area of East London (Charterhouse Street, EC1). The club has three different dance areas and a sound system with speakers situated under the floor. The club features more underground dance music ranging from drum and bass to tech house and trip hop. With both Home and Fabric expect big queues to get in particularly at the weekends. ▶▶ *Go to page 426*

London's most popular brand of home-grown dance music is UK Garage or 'Underground Garage', 'Speed Garage', '2 Step Garage' as it's also known. Taking elements from dance music, US R&B and reggae, UK Garage is immediately identifiable by its strange off-beat rhythm, speeded up vocals and heart shuddering bass. If you turn on a radio in London you will hear up to a dozen pirate radio stations playing nothing else, and this uniquely British sound is by far the music of choice for London's multicultural suburban youth.

You'll find a variety of clubs featuring this music all over London, particularly in the suburbs but probably the best is *Twice As Nice* which happens in Central London at **The End** (West Central Street, WC2) every Sunday night. Expect to see one of the most dressed up crowds in London, with the designer clothes being worn matched by the cars parked outside the club and the flow of champagne within. So make sure you dress up. On other nights The End usually features an excellent selection of dance music and is worth a visit as it is generally regarded as one of the best designed and run clubs in the capital. ▶▶ *Go to page 420*

For black American music like hip hop and R&B there are a number of excellent long-running club nights. Two of the best are *Rotation* on Friday nights at the **Subterania Club** in Labroke Grove, West London (see page 434) and *Fresh & Funky* on Wednesday at the **Hanover Grand** in the West End (Hanover Street, WC1). Both feature young mixed crowds and a party atmosphere. The Subterania Club also plays host to one of the best reggae nights in London on Wednesday hosted by the world famous reggae DJ David Rodigan.

Clubs aren't the only places to hear good dance music and DJ's. Bars have become increasingly popular since London relaxed its entertainment licensing laws in the mid-90s. Across London there are dozens of bars which now open until 0100 or 0200 and feature DJs and club music. Without a doubt the best place to experience this thriving bar culture is in Old Street, just east of central London. Previously a commercial area, in the 90s many young people moved into the neighbourhoods around Old Street such as Hoxton and Shoreditch when old warehouses and offices were turned into loft apartments. The area ▶▶ *Go to page 279* also began to see bars opening. Travel to Old Street tube station and you will have the choice of around a dozen trendy small bars within five minutes walk such as The **Dragon Bar** (Leonard Street, EC1), The **Electricity Show Room** (Shoreditch High Street, EC1), The **Lux** (Hoxton Square, EC1) and The **Home Bar** (Curtain Road).

▶▶ Go to page 430 The Old Street area also has its own clubs like the newly opened and very good **Cargo** (Rivington Street, EC1) and The **333** (Old Street) which is perhaps the quintessential Old Street clubbing experience.

Cinema – the movies in London

Expect to pay £6-10 for screenings in the West End; less before 1700. It's a good idea to book by credit card for the first weekend of a film's release. There's often a small handling fee when booking by phone Like Londoners themselves, cinemas come in every conceivable shape and size. There are small, sweaty booths at the back of seedy bookshops, and seats for nearly 2000 at the Odeon Leicester Square. At the **Institute of Contemporary Arts** (known locally as the ICA; see page 422) you will find cutting-edge epics projected on to screens that put one in mind of bed sheets. Size does matter. But one can go over the top. The screen in the **IMAX Cinema**, planted on a roundabout at Waterloo Station, inspires vertigo. It's so preposterously large that it is impossible to view everything on it at the same time. Not that one would necessarily want to. Due to the size, weight, and sheer expense of the film stock needed to feed the IMAX projectors, there is barely anything worth watching that doesn't involve a Disney cartoon or the mating habits of humpback whales (see page 428).

▶▶ Go to page 417 The user-friendly picture palaces with state-of-the-art sound systems and satisfyingly chunky screens congregate around Soho and the West End. Here the latest blockbusters do battle with the best of the independents. For most visitors, **Leicester Square** satisfies all their needs. Three *Odeon Cinemas* (T0870-5050007), the *Warner Village West End* (T020-7437 3484) and the *Empire* (T020-7437 1234) showcase the crop of current releases. Seats are pricier here than at local cinemas but the rumbling special effects look, sound, and feel better simply because of the scale and sophistication of the equipment. Cinemas like these hardly vary from one continent to another. The airport foyers, the popcorn counters, the plastic hotdogs ... it can seem all too dismally familiar.

More challenging experiences are to be found in London's excellent network of repertory cinemas which specialize in themes, seasons, festivals, and retrospectives. They aren't grouped in one nicely accessible square, but then they aren't miles away either. The atmosphere is more interesting, the buildings are more unusual and they tend to come with bookshops, superior café-bars, often a restaurant, and always a better class of audience.

London Film Festival: T020-7928 3232, www.lff.org.uk, or www.bfi.org.uk
▶▶ *Go to page 428* The obvious starting point is the **National Film Theatre** (T020-7928 3232), a power house on the South Bank nestling between the National Theatre and the Royal Festival Hall (a premier classical music venue). Many British films, like Anthony Minghella's first major movie, *Truly, Madly, Deeply* (with Alan Rickman and Juliet Stevenson), feature riverside views of the Thames shot on the walkways in front of these buildings. In any given week it's not unusual for the NFT's three auditoria to screen over 30 different movies; even more in November when the London Film Festival comes to town. The building's chief attraction is not just the formidable range, but the quality of the programming. The NFT is home to the British Film Institute, itself the spiritual

Entertainment & nightlife

Film festivals

🖐

London has an embarrassment of festivals; many organised in main or part by sundry foreign embassies. Try these ones.
Apart from the **London Film Festival***, the NFT also stages the* **London Lesbian and Gay Film Festival** *in April (T020-7928 3232, www.llgff.org.uk). The Metro hosts the* **Raindance festival** *(T020-7287 3833,*

www.raindance.co.uk) in October which is Britain's largest festival devoted exclusively to independent films, mostly directed by first timers. And for something a little different, you could explore the **British Short Film Festival** *in September (T020- 8743 8000, extension 6222) with screenings all over Soho and Leicester Square.*

home of British film culture, and it's to their great credit that their programmes and seasons range so widely across the international (and historical) spectrum.

But you don't have to cross the Thames to enjoy a more esoteric type of movie. In fact you don't need to stray far from Leicester Square at all. The **Curzon Soho** (see page 417), the **Metro** (see page 417), and the **ICA** (see page 422) are run by organizations who champion the weird and wonderful. The rule of thumb is this: the Curzon Soho normally showcases the most recent big arthouse releases; the Metro fields a short, but usually strong, selection of independent movies; and the ICA finds the most unlikely gems from 'world cinema' – notably the best of the new directors from Japan, China, Russia and the Middle East. They are also interesting venues to visit for themselves.

To this select list can be added a trio of further-flung cinemas with like-minded programmes. The **Everyman** at 1 Hollybush Vale, Hampstead, NW3 (see page 431), turns into a nightclub at weekends. The **Renoir** in Brunswick Square, WC1 (see page 426), is a student oasis; and the **Notting Hill Coronet**, Notting Hill Gate, W11 (see page 434) is one of the prettiest and architecturally most interesting locals in London.

London theatre, dance and comedy

Theatre

On the surface, London must be one of the least theatrical cities in the world. Most of its inhabitants are undemonstrative, don't enjoy being watched and can't bear a scene; many parts of the the city are no stage painting either. And yet the phenomenal vitality of the theatre here continues to amaze Londoners and visitors alike. From record-breaking blockbusting musicals such as the *Lion King* at the Lyceum to the tiniest two-handers in the back rooms of pubs for one week only, almost every day of the year except Sundays the city gears up for an astonishing variety of stage performances on a scale unmatched anywhere else on the planet.

The heart of all this activity is still very much the West End, where about 40 venerable old theatres put on a surprisingly diverse range of shows. Long criticised for pandering to the bottom denominator with a numbing array of tacky musicals, the competition for audiences has become so fierce that producers are now often much more adventurous. A typical night might see new Irish monologues rubbing shoulders with Greek tragedy, all singing and dancing

The best place to discover the latest on what's just opened where are the reviews and listings in Time Out, available weekly in central London on Tue

For details of where to buy theatre tickets, see page 79

spectaculars next door to a modern take on Shakespeare, as well as thrillers, farces and inevitably, *The Mousetrap*, the Agatha Christie whodunnit that has been running like clockwork for almost half a century. Other long-runners include the musicals *Les Miserables*, *Cats*, and *Starlight Express*, along with the spine-chilling *Woman in Black*, and Stephen Daldry's state of the nation production of Priestley's *An Inspector Calls*. Likely to challenge or come near their staying power are Yasmin Reza's brief multicast three-hander on male friendship, *Art*; the sassy Kander and Ebb musical *Chicago*; and the hugely popular Abba revival *Mamma Mia!* Unfortunately new writing still struggles to find space on large London stages in the West End, but it receives important support at theatres like the Royal Court in Chelsea, the Lyric in Hammersmith and also at the Royal National Theatre on the South Bank. Meanwhile, at the Barbican in the City, the Royal Shakespeare Company's repertory seasons usually include at least one sell-out hit.

Many of the smaller theatres and production houses categorized by *Time Out* as 'Off West End' are the places to take the pulse of current theatre practice, generally staging more challenging work. Sam Mendes' **Donmar Warehouse** in Covent Garden (see page 420), the **Almeida Theatre** (see page 433) in its temporary home near King's Cross, the **Young Vic** (see page 428) in Waterloo, **Bush Theatre** in Shepherd's Bush (see page 434) and **BAC** in Battersea (see page 436) all regularly tap into the hottest new acting, writing and directing talent. A relatively recent and hugely welcome addition to this line-up is the **Soho Theatre** (see page 419), bang in the middle of town. Alternatively, during the summer the **Globe Theatre** on Bankside (see page 428) has developed a good reputation for injecting new life into Elizabethan and Jacobean drama by staging jolly productions in their repro period theatre. Meanwhile the Fringe embraces anything and everything from large scale touring productions at the Bloomsbury Theatre to obscure one-offs mounted above a pub in north Clapham. The larger, more professional and high profile venues include the **Pleasance**, marooned off the Caledonian Road (see page 433), the **Southwark Playhouse** (see page 428), the **New End** theatre in Hampstead (see page 431) and the extraordinary **Bridewell Theatre** in Holborn (see page 426). Just a few of the smallest spaces with strong track records include the **Finborough Theatre** in Earl's Court (see page 435), and the **Etcetera** in Camden (see page 432), but the real joy of a trip to the Fringe – apart from the fact that it's usually quite cheap – is the individual character of the different venues and the slim chance of discovering something really spell-binding. If so, the audience – if not the cast – congratulates itself that only a handful of other people will ever be lucky enough to catch it.

Dance

Everyone knows that London has easily one of the most vibrant dance scenes in England, if not the world. The dance form most reported in the entertainment sections of the press is undoubtedly ballet, reflecting the mawkish pride that London takes in its terribly elegant ballet tradition, epitomised most recently in the film *Billy Elliot*. Whatever, the Royal Ballet Company still performs regularly at the **Royal Opera House** in Covent Garden (see page 420). Performances range from traditional classical favourites like *The Nutcracker* or *Swan Lake* to recent innovative and rule-breaking choreographic works, sometimes devised within the company. Look out too for the new breakaway touring group of ex-Royal Ballet dancers called 'K Ballet'. The English National Ballet can also be seen in lavish productions at the **London Coliseum** (see page 418), and high quality touring productions can regularly be seen at the state-of-the-art **Sadler's Wells Theatre** (see page 426).

Contemporary dance is most at home at **The Place Theatre**, currently undergoing a major refit at Dukes Road near Euston (see page 426). Like fringe theatre though, contemporary and experimental dance takes place throughout London. Major venues include the **Lillian Baylis Theatre** at Sadlers Wells, **Watermans Theatre** in Brentford (see page 437), **Jacksons Lane Arts Centre**, and further afield at **The Bull Theatre** in Barnet. Adventures in Motion Pictures is a company that started on London's dance fringe and then stormed the West End with innovative work such as Matthew Bourne's reworking of Swan Lake.

For participants, most of the world's dance forms can be learned at classes throughout London. Excellent Adult Education Centres provide classes in the most popular styles. For enthusiasts of all styles, from jazz and contemporary through to ballet, there's the **Urdang Dance Academy**, T020-7836 5709, and **Pineapple Dance Studios**, T020-7836 4004, both in Covent Garden, as well as the **Dance Attic** in Fulham, T020-7610 2055, and the **London Studio Centre**, T020-7837 7741, and the **London Contemporary Dance Evening School**, T020-7387 0152, both near King's Cross; also **Danceworks** off Oxford Street, and the **Laban Centre** near New Cross, T020-8692 4070, are some of the many that provided classes day and evening on a drop-in basis. The *Laban Centre* is also about to undergo significant extension as a result of new funding from the National Lottery.

For non-professional dancers with a nocturnal and social inclination, the range of London clubs blasting their eclectic range of dance and trance music are honey pots. Salsa is probably the most widespread and popular form, taught in bars where classes are closely followed by disco nights. Londoners jostle with visitors in a vibrant, heady, noisy atmosphere, very conducive to meeting new friends and learning something of the Latin dance form. Look out for these bars throughout London, such as **Salsa!** (see page 420).

One of the latest crazes is Ceroc, but Ballroom, Scottish, Square and Line dance are also some of the other forms taught in open classes at bars, hotels, and community centres throughout London. Information on Ceroc classes is available from *Ceroc*, T020-8846 8653. Venues include the **Jive Bar**, Russell Square on Tuesday, Wednesday and Thursday evenings at 1930 for beginners, £7.50, or the **Jongleurs** in Clapham on Monday, Wednesday, and **Fulham Town Hall** on Thursdays. Whatever way you want to move your bootie in London, it's ready and waiting for you.

Comedy

Jongleurs in Camden is also a major venue on London's comedy circuit. On almost any night of the week you are guaranteed a good laugh somewhere in this comedy-mad city. King of the comedy venues is the legendary **Comedy Store**, off Leicester Square (see page 417).

See Time Out magazine for listings

Entertainment & nightlife

Listings

The West End

Trafalgar Square

Apart from the lectures, slide shows and music evenings in the galleries, or the drifting streetlife, there's not much in the way of entertainment in Trafalgar Square in the evenings.

Festivals Most festivals in Trafalgar Square are best avoided, including the one at New Year. The Sea Cadets parade on **Trafalgar Day**, Sat nearest to Oct 21, celebrating Nelson's victory. St Martin-in-the-Fields hosts the Pearly Kings and Queens at the **Costermongers' Harvest Festival Service** in early Oct, a good-natured Cockney fancy-dress knees-up. The lights on the **Christmas Tree**, an annual gift from Norway in gratitude for British help during the Second World War, are switched on some time in Nov.

Music Free lunchtime concerts on Mon, Tue and Fri at 1305 at *St Martin-in-the-Fields*, also Candlelit Baroque concerts on Thu, Fri and Sat 1930, choral evensong on Sun at 1700. £6-15. T020-7839 8362.

The Strand, Embankment and Aldwych

Dance Tea dances at the *Waldorf* on Sat from 1430-1700 on Sun 1600-1830. Need to book, £25 per person including tea, with scones and cakes. Different big bands.

Music **Rock, folk and jazz** Jazz at *Smollensky's*, and in Palm Court of the *Waldorf*. Jazz brunch on Sun 1200-1430, £40 per person, need to book.

Nightclubs *Heaven*, under the arches, off Villiers St, WC2, T020-7930 2020, www.heaven-london.com Once the foremost gay nightclub in the city, Heaven has been joined by many others but is still going strong. Mon 1030-0300 is *Popcorn*, a disco mix, indie music and house. Wed 1030-0300 is *Fruittmachine*, hard house, disco, soul. Fri (£10) a mixed night, *There*, 1030-0600 hard house. Sat (£5) 1000-0500, commercial house, funky house. Three different rooms, 1 members bar (7 bars). First Thu every month *Bedrock* (£7-8), which is a straight night of hardtrance. All are cheaper before 1130 with a flyer, no booking, just queue. Bedrock and Sat are the busiest.

Theatres *Savoy Theatre*, Strand, WC2, T020-7836 8888. Older than the hotel, the theatre was built in 1881 by Richard d'Oyly Carte for Gilbert and Sullivan's operas. It was the first public place in London to be electrically lit. More recently it stage nearly 2000 performances of Michael Frayn's *Noises Off*. The art deco interior was fully restored after a fire in 1990.

    Adelphi Theatre, Strand, WC2, T020-7344 0055. Opened in 1806, making it the oldest theatre still standing on the Strand, it has been rebuilt 3 times since then, most recently in 1900. Famous for its melodramas and adaptations of Dickens in the 19th century. *Me and My Girl* played here for a long time in the late 80s and 90s. *Chicago* is its current hit. Box Office open Mon-Sat 1000-2000.

    Vaudeville Theatre, Strand, WC2, T020-7836 9987. Opened in 1870, this attractive little theatre was given a make-over in the 20s. Since then it has staged a successful variety of musicals and comedies, including a 6-year run of *Salad Days* in the late 50s.

Strand Theatre, Aldwych, WC2, T020-7930 8800. Opened in 1905 as one of a pair with the Aldwych Theatre. Donald Wolfit performed Shakespeare here at lunchtimes during the Blitz, and more recently Tom Stoppard's *The Real Thing* enjoyed at 2-year run. Box Office open Mon 1000-1800, Tue-Sat 1000-2000, Sun 1230-1600.

Aldwych Theatre, Aldwych, WC2, T020-7416 6003. Built as a pair with Strand Theatre to the south in 1905, the 2 theatres stand either side of the Waldorf. Before the Second World War it staged Ben Travers' farces and became the London home of the Royal Shakespeare Company in 1960 before the company moved to the Barbican in 1982. Box office open Mon-Sat 1000-2000.

Playhouse Theatre, Northumberland Av, WC2, T020-7839 4292.

Leicester Square and around

The 2 big picture palaces in Leicester Square are the 3-screen *Empire*, T020-7437 1234 (bookings T0870-1020 030 plus 50p booking fee), on the north side of the square, where most world and national premieres take place, and the huge-screen *Odeon Leicester Square,* WC2, T0878-5050 007 (plus 40p booking fee), on the east side, formerly the Alhambra Music Hall, now the largest cinema in the West End.

Cinemas
Leicester Square & the surrounding area boasts the densest population of cinemas, theatres & clubs in London

Next door to it is the much less grand 5-screen *Odeon Mezzanine*, T0870-5050 007. On the south side of the square, and much more pleasant, is the *Odeon West End,* T0870-5050 007. *Screen 2 is larger than Screen 1.*

Warner Village West End, Leicester Square (programme information T020-7437 4347; enquiries T020-7437 3484; advance booking T020-7437 4343), is a refurbished 9-screen multiplex. The *ABC Swiss Centre*, Leicester Square, WC2, T020-7439 4470, is a 4-screen cinema that often shows more offbeat releases.

Just off the square itself, the *ABC Panton St*, SW1, T020-7930 0631, is a small 4-screen cinema, while the *UGC Haymarket*, T0870-907 0712, shows mainstream new releases on its 3 screens. The *Odeon Haymarket* T0878-5050 007, further up is being renovated. All the cinemas above show a wide variety of new releases.

Altogether different is The *Prince Charles*, Leicester Place, WC2 (today's films T020-7734 9127; this week's films T0901-2727 007), a popular inexpensive cult repertory cinema club with regular theme nights and late night screenings.

The *Metro*, 11 Rupert St, W1, T020-7734 1506, is a very comfortable 2-screen arthouse, while the *Curzon Soho*, 93-107 Shaftesbury Av, W1, T020-7734 2255 (recorded information T020-7439 4805), does fashionable first-runs, private screenings, and has a good coffee shop and bar.

The trailblazing comedy venue that's now almost too popular for its own good is the *Comedy Store*, 1a Oxendon St, SW1, T020-7344 0234, unreserved, Tue-Sun 1830 for 2000; Fri, Sat midnight, doors open 2300. Each show 2¼ hrs. £12-15, few tickets on the door. Food and bar. Best arrive early to get a good seat at this now legendary and often sold-out comedy dive.

Comedy

Nearby the *Comedy Pub*, 7 Oxendon St, SW1, T020-7839 7261, follows in its footsteps fortnightly Mon and every Tue. Mon at 2000, £4, usually sold out (www.sitcomvacant.com); Thu £6 admission not as busy (www.zoo42.com)

More pub comedy can be found for free at the *Round Table*, 26 St Martin's Court, SW1, T020-7836 6436, on Tue and Sun at 2030.

During Dec, the gardens are taken over by a Christmas fair ground, with all the traditional rides like dodgems and roundabouts but sadly no ferris wheel. **Chinese New Year**, in Jan or Feb, is celebrated in Chinatown with a procession down Gerrard St with masks reflecting whichever Chinese year is being ushered in. The **Chinese mid-Autumn Festival**, in mid-Sep, sees the area lively up itself with stage performances and dancing.

Festivals

Entertainment & nightlife

Music **Classical and opera** The *London Coliseum*, St Martin's Lane, T020-7632 8300, www.eno.org, is the home of English National Opera, and all operas are sung in English. One of the largest theatres in London it also stages ballet and full-scale touring productions. £3-22 with standbys for students.

Rock, folk and jazz Live music happens in some of the clubs, like *Sound*, 10 Wardour St, W1, T020-7287 1010, on Fri nights with Talent Scout £5, 1930-2200 (see below). And the *Wag Club*, 35 Wardour St, W1, T020-7437 5534, with *Blowup* 1000-0500 on Sat, live band, often 60s northern soul (see below).

Nightclubs Two massive dance clubs have long been synonymous with Leicester Square, and both are usually avoided by most Londoners, the *Equinox*, Leicester Square, WC2, T020-7437 1446, and the *Hippodrome*, T020-7437 4311. These mega party venues are popular with tourists and Brits who've come into town for the night.

Recently they've been joined by *Home*, 1 Leicester Square, WC2, T020-7909 0000 (booking tickets T0115-9129225) www.homecorp.com Open Thu-Sat 2200-0300, Thu £7, Fri £10, Sat £15. This 7-storey dance block, complete with restaurant, internet café and coffee shop, cost millions and looks set to make them back double quick. Beat, breaks and underground house set the 3 dancefloors jumping on Thu, while Fri are more funky and Sat are more mainstream and more expensive. With its resident DJs famous, infamous and unknown, Home holds its head up high with megaclubs in Leeds, Manchester and Europe.

Much smaller and more of an old-timer but relatively as popular for commercial house, dance and garage, with soul, swing and R&B in the basement bar and a gay teanight on Sun, is the *Limelight*, 136 Shaftesbury Av, WC2, T020-7434 0572 www.thelimelightclub.com Open Mon-Thu 2200-0300, Fri and Sat 2100-0330. Mon £4 admission after 2300; Tue and Wed £5 admission after 2300; Thu £6 admission after 2300; Fri £3 admission 2100-2200, £5 admission 2200-2230, and £10 admission after 2230; Sat £6 admission before 2200 and £12 after.

If it's funk you're after, check into the *Clinic*, 13 Gerrard St, W1, T020-7734 9836. Open Wed-Sat 2200-0300; £4 admission after 2200. *Operation Funk* stirs things up on Wed, Fri is for twisted house, and Sat sees in the dawn with the *First Church of Funk*. Back on a much bigger scale, *Sound*, 10 Wardour St, W1, T020-7287 1010, is open Mon-Wed until 2400, Thu-Sat, 2200-0400. DJs spin funk and R&B on Fri til 0400, Sat is *Carwash*, the famous 70s disco night.

Two smaller clubs are also worth trying: the *Gass Club*, Whitcomb St, WC2, T020-7839 3922, £10 after 2300 on Fri, no sportswear, and the *Wag Club*, 35 Wardour St, W1, T020-7437 5534. *Blowup* 2200-0500 with live band and 60s northern soul; £10 admission, £8 before 2300. On Tue house, Wed rock and indie, Thu classic 60s-90s, Fri 80s.

Theatres The official half-price ticket booth (see page 79) is on the south side of Leicester Square. Run by the Society of London Theatre (SOLT), T020-7557 6700, it offers discounted tickets, first-come-first-served so there's usually a queue.

Haymarket Theatre Royal, Haymarket, SW1, T020-7930 8800. There's been a theatre on this site since 1720, famous for staging Oscar Wilde's *Ideal Husband* and in 1914 the first London production of Ibsen's *Ghosts*.

Her Majesty's, Haymarket, SW1, T020-7494 5400. Originally built by Sir John Vanbrugh in 1704, managed by William Congreve, and later staged many of the first performances of Handel's work. Burnt down in 1789, then rebuilt as an opera house, witnessing London premieres of *Fidelio, Carmen,* and Wagner's *Ring* cycle. Rebuilt again in 1897 under the management of Herbert Beerbohm Tree, founder of RADA. Lloyd Webber's *Phantom of the Opera* has been running here since 1986.

Comedy Theatre, Panton St, SW1, T020-7369 1731. A little late 19th-century theatre most famous recently for staging the *Little Shop of Horrors*.

Prince of Wales Theatre, Coventry St, W1, T020-7839 5972. Since 1884 this large theatre has been dedicated to musicals and vaudeville.

The following are all on Shaftesbury Av, between Piccadilly Circus and Cambridge Circus: *Apollo*, T020-7494 5070. Nearest to Piccadilly Circus, majors on musicals.

Lyric Shaftesbury, T020-7494 5045. Built in 1888, famous in the 50s for staging plays by TS Eliot and later Alan Bennett, now tends towards West End dramas and star vehicles.

Gielgud Theatre, T020-7494 5065. Built in 1906, now usually shows straight plays, casting as the name suggests (was called *The Globe*).

Queen's Theatre, T020-7494 5040. Built as twin to The Globe, now stages a wide mix of classics, musicals and new plays.

Palace Theatre, T020-7434 0909. Built as an opera house in 1888, staged the *Sound of Music* in the 60s, *Jesus Christ Superstar* in the 70s, and, since 1985, *Les Miserables*.

New Ambassadors, West St, T020-7836 6111. Strong on drama, especially since the recent departure of Royal Court which used it as a temporary space while its home in Sloane Square was refurbished.

St Martin's, West St, WC2, T020-7836 1443. *The Mousetrap*, 5th decade of Agatha Christie's whodunnit, staged here since 1974, sharing its title with the play that catches the conscience of the king in *Hamlet*.

Wyndham's Theatre, Charing Cross Rd, T020-7369 1736. Built in 1899, famous for its radical dramas, now reduced to the ever-changing cast of *Art*.

Garrick Theatre, Charing Cross Rd, WC2, T020-7494 5085. Also built in 1889, famous for a long run of *No Sex Please We're British*, now home to Stephen Daldry's striking production of JB Priestley's *An Inspector Calls*.

Duke of York's, St Martin's Lane, T020-7836 5122. First theatre in St Martin's Lane, originally called the *Trafalgar Square Theatre*, now usually shows straight plays.

Albany Theatre, St Martin's Lane, T020-7369 1730. Opened in 1903 as the *New Theatre*, where Gielgud made his name before the war, Eliot's *Cocktail Party*, Dylan Thomas' *Under Milk Wood*, 60s Lionel Bart's *Oliver* drama.

Arts Theatre, 6-7 Great Newport St, WC2, T020-7836 3334. Opened in 1927 as theatre club, most famous for staging *Waiting for Godot* in 1955. The much-loved Arts Theatre Café has now been reopened as a tapas bar.

Soho

Bar Aquarius, 153 Charing Cross Rd, WC2, T020-7439 9730. Every night, 2000 for 2100, admission £3-5 in basement bar. **Comedy**

The *Soho Jazz Festival* takes place in the last week of Jul each year, bringing a host of top names into the area for some smokin' sounds in a variety of venues. **Festivals**

Rock, folk and jazz The legendary jazz club *Ronnie Scott's*, 47 Frith St, W1, T020-7439 0747, opens at 2030, admission Mon-Thu £15, Fri and Sat £20, still smokin' like a train and often needs to be booked at least a fortnight in advance. Less well-known is the *Blues Bar*, on Kingly St, WC1. The grunge brigade head to *The Mean Fiddler* (formerly *LA2*), 157 Charing Cross Rd, T020-7434 9592 (T020-7344 0044 for bookings), for their doses of live indie and rock (admission £8-20), while next door the *London Astoria* is twice the size hosting more mainstream indie and rock bands. **Music**

Nightclubs For the lastest dance sounds in Soho there's The *Emporium*, 62 Kingly St, W1, T020-7734 3190, www.emporiumlondon.com Admission Fri £10 before 2330, £15 after, Sat £15 ladies, £20 guys, Mon-Thu till 0300, Fri and Sat till 0430 usually dance, UK garage, house and R&B. Another good place is the *Velvet Room*, 143 Charing Cross Rd, WC2, T020-7734 4687, www.velvetroom.co.uk Home to big-name DJs, Mon is a gay R&B soul night, Tue *Syndicate* UK Garage, Wed *Swerve* drum'n'bass, Thu techno night, Fri *whoop it up* progressive house and trance, Sat *big and clever*, funky US house and garage (smart dress only), Sun for jazzy breakbeats, at this plush venue for happening dance music.

Also on Charing Cross Rd, beneath Waterstone's bookshop, is one of London's best Latin nights, *Salsa!* 96 Charing Cross Rd, WC2, T020-7379 3277. Mon Salsa, Tue Brazilian, Wed Introduction to Latin dance with free lesson, Thu Cuban Salsa, Sat and Sun Salsa club nights. From 2100 £4 during the week, weekends £2 at 1900, £4 at 2000, £8 at 2100. Until 0200. No trainers.

Back in deepest Soho, *Madam JoJo's*, 8-10 Brewer St, W1, T020-7734 3040, provides velveteen upholstered seedy basement easy-listening and drag acts until 0300. Bars that are more like clubs include the *Candy Bar*, 23 Bateman St, W1, T020-7437 1977, till 0300, and *Pop*,14 Soho St, W1, T020-7734 4004, till 0500 on Sat £10 after 2100, till 0400 on Fri £10 after 2100, and till 0330 Mon to Thur £5 after 2100, an expensive retro designer bar with live acid jazz bands on Tue and Wed.

Theatres The *Prince Edward Theatre*, Old Compton St, W1, T020-7447 5400, is a large 1930s theatre, now usually staging blockbusting musicals.

The *London Palladium*, Argyll St, W1, T020-7494 5400, a vast entertainment house since 1910 that now specializes in musical spectaculars.

The *Soho Theatre and Writer's Centre*, 21 Dean St, W1, T020-7478 0100, is an excellent brand new base for new playwriting in the West End.

Covent Garden

Dance *The Royal Opera House* is the home of the Royal Ballet, and the new building includes the Clore Studio for workshops and small scale performances (for details see below).

Pineapple Dance Studio, 7 Langley St, WC2, T020-7836 4004. Open 1000-2000 runs regular dance classes in a wide variety of styles catering for most levels of ability. It also has a little café and a gym. Day membership (approximately £4) required and classes cost about £6 an hour.

Festivals The **BOC Covent Garden Festival of Opera, Music and Theatre**, T020-7413 1410, takes place annually mid-May to early Jun, at venues like Bow Street Magistrates Court, St Paul's Church, the Peacock Theatre and the Freemasons' Hall, www.cgf.co.uk The **May Fayre and Puppet Festival**, T020-7375 0441, happens on a Sun early in May in the garden of St Paul's Church, celebrating the first time Samuel Pepys saw a Punch and Judy show in the area in 1662. Not to be confused with the **Punch and Judy Festival** in Oct that takes place in the Piazza, like various other festivals throughout the year, some much better than others. The **Festival of Street Theatre** in mid-Sep sees the jugglers, performance artists, magicians and musicians that usually enliven the Piazza upstaged by some considerably more professional acts. Others have themes like German food, or the **Food Lovers Fair** in the 1st week of Nov (T020-7836 9136 for information on them all).

Music **Classical and opera** *Royal Opera House*, Bow St, WC2, T020-7240 1200, box office/information T020-7304 4000, www.royaloperahouse.org The redeveloped Opera House has left the auditorium and stage almost untouched, but front of house and backstage have had a much-needed revamp. And what a revamp it is: the Floral

Hall is a spectacular space with a bar and restaurant open all day and most the night, while an escalator sweeps elegantly up to the terrace where there are more eating and drinking options, including an outside seating area overlooking the old market. As for the productions, the management of the country's flagship opera house is still giving the government a real headache although the promised reduction in ticket prices has made the place more accessible.

Rock, folk and jazz   On the Piazza itself, the *Rock Garden*, The Piazza, Covent Garden, WC2, T020-7240 3961, and the *Roadhouse*, Jubilee Hall, 35 The Piazza, WC2, T020-7240 6001, open until 0300 Mon-Sat, are probably both best avoided unless you want to let mediocre bands on the make give you earache. The *12 Bar Club* Denmark Pl, Denmark St, WC2, T020-7916 6989, tickets T020-7209 2248, is a very intimate and atmospheric venue for small-scale performances of high-class folk and rock. *The Africa Centre*, 38 King St, WC2, T020-7836 1973, 2130-0300, Fri-Sat, £6-8.

The Gardening Club, The Piazza, Covent Garden, WC2, T020-7497 3154 and *The End*, 18 West Central St, WC2, T020-7419 9199, are 2 of the best clubs in London for techno, garage and house music. **Nightclubs**

   Stringfellows, 16-19 Upper St Martin's Lane, WC2, T020-7240 5534, continues to draw in older, more jaded punters with its cocktail of flashy glamour girls on the dancefloor and a worldwide reputation for 'good clean fun'.

Drury Lane Theatre Royal, Catherine St, WC2, T020-7494 5000. One of London's oldest theatres, founded in 1663, managed by David Garrick in the 18th century, and rebuilt in the early 19th century after 2 disastrous fires. Now usually stages large-scale musicals, currently the *Witches of Eastwick*. Enjoyable backstage tours, which involve actors encouraging audience participation, tell the history of the theatre. Taking about 1 hr, they are at 1230, 1415, 1645 on Mon, Tue, Thu and Fri, and at 1100 and 1300 on Wed, Sat matinee days. £7.50 per person, bookable on box office number. **Theatres**

   Lyceum, Wellington St, WC2, T020-7243 9000. Founded in 1771 but erected on this site in 1834, demolished in 1903 saving the front portico, and rebuilt in 1904. After a difficult century, it was finally fully refurbished and re-opened in the 1990s. Now showing *The Lion King*.

   New London, 167 Drury Lane, WC2, T020-7404 4079. The most recent addition to West End's theatreland, opened in 1973 with a Peter Ustinov production. Andrew Lloyd Webber's *Cats* has been playing here since 1981.

   Cambridge Theatre, Earlham St, WC2, T020-7494 5083. Erected in 1930, famous for its offbeat musicals and drama, including *Return to the Forbidden Planet*, and now staging Lloyd Webber's footballing romp *The Beautiful Game*.

   Duchess, Catherine St, WC2, T020-7494 5075. Relatively small mock-Elizabethan theatre built in 1929, now staging Michael Frayn's excellent anatomy of atomic powerbroking *Copenhagen*.

   Shaftesbury Theatre, Shaftesbury Av, T020-7379 5399. Opened in 1911 and fully reconstructed in the 1920s, this prominent grand theatre on the edge of 'theatreland' now usually stages big musicals, most recently *Napoleon*.

   Donmar Warehouse, 41 Earlham St, WC2, T020-7369 1732. The most innovative, fashionable and exciting small-scale theatre in the West End, run by Sam *American Beauty* Mendes who still directs some productions here, as well as welcoming top-class touring companies. Seats are usually at a premium and need to be booked well in advance.

   The Tristan Bates Studio, The Actors' Centre, 1a Tower St, WC2, T020-7240 3940, is a small fringe theatre named in memory of Alan Bates' son that regularly stages promising new work.

Entertainment & nightlife

Mayfair and Regent Street

Casinos The *Palm Beach*, 30 Berkeley St, W1, T020-7493 6585. Open 1330-0400 daily. Notice needed 24 hrs before you want to play for free membership on production of a passport or driving licence. Members can take up to 6 guests to try their hand at poker, roulette, ponte banco or blackjack. Also one-armed bandits, restaurant and bar.

Cinemas The *Curzon Mayfair*, 38 Curzon St, W1, T020-7465 8865, is probably the most comfortable cinema in London and not as expensive as you might expect for such cosseting. It generally shows middle to highbrow mainstream movies on its 1 screen.

Music Mayfair is not a great destination for live music, with Soho so close, but the *Dover Street Winebar*, 8-10 Dover St, W1, T020-7629 9813, has become one of the biggest and busiest jazz restaurants in the city. It's open Mon-Thu 1200-1530 and 1730-0300, Fri 1200-1530 and 1900-0300, Sat 0700-0300. Live bands Mon-Wed 1015-2300, 2400-0100, Thu-Sat 2230-2320; DJs Mon-Sat 0100-0300. Admission £5 Mon (free before 2130), £6 Tue, £7 Wed, £10 Thu (free before 2200 Tue-Wed); Fri, Sat diners only before 2200, and £10 after.

Nightclubs *Eve Club*, 189 Regent St, opposite *Hamleys*, T020-7734 4252. Open Wed-Sat until 0300, individual nights in louche surroundings by party organizers. Needs phoning and faxing for admission.

The *Hanover Grand*, 6 Hanover St, W1, T020-7499 7977, is a spectacularly cool venue, with state-of-the-art lighting, a large dancefloor, balconies and air conditioning. Unsurprisingly it gets crammed. The glamorous and beautiful brigade turn up in force for funky R&B on Wed, fashionable dance music Thu to Sat. Dress up and look gorgeous or you won't get in.

Legends, 29 Old Burlington St, W1, T020-7437 9933, is a long-running fashionista favourite with house and dance nights Thu 2200-300 (no food served) £5, Fri 1800-400 £10, Sat 2100-0500 £12.

The *Chocolate Bar*, 59 Berkeley Square, W1, T020-7499 7850 runs a basement dance club at weekends. Phone for details.

Piccadilly and St James's

Piccadilly is on the edge of the West End's entertainment hotspots, Soho and Leicester Square. St James's is more staid.

Cinemas *Virgin Cinema* 13 Coventry St, T020-7434 0032. £7.50, £4.50, Mon and before 1700, in Trocadero.

Pepsi IMAX Theatre, Trocadero, W1, T020-7494 4153. Huge screen but with a smaller audience capacity than the BFI's IMAX in Waterloo.

ABC Piccadilly, T020-7437 3561. Two screens, small and a bit of a dive.

Plaza, 17-25 Lower Regent St, W1, T020-7930 0144; recorded info and bookings T0870-603 4567.

ICA Cinema, Nash House, The Mall, SW1 (T020-7930 6393 for recorded information, T020-7930 3647 for credit card bookings, www.ica.org.uk) is the place for very rare or independent films.

Music **Classical and opera** *St James's Church* puts on regular concerts. Contact the Concert Managers T020-7381 0441 for details.

The *Café de Paris*, 3 Coventry St, T020-7734 7700, is a sumptuous venue for a big night **Nightclubs**
out. Wed is *Elite*, a House and Garage night popular with tourists. Thu is *Merge*, a popular corporate night out. Fri *Pornstar*, and Sat always the busiest night. Book for the restaurant to guarantee entry, for a meal from £15-35. *Bar Rumba*, 36 Shaftesbury Av, W1, T020-7287 2715, admission after 1000, is a very popular salsa venue.

For somewhere more discreet with a middle eastern flavour, try the Fri or Sat night disco until 0330 at **Ormond's Restaurant and Club**, 6 Ormond Yard, T020-7930 2842, www.ormonds.co.uk   DJs open until 0330 Fri and Sat. The club is on the site of the old Jermyn St baths.

The Jermyn St Theatre, 16b Jermyn St, SW1, T020-7287 2875, is a plush little basement **Theatres**
theatre that stages a wide variety of fringe shows, from miniature musicals to intimate stagings of the classics. Shows usually start at 1930 and cost about £15. Booking advisable. The emphasis at the *ICA Theatre* is firmly on the avante-garde and experimental.

Criterion Theatre, Piccadilly Circus, T020-7413 1437, currently showing the Reduced Shakespeare Company's lamentable abridgements of Shakespeare an American history.

Piccadilly Theatre, Denman St, W1, T020-7369 1734. Large and fairly modern playhouse that regularly gives space to successful productions transferred from more remote stages.

Oxford Street and Marble Arch

Odeon Marble Arch, 10 Edgeware Rd, W2, National Film Line, T0870-5050 007. Five **Cinemas**
screens, before 1700 £5, £7.50 after.

100 Club, 100 Oxford St, W1, T020-7636 0933, www.the100club.co.uk Open Mon-Thu **Music**
1930-2400, Fri 1200-1500, 2030-0200, Sat 1930-100, Sun 1930-2330. Famous for its nights of punk in the 70s and before that for hosting the Stones, a longplayer of a place that now majors in jazz and blues, with the occasional indie rock band. Unbeatable atmosphere though, depending on the band, and best to arrive early to get a good view of the stage. Admission £7-10. Free lunchtime jazz 1130-1500 in summer.

The *Costa Dorada Spanish Restaurant*, 47-55 Hanway St, W1, T020-7631 5117, is a very lively, atmospheric venue for live Spanish music and flamenco displays. It's open Mon-Sat 1730-300 with dance performances at 2130 and 2330 Mon-Thu and 2200 and 2400 Fri and Sat.

Central London

Westminster and Whitehall

Classical and opera *St John's*, Smith Square, T020-7222 1061. Grand but spartan **Music**
concert hall staging a wide variety of choral, orchestral, and chamber performances both amateur and professional. Tickets £5-35.

Westminster Theatre, 12 Palace St, SW1, T020-7834 0283. Originally a chapel, the thea- **Theatres**
tre was reconstructed in the 60s and is now a small West End theatre.

Whitehall Theatre, Whitehall, SW1, T020-7369 1736. A 1930s building that has long had a reputation for farce and sex comedies, now increasingly playing to audience's baser instincts.

Entertainment & nightlife

Victoria, Belgravia and Pimlico

Nightclubs *The Colosseum*, 1 Nine Elms Lane, SW8, T020-7720 3609. Near Vauxhall tube. Quite a large venue that usually hosts house and trance nights.

Theatres **Victoria Palace Theatre**, Victoria St, SW1, T020-7834 1317. Opposite Little Ben, was built as a music hall in 1911 and now stages big musicals (currently *Fame*).
    Apollo Victoria, Wilton Rd, 0870-400 0870, was purpose-built for musicals in 1901 and has returned to its roots by being completely refitted for Lloyd Webber's long-running rollerskating spectacular, *Starlight Express*.

Knightsbridge, South Kensington and Hyde Park

Cinemas *Goethe Institut*, 50 Princes Gate, SW7, T020-7596 4000. Has undergone a major refurbishment and shows mainly German films with subtitles or surtitles.
    Cine Lumière, 17 Queensberry Pl, SW7, T020-7838 2144. The well-appointed cinema in the French Institute shows European classics and recent releases, most with English subtitles.

Festivals **Creating Sparks** was the South Kensington Festival's title in Sep 2000, a major science and arts jamboree organized by the big museums and colleges which may well be repeated. www.creatingsparks.co.uk

Music **Classical and opera** *Royal Albert Hall*, Kensington Gore, SW7, T020-7589 8212. Grand setting for just about any and every type of entertainment spectacular from high to lowbrow. The BBC Henry Wood Promenade Concerts, aka The Proms, are a huge and ever-popular classical music festival with a jingoistic 'last night', taking place at the Albert Hall every year between Jul and Sep; £3 for a promenading ticket on sale an hour before each concert.
    Royal College of Music, Prince Consort Rd, SW7, T020-7589 3643. Lunchtime concerts daily at 1305, Fri evening concert throughout term-time in St Mary Abbots Church, South Kensington. www.rcm.ac.uk

    Rock, folk and jazz *The Pizza on the Park*, 11 Knightsbridge, SW5, T020-7235 5273, has live jazz (£10-18) downstairs every night, often with top names best booked well in advance.

Chelsea

Cinemas The *Chelsea Cinema*, 206 King's Rd, SW3, T020-7351 3742, next to *Habitat*, has 1 screen usually showing the kind of new releases the good burghers of Chelsea might enjoy.
    UGC Chelsea, 279 King's Rd, SW3, T0870-907 0710. Four screens of major new releases, screens 3 and 4 the smaller pair.
    UGC Fulham Rd, 142 Fulham Rd, SW10, T020-7370 2110. Six screens of new releases, with greater capacity than the one on the King's Rd.

Festivals The **Chelsea Festival**, 18 Cadogan Gdns, SW3 2RP, T020-8878 8944, takes place over 2 weeks from the middle of Jun, involving classical music concerts in various churches morning and evening, exhibitions on local history and by local artists, and a programme of guided tours and special openings of the area's sights.

Music **Rock, folk and jazz** The *606 Club*, 90 Lots Rd, SW10, T020-7352 5953, www.606club.co.uk Mon-Wed 0730-0100, Thu 0930-0130, Fri, Sat 1000-0200, Sun

2000-2400. Admission: Sun-Thu £5, Fri, Sat £6. Always book at weekends. A basement jazz and blues bar that had a long and illustrious beatnik history in its old premises on the King's Rd. Now it's more mainstream and requires punters to eat a full, fairly reasonably priced meal.

Havana SW6, 490 Fulham Rd, SW6, T020-7381 5005. Open 1700-0200, Salsa classes Mon, Tue, Thu at 2030. Smaller and more intimate branch of the Hanover Square Latin music cocktail bar.

Most of the late-night drinking in Chelsea happens behind closed doors in private **Nightclubs** members clubs. The *Po Na Na Souk Bar*, 316 King's Rd, SW3, T020-7352 7127, is a loud, late and lively party venue. The *Vingt-Quatre*, 325 Fulham Rd, SW10, T020-7376 7224, is not really a club, but a 24-hr café bar (alcohol served till midnight) that's a long-standing late-night institution in the area doing decent continental cuisine.

The *Royal Court Theatre*, Sloane Square, SW1, T020-7565 5000, most famous for start- **Theatres** ing the 'kitchen sink' school of drama under George Devine in the 50s with plays like Osborne's *Look Back in Anger* (although it had already carved out a reputation for radicalism by staging the first productions of many of GB Shaw's plays). It has recently been fully refurbished and still pursues an adventurous policy of commissioning new writing. The refurbishment includes an atmospheric and happening restaurant and bar in the basement (T020-7565 5061). The *Royal Court Theatre Upstairs* stages experimental small-scale work (same box office as main theatre).

The *Chelsea Centre*, World's End Pl, SW10, T020-7352 1967, is quite a large fringe theatre with an eclectic mix of shows, and it too has had a major revamp, now featuring *The Brothers Green at the Chelsea Centre* (T020-7352 3535) doing freshly made organic vegetarian breakfasts and lunches, and evenings until 2000.

The Man in the Moon, 392 King's Rd, SW3, T020-7351 2876 is a tiny fringe theatre behind a busy pub that fairly often stages the odd gem.

Marylebone and Regent's Park

Screen on Baker St, 96 Baker St, NW1, T020-7935 2772. Two screens showing first-runs **Cinemas** from the artier side of the spectrum.

Classical and opera *Wigmore Hall*, 36 Wigmore St, W1, T020-7935 2141, **Music** www.wigmore-hall.org.uk One of London's premier small concert halls, pur- *Café 36 (closed Sat* pose-built in 1901 by the piano-maker Bechstein, stages a huge variety of world-class *lunchtime) is the* performances of chamber music and song, lunchtimes at 1300 and evenings at 1930 *pleasant restaurant* Mon-Sat, 1600 and 1900 Sun, and popular hour-long coffee concerts at 1130 on Sun, *& bar downstairs* tickets £8-30.

The *Open Air Theatre*, Queen Mary's Gdns, Regent's Park, NW1, T020-7486 2431 (sum- **Theatres** mer only). Shakespeare's comedies and pastorals have been performed here since 1933, although recently the seasonal repertoire has also included modern musicals. The more than 1000-seat auditorium, exposed to the elements, along with a good restaurant and bar, always generates a sense of occasion. Booking well in advance is advisable.

Euston, St Pancras and King's Cross

Rock, folk and jazz *The Water Rats*, 328 Gray's Inn Rd, WC1, T020-7837 7269, is a **Music** basic boozer with an even more basic back bar that hosts 3 bands a night 6 nights a week, 1st set at about 2045, £5 admission.

Entertainment & nightlife

Nightclubs
Clubnights are the area's strong point at weekends

The old cinema at *The Scala*, 278 Pentonville Rd, N1, T020-7833 2022, now hosts the regular Fri mixed gay night *Popstarz* (£3 before 2300, more after), its 4 different rooms dedicated to indie music, sounds of the 60s and 70s, and pop trash, and on Sat *We Are You*, an American house and tech-house night. During the week there are one-off clubnights and live bands.

The megaclubs in the area are the Ibiza of North London: *The Cross*, The Arches, 27-131 King's Cross Goods Yard, off York Way, N1, T020-7837 0828, www.the-cross.co.uk On Fri for house music *Fiction* £12, and different house nights on Sat, till 0500, 0600 and on alternate Suns *Vertigo* for Italian house, £12.

A slightly younger crowd tend to favour *Bagley's Studios*, King's Cross Goods Yard, off York Way, N1, T020-7278 2777, www.bagleys.net Fri different, Sat *Freedom*, £14 on the door. House again as well as garage.

Theatre *The Courtyard Theatre*, 10 York Way, N1, T020-7833 0870, is a small fringe theatre in a quaint old courtyard that sometimes stages good productions of contemporary classics.

The Camden People's Theatre, 58-60 Hampstead Rd, NW1, T020-7916 5878, is another small community fringe theatre which quite often turns up interesting plays.

Bloomsbury and Fitzrovia

Cinemas *Odeon*, Tottenham Court Rd, W1, T020-7636 6148, booking line 020 8795 6400. Three first-run screens, one often given to more offbeat releases.

Renoir, Brunswick Centre, Brunswick Square, WC1, T020-7837 8402. Usually foreign films, 4 screenings a day on 2 screens, excellent café and bar.

Dance *The Place*, 17 Duke's Rd, WC1, T020-7380 1268. London's premier small-scale contemporary dance venue reopens end of Sep 2001 after hefty refurbishment with new restaurant and reception.

Music *ULU*, University of London Union, Manning Hall, Malet St, WC1, T020-7664 2000. Open 2030-2300, nights vary. Admission £5-10.

Theatres *Dominion*, Tottenham Court Rd, W1, T0870-607 7460. Large West End theatre, expanded for Disney's *Beauty and the Beast* and almost exclusively devoted to blockbusting musicals.

Drill Hall, 16 Chenies St, WC1, T020-7637 8270. London's foremost gay and lesbian theatre and cabaret venue. Mon women only after 1800. Thu no smoking night. Vibrant vegetarian café and bar.

Cochrane Theatre, Southampton Row, WC1, T020-7242 7040. Smallish fringe theatre, part of the London Institute.

Bloomsbury Theatre, 15 Gordon St, WC1, T020-7388 8822. Middle-scale fringe theatre, part of UCL, often hosts good touring productions.

Holborn and Clerkenwell

Dance *Sadler's Wells*, Rosebery Av, EC1, T020-7863 8000, and *Lilian Baylis Theatre* (nearest tube Angel Islington). Superb state-of-the-art new North London base for large scale dance and opera, and a smaller studio space for adventurous new work, both sadly struggling financially. Also runs *The Peacock Theatre*, Portugal St, WC2 a smaller theatre for the same sort of thing.

Festivals **Clerkenwell Festival**, mid-Jul, communtiy festival focused on Clerkenwell Green with a big Fri music night at Smithfield Market and a Sun event on the Green, a celebration of local history. Organized by Clerkenwell.org, 53 Clerkenwell Close, EC1, T020-7251 6311, local history information point and outlet for local crafts.

Also **Clerkenwell Literary Festival**, usually some time in late Jul or early Aug, at the *Tardis*, Turnmill St, T020-7336 6366, and other venues.

Sadler's Wells (see Dance above). *St James's*, Clerkenwell Close, EC1, T020-7251 1190. Bach organ recitals on the 3rd Thu of the month at 1310. **Music**

The End, 18a West Central St, WC1, T020-7419 9199. Open Mon 2200-0300 *Trash* for indie £4, Thu 2100-0330, *Atelier* for house £5, Fri 2200-0600, Sat 2200-0600, *End Saturdays* tech house, £10-15. Owned by Mr C of the Shaman and Leo. Techno driven lounge and main room are the last words in cool. **Nightclubs**

Fabric, 77a Charterhouse St, EC1, T020-7336 8898. Open Fri 2200-0500 *Fabric live*, hiphop break drum 'n' bass, and live acts, £10; Sat 2200-0700 deep house, techno, tribal house, £15; Sun *DTM* mixed gay night, 2200-late. One of the most cutting-edge clubs in London.

Turnmills, 63 Clerkenwell Rd, EC1, T020-7250 3409. Salsa on Tue, 1830-2400, £6 for the class, admission free; Fri *The Gallery* 2230-0730, £10 before 2400, more after, for House music; Sat *Headstart* free before 2200, £5 before 2300, £10 after, techno gaynight. Two floors, with 3 DJs on each. Long queues form after 2100.

The Bridewell, Bride Lane, Fleet St, EC4, T020-7936 3456, is a wonderful old converted swimming baths, a fringe theatre that maintains a pretty high standard, especially on the musical front. **Theatre**

The City

City of London Festival (T020-7377 0540, www.colf.org), Jun and Jul, within the Square Mile, and also at the Spitz in Spitalfields Market, box office Barbican (T020-7638 8891), a classical music, jazz, gospel and world music festival in a variety of City churches including St Paul's. **Festivals**

The Lord Mayor's Show takes place on the 2nd Sat in Nov, usually taking a theme chosen by the Lord Mayor to raise funds for charity, with floats, bands and formal receptions at Mansion House. For more information: T020-7332 1456.

Apart from the lunchtime concerts during the week in many of the City churches (contact the City Information line for details), the bewildering **Barbican Centre** (T020-7638 8891, www.barbican.org.uk) is just about the only place around to see an art show, listen to live music or catch a film or play. The *Royal Shakespeare Company* (RSC) is resident here, with 1 large theatre for its Shakespeare productions and classic revivals, and also the *Pit*, a subterranean studio theatre that sometimes stages more adventurous work. Shows often sell out well in advance and usually begin at 1915. Tickets £5-29. The Barbican Cinema has 2 screens showing first-run and arthouse films, often with excellent special seasons and themed weekends, and a Sat children's cinema club. Tickets £6.50, £4 on Mon. The Barbican Hall is one of London's major middle-scale live music venues hosting a huge variety of different orchestras, bands, and choirs. Tickets £6.50-35. The centre also stages outdoor theatre festivals and events during the summer. **Music** *For news on RSC productions & to buy tickets online, log on to www.rsc.org.uk*

Next door to the Barbican is the *Guildhall School of Music and Drama*, Silk St, EC2, T020-7628 2571, box office T020-7382 7192, with its own theatre and concert hall for regular student performances, often of a very high calibre.

Entertainment & nightlife

Bankside and Southwark

Festivals **The Southwark Festival** usually takes place in the 1st 3 weeks of Oct, an interesting array of community fringe events – plays, poetry, art, food, and music in Southwark Cathedral, Borough Market, Hays Galleria, and Guy's Hospital Chapel.

In 2000, for the first time there was also a **Southwark Literary Festival** in late Oct and Nov, also administrated by the *Southwark Festival Association*, 16 Winchester Walk, SE1, T020-7403 7474, www.southwarkfestival.org.uk

Theatres The *Southwark Playhouse*, 62 Southwark Bridge Rd, SE1, T020-7620 3494, *For details on the* www.southwark-playhouse.co.uk, is a cosy fringe theatre with a strong track record of *Globe Theatre,* innovative and challenging productions, its stage designs often making startling trans- *see page 247* formations to the limited space at its disposal. Front of house there's a bright and cheerful restaurant.

The Jerwood Space, 171 Union St, SE1, T020-7654 0171, is a newish contemporary art gallery, with decent café (open 0930-1800) attached, alongside rehearsal rooms for top theatre companies.

South Bank and Waterloo

Dominating the entertainment scene here is the **South Bank Centre**. Together with the National Film Theatre and the Royal National Theatre, it adds up to a complex compara- ble with the Lincoln Center in New York, with the Kennedy Center in Washington, and perhaps most of all with the South Bank Centre in Melbourne. By no means solely the preserve of 'high art', the complex has fought off accusations of being a cultural ghetto to establish itself as the liveliest concentration of arts venues in the city.

Cinemas The *National Film Theatre* (NFT), South Bank, T020-7928 3535, will eventually be *For more details on* moving to the BFI complex under development in Jubilee Gardens. Until then it is to *London Film Festivals,* be hoped that it continues to fulfull its role as London's flagship repertory cinema, *see page 413* showing a truly international selection of rare, first-run and classic films on its 3 screens. Every Nov it forms the focal point of the increasingly prestigious **London Film Festival**.

The *British Film Institute IMAX cinema/theatre* (see also page 412) is quite tricky to reach, marooned in the middle of a busy roundabout. It's best approached from Belve- dere Rd through a tunnel studded with blue stars. Inside, the IMAX screen is the size of a large house and quite mind-blowing. Unfortunately few proper dramatic movies have yet been made in the format, leaving the screen to travelogues and other sensationalist stuff, although a recent run of a special edition of Disney's *Fantasia* promises well for the future. Daily showings from 1210 onwards T020-7902 1234; £8.50, concession £6.50.

Festivals Almost every Sun from May to Sep, and often during the week as well, the area around *For details T020 -7401* the Oxo Tower Wharf is given a shot in the arm by the annual **Coin Street Festival**. *2255 or visit the Coin* Billed as the largest free festival in the city, it's an invigorating multicultural jamboree of *St Information Centre* food, music, theatre and dance, usually taking place around Bernie Spain Gardens and *in Oxo Tower Wharf* along the river. The festival culminates in the enormously popular **Thames Festival**, on a Sun in the middle of Sep, with an illuminated procession, river-related events and shows, finishing up with a spectacular firework display.

The **Waterloo Festival** in the middle of May is centred around the Church of St John, presenting a week of music and drama (T020-7633 9819, www.stjohnswaterloo.ukf.net).

Classical and opera The 3 concert halls of the South Bank Centre (SBC), the *Royal Festival Hall*, *Purcell Room*, and *Queen Elizabeth Hall*, are without doubt the first stop for classical music lovers in London. Their programme manages to embrace an astonishingly wide range of different musical styles, often played by world-beating orchestras, ensembles, bands, groups and soloists. The Royal Festival Hall's perfect acoustics have been accused of being deadening, but that doesn't seem to put people off. Tickets for concerts often sell out way in advance. The Purcell Room is a more intimate venue, while the Queen Elizabeth Hall is a much-loved space that blends the best qualities of the other two.

The Warehouse is a small, new, fairly trendy concert venue at 13 Theed St, T020-7928 9251, www.lfo.co.uk The brainchild of the London Festival Orchestra. Concerts open to the public are usually given about twice a month.

St John's Church, at the top of Waterloo Rd, T020-7366 9279, runs a good programme of free lunchtime concerts.

Music
South Bank Centre, T020-960 4242, www.sbc.org.uk

Rock, folk and jazz *Bar Cubana*, T020-7928 8778, on Lower Marsh sometimes has live Latin music. Several restaurants in the area also have live music but otherwise the South Bank Centre is once again the best bet.

The mother of all mega-clubs, once the hippest night in the city, is the relentless *Ministry of Sound* in Elephant and Castle, at 103 Gaunt St, SE1, T020-7378 6528; Elephant and Castle tube.

Nightclubs

Royal National Theatre, South Bank, T020-7452 3000. The foundation stone was laid in 1951, but Denys Lasdun's terraced concrete ziggurat only opened in 1976, the new home for the National Theatre Company under the directorship of Peter Hall. It has 3 stages: the *Olivier*, the largest, with an open stage, steeply raked auditorium, and massive revolve. For some productions, the theatre has been brilliantly converted into a vast theatre in the round. The *Lyttelton*, slightly smaller, is the most traditional, with the option of a proscenium arch. The *Cottesloe*, round the side, is a much more intimate studio theatre for experimental productions. Director Trevor Nunn has continued the successful mix of popular classics, a summer musical, and more offbeat productions pioneered by his predecessor Richard Eyre.

Old Vic, The Cut, SE1, T020-7928 7616. Built in 1817 as Royal Coburg Theatre, and later known as the 'Bucket of Blood' because of the cheap melodramas staged here, the Old Victoria theatre was taken over for 25 years from 1912 by Lilian Bayliss, the founder of Sadlers Wells. In 1962, it became the birthplace of the National Theatre Company under the directorship of Laurence Olivier. More recently, following sympathetic restoration by Canadian Ed Mirvish, the theatre was home to Sir Peter Hall's own company, unfortunately a short-lived experiment. It narrowly avoided being turned into a lap-dancing venue and is now run by a board of affectionate trustees.

Young Vic, 66 The Cut, SE1, T020-7928 6363. The best middle-scale experimental theatre in the country.

Union Theatre, 204 Union St, SE1, T020-7261 9876. A small fringe theatre under the arches that occasionally shows interesting new work.

Theatres

Entertainment & nightlife

East London

East End

Cinemas *Lux*, 2-4 Hoxton Square, N1, T020-7684 0201. One-screen BFI arthouse.

Rio Cinema, 107 Kingsland High St, Hackney, E8, T020-7241 9410 (Dalston Kingsland BR). One-screen repertory and mainstream.

Stratford East Picture House, Gerry Raffles Square, T020-8555 3311 information. Multiscreen mainstream.

Genesis Cinema, 93-95 Mile End Rd, T020-7780 2000, www.genesiscinema. co.uk Five-screen independent multiscreen.

Festivals **Brick Lane Festival** in Sep, weekend festival of Bangladeshi culture.

Shoreditch Festival local community festival held in Jul, especially on Hoxton St on Sun 15. Details from 182 Hoxton St, N1, T020-7613 2727.

Music **Classical and opera** *Ocean*, 270 Mare St, Hackney, E8, T020-8986 5336, www.ocean.org.uk Brand new large-scale live music venue with 3 stages dedicated to all types of music, classical, jazz and rock.

Rock, folk and jazz *Vibe Bar*, Truman's Brewery, Brick Lane, E1, T020-7377 2899, for occasional live bands, and regular sound system sessions.

Central Bar, 58 Old St, EC1, T020-7490 0080. Jazz every Tue and Thu, £4 before 2030, £5 after. Mon-Thu open till 2445, Fri, Sat 0145. Hectic cocktail bar.

Arts Café, 28 Commercial St, E1, T020-7247 5681. Live indie and electronic sounds generally on Fri at this pizza and pasta joint.

Spitz, Old Spitalfields Market, 109 Commercial St, E1, T020-7392 9032. Live jazz in bistro on Fri nights, as well as a variety of other music and art events.

Nightclubs *333*, 333 Old St, EC1, T020-7739 5949, Fri 2200-0500 , Sat 2200-0500, Sun £5 before 2300, £10 after. Three floors for various enormously popular and hip dance nights, including *Offcentre*, *Revolver*, and *Perverted Science*. The *Mother Bar* àbove is open until 0300 most nights.

Soshomatch, 2a Tabernacle St, EC2, T020-7920 0701, nu-jazz, deep house, funk and soul, very hip, open Thu, Fri, Sat until 0200, admission £5 after 2200 Sat, after 2100 Fri.

Plastic People, 147 Curtain Rd, EC1, T020-7739 6471. Disco nights Mon, Thu, Fri-Sat.

The Aquarium, 256 Old St, EC1, T020-7251 6136, www.clubaquarium.co.uk Large dance bar and club. Thu night Russian night £8, Fri house and disco, Sat US house and garage £15, 2 dance areas, a swimming pool and jacuzzi.

Katabatic, 89 Great Eastern St, EC2 T020-7739 5173, www.katabatic.co.uk Large new bar-club, formerly *Propaganda*, now plays party house tunes on Fri and Sat.

Cargo, Rivington St, EC2, T020-7354 9611, www.cargo-london.co.uk. Latin house, jazzy house bar-club.

Theatres *Hoxton Hall*, 130 Hoxton St, N1, T020-7684 0060 (booking T020-7739 5431), www.hoxtonhall.dabsol.co.uk, workshops, lectures and visits on Victorian Music Halls, digital experimental theatre.

Brick Lane Music Hall, T020-7739 9996, www.brick-lane-music-hall.co.uk Old-time East End saucy cabarets currently looking for a new home.

The Circus Space, Coronet St, N1, T020-7613 4141, www.thecircusspace.co.uk London's only circus school, doing a 2-year degree course, founded in a training centre with occasional shows.

Chats Palace, 42-44 Brooksbys Walk, E9, T020-8986 6714. Music, physical theatre, dance and comedy on the fringe in deepest Homerton.

Hackney Empire, 291 Mare St, E8, T020-8985 2424. Superb Victorian theatre staging a vibrant mix of community theatre, panto, touring productions and comedy.

Docklands

UGC Cinema, Hertesmere Rd, E14, T0870-9070722. Standard Multiplex.

Cinemas

Rock, folk and jazz *Cabot Hall,* Cabot Place West, E14, T020-7481 2783. Courtney Pine played here recently, and the hall is beginning to attract other big names.

London Arena, Limeharbour, E14, T020-7538 1212. Tends toward trashy mainstream pop and rock. Recent shows by Boyzone and Erasure.

The Space, 269 Westferry Rd, T020-7515 7799. Ballroom and tango. Weekly jazz night on Mon.

Pizza Express, Floor 2, Cabot Pl, E14, T020-7513 0513. Specializes in occasional jazz, check listings for time.

Music
A few of the pubs around Island Gardens have weekly live music nights

The Space, 269 Westferry Rd, E14, T020-7515 7799. Live music and DJs at weekends.

Club Excel E16 Vast modern nightclub planned for the redevelopment at North Woolwich, due to open spring/summer 2001.

Nightclubs

Cabot Hall, Cabot Place West, E14, T020-7481 2783. Diverse but mainstream dance, comedy, music and live bands.

London Arena, Limeharbour, E14, T020-7538 1212. Large-scale shows and concerts.

The Octagon, 1 Harbour Exchange Square, E14, T020-7410 0770. Smaller independent theatre.

The Space, 268 Westferry Rd, T020-7515 7799. One of Docklands' few fringe venues. Features small-scale theatre and variety. Convenient restaurant for a pre-show bite.

Theatres

North London

Hampstead and Highgate

The Everyman Hampstead, 1 Hollybush Vale, Hampstead, NW3, T020-7431 1777. Famous independent local cinema repeatedly saved from extinction by passionate local support. Offers a mix of mainstream and repertory films in a recently refurbished beautifully luxurious space. Standard, deluxe and 'love seats' available. Bar for drinks. Sat morning kids' club.

Cinemas

Screen on the Hill, 203 Haverstock Hill, NW3, T020-7435 3366 (Belsize Park tube). Part of a small cinema group offering mainly arthouse films and often arranging talks by the director. Comfortable cinema with small bar area.

Finchley Road Warner Village, O2 Centre, Finchley Rd, NW3, T020-7604 3110. Multiscreen American-style cinema within the O2 Shopping and Entertainment complex. Mainstream films in state-of-the-art auditoriums.

Classical and opera *Music on a Summer's Evening* Concert series at Kenwood Lakeside on Sats during Jul and Aug. T020-8233 5892 for details.

Regular concerts are also given throughout the year at *Lauderdale House* T020-8348 8716.

Music

Entertainment & nightlife

Theatres *Hampstead Theatre*, Avenue Rd, NW3, T020-7722 9301. Located near Swiss Cottage tube, this esteemed theatre offers West End type productions of a high quality.

New End Theatre, 27 New End, NW3, T020-7794 0022. Small, intimate theatre with an interesting repertoire of new and established plays and attracting loyal audiences.

The Pentameters, Three Horseshoes Pub, 28 Heath St, NW3, T020-7435 3648. Small theatre space upstairs from the pub, well deserving of notice.

Upstairs at the Gatehouse, Hampstead Lane, N6, T020-8340 3488. Relatively large pub theatre with an interesting variety of visiting productions.

Jacksons Lane Community Centre, 269a Archway Rd, N6, T020-8341 4421. Small cutting-edge community theatre with a lively café.

Camden and Kentish Town

Cinemas *Odeon Camden Town*, Parkway, NW1, T0870-5050007. Standard mainstream multiscreen. Does exactly what it says on the cover.

Phoenix, High Rd, East Finchley, N2, T020-8883 2233, bookings T020-8444 6789. Nearest tube East Finchley, a short haul from Camden. One of London's last remaining single-screen reps.

Music **Rock, folk and jazz** *Kentish Town Forum*, 9-17 Highgate Rd, NW5, T020-7344 0044. Excellent mid-sized rock venue, and flagship of the Mean Fiddler chain. Most now-famous bands (Radiohead, Blur, etc) have played here before hitting the really big time. Good acoustics and an enthusiastic crowd.

The Bull & Gate, 389 Kentish Town Rd, NW5, T020-7485 5358, gigs 2030-2300 Mon-Sat, 2030-2230 Sun, £2-5.

The Electric Ballroom, 184 Camden High St, NW1, T020-7485 9006. Long-established venue for young folk with guitars on the verge of greatness.

The Monarch, 49 Chalk Farm Rd, NW1, T020-79161049; Dingwalls, Middle Yard, off Camden Lock, NW1, T020-7267 1577; and *Dublin Castle*, 94 Parkway, NW1, T020-74851773. All 3 are diminutive venues for up and coming indie/rock/punk outfits.

The Jazz Café, 3 Parkway, NW1, T020-79166060. Well-established venue specializing in modern jazz, with a hint of blues, soul and hip-hop. For traditional folk, there's the *Cecil Sharp House*, 2 Regent's Park Rd, NW1, T020-7485 2206, open at 1900, nights vary, £3-6.

Nightclubs *Camden Palace*, 1a Camden High Rd, NW1, T020-73870428. Diverse venue tending toward guitar/indie stompalongs during the week. Resident DJs at weekends spin house and trance epics.

Underworld, 174 Camden High St, NW1, T020-74821932. A wide selection of mainstream and more underground rock sounds.

HQs, West Yard, Camden Lock, NW1, T020-7681 6044. Weekends described as 'Glam PunkVampSex' Trash. Lock up your daughters.

WKD, 18 Kentish Town Rd, NW1, T020-7267 1869. Open till 0200 Mon-Thu, till 0300 Fri and Sat. Everything from funk to trance to UK garage keep regulars and visitors dancing into the small hours at this vital old-timer.

Theatres *The Etcetera Theatre Club*, Camden High St, NW1, T020-7482 4857. Located above a busy pub with a beer garden (the *Oxford Arms*), the productions here frequently showcase new writing with its finger on the pulse.

Theatro Technis, 26 Crowndale Rd, NW1, T020-7387 6617, is a surprisingly roomy fringe theatre specializing in Greek classics and contemporary political issues.

Round House 40-42 Chalk Farm Rd, NW1, T020-7424 9800. Still hosts the odd production, tending toward the 'experimental.'

Highbury and Islington

Screen on the Green, 83 Upper St, N1, T020-7226 3520. Single-screen fashionable arthouse and mainstream.   Cinemas

Holloway Odeon, 417 Holloway Rd, N7, T0870-5050 007. Mainstream multiscreen.

Islington International Festival in Jun. **Stoke Newington Festival** in Jul. **Angel Canal Festival** in Sep.   Festivals

Rock, folk and jazz *The Hope*, 207 Upper St, N1, T020-7354 1312. Live bands in a   Music & dance
bricky basement almost every night beneath an animated old pub.

The Red Eye, 105 Copenhagen St, N1, T020-7837 1514. Grungy indie bands off the beaten track.

The Garage, 20-22 Highbury Corner, N5, T020-8963 0940. Mean Fiddler outfit: live bands famous, infamous and unknown almost every night

The Rocket, 166-220 Holloway Rd, N7, T020-7753 3200. Regular reggae and club music nights in a large University of North London venue.

Bar Latino, Upper St, N1, T020-7704 6868. Open 2100-0200 Mon-Sat. Thumping bass   Nightclubs
sounds and Latin music until late.

Elbow Room, Chapel Market, N1, T020-7278 3244. Open noon until 0200 Fri, Sat, 10 pool tables £9 per hr. Very lively and late pool hall and dance club.

Embassy Bar, 119 Essex Rd, N1, T020-7226 9849, fashionable vaguely art deco music bar where the dancing is tight.

Old Red Lion, 418 St John St, EC1, T020-7837 7816. Long-standing small theatre with a   Theatres
very good reputation above a busy drinking hole.

Almeida, Almeida St, N1, T020-7359 4404, www.almeida.co.uk, is moving to Omega Pl, off the Caledonian Rd, in late 2002. Islington will miss its mix of high-class productions and glamorous casts.

King's Head, 115 Upper St, N1, T020-7226 1916. Solid and adventurous trooper that pioneered the concept of dinner theatre in its amazingly uncomfortable back room. Productions are often of a high standard.

Little Angel Theatre, 14 Dagmar Passage, N1, T020-7226 1787, www.littleangeltheatre.com Old-time puppet theatre with shows for kids at weekends, term-times, and also occasional adult puppetry.

Tower Theatre, Canonbury Pl, N7, T020-7226 3633; box office 1400-2000, shows Jun, Jul and Sep, plays by the resident amateur Tavistock Rep Company, a mixture of mainstream classic and contemporary drama in a historic building.

Hen and Chickens, 109 St Paul's Rd, N1, T020-7704 2001. Lively drama and comedy pub theatre on Highbury Corner.

Pleasance Theatre, 41 North Rd, N7, T020-7609 1800. Large and very well-appointed fringe theatre in converted warehouse near Caledonian Rd tube that often mounts exciting touring productions, located above a bustling bar and brasserie called *Shillibeers*.

Rosemary Branch, 2 Shepperton Rd, N1, T020-7704 6665. Tiny theatre above an arty pub near the canal.

Entertainment & nightlife

West London

Notting Hill and Holland Park

Cinemas

The Coronet is the only cinema in London where you can still smoke

The Gate Cinema, 87 Notting Hill Gate, W11, T020-7727 4043. £6.50, £3.50 for 1st showing Mon-Fri, £3 concession with ID before 1800 Mon-Fri and late nights 2300 Fri and Sat. An excellent arthouse cinema – uncomfortable but worth it – with delicious ice-cream and snacks – special old screenings at the weekend through Video City. Cult and popular programmes. Book up quick – but they'll try and find you a chair even in the first weekend if you hit the late-night screening.

The Coronet, Notting Hill Gate, W11, T020-7727 6705. The best complement to the Gate – only a few doors down and not at all arty – offering a mainstream Hollywood diet but its old musical hall seating, proscenium arch screen and popular smoking policy, as well as its star turn in the movie *Notting Hill* make it a popular dating spot and even quite *Cinema Paradiso* in atmosphere. Worth travelling to find.

The Electric Cinema, Portobello Rd, T020-7229 8688. The lovely old art deco cinema on the Portobello Rd has been fully restored once again, redesigned by the team responsible for hip restaurant *192*, and run by Cityscreen, also responsible for the popular Clapham Picture House and Stratford Green (T020-7734 4342).

Music

Classical and opera   *Holland Park Open-Air Opera* Annually every Jul-Aug. London's answer to Glydebourne. Mixed excellence – but always very ambitious … stroll and picnic outside with the dogwalkers and hear the wafting arias for free during the dusk instead. Makes visitors to the YHA even luckier (unless they prefer techno).

Rock, folk and jazz *Blues West 14*, 11 Russell Gdns, W14, T020-7603 7878, west14@talk21.com http://listen.to/blues.west14 Your classic blues and jazz Soho dive – only tucked away in residential Holland Park/Olympia. Opens strange hours but i've benn unable to check (visited and went inside – place completely empty!)..It's got a sign saying in before 10.30 cheaper than afterwards...the leaflet has special offers eg wed/thu free entry before 9.30 plusfree drink – "Creole Tapas menue" all taps £2.50. Fri/Sat for every 4 people dining get 1 free entry and a bottle of wine...but need the card...(my old flatmate loved it but said drinks expensive but very Ronnie Scotts).

Shepherd's Bush Empire, Shepherd's Bush Green, W12, T020-7771 2000, box office open Mon-Fri 1000-1800, Sat 1200-1800. One of the best venues in London for rock acts – everything from Iggy Pop to Beck. Admission £5-20.

Nightclubs

Notting Hill Arts Club, 21 Notting Hill Gate, W11, T020-7460 4459 (closed Mon). Very lively and late post-industrial basement club, regularly sweaty and packed. Expect to queue even on a Wed.

Subterania, 12 Acklam Rd, W10, T020-8960 4590. Notting Hill's other main club, under the Westway, with a balcony bar overlooking the dance floor and serious dance and reggae nights.

Woodys, 41-43 Woodfield Rd, W9, T020-7266 3030, www.woodysclub.com A little way off the beaten track but possibly the most fashionable of all.

Theatres

The Gate Theatre, 11 Pembridge Rd, W11, T020-7229 5387. Long narrow fringe theatre above a busy pub with a strong reputation for innovative takes on the classics as well as new writing.

The Tabernacle Community and Arts Centre, Powis Square, W11, T020-7565 7800, www.tabernacle.org.uk Open Fri, Sat until 0100. Temporary art shows and events.

The Bush Theatre, Shepherd's Bush Green, W12, T020-8743 3388. One of London's most exciting small-scale studio theatres, more comfortable since being upholstered in Oct 2000.

High Street Kensington and Earl's Court

Odeon Kensington, Kensington High St, opposite The Commonwealth Institute. Mainstream refurbished multiscreen. T0870-5050 007. **Cinemas**

Classical *St Mary Abbots Church*, Kensington Church St, W8, Fri lunctime concerts 1310-1350 given by students of Royal College of Music, admission free. **Music**

The Finborough Theatre, 118 Finborough Rd, SW10, T020-7373 3842, above a busy Irish pub this small fringe theatre has an excellent reputation for promising new work. **Theatres**

Bayswater, Paddington and Little Venice

Ladbroke Golden Horseshoe Casino, 79-81 Queensway, W2, T020-7221 8788. Daily 1400-0400. Cheesy and swanky gambling den, one of a chain of 5. The pictures make it look more like Butlins than Monte Carlo or Las Vegas. "The sheer size of the gaming room will impress" they delare. Casino Restuarant open 1900 or late-night fix is the £5 Breakfast available from midnight to 0200. There is also *Bobby's Bar*, *Sky TV*, car jockey and free parking. Presumably you pay more to get out than you pay to get in... . **Casinos**

UCI Whiteleys, top floor of the Shopping Centre, T0870-102030. Eight-screen mainstream multiplex. **Cinemas**

Ice Disco at Queens Ice Bowl, 17 Queensway, W2, T020-7229 0172. Admission £6.50 including skate hire. 1930-2300 with Live DJs, giveaways and more, also every Sun 1930-2200. £5 including skates. **Nightclubs**

Café Theatre, T020-8960 7654, quirkly little theatre, comedy and cabaret venue above a canalside pub in Little Venice. **Theatres**

Fulham, Hammersmith and Putney

Riverside, Crisp Rd, W6, T020-8237 1111. Excellent single-screen repertory arthouse. *Putney ABC*, T020-8788 3003. *Hammersmith UGC*, T0870-907 0718. **Cinemas**

Dance Attic, 368 North End Rd, SW6, T020-7610 2055. Dance classes as well as Sat night entertainment 1845-2030, free admission to cabaret and theatre bar. **Dance**

Rock, folk and jazz *London Apollo*, Queen Caroline St, W6, T0870-606 3400, medium scale live pop concerts. *Hammersmith & Fulham Irish Centre*, Blacks Rd, W6, T020-8563 8232, gigs from 2000, nights vary, £3-6. **Music**

Hammersmith Palais, 242 Shepherd's Bush Rd, W6, T020-8600 2300. Mainstream dance club with occasional live events. **Nightclubs**
   Po Na Na Fez, 222 Fulham Rd, SW10, T020-7352 5978. Mon-Sat till 0200. Funk to garage to disco.
   Havana, 490 Fulham Rd, SW6, T020-7381 5005. Very loud, lively and late (until 0200 Fri, Sat) salsa bar.

Theatres   *The Lyric Theatre*, King St, W6, T020-8741 2311, and *Lyric Studio Theatre* are two of London's most exciting stages, housed in the unpromising looking King's Mall.

   The Riverside Studios, Crisp Rd, W6, T020-8237 1111, have a tiny studio stage and also a larger main theatre for interesting touring productions.

   The Baron's Court, 28A Comeragh Rd, W14, T020-8932 4747, is a quirky little dive for experimental productions beneath a loud Irish pub.

South London

Brixton, Battersea and Clapham

Cinemas   *Clapham Picture House*, Venn St, SW4 (information T020-7498 2242; booking: T020-7498 3323). Pleasant independent cinema just off Clapham High St showing the old, the new and the cult.

   Ritzys, Brixton Oval, Coldharbour Lane, SW2 (information T020-7737 2121; booking: T020-7733 2229). Classy 5-screen cinema offering the best of both arthouse and mainstream and something of a Brixton institution.

Music   **Rock, folk and jazz** *Brixton Academy*, 211 Stockwell Rd, SW9. Box Office: T020-7771 2000. One of London's best medium-scale venues staging renowned acts from the world of rock and pop.

   Bread and Roses, 68 Clapham Manor St, SW4, T020-7498 1779. Wonderful pub with music from a different African country every Sun (see above) and occasional folk and alt country gigs.

   Souls of Black Folks, 407 Coldharbour Lane, SW9, T020-7738 4141. Café and bookshop with jazz bands playing on a tiny stage most nights of the week.

   The Swan, 215 Clapham Rd, SW9, T020-7978 9778, gigs from 2130 daily, £1.50-6 (usually free Mon-Wed and before 2100 Thu and Sun).

Nightclubs   *Jongleurs*, 49 Lavender Gdns, SW11, T020-7564 2500. The original branch of this expanding comedy chain, *Jongleurs Battersea* plays host to some of the biggest names on the UK comedy circuit. With 2 adjoining bars, *Bar Risa* and *Bar Risa Late*, a varied and riotous night is assured and booking essential.

   Clapham Grand, Severus Rd, SW11, T020-7978 4618. A notable music venue back in the early 90s, this recently reopened converted theatre is now dedicated to playing cheesy hits from the 70s and 80s to a slightly over-exuberant crowd of hipsters in shirts and skirts. All good fun, but more serious clubbers are better off heading to Brixton.

   Fridge, Town Hall Parade, Brixton Hill, SW2, T020-77326 5100. Banging trance and techno is the staple of Brixton's largest club, though it also hosts several popular gay nights. Admission is generally between £8 and £12.

   Mass, St Matthews Church, Brixton Hill, SW2, T020-7738 5255. Situated above the *Bug Bar*, this dark and dingy converted church is renowned for its weekend hard house nights. Despite the mammoth exterior it can appear deceptively small and fills up quickly after midnight.

   Dogstar, 389 Coldharbour Lane, SW9, T020-7733 7515. Technically a bar/club crossover in the *Bug Bar* mould, the Dogstar is one of Brixton's most popular after hours venues, with decent DJs throughout the week and dodgy disco classics at the weekend. Furthermore, the beer is excellent.

   Schooldisco.com, sometimes at Vauxhall Grammar School, 137b Wandsworth Rd (near Vauxhall tube), schooldisco.com School uniform Sat 2230-0300 £10 entry.

Battersea Arts Centre, Lavender Hill, SW11 (T020-7223 2223), BAC is the second largest **Theatres** arts centre in the country and enjoys a formidable reputation for fostering new and experimental theatre under the inspired artistic directorship of Tom Morris. Performances by touring companies include everything from stand-up comedy to opera and the centre's off-beat seasons of visual theatre, and even 'theatre in the dark', always turn up some surprising and challenging work.

The Grace Theatre, Latchmere Pub, 503 Battersea Park Rd, SW11, T020-7794 0022. A small middle-of-the-road theatre often staging fairly impressive productions, many of which later migrate to the more fashionable North. The *Latchmere* pub below is a luxurious and comfortable place for a pre-play pint with an internet booth.

Upstairs at the Landor, 70 Landor Rd, SW9 9PH, T020-7737 7276. A popular stopping off point for young writers showcasing their products. A good stage for new and innovative productions and a busy local with a strange nautical theme below.

The White Bear, 138 Kennington Park Rd, SE11, T020-7793 9193. A tiny theatre with an adventurous record behind a punk Irish pub.

Up and down the river

Hampton Court

Kingston Option ABC, T020-8546 0404, booking T0870-902 0409. Five-screen main- **Cinemas** stream multiscreen.

Hampton Court Flower Show, 3-8 Jul, T020-7834 4333. Royal Horticultural Society's **Festivals** annual flowerfest in the grounds.

Hampton Court Music Festival, 7-16 Jun, T020-8233 5000, in the Base Court of the Palace, kicked off in 2001 by José Carreras, also music from the West End musicals, Vivaldi fireworks, opera, Jools Holland, R&B and Royal Philarmonic classic fireworks finale. £32-75. www.hamptoncourtfestival.com Booking on T020-7420 1030.

Rose and Crown, 61 High St, Hampton Wick (near Kingston Bridge), T020-8296 9100. **Theatres** Small fringe theatre above an excellent pub.

Richmond and Kew

Richmond Filmhouse, 3 Water Lane, Richmond, Surrey, T020-8332 0030. Popular **Cinemas** arthouse cinema showing modern and classic films. *Odeon Hill Street*, 72 Hill St, Richmond, Surrey. *Odeon Studio*, 6 Red Lion St, Richmond, Surrey. Both T0870-505 0007.

Waterman's Arts Centre, High St Brentford, Middlesex, TW8 DS, T020-8847 5651. **Theatres** Closed for refurbishment and 'artistic refocussing' until Sep 2001, this is a picturesque but sadly dilapidated modern location for dance, theatre and the visual arts.

The Orange Tree, 1 Clarence St, Richmond, Surrey, T020-8940 3633. Popular theatre in-the-round which regularly wins widespread critical acclaim for its treatment of old, new and neglected.

Richmond Theatre, The Green, Richmond, Surrey, T020-8940 0088. Well-respected theatre showing a varied range of productions, from Shakespeare to musicals to comedy, now often hosting touring productions. Laurence Olivier, Helen Mirren and Derek Jacobi have all graced the boards here in their time.

Entertainment & nightlife

Greenwich

Cinemas *Greenwich Cinema*, 180 Greenwich High Rd, SE10, T01426-919020. Three-screen mainstream new releases.

Festivals *Greenwich Artists Open Studios*, on 2 weekends in June, T020-8692 3239

Music **Classical and opera** *Blackheath Concert Halls*, 23 Lee Rd, SE3, T020-8463 0100, www.blackheathhalls.com Resident Orchestra of St John's. Very fashionable and lively concert halls.

Nightclubs *Up the Creek*, 302 Creek Rd, SE10, T020-8858 4581. Quality comedy, dodgy cabaret and disco dancing till 0200 as well as very cheap food Fri-Sun. Tickets about £14, £10 concession.

Theatres *Greenwich Theatre*, Crooms Hill, SE10, T020-8858 7755. Old-fashioned and much-loved theatre in a modern building that has been struggling to stave off closure, so far with some success. Hosts middle-scale touring productions.

Sleeping

11

Sleeping

Hotel price guide

AL over £300	**D** £50-£70	*Prices are for two people sharing a double*
A £200-£300	**E** £20-£50	*or twin room with private bathroom in high*
B £100-£200	**F** under £20	*season. Prices in the more expensive hotels*
C £70-£100		*include breakfast, unless stated otherwise.*

West End

AL *The Savoy*, Strand, WC2, T020-7836 4343, www.savoy-group.co.uk 207 rooms, single £329, double £393-£417, suite £535-£1610. Opened by Richard D'Oyly Carte in 1889, retains reputation for grandeur and traditional British style. The great Escoffier was the first chef, inventing the Peach Melba for Australian Dame Nellie Melba after she had been singing in Manon Lescaut at Covent Garden. Cesar Ritz was its first manager. **AL** *One Aldwych*, 1 Aldwych, WC2, T020-7300 1000, www.onealdwych.co.uk Award-winning modern designer hotel with 105 rooms, complete with an extensive art collection, huge swimming pool and plenty of subtle and not-so-subtle style notes.

A *Waldorf Meridien*, Aldwych, WC2, T020-7836 2400. Palm Court is the main attraction, with power breakfasts, tea dances, and later jazz.

B *Strand Palace*, Strand, WC2, T0870-4008702. 784 rooms.

C *Royal Adelphi*, 21 Villiers St, WC2, T020-7930 8764, F020-7930 8735. Very central, small hotel with 47 rooms, not much changed since 60s.

E *Strand Continental*, 142 Strand, WC2, T020-7836 4880. Very basic, cash-only Indian hotel with running hot and cold water in 24 bedrooms. Shared bathrooms. Above the *India Club* restaurant.

The Strand, Embankment & Aldwych
■ *on map, page 69*

AL *The Radisson Edwardian Hampshire*, Leicester Square, WC2, T020-7859 9399, F020-7930 8122, once the Dental Hospital but now a plush five-star hotel with great views from the Penthouse Suite. No single rooms. **AL** *St Martin's Lane*, 45 St Martin's Lane, WC2, T0800-634 5500, F020-7300 5501. Ian Schrager's media favourite, designed by minimalist Philippe Starck, with restaurant doing classic French and modern European on side, the awesome *Light Bar* and the *Seabar* for seafood.

C *Manzi's*, 1/2 Leicester St, WC2, T020-7734 0224, F020-7437 4864. 15 smallish, clean, en-suite rooms, 70 years old, above the famous fish restaurant, popular with business travellers as well as tourists.

Leicester Square & around
■ *on map, page 78*

AL *Sanderson*, 50 Berners St, W1, T020-7300 9500, F020-7300 1400. 150 rooms. The latest in the ultra-modern Philippe Starck-designed chain that includes the *St Martin's Lane Hotel*. Ultra-chic *Spoon Plus* restaurant, *Purple Bar* for residents only, and *Lobby Bar* open to the public until 0100 nightly.

A *Hazlitt's*, 6 Frith St, W1, T020-7434 1771, F020-7439 1524, reservations@hazlitts.co.uk, www.hazlittshotel.com 23 period rooms, in memory of the great essayist, many people's favourite London hotel.

Soho
■ *on map, page 86*

A *Covent Garden*, 10 Monmouth St, WC2, T020-7806 1100. 50 individually decorated rooms, popular with the media set, including *Brasserie Max*, a stylish cocktail bar. **A** *Radisson Mountbatten*, 20 Monmouth St, WC2, T020-7836 4300, F020-7240 3540. 128 rooms, four-star deluxe.

B *Drury Lane Moat House*, 10 Drury Lane, WC2, T020-7208 9988, F020-7831 1548. 163 rooms, 4-star, often fully booked, breakfast included in price, popular corporate choice.

Covent Garden
■ *on map, page 94*

Sleeping

C *Seven Dials*, 7 Monmouth St, T020-7241 0823, F020-7681 0792. 10 rooms, once a picture frame shop, now a clean, convenient and friendly Italian family-run place. **C** *Fielding Hotel*, 4 Broad Court, Bow St, WC2, T020-7836 8305. **C** *Jubilee Hotel*, 11 Upper St Martin's Lane, WC2, T020-7240 1373, F020-7240 4302. 12-room basic budget hotel. Double glazed. No bar or restaurant. Reasonable last-minute option.

Mayfair &
Regent Street
■ *on map, page 106*

AL *Brown's*, 30-34 Albemarle St, W1, T020-7493 6020, F020-7493 9381, www.brownshotel.com Founded by Byron's butler, this Raffles International hotel is the most popular place to take sumptuous English teas in calm, tinkling comfort. A family hotel with impeccable service and bags of character. **AL** *The Connaught*, Carlos Pl, W1, T020-7499 7070, F020-7495 3262, www.savoy-group.com The famous restaurant has recently been refurbished in red. A quiet country-house atmosphere prevails. **AL** *Claridge's*, Brook St, W1, T020-7629 8860, F020-7499 210, www.savoy-group.com The front lobby of Mayfair's most glamorous hotel is being restored to its 1920s state. The bar has won design awards. **AL** *The Dorchester*, 54 Park Lane, W1, T020-7629 8888, F020-7495 7342, www.dorchesterhotel.com Owned by the Sultan of Brunei, has been refurbished in dazzling style and is now a strong contender for the title of London's finest hotel. **AL** *The London Hilton*, 22 Park Lane, W1, T020-7493 8000, F020-7208 4142, www.hilton.com A towering hive of activity, with 4 different restaurants and everything an international jet-setter might require. Spectacular views from the top rooms and *Windows* bar. **AL** *The Metropolitan*, Old Park Lane, W1, T020-7447 1000, F020-7447 1100, www.metropolitan.co.uk Probably still the most fashionable 5-star hotel in London, despite swanky new arrivals at the Aldwych and on St Martin's Lane. Not for wallflowers.

A *Berkeley Plaza*, 39 Hill St, W1, T020-7499 4121. Same sort of thing as the *Curzon Plaza*. **A** *The Chesterfield*, 35 Charles St, W1, T020-7491 2622, F020-7491 4793 www.redcarnationhotels.com Close to Berkeley Square, the *Conservatory* restaurant and bar here have won awards. **A** *Curzon Plaza*, 56 Curzon St, W1, T020-7499 4121, www.curzonplaza.co.uk Serviced apartments, double studio £132 per night. **A** *Flemings Mayfair*, Half Moon St, W1, T020-7499 2964, F020-7629 4063, www.flemings-mayfair.co.uk/flemings Good-value family-run hotel in Georgian buildings with Green Park just over the road. **A** *Millennium Britannia Hotel*, Grosvenor Sq, T020-7629 9400. **A** *No 5 Maddox Street*, 5 Maddox St, W1, T020-7647 0200, F020-7647 0300, www.living-rooms.co.uk Luxurious apartments in a newish boutique hotel fitted out with distinctive flair. **A** *Westbury Hotel*, Bond St, W1, T020-7629 7755, F020-7495 1163, www.westbury-london.co.uk More laid-back than many of Mayfair's finest. Service with a smile and excellent cocktails in the *Polo bar*.

Piccadilly &
St James's
■ *on map, page 118*

AL *Le Meridien*, 21 Piccadilly, W1, T0870-400 8400, F020-7437 3574, LMPICCRES@forte-hotels.com With *Champneys* and Marco Pierre White's *Oak Room*. **AL** *The Ritz*, 150 Piccadilly, W1J, T020-7493 8181, F020-7493 2687. 131 rooms. One of the world's most famous hotels. Tea in Italian Garden for £27.

A *Athenaeum Hotel and Apartment*, 116 Piccadilly, W1V, T020-7499 3464. *Whisky Bar*, *Windsor Lounge*, haute cuisine in *Bullochs* restaurant. 157 rooms, cheaper at weekend. **A** *The Stafford*, St James's Pl, SW1, T020-7493 0111, F020-7493 7121. Converted Carriage House apartments. Expensive restaurant with classic English menu, American bar festooned with hats and baseball helmets, a convivial spot. **A** *Dukes Hotel*, St James's Pl, SW1, T020-7491 4840, F020-7493 1264. 89 rooms. Health club, luxury small hotel tucked away in a quiet backstreet with a cosy bar. **A** *No 22*, 22 Jermyn St, SW1, T020-7734 2353, F020-7734 2353, www.22jermyn.com 18 club-like rooms or small room with a studio. No public areas, 24-hr room service.

A *The Berkshire*, 350 Oxford St, W1, T020-7629 7474, F020-7629 8156, resberk@radisson.com 147 rooms. Prime location, corporate comfort. A Radisson Edwardian hotel.

Oxford Street & Marble Arch

B *Cumberland Hotel*, Marble Arch, W1, T0870-400 8701, F020-7724 4621. Built around Marble Arch tube, busy shopping centre on ground floor at reception. Huge Forte/Meridien place with hundreds of clean, well-appointed rooms.

C *The Ivanhoe Suites*, 1b St Christopher's Pl, W1, T020-7935 1047, F020-7722 0435. 8 rooms, very clean, must book about a week in advance.

Central London

B *Hilton London St Ermin's*, Caxton St, SW1, T020-7222 7888, F020-7222 6914, www.stermins.hilton.com 290 rooms, breakfast included in price. Erstwhile Edwardian splendour in a baroque fantasy of a building. **B** *Sanctuary House Hotel*, 33 Tothill St, SW1, T020-7799 4044, F020-7799 3657. 34 clean rooms above a Fuller's Ale and Pie House.

Westminster & Whitehall
■ on map, page 141

AL *The Berkeley Hotel*, Wilton Pl, SW1, T020-7235 6000, F020-7235 4340, www.savoy-group.co.uk 168 rooms. Home of the superlative French cuisine of *Tante Claire* (T020-7823 2003) amid one of the last words in genteel jet-set accommodation. **AL** *The Lanesborough*, Hyde Park Corner, SW1, T020-7259 5599, F020-7259 5606. 95 rooms. Once the St George's Hospital although you'd never know it, now done up in restrained Regency style incorporating the discreet pleasures of the *Library Bar*. **AL** *Halkin Hotel*, 5-6 Halkin St, SW1, T020-7333 1000, F020-7333 1100. Ultra-contemporary design also boasting a top-class restaurant (T020-7333 1234).

Victoria, Belgravia & Pimlico
■ on map, page 152

B *Lime Tree Hotel*, 135 Ebury St, SW1, T020-7730 8191. Small neat little B&B. **B** *Tophams*, 28 Ebury St, SW1, T020-7730 8147, F020-7823 5966. Charming small country-house style hotel, family-run with friendly service.

C *Collin House*, 104 Ebury St, SW1, T/F020-7730 8031. Small, clean hotel at surprisingly reasonable rates considering its location. **C** *The Blair Victoria Hotel*, 78-84 Warwick Way, SW1, T020-7828 8603, F020-7976 6536, sales@blairvictoria 50 rooms. Most recommended of the area's countless small hotels, for its warm welcome and efficient service. **C** *The Victoria Inn*, 65-67 Belgrave Rd, SW1, T020-7834 6721, F020-7931 0201, www.victoriainn.co.uk 43 rooms. No-nonsense place on the busy Belgrave Rd. **C** *Winchester Hotel*, 17 Belgrave Rd, SW1, T020-7828 2972, F020-7828 5191. Another reasonable alternative that prides itself on being a cut above the rest.

D *Enrico Hotel*, 79 Warwick Way, SW1, T020-7834 9538, F020-7233 9995. 26 rooms. Tiny and basic but still good value.

E *Oak House*, 29 Hugh St, SW1, T020-7834 7151. 6 rooms, beside Victoria Station. More than 5 days bookable (no advance booking for 1 or 2 nights only). Tea and coffee provided.

Sleeping

AL *Blakes*, 33 Roland Gdns, SW7, T020-7370 6701, www.smallchichotels.com 50 rooms. Celebrity and honeymooner favourite without self-consiousness, a place to be pampered, private, recherché and cramped. Each room is different. **AL** *Mandarin Oriental Hyde Park Hotel*, 66 Knightsbridge, SW1, T020-7235 2000, www.mandarinoriental.com 200 rooms. Underrated luxury hotel, good for genteel teas, with an excellent restaurant.

Knightsbridge, South Kensington & Hyde Park
■ on map, page 162

A *Basil Street Hotel*, 8 Basil St, SW3, T020-7581 3311, www.thebasil.com 87 rooms. A nostalgic piece of the Algonquin in old Edwardian Knightsbridge, great for quiet afternoon teas, and cosy basement winebar. **A** *Copthorne Tara*, Scarsdale Pl, T020-7937 7211. **A** *Franklin Hotel*, 28 Egerton Gdns, SW3, T020-7584 5533, www.franklinhotel.co.uk 46 rooms, Quiet, other-worldly very 'English' hotel out of the way just off Brompton Rd. **A** *The Gore*, 189 Queen's Gate, SW7, T020-7584 6601,

www.gorehotel.com 53 rooms. Wood-panelled, family-run and with that certain something for special occasions. No restaurant. **A** *Millenium Bailey's*, 140 Gloucester Rd, T020-7373 6000. **A** Millenium Gloucester, 4-18 Harrington Gdns, T020-7373 6030. **A** *Pelham Hotel*, 15 Cromwell Pl, SW7, T020-7589 8288, www.firmdale.com 50 rooms. Genuinely warm and effortlessly gracious staff, a decent rival to Blakes with untrendy but delicately tasteful rooms, 2 lobbies and nestling spots just for visitors.

B *Aster House*, 3 Sumner Pl, SW7, T020-7581 5888, www.asterhouse.com 14 rooms. Sweet little place with a garden and conservatory. **B** *Diplomat*, 2 Chesham St, SW1, T020-7235 1544, www.btinternet.com/~diplomat.hotel 26 rooms. Beautiful staircase, old building, near *Harrods*. **B** *Five Sumner Place*, 5 Sumner Pl, SW7, T020-7584 7586, F020-7823 9962, www.sumnerplace.com Another cosy, chintzy and award-winning hideaway. **B** *The Gallery Hotel*, 10 Queensberry Pl, South Kensington, SW7, T020-7915 0000, www.eeh.co.uk Five-diamonds (ie no restaurant) but very smart bar and lobby. Breakfast included in price. Part of the same group is the equally comfortable **B** *The Gainsborough Hotel*, 7-11 Queensberry Pl, T020-7957 0000, F020-7957 0001. **B** *Number Sixteen*, 16 Sumner Pl, SW7, T020-7589 5232, www.numbersixteenhotel.co.uk 36 rooms. Elegant privacy and the most salubrious (and expensive) of the set in this dainty little stucco street. **B** *The Regency*, 100 Queen's Gate, SW7, T020-7373 7878, www.regency-london.co.uk 198 rooms. Efficient, clean, corporate, ready and waiting in an old building.

E *Albert Hotel*, 191 Queen's Gate, SW7, T020-7584 3019. Student halls let in the summer holiday, 70 beds, 6-bed dorm £20 a night, 10-bed dorms £15 a night, all including breakfast, bookable from May (probably). **E** *Linstead Hall* on Imperial College Campus, Watts Way, Prince's Gdns, SW7, T020-7594 9507 (Accommodation Link), www.imperialcollege-accommodationlink.co.uk More student rooms.

Holiday Serviced Apartments, 273 Old Brompton Rd, SW5, T020-7373 4477, www.holidayapartments.co.uk From £450 a week self-catering serviced apartments a week upwards in central London.

A *Millenium Chelsea*, 17 Sloane St, T020-7235 4377. **B** *The Claverley*, 13-14 Beaufort Gardens, Knightsbridge, SW3, T020-7589 8541, www.claverleyhotel.co.uk Comfortable and classy small hotel. Breakfast included in price.

Chelsea
■ *on map, page 176*

E *Oakley Hotel*, 73 Oakley St, SW3, T020-7352 5599, F020-7727 1190. Small, clean, friendly and excellent value on the approach to Albert Bridge (£42 including breakfast with shared bathrooms, £56 for the 1 en-suite bedroom).

Nell Gwynne House Apartments, Sloane Ave, SW3, T020-7589 1105. £440-£580 per week for decent self-catering studio apartments in Nell Gwynne House on Sloane Av.

A *Langham Hilton*, 1 Portland Pl, W1, T020-7636 1000, F020-7323 2340, www.langham.hilton.com 429 rooms. One of the oldest grand hotels in London, fully refurbished in the 90s and now a corporate favourite.

Regent's Park & Marylebone
■ *on map, page 186*

C *Hart House Hotel*, 51 Gloucester Pl, Portman Square, W1, T020-7935 2288, F020-7935 8516, reservations@harthouse.co.uk 15 spacious rooms with shower in an attractively converted townhouse. Book at least 2 weeks in advance. **C** *Hallam Hotel*, 12 Hallam St, Portland Pl, W1, T020-7580 1166, F020-7323 4527. 25 rooms in a genteel townhouse. **C** *Georgian House Hotel*, 87 Gloucester Pl, W1, T020-7935 2211/7486 3151, F020-7486 7535. 19 rooms with bathroom.

D-E *Indian Student YMCA*, 41 Fitzroy St, WC1, T020-7387 0411. Anyone can stay. 109 rooms, dinner and breakfast included in an Indian canteen.

E *Carr Saunders Hall*, 18 Fitzroy St, W1, T020-7580 6338. LSE hall of residence just beneath Telecom Tower. 10 twin rooms available during Easter and summer holidays. Book as early as possible. **E** *International Students House*, 229 Great Portland St, W1, T020-7631 8300, F020-7631 8315. Not necessary to be a student, 275 rooms, open to

Sleeping

public throughout, but very full at all other times. Restaurant with international food in the basement, refurbished bar open late to residents. Laundry, cyber-café, microwave.

Euston, St Pancras & King's Cross
■ on map, page 196

B *Shaw Park Plaza*, 100-110 Euston Rd, NW1, T020-7666 9000, www.parkhtls.com 312 rooms with a panoramic elevator. On the site of the once radical *Shaw Theatre*, which has been preserved inside, and where shows are promised for the summer.

C *Euston Travel Inn Capital*, 1 Duke's Rd, WC1, T020-7554 3400, www.travelinn.co.uk 220 rooms. Clean, safe, modern and impersonal.

D *The Carlton Hotel*, Birkenhead St, WC1, T020-7916 9697. 32 clean rooms in what was once a NatWest bank.

E-F *Ashlee House*, 261-265 Gray's Inn Rd, WC1, T020-7833 9400. Clean, secure and bright budget hostel. Twin room £50, dormitory £15. **E-F** *The Generator*, 37 Tavistock Pl, WC1, T020-7388 7666. 217 funky cell-like bunk rooms £23 per person, 8-bed dormitories £15 a night, busy bar in old police station.

Bloomsbury & Fitzrovia
■ on map, page 204

A *Charlotte Street Hotel*, 15-17 Charlotte St, W1, T020-7907 4000, F020-7806 2002. 52 rooms, Super-fashionable, restaurant and bar *Oscar* Popular with film people. **A** *myHotel*, 11-13 Bayley St, WC1, T020-7667 6000, F020-7667 6044. 76 rooms, brand new, Conran-designed feng shui.

●●●

Youth hostels in London

The seven YHA London hostels are well spread out around the city. All are open 24 hours and charge between £20 and £24 per night. Some include breakfast in the price; some provide rooms with en suite facilities. **City** (opposite St Paul's Cathedral): 36 Carter Lane, EC4V 5AB, T020-7236 4965 F020-7236 7681. Meals available; facilities include restaurant, TV lounge, internet access, showers, luggage room and laundry. **Earl's Court** (near Olympia and the Kensington Museums): 38 Bolton Gardens, SW5 0AQ, T020-7373 7083, F020-7835 2034. Meals available; facilities include TV lounge, self-catering kitchen, showers, luggage store, laundry room, cycle store, foreign exchange, internet access, travel desk and garden. Breakfast included. **Hampstead Heath**: 4 Wellgarth Road, Golders Green, NW11 7HR, T020-8458 9054 F020-8209 0546. Meals available; facilities include lounges with TV and video games, showers, luggage room, laundry facilities, garden, internet access. Breakfast included. **Holland House** (overlooking Holland Park, near the Royal Albert Hall): Holland Walk, Kensington, W8 7QU, T020-7937 0748, F020-7376 0667. Meals available; facilities include lounge, TV room, games

room, self-catering kitchen, showers, luggage store, lockers, laundry facilities and grounds. Breakfast included. **Oxford Street** (city centre, close to Soho): 14 Noel Street, W1F 8GJ, T020-7734 1618, F020-7734 1657. Packed breakfast and self-catering only. Facilities include lounge with TV, self-catering kitchen, laundry, internet access, lockers and showers. Breakfast not included in price. **St Pancras** (convenient for King's Cross, Euston and St Pancras train stations): 79-81 Euston Road, NW1 2QS, T020-7388 9998, F020-7388 6766. Evening meals available; facilities include lounge with TV and games area, self-catering kitchen, dining room, cycle store, luggage store, showers, lockers and laundry. Premium rooms available at a higher price. Breakfast included. **Rotherhithe** (close to Greenwich Meridian, Observatory and other South Bank attractions): 20 Salter Road, SE16 5PR, T020-7232 2114, F020-7237 2919. Evening meal available; facilities include licensed bar, TV lounge, self-catering kitchen, laundry room, showers, cycle store and access for wheelchairs. Breakfast included. For **information and reservations** at any of the London hostels, T020-7373 3400, F020-7373 3455.

Sleeping

B *Blooms*, 7 Montague St, WC1, T020-7323 1717, F020-7636 6498. Behind the British Museum, 18th century house and furniture to match, walled garden. **B** *Hotel Russell*, Russell Square WC1, T020-7837 6470, T020-7837 2357, www.principalhotels. co.uk 336 rooms, not including breakfast. Extraordinary Edwardian bar. **B** *Academy*, 21 Gower St, WC1, T020-7631 4115, T020-7636 3442, www.etontownhouse. com Georgian townhouse, library and conservatory, charming staff, with breakfast, bar open to non-residents

C *The Crescent Hotel*, 49-50 Cartwright Gdns, WC1, T020-7387 1515, F020-7383 2054, www.crescenthoteloflondon.com 27 rooms. **C** *Harlingford*, 61-63 Cartwright Gdns, WC1, T020-7387 1551. 43 rooms, refurbished old house. **C** *Mentone Hotel*, 54-56 Cartwright Gdns, WC1, T020-7387 3927, F020-7388 4671. En suite bathrooms, tastefully decorated, family-run hotel. Breakfast included in price. **C** *Morgan*, 24 Bloomsbury St, WC1, T020-7636 3735, F020-7636 3045. 20 rooms, opposite the British Museum Shop on corner. Breakfast included in price. **C** *St Margaret*, 26 Bedford Pl, WC1, T020-7636 4277, F020-7323 3066. 60 rooms.

D *The Jesmond*, 63 Gower St, WC1, T020-7636 3199, F020-7323 4373, www.jesmondhotel.org.uk 16 rooms. Excellent value, with a garden.

A-B *The Rookery*, Peter's Lane, Cowcross St, EC1, T020-7336 0931, F020-7336 0932, www.rookeryhotel.com Newish old-fashioned hotel in an antique building with an eyrie for a penthouse.

Holborn & Clerkenwell
■ *on map, page 220*

AL *Great Eastern Hotel*, Liverpool St, EC2, T020-7618 5000, F020-7618 5001, www.great-eastern-hotel.co.uk 267 rooms. Sir Terence Conran's first hotel, right on top of Liverpool St Station, with an excellent restaurant and tranquil bars. **AL** *The King's Wardrobe*, Carter Lane, EC4, F020-7792 2202, www.bridgestreet.com Superior serviced apartments in a secluded historic courtyard near St Paul's.

The City
■ *on map, page 234*

E *Barbican YMCA*, 2 Fann St, EC2, T020-7628 0697, Tx020-7638 2420. Single and double rooms for 240 people, £52 including breakfast. Admin@barbican.ymca.org.uk **E** *London City YMCA*, 8 Errol St, EC1, T020-7628 8832, F020-7628 4080. Breakfast included.

B *Mercure London City Bankside Hotel*, 75-79 Southwark St, SE1, T020-7902 0800, F020-7902 0810. New '3-star deluxe', 144 rooms part of the Novotel chain, £12 breakfast, mainly corporate custom, halfway down Southwark St.

Bankside & Southwark
■ *on map, page 244*

C *Holiday Inn Express*, 103-109 Southwark St, SE1, T020-7401 2525. Continental breakfast included. 88 rooms all en suite, internet access, small bar, book weeks in advance.

D *Bankside House*, 24 Sumner St, SE1, T020-7633 9877. LSE hall of residence behind Tate Modern, beds in 4-bed rooms for £55 double including breakfast, own shower, 30 Jun-21 Sep only, book as early as possible.

F *St Christopher's Inn Backpackers Village*, 161-163, 121 and 57 Borough High St, SE1, T020-7407 1856. 160 beds; £10 beds in four 12-bed dorms, internet access, laundry, sauna £1 a day, no kitchen, book a week in advance for weekends. Sweaty discos downstairs on Fri and Sat, about £5 admission.

AL-A *London Marriot County Hall Hotel*, T020-7928 5200. 5-star, 200 rooms, majority with river views, from £245 excluding VAT, up to £750 for the Westminster suite. *County Hall Restaurant*, cocktail area, *Leader's Bar*, open to the public.

South Bank & Waterloo
■ *on map, page 257*

C *Days Inn*, 54 Kennington Rd, SE1, T020-7922 1331, F020-7922 1441, waterloo@premierhotels.co.uk/www.daysinn.com Freephone UK reservations T0800-0280 400. 162 rooms, limited free parking.

D *London Country Hall Travel Inn Capital*, Belvedere Rd, SE1, T020-7902 1600. 313 rooms. **D** *The Mad Hatter*, 3-7 Stamford St, SE1, T020-7401 9222, F020-7401 7111, Madhatter@fullers.demon.co.uk Bright new rooms above a Fuller's pub, largish, double-glazed against noise from the busy road junction outside. **D** *Wellington Inn*, 81-83 Waterloo Rd, SE1, T020-7928 6083, F020-7928 6084. Small, clean rooms above a busy refurbished pub. Quite noisy, right next to the railway, but very convenient location. 4 double rooms, 2 twins and 6 singles. Booking at least 2 weeks ahead is advisable. Good for singles and business travellers. Breakfast not included.

East London

East End
■ *on map, page 276*

B *Holiday Inn Express London-City*, 275 Old St, EC1, T020-7300 4300, F020-7300 4400, www.hiexpress.com Over 200 rooms. Functional and efficient new branch of the hotel chain.

C *City Hotel*, 12 Osborn St, E1, T020-7247 3313, F020-7375 2949, www.rcahotels.co.uk 50 rooms.

F *Lea Valley Campsite*, Sewardstone Rd, E4, T020-8529 5689. Open Apr-Oct only. **F** *Tent City Hackney*, Millfields Rd, E5, T020-8985 7656, www.tentcity. co.uk June-September only. £5 per person.

The Tower
& around
■ *on map, page 284*

B *Novotel London Tower Bridge*, 10 Pepys St, EC3, T020-7265 6000, F020-7265 6060. Brand new, 203 rooms, *Pepys Bar*, garden brasserie and fitness centre. **B** *Thistle Tower*, St Katherine's Way, E1W, T020-7481 2575, F020-7488 4106, www.thistlehotels.com 801 a/c rooms.

E *Butler's Wharf Residence*, Gainsford St, SE1, T020-7407 7164. For self-catering flats next to Design Museum, another LSE property, approx £22.50 per person per night, each flat for 6/7 people, own room, not right on the river, needs booking well in advance.

Docklands
■ *on map, page 292*

A *The Four Season's Hotel, Canary Wharf*, 46 Westferry Circus, E14, T020-7510 1999, F020-7510 1998. Giant space-age structure for the wheeler-dealers of Canary Wharf. In-room facilities include multiline telephones and CD players, in-house hydrotherapy centre and fitness suite. Doubles range from £260 to £310, but the presidential suite is on offer for £1500 if sir is feeling opulent.

B *The International Hotel*, *Brittania Group*, 163 Marsh Wall, E14, T020-7515 1551. Clean and modern with superb views of the tower and waterfront. 3 restaurants and in-house gym and swimming pool.

D *Ibis, Isle of Dogs*, Prestons Rd, E14, T0207-517 1100. Standard chain fare. Near Canary Wharf and shopping complex. **D** *Travelodge Docklands*, Coriander Av, E14, T020-7531 9705. Not as spicy as the address suggests but good budget accommodation.

E *Urban Learning Foundation*, 56 East India Dock Rd, E14, T020-7987 0033. Single beds in shared self-catering flats. £22.50 per person per night. Bargain for the area.

North London

Hampstead
& Highgate
■ *on maps,*
pages 302 & 306

B *Forte Posthouse*, 215 Haverstock Hill, Hampstead, NW3, T0870-4009037, F020-7435 5586. Recently renovated and given a tourist board 4-crown commendation. Offers weekend room rates. The newly opened hotel restaurant is run by Marco Pierre White. **B** *The Sandringham Hotel*, 3 Holford Rd, NW3, T020-7435 1569, F020-7431 5932. Comfortable 'chintzy' rooms in a large period Hampstead House. Singles, Doubles and suites. Pleasant breakfast room and garden.

C *The House Hotel*, 2 Rosslyn Hill, NW3, T020-7431 3873, F020-7433 1775. 27 rooms. Refurbished small hotel at the foot of Rosslyn Hill. **C** *The Langorf Hotel and Self-Catering Apartments*, 20-22 Frognal, NW3, T020-7794 4483, F020-7435 9055. The hotel offers a variety of singles and doubles with an executive range available too. Given a 2-crown commendation. The apartments range from 1-2 beds at nightly and weekly rates.

D *La Gaffe*, 107-111 Heath St, NW3, T020-7435 8965, F020-7794 7592. A small family-run hotel offering cosy rooms in a period house with its own locally favoured Italian restaurant. AA and RAC graded.

E *Belsize*, 40 Belsize Park Gdns, NW3, T020-7722 8131, F020-7483 7146. Group rooms and doubles available at varying rates.

A *London Marriot Regent's Park*, 128 King Henry's Rd, NW3, T020-7722 7771. Standard superior chain fare, health club, sauna, solarium, swimming pool. **A** *Thistle Euston*, 190-198, North Gower St, NW1, T020-7387 4400. A lack of accommodation in this bracket might tempt the comfort-hungry nearer to Euston, with all the usual big-chain perks.

Camden
■ *on map, page 314*

C *The Camden Lock Hotel*, 89 Chalk Farm Rd, NW1, T020-7267 3912. Despite looking like a motel somewhere off a motorway in the Midlands, this is a safe, clean bet for those wishing to stay in the middle of Camden.

D *Ibis*, 3 Cardington St, NW1, T020-7388 7777. Cheap(ish) and cheerful branch of the budget chain convenient for the delights of Camden High Rd.

B *Hilton London Islington*, 53 Upper St, N1, T020-7354 7700, F020-7354 7711, www.islington.hilton.com Large chain hotel bang next to the Business Design Centre.

Islington
■ *on map, page 320*

C *Jurys London Inn*, 60 Pentonville Rd, N1, T020-7282 5500, F020-7282 5511. Another large budget chain hotel, clean and safe, at the top of the hill above King's Cross.

D *Kandara Guest House*, 68 Ockenden Rd, N1, T020-7226 5721, F020-7226 3379, www.kandara.co.uk 11 rooms, 5 shared bathrooms. Full English breakfast included. Non-smoking.

West London

A *Portobello Hotel*, 22 Stanley Gdns, W11, T020-7727 2777, F020-7792 9641, www.portobello-hotel.demon.co.uk Internationally trendy hotel to the stars. Johnny Depp and Kate Moss allegedly bathed in champagne here.

Notting Hill & Holland Park
■ *on map, page 330*

A-B *Westbourne Hotel* 163-165 Westbourne Gr, W11, T020-243 6008, F020-7229 7201, enquires@westbournehotel.com Portrait Rooms, Landscape Rooms and Garden rooms available. Fabulously chic – trying to beat the *Portobello* – very Greenwich Village New-Yorky. Stuffed full of contemporary art and "subtle luxury".

B *The Abbey Court Hotel*, 20 Pembridge Gdns, W11, T020-7221 7518, F020-792 0858. The cleanest and most luxurious of the this street packed with modest hotels. The breakfast is served ad lib in the conservatory in its quiet garden. Breakfast included in price. **B** *Holland Court Hotel*, 31-33 Holland Rd, W14, T020-7371 1133, F020-7602 9114. Buffet breakfast included. Clean, friendly and cheap for the area. Close to Olympia, and the far end of Kensington High St (and a wealth of Persian cafés).

D *London Visitors Hotel*, 42-44 Holland Rd, W14, T020-7602 1282, F020-7602 0736, reservations T020-7603 9060. Big double-fronted, cheap hotel. Round corner from Olympia and nearby Holland Park.

A *The Royal Garden Hotel*, 2-24 Kensington High St, W8, T020-7937 8000. This huge modern monstrosity next to Diana's old Kensington Palace is a popular international stopover as well as for weddings and bar mitzvahs. Expensive and not as glitzy as its rivals the other end of Hyde Park, it offers easy access to Central London and limo parking for nipping back to Heathrow … the jetset often stay here. It has luxury dining, and all the usual international and business facilities, as well as spectacular views from the bar on the 10th floor.

In Earl's Court, Barkston Gdns, very close to the tube, has a long row of perfectly pleasant hotels, all of which seem individual but clean and welcoming. Nearest the corner with the main Earl's Court Rd is **B** *The Burns Hotel*, 18-26 Barkston Gdns, SW5, T020-7373 3151. Price excludes breakfast (English £8.75 per person/Continental £5.75per person) The biggest and briskest of the row. **B** *Albany Hotel*, 4-12 Barkston Gdns, SW5, T020-7370 6116, F020-7244 8836, albany@realco.co.uk Rooms for 1-4 people. **B** *Barkston Gdns Hotel*, 34-44 Barkston Gdns, SW5, T020-7373 7851. Less fancy, and more businesslike, offers conference facilities. Breakfast extra (Continental £6.25, English £8.50).

B-C *Henley House Hotel*, 30 Barkston Gdns, SW5, T020-7370 4111, henleyhse@aol.com With bookshelves and tartan sofas, this hotel appeals to the olde-worlde visitor. More individual and charming than the rest of the row.

C *Maranton House Hotel*, 14 Barkston Gdns, SW5, T020-7373 5782, F020-7244 9543. Single, double and triple rooms available. Breakfast included.

D *Merlyn Court Hotel*, 2 Barkston Gdns, SW5, T020-7370 1640. Must be the cheapest – certainly the plainest – out of the row of hotels.

F *The Court Hotel*, 194-196 Earl's Court Rd, SW5, T020-7373 0027, F020-7912 8500. Right beside the tube station tucked above the newsagents, this must be the bargain of the century. Frequented by Ozzie backpackers, offering 15 rooms with TV, a kitchen and a microwave to share. Visitors share and stay for weeks at £15 for 4 or £30 for a single room. "All is negotiable – depending upon availability".

A *The Hempel*, 31-35 Craven Hill Gdns, W2, T020-7298 9000, F020-7402 4666, www.the-hempel.co.uk 41 rooms, 6 apartments. The smartest hotel in the area is still this elegant extravagance designed by the Queen Bee of designer hotels – former model Anouska Hempel aka Lady Weinberger. Very different from her own hotel, *Blakes*, although it too occupies one whole side of a white stucco square. The minimalist Japanese-design with its exquisite interiors defies the Regency architecture outside – every wall, window and portal is different and chic. The central garden holds a pool amongst the shaken-but-never-stirred bay trees amid lots of pebbles. The *Oriental* restaurant and a new bar, the *H Bar*, are open to non-residents.

B *Byron Hotel*, 36-38 Queensborough Terr, W2, T020-7243 0987, F7792 1957, www.capricornhotels.co.uk 45 rooms. English breakfast included.

C *Fairways Hotel*, 186 Sussex Gdns, W2, T/F020-7723 4871, www.fairways-hotel.co.uk 18 rooms, B&B, en suite. **C** *Lancaster Hall Hotel*, 35 Craven Terr, W2, T020-7723 9276, F020-7706 2870, www.lancaster-hotel.co.uk 103 rooms. Tucked away, this large, concrete block is surprisingly quiet in the heart of Bayswater backstreets, between the hub of Queensway and Paddington, only a stone's throw from Lancaster Gate entrance to the park. Very pleasant despite it's 60s concrete exterior and being a corporate favourite.

D *Border Hotel*, 14 Norfolk Square, W2, T020-7723 2968, F020-7402 9061, www.stdavidshotels.co.uk 74 rooms. English breakfast included.

E-F *Dean Court Hotel*, 57 Inverness Terr, W2, T020-7229 2961, F020-7727 1190. Australian-managed. 3-4 to a room, £15 a night, £75 a week, including breakfast. Single sex. Double £45. Dorm room only bookable 2 nights.

South London

C-D *Lavender Guest House*, 18 Lavender Sweep, SW11, T020-7585 2767. Picturesque
Victorian building with a pretty garden for guests' use. A standard double costs £60 a
night with breakfast, though the lavish Executive Room, which might cost around
£300 in the centre, is a snip at £85. **C-D** *Compass Travelodge Battersea*, 200 York Rd,
SW11, T020-7228 5508. Part of a large national chain, Travelodge Battersea offers reliable and comfortable family and standard accommodation. One drawback is the lack
of proximity to a tube station, although Clapham Junction train station is 10 mins walk
down the road.

Battersea
■ *on map, page 368*

   D *Barclay Court Hotel*, 12-14 Hafer Rd, off Battersea Rise, SW11, T020-7228 5272. A
friendly 3-Crown hotel, the *Barclay Court* is ideally located next to the bohemian end
of Battersea Rise and a short walk from Clapham Common. Breakfast is included and
most rooms have showers.

B *Windmill on the Common*, Clapham Common Southside, SW4, T020-8673 4578,
windmillhotel@youngs.co.uk A view over the Common, well-furnished rooms and a
fancy restaurant make the *Windmill* a great base from which to see London. It is not
cheap however (reduced rates weekends).

Clapham
■ *on map, page 370*

   C *Dudley Hotel*, 80-81 Clapham Common Southside, SW4, T020-8673 3534. With
the *Dudley* you pay for location, right next to the Common and very close to Clapham
South tube station. The rooms are all en suite and include a full English breakfast.

   D *The Abbeville*, 89 Abbeville Rd, SW4, T020-7622 5360. Small and friendly bed
and breakfast (7 rooms) on upmarket Abbeville Rd. **D** *Dufort Guest House*, 20
Poynders Rd, SW4, T020-8673 2043, beltwood@bigfoot.com This venerable guesthouse was lovingly restored to its former glory by its Canadian owners and is now
resplendent with chandeliers and fine art. Double rooms with shared facilities or an
en suite triple are available.

C *Beltwood*, 41 Sydenham Hill, SE26, T020-8693 3030. Several dozen rooms in a
Regency mansion house with a terrace above 3½ acres of gardens landscaped by
Paxton, right at the top of the hill. A glass conservatory under construction overlooks
the treeline and splendid views of the city.

Dulwich

Up and down the river

B *The Carlton Mitre Hotel*, Hampton Court Rd, Surrey, KT8 9BN, T020-8979 9988, F8979
9777, www.carltonhotels.co.uk Doesn't include breakfast. *Landings Brasserie* on the
river. Convenient but otherwise not particularly special hotel right opposite the main
gates of the Palace.

**Hampton
Court**

   B-C *Kingston Lodge Hotel*, 94 Kingston Hill, Kingston, KT2 7NP, T0870-4008115,
www.heritage-hotels.com Price includes breakfast. A reasonable chain hotel.

B *Richmond Gate Hotel*, Richmond Hill, Richmond, TW10, T020-8940 0061, F020-8332
0354, www.corushotels.com/richmondgate With 68 bedrooms, an award-winning
restaurant, well-equipped leisure club with sizeable indoor swimming pool and, to cap
it all, a beautiful position at the top of Richmond Hill, the *Richmond Gate* is a treat.
Expensive but better value than many in the centre of town. Price depends on date.
B *Richmond Hill Hotel*, Richmond Hill, Richmond, TW10, T020-8940 2247, F020-8940
5424, www.corushotels.co.uk/richmondhill The *Richmond Hill* dates from 1726 and
retains much of its original grandeur. With an astonishing view over the Thames Valley

**Richmond
& Kew**
■ *on map, page 388*

Sleeping

and convenient proximity to Richmond Park it offers impressive facilities. Owned by the same company though slightly cheaper than the *Richmond Gate*. Price depends on date. **B** *Richmond Inn Hotel*, 50-56 Sheen Rd, Richmond, TW9, T020-8940 0171, F020-8332 2596. Friendly and well located within a couple of minutes walk from the tube. Modern facilities do nothing to detract from its charm.

C *Hobart Hall Hotel*, 43-47 Petersham Rd, Richmond, TW10, T020-8940 0435, F020-8332 2996, www.smoothhound.co.uk/hotels/hobarthall In its time *Hobart Hall* has seen Royalty staying within its 4 walls. Well served by public transport, the hotel is within easy walking distance of the tube and train station, and Richmond Park. It also boasts cut-price student rooms. **C** *Doughty Cottage*, 142a Richmond Hill, Richmond, TW10, T/F020-8332 9434, www.smoothhound.co.uk/hotels/doughtycottage Consisting of 3 sumptuous rooms, *Doughty Cottage* is a luxurious home offering every comfort. The Florentine and Venetian rooms have access to a private patio garden, whilst the Sienna comes with a remarkable vista over Surrey.

D *Chelwood House*, 1 Chelwood Gardens, Kew, TW9, T020-8876 8733. Tucked away down a sleepy cul-de-sac, *Chelwood House* is a small, accessible and welcoming bed and breakfast. Can also recommend others in the area. **D** *Mr and Mrs Leach*, 15 Pensford Av, Kew, TW9, T020-8876 3354. Quiet B&B with 4 rooms.

Greenwich
■ *on map, page 394*
D *Ibis Hotel*, 30 Stockwell St, SE10, T020-8305 1177, F020-8858 7139, www.ibishotel.com 82 rooms all en suite in standard, clean and newish branch of the budget chain. Breakfast £4.25 extra.

Sleeping

Background

12

454

Background

History

One hundred years ago, the novelist HG Wells wrote that "it is not too much to say that the London citizen of the year 2000 AD may have a choice of nearly all England and Wales south of Nottingham and east of Exeter as his suburb... And so the [city] centre will ... be essentially a bazaar, a great gallery of shops and places of concourse and rendezvous, a pedestrian place ... and altogether a very spacious, brilliant and entertaining agglomeration." His vision clearly overestimated the extent to which the urban sprawl of London would expand – the planning regulations of the Green Belt around the city have played their part – and it is neither spacious nor particularly friendly to the pedestrian, but much of what he says does ring true. The commuter belt now extends into the West Country. London has over 5000 pubs and bars and 30,000 shops, and 12,000 restaurants and cafés, and 28 million visitors arrive annually to sample the "brilliant and entertaining agglomeration". It is fitting that so many foreigners should visit the city, because ever since its founding 2000 years ago, London has been a prize and a haven for invading armies and fleeing refugees alike. It is, and has always been, "the mart of many nations".

The Romans are popularly believed to have established the first settlement where the City now lies, but prehistorians have uncovered evidence of habitation in this part of the Thames valley dating back half a million years. The Thames originally flowed through the Vale of St Albans, but was pushed south to its current position by the Ice Age. Flint handaxes have been found in Hillingdon, but perhaps its most fertile prehistoric era was during a warmer spell (about 130,000 BC-110,000 BC), when the landscape was brimming with exotic wildlife. Elephants and hippopotami grazed in what is now Trafalgar Square, lions in Charing Cross, buffaloes in St Martin-in-the-Fields, and wild bears in Woolwich. Remains of giant beavers and hyenas have also been found, and such was the broader nature of the Thames that shark remains have been found in Brentford.

Swamps, lagoons and marshes lined the river's course, fed by a series of rivers emerging from springs in the hills around, rivers that still flow below Londoners' feet. The Fleet rises in Hampstead, flowing from the ponds here and in Highgate down through King's Cross and Clerkenwell to spill into the Thames at Blackfriars. To the east, the Walbrook runs between Moorfields and Bishopsgate, and the more substantial river Lea down to Canning Town. To the west, the Tyburn runs through Regent's Park and under Buckingham Palace; the Westbourne through Hyde Park to Chelsea.

South of the Thames, the rivers Peck, Effra, Falcon and Wandle flows through what was once marshland to the winding Thames. In total some 100 springs gave rise to over 100 miles of rivers beside which communities settled, to grow into villages and then suburbs, such that eventually most of the rivers were covered over by the ever-expanding city. The Thames itself seems to have been venerated by the people around – it has thrown up countless weapons and ceremonial artefacts (most notably the Battersea Shield and Waterloo Helmet), suggesting they were religious offerings made to the river.

By 3800 years ago there were farming settlements on Hampstead Heath, and remnants of Iron Age life have been found in places such as St Mary Axe, Gresham Street and Austin Friars, indicating that the Romans were not the first to settle here. Certainly, what with the abundance of fresh spring waters and fertile hillsides (Tower, Ludgate, Corn) surrounded by marshland, fens and the Thames, the site offered both natural protection and productive soil that was unlikely to have been overlooked by the generations that preceded the Roman invasion. Legend has it that a certain King Lud, buried by Ludgate, set out the original roads and walls of the city in the century before Caesar's first arrival and that the various hills around London spilling forth their waters were holy sites for Druid ritual.

Roman London Whatever the degree of prehistoric settlement here, it was the Romans who first established the town of Londinium as a major trading port, a role it played for almost two millennia. Despite distractions in further-flung regions of Britannia, such as the Scots spilling over the northern border or the Druids in Anglessey, and the city being razed to the ground by Boudicca, Queen of the Iceni, in AD 61, Roman London flourished in the second and third centuries.

A 20 ft wall and ditch surrounded the city, running from the Tower (a later addition) to roughly Blackfriars (the medieval City extended the walls to Temple), interspersed with gates, (the medieval Ludgate, Newgate, Aldersgate, Cripplegate, where there was also a fort, Bishopsgate and Aldgate). The river Walbrook and its tributaries ran down the middle, leaping with salmon and trout. A huge marble-faced basilica, some 70 ft high, stood on the higher land at Cornhill, dominating the skyline; in its shadow business and trade would be conducted in the forum. Houses spread out from here, most made of a mixture of wood and thatch, but also some five-storey villas with courtyards and salmon-painted interiors.

To the north, an amphitheatre held gladiatorial contests and spectaculars, and shops, taverns and other commercial buildings ran down to the governor's palace on the banks of the river (at modern Cannon Street Station). Here the wharves and jetties were lined by ships laden with goods from the Continent, North Africa and the Middle East. Warehouses brimming with anything from olive oil to bronze tableware, or ivory to dried fruit lined the banks. A wooden bridge, wide enough for traffic to pass both ways, spanned the river to Southwark, where commercial and industrial areas shared the land with homes and military bases.

Beyond the walls were farms and cemeteries, both growing in demand as the population reached 60,000 by the fourth century. Londinium was the fifth largest city in the Western Empire, and its reputation earned it the honorific title of 'Augusta'. Over the next 150 years, however, its prosperity declined with that of the Empire as a whole. When Saxons and Angles from northern Europe chose to establish settlements rather than simply make audacious raids, and pirate attacks on trading ships in the Channel became increasingly frequent, it signalled an end to Roman rule.

Saxon London The new settlers, the Saxons, left Roman London abandoned for almost 200 years, and little record remains of the city until about the time of the first building of St Paul's in 604. They preferred to set up farms and villages in the land around such as Barking, Greenwich, Kingston or Hammersmith. By the mid-eighth century, however, the Venerable Bede could describe London as "the mart of many nations resorting to it by land and sea". He was referring to Lundenwic (London port), a town that grew up west of the River Fleet along the modern day Strand and Covent Garden (Aldwych maybe refers to the Saxon 'old-town'). Its flourishing trade invited unwanted attention as Viking raids in the mid-ninth century reduced the city to glowing embers.

Soon after, however, the Saxon King Alfred drove the Danes out, and began to rebuild London on the site of the Roman city. The Roman walls were repaired, jetties restored, streets laid out and markets established. Trade revived, mostly with the northern European and Scandinavian countries, as did industry, particularly metalwork (the abundance of water was a factor) and cloth-making. Further Danish raids in the 10th century resulted in Danish rule again, but not the destruction of the city (many settled in Hackney and Clapham). When Edward the Confessor moved his residence from the 'Wardrobe' in the City to Thorney Island in order to supervise his grand project, Westminster Abbey, politics and commerce were forever separated by the bend in the river. The merchants of the City could now concentrate on their own affairs secluded from court, an independence they have fiercely protected ever since. Tragically for Edward, when the Abbey was consecrated on Christmas Day 1065, he was too ill to attend, and just weeks later he was buried within.

It wasn't long before the Norman conqueror, William, having announced his arrival by burning Southwark, was being crowned at the abbey. He granted privileges to the citizens of the City, being especially careful to keep the merchants sweet, but he was nonetheless wary enough of their independent streak to build three forts within the city walls – Montfichet's Tower, Baynard's Castle, and The White Tower. He introduced the Domesday Book, now the historian's guide to the state of Norman England, in 1086, documenting the size and livestock of each community. Although the City was granted exclusion from such investigations, it leaves us with a picture of a medieval city surrounded by hamlets and farms, fields and market gardens. **Norman London**

William, and many of his successors, held court at Westminster Palace, and the city within the walls was left largely as the residential and commercial heart of London. Ample mansions within spacious walled grounds housed the aristocrats, market gardens and orchards stretched either side of the city walls, and meadows, springs and babbling brooks spread beyond. Vibrant street markets sold imported wares and goods produced by craftsmen and artisans (both natives and Flemish, French, German and Dutch) working from home in the all parts of the city. Fairs and sports were regular events in the fields beyond the city walls, and miracle-plays, cock- and dog fights, bear-baiting and the countless taverns provided the evening entertainment. But the aristocratic mansions propped up shacks, the babbling brooks were virtual sewers, and in the maze of streets the gutters and drains ran with offal. Although some tried to keep the stench at bay with perfumes and posies, it was often futile. Criminals were still left to slowly drown with the tide at Execution Dock in Wapping, refuse would at best be dumped outside the city walls in swamps such as Moorfields, and dead dogs were thrown aside in Houndsditch.

Wealth and poverty lived cheek by jowl, a feature of London throughout the centuries. Two markets, Eastcheap and Westcheap dominated the centre, the latter under the shadow of St Paul's. Eastcheap lay east of Poultry (another market), and was where the finer provisions were sold; Westcheap, now Cheapside, was a muddle of open stalls and kiosks lining the street, where frequent brawls would break out. On the river bank, Billingsgate, perhaps the oldest market, was where the 'wives' of Billingsgate drank and smoked and used foul language and earned the nickname the 'fish-fags'. **Medieval London**

Smaller markets specialized in different provisions – Bread, Wood, or Milk Streets – while the fields at Smoothfield (Smithfield) became famed for the horse market. Laws were regularly passed to try to regulate the size, noise and criminal activity, but their regularity suggests they weren't very effective, as the bustling energy of the medieval city continued unabated. St Paul's, one of the largest covered spaces in the city, also played a part. Shops were set up in the portico (which became known as Paul's Walk), and attempts were made to prevent ball-playing. In 1560 it was described as a place for "all kinds of bargains, meetings, brawlings, murders and conspiracies".

The sound of eager tradesmen and industrious craftsmen resounded throughout the city. Cries of "Dumplins! Dumplins! Diddle, diddle, Dumplins Ho!"or "Buy! Buy! Buy! What d'ye lack? What'll you buy? What'll you buy?" would share the airwaves with the beating of the hammers and the pounding of the metal foundries, all riding over the steady hum of rushing water as the streams flowed through.

Craftsmen gathered in their own localities, eventually forming guilds to maintain the quality of their work and to support their own. They built halls and churches, making the spiritual health of their members one of their principal concerns. While

Background

their relations with God may have prospered, and their rights were firmly protected, the guilds were nevertheless constantly at odds with each other. Clubbings, stabbings, brawls and battles would regularly break out between rival apprentices, each often armed with the tool of his trade.

Some respite from the maelstrom could be found in the religious houses both within and without the city. Most of the monastic orders had established themselves in the 13th century – among them the White Friars, Black Friars and Grey Friars, named in accordance with the colour of their habits – and they were among the chief landowners in and around London. Church lands were everywhere – the farmlands of Soho, for instance, were owned by the Abbey at Abingdon, and the pasture and market gardens north of the Strand by St Peter's Convent. Bishops' inns (in fact, large mansions and palaces) lined the road to Westminster, their gardens sweeping down to the river. Within the city, monastic orders settled among the poorer districts to do their good works, while the spires and towers of over a hundred churches pricked the skyline.

Good works were much needed. Although the hospitals (St Bartholomew's and St Thomas's) provided some form of medical care, plagues were a regular threat, notably the Black Death, a bubonic plague brought by trading ships in 1348. It tormented the citizens in an agonizing and delirious death, swollen buboes growing in their armpits and groin, such that "after Easter in a newly made cemetery next to Smithfield more than two hundred bodies were buried almost every day". Further outbreaks in the following decades ensured London lost up to two-thirds of its people. Those labourers that survived soon began to exploit their relative scarcity, and challenged the old feudal order.

The Peasants' Revolt of 1381, led by Wat Tyler from Kent and Jack Straw from Essex, involved up to 60,000 people laying waste to much of London in pursuit of airing their grievances to the king. Aided by the many city apprentices who joined the crowd, they dragged the Archbishop of Canterbury out of the Tower and beheaded him, burned down the Savoy Palace on the Strand, and ran amok in Clerkenwell where they opened the prisons and recruited the inmates. Wat Tyler finally perished on the dagger of the Mayor outside St Bartholomew's Hospital, and Jack Straw was beheaded at Smithfield.

The Peasants' Revolt presented, briefly, a genuine threat to government, but should be set against the backdrop of a London that often saw outbreaks of fights and small riots. Sometimes it might arise out of a scramble for the body dangling at Tower Hill or Tyburn Gallows, the relatives desperately fighting off those seeking to capitalize on the trade in bodies. Often it would be directed against foreigners, whether Dutch merchants in Westcheap or the Flemish in St Martin's, Vintry. In 1262 over 400 Jews were attacked and killed throughout the city (they were expelled in 1290 until the 17th century), and the Evil May Day Riots in 1517 were directed against the shops and houses of foreign merchants. Wrestling matches between the City and Westminster were known to break out into a full scale fights. Nevertheless, despite the explosions of violence, poor public health, and the virulent plagues, by the end of the 15th century when the Tudors came to power the population was almost 50,000 and growing.

Tudor London The Tudors liked their palaces. Henry VIII, the most ostentatious, had about fifty residences spread throughout the country, most around the capital. Whitehall, Greenwich, Hampton Court and Richmond all found royal favour, each enhanced to display the magnificence of monarchy. Tilt-yards, bowling greens and tennis courts were built, chapels erected, extensions built, and land such as modern Regent's Park and Soho given over to hunting. But his most lasting contribution to the development of the city, and indeed the country, came with his split with the Roman church, and his assumption as the Head of the Church in England.

Although this was prompted by his wish to father a healthy male heir, it also enabled him to claim the church lands as his own. Countless monasteries were 'dissolved', their treasures, buildings and lands either given or sold to courtiers and cronies. Religious houses were torn down and built on, empty sites taken over by tenements and chapels turned into taverns. Outside the city, the monastic lands were now in private hands so grand mansions emerged and land was sold off for building. Chelsea became known as the 'Village of Palaces' due to the grand houses built there. Within the city, migrants from the provinces and refugees from Catholic Europe swelled the numbers. Tressle tables in the markets increasingly turned to shacks and then to homes, thereby narrowing the streets such that the overhanging first floors almost touched over the street. There was some overspill outside the city, particularly to the east, around Whitechapel, Wapping and Spitalfield, and communities had grown around the various royal residences, and at the docks at Greenwich and Woolwich, such that by 1600 the population was 200,000, twice its number just forty years earlier.

Nevertheless, life was no less colourful. Fields outside the city walls were alive with archers firing their arrows, wrestlers facing up, and any number of ball games – "hand-ball, foot-ball, bandy-ball, cambuck or cock-fighting". Moorfields, Lincoln's Inn and Gray's Inn Fields, Finsbury Park and Hyde Park all served as recreation grounds, protected by the crown from farmers' encroachment. In the winter, when the swamp of Moorfields froze, young men would tie animal bones to their feet and go skating; in the summer "the youths are exercised in leaping, dancing, shooting, wrestling, casting the stone and practising their shields". On the river, boats would charge towards each other in a jousting match, adversaries standing at the prow.

Fairs sprinkled the calendar, although they sometimes had to be closed down due to debauched behaviour. St Bartholomew's Fair, held on Smoothfields (Smithfield), was the longest established, Our Lady Fair in Southwark the most congested, and May Fair in Shepherd Market possibly the most unruly (it was eventually suppressed in 1708 for "drunkenness, fornication, gaming and lewdness"). Boxing, wild animals, plays and baiting competed for custom for up to six weeks a year.

Theatres opened up, notably the Globe and the Rose in Southwark, beyond the City's jurisdiction. Here was a sinner's paradise, where Winchester Geese (prostitutes) served the men spilling out from the raucous spews (taverns), theatres and bear or cock pits. Frost Fairs were held below London Bridge which so slowed the Thames' flow that the river froze over (it was wider and shallower than it now is). Booths and tents, cook-shops and barbers' shops were erected beneath the bridge, while youths skated and chased across the ice. This "bacchanalian triumph, or carnival on the water" eventually died a natural death in the 19th century when a new London Bridge allowed a faster flow of water beneath its arches, and with the subsequent building of the Embankment, making the river deeper and faster, we are unlikely to see such sights again.

London Bridge itself was a fragile but magnificent sight. Rebuilt in stone in the 13th century, houses and shops clung to its edges, often arching over the road itself. A chapel dedicated to Thomas Becket was built in the middle, and criminals' heads were left to rot on spikes above the gatehouse at the Southwark end to serve as a constant reminder to those entering the city that retribution could be swift. Houses on the bridge were much coveted for the healthy air and spectacular views, although stalls, animals and traffic clogging up the thoroughfare and regular repair bills for the bridge meant living there was a mixed blessing.

Back on the shore, development tended to follow the movements of the monarch. As the 17th century passed, so building beyond the city walls increased, and the several-storey townhouse was born. Initially these were grand houses, along modern Piccadilly, in current Leicester Square, or along Great Russell Street, and a piazza, designed by Inigo Jones, in Covent Garden. His grand designs for Whitehall Palace were never fully executed, but the Banqueting House is a magnificent suggestion of what might have been.

During the Civil War, London sided with Parliament, forcing King Charles I to raise his army from Nottingham. Barricades were erected on all major roads in and out of the capital, and forts, batteries and ramparts built around the city. Troops turned out in numbers at Turnham Green to face off the king's army, and London was never threatened again. After Charles's defeat, the new regime under Oliver Cromwell confiscated royal treasures and property, and executed the king. One cold January morning in 1649, Charles walked out of Banqueting House to be beheaded. When the blow fell, there was "a dismal groan amongst the thousands of people who were in sight of it as I never heard before, and desire I may not hear again". The puritanical nature of Cromwell's rule, however, in which theatres were closed and Christmas celebrations banned, meant that following the restoration of the monarchy in 1660, his exhumed and rotting head remained on a spike on Westminster Hall for twenty-five long years without public protest.

Charles II entered the city to a carnival of welcome, "the ways strewed with flowers, the bells ringing, the streets hung with tapestry, fountains running with wine". But **Restoration London** soon faced a succession of disasters. Records of epidemics in London date back to the 7th century, whether the bubonic plague, or the 'ague' (malaria) which thrived in the open sewers and swamps caused by blocked gutters. The Black Death had swept away the majority of the city's population, and in the 16th century one outbreak of the plague "visited London with such violence that it carried off thousands in the space of five or six hours".

Towards the end of 1664 plague struck again. Beginning in the "deepe foul and dangerous" courtyards around Drury Lane, the 'sweating sickness' spread, reaching the City in July 1665. Shops closed and people retreated behind their doors, on which a red cross would be daubed if an inhabitant died. There was little traffic on the streets or on the river, only the sounds of the 'dead-carts', the "continuall ringing and tolling of bells", or people venturing out for supplies, sometimes collapsing in mid-transaction.

Fires burned at all major junctions to cleanse the air, and the Mayor ordered the killing of thousands of cats and dogs, thereby unwittingly ridding the flea-carrying rats of their principal predator. Those that could fled to outlying areas, particularly Hampstead and Clapham, but by September 1665, 8000 bodies a week were being thrown into the plague pits scattered outside the city, in some instances voluntarily joined by loved ones who had lost all hope of survival.

Superstitious remedies and quack potions were everywhere – amulets to ward off the evil spirits, potions, treacles and, immortalized in the children's nursery rhyme, pocketfuls of posies (they also stored posies in a large beak held over the nose). The citizens, according to Daniel Defoe, became "raving and distracted" making deathbed confessions while still healthy, and provided easy meat for the wealth of astrologers, fortune-tellers, "conjurors and witches" that capitalized on the people's fear. The plague finally subsided with the winter cold, such that Charles II felt safe to return in February 1666, but he returned to a city mourning almost half its population, some 100,000 dead.

Some notion of normal life was returning to the city when disaster struck again. As London suffered repeated visitations of the plague, so was it regularly alight. Fires often devastated huge areas of the city – in the 10th century what little that was left of Roman London was swept away in the flames, and in the 11th century the whole city from the River Fleet to the bridge was reduced to embers. Fires have destroyed huge palaces – Whitehall, Westminster and Crystal, as well as St Paul's countless times. Smaller conflgrations were more common still, often burning themselves out or being doused by the buckets of water kept outside every home.

Great fire of London

So when a small fire began in the king's baker's in Pudding Lane, the Mayor's reaction – "Pish! A woman might pisse it out" – was not considered overly complacent. But aided by the dry summer and a fresh easterly wind, the fire spread out of control. Panicked residents brought their furniture and treasured items out onto the street, hampering the efforts of the chain of firefighters armed only with leather buckets and crude water hoses. A rush of refugees once more sought sanctuary outside the city in Islington and Highgate, or loaded their possessions onto boats and took to the river from where they could watch the blaze spread.

After four days and much prevarication by the authorities, streets were blown up to create a wasteland that the flames and sparks could not breech. The wind dropped, and the fire turned to smouldering embers. John Evelyn visited the site two days later, and found himself lost, bereft of accustomed landmarks while "clambering over heaps of smoking rubbish". The fire's impact was overwhelming. Not only were countless manuscripts and books destroyed when the roof of St Paul's collapsed, but also over 80 churches, 44 livery halls, and 13,000 houses. Although only six people were reported dead, thousands were made homeless, settling in tented villages in the fields and meadows north of the city.

The fire, however, did provide the opportunity for the city to be rebuilt. Several plans were submitted, most proposing some form of grid street-plan, but merchants and residents alike could not afford to wait for these artistic visions to be approved. Greater thought was given to the style of house – the timber-frame overhanging Tudor houses were replaced by simpler stone and brick designs, and the streets were wider – but the familiar network of streets soon began to re-emerge. Sir Christopher Wren, the great architect of his time, devoted his energy to overseeing the construction of more than 50 churches, his signature piece being a further incarnation of St Paul's Cathedral, towering over the city with a splendour befitting the world's first Protestant cathedral. Beyond the city walls building also continued in earnest.

Redevelopment of London

Charles II favoured St James's Palace, so the area around spawned squares, streets and grand mansions (Buckingham, Arlington and Clarendon houses) to accommodate the courtiers. Aristocrats moved west, so their previous residences were torn down and replaced by town houses as happened along the Strand, or taken over by merchants, as happened in Clerkenwell. Soho, swollen by the influx of Huguenots from France, developed around King's (now Soho) Square, and by the end of the century Bloomsbury (with Red Lion Square), and the area around the Seven Dials were established.

The West End continued to spread as the new century dawned. Squares, such as Hanover, Berkeley, and Grosvenor in Mayfair became fashionable, while Kensington drew greater interest following William III's decision to settle there. Proximity to the court did not preoccupy the East End so much. Huguenot refugees from France arrived in force following a clampdown by Catholic Europe, and Irish, Dutch and Jewish immigrants brought their varied crafts and trades to Spitalfields and Whitechapel, but were forced to settle among the small courtyards, dark alleys and low tenements notorious for crime and poverty.

Background

This was a time of true Bacchanalian indulgence. Prostitutes were plentiful, drink overflowing, and rioting frequent. Sex for sale was of course as old as the city, from the Roman 'fornixes' (shacks set up below arches) to medieval street names such as Maid, Cock and Love Lanes. Slang terms for prostitutes ran from the faintly sentimental 'Mother Midnights' to the plain infantile 'Trugmoldies'. In the 18th and 19th centuries business boomed. Whitechapel, Wapping and Spitalfields worked the lower end of the market, while The Strand, Covent Garden and Drury Lane weren't quite the match of the brothels in James and Curzon Streets in Mayfair.

Tourists could consult Harris's *New Atlantis* or Henry's *List of Covent Garden Ladies* for further details. Gays were served by 'Mollie' houses such as the Mother's Clap in Holborn, at alehouses such as the Fountain in the Strand, or by cruising the Royal Exchange. Those of better means kept mistresses in nearby hamlets like Brompton, and those seeking a mistress or a lover might hover under the portico of St Paul's church in Covent Garden. Haymarket and St James's Park were popular night haunts, where James Boswell met with "ugly and lean" and "monstrous big" prostitutes, or "a strong, jolly young damsel" and "a little girl". Child prostitution was common.

In the 19th century the number of 11 to 16 year olds with syphillis in any one year exceeded two thousand, and Dostoevsky commented on mothers encouraging their daughters "to ply the same trade" in Haymarket. Some would be child mistresses – funded through school and put up in accommodation, in return for their sexual favours. Violence against prostitutes also proliferated, whether by Mohocks (gangs of youths) or in attacks on brothels, and gays had the added threats of blackmail or arrest. It was a century "dedicated to venereal pleasures", as one foreign observer put it, and by the mid-19th century there were estimated to be 80,000 prostitutes, the majority streetwalkers, and 3000 brothels.

If they weren't rutting, they were rioting. Scapegoating attacks on foreigners, price riots in theatres, brawls after football matches, food riots among workers and assaults on prisons. In 1780 the Gordon Riots ran a rampage of drunken thuggery through London over a number of days. Gathering in St George's Fields, it was intended as an anti-Popery march on Parliament to protest against the Catholic Relief Act. But the reality was much less contained. Gathering extras as they went, (many of whom were simply along for the ride), they attacked Irish labourers and looted Catholic chapels in the East End, and attacked Downing Street, the Bank of England and prisons in Clerkenwell and Newgate. En route, they raided and set alight to a distillery. Many died in the smoke and flames when they ran into the cellars to grab gin, and others drank themselves to death in the rum running in the gutters. The government was worried, but the very substance that helped fuel the rioters was also a factor in their undoing. While approaching their next target, Kenwood House on Hampstead Heath, the mob were distracted by the offer of a free drink from the landlord of the Spaniard's Inn. The delay was sufficient to give time for the army to arrive.

Drink fuelled much of London life. Brown or pale ale, bitter beer or mellow porter, or the hangover remedy, 'saloop', were all served in a series of small rooms in private houses that acted as taverns and beer houses. In the early 18th century there were estimated to be over 6000 taverns, inns and beer houses, while in the cellars and workshops were gin-houses', serving the favourite spirit of the time. Many people would have a mug of ale for breakfast not least because it was probably 'cleaner' than the water and because drinking tea was considered "one of the worst habits". Beer was also not exclusively an adult pleasure. Children were often to be seen in taverns with a mug of ale, refilling their clay pipes with casual assurance.

A slightly more refined experience was to be had in the wealth of coffee-houses brewing up all over the city. A Swiss observer commented on them as where "you can partake of chocolate, tea or coffee, and all sorts of liquors served hot", but they also served as anything from auction rooms to postal addresses for the regulars. Charles II tried to have them banned, complaining that this was "where the disaffected meet and spread scandalous reports", but had to bow to public pressure to revoke the order.

Certainly they were important meeting places – the clergy in Child's (St Paul's Churchyard), Frenchmen in Giles (St Giles), artists in Old Slaughter (St Martin's Lane) or wits and authors at Will's in Covent Garden (Samuel Pepys, John Dryden, Aphra Benn and Jonathan Swift were among the regulars). Whigs met at St James's, the Tories at the Cocoa Tree. Batson's on Cornhill became a virtual doctor's consulting room, and Button's in Covent Garden became the editorial offices for the *Guardian* periodical. A French visitor described them as "the seats of English liberty" on account of the newspapers that lay on the tables, and the heated discussions that prevailed. Some houses, however, were less troubled by the state of the nation. Those that doubled as "temples of Venus" could be found where there hung the tell-tale sign of a woman's arm holding a coffee-pot, and others advertised auctions of slave boys.

By the end of the 18th century, London had grown significantly, reaching a population of almost one million. Putney, Westminster and Blackfriars became the first bridges over the Thames since the Roman settlers built the stilted wooden affair across to Southwark. The New Road, now the Marylebone Road, was created as a ring road round the north of London for the traffic of cattle and sheep being driven to Smithfield Market. Bloomsbury, Fitzrovia, Mayfair and Marylebone all became fashionable, a multitude of Georgian terraces interspersed with grand squares.

Further developments

Buckingham Palace became one of George III favoured residences, although it was only later under Queen Victoria that it became established as the monarch's primary London residence. After the Tyburn Gallows had been removed from what is now Marble Arch in 1783, Oxford Street showed the early signs of its current role as a shopping street. With this expansion came slums. Intended developments such as Somers Town stopped abruptly when funds ran out, only to grow into dirty and dangerous slums with the arrival of French émigrés fleeing the Revolution. Nevertheless, the likes of Bow, Hackney, Islington and Chelsea remained as villages surrounded by fields and market gardens.

Regency London bacame grander still. In the West End architect John Nash linked St James's to Marylebone Park (later Regent's Park) with the broad and sweeping Regent's Street, and Thomas Cubitt built stuccoed squares, terraces and villas behind Buckingham Palace in Belgravia. In the East End, expansion continued apace with the development of the docks, and the digging of the Regent's Canal from the Thames at Limehouse to Paddington. The London, East India, Surrey, St Katharine's and West India Docks were all dug by 1830, many protected by 30-ft walls and marine police such was the threat of criminal activity. Whitechapel was one of the most populous areas, close on the heels of fashionable Marylebone. A ribbon of industrial developments, warehouses and small factories sprung up along the Canal – in Camden, Islington, King's Cross and Paddington – and a new London Bridge was built across the Thames in 1831.

By the time Victoria came to the throne in 1837, London was at the centre of an Empire spanning one-fifth of the globe, its spoils contributing wealth and employment to the capital at its heart. Docks and warehouses blossomed with the growing trade and

Victorian London

business boomed as goods were exported to all corners of the world. Large industry included the likes of ship building (Brunel's *Great Eastern*, the largest ship of its time, was built in Millwall docks), breweries and iron foundries, and Bryant & May's matchbox factory in Bow, employing some 5,600 people, but in 1851 over four-fifths of the capital's manufacturers employed 10 people or less. These businesses grew along the newly laid railway lines and the slightly older canals, or in the sweatshops of dark, damp and dingy basements and cellars, or in the one or two rooms that also served as the family home. At the other end of the scale, commercial enterprises such as banks, insurance and investment companies built fine offices in the City, slowly marking out their territory in what was to become the finance capital of the world.

By far the greatest transformation to the city's landscape was brought about by the transport revolution, particularly the arrival of the railways. In 1836 the first railway in London ran between the *Bricklayer's Arms* in Southwark and Deptford, although it was soon extended to London Bridge and Greenwich.

Over the next 20 years stations and large termini began cropping up across the city. Euston, Paddington, and King's Cross stations opened, and anything from shunting yards and engine huts to hotels sprung up nearby. Thousands were displaced as slums were cleared to lay tracks. Warehouses, small industries, and above all slum housing developed along the line of the tracks, and the population grew exponentially with the greater ease of movement. The railway opened up the suburbs, encouraging the growth of the likes of Norwood and Highgate.

In 1863 the Metropolitan Line, the world's first underground line, opened, ferrying a mixture of excited and sceptical Londoners across the city under the New Road from Paddington to Farringdon Road. Some feared that the tunnels would collapse, others considered the "mixture of sulphur, coal dust and foul fumes" unhealthy, although the Duke of Wellington's fear that an invading French army could now arrive unannounced at a station had less basis in reality.

Above ground, London's streets were awash with a multitude of vehicles. Horse-drawn trams and buses fought for right of way with hansom cabs, broughams, landaus and gigs, in a city still lit by gas and oil lamps. The advent of electricity, however, further transformed the city above and below ground. The first electric line, part of what became the Northern Line, opened in 1890, two years after, Electric Avenue in Brixton blazed electric light along its length. Horse-drawn trams soon turned electric, and continued to distribute commuters to their homes in the suburbs.

Omnibuses, horse drawn when first introduced in 1829, grew in popularity – by 1900, there were 3000 of them carrying up to 500 million passengers a year, even though the motorized bus only chugged for the first time in 1904. By 1902, as Sir Halford Mackinder observed, London exhibited "the daily throb of a huge pulsating heart", whereby every morning and evening "half a million men are sent in quick streams, like corpuscles of blood through arteries, along the railways and the trunkroads".

Mile upon mile of Victorian terraces went up to accommodate the growing population of commuters. Victoria, Notting Hill, Holland Park, Camden, Islington and Finsbury in the north, and Brixton, Battersea, Lambeth and Kennington in the south all grew, the market gardens and fields slowly turning to brick fields and then streets and houses. The railway also brought shoppers to *Harrods*, *Liberty's*, and *Whiteleys*, and visitors to the Great Exhibition of 1851, a magnificent display of imperial power and confidence housed in a sparkling glass palace in Hyde Park. The Oval Stadium in Kennington hosted the first soccer cup final in 1871, soon followed by the first rugby international and cricket Test Match.

While the 19th century saw the most rapid expansion of London's suburbs to date, inner city slums continued to fester. The rapid expansion in the city's population meant huge overcrowding in the tenements – a census in Westminster uncovered an average of 40 people per house in the worst areas, while lodging-houses earned disapproval for the bed-sharing that was necessary to accommodate all the tenants

Many slums were houses vacated by wealthier Londoners, still displaying their 'decayed glory' through the mould and crumbling 'stately edifices'. Others such as Agar Town, were virtual shanty towns, decried by Londoners as "a disgrace to the metropolis". The Seven Dials was particularly notorious for its criminal element, a crowd of alleys and courtyards and "dirty, straggling houses" (Dickens) hiding a network of escape routes carved through the buildings. One observer described London as "rattling, growling, smoking, stinking...pouring out poison at every pore".

Underneath most houses were cesspits to hold the pungent mixture of household and human waste. Streets were used as toilets, and the overflowing pits often seeped into the homes above. The sewage and water systems were part of the same cycle, with the former being tipped into the city's streams and rivers, only to be piped back through the street's water pumps.

Disease once again plagued the city. Cholera epidemics were severe and frequent, aided by the authorities' conviction that the carrier was a 'miasma' in the air that could best be solved by washing the streets' detritus into the very same waterways that were feeding the disease.

Public health campaigners such as Dr John Snow and Edwin Chadwick fought a sceptical and sluggish establishment to wake up to the links between poverty and disease, water and drainage. Countless studies and surveys put pressure on the authorities to take action, but it needed the 'Great Stink' of 1858 that infected the city with a stench previously unrivalled to force action.

The Metropolitan Board of Works constructed a drainage system that still forms the basis for London's drainage today. As one contemporary newspaper put it in Chadwick's obituary: "had he killed in battle as many as he saved by sanitation, he would have had equestrian statues by the dozen put up to his memory."

Nevertheless in 1883 Andrew Mearns still entered "courts reeking with poisonous and malodorous gases arising from accumulations of sewage and refuse scattered in all directions", and passed through "passages swarming with vermin" to "gain access to the dens in which these thousands of beings...herd together."

Housing programmes were enacted by parliament but it still required the diligence, money and concern of the likes of Lord Shaftesbury to really effect change. Slum clearances merely moved the problem to another part of the city, creating still more overcrowding there. Charities and philanthropists gave money, time and thought to easing the burden. George Peabody, an American millionaire and London resident, built model dwellings for the working classes; Angela Burdett-Coutts built blocks in Bethnal Green for "the very poorest", and Octavia Hill restored delapidated cottages for the poor inhabitants. Some, such as John Hollingshead, felt the charity was misplaced : "they have wasted their means on a class well able to help themselves...the industrious poor are still rotting up their filthy, ill-drained, ill-ventilated courts", in the likes of Somers Town and Agar Town. Ragged children still slept in alleys and under bridges, and most nights there were up to 400 people camped out in Trafalgar Square.

Alongside practical support, there was often spiritual and moral guidance to boot. The Society for Suppression of Vice, the Reformatory and Refuge Union , or the Christian Mission to the Heathen of our own Country (or the Salvation Army) all did good works in an attempt to steer their charges along the straight and narrow. Inspired by the horrors of St Jude's slum in Whitechapel, Canon Barnett founded the East London Dwelling's Company and the educational establishment at Toynbee Hall, while

Background

declaring that the "principle of our work is that we aim at decreasing not suffering, but sin!" Others opted for a more hands-on attempt at reform, such as Prime Minister Gladstone who took prostitutes home in order to try to rectify their wayward ways.

Nevertheless, the housing shortage was rarely solved, merely moved. In 1901, a survey in Finsbury recorded that 45% of families still lived in one or two rooms, while in 1925 a Czech visitor described the East End as "miles and miles of grimy houses, hopeless streets...a superfluity of children, gin palaces and Christian shelters".

Immigration This was what greeted many of the immigrants who reached London's streets in the 19th century. Chinese sailors settled in Limehouse in the 1850s, and in the following decades Russian and Polish Jews, escaping the pogroms in Eastern Europe, settled in Stepney. Italians congregated in Finsbury, the Irish in Docklands, and Germans in and around Camden. Elsewhere, Swedes, French, Spaniards, Americans and Turks sought to make a new home here.

London has had a history of ambivalence towards the immigrant population, not least because most of its residents were of immigrant stock themselves. Richard of Devizes' complaint that in London "all sorts of men crowd there from every country under the heavens. Each brings its own vices and its own customs to the city", is one that in its various forms has been echoed through time. Attacks on Jews were frequent until their expulsion in 1290, and were repeated over the centuries following their return under Cromwell; the Irish were also a particular source of suspicion, and subject to violent attacks for either being Catholic, or being prepared to work for less wages that an Englishman.

Bottom of the pile were blacks. By the late 18th century there were up to 20,000, most in domestic service, either as slaves or servants, having been brought over by plantation owners, sold in the coffee houses, or given as a 'presents' to wealthy friends. But many were discarded by their owners or employers, and left scraping for a living in the likes of Wapping and St Giles. They were often the last to be given employment, and could be seen scavenging on the streets at dusk, keen to keep a low profile.

London also became a haven for radical thinkers and activists from abroad. Karl Marx lived in poverty in Soho (although aided by Freidrich Engels, a resident of Camden), plodding to the Reading Room at the British Museum to work on his pot-boiler, *Das Kapital*. Mahatma Gandhi and Mohammed Ali Jinnah both studied law here towards the end of the century; Jawarharlal Nehru (also a student at Harrow and Cambridge) completed the trinity when he studied at the bar at Inner Temple in 1910. Revolutionaries studied or worked here before returning to their homeland to act out their destiny. Sun Yat Sen (China), Marcus Garvey (West Indies), Michael Collins (Ireland) and Lenin (Russia) could all be found here in the early years of the century; Ho Chi Minh washed up dishes at the Carlton Hotel before doing much the same to American forces in his native Vietnam some 60 years later.

20th-century As the end of the century approached, much of London flourished. The growth of
London the railway network drew not only suburban commuters but also visitors from the country and abroad. Hotels sprung up in numbers – the *Westminster Palace*, the *Savoy*, the *Ritz* (often with shared bathrooms; at the Westminster Palace, 14 bathrooms served 300 rooms). Theatres boomed, and the likes of Henry Irving or Ellen Terry trod the boards at new theatres such as The Strand, Aldwych, or Lyric. In the musichalls the bawdy songs, dance and comedy routines of Max Miller or Marie Lloyd would also pack in the crowds.

The Olympics were held at White City in 1908. Piccadilly Circus glowed under neon lights in 1910, a more glamorous addition to a city now bathing in electric light. Cinemas began screening throughout the capital, and the Lyon's Corner

House in Coventry Street offered more than palatable fare to over 4,500 people within many working men's budget. The *Café Royale* attracted the fashionable set, such as Oscar Wilde, Audrey Beardsley and Whistler, and London clubs in St James's basked in their exclusivity. The electric tram, the motorized bus and the motorcar began appearing on the streets, ferrying a population now grown to 6½ million.

The peace was broken by the outbreak of war in 1914. Young men turned up at recruitment offices across the capital, eager to fight for King and Country, unaware of the carnage that lay in wait. In 1915 London suffered its first air raid, when Zeppelins dropped incendiaries on Stoke Newington and Hackney. A few months later 39 people were killed near the Guildhall, and by the end of the war 650 had died in attacks from the air. Waterloo and Victoria stations became the setting of tearful and often final farewells by troops bound for the trenches, and Alexandra Palace took the German POWs. German and Austrian residents were rounded up as a precaution, and factories were given over to munitions production.

First World War & after

Due to the shortage of male labour, the women of the city took over half the factory jobs. In the build up to war, the Suffragette movement (a *Daily Mail* name) had moved to London from Manchester, setting up headquarters in Westminster, closer to government. From here, Emmeline Pankhurst and her two daughters Sylvia and Christabel orchestrated a campaign ranging from window-smashing in Parliament and Oxford Street, to chaining themselves to railings at Downing Street and Buckingham Palace, and slashing the *Rokeby Venus* in the National Gallery. With the outbreak of war, however, the campaigners were keen to demonstrate their patriotism, and they suspended the campaign and set to working for the war effort. There was some reward in legislation passed after the end of the war, but it was 1928 before they achieved parity with men.

Women continued to work in the factories such as Hoover and Firestone after the war, partly because the male labour force was depleted by casualties (some 125,000 Londoners are estimated to have died). Domestic service, however, was their main source of employment. Nannies, butlers, maids, sometimes all three, would live in the attic rooms of tall villas and terraces, Mary Poppins-like, or, if attached to any of the Mayfair mansions, from mews houses nearby.

Between the wars

American culture, promoted largely through the cinema, began to take grip. Cocktail and milk bars, jazz and the Charleston became a feature of the West End and in 1924 *Woolworths* opened a store on Oxford Street. Greyhound racing, another American import, was held at White City, no longer London's master stadium after Wembley opened in 1923.

Meanwhile, the London County Council set about improving the city's environment. Slums were cleared, houses built and parks extended. Nevertheless, Sir Arthur Conan Doyle was still moved to describe London as "a great cesspit into which all the loungers of the Empire are irresistably drained".

Elsewhere in the country, a slump in industries such as steel and textiles brought the government into conflict with the unions, and in 1926 the General Strike saw London almost grind to a halt. For several days volunteers and the army took over essential services – students tried to run the tube, volunteers to drive the buses, while the army escorted food convoys. But perhaps its most significant contribution was to establish the radio as a source of information and entertainment.

Home for many was now in the suburbs, in developments advertised in the enticingly titled *Metroland*. "Vast new wildernesses of glass and brick" sprung up in Cedars Estate in Rickmansworth, Becontree Estate at Dagenham (where there were just six pubs for 120,000 people), Ruislip, Edgware and Finchley, in the process swallowing up the market gardens and fields that hitherto surrounded London. One million new houses were built for a population fast approaching 8.7 million, a figure never matched before or since, such that in 1938 the notion of a 'Green Belt' of protected countryside around the growing city was widely welcomed. JB Priestley described an urban culture "of arterial and by-pass roads, of filling stations and factories..., of giant cinemas and dance halls and cafés, bungalows with tiny garages, cocktail bars, Woolworths, motor coaches, [and] wireless".

It was all that, but it was also a city facing war. Londoners were not unfamiliar with fascism. Sir Oswald Moseley, leader of the 'blackshirts', had held rallies at major venues such as the Albert Hall and Olympia, and then led his troops through the East End, creating a riot in Cable Street.

Second World War The threat to the average Londoner was not from the ground, however, but from the air. In the year that followed, while the country armed itself for war, London prepared itself for imminent destruction. Schoolchildren and toddlers with mothers were evacuated north and west, some as far as Canada or Australia. Vacated buildings were taken over as reception centres for those bombed out, and the nations treasures carefully stored. The army moved into the parks, setting up anti-aircraft guns to scan the skies.

"Britain's finest hour", as Churchill called it, began on Black Saturday, 7 September 1940. A raid of 400 bombers signalled the start of a bombardment that was to kill 20,000 Londoners, leave another 25,000 injured, and at its most intense, run for 57 consecutive days. The Docks, Law Courts, The Tower, the House of Commons, Westminster Abbey, and even St Paul's, where "London was burning and the dome seemed to ride the sea of fire", all suffered some damage. After perhaps the severest night, December 29th 1940, a visitor commented that the "air felt singed. The air itself, as we walked smelt of burning", recalling images of John Evelyn in the rubble after the Great Fire.

Londoners' reaction was mixed – some were hysterical (there was an increased incidence of suicide), but many were defiant. They continued to go to work, stumbling across debris en route if necessary, and a Mass Observation survey held in the winter of the Blitz recorded more Londoners to be depressed by the weather than by the bombing. During raids most people sought shelter in a basement or cellar, or under the stairs.

Many took refuge in the government sponsored 'Anderson' shelters built out of soil and corrugated iron at the end of the garden. Railway arches became popular havens, and a network of trenches was built under Lincoln's Inn Fields, and in Bloomsbury and Russell squares. Almost 150,000 people took to the underground itself. The platforms, corridors and stairs were swollen with people, but this "lice to lice" as some called it, gave people an attachment and loyalty to their shelter. Stations had their own libraries and canteens, there was underground theatre and at Swiss Cottage they produced a newsletter, the *Swiss Cottager*. One observer commented "the danger here is not bombs, or even burial or typhus, but of going native and not coming up again till after the war, when you will emerge with a large family and speaking another language".

East Enders took over massive subterranean warehouses, such as 'Mickey's Shelter' under Stepney. Mickey Davies, a dwarf hunchback, gave the shelter such a celebrity status that the American Presidential candidate paid a visit on his tour of London. Further shelters were excavated under a number of underground stations, most for the use of the public, although Stockwell was given over to American troops, and Goodge Street as General Eisenhower's headquarters.

The government moved underground too, Churchill's Cabinet War Rooms taking up just a fraction of the huge complex of rooms under Storey's Gate just off Parliament Square. But being underground did not guarantee safety. 600 people were drowned at Balham Station when a bomb burst a water main and flooded the tunnel, and at Bank 117 people were killed by a bomb that bounced its way down the escalator and exploded on the platform.

Even when the 'Blitz' ended the following May, air raids were still a threat. In 1944, the VI, or 'doodle-bug', a pilotless plane of explosives that fell when its engines cut out, terrorized the capital. Witnesses recalled "holding one's breath, praying that they will travel on". Its successor, the V2, was still more destructive, killing scores of Saturday-afternoon shoppers in Woolworths on its first flight. The doodle-bugs damaged half the city's housing stock, some 1¼ million homes, but were cut short by the end of the war in May 1945.

Some 30,000 people had died in London in the course of the war, and another 50,000 had been injured. About a third of the City had been destroyed, including twenty churches and 18 livery halls on that December night alone. Large areas of the East End were devastated (Poplar and Stepney were largely flattened), such that when Buckingham Palace was hit in September 1940, Queen Elizabeth, now the Queen Mother, is reputed to have said "now we can look the East End in the face". Communities had been disrupted, not only by the devastation from above, but by the mass exodus of residents to the suburbs, some of whom never returned. On top of this there were 1½ million Londoners who simply didn't have a home anymore.

The housing problem was given some temporary relief by the 'prefab' houses issued by the government, and by the unilateral actions of squatters who took over empty properties in the likes of Marylebone and Kensington. New towns such as Basildon, Stevenage and Harlow sprung up beyond the Green Belt as London raised itself from the ashes. The Olympics at Wembley in 1948, the Festival of Britain in 1951 and the Coronation of Queen Elizabeth II two years later all lent some sparkle to a time made lean by rationing. To add to the gloom, London suffered a particularly acute year of smog in 1952, causing up to 4000 deaths in associated illnesses. But theatres and cinemas were buoyant, football matches were well attended, and jazz could be heard in the pubs and clubs of Soho.

Post-war London

Heathrow and Gatwick both opened in the 1950s, and by 1956 the dockyards were dealing with up to 1000 ships a week. A skilled labour shortage prompted the likes of London Transport and the health service to seek employees from abroad. The 492 Jamaicans who disembarked from the *Empire Windrush* in 1948 had been broadly welcomed, but as economic pressures intensified and the West Indian population grew, local relations became strained. Riots in Notting Hill in 1958, where the homes of Trinidadians and Barbadians were attacked by "a crowd of a thousand white men and some women….tooled up with razors, knives, bricks and bottles", gave a different message to the thousands of immigrants who had been actively encouraged to come here.

In the 1960s many of Britain's colonies achieved independence, and were free to seek other markets. London's trade with the Commonwealth halved. Dockyards such as The East India and St Katharine closed, often in the wake of union struggles that protected the workers' rights in the short term, but lost them their jobs in the long term. Pear's Soap closed its Isleworth factory in its centenary year of 1962, as unemployment in inner city areas such as Tower Hamlets grew. Between 1966 and 1976, London lost half a million manufacturing jobs, and over ⁷% of its population.

The laxness of planning authorities allowed over 400 tower blocks to be built across the city, a transformation of London's skyline comparable with that achieved

Background

by Wren. The result was hardly as picturesque, and the soulless blocks were regularly subject to vandalism, effectively imprisoning residents with the broken lifts and the fear of violence. The architectural, let alone social, failings of the towers were confirmed in 1968 when several storeys of a block collapsed in Ronan Point.

Meanwhile, in 1966, *Time* magazine confidently reported that London "swings, it is the scene". From the tentative appearance of the first coffee bar in Soho in 1953, and the bistros and the Mary Quant boutique in Chelsea, London was becoming the music and fashion capital of the world. Soho was invaded by media and music companies, and at its peak some quarter of a million Londoners were involved in photography, modelling, magazine publishing or advertising. Art-deco was undergoing a renaissance at Barbara Hulanicki's boutique, *Biba* in Kensington, and Terence Conran's *Habitat* store in Fulham brought a sense of design to the home. The King's Road in Chelsea and Carnaby Street in the West End became the place to be seen.

The London music scene took off, fed by a vibrant student art scene in a London teeming with the young (some estimate that 40% of London's population were under 25). The Rolling Stones, The Who, the Small Faces and the Yardbirds all played in London venues, most notably on Eel Pie Island in the Thames by Twickenham. The club formed in the hotel that once stood here boasted 30,000 membership (that number would scarcely fit on the island itself), and became a magnet for that unholy trinity of the 1960s, sex, drugs and Rock & Roll.

Meanwhile, demonstrations against the Vietnam War in 1968, and concerts in Hyde Park for some half a million people, represented a youth culture that challenged the establishment and dreamt of a life free of the threat of nuclear annihilation and at peace with itself. Cultural heroes, from 'Twiggy' in modelling, and East Enders David Bailey in photography or Vidal Sassoon in hair-styling, shared the spotlight with other photographers such as lords Lichfield and Snowdon, as fashion became less trammelled by concerns over class and status.

Late 20th-century London

Thirty years later, in 1996, another American publication, *Newsweek*, announced that London was "the world's coolest city", a claim that for many was as ignorant as it was meaningless. Certainly many people had seen wealth and an improved lifestyle in the 1970s and 80s. The financial institutions in the City had adapted well to the decline of the Empire, and in the 1960s London became the world's largest source of borrowing. The Stock Exchange moved into a new building in 1972, and by the 1980s there were more foreign banks located within the square mile than anywhere else in the world. Prime Minister Margaret Thatcher favoured deregulation, and when in 1986 the Stock Exchange opened its doors to overseas members, businesses rushed to invest.

House prices reached a peak in 1988 as 'yuppies' (Young Urban Professionals), and 'dinkies' (Double Income, No Kids) helped fuel property prices. Georgian and Victorian properties were restored as fine family houses, or remodelled into smart bachelor pads, in areas as far afield as Clapham and Camberwell, Highbury and Paddington.

The story wasn't so sweet for everybody. Between 1973 and 1983 London lost half its manufacturing jobs. British Aerospace and the General Electric Company shed jobs in Hayes and Willesden. Companies sought out the cheaper labour and more efficient transport links offered by development along new motorway corridors such as the M4, around Reading, Swindon and Bristol. The last of the docks finally closed in 1981 – only Tilbury, further east, survived.

By 1990, 20% of the residents in Hackney & Haringay were unemployed, and 10% of all Londoners were on income support. Local councils became political footballs, having their central government subsidies cut or capped by successive governments from 1975. Conservative councils in Westminster and Wandsworth and Labour councils in Tower Hamlets and Hackney became flagbearers for their respective ideologies, though not without more than a whiff of corrupt practices.

In 1986 Margaret Thatcher abolished the Greater London Council, citing inefficiency and profligacy among its crimes, a decision no doubt made easier by the ideological gulf between the 'Iron Lady' and the council leader 'Red' Ken Livingstone. London was now the only major European capital without its own central authority (a situation only rectified by the incoming Labour government in 2000, when Londoners voted Livingstone back in as Mayor in a new Greater London Authority).

Reported crime rose, schools closed or awaited building repairs, and the underground and sewers, both in need of urgent investment, were left to age. Housing stock fell as government legislation forced councils to sell their homes to the tenants, but prevented them from building replacements with the proceeds.

By 1990, there were only 302 housing new starts, compared with over 9000 in 1979. Homelessness became apparent across the city, with up to 65,000 single homeless people seeking shelter in emergency accommodation. Cardboard cities grew up in Lincoln's Inns Fields, Waterloo Bridge or off the Strand, and isolated figures in sleeping bags dotted the shop doorways. The *Big Issue*, written and sold by homeless people, attempted to give a leg up to those still awaiting the promised 'trickledown' effect of the 'economic miracle'.

Clashes between blacks and the police in Brixton and the Broadwater Farm Estate in Tottenham in the 1980s gave vent to simmering racial tensions. In 1986, a church report entitled *Faith in the City*, expressed concern over the degeneration of areas that "has now gone so far that they are in effect 'separate territories' outside the mainstream of our social and economic life". The Poll Tax riots of 1990 were partly sparked by a resentment at the widening gap between the 'haves' and 'have-nots', and Thatcher's resignation later in the year left John Major with an economy in recession and a party split over the touchy issue of Britain's role in Europe. Paradoxically, perhaps, a 1991 a survey revealed that 48% of Londoners wanted to leave the city, at a time when tourism was booming (25 million tourists visited in 1990). The Conservative government squeezed through one further election, and then limped to sleaze-ridden defeat in 1997, as New Labour swept to victory on a wave of optimism.

21st-century London

So when future historians attempt to describe London in the year 2000, as they most surely will, what will they say? They may marvel at the 200 museums and galleries, a staggering array of treasures bought, donated and appropriated from around the world, and envy the vast choice of food and drink available in the thousands of pubs and restaurants. They will paint colourful pictures of the theatre, the music, the lights and the sights, and show incredulity at the number and variety of shops.

They might gasp at the London Eye, puzzle over the Dome, snigger at the Millennium Bridge or admire the Great Court at the British Museum. They may salute the City as the capital of commerce, where one-third of the world's dealings pass through, and will no doubt celebrate the 300 languages that can be heard on the streets or in the homes. There will be tales of clubbing, dancing, drinking and drugs, of fast cars, fast living and above all fast spending.

But they will also record the estates and tower blocks, the bedsits and the shelters, the doorways and the underpasses where many people still live. They will note the slowing beat of manufacturing, the stillness of the waters in the docks, and the creaking of the Underground. There will be tales of stabbings and muggings, of struggling schools and hospitals, of dirty air and the choking roads. But they will also recognize that such contrasts have been apparent throughout the ebb and flow of the city, perhaps all great cities. That slums have always rubbed shoulders

Background

with mansions, that business and manufacturing has constantly reinvented itself to adapt to changing circumstance, and that London will always regenerate.

One way or another, London will always to be the object of much comment. It has been eulogized in poetry as "the fairest capital", and as "the flower of cities all". It has been labelled "the clearing-house of the world", and "the mansion-house of liberty". It is "immutable" and "eternal", "scattered" and "haphazard", "beautiful" and "uniquely seductive". One can speculate endlessly as to how and why London came to be as it is, but certainly the safest, and perhaps the wisest conclusion is given by the social historian Roy Porter in 1994 when he wrote: "London was always a muddle that worked".

Architecture

London is one of the world's most miasmic cities. It is at once ordered and chaotic, old fashioned and ultra-modern, opulent and squalid. It is also, for all its fine tailoring, gunmakers, fine tailoring, hand-made shoes and posh accents, something of a mongrel: it has pretty much always been a home for successive waves of invaders and refugees, who over the centuries, have given the city its extraordinary global character. To see the world, and its architecture, in a single capital city, come to London.

Founded essentially by the Romans in the first century AD – certainly from an architectural perspective – London has always been like this. It had only just got into its first stride when Boudicca and her East Anglian warriors burned the place down. After that it rose to become one of the major cities of the western Empire, although, as far as we can tell, its architecture was often fairly crude and provincial compared with that of Rome or the great classical cities of what are now Turkey, Syria and Libya.

London declined after the Roman legions left in 410 AD, yet we know that Saxon architects travelled to Rome to study masonry and that the city was never as cut off from stylistic and technical developments during the Dark Ages as we were taught at school. In fact, what makes London such a delightful mongrel city is the way in which architectural currents lapped against the banks of the Thames on their way from other parts of the world. Always a little late and always reinterpreted for the London market.

So, Gothic architecture (born in France) came late to London and was never as flamboyant as its continental precursors unless made for kings who were often French speaking and who ruled much of France. Renaissance architecture was also slow of the mark, not really making much impact – with the exception of the works of Inigo Jones (the **Banqueting Hall, Whitehall**, from where Charles I walked out of a first storey window to the scaffold and his execution in 1649; **St Paul's Church, Covent Garden** – "the handsomest barn in England" the architect promised the Earl of Bradford; the **Queen's House, Greenwich**), until after the Great Fire of 1666 when Christopher Wren began to rebuild the City with a necklace of imaginative parish churches gathered around the defining dome of his masterwork, **St Paul's Cathedral** (1675-1710). Even then, look how St Paul's is really an old fashioned Gothic cathedral in plan (which is what Wren's client, the Church Commission, wanted) clad in Renaissance garb and capped with that peerless dome. In other words St Paul's was a compromise – a brilliant one – and a grand example of London's mongrel spirit.

London came into its own, architecturally, from Wren. His own unmissable buildings here are nearly all in the old City of London, with the exception of the exquisitely mannered **Royal Hospital, Chelsea** – home of the Chelsea Pensioners – and the magnificent Royal Naval complex downriver at Greenwich. This is now the **University of Greenwich**. This great gathering of Baroque towers, domes, courtyards, colonnades and painted halls overlooking the Thames is one of Europe's greatest architectural set pieces. Built over many decades, it includes work by Wren's famous assistants, Nicholas Hawksmoor and Sir John Vanbrugh, a former playwright and soldier whose exotic designs were inspired partly by extensive travels that took him as far as India.

Hawksmoor was quite simply one of the greatest architects of all time. A broody introspective man from a humble background, but of great learning, he was very different from the urbane and gentlemanly Wren and the flamboyant and funny Vanbrugh. The character of his powerfully sculpted designs reflect his brilliant intensity. They include the nearly restored **Christ Church, Spitalfields**, its skypiercing Portland stone tower soaring above gentrified streets of handsome Georgian terraced houses just a trader's shout from the brash new Post-Modern banks of the City of London and the organic foodstalls of the revitalised Spitalfields Market. His other great London designs are the churches of **St Mary Woolnoth** near the Mansion House and Royal Exchange, **St George's Bloomsbury** (which once featured a lion and unicorn chasing one another around its curious stepped tower based on the ancient Greek Temple of Helicarnassus; sadly there's only a statue of George I today) and a sequence of grand stone churches in London's Docklands.

London's Georgian streets lined with abstemiously decorated brick houses remain a quiet visual treat and some of the most sought after homes and offices in the capital. There are many to choose from, most designed by surveyors and builders working to designs reproduced from the prescriptive pages of 18-century pattern books. But, no one would want to miss Bedford Square, Bedford Row, Doughty Street and Great James Street (Bloomsbury), Fournier Street (Spitalfields) or the dignified streets that constitute much of Marylebone and Mayfair, including Harley Street with its legion of private doctors.

Notable buildings of this long period of text-book Georgian good manners include **Somerset House**, a civic palace built around a grand courtyard overlooking the Thames on one side and facing the Strand with its ceaseless traffic on the other. Designed by Sir William Chambers, who acted as King George III's architectural tutor, Somerset House is, in fact, the first purpose-built office block in London. It was built for the Navy and other government offices and until recently was crammed with civil servants who parked their cars in the courtyard. Today the officials are on their way out; their cars have already gone. Their place is being taken by a mix of museums, including an outpost of the Hermitage (St Petersburg), the Courtauld Institute (a posh fine arts finishing school for impossibly grand young men and women) and at least one very smart restaurant, The Admiralty.

The greatest talent of the late Georgian period was that of the manic depressive Sir John Soane (1757-1837). He designed the labyrinthine **Bank of England**, but, sadly, this was largely demolished, except for its superb defensive walls, in the 1920s. A part of Soane's magical interior has been rebuilt and is well worth a visit. Few architects before or since have handled the play of daylight inside buildings so well. Luckily, Soane's own truly fantastic house which was also his personal museum has survived inside three customised Georgian terraced houses in Lincoln Inn's Fields. The **Sir John Soane Museum** is an architectural sonnet. A time machine and shaper of dreams, it remains one of the best kept secrets in London. Because it's a house, visitors have to ring the bell to gain admittance and sign the visitors' book; it's as if Soane is still in residence even though he lies buried in a curious Greek Revival tomb in old St Pancras churchyard, a haunt of drug-addicts and prostitutes alongside the Midland main-line railway today.

Yet, for all its Georgian inheritance, London, has has largely been made by the Victorians. Grand Gothic Revival churches, the **Palace of Westminster** by Charles Barry and Augustus Welby Northmore Pugin, the **Grand Midland Hotel at St Pancras** by Sir George Gilbert Scott are the pinnacles of a wave of almost over-confident design that swept over London as the British Empire reached its peak. This wave kept on rolling up until the First World War. Modern architecture shuffled, soft-shoed, into London from the Continent in the 1930s. At first it was the work of emigre architects, from Russia, Hungary and other points east. The Modern Movement in London was a refugee movement to begin with, yet, after the Second World War, was to sweep through the capital with its challenging concrete forms from giant housing estates to the National Theatre. Modern architecture was largely despised in London until the 1980s when not only did it become more glamorous - it had been a little on the wholemeal side before before then - but it also became fashionable. By the beginning of the new century (the much vaunted new millennium), Londoners, and visitors to London, actually looked forward to see the latest addition to this complex and contradictory cityscape.

An architectural tour of modern London

The London Eye (2000) Not really architecture, but a very fine, if rather highly strung, big wheel has been brought up to date for London's millennium celebrations by the architects David Marks and Julia Barfield. An immensely tall, yet remarkably unobtrusive Big Wheel from which London's streetscape, its parks and architecture can be admired night and day (see page 258).

Waterloo International (1993) Prognathous Eurostar trains glide in and out under the great glazed roof of this super sleek modern-day railway terminus, linking London and Paris via the Channel Tunnel in just three tantalizing hours. The roof and platforms snake away from the airport-style concourse and ticket barriers following the line of the former Southern Railway main line towards Clapham Junction, still the world's busiest station. The only sad thing is that passengers are only allowed up to the platforms at the last moment so that the glory of Nicholas Grimshaw's fine roof is mostly experienced from outside the station.

Royal Festival Hall (1951) The handsome and popular music venue on the South Bank was designed by London County Council architects under Sir Leslie Martin; a showpiece of Festival of Britain design, it's public spaces are awash with shimmering Thames' light. A building, with roots in Scandinavian and Revolutionary Russian ideas, that brought modern architecture and design to a wide audience (see page 259).

Hayward Gallery (1967) Still controversial, this, the most brutal of Brutalist buildings was designed by the former London County Council's architects' department from the late 1950s. Like some kind of Mayan temple realised in mossy concrete, it is loved and loathed in equal measures. Its thick concrete walls were meant to baffle the noise of the London Heliport that was to have been built virtually alongside. It never happened. Despite its rough-hewn appearance, the Hayward Gallery is beautifully built; just look at all that bronze and brass inside. The gallery is soon to be rebuilt to make it easier to put on exhibitions, which are normally very good indeed, (see page 260).

Royal National Theatre (1967-77) The vast geological outcrop of concrete terraces and towers on the South Bank houses the Olivier, Lyttleton and Cottesloe theatres. The serious-minded and magnificent masterpiece of Denys Lasdun (1914-2000), it remains a great meeting place and is a fine institution with terraces which offer inspiring views of London's peerless riverscape.

This is Mongrel London at its most heroic. Here the former Bankside Power Station, sited slap, bang opposite St Paul's Cathedral, has been transformed into Britain's leading gallery of 20th century and contemporary art. The heroic scale of the project demonstrates London's extraordinary commitment to modern art in recent years. The brobdingnagian power station, finally completed in 1955, was given a handsome brick façade by Sir Giles Gilbert Scott, architect of Waterloo Bridge, Battersea Power Station (currently in ruins but possibly to be rebuilt as a culture and entertainment venue) and the Guinness Brewery in Park Royal, West London. This temple of power was converted into a cathedral of art by the Swiss architects Herzog and de Meuron (designers of the Laban Dance Centre, Deptford, due to open in 2003). The Tate has opened up the old and long-neglected borough of Southwark to Londoners and visitors alike; it is as much a place to crowd into on rainy Sundays as it is a huge vote of confidence in London's role as munificent patron of modern art (see page 243).

Tate Modern (2000)

The famous - or is it infamous? - 'Wobbly Bridge'. Long awaited, London's first pedestrian Thames crossing wobbled dramatically as a vast crowd surged across when it first opened in May 2000. Modifications have been made and this exquisite suspension bridge, designed by Norman Foster, the sculptor Anthony Caro and the engineers Ove Arup & Partners, will soon enough be taking people across from St Paul's Cathedral to the Tate Modern.

Millennium Bridge (2000)

A vast concrete ocean liner of a housing estate and arts complex designed by architects Chamberlin Powell & Bon and come to berth in the City of London. Dominated by three 412-ft residential towers – Cromwell, Lauderdale and Shakespeare – the Barbican was originally built as affordable homes to rent; since its completion it has become a much-fêted middle-class bastion, offering well-built flats, many with inspiring views, minutes from the City's computer-driven counting houses. It also boasts an Arts Centre, famous for being more difficult to navigate than the Labyrinth (even Theseus would have missed the first act of the latest RSC production).

Barbican (1958-1981)

Ambitious US-style office scheme built to coincide with the deregulation of the City of London in Margaret Thatcher's heyday. This move led to a boom in City financial trading floors. The generously built and lavishly appointed Broadgate offices - acres of shiny marble, miles of polished brass - designed mainly by the US architects Skidmore Owings and Merrill were the answer. This massive development with its impressive public squares and notable artworks rode the roller-coaster of the Britain's economic ups and downs in the 1980s and 90s. It has since proved to be a big success. And, boy, is it BIG.

Broadgate (1984 to date)

Richard Rogers' masterpiece is an astonishing space-age building infused with the spirit of *Blade Runner*, *Aliens* and, no less prosaically, North Sea oil rigs rising above Leadenhall Market. Hard to believe that this titanic hi-tech finance house was commissioned by what was thought to be one of the most conservative bodies in Britain. Upper floors are reached by vertigo-inducing glass lifts that zoom up and down the outside of the building's stainless steel-clad towers. The whole edifice is gathered around a vast, Crystal Palace-style atrium and is full of delightful architectural surprises.

Lloyd's Building, City (1986)

Movie-style Chicago architecture came to London's former Docklands from the late 1980s with this spectacularly banal new office city aimed at dragging the bankers and brokers of the ancient City of London east along the Thames. Well built and thoroughly landscaped, the Post-Modern office towers of Canary Wharf are suitably vacuous symbols for the Thatcherite money culture they continue to celebrate. Canary Wharf Tower, by the New York architect Cesar Pelli is, at 800-ft, the tallest

Canary Wharf (under construction)

Background

building in Britain. This stainless-steel monolith is hard to avoid on the city's skyline; it does look good though at sunrise and sunset when it appears to burst into flames, towering Inferno-style. The Canary Wharf development also includes Norman Foster's superb Jubilee Line station and is home to many water birds.

Jubilee Line Extension (2000) One of the most interesting journeys any visitor can make through East London, both north and south of the Thames, is by the new Jubilee Line Extension from Westminster to Stratford. Without exception the new stations have been designed to an exceptionally high standard under the aegis of the project's Anglo-Italian architect Roland Paoletti (who previously designed the super-efficient Hong Kong Metro). Each is a landmark, each the final fling of publicly funded public architecture in a country crazy about privatization and where trains and buses are now run by cynical cowboys. It's hard to single out the best stations, but Westminster (Michael Hopkins), Canary Wharf (Foster), North Greenwich (Alsop & Stormer) and the train depot west of Stratford with its sweeping arched roof are exceptionally good.

Pumping Station, Millwall (1988) This is Post-Modernism at its best, as wilful architectural folly. John Outram's pumping station enlivens a rather grim stretch of the Thames as it winds eastwards to Greenwich from under Tower Bridge. It is a grandiloquent play of ancient and classical themes. It also serves a very useful purpose. Best seen from a boat.

The Dome (1999-2000) Nancy Banks-Smith, the *Guardian*'s TV critic described this heroic hi-tech tent as looking, by night, like a jellyfish glowing on the banks of the Thames. Designed by the Richard Rogers Partnership to house the deeply embarassing Millennium Experience, a patronizing view of life in Britain in the year leading up to the new millennium, the building itself is a romantic thing, a modern cross-breeding of the two most celebrated structures at the 1951 Festival of Britain; these were the Skylon, an ethereal space-age tower by Powell & Moya, and the Dome of Discovery, a kind of Boy's Own flying saucer filled with the latest post-war British technology. The Festival of Britain was much more popular than the Millennium Experience; its legacy includes the cultural buildings on the South Bank. The future of the Dome hangs in the balance. Most extravagant national exhibitions championed by governments have tended to vanish in a puff of costly smoke.

Sainsbury Wing, National Gallery (1987) Limp-wristed attempt by US Post-Modern architects Robert Venturi and Denise Scott-Brown to add a bit of Classical wit to the rather damp façade of William Wilkin's Neo-Greek National Gallery. As for the paintings this otherwise well-planned gallery houses, what can anyone say that would deflate a Bellini or give umbrage to a Uccello?

Charing Cross Station (1990) Big, brash, Post-Modern railway terminus remodelled by Terry Farrell. Overscaled and finished in vile colours, the redevelopment of Charing Cross was significant not so much for the way it intruded aggressively into the romantic Thames riverscape, but because it showed how, if they could, developers would build masses of office space above public buildings, stations especially, and leave those who needed to use them, like commuters, in dismal dark spaces below. Great, eh?

Portcullis House, Westminster (2000) Hard to believe this ugly, bloated monster is by the same architects as the fine underground station beneath it. Designed as offices for members of parliament, previously squeezed indecorously into the Gothic Revival corridors of the Palace of Westminster opposite (Barry & Pugin, 1837-60), Portcullis - even its name - is symbolic of Britain's politicians desire to hide themselves away from those dumb enough to elect them. Gathered around a glazed courtyard lined with fig trees, MPs while away their days in a kind of bombastic and lavish splendour. The chimneys on top of the building are simply ugly.

Tall, slim beehive-style office tower at the eastern end of London's busiest shopping street. An icon of Pop architecture, designed by Colonel Richard Seifert, it seems odd now that it was much despised for many years, a symbol of aggressive high-rise property development. Fun to look at, it generates gale-force winds and so is hard to walk by. There is a bar low-down, but Londoners flock to a stylish bar on the tower's coveted top (35th) floor.

Centre Point (1967)

Standing like some giant robot in the heart of Bloomsbury, the Telecom Tower was the showcase of Britain's white hot technological 'revolution' championed by the Labour government of Harold Wilson in the 1960s. It beams zillions of telephone calls by microwave (keep your poodle well away) to lesser towers installed across the country. At 580-ft, it was until 1981 the tallest building in London. Visitors used to zoom up to the viewing galleries and revolving restaurant at its top. Sadly, these were closed permanently after the IRA exploded a bomb high in the tower. It was designed by the architects' section of the Ministry of Works, the team led by Eric Bedford.

London Telecom Tower (1966)

The breathtaking covered courtyard - Europe's largest - is at the heart of London's busiest museum (built, originally, to the designs of Robert Smirke between 1823 and 1847). The courtyard was a secret from 1857 when the famous circular Reading Room (by Smirke's younger brother, Sydney) was built inside it; the space left over was devoted to bookstacks. Now the courtyard, together with the Reading Room, has been opened up to the public, protected by a billowing and beautiful glazed roof. Under it you might like to try and identify the infamous South Portico, a classical design by the hi-tech Foster team; the design hasn't been in question - it is coolly elegant - but it is made of a French rather than good old English Portland stone from Purbeck in Dorset. This led to much huffing and puffing among those who felt the overcrowded museum should have been left as it was. A storm in an antique drinking vessel whipped up by the media, the South Portico will soon blend intrusively into this ambitious and truly grand design.

Great Court, British Museum (2000)

Britain's most expensive building, the British Library, designed by Colin St John Wilson and Partners, took many years to plan and build. A red-brick colossus, it is pretty indigestible as seen from the street, yet the noble interiors are beautifully made, generous and a pleasure to use.

British Library, Bloomsbury (1997)

Post-Modern architecture came to London with this brash, flash and rather endearing broadcasting studio and offices for TV-am, a short-lived breakfast channel. A former garage, it was converted by Terry Farrell & Co into an entertaining three-dimensional map of the world (well, the flamboyant lobby at least). It was all done on a shoestring at a time when the British economy was still struggling out of a rut. It became known as Eggcup House, because of decorative glass-fibre eggcups (breakfast imagery, don't you know) set along its cornice lines. And the overall style? 'Depression Deco'.

TV-am Camden Town (1982)

The surreal housing scheme, comprising 520 homes, lined along one giant carless street, is hidden away from the world of elegant white-stucco clad early Victorian houses all around. This is the last of London's major public-housing schemes, designed by the Greater London Council architectural team led by Neave Brown, and it's quite mind-bending.

Alexandra Road, Camden (1969-79)

Background

1-3 Willow Rd, Hampstetad (1940) Pre-war, but this was the home of the Brutalist architect Erno Goldfinger who designed the now fashionable Trellick Tower housing brooding over Portobello Road (see below) and the former Sanderson Wallpapers office, Fitzrovia, now the intensely fashionable Sanderson Hotel. Goldfinger (his friend Ian Fleming borrowed the Hungarian architect's name and accent for his famous Bond baddie) designed the house, one of a terrace of three, for himself and his wife Ursula and lived here until his death in 1987. In 1994, the house was bought by the National Trust. It is open to the public and is much as its designer left it.

Lord's Cricket Ground (1984-2000) Another old London institution - the home of half-cut old gents asleep on summer days sporting panamas and salmon-and-custard ties pretending to watch Test Matches – which invested, all of a sudden, from the mid-1980s in adventurous new design. The white, tented Mound Stand by Michael Hopkins set the tone for a pavilion with unobstructed views and real elegance. The Press Pavilion by Future Systems is almost sensational: Britain's first large-scale monocoque building (its structure is all of a piece), it seems quite happy here in Marylebone even though it would be equally at home on Mars.

Trellick Tower, North Kensington (1973) The now fashionable Brutalist high-rise concrete housing block designed by Erno Goldfinger overshadows Portobello Road and its famous market. Highly expressive and not a little frightening, the flats are gained by lifts running up a detached tower. The views from the flats are breathtaking.

Peckham Library (2000) The colourful new public library appears to stand on stilts set at crazy angles and to be made of copper and stained glass. Designed by architects Alsop & Stormer it is quite simply one of the most enjoyable new buildings in London, set in one of its poorest quarters. The interior is a treat with its Sci-Fi reading rooms housed in 'pods'. The views across north London from the London Eye to the Greenwich Dome are dazzling.

Designed restaurants It's hard to single out London's best architect-designed restaurants, but Tess and Julyan Wickham's **Kensington Place** (1987) is among those that take pride of place. A sweeping, bright and sociable space, it was a deservedly popular symbol of the moment when London began to fall in love with good modern food and good Modern architecture. It is still a fine, if noisy, place to eat.

The Avenue (1998) Rick Mather's design rivals the Wickhams as one of the essential architect-designed London restaurants. Big, classy and refined, it is also sociable and an easy place to dine. Set in the heart of gloriously old-fashioned St James's - Lock's the hatter and Lobb's the shoemakers - are next-door neighbours, The Avenue shows how class can take many forms.

Sanderson Hotel (1999) An Erno Goldfinger office building transformed by the New York hotelier Ian Schrager and Parisian designer Philippe Starck into one of the most stylish new hotels in London. Wonderfully over-the-top furniture, a dazzling white bar matched by a dark, sensual counterpoint elsewhere off the lobby and a fine garden bar and café, it is a fine and fashionable place to meet as long as you pass the doormen's intelligently astute gaze. Look like a star (or just a wannabe star) and you're indon in the movies.

Contemporary Art

In 1976 the American artist RB Kitaj, then resident in London, coined the term 'School of London' to describe the "artistic personalities in this small island more unique and strong and I think numerous than anywhere in the world outside America's jolting artistic vigour". At a time when radical conceptual and minimal art by the likes of Richard Long (going on walks) or Gilbert & George (living sculpture) ruled the roost, Kitaj's polemic instead embraced primarily figurative artists of earlier generations such as Francis Bacon or David Hockney. For years art had barely figured in the wider cultural life of this island; it was thought to be something the French or Americans did better (a state of affairs that Kitaj was trying to redress).

In the 1990s things really seemed to change: the media fêted artists like Tracey Emin or Damien Hirst as if they were popstars and in the words of too many glossy magazine headlines 'London Swings Again'. Collected, anthologized, celebrated and promoted with an ad man's zeal, probably one of the best places to see art of the 90s is the vast space of Charles Saatchi's Saatchi Gallery in St John's Wood. However, it was with the opening in May 2000 of Tate Modern in the giant landmark building of Gilbert Scott's Bankside Power Station that the British public's interest in art – particularly contemporary art – was confirmed by the millions of visitors attracted to the new museum. The original Tate Gallery, now renamed Tate Britain and situated on the north side of the river at Millbank, at first suffered from the attention given to the opening of Tate Modern, but its collection is still unrivalled and well worth a look (it's quieter there too).

The art map of London has always been determined by fashion and money, and in this it is no different from any other city. A century ago and until the 1930s, artists congregated in Chelsea in the triangle formed by Cheyne Walk and the Chelsea Embankment to the south, Sloane Street to the east and Fulham Road to the west and north. Although the purpose-built studio houses in the area are studded by blue plaques with the names of many distinguished artists of days gone by, very few artists today live and work in the area. The Chelsea Arts Club – for members only – is not the local it once was. Chelsea, however, was never really the place for the poor and starving artist.

In the first decades of the 20th century artists also lived and worked in what were then decidedly grubby and disreputable areas such as Fitzrovia (home to Wyndham Lewis and the Vorticists) or Bloomsbury (home to Virginia Woolf and the Bloomsbury Group). Other artists, especially in the 30s, opted for the rather more genteel atmosphere of Hampstead, home to many artist exiles from the continent, such as Piet Mondrian, who settled easily into what was described as a "gentle nest of artists" feathered by the likes of Henry Moore, Barbara Hepworth and Ben Nicholson. Now the area is home to the Camden Arts Centre (Arkwright Road), justly renowned for its exhibitions of contemporary and 20th-century art.

The 40s and 50s saw the rise of the louche dives and pubs of Soho and Fitzrovia as the backdrop for artists and poets at play from Francis Bacon to Dylan Thomas. In the 50s and 60s most young artists colonized the run-down territory of Notting Hill and Ladbroke Grove before moving east in the 70s and 80s to the still-deserted loft spaces of Docklands. In the 90s the location of choice was the run-down spaces of Shoreditch – now the grooviest place in London to live and one of the most expensive; Shoreditch is now almost completely devoid of artists who have all been forced out by soaring rents.

For generations the centre of the commercial art world in London has been Cork Street and Bond Street on the edge of Mayfair and close to the Royal Academy. Save

Background

But is it art?

It is thought that the typical young British artist (yBa) – be it Chris Ofili, Jake & Dinos Chapman or Tracey Emin – is a product of the east London areas of Hoxton and Shoreditch, but the birth of yBa actually took place, variously, in the opportunistic wastelands of soon to be developed Docklands (where Damien Hirst organized the alternative degree show 'Freeze' in 1988 which launched many of the artists), the South London borders of New Cross (where they studied at Goldsmiths College and had their first studios), and the leafy roads in St Johns Wood where, through the 1990s, advertising mogul and collector Charles Saatchi mounted exhibitions of their work (most famously Hirst's tiger shark pickled in

formaldehyde – The Physical Impossibility of Death in the Mind of Someone Living – in 1992). The flowering of British art under the label of the Goldsmiths Generation (even though many neither studied at Goldsmiths nor are the same age) was typified as media friendly by a supposedly punk aesthetic alongside the embrace of big subjects (such as 'life' and 'death') which were easy to get if difficult to pin down. Indeed much of the media hype has ignored the fact that there were many artists, such as Mark Wallinger, Langlands & Bell, or Simon Patterson, who were making work in the 1990s that was just as powerful if much quieter in tone and belied the tabloid characterisation of yBa as slasher art.

for a few survivors, most contemporary art galleries have moved away, or closed, long ago. It is the place where rich people shop and is where Sotheby's has its auction rooms (always worth a look). Few contemporary art galleries can afford the rents or deal with the historical baggage of staying in the area. Those worth seeing are Stephen Friedman (Old Burlington Street), Asprey Jacques (Clifford Street), Waddingtons and Mayor Gallery (Cork Street), Anthony d'Offay Gallery and Anthony Reynolds (Dering Street). For a taste of a new way with an old style the Helly Nahmed Gallery (Cork Street) is breathtaking for the sheer range and quality of its stock, from Impressionist and Post-Impressionist classics through to the Britart of Damien Hirst. For a slower pace one should move through the stately velvet-draped spaces of Agnews Gallery (between Old Bond Street and Albermarle Street) – don't miss the upstairs gallery.

One oddity is the existence of White Cube, a small project space in Duke Street, St James's. Amid old master dealers, private gentlemen's clubs, tailors and the auction rooms of Christie's resides the tiny space from which Jay Jopling has supported and promoted the careers of some of the most talked-about artists of the 90s. Realizing that the size of his gallery was disproportionate to the profile of his artists, he has recently opened White Cube[2] in the epicentre of Shoreditch: Hoxton Square.

Similarly in 2000, Victoria Miro, dealer to Peter Doig and Chris Ofili, closed her small boutique space in Cork Street and moved to a huge warehouse building in Wharf Road on the edge of Shoreditch. East London has, indeed, been going through one of its periodic booms. One of the first dealers to open up shop in Hackney was the American Maureen Paley. Recently both Anthony Wilkinson and the Approach Gallery have also moved in to this area, which has always been rich in publicly funded and artist-run galleries such as the Whitechapel Gallery, Matt's Gallery, the Showroom and the Chisenhale Gallery.

If it seems strange to see the White Cube in St James's, perhaps the location of the Institute of Contemporary Arts on the Mall, just down the road from Buckingham Palace, is even odder. Described as "an adult play centre" by one if its founders in the 1940s (when it had premises in Dover Street), things can still get quite anarchic there, with much to choose from between the bar, café, cinema, theatre and gallery.

Similarly incongruous is the Serpentine Gallery in a much-converted pavilion in the middle of Kensington Gardens. Its programme of young contemporary artists, 20th-century classics and timely group shows is outstanding and celebrated around the world. However, one of the most sympathetic public galleries, despite its uncompromising brutalist architecture, is the Hayward Gallery on the South Bank, a short walk westwards along the river from Tate Modern. Since it opened in 1968, the Hayward has produced some of the most exciting, significant and thought-provoking exhibitions to be mounted in London.

London in the movies

The city of London has never quite matched the celluloid magic of New York's skyscrapers or Hollywood's neon thrills. We try. James Bond launched a speed boat from the MI6 building by Vauxhall Bridge, and pursued yet another underdressed female kick-boxer all the way to that doomed symbol of modernity, the Greenwich Dome, in 1999. Michael Apted's opening sequence for The World Is Not Enough *is the most frantic river trip through London any of us had ever seen, yet it wasn't quite enough after all. The film promptly ditched London and set off in search of other more interesting bits of the globe.*

American cities seem to have it easier. Perhaps it's all that shimmering glass and heli-copter-eye views of serial killers, stars and romance. The making and breaking of the American Dream is stitched into the very fabric of the buildings. The effortless glamour of it all is still Hollywood's hottest ticket, despite the complacency with which it is now served up. In the wrong hands, London can still look like a patchwork quilt of colloquial views and foggy heritage. And London is frequently in the wrong hands. Even now there are some whose celluloid view of the city is a caper comedy with randy cab drivers and saucy spinsters. For others, it's a starchy arrogant city full of stuffy drawing rooms, cobbled streets, and stiff upper lips. For an older generation of cinema-goers, the city was Boris Karloff in *Corridors of Blood* (1958), and Ingrid Bergman losing her marbles in *Gaslight* (1944). Fifty years later John Schlesinger wasn't doing much to change the tune with his 1997 version of *Sweeney Todd* complete with Ben Kingsley as the demon barber and Joanna Lumley with black teeth and grimy knickerbockers.

The 1960s provide rich pickings. Michelangelo Antonioni's *Blow-Up* (1966) is the vintage Swinging Sixties movie revolving around David Hemmings's strange adventures in Maryon Park off the Woolwich Road, and what he may or may not have seen there. The film ends with mime artists playing tennis without a ball. The park itself has barely changed since Hemmings went mad there. Michael Winner swung through London like Tarzan, perhaps most memorably with Oliver Reed and Michael Crawford in *The Jokers* (1967), a movie that moved seamlessly from Winner's South Kensington flat to the Tower of London via Tramp's nightclub and the old Stock Exchange. In a coup that belies the quality of this rough gem, Winner managed to get permission to hide the stolen jewels in the Scales of Justice on top of the Old Bailey. They don't make 'em like that anymore.

The current sledge of ultra-violent gangster capers that stretch from Guy Ritchie's *Lock, Stock and Two Smoking Barrels* (1998) to Guy Ritchie's *Snatch* (2000) (with Brad Pitt as a gypsy bare-knuckle boxer), has created yet more cock-eyed views of the city. Maybe we should blame the late great Stanley Kubrick for making London gangsters both hip and ridiculous when he banned his own film, *A Clockwork Orange* (1971), from being screened in Britain. Parts of it were shot in the basement of the Barbican Centre (as it was being built); other parts in the mean streets of the East End.

Background

Ah the East End. In Peter Medak's *The Krays* (1990), about London's two most infamous mobsters, the Krays's home turf turned out to be Caradoc Street in leafy Greenwich on the other side of the Thames. Fans of Meryl Streep and Charles Dance will doubtless remember the dilapidated lovebirds tottering down the same street in David Hare's *Plenty* five years earlier. Where would the East End be without Cheney Road, NW1 (note the post code). An amazing number of films (by British standards) have been shot on this cobbled street, one of the last in London. It lies in the gloomy hinterland behind King's Cross, next to a sprinkling of old warehouses and gasometers. The street starred in *Alfie* (1966) with Michael Caine, *Shirley Valentine* (1989) with Pauline Collins, and most memorably in *Chaplin* (1992) with that clean cut young American actor, Robert Downey Jr. Yes, it's a terrifying place. Here is where Alec Guinness pulled off a violent heist in *The Ladykillers* (1955).

That London is able to reveal so many conflicting faces is perhaps the greatest compliment one can pay the city. But the best way of discovering the myths behind the movies is to explore the locations yourself. The possibilities are endless. Films like Merchant Ivory's *Howards End* (1992) are so stuffed with beautifully appointed location shots that they deserve an entire chapter to themselves: Roast beef at Simpson's-in-the-Strand; shopping at Fortnum and Mason's; a conversation by Admiralty Arch; a train to St Pancras; St James Court Hotel in Buckingham Gate doubling as a flat; and a hero's down-at-heel digs in Park Street in Southwark (home to Borough Market the best food market in London), all these locations feature in this Oscar-winning Merchant Ivory film which starred Helena Bonham Carter, Anthony Hopkins, Vanessa Redgrave, Sam West, and Oscar-winner Emma Thompson.

Young female romantics will probably find the journey to the Travel Bookshop (13 Blenheim Crescent, W11) a greater thrill. It's here that the shy Portobello bookshop owner, Hugh Grant, accidentally spills fruit juice over browsing superstar, Julia Roberts, in Roger Michell's *Notting Hill* (1999). The area has never quite recovered its bohemian cool, made famous by Hanif Kureshi's drug-dealing hero Clint (Justin Chadwick) in the 1991 film, *London Kills Me*.

An actor responsible for a lot more juicy slaughter is David Naughton in *An American Werewolf in London* (1981). The extensive filming in some of London's busiest parts put a sharp comic chill on John Landis's cult classic. One of the most memorable meals was witnessed on the escalator at Aldwych tube station courtesy of an unwary passenger and a ravenous toothy Naughton. Naughton wakes up in a cage in London Zoo, Regent's Park the following morning, then brings Piccadilly to a standstill by running amok taking bites out of anything in sight. Eros has never before or since played host to a 20-car pile-up.

The most unusual new angle on London has arguably been pinched by Julian 'The Filth and the Fury' Temple who manages the remarkable feat of bringing Coleridge (Linus Roache) and Kubla Khan to life inside a Millennium Wheel pod in his recent release, *Pandemonium* (2000). The chronicler of the Sex Pistols claims to be the first director to shoot scenes inside the London Eye with its spectacular views over the city. But I doubt he or any other director will be able to top Kubrick's *Full Metal Jacket* (1987). Perhaps only Kubrick had the nerve to recreate the Vietnam War in the derelict Beckton Gas Works just beyond Docklands on the north bank of the Thames. Matthew Modine and his lads blew up so much of the property, and left so many of the old derelict office buildings unsafe, that the area had to be sealed off from the public. Much like Vietnam itself. Enjoy.

London books

Contemporary fiction

Ackroyd, Peter *Hawksmoor* (Penguin, 1993). Mystery chiller about rebuilding London after the Great Fire. **Arnott, Jake** *The Long Firm* (Hodder and Stoughton, 1999), Cockney gangster novel set in the 60s and *He Kills Coppers* (Sceptre 2001), another London gangster story set in 60s Soho. **Baron, Alexander** *The Lowlife* (Harvill Press, 2001). Guilt-racked life of an East End Jewish gambler. **Boyd, William** *Armadillo* (Penguin, 1998). Accomplished comic thriller about a Pimlico loss-adjuster. **Duffy, Maureen** *Capital* (Harvill Press, 2001). An amateur archaeologist looks to the city's future while searching for clues to its destruction in the Dark Ages. **Dunn, Nell** *Steaming* (Amber Lane 1981). Very funny play about five women in an East London Turkish bath. **Emecheta, Buchi** *Head Above Water* (Heinemann, 1994). Autobiographical account of a Nigerian woman settling in north London. **Frewin, Antony** *London Blues* (No Exit Press, 2000). Black and white blue movies and the Profumo scandal.

Green, Henry *Caught* (Panther 2001). A story of male friendship on active service with the Auxiliary Fire Service during the Blitz. **Hill, Tobias** *Underground* (Faber & Faber, 1999). Punchy thriller located on the tube system. **Hornby, Nick** *Fever Pitch* (Penguin, 2000), modern love among the Arsenal terraces and *High Fidelity* (Penguin, 2000), modern love among the Holloway Road record stacks. **Kersh, Gerald** *Fowlers End* (Panther, 2001). Picture house politics in a run-down London community. **Kureishi, Hanif** *Buddha of Suburbia* (Faber and Faber, 1991) South London mixed race life. **Kureishi, Hanif** *London Kills Me* (Faber and Faber 1991). Drug dealer tries to improve himself in Notting Hill. **Lanchester, John** *Mr Philipps* (Faber and Faber, 2001) A newly unemployed accountant goes walkabout round modern London. **Lott, Tim** *White City Blue* (Viking, 1999). Comic west London buddy buddy novel.

Moorcock, Michael *King of the City* (Scribner 2000), a washed-up 60s waster recollects his London high life and *Mother London* (Scribner, 2000), four 'mental patients' eavesdrop on the margins of the city. **Palliser, Charles** *The Quincunx* (Penguin 1995). Contemporary 19th-century murdery mystery novel set in London. **Petit, Chris** *Robinson*. Idiosyncratic Soho low life and high life. **Raban, Jonathan** *Soft City* (Harvill Press, 1998). Early work on metropolitan life focusing on London and New York. **Richards, Ben** *A Sweetheart Deal* (Review, 2000). Baroque love story set in the underbelly of the city. **Royle, Nicholas** *The Director's Cut* (Abacus, 2000). Strange murder mystery in a cinematic West End. **Self, Will** *Grey Area* (Penguin 1996). Very articulate and funny divertimenti on Soho and London life. **Sinclair, Ian** *Downriver* (Vintage, 1995). The legacy of Thatcherism with a Thames perspective. **Spark, Muriel** *The Ballad of Peckham Rye* (Penguin, 1970). The devil arrives to shake up Peckham in the 50s. **Swift, Graham** *Last Orders* (Picador, 1997) Smithfield and East London grit and grime. **Thorne, Matt** *Dreaming of Strangers* (Weidenfeld and Nicolson, 2000). A movie reviewer and movie buff meet in comedy of London manners. **Tiffin, George** *Mercy Alexander* (Picador, 2001). Contemporary thriller about Thameside prostitution. **Williams, Nigel** *Fortysomething* (Viking, 1999). A sacked soapstar faces being 50 in Wimbledon.

London non-fiction

Ackroyd, Peter *London, The Biography* (Chatto & Windus, 2000). The story of the capital told with endless imagination, thought and humour. The best. **Barker, Felix**

London – a literary odyssey

My literary London began in the mud of the Thames' Embankment at **Vauxhall** with an old jetty. No inscription. Just a log of wood that jutted up at low tide alongside the greening debris of abandoned wharves. I thought it must be at least Victorian, and probably slippery with ghosts: a mooring for Charles Dickens' Our Mutual Friend *in which the boatman and his daughter live by dredging corpses from the river. Later, when Joseph Conrad's* Heart of Darkness *opened on a boat moored on the Thames – "one of the dark places of the earth" – I felt myself slipping off from the jetty on to the muddy, swollen, brown river of the Congo. London's tidal river has always been among the most interesting – and mysterious – of London's literary characters.*

Geoffrey Chaucer's The Canterbury Tales *opens just south of* **London Bridge** *with a gathering of medieval pilgrims at the Tabard Inn in* **Southwark**. *Chaucer's great claim to wealth in life was as customs officer on the river – an early example of Londoners being rude about people and getting their money off them. The Host of the Tabard, Harry Bailly – who jollys along the story-telling after everyone has paid their bill – has the name of an actual Southwark innkeeper and member of parliament of the period. The Tabard burned in 1679 and was replaced by The Talbot. I've heard that in some form it's still*

standing; perhaps it's worth a legless pub-crawl to try and find it. Chaucer himself leased a house at Aldgate in the City. The southeast Midland dialect of English, as spoken by Chaucer's London, became the dominant form of English.

"Sweet Thames run softly till I end my song", wrote Edmund Spenser of The Faerie Queene, *but unfortunately for him he was exiled to Ireland to face the likes of the great, Gaelic bandit Queen, Grace O'Malley, who herself sailed up the Thames to sue for peace with Elizabeth I in Latin, their only shared language. There's a pavement to Spencer – who was educated at Merchant Taylors' School, London – along by the Southbank's* **Jubilee Walk** *which is engraved with an extract from his* Prothalamion *to give him a foot back in the place. He was buried in Westminster Abbey in 1599, which has, of course, its famous 'poet's corner'.*

The South Bank Arts Centre, with its complex of theatres, concert halls, poetry library and galleries, is a modern descendent of **Bankside** *further to the east and scene of the greatest out-pouring of literature London has known. Outside the remit of the City magistrates, this south-of-the-river stretch catered for the London overspill of bawdy revellers, bear-baiters and play-goers (and boasted its own prison, The Clink, for when things got out of hand). The working*

& Jackson, Peter *A History of London in Maps* (Barrie & Jenkins, 1990). Fascinating insights into urban growth, illustrated by contemporary maps from the 16th century onwards. **Glinert, Ed** *A Literary Guide to London* (Penguin, 2000). The movements of writers of all kinds systematically traced through the streets. **Hibbert, Christopher and Weinreb, Ben** (Ed) *The London Encyclopaedia* (Macmillan, 1983). The history of any building, park, street, statue that ever was part of London, or still is. A tome. **Hibbert, Christopher** *London: The Biography of a City* (Longmans, Green & Co, 1977). An entertaining and fluent account of the city's history, finely illustrated. **Jones, Edward & Woodward, Christopher** *A Guide to the Architecture of London* (Weidenfeld & Nicolson, 1992). The A-Z (with photographs) of London's architecture, building by building, area by area.

Piper, David *The Companion Guide to London* (Spectrum, 1964). A personal and engaging walking tour of the historic areas of the capital. **Porter, Roy** *London A Social History* (Hamish Hamilton, 1994). A lively, detailed and refreshing history of the

reconstruction of The Globe Theatre, Bankside, is your mecca for Shakespeare-wallahs. Built originally in 1599 by the theatrical impresario, James Burbage – who moved there from Shoreditch and cleverly gave Shakespeare a tenth share in the place – The Globe was in stiff competition with Burbage's rival, Philip Henslowe, who ran the Rose Theatre and a number of 'stews', or brothels, on Bankside. Among the many images Shakespeare offers of his Bruegelesque working environment is the glimpse in Measure for Measure of people "groping for trout in a peculiar river".

The divine John Donne was dean of **St Paul's Cathedral**, visible on the other side of the river. For the intrepid literary pilgrim you could knock on the door of the deanery and ask to see his portrait in the study. But moving swiftly on, the theatres closed under the plague and the puritans were opened again with the Restoration by Charles II who licensed the King's Men and the Duke's Men for public performance in painted theatres – with actresses! From William Congreve, John Vanbrugh, John Gay and George Farquhar to Oliver Goldsmith and Richard Sheridan, the theatres of **Drury Lane** by Covent Garden became microcosms of society London – having turned their back on poor, blind old Milton buried obscurely somewhere over by St Giles', **Cripplegate**.

The new money of commercial, 18th-century London was reflected in Steele and Addison's The Spectator, published out of the **Fleet Street** scene of coffee-houses to the east of Drury Lane – one of which is still partially visible in The City of York pub on **High Holborn** near Chancery Lane. Living to the west of Drury Lane, off the **Strand**, was the oracular and extraordinary Dr Samuel Johnson ("a dangerous man to disagree with") who brought to writing the important business of earning money – since who, but a fool, according to Dr Johnson, ever wrote for anything else?

The visionary poet and illustrator, William Blake, hardly turned a penny his whole life – which might, partly, be explained by the very singular circumstance of having seen angels in a tree on Peckham Rye in Southwark as a young man. Safely back in South London, a blue plaque – watch out for them! – in **Hercules Road** by Lambeth North tube station marks the spot of Blake's old house. You could go north of the river to look up Keats' House museum in **Hampstead**, wander around **Bloomsbury**, home of the eponymous group of writers which included the likes of Virginia Woolf, Lytton Strachey and Vita Sackville-West, or visit St. Giles in **Covent Garden**, setting for Incomparable World, S I Martin's novel of 18th-century black London.

Londoner. **Rasmussen, Steen Eiler** London The Unique City (MIT Press, 1982). A study of the city and its people that has become a minor classic. **Rennison, Nick** The London Blue Plaque Guide (Sutton, 1999). An alphabetical guide to those distinguished residents of London, and where they live. **Russan Simpkin, Lilian and Ashmore** Historic Streets of London (Marshall, Hamilton 1923). The historic and etymological origin of the capital's street-names. **Seatrobe, JB** Political London (Politico's, 2000). A clear and simple guide to some of the locations of scandal, intrigue and historic events. **Trench, Richard and Hillman, Ellis** London under London (John Murray, 1993). A wonderful study of the people, pipes, tunnels, and lost rivers of a fascinating subterranean world. **Wilson, AN** (Ed) The Faber Book of London (Faber & Faber, 1993). An anthology of writing about London. **Wittich, John** Discovering London Street Names (Shire, 1996). The historic and etymological origin of the capital's street-names.

Background

Footnotes

13

Footnotes

Index

Footnotes

Map index

Shorts

Five of the best

Footprint travel list

Footprint publish travel guides to over 120 countries worldwide. Each guide is packed with practical, concise and colourful information for everybody from first-time travellers to travel aficionados . The list is growing fast and current titles are noted below. For further information check out the website **www.footprintbooks.com**

Andalucía Handbook
Argentina Handbook
Bali & the Eastern Isles Hbk
Bangkok & the Beaches Hbk
Bolivia Handbook
Brazil Handbook
Cambodia Handbook
Caribbean Islands Handbook
Chile Handbook
Colombia Handbook
Cuba Handbook
Dominican Republic Handbook
East Africa Handbook
Ecuador & Galápagos Handbook
Egypt Handbook Handbook
Goa Handbook
India Handbook
Indian Himalaya Handbook
Indonesia Handbook
Ireland Handbook
Israel Handbook
Jordan Handbook
Jordan, Syria & Lebanon Hbk
Laos Handbook
Libya Handbook
London
Malaysia Handbook
Myanmar Handbook
Mexico Handbook
Mexico & Central America Hbk
Morocco Handbook
Namibia Handbook
Nepal Handbook

Pakistan Handbook
Peru Handbook
Rio de Janeiro Handbook
Scotland Handbook
Singapore Handbook
South Africa Handbook
South American Handbook
South India Handbook
Sri Lanka Handbook
Sumatra Handbook
Thailand Handbook
Tibet Handbook
Tunisia Handbook
Turkey
Venezuela Handbook
Vietnam Handbook

In the pipeline – Edinburgh, Rajasthan, Scotland Highlands & Islands, Syria & Lebanon

Also available from Footprint
Traveller's Handbook
Traveller's Healthbook

Footnotes

Available at all good bookshops

London by cuisine

A quick reference guide to help you locate a restaurant to suit your taste and budget near to you.
Further details can be found by turning to the page ▸▸

Codes are **£** under £20; **££** £20-40; **£££** over £40 (Three-course meal plus drink for one)

Afghan

Bayswater	*Mandola*	£	
	T020-7229 4734		▸▸ 352
Covent Gdn	*Calabash at the Africa Centre*	££	
	T020-7836 1976		▸▸ 98
Islington	*The Afghan Kitchen*	£	
	T020-7359 8019		▸▸ 323
Mayfair	*Momo*	££	
	T020-434 4040		▸▸ 112

Arabian

Bayswater	*The Baghdad Restaurant*	£	
	T020-7229 3048		▸▸ 352

Argentine

Mayfair	*Gaucho Grill*	££	
	T020-7734 4040		▸▸ 111

Asian

The City	*Singapura*	££	
	T020-7329 1133		▸▸ 239
Docklands	*The Elephant Royal*	££	
	T020-7987 7999		▸▸ 296
East End	*East*	££	
	T020-7729 5544		▸▸ 279
Fitzrovia	*Bam-Bou*	£££	
	T020-7323 9130		▸▸ 212
Mayfair	*Cassia Oriental*	££	
	T020-7629 8886		▸▸ 111
Notting Hill	*Rain Bar & Restaurant*	££	
	T020-8968 2001		▸▸ 334
	Ulli	£	
	T020-7727 7511		▸▸ 335

Belgian

Covent Gdn	Belgo Centraal	£	
	T020-7813 2333		▸▸ 99
Sth Kensington	*Abbaye*	£	
	T020-7373 2403		▸▸ 171

Brazilian

Highgate	*Sabor do Brasil*	£	
	T020-7263 9066		▸▸ 308

British (see also Modern British)

Chelsea	*Chelsea Bun*	£	
	T020-7352 3635		▸▸ 181
	Chelsea Farmer's Market	£	
			▸▸ 181
	The Chelsea Kitchen	£	
	T020-7589 1330		▸▸ 181
Clerkenwell	*Smiths of Smithfield*	££	
	T020-7236 6666		▸▸ 226
	St John	££	
	T020-7251 0848		▸▸ 226
	The Quality Chop House	££	
	T020-7837 5093		▸▸ 227
Covent Gdn	*Alfred*	££	
	T020-7240 2566		▸▸ 98
	Plummers	£	
	T020-7240 2534		▸▸ 99
	Rules	£££	
	T020-7836 5314		▸▸ 98
Leicester Sq	*Stockpot*	£	
	T020-7839 5142		▸▸ 81
	West End Kitchen	£	
	T020-7839 4241		▸▸ 81
Mayfair	*The Guinea Grill*	££	
	T020-7499 1210		▸▸ 111
Pimlico	*Peter's Café*	£	
	T020-7730 5991		▸▸ 157
St James's	*@ venue*	£££	
	T020-7321 2111		▸▸ 127
	Greens	£££	
	T020-7930 4566		▸▸ 127
	Wiltons	£££	
	T020-7629 9955		▸▸ 126
Sth Kensington	*Stockpot*	£	
	T020-7589 8627		▸▸ 171
Southwark	*Cathedral refectory*	£	
			▸▸ 252
	The Honest Cabbage	£	
	T020-7234 0080		▸▸ 252
The Strand	*Savoy Grill*	£££	
	T020-7836 4343		▸▸ 73
	Simpsons-in-the-Strand	£££	
	TT020-7836 9112		▸▸ 73
Tower	*Butler's Wharf Chop House*	££	
	T020-7403 3403		▸▸ 289

British cont.

	The Vineyard	£	
	T020-7480 6680		▸▸ 289
Trafalgar Sq	*Hampton's Wine Bar*	£	
	T020-7839 2823		▸▸ 65
Waterloo	*Bar and Restaurant*	££	
	T020-7620 2226		▸▸ 263
	R Cooke	£	
	T020-7928 5931		▸▸ 264
	The Archduke	£	
	T020-7928 9370		▸▸ 264
Westminster	*Shepherd's*	£££	
			▸▸ 149

Cantonese

The City	*Imperial City*	££	
	T020-7626 3437		▸▸ 239
Docklands	*Tai Pan*	££	
	T020-7791 0118		▸▸ 296
Knightsbridge	*Oriental Canteen*	£	
	T020-7581 8831		▸▸ 171
Leicester Sq	*1997*	£	
	T020-7734 2868		▸▸ 81
	Aroma II	££	
	T020-7437 0377		▸▸ 80
	Canton Restaurant	£	
	T020-7437 8193		▸▸ 81
	China City	££	
	T020-7734 3388		▸▸ 80
	Fung Shing	££	
	T020-7437 1539		▸▸ 80

Caribbean

Camden	*Mum's Kitchen*	££	
	T020-7428 0820		▸▸ 313

Chinese

Bayswater	*Hung To*	£	
	T020-7727 5753		▸▸ 351
	Mandarin Kitchen	££	
	T020-7727 9012		▸▸ 351
	Royal China	£££	
	T020-7221 2535		▸▸ 351
Belgravia	*Jenny Lo's Teahouse*	£	
	T020-7823 6331		▸▸ 157
Chelsea	*Wok Wok*	£	
	T020-7370 5355		▸▸ 182
Docklands	*Jade Harbour*	£	
	T020-7987 0771		▸▸ 296
Fulham	*Mayflower*	£	
	T020-7386 0657		▸▸ 359
Greenwich	*Noodle Time*	£	
	T020-8293 5263		▸▸ 400

Chinese cont.

Hampstead	*Dim T café*	£	
	T020-7435 0024		▸▸ 307
	ZenW3	££	
	T020-7794 7863		▸▸ 306
Hampton Ct	*Chu Chin Chow*	£	
	T020-8979 5993		▸▸ 384
Holborn	*Sheng's Tea House*	£	
	T020-7405 3697		▸▸ 227
Kensington	*Mr Wing*	££	
	T020-7370 4450		▸▸ 344
	The New Ho Ho	£	
	T020-7937 4898		▸▸ 344
Knightsbridge	*Mr Chow*	££	
	T020-7589 7347		▸▸ 171
Leicester Sq	*Jen*	£	
	T020-7287 8193		▸▸ 81
	Jen Café Tea Specialist	£	
	T020-7287 9708		▸▸ 81
	Lee Ho Fook	£	
	T020-7734 0782		▸▸ 81
	Mr Kong	£	
	T020-7437 7923		▸▸ 81
Mayfair	*Zen Central*	££	
	T020-7629 8089		▸▸ 111
	Zen Garden	££	
	T020-7493 1381		▸▸ 111
Notting Hill	*The New Cultural Revolution*	£	
	T020-7313 9688		▸▸ 335
Piccadilly	*China House*	£	
	T020-7499 6996		▸▸ 128
Richmond	*Four Regions*	££	
	T020-8940 9044		▸▸ 390
Soho	*Wok-Wok*	£	
	T020-7437 7080		▸▸ 89
South Bank	*Four Regions*	££	
	T020-7928 0988		▸▸ 263
Tower	*Poons in the City*	££	
	T020-7626 0126		▸▸ 289

European

Chelsea	*Piccasso's*	£	
	T020-7352 4921		▸▸ 181
Hammersmith	*River Café*	£££	
	T020-7381 8824		▸▸ 359
Holborn	*October Gallery Café*	£	
	T020-7242 7367		▸▸ 227
Kew	*The Glasshouse*	£	
	T020-8940 6777		▸▸ 390
Marylebone	*ITS*	£	
	T020-7224 3484		▸▸ 192
Notting Hill	*Kensington Place*	£££	
	T020-7727 3184		▸▸ 333

European cont.

Piccadilly	*Chubbie's*	£	
	T020-7839 3513	▸▸ 128	
Soho	*Alastair Little*	£££	
	T020-7734 5183	▸▸ 88	
	Amato	£	
	T020-7734 5733	▸▸ 89	
	Café Emm	£	
	T020-7437 4123	▸▸ 89	
	Garlic & Shots	££	
	T020-7734 9505	▸▸ 89	
Sth Kensington	*Bibendum*	£££	
	T020-7581 5817	▸▸ 170	
Southwark	*The Leather Exchange*	£	
		▸▸ 252	
Trafalgar Sq	*Café in the Crypt*	£	
	T020-7839 4342	▸▸ 65	
Westminster	*Bagel Express*	£	
		▸▸ 149	
	Tevere Restaurant	£	
		▸▸ 149	

Fish & Seafood

Camden	*Monkey Chews*	££	
	T020-7267 6406	▸▸ 315	
The City	*The Place Below*	£	
	T020-7329 0789	▸▸ 240	
	Sweetings	£	
	T020-7248 3062	▸▸ 240	
Clerkenwell	*Abbaye*	££	
	T020-7253 1612	▸▸ 227	
	The Fryer's Delight	£	
	T020-7405 4114	▸▸ 227	
	Stream Bubble and Shell	££	
	T020-7796 0070	▸▸ 227	
Covent Gdn	*Livebait*	££	
	T020-7836 7161	▸▸ 98	
	The Rock and Sole Plaice	£	
	T020-7836 3785	▸▸ 99	
Docklands	*Fish!*	£	
		▸▸ 296	
Fitzrovia	*Back To Basics*	££	
	T020-7436 2181	▸▸ 213	
	North Sea Fish Restaurant	£	
	T020-7387 5892	▸▸ 213	
Hampton Ct	*Café Society*	£	
	T020-8977 7691	▸▸ 384	
Islington	*Sariyer Balik*	£	
	T020-7275 7681	▸▸ 323	
Kensington	*Lou Pescadou*	££	
	T020-7370 1057	▸▸ 344	
Leicester Sq	*J Sheekey*	£££	
	T020-7240 2565	▸▸ 80	

Fish & Seafood cont.

Marylebone	*Bentley's*	££	
	T020-7734 4756	▸▸ 111	
	The Golden Hind	£	
	T020-7486 3644	▸▸ 192	
Notting Hill	*Geales*	£	
	T020-7727 7528	▸▸ 335	
Soho	*Randall & Aubin*	££	
	T020-7287 4447	▸▸ 88	
	Zilli Fish	££	
	T020-7734 8649	▸▸ 88	
Southwark	*Balls Brothers*	££	
	T020-7407 4301	▸▸ 251	
	fish!	££	
	T020-7234 3333	▸▸ 251	
Waterloo	*Livebait*	£££	
	T020-7928 7211	▸▸ 263	
	Masters Super Fish	£	
	T020-7928 6924	▸▸ 264	
Victoria	*Seafresh Fish Restaurant*	£	
	T020-7828 0747	▸▸ 157	
Westminster	*The Laughing Halibut*	£	
	T020-7799 2844	▸▸ 149	

French

Bankside	*Petit Robert*	££	
	T020-7357 7003	▸▸ 251	
Bloomsbury	*Savoir faire*	£	
	T020-7436 0707	▸▸ 213	
	Townhouse Brasserie	£	
	T020-7636 2731	▸▸ 213	
Clapham	*Gastro*	££	
	T020-7627 0222	▸▸ 371	
Camden	*Camden Brasserie*	££	
	T020-7482 2114	▸▸ 313	
Chelsea	*Thierry's*	££	
	T020-7352 3365/9832	▸▸ 181	
The City	*Chez Gerard Bishopsgate*	££	
	T020-7588 1200	▸▸ 239	
Clerkenwell	*Club Gascon*	£££	
	T020-7796 0600	▸▸ 226	
Covent Gdn	*Café des Amis*	££	
	T020-7379 3444	▸▸ 98	
	Incognito	£££	
	T020-7836 8866	▸▸ 98	
	Le Palais du Jardin	££	
	T020-7379 5353	▸▸ 98	
	Mon Plaisir	£££	
	T020-7836 3969	▸▸ 98	
Earl's Court	*The Little French Restaurant*	£	
	T020-7370 0366	▸▸ 344	
Embankment	*RS Hispaniola*	££	
	T020-7839 3011	▸▸ 74	

French cont.

Fitzrovia	*Chez Gerard*	£££
	T020-7636 4975	▸ 263
	Elena's L'Etoile	£££
	T020-7636 4975	▸ 213
	Pied-à-terre	£££
	T020-7636 1178	▸ 212
Hampstead	*Le Cage Imaginaire*	££
	T020-7794 6674	▸ 307
Hampton Ct	*Monsieur Max*	££
	T020-8979 5546	▸ 384
Holborn	*High Holborn*	£££
	T020-7404 3338	▸ 226
Islington	*Le Mercury*	£
	T020-7354 4088	▸ 323
Kensington	*La Brasserie*	££
	T020-7581 3089	▸ 171
	Maggie Jones	£££
	T020-7937 6462	▸ 343
Marylebone	*Villandry*	£££
	T020-7631 3131	▸ 192
Mayfair	*Chez Nico at 90 Park Lane*	£££
	T020-7409 1290	▸ 110
	The Mirabelle	£££
	T020-7499 4636	▸ 110
	The Square	£££
	T020-7839 8787	▸ 110
Notting Hill	*Brasserie du Marché*	£
		▸ 335
Piccadilly	*The Criterion*	£££
	T020-7930 0488	▸ 126
Putney	*Putney Bridge*	£££
	T020-8780 1811	▸ 359
Richmond	*Chez Lindsay*	£
	T020-8948 7473	▸ 391
St James's	*Le Caprice*	£££
	T020-7629 2239	▸ 127
	L'Oranger	£££
	T020-7839 3774	▸ 126
	Quaglino's	£££
	T020-7930 6767	▸ 127
Soho	*Qua Vadis*	£££
	T020-7437 9585	▸ 88
South Bank	*Chez Gerard*	£££
	T020-7202 8470	▸ 213
	The People's Palace	£££
	T020-7928 9999	▸ 263
	RSJ	£££
	T020-7928 4554	▸ 263
Sth Kensington	*Brasserie de l'Institut*	£
	T020-7838 2144	▸ 171
	Hilaire	£££
	T020-7584 8993	▸ 170

French cont.

	Le Suquet	££
	T020-7581 1785	▸ 171
The Strand	*The Admiralty*	££
	T020-7845 4646	▸ 73
Trafalgar Sq	*Prêt à Manger*	£
		▸ 65
Victoria	*Justin de Blank*	££
	T020-7828 4111	▸ 157

Fusion

Battersea	*La Pampa Grill*	££
	T020-7924 4774	▸ 371
Camden	*Café Delancey*	££
	T020-7387 1985	▸ 313
	The Engineer	££
	T020-7722 0950	▸ 314
	Saucebarorganic Diner	££
	T020-7482 0777	▸ 316
The City	*Prism*	££
	T020-7256 3888	▸ 239
Docklands	*Browns*	££
		▸ 296
Greewich	*The Wardroom*	££
	T020-8269 4797	▸ 400
Hampstead	*Giraffe*	£
	T020-7435 0348	▸ 307
	Gresslins	££
	T020-7794 8386	▸ 306
	The House on Rosslyn Hill	£
	T020-7435 8037	▸ 307
	Toast	££
	T020-7431 2244	▸ 305
Hampton Ct	*Blubeckers*	£
	T020-8941 5959	▸ 384
Holborn	*Bleeding Heart*	£££
	T020-7242 2056	▸ 226
Islington	*Browns*	££
	T020-7226 2555	▸ 323
	Lola's	££
	T020-7359 1932	▸ 322
	Mesclun	££
	T020-7249 5029	▸ 323
	Monitor	£
	T020-7607 7710	▸ 323
Kensington	*Arcadia*	£££
	T020-7937 4294	▸ 344
	Ashee's Wine Cellar bar	£
	T020-7373 6180	▸ 344
Leicester Sq	*Asia de Cuba*	££
	T020-7300 5588	▸ 80
Mayfair	*The Loop*	£
	T020-7493 1003	▸ 112

Fusion cont.

	Nobu	£££
	T020-7447 4747	▸▸ 110
Notting Hill	The Pharmacy	£££
	T020-7721 2442	▸▸ 333
Richmond	Ocean	£
	T020-8948 8008	▸▸ 391
	Prego	£
	T020-8948 8508	▸▸ 390
Soho	The Sugar Club	£££
	T020-7437 7776	▸▸ 88
Tower	Vestry Restaurant	££
	T020-7488 4933	▸▸ 289
	Wine Library	£
	T020-7481 0415	▸▸ 289

Greek

Bayswater	Angelo's	££
	T020-7221 8843	▸▸ 351
Bloomsbury	Yialousa Greek Taverna	£
	T020-7278 4945	▸▸ 213
Camden	Andy's Taverna	££
	T020-7482 0777	▸▸ 316
	Lemonia	££
	T020-7586 7454	▸▸ 315
East End	The Real Greek	££
	T020-7739 8212	▸▸ 278
Holland Park	Costas Grill	£
	T020-7229 3794	▸▸ 335
Soho	Jimmy's	£
	T020-7437 9521	▸▸ 89

Hungarian

Soho	Gay Hussar	£££
	T020-7437 0973	▸▸ 88

Indian

Bayswater	Khans	£
	T020-7727 5420	▸▸ 351
Camden	Mango Rooms	££
	T020-7482 5065	▸▸ 316
Chelsea	Chutney Mary	££
	T020-7351 3113	▸▸ 181
	Vama	££
	T020-7351 4118	▸▸ 181
	Zaika	££
	T020-7351 7823	▸▸ 181
City	Bengal Tiger	£
	T020-7248 6361	▸▸ 240
Covent Gdn	Punjab	££
	T020-7836 9787	▸▸ 98
Docklands	Tabla	££
	T020-7345 0345	▸▸ 296

Indian cont.

East End	Bengal Village	££
	T020-7366 4868	▸▸ 279
	Brick Lane Brasserie	££
	T020-7377 8072	▸▸ 279
	Café Naz	££
	T020-7247 0234	▸▸ 279
	Café Spice Namaste	££
	T020-7488 9242	▸▸ 289
	Le Taj	££
	T020-7247 4210	▸▸ 279
	Saffron	££
	T020-7247 2633	▸▸ 279
Euston	Diwana Bhel Poori House	£
	T020-7387 5556	▸▸ 200
	Ravi Shankar	£
	T020-7388 6458	▸▸ 200
Fitzrovia	Rasa Samudra	££
	T020-7637 0222	▸▸ 213
Fulham	Nayab	£
	T020-7731 6993	▸▸ 359
Marylebone	Kerela	£
	T020-7580 2125	▸▸ 192
Mayfair	Tamarind	££
	T020-7629 3561	▸▸ 111
Notting Hill	Malabar	££
	T020-7727 8800	▸▸ 334
Oxford Street	Rasa W1	££
	T020-7629 1346	▸▸ 133
Regent Street	Veeraswamy	££
	T020-7734 1401	▸▸ 111
Soho	The Red Fort	££
	T020-7437 2115	▸▸ 89
	Soho Spice	££
	T020-7434 0808	▸▸ 89
The Strand	India Club	£
	T020-7836 0650	▸▸ 74
Tower	The India Raj	£
	T020-7481 1022	▸▸ 289
Westminster	The Cinnamon Club	££
	T020-7517 9898	▸▸ 149

International

Bankside	Bankside Restaurant	££
	T020-7633 0011	▸▸ 251
Brixton	Helter Skelter	££
	T020-7274 8600	▸▸ 371
Chelsea	Gasworks	££
	T020-7736 3830	▸▸ 181
	Gordon Ramsay	£££
	T020-7352 4441	▸▸ 181
Covent Gdn	The Ivy	£££
	T020-7836 4751	▸▸ 98

International cont.

Docklands	The Quadrato Restaurant	£££	
	T020-7510 1999	▶▶ 296	
Knightsbridge	Fifth Floor	£££	
	T020-7235 5250	▶▶ 170	
Piccadilly	Oak Room	£££	
	T020-7851 3140	▶▶ 126	
Pimlico	Pomegranates	£££	
	T020-7828 6560	▶▶ 157	
St James's	Petrus	£££	
	T020-7930 4272	▶▶ 127	
Soho	Circus Restaurant & Bar	£££	
	T020-7534 4000	▶▶ 88	
	Spoon Plus	£££	
	T020-7245 0896	▶▶ 88	
	Titanic	£££	
	T020-7437 1912	▶▶ 88	
Sth Kensington	The Collection	£££	
	T020-7225 1212	▶▶ 170	
Waterloo	The Fire Station	££	
	T020-7620 2226	▶▶ 263	
	Honest Goose	£	
	T020-261 1221	▶▶ 263	

Iranian

Holland Park	Alounak	£	
	T020-7603 7645	▶▶ 336	

Irish

Marylebone	O'Conor Don	££	
	T020-7935 9311	▶▶ 192	
Mayfair	Mulligan's of Mayfair	££	
	T020-7409 1370	▶▶ 111	
Soho	Toucan	£	
	T020-7437 4123	▶▶ 89	

Italian

Battersea	Basilico	££	
	T020-7924 4070	▶▶ 372	
	Buona Sera at Battersea	££	
	T020-7228 9925	▶▶ 372	
	Verso 84	££	
	T020-7720 1515	▶▶ 373	
Brixton	Eco	££	
	T020-7738 3021	▶▶ 371	
	Pangaea	££	
	T020-7737 6777	▶▶ 373	
Bayswater	L'Accento	££	
	T020-7243 2664	▶▶ 351	
Belgravia	Oliveto	££	
	T020-7730 0074	▶▶ 157	
	Olivo	££	
	T020-7730 2505	▶▶ 157	

Italian cont.

Bloomsbury	Pizza Express	£	
		▶▶ 213	
Camden	Marine Ices	££	
	T020-7485 3132	▶▶ 316	
	Pizza Express	££	
	T020-7267 2600	▶▶ 316	
	Trattoria Fiorentina	££	
	T020-7419 7163	▶▶ 313	
Chelsea	Buona Sera at The Jam	££	
	T020-7352 8827	▶▶ 181	
	Daphne's	£££	
	T020-7584 6883	▶▶ 181	
	Elystano Restaurant	££	
	T020-7584 5248	▶▶ 181	
	King's Road Café	£	
	T020-7351 6645	▶▶ 181	
	Pellicano	££	
	T020-7589 3718	▶▶ 181	
	The Pheasantry	£	
		▶▶ 181	
	Pizza Express	£	
	T020-7351 5031	▶▶ 181	
	Ristorante La Bersagliera	£	
	T020-7352 5993	▶▶ 182	
The City	Pizza Express	£	
	T020-7600 8880	▶▶ 240	
Covent Gdn	Bertorelli's	£££	
	T020-7836 3969	▶▶ 98	
	Orso	££	
	T020-7240 5269	▶▶ 98	
Docklands	Amerigo Vespucci	££	
	T020-7513 0288	▶▶ 296	
	Pizza Express	££	
		▶▶ 296	
Earl's Court	Bistro Benito	£	
	T020-7373 6646	▶▶ 344	
East End	Bluu	££	
	T020-7613 2793	▶▶ 279	
	Great Eastern Dining Room	££	
	T020-7613 4545	▶▶ 278	
Fulham	Basilico	£	
	T020-7384 2633	▶▶ 359	
	Miraggio Club	£	
	T020-7384 3142	▶▶ 359	
Hampstead	Pizza Express	£	
	T020-7433 1600	▶▶ 308	
	Villa Blanca	££	
	T020-7435 3131	▶▶ 307	
Hampton Ct	Vecchia	£	
	T020-8941 5337	▶▶ 384	
Holborn	Mangiare	£	
	T020-7831 9268	▶▶ 227	

Italian cont.

Holland Park	Cibo	££
	T020-7371 6271	▸▸ 335
	Il Carratto Restorante	£
	T020-7229 9988	▸▸ 335
Islington	Casale Franco	££
	T020-7226 8994	▸▸ 322
	La Porchetta	£
	T020-7288 2488	▸▸ 323
	Ristorante Portofino	££
	T020-7226 0884	▸▸ 323
	Strada	£
	T020-7226 9742	▸▸ 323
	Trattoria Aquilino	£
	T020-7226 5454	▸▸ 323
Kensington	Dall' Artista	£
	T020-7373 1659	▸▸ 344
	Il Portico	£
	T020-7602 6262	▸▸ 344
	La Pappardella	£
	T020-7373 7777	▸▸ 344
	Scoffs	£
	T020-7602 6777	▸▸ 344
Knightsbridge	Osteria d'Isola	£££
	T020-7838 1044	▸▸ 170
	The Pizza on the Park	£
	T020-7235 5273	▸▸ 171
	Zafferano	£££
	T020-7235 5800	▸▸ 170
Leicester Sq	Manzi's	££
	T020-7734 0224	▸▸ 80
	Pizzico	£
	T020-7839 3641	▸▸ 81
Marylebone	Ibla	£££
	T020-7224 3799	▸▸ 192
Mayfair	The Marquis	£
	T020-7499 1256	▸▸ 112
	Rocket	£
	T020-7629 2889	▸▸ 112
	Sartoria	£££
	T020-7534 7000	▸▸ 111
Notting Hill	Assaggi	£££
	T020-7792 5501	▸▸ 333
	Mediterraneo	£
	T020-7792 3131	▸▸ 336
	Osteria Basilico	£
	T020-7727 9372	▸▸ 335
Pimlico	Pizza Express	£
	T020-7592 9488	▸▸ 157
St James's	Al Duca	££
	T020-7839 3090	▸▸ 127
	Il Viccolo	££
	T020-7839 3960	▸▸ 127

Italian cont.

	Mokaris	£
	T020-7495 5909	▸▸ 128
Soho	Centrale	£
	T020-7437 5513	▸▸ 89
	Il Forno	££
	T020-7734 4545	▸▸ 88
	Kettners	£
	T020-7734 6112	▸▸ 89
	L'Arena	££
	T020-7734 2334	▸▸ 88
	Luigi's	££
	T020-7437 6527	▸▸ 88
	Pizzeria Malleti	£
	T020-7439 4096	▸▸ 89
	Pollo	£
	T020-7734 5917	▸▸ 89
	Spiga	££
	T020-7734 3444	▸▸ 88
South Bank	Gourmet Pizza Company	£
	T020-7928 3188	▸▸ 263
	Pizza Express	£
	T020-928 4091	▸▸ 263
Sth Kensington	Il Falconiere	£
	T020-7589 2401	▸▸ 171
	Monza	££
	T020-7591 0210	▸▸ 171
Southwark	The Blue Olive	£
	T020-7407 6001	▸▸ 252
Tower	Cantina del Ponte	££
	T020-7403 5403	▸▸ 289
	Il Bordello	£
	T020- 7481 9950	▸▸ 289
Victoria	L'Incontro	£££
	T020-7730 6327	▸▸ 157
Westminster	The Atrium	££
	T020-7233 0032	▸▸ 149
	Sorriso	££
	T020-7222 3338	▸▸ 149

Japanese

Bankside	Feng Sushi	£
	T020-7407 8744	▸▸ 252
Bloomsbury	Abeno	£
	T020-7405 3211	▸▸ 213
	Hare and Tortoise	£
	T020-7278 4945	▸▸ 213
	Wagamama	£
	T020-7323 9223	▸▸ 213
Camden	Asakusa	££
	T020-7388 8533	▸▸ 316
	Wagamama Camden	££
	T020-7428 0800	▸▸ 316

Japanese cont.

The City	Japanese Canteen	£	
	T020-7329 3555	▸▸ 240	
Clerkenwell	Japanese Canteen	£	
	T020-7833 3521	▸▸ 227	
Fitzrovia	Ikkyu	£	
	T020-7636 9280	▸▸ 213	
Hampstead	Jin Kichi	££	
	T020-7794 6158	▸▸ 307	
Knightsbridge	It'su	££	
	T020-7584 5522	▸▸ 171	
Leicester Sq	Tokyo Diner	£	
	T020-7287 8777	▸▸ 81	
	Zipangu	£	
	T020-7437 5042	▸▸ 81	
Marylebone	Wagamama	£	
	T020-7224 3484	▸▸ 192	
Mayfair	Benihana	££	
	T020-7494 2525	▸▸ 112	
	San Sui	££	
	T020-7229 7136	▸▸ 335	
	Yoshino	££	
	T020-7287 6622	▸▸ 112	
Soho	Kulu Kulu	£	
	T020-7734 7316	▸▸ 89	
	Misato	£	
	T020-7734 7316	▸▸ 89	
	Ramen Sato	£	
	T020-7434 0309	▸▸ 89	
	RYO	£	
	T020-7287 1318	▸▸ 89	

Korean

Mayfair	Kaya	££	
	T020-7499 0622	▸▸ 112	

Kurdish

Islington	Halkevi	£	
		▸▸ 323	

Lebanese

Bayswater	Al-Omaraa	£	
	T020-7221 8045	▸▸ 351	
Mayfair	Al Hamra	££	
	T020-7493 1954	▸▸ 111	

Mediterranean

Fulham	The Atlas	£	
	T020-7385 9129	▸▸ 359	
Hampstead	Base	£	
	T020-7435 0348	▸▸ 307	

Mexican

Mayfair	El Pirata	£	
	T020-7491 3810	▸▸ 112	
	Havana	£	
	T020-7629 2552	▸▸ 112	
Sth Kensington	Cactus Blue	££	
	T020-7823 7858	▸▸ 171	

Middle Eastern

Covent Gdn	Sarastro	£	
	T020-7836 0101	▸▸ 99	
Earl's Court	Moshsen	£	
	T020-7603 9888	▸▸ 344	
Marylebone	Patogh	£	
	T020-7262 4015	▸▸ 192	

Modern British

Camden	Odette's	££	
	T020-7586 5486	▸▸ 315	
	Pie and Mash	££	
		▸▸ 316	
Docklands	The House	££	
	T020-7538 3818	▸▸ 296	
Earl's Court	The Abingdon	£££	
	T020-7937 3339	▸▸ 343	
Fitzrovia	RK Stanley	£	
	T020-7462 0099	▸▸ 213	
Greenwich	Chapter Two	££	
	T020-8333 2666	▸▸ 400	
Holland Park	Aix en Provence	£££	
	T020-7221 5411	▸▸ 333	
	Alastair Little	££	
	T020-7243 2220	▸▸ 334	
	The Belvedere	£££	
	T020-7602 1238	▸▸ 333	
	Julie's bar and restaurant	££	
	T020-7229 8331	▸▸ 335	
Kensington	Bellini	££	
	T020-7937 5520	▸▸ 344	
	The Dome	£	
	T020-7937 6655	▸▸ 344	
	Langans' Coq d'e Or	£££	
	T020-7259 2599	▸▸ 344	
	The Roof Gardens	£££	
	T020-7937 7994	▸▸ 343	
Marylebone	Purple Sage	££	
	T020-7486 1912	▸▸ 192	
Mayfair	The Greenhouse	£££	
	T020-7499 3331	▸▸ 110	
Notting Hill	192	£££	
	T020-7229 0482	▸▸ 333	
	Bali Sugar	££	
	T020-7221 4477	▸▸ 335	

Modern British cont.

	Leiths	£££	
	T020-7229 4481		▶▶ 333
Soho	*Richard Corrigan*	£££	
	T020-7439 0450		▶▶ 88
Sth Kensington	*Kemps*	££	
	T020-7589 8288		▶▶ 171
Southwark	*Delfina Studio Café*	££	
	T020-7357 0244		▶▶ 252
Tower	*Blue Print Café*	££	
	T020-7378 7031		▶▶ 289
Trafalgar Sq	*Portrait Rooftop Restaurant*	££	
	T020-7312 2490		▶▶ 65

Modern European

Aldwych	*Bank*	£££	
	T020-7379 9797		▶▶ 73
Bankside	*Tate Cafés*	££	
	T020-7401 5020		▶▶ 251
Battersea	*Ditto*	££	
	T020-8877 0110		▶▶ 371
Chelsea	*Bluebird*	£££	
	T020-7559 1000		▶▶ 181
The City	*Aurora*	£££	
	T020-7618 7000		▶▶ 239
Covent Gdn	*Café du Jardin*	££	
	T020-7836 4123		▶▶ 98
Earl's Court	*Equals Bar & Restaurant*	£	
	T020-7370 6994		▶▶ 344
East End	*The Cantaloupe*	££	
	T020-7613 4411		▶▶ 278
Greenwich	*Inside*	££	
	T020-8265 5060		▶▶ 400
	Time	£	
	T020-8305 9767		▶▶ 400
Hampstead	*Cucina*	££	
	T020-7435 7814		▶▶ 307
Holborn	*The Eagle*	££	
	T020-7837 1353		▶▶ 227
Islington	*Granita*	££	
	T020-7226 3222		▶▶ 322
Leicester Sq	*Seven*	££	
	T020-7734 0224		▶▶ 80
	Teatro	£££	
	T020-7494 3040		▶▶ 80
Marylebone	*The Orrery*	£££	
	T020-7616 8000		▶▶ 192
Mayfair	*Mash*	££	
	T020-7495 5999		▶▶ 213
	Noble Rot	£££	
	T020-7629 8877		▶▶ 110
St James's	*Che*	£££	
	T020-7747 9380		▶▶ 127

Modern European cont.

Soho	*Andrew Edmonds*	££	
	T020-7437 5708		▶▶ 88
	French House Dining Room	££	
	T020-7437 2477		▶▶ 88
	Leith's Soho	£££	
	T020-7287 2057		▶▶ 88
	Mezzo	££	
	T020-7314 4000		▶▶ 89
South Bank	*Oxo Tower Restaurant*	£££	
	T020-7803 3888		▶▶ 263
Westminster	*Footstall Restaurant*	££	
	T020-7222 2779		▶▶ 144

Moroccan

Mayfair	*Mô*	£	
	T020-7434 4040		▶▶ 112

Nepalese

Euston	*Great Nepalese*	£	
	T020-7388 6737		▶▶ 200

North America

Chelsea	*The Big Easy*	££	
	T020-7352 4071		▶▶ 181
	Ed's Easy Diner	£	
	T020-7352 1952		▶▶ 90
Covent Gdn	*Christophers*	£££	
	T020-7240 4222		▶▶ 98
	Joe Allen	££	
	T020-7836 0651		▶▶ 98
Fitzrovia	*Mash*	££	
	T020-7637 5555		▶▶ 111
Highgate	*Idaho*	££	
	T020-8341 6633		▶▶ 307
Hampstead	*Maxwells*	£	
	T020-7433 1600		▶▶ 308
Holland Park	*Tootsies*	£	
	T020-7229 8567		▶▶ 336
Notting Hill	*Dakota*	£££	
	T020-7792 9191		▶▶ 333
Piccadilly	*Planet Hollywood*	££	
	T020-7287 1000		▶▶ 127
	Rainforest Café	££	
	T020-7434 3111		▶▶ 127
Richmond	*The Canyon*	££	
	T020-8948 2944		▶▶ 390
Soho	*Ed's Easy Diner*	£	
	T020-7434 4439		▶▶ 181
The Strand	*Smollensky's on the Strand*	££	
	T020-7497 2101		▶▶ 74

Oriental

Camden	*Café Bintang*	££	
	T020-7428 9603	▸▸ 313	
	Cheng Du	££	
	T020-7485 8058	▸▸ 313	

Pacific

Mayfair	*Suze in Mayfair*	£	
	T020-7491 3237	▸▸ 112	

Peruvian

Southwark	*Fina Estampa*	£	
	T020-7403 1342	▸▸ 252	

Polish

Hammersmith	*Lowiczanka*	£	
	T020-8741 3225	▸▸ 359	
Sth Kensington	*Daquise*	££	
	T020-7589 8627	▸▸ 171	

Portuguese

Knightsbridge	*O Fado*	££	
	T020-7589 3002	▸▸ 171	

Russian

Mayfair	*Firebird*	££	
	T020-7493 7000	▸▸ 111	

Scottish

Belgravia	*Boisdale*	£££	
	T020-7730 6922	▸▸ 157	

South American

Fulham	*Montana*	££	
	T020-7385 9500	▸▸ 359	
Islington	*La Piragua*	£	
	T020-7364 2843	▸▸ 323	

Spanish

Battersea	*San Miguel's on the River*	££	
	T020-7801 9696	▸▸ 372	
Clerkenwell	*Moro*	£££	
	T020-7833 8336	▸▸ 226	
Docklands	*Baradero*	£	
	T020-7987 0771	▸▸ 296	
Embankment	*El Barco Latino*	££	
	T020-7379 5496	▸▸ 74	
Mayfair	*Down Mexico Way*	££	
	T020-7437 9895	▸▸ 111	
Paddington	*Los Remos*	£	
	T020-7723 5056	▸▸ 351	
Pimlico	*Goya*	££	
	T020-7976 5309	▸▸ 157	

Spanish cont.

Putney	*La Mancha*	£	
	T020-8780 1022	▸▸ 359	
Southwark	*Mar i Terra*	£	
	T020-7928 7628	▸▸ 252	
Waterloo	*Meson Don Felipe*	££	
	T020-7928 3237	▸▸ 263	

Tex-Mex

Piccadilly	*The Hard Rock Café*	££	
	T020-7629 0382	▸▸ 127	

Thai

Bloomsbury	*Thai Garden Café*	£	
	T020-7323 1494	▸▸ 213	
The City	*Silks and Spice*	££	
	T020-7248 7878	▸▸ 239	
Clapham	*Pepper Tree*	££	
	T020-7622 1758	▸▸ 373	
Earl's Court	*Pin Petch*	£	
	T020-7370 1371	▸▸ 344	
Fulham	*206 Café*	£	
		▸▸ 359	
Greenwich	*Thai Chung*	£	
	T020-8858 8588	▸▸ 400	
Islington	*Tuk Tuk*	£	
	T020-7226 0837	▸▸ 323	
Marylebone	*Thai West*	£	
	T020-7224 1367	▸▸ 192	
Notting Hill	*Churchill Arms*	£	
	T020-7792 1246	▸▸ 335	
Soho	*Chiang Mai*	££	
	T020-7437 7444	▸▸ 89	
The Strand	*Thai Pot Express*	£	
	T020-7497 0904	▸▸ 74	

Turkish

Islington	*Baraka*	£	
	T020-7254 1500	▸▸ 323	
	Gallipoli	£	
	T020-7359 0630	▸▸ 323	
	Gallipoli Again	£	
	T020-7359 1578	▸▸ 323	
	Pasha	££	
	T020-7226 1454	▸▸ 323	
	Solen	£	
	T020-7254 6999	▸▸ 323	
Mayfair	*Sofra Bistro*	££	
	T020-7499 4099	▸▸ 111	
Waterloo	*Tas*	£	
	T020-7928 1444	▸▸ 263	

Vegetarian

Covent Gdn	*Food for Thought*	£	
	T020-7836 0239	▶▶ 99	
Hammersmith	*The Gate*	££	
	T020-8748 6932	▶▶ 359	
Soho	*Busaba Eathai*	£	
	T020-7255 8686	▶▶ 89	
	Country Life	£	
	T020-7434 2922	▶▶ 89	
	CTJ Vegan Restaurant	£	
	T020-7287 3714	▶▶ 89	
	Mildred's Wholefood Café	£	
	T020-7494 1634	▶▶ 89	
	Satsuma	£	
	T020-7437 8338	▶▶ 89	
Trafalgar Sq	*Cranks Express*	£	
	T020-7836 0660	▶▶ 65	

Vietnamese

East End	*Viet Hoa Café*	££	
	T020-7729 8293	▶▶ 279	
Fulham	*Zen Bonjour Vietnam*	£	
	T020-7385 7603	▶▶ 359	

What the papers say

"The guides for intelligent, independently-minded souls of any age or budget."
Indie Traveller

"While Wallpaper shies away from the standard handbook when packing our Vuitton, we are prepared to make an exception for the Footprint series when it comes to South America."
Wallpaper

"If 'the essence of real travel' is what you have been secretly yearning for all these years, then Footprint are the guides for you."
Under 26

"The titles in the Footprint Handbooks series are about as comprehensive as travel guides get."
Travel Reference Library

Mail order
Available worldwide in bookshops and on-line. Footprint travel guides can also be ordered directly from us in Bath, via our website **www.footprintbooks.com** or from the address on the imprint page of this book.

Will you help us?

We try as hard as we can to make each Footprint Handbook as up-to-date and accurate as possible but, of course, things always change. Many people email or write to us – with corrections, new information, or simply comments. If you want to let us know about your experiences and adventures – be they good, bad or ugly – then don't delay; we're dying to hear from you. And please try to include all the relevant details and juicy bits. Your help will be greatly appreciated, especially by other travellers. In return we will send you details about our special guidebook offer.

email Footprint at:
lon1_online@footprintbooks.com

or write to:

Elizabeth Taylor
Footprint Handbooks
6 Riverside Court
Lower Bristol Road
Bath
BA2 3DZ
UK

M25 & routes into London

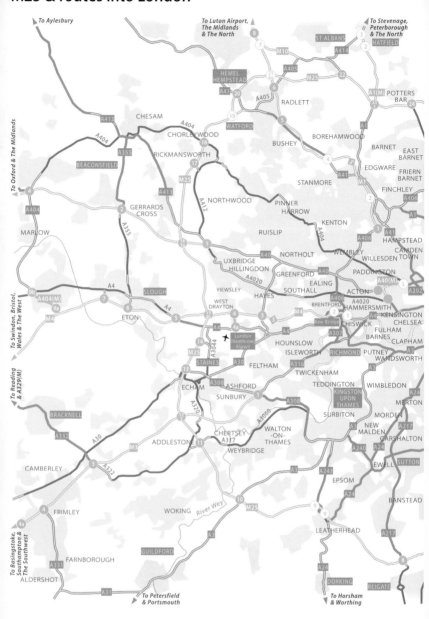

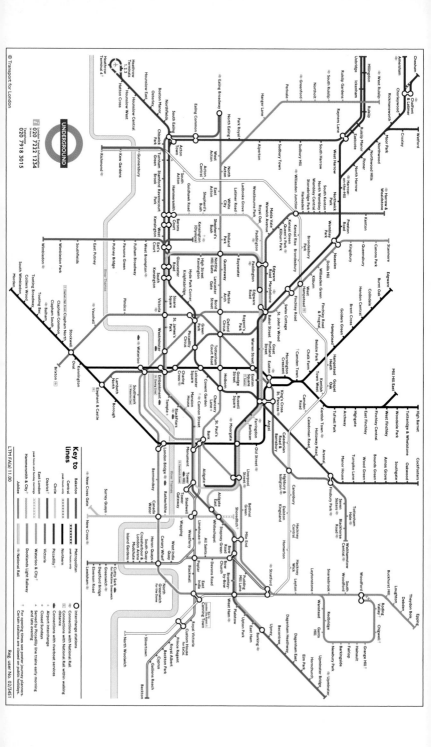

Acknowledgements

Endless thanks to all the Contributors for adding expert breadth and depth to what would otherwise have been very limited coverage of London's bewildering array of entertainment options, in particular to Andrew White for his thorough histories of each area and the city as a whole, and to Jonathan Glancey for the round-up of the city's architecture and the low-down on its wealth of new buildings.

And special thanks also to the book's seven other writers and researchers, especially Lizzie Taylor, along with Chris Moore, Tim Rowbottom, Natasha Plowright, Tim Clark, and Mou Banerjee. All have been very generous with their time and commitment, providing entertaining insights, information and research on several areas north, south, east and west.

Charlie Godfrey-Faussett would like to thank everyone in his home city who has directly made the task of writing about it more easy, bearable and even pleasurable. These include Caro Taverne, Keith Coventry, Paul Baggaley, Dev Mukerjee, Matthew Brett, Ned Bigham, Max Carlish, Clare Hoffmann, Alice Lucas-Tooth, John Ford, Jason Gathorne-Hardy, Jessica Purcell, James Robinson, Alex Studholme, Frances Treanor, Neil Sellas, as well as my family and other friends.

Many press officers, gallery staff, waiters, bar staff, taxi drivers, Beefeaters, cycle couriers, shop assistants and any number of others have also been happy to share their enthusiasm for the city and its attractions.

Finally, many thanks to everyone at Footprint, especially Felicity Laughton for the Essentials chapter and much more, and also to the editor Alan Murphy for his calm and patience, and Rachel Fielding for commissioning the book in the first place.

About the author

Raised in the county of Kent, **Charlie Godfrey-Fausset**t has lived and worked both north and south of the river in London for the last 15 years. As a freelance journalist, he has reviewed theatre in various far-flung parts of town as well as in the West End for *Time Out* magazine, and contributed to other London-based newspapers, magazines and international websites. Charlie also wrote the Cadogan guide to Edinburgh and upon returning to the Big Smoke finds that he only occasionally hankers after long walks in the woods and fields of the Garden of England.

About the contributors

Andrew White (History) is a London-based freelance editor and writer. **Jonathan Glancey** (Architecture), is Architecture and Design editor of *The Guardian*. **James Christopher** (Film) is film critic for *The Times*. **Andrew Wilson** (Contemporary Art) is art historian, critic, curator and deputy editor of *Art Monthly*. **Gabriel Gbadamosi** ('The Clock Room' and 'London – a literary odyssey') is a London-based poet and playwright. **Tony Farsides** (London club scene) is music journalist for *Music* magazine, Worldpop.com, and editor of Thebox.co.uk **Tim Rowbottom** (London music scene) is a freelance journalist and dab hand at the *New Musical Express* crossword.